Lecture Notes in Computer Science

Vol. 245: H.F. de Groote, Lectures on the Complexity of Bilinear Problems. V, 135 pages. 1987.

Vol. 246: Graph-Theoretic Concepts in Computer Science. Proceedings, 1986. Edited by G. Tinhofer and G. Schmidt. VII, 307 pages. 1987.

Vol. 247: STACS 87. Proceedings, 1987. Edited by F.J. Brandenburg, G. Vidal-Naquet and M. Wirsing. X, 484 pages. 1987.

Vol. 248: Networking in Open Systems. Proceedings, 1986. Edited by G. Müller and R.P. Blanc. VI, 441 pages. 1987.

Vol. 249: TAPSOFT '87. Volume 1. Proceedings, 1987. Edited by H. Ehrig, R. Kowalski, G. Levi and U. Montanari. XIV, 289 pages. 1987.

Vol. 250: TAPSOFT '87. Volume 2. Proceedings, 1987. Edited by H. Ehrig, R. Kowalski, G. Levi and U. Montanari. XIV, 336 pages. 1987.

Vol. 251: V. Akman, Unobstructed Shortest Paths in Polyhedral Environments. VII, 103 pages. 1987.

Vol. 252: VDM '87. VDM – A Formal Method at Work. Proceedings, 1987. Edited by D. Bjørner, C.B. Jones, M. Mac an Airchinnigh and E.J. Neuhold. IX, 422 pages. 1987.

Vol. 253: J.D. Becker, I. Eisele (Eds.), WOPPLOT 86. Parallel Processing: Logic, Organization, and Technology. Proceedings, 1986. V, 226 pages. 1987.

Vol. 254: Petri Nets: Central Models and Their Properties. Advances in Petri Nets 1986, Part I. Proceedings, 1986. Edited by W. Brauer, W. Reisig and G. Rozenberg. X, 480 pages. 1987.

Vol. 255: Petri Nets: Applications and Relationships to Other Models of Concurrency. Advances in Petri Nets 1986, Part II. Proceedings, 1986. Edited by W. Brauer, W. Reisig and G. Rozenberg. X, 516 pages. 1987.

Vol. 256: Rewriting Techniques and Applications. Proceedings, 1987. Edited by P. Lescanne. VI, 285 pages. 1987.

Vol. 257: Database Machine Performance: Modeling Methodologies and Evaluation Strategies. Edited by F. Cesarini and S. Salza. X, 250 pages. 1987.

Vol. 258: PARLE, Parallel Architectures and Languages Europe. Volume I. Proceedings, 1987. Edited by J.W. de Bakker, A.J. Nijman and P.C. Treleaven. XII, 480 pages. 1987.

Vol. 259: PARLE, Parallel Architectures and Languages Europe. Volume II. Proceedings, 1987. Edited by J.W. de Bakker, A.J. Nijman and P.C. Treleaven. XII, 464 pages. 1987.

Vol. 260: D.C. Luckham, F.W. von Henke, B. Krieg-Brückner, O. Owe, ANNA, A Language for Annotating Ada Programs. V, 143 pages. 1987.

Vol. 261: J. Ch. Freytag, Translating Relational Queries into Iterative Programs. XI, 131 pages. 1987.

Vol. 262: A. Burns, A.M. Lister, A.J. Wellings, A Review of Ada Tasking. VIII, 141 pages. 1987.

Vol. 263: A.M. Odlyzko (Ed.), Advances in Cryptology – CRYPTO '86. Proceedings. XI, 489 pages. 1987.

Vol. 264: E. Wada (Ed.), Logic Programming '86. Proceedings, 1986. VI, 179 pages. 1987.

Vol. 265: K.P. Jantke (Ed.), Analogical and Inductive Inference. Proceedings, 1986. VI, 227 pages. 1987.

Vol. 266: G. Rozenberg (Ed.), Advances in Petri Nets 1987. VI, 451 pages. 1987.

Vol. 267: Th. Ottmann (Ed.), Automata, Languages and Programming. Proceedings, 1987. X, 565 pages. 1987.

Vol. 268: P.M. Pardalos, J.B. Rosen, Constrained Global Optimization: Algorithms and Applications. VII, 143 pages. 1987.

Vol. 269: A. Albrecht, H. Jung, K. Mehlhorn (Eds.), Parallel Algorithms and Architectures. Proceedings, 1987. Approx. 205 pages. 1987.

Vol. 270: E. Börger (Ed.), Computation Theory and Logic. IX, pages. 1987.

Vol. 271: D. Snyers, A. Thayse, From Logic Design to L Programming. IV, 125 pages. 1987.

Vol. 272: P. Treleaven, M. Vanneschi (Eds.), Future Parallel Com ters. Proceedings, 1986. V, 492 pages. 1987.

Vol. 273: J.S. Royer, A Connotational Theory of Program Struct V, 186 pages. 1987.

Vol. 274: G. Kahn (Ed.), Functional Programming Languages Computer Architecture. Proceedings. VI, 470 pages. 1987.

Vol. 275: A.N. Habermann, U. Montanari (Eds.), System Devel ment and Ada. Proceedings, 1986. V, 305 pages. 1987.

Vol. 276: J. Bézivin, J.-M. Hullot, P. Cointe, H. Lieberman (Ed ECOOP '87. European Conference on Object-Oriented Progr ming. Proceedings. VI, 273 pages. 1987.

Vol. 277: B. Benninghofen, S. Kemmerich, M.M. Richter, Systems Reductions. X, 265 pages. 1987.

Vol. 278: L. Budach, R.G. Bukharajev, O.B. Lupanov (Eds.), Fun mentals of Computation Theory. Proceedings, 1987. XIV, 505 pa 1987.

Vol. 279: J.H. Fasel, R.M. Keller (Eds.), Graph Reduction. Proce ings, 1986. XVI, 450 pages. 1987.

Vol. 280: M. Venturini Zilli (Ed.), Mathematical Models for the Sem tics of Parallelism. Proceedings, 1986. V, 231 pages. 1987.

Vol. 281: A. Kelemenová, J. Kelemen (Eds.), Trends, Techniques, Problems in Theoretical Computer Science. Proceedings, 1986. 213 pages. 1987.

Vol. 282: P. Gorny, M.J. Tauber (Eds.), Visualization in Programmi Proceedings, 1986. VII, 210 pages. 1987.

Vol. 283: D.H. Pitt, A. Poigné, D.E. Rydeheard (Eds.), Categ Theory and Computer Science. Proceedings, 1987. V, 300 pag 1987.

Vol. 284: A. Kündig, R.E. Bührer, J. Dähler (Eds.), Embedd Systems. Proceedings, 1986. V, 207 pages. 1987.

Vol. 285: C. Delgado Kloos, Semantics of Digital Circuits. IX, 1 pages. 1987.

Vol. 286: B. Bouchon, R.R. Yager (Eds.), Uncertainty in Knowled Based Systems. Proceedings, 1986. VII, 405 pages. 1987.

Vol. 287: K.V. Nori (Ed.), Foundations of Software Technology a Theoretical Computer Science. Proceedings, 1987. IX, 540 page 1987.

Vol. 288: A. Blikle, MetaSoft Primer. XIII, 140 pages. 1987.

Vol. 289: H.K. Nichols, D. Simpson (Eds.), ESEC '87. 1st Europe Software Engineering Conference. Proceedings, 1987. XII, 404 ges. 1987.

Vol. 290: T.X. Bui, Co-oP A Group Decision Support System Cooperative Multiple Criteria Group Decision Making. XIII, 250 ges. 1987.

Vol. 291: H. Ehrig, M. Nagl, G. Rozenberg, A. Rosenfeld (Eds Graph-Grammars and Their Application to Computer Science. V 609 pages. 1987.

Vol. 292: The Munich Project CIP. Volume II: The Program Transf mation System CIP-S. By the CIP System Group. VIII, 522 pag 1987.

Vol. 293: C. Pomerance (Ed.), Advances in Cryptology – CRYPT '87. Proceedings. X, 463 pages. 1988.

Vol. 294: R. Cori, M. Wirsing (Eds.), STACS 88. Proceedings, 198 IX, 404 pages. 1988.

Vol. 295: R. Dierstein, D. Müller-Wichards, H.-M. Wacker (Eds Parallel Computing in Science and Engineering. Proceedings, 198 V, 185 pages. 1988.

Lecture Notes in Computer Science

Edited by G. Goos and J. Hartmanis

329

E. Börger H. Kleine Büning
M. M. Richter (Eds.)

CSL '87

1st Workshop on Computer Science Logic
Karlsruhe, FRG, October 12–16, 1987
Proceedings

Springer-Verlag
Berlin Heidelberg New York London Paris Tokyo

Editors

Egon Börger
Dipartimento di Informatica, Università di Pisa
Corso Italia, 40, I-56100 Pisa, Italia

Hans Kleine Büning
Fachbereich 11, Praktische Informatik, Universität Duisburg
Postfach 101629, D-4100 Duisburg 1, FRG

Michael M. Richter
Fachbereich Informatik, Universität Kaiserslautern
Postfach 3049, D-6750 Kaiserslautern, FRG

CR Subject Classification (1987): D.3, F, G.2, H.2.1, I.1, I.2.2–8

ISBN 3-540-50241-6 Springer-Verlag Berlin Heidelberg New York
ISBN 0-387-50241-6 Springer-Verlag New York Berlin Heidelberg

Printed in Germany

Printing and binding: Druckhaus Beltz, Hemsbach/Bergstr.
2145/3140-543210

Preface

This volume contains the papers which were presented to the workshop "Logik in der Informatik" held in Karlsruhe, from October 12 - 16, 1987.

The broad resonance of the workshop confirmed our impression that the time was ripe for such a gathering. It encouraged us to institutionalize this meeting on "Computer-Science Logic" and to hold it regularly every year in the fall.

What is the content and the program of "Computer-Science Logic"? Traditionally Logic, or more specifically, Mathematical Logic splits into several subareas: Set Theory, Proof Theory, Recursion Theory, and Model Theory. In addition there is what somestimes is called Philosophical Logic which deals with topics like nonclassical logics and which for historical reasons has been developed mainly at philosophical departments rather than at mathematics institutions.

Not all of these branches of Logic have been there from the very beginning. They grew out to solve fundamental problems which had come up mainly in mathematics and philosophy, and only the future can tell what will last and what not.

Today Computer Science challenges Logic in a new way. In the 1940's logic was one of the sources of development of computers and their theory, as became manifest in persons like A.T. Turing and K. Zuse. But this is not our point here, since after the advent of computers mathematical logic developed in quite a different direction. What we have in mind is the phenomenon that the theoretical analysis of problems in computer science for intrinsic reasons has pointed back to logic. A broad class of questions became visible which is of a basically logical nature.

These questions are often related to some of the traditional disciplines of logic but normally without being covered adequately by any of them. The novel and unifying aspect of this new branch of logic is the algorithmic point of view which is essentially based on experiences people had with computers.

The aim of the "Computer-Science Logic" workshop and of this volume is to represent the richness of research activities in this field in the German-speaking countries and to point to their underlying general logical principles.

The workshop in Karlsruhe was made possible by a generous grant of the "Stiftung Volkswagenwerk" which we gratefully acknowledge.

E. Börger H. Kleine Büning M.M. Richter

Table of Contents

DIAGONALIZING OVER DETERMINISTIC POLYNOMIAL TIME

Klaus Ambos-Spies
Hans Fleischhack
Universität Oldenburg

Hagen Huwig
Universität Dortmund

In [3] the authors have introduced two formal concepts covering certain diagonalizations over polynomial time computable sets, functions, and reductions. In the present paper we embed these notions into a sequence of diagonalization concepts of growing strength. The power of the individual concepts will be characterized by the type of redundancies in a language which can be eliminated.

Though some of our concepts will be defined for arbitrary complexity classes, we are only interested in diagonalizing over deterministic polynomial time. (In particular, we do not consider the polynomially bounded classes for other complexity measures like nondeterministic time (**NP**), (bounded) alternating time (**PH**), or space (**PSPACE**).) We say that a diagonalization concept *D* pertains to deterministic polynomial time (or **P**) if the following holds. First, the concept is sufficiently strong to diagonalize over **P**, i.e., to construct a recursive set $D \notin$ **P**. Second, we obtain diagonals of (essentially) arbitrarily low hyperpolynomial deterministic time complexity, i.e., any property Q which can be enforced by a diagionalization of type *D* is shared by some set in **DTIME**(f(n)), f any "natural" hyperpolynomial function. Our interest was in finding as powerful as possible diagonalization concepts which still pertain to **P**. From the concepts discussed here, only some will pertain to P. Other ones will be too powerful, that is they will also allow certain diagonalizations over deterministic exponential time or nondeterministic polynomial time.

In Section 1, starting from effective Cantor style diagonalizations, i.e., diagonalizations over recursively presentable classes, we introduce the framework within which our diagonalization concepts will be developed.

In Section 2 we introduce our first concept: **P**-1-diagonalizations (2.1). We show that **P**-1-diagonalizations pertain to **P** (2.7). Moreover, like for all the following diagonalization concepts, there is a strongest property forcible by **P**-1-diagonalization, called **P**-1-genericity (2.5,2.6). The power of **P**-1-diagonalizations is characterized by showing that **P**-1-genericity and bi-**P**-immunity coincide (2.9). Hence **P**-1-diagonalizations can exactly eliminate infinite polynomial time computable subsets in a set and in its complement. This diagonalization concept is to weak, however, to eliminate efficiently describable functional or relational dependencies in a set (2.11). To eliminate redundancies of the latter type, we introduce two stronger diagonalization concepts: **P**-2-diagonalizations (3.1) and **P**-3-diagonalizations (4.2).

The **P**-2-diagonalizations of Section 3 are designed to eliminate relational dependencies which can be efficiently discovered by a *backward* search. This concept applies to diagonalizations over **P**-many-one reductions or, more generally,

P-bounded-truth-table reductions. **P**-2-diagonalizations, however, include certain diagonalizations over **EXPTIME** = ∪ {**DTIME**(2^{cn}) : c≥1}, whence **P**-2-diagonalizations do not pertain to **P** (actually **P**-2-diagonalizations subsume **EXPTIME**-1-diagonalizations and they pertain to **EXPTIME** (3.6 and 3.8)). Still we can show that, relative to some oracle, **P**-2-diagonalizations can be carried out within **NP** (3.7), whence properties enforcable by **P**-2-diagonalizations may serve for strong separation results for relativized **P** and **NP**.

The situation becomes more satisfying if we consider only such properties which are shared by some tally set: **P**-2-tally-diagonalizations are diagonalizations of the power of **P**-2-diagonalizations but limited to diagonals in $\{0\}^*$ (3.9): **P**-2-tally-diagonalizations eliminate exactly relational dependencies (relative to $\{0\}^*$) which can be efficiently discovered by a backward search (3.13), and, in contrast to **P**-2-diagonalizations, **P**-2-tally diagonalizations pertain to **P** (3.11). In [3] **P**-2-diagonalizations are called p-standard diagonalizations. Various examples demonstrating the power of this diagonalization concept can be found there.

Finally, in Section 4, we introduce **P**-3-diagonalizations, which are designed to eliminate relational dependencies which can be efficiently discovered by a backward and *forward* search. Such diagonalizations are required for diagonalizing over **P**-Turing reductions (4.3.1). Since **P**-3-diagonalizations subsume **P**-2-diagonalizations, they do not pertain to **P**. Now even the tally diagonalization variant, **P**-3-tally-diagonalizations, does not pertain to **P** unless **P**=**NP**: There are no **P**-3-tally-generic sets in **NP** (4.4).

Due to space limitation, most proofs are only sketched, some omitted. We assume the reader to be familiar with Sections 1-4 of [3]. Unexplained notation can be found there. The notions set, problem and language are synonymously used for subsets of Σ^*, where $\Sigma=\{0,1\}$. The (n+1)st string of Σ^* with respect to the lexicographical ordering is denoted z_n. The concatenation of two strings x and y is denoted by x^*y or xy. The length of x is denoted by $|x|$, and we do not distinguish between an element i of Σ and the string of length 1 consisting of the letter i. The (n+1)st letter of a string x is denoted by x(n). The join of two sets A and B is the set $A \oplus B = \{0x : x \in A\} \cup \{1x : x \in B\}$ and $A^c = \Sigma^* - A$ is the complement of A. In our notation we do not distinguish between a set and its characteristic function and between a machine and the language accepted by it (i.e., $x \in A$ iff $A(x)=1$ and M accepts x iff $x \in M$ iff $M(x)=1$).

In the following $\{P_e : e \in N\}$, $\{f_e : e \in N\}$ and $\{M_e(X) : e \in N\}$ are some fixed recursive enumerations of the polynomial time computable sets, the polynomial time computable functions f: $\Sigma^* \to \Sigma^*$, and the polynomial time bounded deterministic oracle Turing machines (p-OTM for short) with oracle set X, respectively. Moreover, we assume that the polynomial p_e bounds the computation time of P_e, f_e and $M_e(X)$. $\lambda x,y.\langle x,y\rangle : \Sigma^* \times \Sigma^* \to \Sigma^*$ is a polynomial time computable and invertible pairing function. For any set A, the (n+1)st row of A is defined by $A^{(n)} = \{x : \langle z_n, x\rangle \in A\}$.

1. Effective Diagonalizations

Recall that a class **C** of recursive sets is *recursively presentable (r.p.)* if there is a recursive enumeration $<C_n : n\in N>$ of the members of **C**. More formally, **C** is r.p. if there is a recursive set U such that $\mathbf{C} = \{U^{(n)} : n\in N\}$. U is called a *universal set* for **C**. Note that the standard complexity classes like **P**, **NP**, **EXPTIME** etc. are r.p. (see e.g. [2]). Based on a universal set U of an r.p. class **C**, we can use a Cantor style diagonalization to construct a recursive diagonal D for **C**, i.e. a recursive set $D\notin \mathbf{C}$, by letting

$$D(z_n) = 1-U^{(n)}(z_n).$$

Here the definition of D on z_n ensures that D differs from the (n+1)st member $U^{(n)}$ of **C**.

This diagonalization can be visualized as follows: The global task of the diagonalization, namely to build a set $D\notin \mathbf{C}$, is split up in an infinite sequence $<R_e : e\in N>$ of subtasks *(requirements)*, namely

$$R_e : D \neq U^{(e)}.$$

Then any set satisfying all requirements will meet the global task. Moreover the individual requirements are *finitary*. That means by appropriately defining some finite interval of (the characteristic function of) D, we can force that R_e will be met, no matter how D will look like outside this interval. In our example it suffices to appropriately define D on any arbitrary string x to enforce R_e (namely let $D(x)=1-U^{(e)}(x)$):

(1.1) $\quad \forall x\ \exists i\in\Sigma\ (\ D(x) = i \Rightarrow R_e$ is met)

Any property Q of languages which can be characterized by a sequence $<R_e : e\in N>$ of requirements of type (1.1) can be enforced by a Cantor diagonalization as follows:

1.1. Construction. A set D with property Q is inductively defined in stages $n\in N$. At stage n, $D(z_n)$ will be defined.

Stage n: According to (1.1) fix the least $i\leq 1$ such that $D(z_n)=i$ ensures that R_n is met, and let $D(z_n)=i$.

Then $D(z_n)$ will witness R_n, whence D has property Q. Moreover, if the function

$$w(e,x) = \mu i\in\Sigma\ (\ D(x)=i \text{ ensures that } R_e \text{ is met})$$

is recursive, then the diagonal D is recursive too. Furthermore, the complexity of D depends on the complexity of an algorithm for computing w. The complexity of w in turn depends on the complexity of the sets in the class C over which we diagonalize. For instance, if we let **C**=**P** and $U^{(e)}=P_e$, then for the requirements above the function w becomes

$$w(e,x) = 1-U^{(e)}(x) = 1-P_e(x).$$

Hence, for a fixed requirement R_e the witness function $\lambda x.w(e,x)$ is polynomial time computable, where a polynomial bound p_e depends on e. It follows that $D(z_n)$ can be computed in $O(p_n(z_n))$ steps, that is the complexity of D also depends on the chosen universal set U for **P**.

For any "natural" hyperpolynomial function f we can choose a universal U for **P** yielding a diagonal $D\in$ **DTIME**(f(n)). For given U we can achieve the same by *slowing down* the diagonalization.

1.2. Proposition. Let f be any nondecreasing, fully time constructible function f which majorizes all polynomials. There is a set $D \in$ **DTIME**(f(n))-**P**.

Proof (sketch). The graph of the characteristic function of D is effectively enumerated in increasing order, $D(z_n)$ being defined at stage n. Simultaneously, a list SAT of indices is enumerated, such that at the end of stage n, SAT contains the indices of those requirements which have been met by the end of this stage.

Stage n. The stage consists of two parts. The action of each part is limited to $f(|z_n|)$ steps (whence D is computable in O(f) steps).

Part 1: For up to $f(|z_n|)$ steps, by looking back to stages 0, 1, 2, ... of the construction, compute an initial segment $SAT_n = (e_1, \ldots, e_m)$ of the list SAT. Then let $e = \mu k(\, k \notin SAT_n)$.

Part 2: If $P_e(z_n)$ can be computed in $f(|z_n|)$ steps, then let $D(z_n)=1-P_e(z_n)$ and add e to SAT. Otherwise let $D(z_n)=0$.

By choice of f, an easy induction on n shows that the numbers $e=e_n$ are nondecreasing and unbounded in n. Hence D meets each requirement eventually, though in general R_e will not be ensured at stage e (i.e. witnessed by z_e) but at some later stage (i.e. witnessed by z_m for some m>e). (Also it might happen that successful action to meet R_e is taken at several (successive) stages, since, due to lack of time, the succesful action of stage $t \leq s$ cannot be recognized in part 1 of stage s+1.) □

Diagonalizations of the just described type are called *slow* or *delayed* diagonalizations. (In an interesting variant of the delayed diagonalization technique, which we will not discuss here, one constructs a diagonal D for the union $\mathbf{C}_1 \cup \ldots \cup \mathbf{C}_n$ of r.p. classes from given diagonals D_i for the individual classes $\mathbf{C}_i$. This is achieved by letting D sufficiently look like D_i (i.e. $D = D_i \cap E_i$ for some appropiate $E_i \in \mathbf{P}$) thereby ensuring $D \notin \mathbf{C}_i$. See e.g. [2,12].)

Since requirements of type (1.1) can be attacked at any point of the construction, we can build diagonals inside any given set which is infinite. For instance the set D in Proposition 1.2 can be chosen to be tally by replacing z_n by 0^n in the proof. As we will show next, this will not be true for more sophisticated requirements. We give an example.

1.3. Definition (cf. [5,10]). Let **C** be a class of languages. An infinite set A is ***C-immune*** if no infinite subset of A belongs to **C**. (Hence, in particular, $A \notin \mathbf{C}$). A is *bi-**C**-immune* if A and A^c are **C**-immune.

For any r.p. class **C**, given an enumeration $\{I_e : e \in N\}$ of all infinite sets in **C**, the following construction yields a **C**-immune set D.

1.4. Construction. We define a strictly increasing function $f\colon N \to \Sigma^*$, by letting $f(n) = \mu x\ (\ |x| > |f(n-1)|\ \&\ x \in I_n\ )\ (f(-1)=\varepsilon)$, and let $D = \Sigma^* - \text{range}(f)$.

Then, since range(f) contains at most one string of each length, D is infinite, and, by definition of f, $f(n)\in I_n-D$, whence D does not contain an infinite **C**-set. Though we have assumed **C** to be r.p., in general we cannot decide, however, whether a **C**-set is infinite, whence Construction 1.4 is not effective. In an effective construction of a **C**-immune set we work with a recursive enumeration $\{C_e: e\in N\}$ of all **C**-sets and meet the the following requirements of conditional form

$$R_e : \text{If } C_e \text{ is infinite, then } D^c \cap C_e \neq \emptyset.$$

Note that any infinite set D meeting these requirements is **C**-immune.

1.5. Construction. D is inductively defined, $D(z_n)$ being defined at stage n. Simultaneously with D we enumerate a set SAT containing the indices of requirements which have been previously satisfied.

Stage n. If there is a number $e\leq n/2$ such that e is not yet in SAT and $z_n\in C_e$, then let $D(z_n)=0$ and add e to SAT. Otherwise, let $D(z_n)=1$.

Obviously the construction is effective, whence D is recursive. Moreover, if C_e is infinite then, for the least string $z_n\in C_e$ with $n>2e$, $D(z_n)=0<1=C_e(z_n)$ by construction, whence requirement R_e is met. Finally, the clause "$e\leq n/2$" in the construction ensures that there are at least n strings $\leq z_{2n}$ in D, whence D is infinite.

The crucial difference between Constructions 1.4 and 1.5 is that in 1.4 we *search* for a diagonalization candidate f(e) for a requirement R_e, whereas in 1.5 we *wait* for such a candidate, i.e., at any sufficiently large stage n we check whether the current string z_n may serve as a diagonalization witness. [This difference is reflected by the order in which the requirements are satisfied: In 1.4 requirements are satisfied in increasing order, whereas the order in 1.5 depends on the structure of the sets C_e (and here, in general, we cannot decide whether a requirement will be met by some diagonalization action or whether it will trivially hold since its hypothesis fails).]

Construction 1.5 is a simple example of a *wait-and-see* argument. Such diagonalizations play a fundamental role in recursive function theory (see e.g. [11,13]) and computational complexity theory. Here we will formalize 3 types of wait-and-see arguments of increasing power for diagonalizing over deterministic polynomial time. These diagonalizations are classified by the form of the requirements. The fact that we diagonalize over **P**, will be reflected by the fact that the objects occuring in the requirements are polynomial time computable.

Our first notion will be obtained by formalizing requirements of the immunity type. Note that the immunity requirements R_e are of the logical form

(1.2) If there are infinitely many x such that, for some $i\leq 1$, by letting $D(x)=i$, the goal of R_e will be achieved, then for some y, D(y) has to be chosen appropriately.

Moreover, if we consider **C**=**P** (i.e. $C_e=P_e$), then for a fixed requirement R_e the action pertaining to R_e can be performed in polynomial time. Namely, for $C'_e = \{<x,0> : P_e(x)=1\}$, $C'_e \in$ **P** and the fact that the choice of $D(y)$ ensures the **P**-immunity requirement R_e is equivalent to $<y,D(y)> \in C'_e$. Hence the e-th **P**-immunity requirement can be rephrased as

R_e : If there are infinitely many x such that, for some $i \leq 1$, $<x,i> \in C'_e$, then, for some y, $<y,D(y)> \in C'_e$.

2. P-1-diagonalizations

2.1. Definition. Let **C** be any class of recursive sets. A property Q of languages can be enforced by a **C**-*1-diagonalization* if there is a recursive sequence $<C_e : e \in N>$ of languages $C_e \in$ **C** such that, for any set D satisfying

(2.1) If for infinitely many strings x there is a number $i \leq 1$ such that $<x,i> \in C_e$, then $<y,D(y)> \in C_e$ for some string y.

for all numbers e, D has property Q. In this case we say $<C_e : e \in N>$ **C**-*1-forces* Q, and we call C_e a *condition* set (for Q).

2.2. Examples. 1. The condition sets $C_e = \{<x,1-P_e(x)> : x \in \Sigma^*\}$ **P**-1-force intractability, i.e., not being polynomial time computable.

2. **P**-immunity is forced by the sequence $<C_e : e \in N>$ of the **P**-sets $C_{2e} = \{<x,0> : P_e(x)=1\}$ and $C_{2e+1} = \{<z_n,1> : n \geq e\}$. (Note that the even condition sets ensure that any set D satisfying (2.1) has no infinite polynomial time computable subset, while the odd conditions make D infinite.)

3. Similarly, bi-**P**-immunity is **P**-1-forced by the sequence $<C_e : e \in N>$ where $C_{2e+i} = \{<x,i> : P_e(x)=1\}$ $(i=0,1)$.

2.3. Remark. The preceding examples carry over to arbitrary r.p. classes **C** in place of **P** with sufficient closure properties. For instance are not being in **EXPTIME** and bi-**EXPTIME**-immunity enforcable by **EXPTIME**-1-diagonalizations. Furthermore, the results of 2.2 relativize to any oracle **A**.

As we shall show next, any property enforcable by a **C**-1-diagonalization is shared by some recursive set.

2.4. Proposition. Let **C** be any class of recursive sets and let Q be a property of languages enforcable by **C**-1-diagonalization. There is a recursive language with property Q.

Proof (sketch). Let $<C_e : e \in N>$ be a recursive sequence of **C**-sets which forces Q. A recursive set D satisfying (2.1) is defined inductively as follows. Given $D(z_m)$ for all $m<n$, for the definition of $D(z_n)$ we distinguish two cases:

Case 1: There are numbers $e \leq n$ and $i \leq 1$ such that $<z_n,i> \in C_e$ and $<z_m,D(z_m)> \notin C_e$ for all $m<n$.

Then choose the least such numbers e and i (in this order) and let $D(z_n)=i$.

Case 2: Otherwise. Then let $D(z_n)=0$. □

For any r.p. class **C**, there is a strongest property which can be enforced by **C**-1-diagonalization.

2.5. Definition. A set G is ***C**-1-generic* if for any set $C \in$ **C** the following holds

(2.2) If for infinitely many strings x there is a number $i \le 1$ such that $\langle x,i\rangle \in C$, then $\langle y,G(y)\rangle \in C$ for some string y.

2.6. Proposition. Let **C** be an r.p. class.

(i) **C**-1-genericity can be enforced by **C**-1-diagonalization.

(ii) If G is **C**-1-generic, then G has all properties which can be enforced by **C**-1-diagonalizations.

Proof. (i) Given a universal set U of **C**, the sequence $\langle U^{(e)}: e \in N\rangle$ forces **C**-1-genericity. (ii) Immediate by Definitions 2.1 and 2.5. □

By Propositions 2.4 and 2.6 there are recursive **P**-1-generic sets, i.e., recursive sets which have all properties enforcable by **P**-1-diagonalizations. By 2.2.1, **P**-1-generic sets are intractable. On the other hand, by slowing down the diagonalization in the proof of Proposition 2.4 (cf. Proposition 1.2), we get **P**-1-generic sets of arbitrarily low hyperpolynomial deterministic time complexity. Moreover, we obtain such sets of polynomial density. (By 2.2.3, however, no **P**-1-generic set is tally.)

2.7. Theorem. Let f be any nondecreasing, fully time constructible function which majorizes all polynomials. There is a sparse **P**-1-generic set G in **DTIME**(f).

Proof. Omitted.

By Theorem 2.7, **P**-1-diagonalizations pertain to **P**. By relativizing this observation, we can show that relative to some oracle there are **P**-1-generic sets in **NP**-**P**.

2.8. Corollary. There is an oracle A such that $\mathbf{NP}^A$ contains a (sparse) $\mathbf{P}^A$-1-generic set.

Proof. The proof of Theorem 2.7 relativizes, whence, for any oracle A and for any hyperpolynomial, nondecreasing and fully time constructible function f, there is a sparse $\mathbf{P}^A$-1-generic set in $\mathbf{DTIME}^A(f(n))$. The claim follows, since Gasarch and Homer [8] constructed an oracle A such that $\mathbf{DTIME}^A(2^n) \subseteq \mathbf{NP}^A$. □

Note that not for all oracles A separating **P** and **NP** there are $\mathbf{P}^A$-1-generic sets in $\mathbf{NP}^A$. Homer and Maass [10] have constructed an oracle A such that $\mathbf{P}^A \ne \mathbf{NP}^A$ but $\mathbf{NP}^A$ does not contain a $\mathbf{P}^A$-immune set.

The power of **P**-1-diagonalizations is limited by the following characterization of **P**-1-generic sets.

2.9. Proposition. A set is **P**-1-generic if and only if it is bi-**P**-immune.

Proof. By 2.2.2 and 2.6(ii), **P**-1-generic sets are bi-**P**-immune. For a proof of the converse, let A be bi-**P**-immune and let C be any polynomial time computable set such that for infinitely many strings x there is a number $i \le 1$ with $\langle x,i \rangle \in C$. We have to show $\langle y,A(y) \rangle \in C$ for some y.
Let $C_i = \{x : \langle x,i \rangle \in C\}$ (i=0,1). Then $C_i \in$ **P** and C_0 or C_1 is infinite. If C_1 is infinite, then, by **P**-immunity of A^c, there is some string $y \in A \cap C_1$; and if C_0 is infinite, then, by **P**-immunity of A, there is some string $y \in A^c \cap C_0$. In either case $\langle y,A(y) \rangle \in C$. □

By Proposition 2.9, **P**-1-diagonalizations can eliminate any infinite easy subsets in a set under construction and in its complement, thereby yielding almost everywhere intractable problems. Other redundancies which may occur in the encoding of the information of a set, namely functional -or, more generally, relational- dependencies, however, cannot be avoided by **P**-1-diagonalizations. We illustrate this by the following example.

2.10. Definition ([1]). A set A is **P**-m-autoreducible if there is a polynomial time computable function f: $\Sigma^* \rightarrow \Sigma^*$ such that $A \le_{pm} A$ via f and $f(x) \ne x$ for all strings x. Otherwise A is non-**P**-m-autoreducible.

For a **P**-m-autoreducible set A, we can efficiently reduce any membership question about A to a different one. Note that, for any set $A \ne \Sigma^*$, $A \oplus A = \{ix : x \in A \ \& \ i \le 1\}$ is **P**-m-autoreducible via f, where $f(ix)=(1-i)x$ and $f(\varepsilon)=0y$, y some element from the complement of A.

2.11. Proposition. Non-**P**-m-autoreducibility cannot be enforced by **P**-1-diagonalization.

Proof. For any bi-**P**-immune set A, $A \oplus A$ is bi-**P**-immune again. The claim follows with the preceding observation and Propositions 2.6 and 2.9. □

3. P-2-diagonalizations

We will now extend our diagonalization concept to be able to avoid any efficient functional dependencies. We start with describing the construction of a non-**P**-m-autoreducible set D. The set D has to meet the requirements

R_e: If $f_e(x) \ne x$ for all strings x, then $D(y) \ne D(f_e(y))$ for some string y.

Note that, if the hypothesis of R_e holds, then there are infinitely many strings y such that

(3.1) $f_e(y) < y$ or

(3.2) $y = f_e(x)$ for some string $x < y$.

So in a recursive enumeration of D in increasing order, there will be infinitely many strings y such that the appropriate choice of D(y) will enforce R_e. Namely, if (3.1) applies, we let

(3.3) $D(y) = 1 - D(f_e(y))$,

and if (3.2) applies, then, for the least x satisfying this condition, we let

(3.4) $D(y) = 1 - D(x)$

(thus ensuring $D(x) \neq D(f_e(x))$). Hence the following inductive definition of D will succeed in making D non-**P**-m-autoreducible. Given $D(z_m)$ for m<n, we choose e<n minimal such that R_e has not been forced previously and it can be forced by $y=z_n$ in the way described above. We then define $D(z_n)$ according to (3.3) or (3.4), thereby satisfying R_e. (If no such e exist, we let $D(z_n)=0$.)

This diagonalization argument differs from the ones in the preceding sections with regard to the action necessary for meeting the individual requirements. First, the choice of D(y) to meet R_e depends on previous values of D (namely, on $f_e(y) < y$ in (3.3) and on $x < y$ in (3.4)). Second, the action required by a fixed requirement R_e cannot be performed in polynomial time (unless **P**=**NP**): To decide whether (3.2) applies, we have to compute $f_e(x)$ for all x<y. Since the number of predecessors of y is exponential in |y|, this requires exponential time relative to |y|, unless we nondeterministically guess some string x with property (3.2). (As one can easily show **P**≠**NP** implies that there are polynomial time computable functions which cannot be inverted in polynomial time; see e.g. Homer and Long [9].) This action remains polynomial (in fact linear), however, if we measure the time in the length of the initial segment of D up to y, i.e. in the number of predecessors of y.

In order to introduce a formal diagonalization notion covering diagonalizations of the just described type we require some notation. Given a set A, we let $A|z_n$ denote the initial segment of A up to z_n. I.e., $y \in A|z_n$ iff $y \in A$ and $y<z_n$. $[A|z_n]$ denotes the characteristic string of $A|z_n$; i.e., $[A|z_n]$ has length n and, for k<n, $[A|z_n](k)=A|z_n(z_k)$. Note that $2^{|x|}-1 \leq [A|x] \leq 2^{|x|+1}-1$.

Using this notation we can define a condition set C_e corresponding to the requirement R_e above:

$$C_e = \{x : \exists n<|x|-1 \ (x(n) \neq x(|x|-1) \ \& \ [f_e(z_{|x|-1})=z_n \text{ or } f_e(z_n)=z_{|x|-1}] \ )\}$$

Then $C_e \in$ **P** and $[D|z_{n+1}] \in C_e$ iff, for $y=z_n$, (3.1) and (3.3) or (3.2) and (3.4) hold. Moreover, the hypothesis of R_e implies that there are infinitely many strings x such that $[D|x]^*i \in C_e$ for some $i \leq 1$. Hence R_e can be rephrased as follows:

If there are infinitely many strings x such that $[D|x]^*i \in C_e$ for some $i \leq 1$, then $[D|y] \in C_e$ for some string y.

We will now analyse diagonalization arguments with requirements of this type.

3.1. Definition. Let **C** be any class of recursive sets. A property Q of languages can be enforced by a **C**-*2-diagonalization* if there is a recursive sequence $<C_e : e \in N>$ of languages $C_e \in$ **C** such that, for any set D satisfying

(3.5) If there are infinitely many strings x such that $[D|x]^*i \in C_e$ for some $i \leq 1$, then $[D|y] \in C_e$ for some string y.

for all numbers e, D has property Q. (Again we say $<C_e : e \in N>$ **C**-*2-forces* Q and we call

C_e a *condition* set for Q).

3.2. Examples. 1. As shown above, non-**P**-m-autoreducibility is **P**-2-forced by the condition sets

$$C_e = \{x : \exists n<|x|-1 \ (x(n)\neq x(|x|-1) \ \& \ [f_e(z_{|x|-1})=z_n \text{ or } f_e(z_n)=z_{|x|-1}] \ )\}.$$

2. A set A is *P-selfdual* if $A \leq_{pm} A^c$. Note that SAT (or any other **NP**-complete problem) is **P**-selfdual iff **NP=co-NP**. Non-**P**-selfduality is **P**-2-forced by the condition sets

$$C_e = \{x : \exists n<|x|-1 \ (x(n)=x(|x|-1) \ \& \ [f_e(z_{|x|-1})=z_n \text{ or } f_e(z_n)=z_{|x|-1}] \ )\}.$$

Like for **C**-1-diagonalizations, we can show that **C**-2-forcable properties are shared by some recursive sets and that there is a strongest property of this kind.

3.3. Proposition. Let **C** be any class of recursive sets and let Q be a property of languages enforcable by **C**-2-diagonalization. There is a recursive language with property Q.

Proof. Like the proof of Proposition 2.4. Case 1 now becomes
Case 1: There are numbers $e\leq n$ and $i\leq 1$ such that $[D|z_n]^*i\in C_e$ and $[D|z_m]\notin C_e$ for all $m\leq n$.

□

3.4. Definition. A set G is *C-2-generic* if for any set $C\in$ **C** the following holds

(3.6) If for infinitely many strings x there is a number $i\leq 1$ such that $[G|x]^*i\in$ **C**, then $[G|y] \in$ **C** for some string y.

3.5. Proposition. Let **C** be an r.p. class.

(i) **C**-2-genericity can be enforced by **C**-2-diagonalization.

(ii) If G is **C**-2-generic, then G has all properties which can be enforced by **C**-2-diagonalizations.

Proof. (i) Given a universal set U of **C**, the sequence $<U^{(e)}: e\in N>$ forces **C**-2-genericity.
(ii) Immediate by Definitions 3.1 and 3.4. □

Using a slow diagonalization, we can improve Proposition 3.3 as follows.

3.6. Theorem. Let f be any nondecreasing, fully time constructible function such that f majorizes the functions $\lambda n.2^{cn}$ for all $c\in N$. There is a sparse **P**-2-generic set G in **DTIME**(nf(n)). In particular there is a **P**-2-generic set G in **DTIME**(2^{n^2}).

Proof. Omitted.

By relativizing Theorem 3.6, we may conclude that relative to some oracle, all properties enforcable by **P**-2-diagonalizations are shared by some **NP**-set.

3.7. Corollary. There is an oracle A such that $\mathbf{NP}^A$ contains a (sparse) $\mathbf{P}^A$-2-generic set.

Proof. By relativizing Theorem 3.6 and by Gasarch and Homer's result in [8] that $\mathbf{DTIME}^A(2^{n^2}) \subseteq \mathbf{NP}^A$ for some oracle A. □

By Corollary 3.7, **P**-2-diagonalizations can be carried out inside **NP** relative to some appropriate oracle. In contrast to the **P**-1-diagonalizations, however, **P**-2-diagonalizations capture certain diagonalization arguments over larger deterministic time complexity classes than **P**.

3.8. Proposition. Let G be **P**-2-generic. Then G is **EXPTIME**-1-generic. In particular, G $\notin$ **EXPTIME**.

Proof. Let $C \in$ **DTIME**(2^{cn}) be given such that for infinitely many strings x there is a number $i \leq 1$ with $<x,i> \in C$. We have to show $<y,G(y)> \in C$ for some string y.
Let $C' = \{x : <z_{|x|-1}, x(|x|-1)> \in C\}$. Then, as one can easily check, $C' \in$ **P** and $[G|z_n]^* i \in C'$ if and only if $<z_n, i> \in C$. By assumption on C and by **P**-2-genericity of G, this implies $[G|z_{n+1}] \in C'$ for some n, whence $<z_n, G(z_n)> \in C$. □

By Proposition 3.8, **P**-2-diagonalizations are too powerful, i.e., do not completely pertain to **P**. If we consider only such properties which are shared by some tally set, however, we obtain a variant of **P**-2-diagonalizations which only capture diagonalizations over **P**. This is possible, since the initial segment of a tally set up to some string y has length |y|. For any (not necessarily tally) set A, we let A||n denote the intersection of A with $\{0^m : m<n\}$. [A||n] denotes the characteristic string of A||n, i.e., [A||n] has length n and, for m<n, $[A||n](m)=A(0^m)$.

3.9. Definition. (i) Let **C** be any class of recursive sets. A property Q of languages can be enforced by a **C**-*2-tally-diagonalization* if there is a recursive sequence $<C_e : e \in N>$ of languages $C_e \in$ **C** such that, for any <u>tally</u> set D satisfying

(3.7) If there are infinitely many numbers n such that $[D||n]^* i \in C_e$ for some $i \leq 1$, then $[D||m] \in C_e$ for some number m.

for all numbers e, D has property Q.

(ii) A tally set G is **C**-*2-tally-generic* if for any set $C \in$ **C** the following holds

(3.8) If for infinitely many numbers n there is a number $i \leq 1$ such that $[G||n]^* i \in C$, then $[G||m] \in C$ for some number m.

In [3] **P**-2-tally diagonalizations and **P**-2-tally sets are called *p-standard diagonalizations* and *p-generic sets*, respectively. There these notions are intensively studied. For instance it is shown that p-generic sets are **P**-immune, non-**P**-m-autoreducible and non-**P**-selfdual. Moreover, the standard strong polynomial time reducibilities, like $\leq_{p1}$, $\leq_{pm}$, $\leq_{p\text{-}k\text{-}tt}$ ($k \in N$) and $\leq_{p\text{-}btt}$ are pairwise different below any p-generic set. Since p-generic sets are tally, p-standard diagonalizations cannot eliminate redundancies in the complement $A^c = \Sigma^* - A$ of a set A under construction but only in $\{0\}^* - A$, i.e., in the complement of A relative to $\{0\}^*$. For instance, a p-generic set G is not bi-**P**-immune, but both G and $\{0\}^* - G$ are **P**-immune.

To show that a p-standard diagonalization does not suffice to diagonalize over any deterministic time complexity class properly extending **P**, we use the following relation between **P**-2-generic and **P**-2-tally generic sets.

3.10. Lemma. A set G is **P**-2-generic if and only if TALLY(G)={0^n : $z_n \in$ G} is **P**-2-tally-generic.

Proof. Since [G|z_n] = [TALLY(G)||n], this is immediate by definition. □

3.11. Corollary. Let f be any nondecreasing, fully time constructible function that majorizes all polynomials. There is a **P**-2-tally-generic set G in **DTIME**(logn f(n)).

Proof. The function g(n)=f(2^n) is nondecreasing and fully time constructible (up to some constant factor). Moreover, since f is hyperpolynomial, for any c, g(n) ≥ 2^{cn} for all sufficiently large numbers n. By Theorem 3.6, this implies that there is a **P**-2-generic set G′ in **DTIME**(nf(2^n)). Hence, for G=TALLY(G′), G∈**DTIME**(lognf(n)) and G is **P**-2-tally-generic by Lemma 3.10. □

We conclude this section by showing that **P**-2-tally diagonalizations can eliminate exactly those redundancies in a tally set A and its complement {0}*-A relative to {0}*, which can be efficiently discovered by a backward search. Recall that a set A is ***P**-selfreducible* if there is a p-OTM M such that A=M(A) and, for any oracle X and on any input, M(X) queries only strings which are shorter than the input (cf. e.g. [4]). Intuitively, if A is **P**-selfreducible then A(x) can be efficiently computed from A|x.

3.12. Definition. An infinite set A is *1-sided **P**-selfreducible* if there is a p-OTM M such that

(i) For any oracle X, in the computation M(X;x) only strings of length less than |x| are queried.

(ii) M(A;x) ≤ A(x) for all x∈Σ*

(iii) M(A;x) = 1 for infinitely many x∈Σ*.

Otherwise A is *strongly non-**P**-selfreducible.*

Note that if A is strongly non-**P**-selfreducible then there is no set C with infinite intersection with A such that there is an efficient procedure, which for x∈C correctly computes A(x) from A|x and for x∉C outputs 0. Hence if A and A^c are strongly non-**P**-selfreducible, then A is *almost everywhere* non-**P**-selfreducible. (Also note that if in Definition 3.12 M is replaced by a Turing machine without oracle, then M defines an infinite polynomial time computable subset of A and vice versa. I.e. strongly non-**P**-selfreducible sets are **P**-immune.)

3.13. Theorem. For a tally set A the following are equivalent.

(i) A is p-generic (i.e. **P**-2-tally generic)

(ii) A and {0}*-A are strongly non-**P**-selfreducible.

Proof. *(i) ⇒ (ii).* Let A be p-generic. Then, as shown in [3], {0}*-A is p-generic too. Hence it suffices to show that A is not 1-sided **P**-selfreducible. Let M be a p-OTM satisfying (i) and (iii) of Definition 3.12. We will show that M(A;x)=1 for some x∉A. If M(A;x)=1 for some x∉{0}* then this is immediate. Hence, by 3.12(iii), we may assume

(3.9) M(A;0^n)=1 for infinitely many n.

Now, let C={[X||n]*0 : M(X||n;0^n)=1}. Then C∈**P**. Note that, by 3.12(i), M(X;0^n)=M(Y;0^n) for any tally oracle sets X and Y satisfying X||n=Y||n, whence in particular M(A;0^n)=M(A||n;0^n). By definition of C this implies that [A||n]*0∈C for all numbers n with $M(A;0^n)=1$. Hence, by (3.9) and by p-genericity of A, $[A||m] \in C$ for some m, whence, by definition of C, $A(0^{m-1})=0$ and $M(A;0^{m-1})=1$.

(ii) $\Rightarrow$ *(i)*. The proof is by contraposition. Assume that A is not p-generic. Then there is a polynomial time computable set C such that, for some $i \leq 1$,

(3.10) $[A||n]^* i \in C$ for infinitely many n

but

(3.11) $[A||n] \notin C$ for all n.

First assume that (3.10) holds for i=0. Define a p-OTM M by letting

$$M(X;x) = \textbf{if } x=0^n \ \& \ [X||n]^*0 \in C \textbf{ then } 1 \textbf{ else } 0 \textbf{ fi}.$$

Obviously, M satisfies 3.12(i). Moreover, if $M(A;x)=1$ then $x=0^n$ and $[A||n]^*0 \in C$, whence $A(0^n)=1$ (since otherwise $[A||n+1]=[A||n]^*0 \in C$ contrary to (3.11)). Hence 3.12(ii) is satisfied. Finally, by (3.10) (for i=0), $M(A;0^n)=1$ infinitely often, whence 3.12(iii) is also satisfied. It follows that M is a 1-sided **P**-selfreduction of A. If (3.10) holds for i=1, then we can construct a 1-sided **P**-selfreduction for $\{0\}^*$-A in a similar way. □

4. P-3-diagonalizations

By Theorem 3.13, **P**-2-tally-diagonalizations can eliminate all relational dependencies which can be discovered by efficient backward searches. In general, however, the discovery of relational dependencies also requires a forward search. In particular this applies to diagonalizations over polynomial-time Turing reductions. To illustrate this we consider the extension of Definition 2.10 to Turing reducibility in place of many-one reducibility.

4.1. Definition ([1]). A set A is ***P**-T-autoreducible* if there is a p-OTM M such that

(i) for any oracle X and on any input x, M(X;x) does not query x and

(ii) A=M(A).

Otherwise A is *non-**P**-T-autoreducible*.

Obviously **P**-m-autoreducible sets and **P**-selfreducible sets are **P**-T-autoreducible. The converse, however, is not true: One can easily construct a **P**-T-autoreducible **P**-2(-tally)-generic set (cf. [3a] for the tally case).

The analysis of the construction of a non-**P**-T-autoreducible set, which we will describe next, will lead us to our final diagonalization concept.

A non-**P**-T-autoreducible set D has to meet the requirements

R_e: If, for all oracle sets X and for all strings x, $M_e(X;x)$ does not query x, then $D(y) \neq M_e(D;y)$ for some string y.

Now, given any initial part D|y of D we can find a finite extension D|y′ of D|y which forces R_e as follows. Compute $M_e(D|y;y)$ and $M_e(D|y \cup \{y\};y)$. If $M_e(D|y;y) \neq M_e(D|y \cup \{y\};y)$ then $M_e(D|y;y)$ and $M_e(D|y \cup \{y\};y)$ query input y, whence the hypothesis of R_e is refuted. Otherwise, since M_e on input y can query only strings of length less than $p_e(|y|)$, we will have

$$M_e(D|y;y) = M_e(D|y \cup \{y\};y) = M_e(D;y),$$

provided that no string z>y of length less than $p_e(|y|)$ will be added to D. Hence, by letting

$$D|0^{p_e(|y|)} = \textbf{if } M_e(D|y;y)=0 \textbf{ then } D|y\cup\{y\} \textbf{ else } D|y \textbf{ fi},$$

we have built a finite extension of D|y guaranteing that R_e is met.

In contrast to the previous diagonalization constructions, here for meeting a single requirement it does not suffice to appropriately define D on a single string but D has to be appropriately defined on a finite interval of strings, where the length of the strings in this interval is polynomially bounded in the length of the string up to which D had been already defined. (This polynomial bound reflects that we diagonalize over **P**-T-reductions.)

We now formalize this type of diagonalization argument, where our formal diagonalization notion will again capture also those requirements which can be attacked infinitely often in the course of the construction (The requirements above can be attacked at every step of the construction). We need the following notion: We say an initial segment $Y|z_n$ *extends* the initial segment $X|z_m$ if m≤n and $X(z_k)=Y(z_k)$ for all k<m (i.e., if the characteristic string $[X|z_m]$ of $X|z_m$ is a prefix of the characteristic string $[Y|z_n]$ of $Y|z_n$). If Y|y extends X|x, then we write X|x ⊑ Y|y and [X|x] ⊑ [Y|y]. Similarly, we say Y||n *extends* X||m, and write X||m ⊑ Y||n and [X||m] ⊑ [Y||n], if m≤n and $X(0^k)=Y(0^k)$ for k<m. In the following definition we will confine ourselves to the case of diagonalizations over **C**=**P**.

4.2. Definition. (i) A property Q of languages can be enforced by a **P**-*3-diagonalization* if there is a recursive sequence $<C_e : e\in N>$ of languages $C_e\in$ **P** such that, for any set D satisfying

(4.1) If there is a polynomial p such that for infinitely many strings x there is an extension X|z of D|x such that |z| < p(|x|) and $[X|z] \in C_e$, then $[D|y]\in C_e$ for some string y.

for all numbers e, D has property Q.

(ii) Property Q can be enforced by a **P**-*3-tally-diagonalization* if there is a recursive sequence $<C_e : e\in N>$ of languages $C_e\in$ **P** such that, for any <u>tally</u> set D satisfying

(4.2) If there is a polynomial p such that for infinitely many numbers n there is an extension X||k of D||n such that k < p(n) and $[X||k]\in C_e$, then $[D||m]\in C_e$ for some number m.

for all numbers e, D has property Q.

(iii) A set G is ***P**-3-generic* if for any set C∈ **P** the following holds

(4.3) If there is a polynomial p such that for infinitely many strings x there is an extension X|z of G|x such that |z| < p(|x|) and [X|z] ∈ C, then [G|y]∈ C for some string y.

(iv) A set G is ***P**-3-tally-generic* if for any set C∈ **P** the following holds.

(4.4) If there is a polynomial p such that for infinitely many numbers n there is an extension X||k of G||n such that k <

p(n) and $[X||k] \in C$, then $[G||m] \in C$ for some number m.

4.3. Examples. 1. Non-**P**-T-autoreducibility is **P**-3-forced by the condition sets $C_e = \{[X|0^{p_e(n)}] : \exists k\ (|z_k|=n\ \&\ M_e(X|0^{p_e(n)};z_k) \neq [X|0^{p_e(n)}](k)\ )\}$ and **P**-3-tally-forced by the condition sets $C_e' = \{[X||p_e(n)] : M_e(X||p_e(n);0^n) \neq [X||p_e(n)](n)\}$.

2. Nonsparseness is **P**-3-forced by the condition sets

$$C_e=\{x : \exists n\geq e\ (|x|=2^{n+1}\ \&\ \forall i\ [2^n\leq i<2^{n+1} \Rightarrow x(i)=1])\}.$$

Here condition C_e ensures that, for some number n≥e, D contains all strings of length n. (Hence, for a **P**-3-generic set G, there are infinitely many numbers n such that G contains all strings of length n. As one can easily check, the class of sets with this property has measure 0 (with respect to the canonical measure on the power set of Σ^*). This is contrasted by the observation that the class of **P**-2-generic sets has measure 1. Hence *random* sets are **P**-2-generic but not **P**-3-generic. Similar results on measure and category of tally-generic sets have been proved by the second author in [6,7].)

In [3] **P**-3-tally diagonalizations and **P**-3-tally-generic sets are called *generalized p-standard diagonalizations* and *strongly p-generic* sets, respectively. Again one can easily show that **P**-3(-tally)-genericity is the strongest property enforcable by **P**-3(-tally)-diagonalizations. For the construction of a recursive **P**-3-tally generic (i.e., strongly p-generic) set, we refer the reader to [3]. The construction given there can be easily modified to build a recursive **P**-3-generic set. Moreover, by analysing the constructions we can show that there are **P**-3(-tally)-generic sets in triple (double) exponential time. As our final theorem shows, however, **P**-3(-tally)-diagonalization cannot be carried out within **NP**. Hence, in contrast to the previous diagonalization concepts, not all **P**-3(-tally)-forcable properties are shared by some **NP** set (relative to any oracle).

4.4. Theorem. (i) There is no **P**-3-tally-generic set in **NP**.

(ii) There is no **P**-3-generic set in $\mathbf{NTIME}(2^{cn})$ (c≥1).

Proof. (i). For a contradiction assume that G is a **P**-3-tally-generic set in **NP**. Since $G \in \mathbf{NP}$, there is a polynomial p and a set $A \in \mathbf{P}$ such that

$$x \in G \Leftrightarrow \exists y\ (\ |y| = p(|x|)\ \ \&\ <x,y> \in A\ ).$$

Let

$$C=\{z0y : |y|=p(|z|)\ \&\ <0^{|z|},y> \in A\}.$$

Then $C \in \mathbf{P}$ and

$$(4.5)\qquad 0^n \in G \quad \Leftrightarrow \quad \exists y\ (\ |y| = p(n)\ \ \&\ <0^n,y> \in A\ )$$
$$\Leftrightarrow \quad \exists y\ (\ |y| = p(n)\ \ \&\ [G||n]0y \in C\ ).$$

By infinity of $G \subsetneq \{0\}^*$, this implies that, for infinitely many numbers n $[G||n]$ can be extended to a string $[X||p(n)+n+1] \in C$, whence, by genericity of G, $[G||m] \in C$ for some m. By definition of C, $[G||m] = [G||k]0y$ for some k <m and some string y of length p(k). Since $[G||m] = [G||k]0y$, $G(0^k)=0$, whence, by (4.5), $[G||k]0y \notin C$. A contradiction.

(ii). For a contradiction assume that G is a **P**-3-generic set in $\mathbf{NTIME}(2^{cn})$. Then, as one can easily check, $\mathrm{TALLY}(G)=\{0^n : z_n \in G\}$ is **P**-3-tally-generic and $\mathrm{TALLY}(G) \in \mathbf{NTIME}(n^c)$. By part (i) of the theorem, this is impossible. □

References

1 K.Ambos-Spies, P-mitotic sets, in "Logic and Machines: Decision Problems and Complexity", Lecture Notes Comput. Sci. 171 (1984) 1-23, Springer–Verlag.

2 K.Ambos-Spies, Polynomial time degrees of NP-sets, in "Trends in Theoretical Computer Science", E.Börger, Ed., Computer Science Press, 1987, 95-142.

3 K.Ambos-Spies, H.Fleischhack and H.Huwig, Diagonalizations over polynomial time computable sets, Theor. Comput. Sci. 51 (1987) 177-204.

3a K.Ambos-Spies, H.Fleischhack and H.Huwig, Diagonalizations over polynomial time computable sets, Tech. Rep. 177 (1984), Dept. Comput. Sci., Universität Dortmund.

4 J.Balcazar, Self-reducibility, Proc. STACS 87, Lecture Notes Comput. Sci. 247 (1987) 136-147, Springer–Verlag.

5 C.H.Bennett and J.Gill, Relative to a random oracle A, $P^A \neq NP^A \neq co\text{-}NP^A$ with probability 1, SIAM J. Comput. 10 (1981) 96-113.

6 H.Fleischhack, On diagonalizations over complexity classes, Tech. Rep. 210 (1985), Dept. Comput. Sci., Universität Dortmund.

7 H.Fleischhack, P-genericity and strong P-genericity, Proc. MFCS 1986, Lecture Notes Comput. Sci. 233 (1986) 341-349, Springer–Verlag.

8 W.Gasarch and S.Homer, Relativizations comparing NP and exponential time, Inform. Control 58 (1983) 88-100.

9 S.Homer and T.J.Long, Honest polynomial degrees and P=?NP, Theor. Comput. Sci. (to appear).

10 S.Homer and W.Maass, Oracle dependent properties of the lattice of NP-sets, Theor. Comput. Sci. 24 (1983) 279-289.

11 M.Lerman, Degrees of Unsolvability, Springer–Verlag, 1983.

12 U.Schöning, A uniform aproach to obtain diagonal sets in complexity classes, Theor. Comput. Sci 18 (1982) 95-103.

13 R.I.Soare, Recursively enumerable sets and degrees, Springer–Verlag, 1987.

Resolution with Feature Unification

K. H. Bläsius, U. Hedtstück

IBM Deutschland GmbH
WT LILOG / Abt. 3504
Postfach 80 08 80
D-7000 Stuttgart 80
Fed. Rep. of Germany

Abstract

A resolution based proof procedure for order-sorted predicate logic is presented where sorts are represented by feature terms. Term unification is extended by feature unification. Soundness and completeness of the calculus presented are reduced to the soundness and completeness results for an order-sorted predicate calculus with a fixed sort lattice containing primitive sorts only.

1. Introduction

Deduction systems are main components of many AI-systems. They are, for example, used to ensure consistency of knowledge bases, to answer questions to expert systems, or to resolve ambiguity in natural language understanding. Since deduction components are called frequently, they must solve subproblems very fast. Furthermore proofs should be short and easy to understand, in order to be able to check the proofs and to construct an explanation.

Order-sorted logic as presented in [Walther 1987] or [Schmidt-Schauss 1988] meets these requirements in a better way compared to ordinary predicate logic, and is therefore applied in theorem proving [Karl Mark 1984] or natural language understanding [Rollinger et al. 1987]. The main advantages of order-sorted logic are more natural and shorter proofs and smaller search spaces.

However, the calculi developed so far for order-sorted logic also have some disadvantages: a fixed set of sorts and subsort relations is necessary and must be present at the beginning of a proof. It is not possible to dynamically create new sorts during the proof. This is an essential weakness of an order-sorted calculus if used in expert or natural language systems. In such applications a huge set of sorts and subsort relations is required to represent concepts and reference objects, for example. Especially in natural language understanding systems such concepts are sometimes computed from the given text, possibly by resolving ambiguities. Using deduction systems to solve ambiguity or anaphora problems the dynamic creation of new sorts and subsort relations would be necessary.

A way out is the use of feature terms and feature unification developed for knowledge representation [Aït-Kaçi 1984] and linguistic processing in the field of computational linguistics (see, e.g., [Kasper/Rounds 1986], [Johnson 1987]). In formalisms like unification grammars [Shieber 1986] feature terms are used in natural language understanding to represent sorts, attributed objects, lexical entries, grammar rules or axioms, and to describe complex objects like sentences: feature terms which represent single words and grammar rules are successively merged by feature unification resulting in a single feature term which represents the whole sentence.

Feature unification may also be used in order-sorted calculi to avoid the disadvantages mentioned above. In order-sorted calculi the unification of terms has to be modified: a GLB (greatest lower bound) - that is the greatest common subsort - of sorts has to be computed. If a fixed set of sorts and subsort relations forming a sort-lattice is used, then the GLB is to be searched for in this sort lattice [Walther 1987].

For feature terms representing sorts, a feature unification algorithm computes the GLB, which represents a new sort, not necessarily predefined. Hence new sorts and the respective subsort relations are dynamically constructed guided by unification. Only a basic set of sorts (primitive sorts) with their subsort relations and a set of features are necessary. Similar to the construction of terms from constants, functions and variables, sorts may be constructed using primitive sorts and features.

The main benefit of using feature terms to represent sorts are more adequate knowledge representations and more efficient inferencing.

Feature terms and unification are also used in the LILOG project of IBM Germany concerning the development of linguistic and logical methods for natural language understanding [Herzog et al. 1986], [Rollinger et al. 1987]. An essential concept for the linguistic processing parts in LILOG are STUF-graphs (Stuttgart Type Unification Formalism) [Uszkoreit 1988], which are rooted directed acyclic graphs and are similar to the feature terms. In the LILOG project the advantages of feature terms to represent sorts are exploited yielding a more powerful calculus for order-sorted predicate logic. It is based on the concepts realized in the knowledge representation language L_{LILOG} [Beierle et al. 1988], a decidable feature logic presented in [Smolka 1988] and an extension of these concepts to predicate logic, as presented in this paper. However, in this paper we do not use the full power of feature logic as proposed for example in [Smolka 1988].

2. Feature Terms

In this section we define feature terms to be used as sorts in order-sorted predicate logic.

The set of all feature terms is determined by a feature term signature $\$ = (S,F)$, which consists of a set S of primitive sorts (also called type symbols), and a set F of features (also called attribute labels). We suppose that the two sets are pairwise disjoint and that on S there is defined a subsort relation, which makes S a partial ordering. In addition, let S have a greatest element, called TOP, and a least element, called BOTTOM.

Definition.

A feature term is defined as follows:

if s is a primitive sort, $f_1, \ldots, f_n$ are pairwise distinct features ($n \geq 0$), $t_1, \ldots, t_n$ are feature terms and s, $t_1, \ldots, t_n$ are different from BOTTOM, then $[s, f_1 => t_1, \ldots, f_n => t_n]$ is a feature term.

For feature terms consisting only of a primitive sort, the square brackets are often omitted, i.e. we write s instead of [s].

The following example represents the set of all persons having an id, which is a name, consisting of a first name and a last name, and having a father, who also is a person, having an id, which is a name and consists of at least a last name. Both first and last names are strings.

Example.

[PERSON , id=>[NAME , first=>STRING , last=> STRING] ,
father=>[PERSON , id=>[NAME , last=>STRING]]]

Since feature terms will be used as sorts the subsort relation postulated for the set of primitive sorts is to be extended to a subsort relation on arbitrary feature terms:

Definition.

For a given feature term signature $\$ = (S,F)$, let $T_\$$ be the set of all feature terms over $\$$, and let $\leq$ be the subsort relation on S. We extend $\leq$ to a partial ordering $\leq$ on $T_\$$, also called subsort relation (or subsumption relation), in the following way:

Let t_1, t_2 be feature terms with $t_1 = [s_1, f_{11} => t_{11}, \ldots, f_{1n} => t_{1n}]$, and $t_2 = [s_2, f_{21} => t_{21}, \ldots, f_{2m} => t_{2m}]$, $(n,m \geq 0)$.

$t_1 \leq t_2$ iff

(1) $s_1 \leq s_2$

(2) $\{f_{11}, \ldots, f_{1n}\} \supseteq \{f_{21}, \ldots, f_{2m}\}$

(3) $f_{1j} = f_{2i}$ implies $t_{1j} \leq t_{2i}$, for $1 \leq i \leq n$, $1 \leq j \leq m$.

BOTTOM $\leq t_1 \leq$ TOP

We say, t_1 is a subsort of t_2 (or t_1 is subsumed by t_2), if $t_1 \leq t_2$. BOTTOM and TOP are the least and the greatest elements in $T_\$$, respectively.

<u>Example (taken from [Aït-Kaçi/Nasr 1986]).</u>

Let STUDENT $\leq$ PERSON, AUSTIN $\leq$ CITYNAME.

Then $t_1 \leq t_2$, for the two feature terms

```
t1 = [STUDENT, id=>[NAME , first=>STRING , last=> STRING] ,
        lives_at=>[ADDRESS , city=>AUSTIN] ,
        father=>[PERSON, id=>[NAME , last=>STRING] ,
                         lives_at=>AUSTIN]]

t2 = [PERSON , id=>[NAME , last=>STRING] ,
        lives_at=>[ADDRESS , city=>CITYNAME] ,
        father=>[PERSON, id=>[NAME , last=>STRING]]
```

In [Aït-Kaçi 1984] it is shown, that if in a feature term signature $\$ = (S,F)$, S is a lower semi-lattice with respect to the subsort relation, then the partial ordering on the set of all feature terms over \$, given by the induced subsort relation, is also a lower semi-lattice, denoted as $S_{\leq}$. In particular, this means, that for any pair of feature terms a greatest lower bound with respect to the subsort relation exists.

Since feature terms are only used as sorts for an order-sorted predicate logic, the semantics of feature terms is given by the subsort relation defined above and an ordinary semantics for sorts in order-sorted logic (usually interpreted as sets).

3. Feature Unification

In this section an algorithm to unify feature terms is given by the definition of a function unifyft (unify feature terms). This function computes the greatest lower bound of sorts represented by feature terms. Other algorithms for feature unification may be found, for example, in [Beierle/Pletat 1988] and [Aït-Kaçi/Nasr 1986].

We presuppose a function glb computing the greatest lower bound for primitive sorts (see [Walther 1987]).

<u>Definition.</u>

1. if s_1 and s_2 are primitive sorts, then $\text{unifyft}(s_1, s_2) = \text{glb}(s_1, s_2)$

2. $\text{unifyft}([s_1, f_1 => t_1, \ldots, f_i => t_i, \ldots, f_n => t_n], [s_2, f_i => t_{n+1}])$

$$= \begin{cases} \text{BOTTOM} & \text{if } \text{glb}(s_1, s_2) = \text{BOTTOM} \\ & \text{or } \text{unifyft}(t_i, t_{n+1}) = \text{BOTTOM} \\ [\text{glb}(s_1, s_2), f_1 => t_1, \ldots, f_i => \text{unifyft}(t_i, t_{n+1}), \ldots, f_n => t_n] & \\ \quad \text{otherwise} & \end{cases}$$

3. if f_{n+1} is different from f_i for $i = 1 \ldots n$ then

$\text{unifyft}([s_1, f_1 => t_1, \ldots, f_n => t_n], [s_2, f_{n+1} => t_{n+1}])$

$$= \begin{cases} \text{BOTTOM} & \text{if } \text{glb}(s_1, s_2) = \text{BOTTOM} \\ [\text{glb}(s_1, s_2), f_1 => t_1, \ldots, f_n => t_n, f_{n+1} => t_{n+1}] & \text{otherwise} \end{cases}$$

4. $\text{unifyft}(t', [s, f_1 => t_1, \ldots, f_n => t_n]) =$
$\text{unifyft}(\text{unifyft}(t', [s, f_1 => t_1]), [\text{TOP}, f_2 => t_2, \ldots, f_n => t_n])$

5. $\text{unifyft}(t', \text{BOTTOM}) = \text{unifyft}(\text{BOTTOM}, t') = \text{BOTTOM}$

The following theorem states that unifyft just computes the greatest lower bound of sorts, if the set of primitive sorts S with the subsort relation $\leq$ is a lower semi-lattice. For a more general case, a proof may be found in [Aït-Kaçi, 1984].

Theorem.

let $S_{\leq}$ be a lower semi lattice, and let $t = unifyft(t', t'')$ then

a) $t \leq t'$ and $t \leq t''$
b) $t''' \leq t'$ and $t''' \leq t''$ implies $t''' \leq t$

Proof.

a) the validity of the theorem is shown by induction on the definition of unifyft. The notation within the proof refers to the definition of unifyft and to the convention that the first argument of unifyft is abbreviated by t′, the second by t″ and the result by t.

1. trivial, since the glb of two primitive sorts returns the greatest common subsort
2. If $t = BOTTOM$ then $t \leq t'$ and $t \leq t''$
   else we have $glb(s_1, s_2) \leq s_1$, $\{f_1, ..., f_i, ..., f_n\} = \{f_1, ..., f_i, ..., f_n\}$,
   and we assume inductively that $unifyft(t_i, t_{n+1}) \leq t_i$,
   hence with the definition of the subsort relation we have $t \leq t'$.
   With $glb(s_1, s_2) \leq s_2$, $\{f_i\} \subseteq \{f_1, ..., f_i, ..., f_n\}$,
   and the inductive assumption that $unifyft(t_i, t_{n+1}) \leq t_{n+1}$,
   we have $t \leq t''$
3. analogous to 2
4. inductively we can assume:
   $t = unifyft(\, unifyft(t', [s, f_1 => t_1]), [TOP, f_2 => t_2, ..., f_n => t_n])$
   $\leq unifyft(t', [s, f_1 => t_1]) \leq t'$.
   We also have $t \leq [TOP, f_2 => t_2, ..., f_n => t_n]$
   and $t \leq [s, f_1 => t_1]$
   hence $t \leq t'' = [s, f_1 => t_1, ..., f_n => t_n]$
5. trivial, since $BOTTOM \leq BOTTOM$ and $BOTTOM \leq t'$

b) let $t = [s, f_1 => t_1, ..., f_m => t_m]$
   $t' = [s', f'_1 => t'_1, ..., f'_k => t'_k]$,
   $t'' = [s'', f''_1 => t''_1, ..., f''_l => t''_l]$ and
   $t''' = [s''', f'''_1 => t'''_1, ..., f'''_n => t'''_n]$
   suppose we have $t''' \leq t'$ and $t''' \leq t''$
   hence we also have $s''' \leq s'$ and $s''' \leq s''$
   From the definition of feature unification we can infer that $s = glb(s', s'')$.
   Since the glb computes just the greatest lower bound of two primitive sorts, we have $s''' \leq s$.
   With the definition of $\leq$ we know:
   $\{f'_1, ..., f'_k\} \subseteq \{f'''_1, ..., f'''_n\}$ and $\{f''_1, ..., f''_l\} \subseteq \{f'''_1, ..., f'''_n\}$.

We can infer by induction over the definition of feature unification, that $\{f_1, \dots, f_m\} \subseteq \{f'_1, \dots, f'_k\} \cup \{f''_1, \dots, f''_l\}$.
Hence we also have $\{f_1, \dots, f_m\} \subseteq \{f'''_1, \dots, f'''_n\}$.
For $f_i = f'''_j$, $1 \leq i \leq m$ and $1 \leq j \leq n$ we can show by induction that t_i is the result of feature unification, hence we can inductively assume that $t'''_j \leq t_i$
With the definition of $\leq$ we now have $t''' \leq t$.

4. Resolution Calculus

Let OSR (order-sorted resolution) be a resolution calculus for order-sorted predicate logic based on a fixed set of primitive sorts S, a subsort relation on the set of primitive sorts $\leq$, such that $S_{\leq}$ is a lower semi-lattice, and a function glb called from term unification to compute the greatest lower bound of sorts (which is not unitary, if the subsort relation doesn't form a lower semi-lattice). Such a calculus is for example given in [Walther 1987].

Definition.

We define an FOSR-calculus for order-sorted predicate logic using feature terms as sorts instead of primitive sorts only and the subsort relation defined in section two. Furthermore in the FOSR the function glb is replaced by the function unifyft, defined in the previous section.

Theorem.

The soundness and completeness results for OSR are also valid for FOSR.

Proof.

In section three we have proven that unifyft just computes the greatest lower bound of two feature terms. Hence the set of all feature terms together with the subsort relation may be regarded as fixed set of primitive sorts with subsort relation for the calculus OSR, where unifyft takes the role of glb, computing just the greatest lower bound for the supposed fixed set of sorts. Hence the soundness and completeness results for OSR are valid.

5. Outlook

During the implementation of the first LILOG-prototype we made the experience that the inference mechine based on order-sorted logic produced very short proofs for our test examples. However, on the other hand we also made the experience, that even in a very restricted application area a large amount of sorts is required for the representation of a natural language text and background knowledge. Our approach of an order-sorted logic, allowing for the dynamical introduction of new sorts, based on feature unification, now meets the demands from the linguists and knowledge engineers for a more powerful representation formalism. The use of feature terms gives us more expressive power for the representation of sorts.

Currently in the LILOG project, several extensions of the concept considered in this paper are being worked out. In [Smolka 88] disjunction and complement operations for feature terms are introduced. Disjunctive feature terms allow for the representation of vague sort information and complements of feature terms give us the possibility to exclude certain sort informations. Further extensions concern the possibility to express if two sorts are disjoint or not and to allow for informations about the features, like partialness or totalness.

The concept of feature terms presented here is also extended by a concept to express relations between subterms. This is done by coreference markers or variables for subterms (see, for example [Aït-Kaçi 1984], [Beierle/Pletat 1988], or [Smolka 1988]). In fact coreference markers are constraints concerning different features of one sort. They are used to specify the equality of the values for certain features occurring in the feature term. The definition of feature terms might be extended to also allow the specification of other constraints, for example given by ordering relations or arbitrary logical formulae. However, an efficient constraint solver would be required, or in case the logic used to formulate constraints is undecidable, a certain kind of partial unification and rather complicated control mechanisms are required.

In the LILOG project the concept of feature structures has been integrated as the "order-sorted part" into the knowledge representation language L_{LILOG}, which is based on order-sorted first order predicate logic [Beierle et al. 1988]. The feature unification based resolution mechanism discussed in this paper forms the basis for the development of a deduction system for L_{LILOG}.

Acknowledgements

We would like to thank Christoph Beierle, Günther Görz, Gert Smolka and Birgit Wesche for their valuable suggestions and comments.

References

[Aït-Kaçi 1984] Aït-Kaçi, H., A Lattice-Theoretic Approach to Computation Based on a Calculus of Partially-Ordered Type Structures, Ph.D. Thesis, Computer and Information Science, Univ. of Pennsylvania, Philadelphia, 1984.

[Aït-Kaçi/Nasr 1986] Aït-Kaçi, H., Nasr, R., LOGIN: A Logic Programming Language with Built-In Inheritance, J. Logic Programming 3, 1986, 185-215.

[Beierle et al. 1988] Beierle, C., Dörre, J., Pletat, U., Schmitt, P. H., Studer, R., The Knowledge Representation Language L_{LILOG}, LILOG-Report 41, IBM Germany, Stuttgart, 1988.

[Beierle/Pletat 1988] Beierle, C., Pletat, U., Feature Graphs and Abstract Data Types: A Unifiying Approach, LILOG Report 39, IBM Germany, Stuttgart, 1988. To appear in: Proc. COLING '88, Budapest, 1988.

[Herzog et al. 1986] Herzog, O., et al., LILOG-Linguistic and Logic Methods for the Computational Understanding of German, LILOG-Report 1b, IBM Germany,Stuttgart, 1986.

[Johnson 1987] Johnson, M.E., Attribute-Value Logic and the Theory of Grammar, PhD Dissertation, Stanford University, 1987. To appear as CSLI Lecture Notes.

[Karl Mark 1984] Karl Mark G. Raph: The Markgraf Karl Refutation Procedure, Internal Report, Memo-Seki-MK-84-01, Fachbereich Informatik, Universität Kaiserslautern, 1984.

[Kasper/Rounds 1986] Kasper, R.T., Rounds, W.C., A logical Semantics for Feature Structures, Proc. of the 24th Annual Meeting of the Association of Computational Linguistics, Columbia University, New York, 1986, 257-265.

[Rollinger et al. 1987] Rollinger, C. R., Studer, R., Uszkoreit, H., Wachsmuth, I., Textunderstanding in LILOG - Sorts and Reference Objects, Proc. 2. Internationaler GI-Kongreß in München, Informatik-Fachberichte 155, Springer-Verlag, Heidelberg et al.,1987.

[Schmidt-Schauss 1988] Schmidt-Schauss, M., Computational Aspects of an Order-Sorted Logic with Term Declaration, Dissertation, University of Kaiserslautern, 1988.

[Shieber 1986] Shieber, S. M., An Introduction to Unification-Based Approaches to Grammar, CSLI Lecture Notes 4, Stanford University, California, 1986.

[Smolka 1988] Smolka, G., A Feature Logic with Subsorts, LILOG-Report 33, IBM Germany, Stuttgart, 1988 .

[Uszkoreit 1987] Uszkoreit, H., STUF: A Description of the Stuttgart Type Unification Formalism, LILOG-Report 16, IBM Germany, Stuttgart, 1987.

[Walther 1987] Walther, C., A Many-Sorted Calculus Based on Resolution and Paramodulation, in Research Notes in Artificial Intelligence, Pitman, London, and Morgan Kaufmann, Los Altos, Calif., 1987.

SURJECTIVITY FOR FINITE SETS OF COMBINATORS BY WEAK REDUCTION[1]

Corrado Böhm and Adolfo Piperno[2]

Dipartimento di Matematica
Istituto "G. Castelnuovo"
Università degli Studi di Roma "La Sapienza"
P.le Aldo Moro 5 , I-00185 ROMA

ABSTRACT

A set $\mathbf{F} \equiv \{F_1,\dots,F_t\}$ of closed λ-terms in β-η-normal form (combinators) is s-t-*surjective* iff the system of equations $F_i X_1 \dots X_s = y_i$ (i=1,...,t), where the y_i's are arbitrary variables, is solvable using only weak (β) reduction. It is well known that $\mathbf{F}$ is s-t surjective if s is sufficiently large.
In this paper sufficient conditions are given for the s-t-surjectivity of $\mathbf{F}$ if s=n, where n is the maximum number of initial abstractions among its elements. An interesting consequence is that $\mathbf{F}$ is unconditionally (n+1)-t-surjective. Another technical result which revealed itself useful for the proof of the main theorem is: if every element of $\mathbf{F}$ has the same number n of initial abstractions, then there are ∞^n ways of finding a set $\mathbf{L} \equiv \{L_1,\dots,L_t\}$ of combinators such that, for i=1,...,t and any given λ-terms $Y_1,\dots,Y_t$, $F_i X_1 \dots X_n = Y_i$ is solvable $\Leftrightarrow$ $L_i X = Y_i$ is solvable.

KEYWORDS: Pure λ-calculus, combinatory algebras, surjectivity, discriminability or X-separability in λ-(β)-calculus.

0. MOTIVATION AND SUMMARY

Combinatory Logic, from the point of view of Computer Science, may be considered as a typeless and pure functional programming language, whose semantics is an algebra (of programs) based on the domain equation $D = D \to D$.
Our main interest, as in [BD 74], is to solve systems of combinatory equations having the shape

$$(0.1) \qquad F_i X_1 \dots X_n = H_i \quad (i=1,\dots,t)$$

where $\mathbf{F} \equiv \{\mathbf{F}_1,\dots,\mathbf{F}_t\}$ is a set of normal combinators (closed λ-terms in β-η-normal form) and $H_1,\dots,H_t$ are *given* combinatory obs (λ-terms) [CuF 58].
Following Statman[3] the solvability of (0.1) is undecidable even in the case n = t = 1, i.e.

$$(0.2) \qquad \mathbf{F} X = H$$

(1) This research has been supported by grants of Ministero della Pubblica Istruzione, Italia.

(2) PhD student in Computer Science.

(3) Private communication.

where we require that both X and H be in normal form.

We are then led to study a property stronger than solvability of (0.1-2). We would like to require an *unconditional* solvability of equations or systems of equations.

For example, in the case of (0.2), we may ask if the combinator **F** is *surjective* on Λ.(4)

Such a problem has been proved solvable in [BD 74] using weak reduction (following [Hin 77] and [Hin 79] this corresponds to reduce **F** X by a head β-reduction(5)).

We try here to extend the definition of surjectivity from a combinator **F** to a set

$$\mathbf{F} \equiv \{\mathbf{F}_1,\ldots,\mathbf{F}_t\} \subset \Lambda^0 N^{(6)}.$$

Since combinators may also be viewed as closed λ-terms, like

$$\mathbf{I} \equiv \lambda x.x \quad , \quad \mathbf{K} \equiv \lambda xy.x \quad , \quad \mathbf{S} \equiv \lambda xyz.xz(yz)$$

a *naive* type assignement would be $\mathbf{I}: \Lambda \rightarrow \Lambda$, $\mathbf{K}: \Lambda\times\Lambda \rightarrow \Lambda$, $\mathbf{S}: \Lambda\times\Lambda\times\Lambda \rightarrow \Lambda$, i.e. we may identify every combinator with a (possibly multidimensional) mapping on Λ. This identification is naive for two reasons:

i) It ignores the λ-K-calculus, where you may abstract variables not occurring in the body of a term.

ii) It ignores the fact that a combinator may be applied to any number of arguments.

A theorem based on the last property is Böhm's theorem [Böh 68] treating the discriminability of a pair of non convertible λ-terms and its extension to a finite set [BDPR 79], here resumed as:

<u>0.3. BASIC THEOREM</u> Given a finite set $\mathbf{F} \equiv \{\mathbf{F}_1,\ldots,\mathbf{F}_t\} \subset \Lambda^0 N$ and a t-tuple of variables $y_1,\ldots,y_t$, there exist $s > 0$ and a Church s-tuple of terms $< X_1,\ldots,X_s >$ such that

$$(0.3.1) \qquad < X_1,\ldots,X_s > \mathbf{F}_i = \mathbf{F}_i X_1 \ldots X_s = y_i \quad (i=1,\ldots,t)^{(7)}. \qquad \square$$

We gain a better insight into the meaning of the Basic Theorem if we look at $\mathbf{F}_1,\ldots,\mathbf{F}_t$ as a sequence(8) defining a mapping $\mathbf{F}: \Lambda^s \rightarrow \Lambda^t$ (called here for brevity *s-t-mapping*). Under this interpretation the theorem means simply:

Every finite set of t combinators corresponds to a *surjective* s-t-mapping, if we choose s large enough.

Since s must not be less than the maximum number n of initial abstractions among the elements of **F**, an interesting question (certainly not naive) is the relationship between n and s .

---

(4) Λ will denote the set of λ-terms.

(5) The question of the surjectivity for a combinator as a mapping on the domain Λ^0 of closed λ-terms is still open even allowing only β-reduction.

(6) $\Lambda^0 N$ will denote the set of closed λ-terms in β-η-normal form.

(7) The reductions here are again head β-reductions [Hin 79].

(8) By "abus de langage" we will denote this sequence by an indexed set.

Let $\mathbf{F} \equiv \{\mathbf{F}_1,\ldots,\mathbf{F}_t\} \subset \Lambda^0 N_{\le n}$[9] and the number of initial abstractions of $\mathbf{F}_i$ be n_i $(i=1,\ldots,t)$, with $n = \max\{n_i\}$. Then it is meaningful to ask if the system

(0.3.2) $\quad \mathbf{F}_i X_1 \ldots X_{n_i} = y_i \quad (i=1,\ldots,t)$

is solvable.

There are two different ways to transform a set of combinators, whose maximum number of initial abstractions is n, into a set of combinators each of which has the same number n of initial abstractions (we are obliged to proceed in this way, in order to preserve the notion of n-t-surjectivity). These two ways correspond exactly to remarks 0.i) and 0.ii).

The first way is to add the lacking number of abstractions, to the right of the current abstractions, to each needy element of **F**; **F** will be transformed into a different **F'** but the possible solutions $X_1,\ldots,X_n$ of (0.3.2) will be preserved.

The second way is to add the lacking number of abstractions to each needy element of **F** by η-expanding it the suitable number of times and obtaining a new set **F''** of combinators. The elements of **F''** are convertible to the old ones, but they are no more in η-normal form. This is equivalent to asking whether the system (0.1) would be solvable for **F** for *any* H_i with $s = n$, or whether the Basic Theorem (corresponding to the system (0.3.1)) would hold with $s = n$.

This paper gives the following answer to this question:

<u>0.4. MAIN COROLLARY</u> (see Section 3)

Let $\mathbf{F} \equiv \{\mathbf{F}_1,\ldots,\mathbf{F}_t\} \subset \Lambda^0 N_{\le n}$ and let n be the maximum number of initial abstractions. Then the Basic Theorem holds with $s = n + 1$.

In other words the given set **F** corresponds to a surjective n+1-t-mapping. ❏

The <u>Main Theorem</u> of this paper constructively characterizes a subset of the class of all **F** corresponding to surjective n-t-mappings.

Obviously each combinator is n-1-surjective (singleton case).

This paper is in some respects a restriction and in some others an extension of [BT 87], where a subset $\Lambda_{X,e,m}$ of Λ was characterized for X-separability, essentially the same notion as surjectivity. The following example, quoted from the just mentioned paper, lies in the intersection of the two sets and has two features:

i) it exhibits a surjective 1-2-mapping, which is an example of the main theorem;

ii) it may be viewed as an example of self-discrimination, a case not directly treatable by the Basic Theorem.

---

(9) $\Lambda^0 N_{\le n} \subset \Lambda^0 N$ and $\mathbf{G} \in \Lambda^0 N_{\le n}$ implies that the number of initial abstractions of $\mathbf{G}$ is $\le n$.

0.5. EXAMPLE

$\mathbf{F}_1 \equiv \lambda x.xx$, $\mathbf{F}_2 \equiv \lambda x.x\mathbf{F}_1$. We ask for Δ s.t. $\Delta\Delta = y_1$, $\Delta\lambda t.tt = y_2$ ❑

Many restrictions are eliminated in [BP 88] which extends the present paper and contains also the characterization of right- and left-invertibility of the combinatory n-t-mappings.

0.6. SUMMARY

Section 1 contains the reduction of any finite system of combinatory equations to a standard form. First, the number of initial abstractions is equalized to n. Secondly, the combinators are replaced by λ-free terms. Thirdly, the number of the unknown terms is reduced to one, without losing the possibility to recover their value, after the resolution of the system of equations.

Section 2 contains the proof of the Main Theorem, whereas the more technical developments are deferred to the Appendix.

The Main Corollary, a refinement of the Basic Theorem, is stated and proved in Section 3 and in Section 4 there are some concluding remarks. ❑

1. SOME STANDARDIZATIONS

1.0. FORCING TO n THE DIMENSION OF THE DOMAIN

In Section 0 we introduced two ways, reached without loss of generality and explained in great details, of forcing to n the dimension of the domain.

Let $\mathbf{F} \equiv \{\mathbf{F}_1,\dots,\mathbf{F}_t\} \subset \Lambda^0 N_n$ (10) be a given set of combinators and let $y_1,\dots,y_t$ be a given t-tuple of variables. In the case that the variables are all different we search sufficient conditions for the surjectivity of the n-t-mapping represented by the set $\mathbf{F}$, i.e. for the solvability of the following system of equations:

$$(1.0.1) \qquad \mathbf{F}_i X_1 \dots X_n = y_i \quad (i = 1,\dots,t).$$ ❑

1.1. REDUCING COMBINATORS TO λ-FREE TERMS

Our aim is to simplify the proofs of the propositions stated in the next two Sections. The choice between the two ways of reaching the elements of $\Lambda^0 N_n$ is rendered implicit if we consider the bijection between $\Lambda^0 N_{\le n}$ and $\Lambda^{\le n} N$, the set of λ-free terms whose number of free variables is $\le n$. In fact, remembering (0.3.2) we have

$$\mathbf{F}_i \in \Lambda^0 N_{\le n} \Leftrightarrow \Lambda^{\le n} N \ni \mathbf{F}_i\, x_1 \dots x_{n_i} \equiv F_i$$

and we may start from a set $F \subset \Lambda^{\le n} N$ instead of $\mathbf{F} \subset \Lambda^0 N_{\le n}$. ❑

(10) $\Lambda^0 N_n \subset \Lambda^0 N_{\le n}$ and every $\mathbf{G} \in \Lambda^0 N_n$ has the same number n of initial abstractions.

1.2. Reducing To One The Dimension Of The Domain

Another way to look at the Basic Theorem is to consider

$$\mathbf{F}^* \equiv \{\lambda x.x\mathbf{F}_1,\ldots,\lambda x.x\mathbf{F}_t\}$$

instead of **F** and to use the solution $<X_1,\ldots,X_s>$ to prove the surjectivity of the 1-t-mapping induced by $\mathbf{F}^*$. This leads us to formulate the following

1.2.0. LEMMA (reduction of n-t-mappings to 1-t-mappings)

Let $\mathbf{G} \equiv \{\mathbf{G}_1,\ldots,\mathbf{G}_n\} \subset \Lambda^0 N$ and $\mathbf{F} \equiv \{\mathbf{F}_1,\ldots,\mathbf{F}_t\} \subset \Lambda^0 N_n$

Then there exists $\mathbf{L} \equiv \{\mathbf{L}_1,\ldots,\mathbf{L}_t\} \subset \Lambda^0 N_1$ such that

F induces a surjective n-t-mapping ⇔ **L** induces a surjective 1-t-mapping. ❑

PROOF:

⇒

"**F** induces a surjective n-t-mapping" implies the existence of terms X_j's (j=1,...,n) such that

$$(1.0.1) \qquad \mathbf{F}_i\, X_1\ldots X_n = y_i \quad (i=1,\ldots,t).$$

Moreover, by the Basic Theorem, there exists a Church s-tuple

$$X^\# \equiv <\mathbf{H}_1 x_1\ldots x_n,\ldots,\mathbf{H}_s\, x_1\ldots x_n>,$$

where $\mathbf{H}_1,\ldots,\mathbf{H}_s$ are combinators, such that

$$(1.2.1) \qquad (\lambda x.\, x\mathbf{G}_j)\, X^\# = x_j \quad (j=1,\ldots,n).$$

It follows that, in particular, there exists a Church s-tuple

$$X \equiv <\mathbf{H}_1 X_1\ldots X_n,\ldots,\mathbf{H}_s\, X_1\ldots X_n>$$

satisfying

$$(1.2.2) \qquad (\lambda x.\, x\mathbf{G}_j)\, X = X_j \quad (j=1,\ldots,n).$$

Let now $\mathbf{L} \equiv \{\mathbf{L}_1,\ldots,\mathbf{L}_t\} \subset \Lambda^0 N_1$ be defined by

$$(1.2.3) \qquad \mathbf{L}_i \equiv \lambda x.\mathbf{F}_i\, (x\mathbf{G}_1)\ldots(x\mathbf{G}_n) \qquad (i=1,\ldots,t).$$

We have then $\mathbf{L}_i X = \mathbf{F}_i\, (X\mathbf{G}_1)\ldots(X\mathbf{G}_n) = \mathbf{F}_i\, X_1\ldots X_n = y_i \quad (i=1,\ldots,t),$

i.e. **L** induces a surjective 1-t-mapping. ⇒❑

⇐

If **L** induces a surjective 1-t-mapping then there exists a term X such that

$$\mathbf{L}_i\, X = y_i \quad (i=1,\ldots,t),$$

i.e., by definition of **L**,

$$\mathbf{F}_i\, (X\mathbf{G}_1)\ldots(X\mathbf{G}_n) = y_i \quad (i=1,\ldots,t).$$

Defining

$$X_j \equiv X\mathbf{G}_j \qquad (j=1,\ldots,n)$$

we deduce

$$\mathbf{F}_i\, X_1\ldots X_n = y_i \qquad (i=1,\ldots,t),$$

i.e. **F** induces a surjective n-t-mapping. ⇐❑

We proved indeed a stronger

<u>1.2.4. THEOREM</u> (on solvability of equations)

Let $\mathbf{F} \equiv \{\mathbf{F}_1,\ldots,\mathbf{F}_t\} \subset \Lambda^0 N_n$ and let $Y_1,\ldots,Y_t \in \Lambda$ be given terms.
Then there exist ∞^n ways to associate to $\mathbf{F}$ a set $\mathbf{L} \equiv \{\mathbf{L}_1,\ldots,\mathbf{L}_t\} \subset \Lambda^0 N_1$ such that for i=1,...,t

$$\mathbf{F}_i\, X_1 \ldots X_n = Y_i \text{ is solvable} \iff \mathbf{L}_i\, X = Y_i \text{ is solvable.}$$ ❑

<u>1.2.5. EXAMPLE</u>

$\mathbf{F}_1 : \lambda x_1 x_2 . x_1 \mathbf{I}(\lambda z. z(x_1 \mathbf{II}))$ $\quad$ $\mathbf{L}_1 : \lambda x. x\mathbf{II}(\lambda z. z(x\mathbf{III}))$

$\mathbf{F}_2 : \lambda x_1 x_2 . x_2 \mathbf{I}(\lambda z. z(x_1 \mathbf{II}))$ $\quad$ $\mathbf{L}_2 : \lambda x. x\mathbf{KI}(\lambda z. z(x\mathbf{III}))$

$\mathbf{F}_3 : \lambda x_1 x_2 . x_2 \mathbf{I}(x_2 \mathbf{KI})$ $\quad$ $\mathbf{L}_3 : \lambda x. x\mathbf{KI}(x\mathbf{KKI})$ ❑

<u>1.2.6. REMARK</u> (preconditioning a 1-t-mapping)

An obvious consequence of the reduction of the domain to one dimension is that each occurrence of x in any subterm belonging to elements of **F'** has a combinator as first son in the Böhm tree representation(11).

If this feature does not hold inside a set $\mathbf{F} \subset \Lambda^0 N_1$, we will define

$$\mathbf{F}'_i \equiv \lambda x . [x\mathbf{I}/x]\,\mathbf{F}_i x \quad (i=1,\ldots,t)\text{ , where } \mathbf{I} \equiv \lambda u.u\ .$$ ❑

<u>1.2.7. EXAMPLE</u> (0.5 continued)

$\mathbf{F}'_1 \equiv x\mathbf{I}(x\mathbf{I})$, $\mathbf{F}'_2 \equiv x\mathbf{I}\,\lambda u.uu$ ❑

<u>1.3. COMBINING THE THREE STANDARDIZATIONS TOGETHER</u>

Since $\Lambda^0 N_{\leq 1}$ means $\Lambda^0 N_1$ and $\Lambda^{\leq 1} N$ means $\Lambda^1 N$, we may conclude this Section by remarking that both the problem of the n-t-surjectivity, represented by the solvability of system (1.0.1), and the solvability of the system (0.3.2) can be suitably treated if we are given a set $F \equiv \{F_1,\ldots,F_t\} \subset \Lambda^1 N$ and we ask if there exists a λ-term X such that

$$[X/x]\,F_i = y_i \quad \text{and } x \neq y_i \quad (i=1,\ldots t).$$

Since the reduction to one dimension or the preconditioning give a special shape to the elements of F we will introduce a new subset of $\Lambda^1 N$ by means of the following

<u>1.3.1. DEFINITION</u> (of $\Lambda^\# N$)

$\Lambda^\# N$ is the set of all λ-free terms in β-η-normal form having x as their only free variable and where each occurrence of x has a closed term (in β-η-normal form) as first son. ❑

(11) If $M \equiv \lambda z_1 \ldots z_n . \zeta M_1 \ldots M_m$ we define the *Böhm tree* of M

$BT(M) \equiv \lambda z_1 \ldots z_n . \zeta$

/ \

$BT(M_1) \ldots\ldots BT(M_m)$

Furthermore, we define ord(M) = n (the *order* of M), deg(M) = m (the *degree* of M) and root(M) = ζ (the *root* of M).

2. A SUFFICIENT CONDITION FOR SURJECTIVITY

2.0. DEFINITION (surjectivity in $\Lambda^{\#}N$)

Let $F \equiv \{F_1,\ldots,F_t\} \subset \Lambda^{\#}N$.

We say that F is surjective iff there exists a combinator **D** (with t initial abstractions) s.t.

$$(2.0.1) \qquad [\mathbf{D}\, y_1 \ldots y_t / x]\, F_i = y_i \quad (i \in \{1,\ldots,t\}),$$

where $y_1,\ldots,y_t$ are arbitrary variables different from x. ❑

2.1. DEFINITION (main definition: self-distinct set)

Let $F \equiv \{F_1,\ldots,F_t\} \subset \Lambda^{\#}N$.

We say that F is self-distinct iff for every $i \neq j$ ($1 \leq i,j \leq t$) F_i does not occur in F_j. ❑

2.2. EXAMPLES

Let $\mathbf{H}_1$ and $\mathbf{H}_2$ be distinct combinators.

$F_1 \equiv \{ F_{1,1}: \mathbf{xH}_1(\mathbf{xH}_1),\ F_{1,2}: \mathbf{xH}_1\ \lambda t.tt \}$ and

$F_2 \equiv \{ F_{2,1}: \mathbf{xH}_1(\mathbf{xH}_2),\ F_{2,2}: \mathbf{xH}_2\ \lambda t.t(\mathbf{xH}_1(\mathbf{xH}_1)(\mathbf{xH}_2)) \}$ are self-distinct sets, while

$F_3 \equiv \{ F_{3,1}: \mathbf{xH}_1(\mathbf{xH}_2),\ F_{3,2}: \mathbf{xH}_2(\mathbf{xH}_1(\mathbf{xH}_2)) \}$ is not self-distinct. ❑

2.3. THEOREM: (Main Theorem)

Let $F \equiv \{F_1,\ldots,F_t\} \subset \Lambda^{\#}N$ be a self-distinct set.

Then F is surjective. ❑

PROOF:

We will divide the proof in two parts:

- we will introduce a substitution for the free variable x in F, inducing a transformation over F and we will prove it to be injective and to preserve the self-distinction of the transformed set.
- this enables us to define an algorithm, which is constituted by a finite composition of such substitutions. The proof of termination of this algorithm will then achieve the proof of the theorem.

Part 1: INTRODUCING A SUBSTITUTION FOR x

We denote:

(2.3.1) $r_1 \equiv \max\{ \mathrm{ord}(T) \mid T$ is the second son of some occurrence of the free variable x in $BT(F_1),\ldots,BT(F_t) \}$.

(2.3.2) $s_1 \equiv \max\{ \deg(U) \mid U$ is some subterm of $F_1,\ldots,F_t \}$.

(2.3.3) $r = s_1 + 3r_1 + 1 \quad ; \quad s = s_1 + 2r_1 + 1$.

Let us consider the following substitution:

(2.3.4) $\quad [\lambda ab.b\mathbf{P}_{s+r+1}\ldots\mathbf{P}_{s+2r+1}\mathbf{B}_1\ldots\mathbf{B}_{s+2r}\mathbf{K}^{s+r-1}\ldots\mathbf{K}^{2(s+r-1)}E_1\ldots E_{2s+2r}ba\,/\,x\,]$ [12] [13],

with

(2.3.5) $\quad \mathbf{B}_j \equiv \lambda z_1\ldots z_{3r+2s}\,.\,z_{3r+2s}\!<\mathbf{K}^{j-1}\,\mathbf{K}^{s+2r-j+1}\,,<z_1,\ldots,z_s>>$ $(j=1,\ldots,s+2r)$

and

(2.3.6) $\quad E_h \equiv\, <A_{h,1},\ldots,A_{h,s+2r+1}>$ $(h=1,\ldots,2s+2r)$, where:

if $h = 2s-1$:

(2.3.7.1) $\quad A_{h,k} \equiv \lambda z_1\ldots z_{2r+3}\,.\,z_1\,(\,z_{2r+3}\,(\,\mathbf{K}^{s+2r+3}(\mathbf{C}_{[s]}X_{1,k}\,)\,)\ldots(\,\mathbf{K}^{s+2r+3}(\mathbf{C}_{[s]}\,X_{s+r+1,k}\,)\,)$

$\qquad (\,\mathbf{K}^{s+2r+2}(\mathbf{C}_{[s]}\,Y_{1,k}\,)\,)\ldots(\,\mathbf{K}^{s+2r+2}(\mathbf{C}_{[s]}\,Y_{r+2,k}\,)\,)\,)$ [14],

otherwise, let $h = 2s-1+p$ $(p \neq 0)$:

(2.3.7.2) $\quad A_{h,k} \equiv \lambda z_1\ldots z_{2r-p+3}\,.\,z_1\,(\mathbf{C}_{[s]}\,Z_{h,k}\,)$.

The $X_{h,k}$'s , the $Y_{h,k}$'s and the $Z_{h,k}$'s are *fresh* variables still at our disposal.

We will now distinguish 3 possible shapes for $M \in F$ showing for each of them the transformation caused by (2.3.4); we denote by M^* the term obtained from M after the substitution (2.3.4):

shape 1:[15] $\quad M_1 \equiv \mathbf{xH}_0(\lambda z_1\ldots z_u.\mathbf{xH}_1)T_2\ldots T_n$ $(u \geq 0\,,\,n \geq 1)$.

$\qquad M_1^* = Y_{u+1,s+u+1}\,\mathbf{H}_1\,\mathbf{Q}_1\ldots\mathbf{Q}_s$ [16] $\mathbf{P}_{s+r+u+2}\ldots\mathbf{P}_{s+2r+1}\mathbf{B}_1\ldots\mathbf{B}_{s+2r}$

$\qquad \mathbf{K}^{s+r-1}\ldots\mathbf{K}^{2(s+r-1)}E_1\ldots E_{2s+2r}S^*$ [17] $\mathbf{H}_0T_2^*\ldots T_n^*$.

shape 2:[18] $\quad M_2 \equiv \mathbf{xH}_0(\lambda z_1\ldots z_v\,.z_i\,G_1\ldots G_w)V_2\ldots V_m$ $(v>0\,,\,0<i\leq v\,,\,w\geq 0)$.

if $v-w \neq 0$: $\quad M_2^* = Z_{2(s+v-w)-1,s+i+v-w}\,\mathbf{H}_0G_1^*\ldots G_w^*\,\mathbf{Q}_1\ldots\mathbf{Q}_{s-w}$ [19] $V_2^*\ldots V_m^*$.

if $v-w = 0$: $\quad M_2^* = X_{i,s+i}\,\mathbf{H}_0G_1^*\ldots G_w^*\,\mathbf{Q}_1\ldots\mathbf{Q}_{s-w}\,V_2^*\ldots V_m^*$.

shape 3: $\quad M_3 \equiv \mathbf{xH}_0(\lambda z_1\ldots z_a.\mathbf{xH}_1U_2\ldots U_b)Z_2\ldots Z_c$ $(a\geq 0\,,\,b\geq 2\,,\,c\geq 1)$.

$$M_3^* = (\lambda z_1\ldots z_a.\mathbf{xH}_1U_2\ldots U_b)^*\mathbf{P}_{s+r+1}\ldots\mathbf{P}_{s+2r+1}\mathbf{B}_1\ldots\mathbf{B}_{s+2r}\mathbf{K}^{s+r-1}\ldots\mathbf{K}^{2(s+r-1)}$$
$$E_1\ldots E_{2s+2r}(\lambda z_1\ldots z_a.\mathbf{xH}_1U_2\ldots U_b)^*\mathbf{H}_0\,Z_2^*\ldots Z_c^* =$$

(2.3.8) $$= x^*\mathbf{H}_1U_2'^*\ldots U_b'^*\mathbf{P}_{s+r+a+1}\ldots\mathbf{P}_{s+2r+1}\mathbf{B}_1\ldots\mathbf{B}_{s+2r}\mathbf{K}^{s+r-1}\ldots\mathbf{K}^{2(s+r-1)}$$
$$E_1\ldots E_{2s+2r}(\lambda z_1\ldots z_a.\mathbf{xH}_1U_2\ldots U_b)^*\mathbf{H}_0\,Z_2^*\ldots Z_c^*$$

where (2.3.9) $\quad U_i' = [\,\mathbf{P}_{s+r+j}\,/\,z_j\,]\,U_i$ $(i=1,\ldots,b\,,\,j=1,\ldots,a)$,

---

(12) Recall that $\mathbf{P}_h \equiv \lambda z_1\ldots z_{h+1}\,.\,z_{h+1}\,z_1\ldots z_h$ and $\mathbf{K}^h \equiv \lambda z_1\ldots z_{h+1}\,.\,z_1$ $(h \geq 0)$.

(13) We mention a more detailed assignment for r and s (see 2.3.3):
it is possible to assign $r \equiv r_1$, $s \equiv s_1$ if the following condition holds: there does not exist a subterm N of some element of F with $N \equiv \mathbf{xH}(\lambda z_1\ldots z_s\,.\,\zeta\,M_1\ldots M_t)N_1\ldots N_u$ $(s,t,u\geq 0)$ and $\zeta \notin \{z_1,\ldots,z_s\} \cup \{x\}$.

(14) Recall [CuF] that $\mathbf{C}_{[h]} \equiv \lambda f z_1\ldots z_{h+1}.f z_{h+1}z_1\ldots z_h$. Notice that $\mathbf{C}_{[h]}\mathbf{I} = \mathbf{P}_h$.

(15) See APPENDIX.

(16) $\mathbf{Q}_1,\ldots,\mathbf{Q}_s$ are the first s elements among $\mathbf{P}_{s+r+1},\ldots,\mathbf{P}_{s+2r+1},\mathbf{B}_1,\ldots,\mathbf{B}_{s+u},\mathbf{B}_{s+u+2},\ldots,\mathbf{B}_{s+2r}$.

(17) Denote $S^* \equiv (\lambda z_1\ldots z_u ab.b\mathbf{P}_{s+r+1}\ldots\mathbf{P}_{s+2r+1}\mathbf{B}_1\ldots\mathbf{B}_{s+2r}\mathbf{K}^{s+r-1}\ldots\mathbf{K}^{2(s+r-1)}E_1\ldots E_{2s+2r}b\mathbf{H}_1)$.

(18) See APPENDIX.

(19) $\mathbf{Q}_1,\ldots,\mathbf{Q}_{s-w}$ are the first s-w elements among $\mathbf{P}_{s+r+v+1},\ldots,\mathbf{P}_{s+2r+1},\mathbf{B}_1,\ldots,\mathbf{B}_{s+i+v-w-1},\mathbf{B}_{s+i+v-w+1}\ldots\mathbf{B}_{s+2r}$.

and where in (2.3.8) $x^*\mathbf{H}_1U_2'^*\ldots U_b'^* \equiv (x\mathbf{H}_1U_2'\ldots U_b')^*$ trivially has shape 1, 2 or 3 again; it follows that the reduction of (2.3.8) goes on until a term having shape 1 or 2 is reached. This leads us to associate to every $F \in \mathcal{F}$ a minimal term in the following way:

$$\text{minterm}(F) = F_{<2>}\ ^{(20)} \qquad \text{if } F \text{ has shape 1 or 2}$$

$$\text{minterm}(F) = \text{minterm}(F_{<2>}') \qquad \text{if } F \text{ has shape 3.}$$

The substitution (2.3.4) actually divides $\mathcal{F}^*$ into the equivalence classes[21] determined by minimal terms of elements of $\mathcal{F}$, i.e. for $i,j=1,\ldots,t$ $(i \neq j)$

(2.3.10) $\quad \text{head}(F_i^*) = \text{head}(F_j^*)$ iff $\text{minterm}(F_i)$ is equivalent to $\text{minterm}(F_j)$.

Notice that the same transformations are performed over subterms of elements of $\mathcal{F}$ having the shapes described before.

We will now turn back to consider the shapes of transformed terms, in order to assign suitable terms to the fresh variables appearing in (2.3.7.1-2).

shape 1^*: $\quad M_1^* = Y_{u+1,s+u+1}\, \mathbf{H}_1\, \mathbf{Q}_1\ldots\mathbf{Q}_s\mathbf{P}_{s+r+u+2}\ldots\mathbf{P}_{s+2r+1}\mathbf{B}_1\ldots\mathbf{B}_{s+2r}$
$\mathbf{K}^{s+r-1}\ldots\mathbf{K}^{2(s+r-1)}E_1\ldots E_{2s+2r}\,S^*\,\mathbf{H}_0T_2^*\ldots T_n^*$:

Let M_u be the set of (not necessarily proper) subterms of elements of $\mathcal{F}^*$ whose head is $Y_{u+1,s+u+1}$, and let $\tau_u = 5s + 6r - u + 2$ (τ_u is the number of terms from $\mathbf{H}_1$ to $\mathbf{H}_0$, $\mathbf{H}_1$ and $\mathbf{H}_0$ included, in M_1^*).

Since the $\tau_u - 2$ terms

$$\mathbf{Q}_1,\ldots,\mathbf{Q}_s,\mathbf{P}_{s+r+u+2},\ldots,\mathbf{P}_{s+2r+1},\mathbf{B}_1,\ldots,\mathbf{B}_{s+2r},\mathbf{K}^{s+r-1},\ldots,\mathbf{K}^{2(s+r-1)},E_1,\ldots,E_{2s+2r},S^*$$

appear in every element of the class M_u, we can erase them. Moreover, we will erase some terms among $T_2^*,\ldots,T_n^*$, under the condition that they also appear in every element of M_u in the same position .

To this purpose, we consider the minimum integer c_u ($c_u \geq 0$) s.t. *at least one* of the following conditions is satisfied:

(2.3.11.i) there is an element L in M_u s.t. $\deg(L) < \tau_u + c_u$;

(2.3.11.ii) there are at least two elements P and Q in M_u s.t.

$$P_{<\tau_u + c_u>} \neq Q_{<\tau_u + c_u>}.$$

It follows that we can assign:

(2.3.12) $\quad Y_{u+1,s+u+1} \equiv \mathbf{B}\mathbf{K}^{\tau_u - 2}(\lambda yz\,.\,\mathbf{K}^{c_u}(\,x < \mathbf{N}_u\,, < y\,, z >>))$ [22],

where $\mathbf{N}_u$ is a *fresh* combinator. Hence we obtain:

(2.3.13) $\quad M_1^* = x < \mathbf{N}_u\,, < \mathbf{H}_1, \mathbf{H}_0 >> T_{2+c_u}^*\ldots T_n^*$.

---

(20) We denote by $F_{<h>}$ $(h \geq 1)$ the h-th son of the root of F in its Böhm tree representation.

(21) Recall [Bar 84] that if $M \equiv \lambda z_1\ldots z_n.\zeta M_1\ldots M_m$ and $N \equiv \lambda z_1\ldots z_{n'}.\xi N_1\ldots N_{m'}$ then M is *equivalent* to N iff: $m - n = m' - n'$ and $\zeta \equiv \xi$.

(22) $\mathbf{B} \equiv \lambda fgx.f(gx)$.

shape 2^*: we proceed in a way similar to shape 1^*:

if $v - w \neq 0$: $\qquad M_2^* = Z_{2(s+v-w)-1,s+i+v-w}\ \mathbf{H}_0 G_1^* \ldots G_w^*\ \mathbf{Q}_1 \ldots \mathbf{Q}_{s-w} V_2^* \ldots V_m^*$.

if $v - w = 0$: $\qquad M_2^* = X_{i,s+i}\ \mathbf{H}_0 G_1^* \ldots G_w^*\ \mathbf{Q}_1 \ldots \mathbf{Q}_{s-w} V_2^* \ldots V_m^*$.

Let $M_{f,g}$ be the set of (not necessarily proper) subterms of elements of F^* whose head is

$$Z_{2(s+g)-1,s+f+g} \qquad \text{if } g \neq 0,$$
$$X_{f,s+f} \qquad \text{if } g = 0.$$

We consider the minimum integer $c_{f,g}$ ($c_{f,g} > 1$) s.t. *at least one* of the following conditions is satisfied:

(2.3.14.i) there is an element L in $M_{f,g}$ s.t. $\deg(L) < c_{f,g}$;

(2.3.14.ii) there are at least two elements P and Q in $M_{f,g}$ s.t.

$$P_{< c_{f,g} >} \neq Q_{< c_{f,g} >}.$$

It follows that we can assign:

(2.3.15) $\quad Z_{2(s+g)-1,s+f+g} \equiv \mathbf{BK}^{c_{f,g}}(\lambda z . x < \mathbf{N}_{f,g}, z >)$,

(2.3.16) $\quad X_{f,s+f} \equiv \mathbf{BK}^{c_{f,0}}(\lambda z . x < \mathbf{N}_{f,0}, z >)$,

where the $\mathbf{N}_{f,g}$'s are fresh combinators. Hence we obtain, denoting by $R_{c_{f,g}+1}, \ldots, R_{m+s}$ the $c_{f,g}$+1-th,...,m+s-th element among $G_1^*, \ldots, G_w^*, \mathbf{Q}_1, \ldots, \mathbf{Q}_{s-w}, V_2^*, \ldots, V_m^*$:

(2.3.17) $\quad M_2^* = x < \mathbf{N}_{f,g}, \mathbf{H}_0 > R_{c_{f,g}+1} \ldots R_{m+s}$.

Let now $P, Q \in F$. It is clear that if P and Q have different shapes, or if they have the same shape but non equivalent minimal terms, then $P^* \neq Q^*$.

To prove the injectivity of the substitution (2.3.4) we consider the case in which P and Q have the same shape and equivalent minimal terms. In this case the problem is reduced to the one of inspecting the transformations caused by (2.3.4) over subterms of P and Q.

Recalling that for every substitution and for any term T the following properties hold:

$$(\lambda u.T)^* = \lambda u.T^* \ ; \ T \equiv yT_1 \ldots T_m \ (y \neq x) \Rightarrow T^* = yT_1^* \ldots T_m^*,$$

we consider, in addition to shapes 1-3, the following 2 possible shapes for subterms of P and Q, together with their transformations by (2.3.4):

shape 4: $\qquad M_4 \equiv x\mathbf{H}_0(\lambda z_1 .. z_j . \zeta R_1 \ldots R_k) S_2 .. S_f \quad (j,k \geq 0,\ f \geq 1,\ \zeta \notin \{z_1, \ldots, z_j\} \cup \{x\})$.

$$M_4^* = \zeta R_1^* \ldots R_k^* \mathbf{P}_{s+r+1} \ldots \mathbf{P}_{s+2r+1} \mathbf{B}_1 \ldots \mathbf{B}_{s+2r} \mathbf{K}^{s+r-1} \ldots \mathbf{K}^{2(s+r-1)} E_1 \ldots E_{2s+2r} (\lambda z_1 \ldots z_j . \zeta R_1 \ldots R_k)^* \mathbf{H}_0 S_2^* \ldots S_f^* .$$

shape 5: $\qquad M_5 \equiv x\mathbf{H}_0$.

$$M_5^* = \lambda b.b\mathbf{P}_{s+r+1} \ldots \mathbf{P}_{s+2r+1} \mathbf{B}_1 \ldots \mathbf{B}_{s+2r} \mathbf{K}^{s+r-1} \ldots \mathbf{K}^{2(s+r-1)} E_1 \ldots E_{2s+2r} b\mathbf{H}_0 .$$

If we compare the shapes of proper subterms of P and Q, then the injectivity of the substitution (2.3.4) follows by induction on the structure of P and Q themselves.

We will now prove that the substitution (2.3.4) preserves the self-distinction of F^*.

Let $F_1, F_2 \in \mathsf{F}$. We will show that F_2^* does not occur as head term either in F_1^* or in some subterm of F_1^*.

Suppose there exist k terms $T_1,\ldots,T_k$ such that:

(2.3.18) $\quad F_2^* T_1 \ldots T_k = F_1^*$.

Since (2.3.19) $\quad F_2^* T_1 \ldots T_k = (F_2 T_1 \ldots T_k)^*$,

it follows from the injectivity of (2.3.4) that $F_1 \equiv F_2 T_1 \ldots T_k$, which is a contradiction.

Hence F_2^* does not occur as head term in F_1^*.

Let $F_1 \equiv x\mathbf{H}\, F_{1,1} \ldots F_{1,\sigma}$. Since

$F_1^* = F_{1,1}^*\, \mathbf{P}_{s+r+1} \ldots \mathbf{P}_{s+2r+1} \mathbf{B}_1 \ldots \mathbf{B}_{s+2r} \mathbf{K}^{s+r-1} \ldots \mathbf{K}^{2(s+r-1)} E_1 \ldots E_{2s+2r}\, F_{1,1}^*\, \mathbf{H}\, F_{1,2}^* \ldots F_{1,\sigma}^*$,

then the preservation of self-distinction follows by induction on the structure of F_1.

(Part 1) ❑

<u>2.3.20. EXAMPLE</u> (1.2.7 continued)

$F_1 \equiv x\mathbf{I}(x\mathbf{I})$ has shape 1 , $F_2 \equiv x\mathbf{I}\, \lambda u.uu$ has shape 2.

<u>Substitution:</u> $[\lambda ab.b\mathbf{P}_3\mathbf{P}_4\mathbf{B}_1\mathbf{B}_2\mathbf{B}_3\mathbf{K}^1\mathbf{K}^2 E_1 E_2 E_3 E_4\, ba / x]$,

where $E_1 \equiv \mathbf{P}_4 A_{1,1} A_{1,2} A_{1,3} A_{1,4}$ and

$A_{1,2} \equiv \lambda z_1 \ldots z_5 . z_1(z_1 (\mathbf{K}^6(\mathbf{C}_{[1]} X_{1,2})) \ldots (\mathbf{K}^6(\mathbf{C}_{[1]} X_{3,2}))\, (\mathbf{K}^5(\mathbf{C}_{[1]} Y_{1,2})) \ldots (\mathbf{K}^5(\mathbf{C}_{[1]} Y_{3,2})))$.

We obtain :

$F_1^* = Y_{1,2}\mathbf{I}\mathbf{P}_3\mathbf{P}_4\mathbf{B}_1\mathbf{B}_2\mathbf{B}_3\mathbf{K}^1\mathbf{K}^2 E_1 E_2 E_3 E_4 (x\mathbf{I})^*\mathbf{I}$

$F_2^* = X_{1,2}\mathbf{I}\mathbf{P}_3$

The assignment: $Y_{1,2} \equiv \mathbf{B}\mathbf{K}^{10}(\lambda yz . x < \mathbf{N}_0 , < y , z > >)$,

$X_{1,2} \equiv \mathbf{B}\mathbf{I}(\lambda z . x < \mathbf{N}_{1,0}, z >)$

where $\mathbf{N}_0$ and $\mathbf{N}_{1,0}$ are distinct combinators

gives: $F_1^* = x < \mathbf{N}_0 , < \mathbf{I} , \mathbf{I} > >$, $F_2^* = x < \mathbf{N}_{1,0}\mathbf{I} >$

The application of the Basic Theorem gives the result. ❑

<u>Part 2: COMPOSITION OF SUBSTITUTIONS</u>

Let us consider the set $\mathsf{F}^* \equiv \{ F_1^*,\ldots,F_t^* \}$ obtained from F after the substitution (2.3.4).

If there exists $F^* \in \mathsf{F}^*$ s.t. $\deg(F^*) = 1$, then $F^* \equiv x\mathbf{H}$, where $\mathbf{H}$ is a combinator which does not occur in $\mathsf{F}^* - \{F^*\}$, by the self-distinction hypothesis.

It follows that we can apply the Basic Theorem to the multiset $\mathbf{L} \equiv \{ \mathbf{L}_1,\ldots,\mathbf{L}_\rho \}$ of first sons of the occurrences of x in F^*, therefore obtaining the transformation:

(2.3.21.i) $\quad x\mathbf{L}_h \rightarrow x\mathbf{L}_h$ if $\mathbf{L}_h \neq \mathbf{H}$ $(h=1,\ldots,\rho)$;

(2.3.21.ii) $\quad x\mathbf{L}_h \rightarrow y$ if $\mathbf{L}_h = \mathbf{H}$, where $y\ (\in \{ y_1,\ldots,y_t \})$ is a fresh variable.

Hence we succeded in eliminating one term from F^*.

It follows that it is not restrictive to suppose that every $F^* \in \mathsf{F}^*$ is s.t. $\deg(F^*) > 1$.

2.3.22. REMARK

Let $F = \{F_1,\ldots,F_t\}$ be a self-distinct set. The substitution

(2.3.22.1) $[\mathbf{BC}_{[k]}x/x]$ $(k < \min\{\deg(F) \mid F \in F\}$

is trivially injective and preserves the self-distiction over the transformed set F' obtained from F after the substitution (2.3.22.1). ❑

Let now $F_\alpha, F_\beta \in F$, with

$$F_\alpha \equiv x\mathbf{H}G_{\alpha,2}\ldots G_{\alpha,m_\alpha}$$

$$F_\beta \equiv x\mathbf{H}G_{\beta,2}\ldots G_{\beta,m_\beta} \ .$$

Our aim is to prove that, if $G_{\alpha,h} \neq G_{\beta,h}$ for some $h \leq \min\{m_\alpha, m_\beta\}$, then we are able to transform F_α and F_β respectively into

(2.3.23.i) $F_\alpha^* \equiv x\mathbf{L}_1 \ldots$

(2.3.23.ii) $F_\beta^* \equiv x\mathbf{L}_2 \ldots$, where $\mathbf{L}_1$ and $\mathbf{L}_2$ are distinct combinators.

We may suppose $h = 2$, otherwise applying the transformation (2.3.22.1) with $k = h - 2$ we obtain:

$$F'_\alpha \equiv x\mathbf{H}G'_{\alpha,h}\, G'_{\alpha,2}\ldots G'_{\alpha,h-1}\, G'_{\alpha,h+1}\ldots G'_{\alpha,m_\alpha}$$

$$F'_\beta \equiv x\mathbf{H}G'_{\beta,h}\, G'_{\beta,2}\ldots G'_{\beta,h-1}\, G'_{\beta,h+1}\ldots G'_{\beta,m_\beta} \ .$$

If minterm(F_α) is not equivalent to minterm(F_β), then (2.3.23.i-ii) are reached, as shown by (2.3.10), hence we limit ourselves to suppose that the minimal terms of F_α and F_β are equivalent, and we distinguish the following cases:

case 1: both F_α and F_β have shape 1, i.e.

$F_\alpha \equiv x\mathbf{H}(\lambda z_1\ldots z_u.x\mathbf{H}_1)G_{\alpha,3}\ldots G_{\alpha,m_\alpha}$, $F_\beta \equiv x\mathbf{H}(\lambda z_1\ldots z_u.x\mathbf{H}_2)G_{\beta,3}\ldots G_{\beta,m_\beta}$

where $\mathbf{H}_1$ and $\mathbf{H}_2$ are distinct combinators. This case is easily settled by (2.3.13).

case 2: F_α has shape 1 and F_β has shape 3: we have

$F_\alpha \equiv x\mathbf{H}(\lambda z_1\ldots z_u.x\mathbf{H}_1)G_{\alpha,3}\ldots G_{\alpha,m_\alpha}$.

If $\text{minterm}(F_\beta) \neq \lambda z_1\ldots z_u.x\mathbf{H}_1$, then the case is reduced to case 1;

otherwise $F_\alpha^* = x\mathbf{H}'G_{\alpha,3}^*\ldots G_{\alpha,m_\alpha}^*$ (see shape 1)

$F_\beta^* = x\mathbf{H}'\mathbf{P}_k\ldots$ for some k (see shape 3),

and $\mathbf{P}_k$ is trivially not equivalent to $G_{\alpha,3}^*$.

case 3: both F_α and F_β have shape 2, i.e.

$F_\alpha \equiv x\mathbf{H}(\lambda z_1\ldots z_{u_\alpha}.z_i\, Y_1\ldots Y_{w_\alpha})G_{\alpha,3}\ldots G_{\alpha,m_\alpha}$,

$F_\beta \equiv x\mathbf{H}(\lambda z_1\ldots z_{u_\beta}.z_i\, \Psi_1\ldots \Psi_{w_\beta})G_{\beta,3}\ldots G_{\beta,m_\beta}$ where $w_\alpha - u_\alpha = w_\beta - u_\beta$.

If $w_\alpha = w_\beta$, then the case is trivially settled comparing F_α^* and F_β^* (see shape 2^*).

Otherwise by the injectivity of the transformation, we have $Y_r^* \neq \Psi_r^*$, for some r.

Furthermore, the <u>distance</u>[23] between Y_r^* and F_α^* (and between Ψ_r^* and F_β^*)

---

(23) Let P be a term and Q a proper subterm of P. We define the *distance* between Q and the root of P to be the length of the path from root(P) to root(Q).

decreases with respect to the distance between Y_r and F_α (and between Ψ_r and F_β) and the case is settled by induction on this distance.

case 4: F_α has shape 2 and F_β has shape 3: similar to case 2.

case 5: both F_α and F_β have shape 3:

If minterm(F_α) $\neq$ minterm(F_β) then the case is reduced to one of the previous cases. Otherwise, there exist non equivalent subterms Y and Ψ respectively of $(F_\alpha)_{<2>}$ and $(F_\beta)_{<2>}$; this case follows by induction on the distance between Y and F_α (and between Ψ and F_β).

2.3.24. SKETCH OF THE ALGORITHM

The algorithm consists of iterating the next two steps until the t combinators, which are the first sons of the roots of the elements of F, become pairwise distinct.

First step.

Replace the second son of the roots of all elements of F, by the h-th son (h may be chosen as the minimum) s.t. not all sons are equal. Since the set F is self-distinct,this is feasible and can always be done in a reversible way by the substitution [$\mathbf{BC}_{[h-2]}$ x / x] (it could also be done by erasing all sons from the second to the (h-1)-th - bounds included -, if they are columnwise equal, for all occurrences of x in F).

Second step.

Apply the substitution (2.3.4), which has two important features:

- it reduces the distance between subterms of elements of F and the roots of Böhm trees in which they appear, bringing them, in a finite number of steps, to the outer level of depth;
- it introduces fresh combinators, only if terms not having shape 3 have nonequivalent minimal terms. ❑

The theorem follows from observing that by self-distinction hypothesis:

i) there exists always an integer h (≥ 1) s.t. for every F_α, $F_\beta \in$ F the h-th sons of the roots of F_α and F_β are not equal;

ii) for every F $\in$ F and for every proper subterm N of some element of F, with head(N) = x, if deg(N) $\geq$ deg(F), then there exists an integer h (≥ 1) s.t. the h-th sons of the roots of N and F are not equal. ❑

2.4. EXAMPLE (1.2.5 continued)

F_1 : $x\mathbf{II}(\lambda z.z(x\mathbf{III}))$	substituting	F_1^* : $x\mathbf{I}(\lambda z.z(x\mathbf{III}))\mathbf{I}$
F_2 : $x\mathbf{KI}(\lambda z.z(x\mathbf{III}))$	$[\mathbf{BC}_{[1]}x/x]$	F_2^* : $x\mathbf{K}(\lambda z.z(x\mathbf{III}))\mathbf{I}$
F_3 : $x\mathbf{KI}(x\mathbf{KKI})$	we obtain	F_3^* : $x\mathbf{K}(x\mathbf{KIK})\mathbf{I}$

Substitution: $[\lambda ab.b\mathbf{P}_5\mathbf{P}_6\mathbf{B}_1..\mathbf{B}_5\mathbf{K}^3..\mathbf{K}^6\mathrm{E}_1..\mathrm{E}_8\, b\, a / x]$, where $\quad E_5 \equiv \mathbf{P}_6 A_{5,1} A_{5,2} A_{5,3} A_{5,4} A_{5,5} A_{5,6}$,

$E_7 \equiv \mathbf{P}_6 A_{7,1} A_{7,2} A_{7,3} A_{7,4} A_{7,5} A_{7,6}$ and

$A_{5,4} \equiv \lambda z_1 \ldots z_5 . z_1(z_5(\mathbf{K}^8(C_{[3]} X_{1,4})) \ldots (\mathbf{K}^8(C_{[3]} X_{5,4}))(\mathbf{K}^7(C_{[3]} Y_{1,4})) \ldots (\mathbf{K}^7(C_{[3]} Y_{3,4})))$

$A_{7,5} \equiv \lambda z_1 \ldots z_3 . z_1(C_{[3]} Z_{7,5})$.

We obtain : $\quad F_1^{**} = X_{1,4}\mathbf{I}(Z_{7,5}\mathbf{I}\mathbf{P}_6\mathbf{B}_1\mathbf{B}_2\mathbf{I})\mathbf{P}_6\mathbf{B}_1\mathbf{I}$

$F_2^{**} = X_{1,4}\mathbf{K}(Z_{7,5}\mathbf{I}\mathbf{P}_6\mathbf{B}_1\mathbf{B}_2\mathbf{I})\mathbf{P}_6\mathbf{B}_1\mathbf{I}$

$F_3^{**} = Z_{7,5}\mathbf{K}\mathbf{P}_6\mathbf{B}_1\mathbf{B}_2\mathbf{K}\mathbf{P}_5 \ldots E_8(Z_{7,5}\mathbf{K}\mathbf{P}_6\mathbf{B}_1\mathbf{B}_2\mathbf{K})\mathbf{K}\mathbf{I}$

The assignment: $\quad X_{1,4} \equiv \mathbf{B}\mathbf{K}^4(\lambda z . x < \mathbf{N}_{1,0}, z >)$,

$Z_{7,5} \equiv \mathbf{B}\mathbf{K}^4(\lambda z . x < \mathbf{N}_{7,5}, z >)$,

where $\mathbf{N}_{1,0}$ and $\mathbf{N}_{7,5}$ are distinct combinators, gives:

$F_1^{**} = x < \mathbf{N}_{1,0}, \mathbf{I} >$, $\quad F_2^{**} = x < \mathbf{N}_{1,0}, \mathbf{K} >$,

$F_3^{**} = x < \mathbf{N}_{7,5}, \mathbf{K} > \mathbf{P}_5 \ldots E_8 (x < \mathbf{N}_{7,5}, \mathbf{K} >)\mathbf{K}\mathbf{I}$.

The application of the Basic Theorem gives the result. ❑

3. A REFINEMENT OF THE BASIC THEOREM

<u>3.0. MAIN COROLLARY</u> (Refinement of the Basic Theorem)

Let $\mathbf{F} \equiv \{ \mathbf{F}_1, \ldots, \mathbf{F}_t \} \subset \Lambda^0 \mathrm{N}_{\leq n}$ and let n_i be the number of initial abstractions of $\mathbf{F}_i$ ($i=1,\ldots,t$), with $n = \max \{n_i\}$.

Then there exists a Church n+1-tuple of terms $< X_1, \ldots, X_{n+1} >$ such that

$$< X_1, \ldots, X_{n+1} > \mathbf{F}_i = \mathbf{F}_i X_1 \ldots X_{n+1} = y_i \quad (i = 1, \ldots, t) .$$ ❑

<u>PROOF:</u>

i) $n > 1$. Proceeding as in 1.0 we first construct from the set $\mathbf{F} \equiv \{ \mathbf{F}_1, \ldots, \mathbf{F}_t \} \subset \Lambda^0 \mathrm{N}_{\leq n}$ a set $\mathbf{F}' \equiv \{ \mathbf{F}'_1, \ldots, \mathbf{F}'_t \} \subset \Lambda^0 \mathrm{N}_n$; then applying the Lemma 1.2.0(⇒) we construct a set $\mathbf{L} \equiv \{ \mathbf{L}_1, \ldots, \mathbf{L}_t \} \subset \Lambda^0 \mathrm{N}_1$. Then we proceed to step iii).

ii) $n = 1$. If necessary, we proceed to the preconditioning of the 1-t-mapping as explained in 1.2.6. obtaining a set $\mathbf{L} \equiv \{ \mathbf{L}_1, \ldots, \mathbf{L}_t \} \subset \Lambda^0 \mathrm{N}_1$.

iii) We apply now 1.1 reducing the set $\mathbf{L} \subset \Lambda^0 \mathrm{N}_1$ to a set $L \equiv \{ L_1, \ldots, L_t \} \subset \Lambda^{*} \mathrm{N}$ of λ-free terms. Since we cannot warrant that $L \subset \Lambda^{\#} \mathrm{N}$, we define a set $L' \subset \Lambda^{\#} \mathrm{N}$ by defining $\quad L'_i \equiv L_i \ (x\mathbf{G}_{n+1}) \quad (i=1,\ldots,t)$, where $\mathbf{G}_{n+1} \in \Lambda^0 \mathrm{N}$, but $\mathbf{G}_{n+1} \notin \mathbf{G} \equiv \{ \mathbf{G}_1, \ldots, \mathbf{G}_n \}$, as defined inside the Lemma 1.2.0(⇒). We may now apply the Main Theorem and prove the surjectivity of L' finding the term X. Finally we apply Lemma 1.2.0(⇐) finding first

$$\mathbf{F}_i (X\mathbf{G}_1) \ldots (X\mathbf{G}_n)(X\mathbf{G}_{n+1}) = y_i \quad (i = 1, \ldots, t),$$

and then, using the definition

$$X_j \equiv X\mathbf{G}_j \qquad (j=1,\ldots,n+1),$$

we obtain the result

$$\mathbf{F}_i X_1 \ldots X_{n+1} = y_i \qquad (i = 1, \ldots, t).$$ ❑

4. CONCLUDING REMARKS AND FURTHER DEVELOPMENTS

Let us review the main ideas and results presented in this paper.
We succeeded in finding sufficient conditions for the solvability of system of equations having the shape

$$(0.1) \qquad \mathbf{F}_i X_1 \ldots X_n = H_i \quad (i=1,\ldots,t)$$

where the $\mathbf{F}_i$'s are combinators in β-η-normal form having n as the maximum number of initial abstractions and the H_i's are arbitrary obs (λ-terms) to be reached, from the l.h.s. terms of (0.1), by weak reduction only.
To this aim the notion of n-t-surjectivity was associated to the finite set $\mathbf{F} \equiv \{\mathbf{F}_1,\ldots,\mathbf{F}_t\}$,and two different ways were described to equalize to the same value n the number of initial abstractions of the elements of $\mathbf{F}$.
The previous results may be considered as a rudimentary type assignment to combinators , without really entering in some type discipline.
The domain paradigm $D = D \rightarrow D$ may be used to give a correct interpretation of two further results of this paper: the Theorem 1.2.4, showing the possibility to reduce n to 1 in (0.1) without loss of information, and the Main Corollary 3.0, where increasing n by one is explained viewing the r.h.s of (0.1) as elements of $D \rightarrow D$.
Viewing all these theorems from the algorithmic point of view, the Main Corollary may be considered as a refinement and an improvement of the Basic Theorem, invoked in the proof of the Main Theorem. Hence the latter one can use the Main Corollary to improve itself. We have here an example of an algorithm improving itself just once!
The problem of the decidability of the n-t-surjectivity, corresponding to the characterization of the surjective t-tuples of λ-free terms with only n free variables, has been faced by the same authors in [BP 88] together with the decidability of the right- and left- invertibility of an n-t-mapping. A still open problem is the solvability of a single system (0.1), where the H_i's are given β-normal forms and the $\mathbf{F}_i$'s satisfy some suitable assumptions.

ACKNOWLEDGMENTS

We are grateful to Mariangiola Dezani-Ciancaglini and Enrico Tronci for helpful discussions on the topics of this paper, and to Dario Fragassi, whose Combinatory Logic computer program gave us a great support in checking the proof of the theorem.

REFERENCES

[Bar 84] Barendregt, H.P., The lambda calculus, North Holland, 1984

[CuF] Curry,H.B. and Feys,R., Combinatory Logic, Vol.1, North Holland,Amsterdam 1958

[BD 74] Böhm, C. and Dezani-Ciancaglini, M., Combinatorial problems, combinator equations and normal forms,in: Lœckx (ed.) Aut.,Langu. and Progr, 2nd Colloquium, LNCS 14,1974, pp. 185-199

[BDPR 79] Böhm, C.,Dezani-Ciancaglini,Peretti,P. and Ronchi della Rocca, S., A discrimination algorithm inside λ-β-Calculus, Theor. Comput.Sci. 8, (1979), pp. 271-291

[Böh 68] Böhm, C., Alcune proprietà delle forme β-η-normali nel λ-**K**- calcolo, IAC Publ. n. 696, Roma ,19 pp., 1968

[BP 88] Böhm,C. and Piperno,A.,Surjectivity and one-side invertibility of λ-β-Ω-mappings, To appear in the Proceedings of LICS 88, Edinburgh

[BT 87] Böhm,C. and Tronci,E., X-Separability and Left-Invertibility in Lambda-Calculus, Symposium on Logic and Computer Science, Ithaca ,N.Y.June 22-25,1987, Computer Soc.of the IEEE, p.320-328

[Hin 77] Hindley,R., Combinatory Reductions and Lambda Reductions compared, Zeitschr.f.math.Logik und Grundlagen d. Math., Bd.23, S.169-180, 1977

[Hin 79] Hindley,R., The Discrimination Algorithm holds for Combinatory Weak Reduction, Theor. Comput.Sci. 8, (1979), pp. 393-394

APPENDIX

$$M_1 \equiv x\mathbf{H}_0(\lambda z_1\dots z_u.x\mathbf{H}_1)T_2\dots T_n .$$

$$M_1^* = (\lambda z_1\dots z_u.x^*\mathbf{H}_1)\mathbf{P}_{s+r+1}\dots\mathbf{P}_{s+2r+1}\mathbf{B}_1\dots\mathbf{B}_{s+2r}\mathbf{K}^{s+r-1}\dots\mathbf{K}^{2(s+r-1)}E_1\dots E_{2s+2r}$$

$$(\lambda z_1\dots z_u ab.b\mathbf{P}_{s+r+1}\dots\mathbf{P}_{s+2r+1}\mathbf{B}_1\dots\mathbf{B}_{s+2r}\mathbf{K}^{s+r-1}\dots\mathbf{K}^{2(s+r-1)}E_1\dots E_{2s+2r}b\mathbf{H}_1)\mathbf{H}_0T_2^*\dots T_n^* =$$

$$(\text{denote } S^* \equiv (\lambda z_1\dots z_u ab.b\mathbf{P}_{s+r+1}\dots\mathbf{P}_{s+2r+1}\mathbf{B}_1\dots\mathbf{B}_{s+2r}\mathbf{K}^{s+r-1}\dots\mathbf{K}^{2(s+r-1)}E_1\dots E_{2s+2r}b\mathbf{H}_1))$$

$$= x^*\mathbf{H}_1\mathbf{P}_{s+r+u+1}\dots\mathbf{P}_{s+2r+1}\mathbf{B}_1\dots\mathbf{B}_{s+2r}\mathbf{K}^{s+r-1}\dots\mathbf{K}^{2(s+r-1)}E_1\dots E_{2s+2r}S^*\mathbf{H}_0T_2^*\dots T_n^* =$$

$$= \mathbf{P}_{s+r+u+1}\mathbf{P}_{s+r+1}\dots\mathbf{P}_{s+2r+1}\mathbf{B}_1\dots\mathbf{B}_{s+2r}\mathbf{K}^{s+r-1}\dots\mathbf{K}^{2(s+r-1)}E_1\dots E_{2s+2r}\mathbf{P}_{s+r+u+1}\mathbf{H}_1$$

$$\mathbf{P}_{s+r+u+2}\dots\mathbf{P}_{s+2r+1}\mathbf{B}_1\dots\mathbf{B}_{s+2r}\mathbf{K}^{s+r-1}\dots\mathbf{K}^{2(s+r-1)}E_1\dots E_{2s+2r}S^*\mathbf{H}_0T_2^*\dots T_n^* =$$

$$= \mathbf{B}_{s+u+1}\mathbf{P}_{s+r+1}\dots\mathbf{P}_{s+2r+1}\mathbf{B}_1\dots\mathbf{B}_{s+u}\mathbf{B}_{s+u+2}\dots\mathbf{B}_{s+2r}\mathbf{K}^{s+r-1}\dots\mathbf{K}^{2(s+r-1)}E_1\dots E_{2s+2r}\mathbf{P}_{s+r+u+1}\mathbf{H}_1$$

$$\mathbf{P}_{s+r+u+2}\dots\mathbf{P}_{s+2r+1}\mathbf{B}_1\dots\mathbf{B}_{s+2r}\mathbf{K}^{s+r-1}\dots\mathbf{K}^{2(s+r-1)}E_1\dots E_{2s+2r}S^*\mathbf{H}_0T_2^*\dots T_n^* =$$

$$= \mathbf{K}^{2s+r-2} < \mathbf{K}^{s+u}\mathbf{K}^{2r-u}, <\mathbf{Q}_1,\dots,\mathbf{Q}_s>>^{(16)}\mathbf{K}^{2s+r-1}\dots\mathbf{K}^{2(s+r-1)}E_1\dots E_{2s+2r}\mathbf{P}_{s+r+u+1}\mathbf{H}_1$$

$$\mathbf{P}_{s+r+u+2}\dots\mathbf{P}_{s+2r+1}\mathbf{B}_1\dots\mathbf{B}_{s+2r}\mathbf{K}^{s+r-1}\dots\mathbf{K}^{2(s+r-1)}E_1\dots E_{2s+2r}S^*\mathbf{H}_0T_2^*\dots T_n^* =$$

$$= <\mathbf{K}^{s+u}\mathbf{K}^{2r-u}, <\mathbf{Q}_1,\dots,\mathbf{Q}_s>> E_{2s-1}\dots E_{2s+2r}\mathbf{P}_{s+r+u+1}\mathbf{H}_1$$

$$\mathbf{P}_{s+r+u+2}\dots\mathbf{P}_{s+2r+1}\mathbf{B}_1\dots\mathbf{B}_{s+2r}\mathbf{K}^{s+r-1}\dots\mathbf{K}^{2(s+r-1)}E_1\dots E_{2s+2r}S^*\mathbf{H}_0T_2^*\dots T_n^* =$$

$$= E_{2s-1}(\mathbf{K}^{s+u}\mathbf{K}^{2r-u}) <\mathbf{Q}_1,\dots,\mathbf{Q}_s> E_{2s}\dots E_{2s+2r}\mathbf{P}_{s+r+u+1}\mathbf{H}_1$$

$$\mathbf{P}_{s+r+u+2}\dots\mathbf{P}_{s+2r+1}\mathbf{B}_1\dots\mathbf{B}_{s+2r}\mathbf{K}^{s+r-1}\dots\mathbf{K}^{2(s+r-1)}E_1\dots E_{2s+2r}S^*\mathbf{H}_0T_2^*\dots T_n^* =$$

$$= A_{2s-1,s+u+1} <\mathbf{Q}_1,\dots,\mathbf{Q}_s> E_{2s}\dots E_{2s+2r}\mathbf{P}_{s+r+u+1}\mathbf{H}_1$$

$$\mathbf{P}_{s+r+u+2}\dots\mathbf{P}_{s+2r+1}\mathbf{B}_1\dots\mathbf{B}_{s+2r}\mathbf{K}^{s+r-1}\dots\mathbf{K}^{2(s+r-1)}E_1\dots E_{2s+2r}S^*\mathbf{H}_0T_2^*\dots T_n^* =$$

$$= <\mathbf{Q}_1,\dots,\mathbf{Q}_s> (\mathbf{P}_{s+r+u+1}(\mathbf{K}^{s+2r+3}(C_{[s]}X_{1,s+u+1}))\dots(\mathbf{K}^{s+2r+3}(C_{[s]}X_{s+r+1,s+u+1}))$$

$$(\mathbf{K}^{s+2r+2}(C_{[s]}Y_{1,s+u+1}))\dots(\mathbf{K}^{s+2r+2}(C_{[s]}Y_{r+2,s+u+1})))\mathbf{H}_1\mathbf{P}_{s+r+u+2}\dots\mathbf{P}_{s+2r+1}$$

$$\mathbf{B}_1\dots\mathbf{B}_{s+2r}\mathbf{K}^{s+r-1}\dots\mathbf{K}^{2(s+r-1)}E_1\dots E_{2s+2r}S^*\mathbf{H}_0T_2^*\dots T_n^* =$$

$$= \mathbf{P}_{s+r+u+1}(\mathbf{K}^{s+2r+3}(C_{[s]}X_{1,s+u+1}))\dots(\mathbf{K}^{s+2r+3}(C_{[s]}X_{s+r+1,s+u+1}))$$

$$(\mathbf{K}^{s+2r+2}(C_{[s]}Y_{1,s+u+1}))\dots(\mathbf{K}^{s+2r+2}(C_{[s]}Y_{r+2,s+u+1}))\mathbf{Q}_1\dots\mathbf{Q}_s\mathbf{H}_1\mathbf{P}_{s+r+u+2}\dots\mathbf{P}_{s+2r+1}$$

$$\mathbf{B}_1\dots\mathbf{B}_{s+2r}\mathbf{K}^{s+r-1}\dots\mathbf{K}^{2(s+r-1)}E_1\dots E_{2s+2r}S^*\mathbf{H}_0T_2^*\dots T_n^* =$$

$$= \mathbf{K}^{s+2r+2}(C_{[s]}Y_{u+1,s+u+1})(\mathbf{K}^{s+2r+3}(C_{[s]}X_{1,s+u+1}))\ldots(\mathbf{K}^{s+2r+3}(C_{[s]}X_{s+r+1,s+u+1}))$$
$$(\mathbf{K}^{s+2r+2}(C_{[s]}Y_{1,s+u+1}))\ldots(\mathbf{K}^{s+2r+2}(C_{[s]}Y_{u,s+u+1}))(\mathbf{K}^{s+2r+2}(C_{[s]}Y_{u+2,s+u+1}))\ldots$$
$$\ldots(\mathbf{K}^{s+2r+2}(C_{[s]}Y_{r+2,s+u+1}))\, \mathbf{Q}_1 \ldots \mathbf{Q}_s\, \mathbf{H}_1\, \mathbf{P}_{s+r+u+2}\ldots\mathbf{P}_{s+2r+1}\mathbf{B}_1\ldots\mathbf{B}_{s+2r}$$
$$\mathbf{K}^{s+r-1}\ldots\mathbf{K}^{2(s+r-1)}E_1\ldots E_{2s+2r}S^*H_0T_2^*\ldots T_n^* =$$
$$= Y_{u+1,s+u+1}\, \mathbf{H}_1\, \mathbf{Q}_1 \ldots \mathbf{Q}_s$$
$$\mathbf{P}_{s+r+u+2}\ldots\mathbf{P}_{s+2r+1}\mathbf{B}_1\ldots\mathbf{B}_{s+2r}\mathbf{K}^{s+r-1}\ldots\mathbf{K}^{2(s+r-1)}E_1\ldots E_{2s+2r}S^*H_0T_2^*\ldots T_n^*$$

$$M_2 = x\mathbf{H}_0(\lambda z_1\ldots z_v.z_iG_1\ldots G_w)V_2\ldots V_m .$$
$$M_2^* = (\lambda z_1\ldots z_v.z_iG_1^*\ldots G_w^*)\mathbf{P}_{s+r+1}\ldots\mathbf{P}_{s+2r+1}\mathbf{B}_1\ldots\mathbf{B}_{s+2r}\mathbf{K}^{s+r-1}\ldots\mathbf{K}^{2(s+r-1)}E_1\ldots E_{2s+2r}$$
$$(\lambda z_1\ldots z_v.z_iG_1^*\ldots G_w^*)\mathbf{H}_0V_2^*\ldots V_m^* =$$
$$= \mathbf{P}_{s+r+i}G_1^*\ldots G_w^*\mathbf{P}_{s+r+v+1}\ldots\mathbf{P}_{s+2r+1}\mathbf{B}_1\ldots\mathbf{B}_{s+2r}\mathbf{K}^{s+r-1}\ldots\mathbf{K}^{2(s+r-1)}E_1\ldots E_{2s+2r}$$
$$(\lambda z_1\ldots z_v.z_iG_1^*\ldots G_w^*)\mathbf{H}_0V_2^*\ldots V_m^* =$$
$$= \mathbf{B}_{s+i+v-w}G_1^*\ldots G_w^*\mathbf{P}_{s+r+v+1}\ldots\mathbf{P}_{s+2r+1}\mathbf{B}_1\ldots\mathbf{B}_{s+i+v-w-1}\mathbf{B}_{s+i+v-w+1}\ldots\mathbf{B}_{s+2r}\mathbf{K}^{s+r-1}\ldots\mathbf{K}^{2(s+r-1)}$$
$$E_1\ldots E_{2s+2r}(\lambda z_1\ldots z_v.z_iG_1^*\ldots G_w^*)\mathbf{H}_0V_2^*\ldots V_m^* =$$
$$= \mathbf{K}^{2s+r+v-w-2}< \mathbf{K}^{s+i+v-w-1}\, \mathbf{K}^{2r+w-v-i+1}, < G_1^*,\ldots,G_w^*, \mathbf{Q}_1, \ldots, \mathbf{Q}_{s-w} > >^{(19)}$$
$$\mathbf{K}^{2s+r+v-w-1}\ldots\mathbf{K}^{2(s+r-1)}E_1\ldots E_{2s+2r}(\lambda z_1\ldots z_v.z_iG_1^*\ldots G_w^*)\mathbf{H}_0V_2^*\ldots V_m^* =$$
$$= < \mathbf{K}^{s+i+v-w-1}\, \mathbf{K}^{2r+w-v-i+1}, < G_1^*,\ldots,G_w^*, \mathbf{Q}_1, \ldots, \mathbf{Q}_{s-w} > > E_{2(s+v-w)-1}\ldots E_{2s+2r}$$
$$(\lambda z_1\ldots z_v.z_iG_1^*\ldots G_w^*)\mathbf{H}_0V_2^*\ldots V_m^* =$$
$$= E_{2(s+v-w)-1}\, (\mathbf{K}^{s+i+v-w-1}\, \mathbf{K}^{2r+w-v-i+1})\, < G_1^*,\ldots,G_w^*, \mathbf{Q}_1, \ldots, \mathbf{Q}_{s-w} > E_{2(s+v-w)}\ldots E_{2s+2r}$$
$$(\lambda z_1\ldots z_v.z_iG_1^*\ldots G_w^*)\mathbf{H}_0V_2^*\ldots V_m^* =$$
$$= A_{2(s+v-w)-1,s+i+v-w}\, < G_1^*,\ldots,G_w^*, \mathbf{Q}_1, \ldots, \mathbf{Q}_{s-w} > E_{2(s+v-w)}\ldots E_{2s+2r}$$
$$(\lambda z_1\ldots z_v.z_iG_1^*\ldots G_w^*)\mathbf{H}_0V_2^*\ldots V_m^* =$$

Case a: $v - w \neq 0$:

$$= < G_1^*,\ldots,G_w^*, \mathbf{Q}_1, \ldots, \mathbf{Q}_{s-w} > (C_{[s]}\, Z_{2(s+v-w)-1,s+i+v-w})\, \mathbf{H}_0\, V_2^*\ldots V_m^* =$$
$$= Z_{2(s+v-w)-1,s+i+v-w}\, \mathbf{H}_0\, G_1^*\ldots G_w^*\, \mathbf{Q}_1 \ldots \mathbf{Q}_{s-w}\, V_2^*\ldots V_m^*$$

End case a

Case b: $v - w = 0$:

$$= A_{2s-1,s+i}\, < G_1^*,\ldots,G_w^*, \mathbf{Q}_1, \ldots, \mathbf{Q}_{s-w} > E_{2s}\ldots E_{2s+2r}$$
$$(\lambda z_1\ldots z_v.z_iG_1^*\ldots G_w^*)\mathbf{H}_0V_2^*\ldots V_m^* =$$
$$= < G_1^*,\ldots,G_w^*, \mathbf{Q}_1, \ldots, \mathbf{Q}_{s-w} >$$
$$(\,(\lambda z_1\ldots z_v.z_iG_1^*\ldots G_w^*)\,(\mathbf{K}^{s+2r+3}(C_{[s]}X_{1,s+i}))\ldots(\mathbf{K}^{s+2r+3}(C_{[s]}X_{s+r+1,s+i}))$$
$$(\mathbf{K}^{s+2r+2}(C_{[s]}Y_{1,s+i}))\ldots(\mathbf{K}^{s+2r+2}(C_{[s]}Y_{r+2,s+i}))\,)\, \mathbf{H}_0\, V_2^*\ldots V_m^* =$$
$$= (\lambda z_1\ldots z_v.z_iG_1^*\ldots G_w^*)\,(\mathbf{K}^{s+2r+3}(C_{[s]}X_{1,s+i}))\ldots(\mathbf{K}^{s+2r+3}(C_{[s]}X_{s+r+1,s+i}))$$
$$(\mathbf{K}^{s+2r+2}(C_{[s]}Y_{1,s+i}))\ldots(\mathbf{K}^{s+2r+2}(C_{[s]}Y_{r+2,s+i}))G_1^*\ldots G_w^*\, \mathbf{Q}_1 \ldots \mathbf{Q}_{s-w}\, \mathbf{H}_0\, V_2^*\ldots V_m^* =$$
$$= \mathbf{K}^{s+2r+3}(C_{[s]}X_{i,s+i})\, G_1^*\ldots G_w^*\, (\mathbf{K}^{s+2r+3}(C_{[s]}X_{v+1,s+i}))\ldots(\mathbf{K}^{s+2r+2}(C_{[s]}Y_{r+2,s+i})$$
$$G_1^*\ldots G_w^*\, \mathbf{Q}_1 \ldots \mathbf{Q}_{s-w}\, \mathbf{H}_0\, V_2^*\ldots V_m^* =$$
$$= X_{i,s+i}\, \mathbf{H}_0\, G_1^*\ldots G_w^*\, \mathbf{Q}_1 \ldots \mathbf{Q}_{s-w}\, V_2^*\ldots V_m^*$$

End case b

❑

Proving Finite Satisfiability of Deductive Databases

François Bry and Rainer Manthey
ECRC, Arabellastr. 17, D - 8000 München 81, West Germany

ABSTRACT *It is shown how certain refutation methods can be extended into semi-decision procedures that are complete for both unsatisfiability and finite satisfiability. The proposed extension is justified by a new characterization of finite satisfiability. This research was motivated by a database design problem: Deduction rules and integrity constraints in definite databases have to be finitely satisfiable.*

1. Introduction

When designing deductive databases, deduction rules and integrity constraints have to be checked for various well-formedness properties in order to prevent deficiencies at update or query time. Current research in deductive databases is focussing mainly on databases with definite deduction rules. A necessary well-formedness property for definite databases is the finite satisfiability (i.e., the existence of a finite model) of the set of all deduction rules and integrity constraints (considered as first-order formulas). A method able to detect finite satisfiability of formulas is therefore highly desirable, e.g. as part of an automated design system for definite databases.

Though finite satisfiability is undecidable [TRAC 50], it is at least semi-decidable (like, e.g., unsatisfiability). Therefore checking methods guaranteed to terminate for every finitely satisfiable input may exist. Finite satisfiability has been studied by logicians only indirectly. Since Hilbert's dream of a solution to the decision problem and Church's proof of its unsolvability, various special classes of formulas for which decision procedures may exist have been investigated. Many of these so-called *solvable classes* are in fact *finitely controllable* (a term introduced in [DG 79]), i.e., satisfiability and finite satisfiability coincide for these classes. [DG 79] provides a systematic and unified study of solvable classes in general and of finitely controllable classes in particular. However, decision methods for most of the finitely controllable classes are not known. Furthermore, these classes are characterized by means of rather strong syntactical restrictions which are too stringent for being acceptable in a database context.

Dreben and Goldfarb in addition provide a *finite model lemma* characterizing finitely satisfiable sets of formulas in general by means of term-mappings. In most cases, these mappings don't have any direct practical relevance either, as they are defined on the whole (usually infinite) Herbrand universe. We therefore give a new characterization of finite satisfiability in terms of Herbrand levels and special term-mappings of these finite subsets of the Herbrand universe. This characterization gives rise to extending refutation procedures based on the Herbrand's theorem - i.e., based on a model-theoretic paradigm - into semi-decision procedures for both, unsatisfiability as well as finite satisfiability. When applied to sets of formulas in a finitely controllable class, this extension is a decision procedure for the respective class.

Although it is well-known that direct implementations of Herbrand's theorem are inherently inefficient - as they are based on exhaustive instantiation - a treatment of finite satisfiability in the context of a Herbrand procedure provides valuable insight into the principle techniques on which efficient procedures may rely. Such a more efficient implementation of an instantiation-based proof procedure and its extension into a semi-decision procedure for finite satisfiability have been developped by the authors. They are documented in [MB 87, BDM 88]. In many cases this approach is competitive even if compared with sophisticated resolution-based techniques [MB 88].

This article consists of six sections. Section 1 is this introduction. Section 2 provides a more elaborate motivation of the relevance of finite satisfiability for databases. In Section 3, the Herbrand's theorem and the Herbrand procedure are recalled. Section 4 contains the above-mentioned characterization of finite satisfiability and the corresponding extension of the Herbrand procedure. In Section 5 the extended method is improved. It is combined in Section 6 with a model building approach to deciding propositional satisfiability. Section 7 is a conclusion.

Terminology and Notations

Where appropriate, we consider clauses instead of formulas. We assume that all function symbols denote Skolem functions. Skolemizing (i.e., replacing existentially quantified variables by Skolem terms) does not preserve logical equivalence. A formula F and one of its Skolem forms Sk(F) do not have the same interpretations, since interpretations of Sk(F) assign functions to Skolem function symbols, while interpretations of F ignore these symbols. However, interpretations of Sk(F) induce interpretations of F, and interpretations of F extend into interpretations of Sk(F): Skolemization preserves satisfiability. The proof of this result (see, e.g., [LOVE 78 ,p. 41]) can easily be adapted to proving that skolemization also preserves finite satisfiability.

The character S will always be used for denoting a *finite* set of clauses. H_S denotes the Herbrand universe of S, $H_S{}^i$ the ith level of H_S. $\Delta_S{}^i$ denotes the difference set $H_S{}^i \setminus H_S{}^{i-1}$. Given a subset T of H_S, T[S] denotes the saturation of S over T, i.e., the set of all ground clauses obtained by instantiating variables in clauses in S with terms in T.

Given a clause C and a set of pairs of (possibly ground) terms $\sigma=\{(t_1,u_1), (t_2,u_2), ..., (t_i,u_i), ...\}$ the clause $C\sigma$ is obtained by replacing simultaneously for all i each occurrence of a u_i in C by t_i. E.g., $p(f(a), x)\{(a,f(a))\} = p(a, x)$. The set σ is called a *substitution*.

If a set A is the union of two disjoint sets B and C, we write A = B + C. For other notions, refer to [MEND 69, LOVE 78].

2. Databases and Finite Satisfiability

A deductive database can be formalized in logic [GMN 84, REIT 84] as a triple DB = (F,DR,IC) where:

1. F is a finite set of variable-free atomic formulas.
   (The set of *facts*, or *extensional database*.)
2. DR is a finite set of closed first-order fromulas, used to derive new facts from F.
   (The set of *deduction rules*, or *intentional database*.)
3. IC is a finite set of closed first-order formulas expressing conditions imposed on the extensional as well as intentional databases.
   (The set of *integrity constraints*.)

If DR is empty, DB is a conventional relational database.

In order to preclude derivation of irreducible disjunctive formulas - a formula $F_1 \vee F_2$ is irreducible if neither F_1 nor F_2 are provable - the class of *definite* deduction rules has been defined [KUHN 67]. A formula is *definite* if:

1. all its variables are universally quantified
2. each conjunct of its conjunctive normal form contains exactly one non-negated atom.

A *definite deductive database* is a database the deduction rules of which are definite. In a definite database DB, F$\cup$DR is necessarily satisfiable (a set of definite formulas is always satisfiable). Since F$\cup$DR contains only formulas of the Bernays-Schoenfinkel class, it is even *finitely satisfiable*.

A database DB *satisfies its integrity constraints* if F$\cup$DR $\vdash$ IC, i.e., if all models of F$\cup$DR are models of IC. Therefore, finite satisfiability of IC and moreover of DR$\cup$IC is a necessary condition for definite deductive database [BM 86]. The importance of finite satisfiability for conventional as well as definite deductive databases has already been explicitly mentioned in [FV 84], implicitly in [NG 78].

3. The Herbrand Procedure

Most refutation procedures are justified by means of the following result:

Theorem 1: [Herbrand's Theorem]
S is unsatisfiable iff there is a Herbrand level H_S^i such that $H_S^i[S]$ is unsatisfiable.

This version of the Herbrand's theorem induces a basic refutation procedure - called the Herbrand procedure - that successively generates the level-saturations $H_S^i[S]$ and checks them for propositional unsatisfiability (which is a decidable property). If an unsatisfiable saturation is found, the procedure terminates: Unsatisfiability of S has been shown. In case all Skolem terms in S are constants (i.e., S corresponds to a formula of the Beranys-Schoenfinkel class), H_S is finite and all H_S^i are identical. In this case, satisfiability of H_S^0 implies finite satisfiability of S. Otherwise there are infinitely many levels to be considered, and the Herbrand procedure runs forever if S is satisfiable. All procedures introduced in the following are based on the Herbrand procedure:

Herbrand Procedure:

1. **Initialization**

i := 0,
if H_S^0 is unsatisfiable
then report unsatisfiability of S and stop
else if $H_S^0 = H_S^1$
    then report finite satisfiability of S and stop
    else goto 2.

2. **Unsatisfiability Check**

i := i+1,
if $H_S^i[S]$ is unsatisfiable
then report unsatisfiability of S and stop
else goto 2.

4. A Characterization of Finite Satisfiability

The Herbrand procedure detects finite satisfiability only if the Herbrand universe H_S is finite. There are, however, finitely satisfiable sets of clauses with infinite Herbrand universe. Proposition 3 characterizes these sets by means of the concept of *term-mapping* we first define:

Definition 2:

Let T be a subset of H_S.

A *term-mapping* σ *of* T is a surjective function from T onto T.

A term-mapping σ of a set $T \subseteq H_S$ induces a substitution $\{(\sigma(t),t) \mid t \in T\}$. This substitution is also denoted by σ.

Proposition 3: [Finite Model Lemma]

S is finitely satisfiable iff there is a term-mapping σ of H_S such that $\sigma(H_S)$ is finite and $H_S[S]\sigma$ is satisfiable.

This is the the characterization by Dreben and Goldfarb mentioned in the introduction. A method able to detect finite satisfiability must necessarily provide a feature that corresponds to the search for a term-mapping with finite range. Instead of searching for term-mappings of the Herbrand universe as a whole, we can restrict attention to special mappings of Herbrand levels only.

Definition 4:

A term-mapping σ of an Herbrand level $H_S{}^i$ is *regular* iff

1. $\sigma(H_S{}^i)$ is subterm-closed
   (i.e., if $t \in \sigma(H_S{}^i)$, then all subterms of t are in $\sigma(H_S{}^i)$ as well)
2. $\sigma(t) = t$ for all $t \in \sigma(H_S{}^i)$

Proposition 5:

S is finitely satisfiable iff there is a Herbrand level $H_S{}^i$ and a regular term-mapping σ of $H_S{}^{i+1}$ such that $\sigma(H_S{}^{i+1}) \subseteq H_S{}^i$ and $H_S{}^i[S]\sigma$ is satisfiable.

[Proof: (sketched) Necessary condition: If a regular term-mapping of $H_S{}^{i+1}$ is given, it extends naturally into a mapping of H_S. By Proposition 3, S is finitely satisfiable.

Sufficient condition: Assume S is finitely satisfiable. Consider a term-mapping σ of H_S such that $\sigma(H_S)$ is finite and $H_S[S]$ is satisfiable, the existence of which follows from Proposition 3.

Let < be a total order on H_S compatible with the Herbrand level hierarchy, i.e., such that:

1. $t^i < t^j$ if $t^i \in H_S{}^i$, $t^j \in H_S{}^j$, and $i \leq j$
2. $f(t_1{}^1,\dots,t_n{}^1) < f(t_1{}^2,\dots,t_n{}^2)$ if f is an n-ary function symbol, the $t_k{}^l$ are in H_S and $(t_1{}^1,\dots,t_n{}^1) <_L (t_1{}^2,\dots,t_n{}^2)$ in the lexicographical order $<_L$ induced by <.

Let ~ the equivalence relation on H_S defined from σ by $t^1 \sim t^2$ iff $\sigma(t^1) = \sigma(t^2)$.

Since $\sigma(H_S)$ is finite, $H_S/_\sigma$ is finite. Let $H_S/_\sigma = \{C_1,\dots,C_n\}$ and let c_k be the <-smallest element of C_k, for all $k = 1,\dots,n$. Define a term-mapping τ by $\tau(t) = c_k$, if $t \in C_k$. Let i be the smallest integer such that $H_S{}^i$ contains all c_k; i exists because there are only finitely many c_k.

• τ is regular:

$\tau(H_S{}^i)$ is subterm-closed because of the definiton of <.

$\tau(t) = t$ for all $t \in \tau(H_S{}^{i+1})$ by definition of τ and since $\tau(H_S{}^{i+1}) = \{c_1,\dots,c_k\}$.

• $\tau(H_S^{i+1}) \subseteq H_S^i$:
by definition of i.
• $H_S^i[S]\tau$ is satisfiable:
By definition of i and ~, $H_S^i[S]$ is isomorphic to $H_S/_{\sim}[S]$. $H_S^i[S]\tau$ is therefore isomorphic to $H_S/_{\sim}[S]\sigma$. Since the quotient of H_S by ~ preserves σ, $H_S/_{\sim}[S]\sigma$ is satisfiable like $H_S[S]\sigma$. $H_S^i[S]\tau$ is therefore satisfiable as well.]

Proposition 5 motivates the following first extension of the Herbrand procedure.

Procedure 1:

1. **Initialization**

i := 0,
if H_S^0 is unsatisfiable
then report unsatisfiability of S and stop
else if $H_S^0 = H_S^1$
    then report finite satisfiability of S and stop
    else goto 2.

2. **Finite Satisfiability Check**

for each regular term-mapping σ of H_S^{i+1} such that $\sigma(H_S^{i+1}) \subseteq (H_S^i)$
    if $H_S^i[S]\sigma$ is satisfiable
    then report finite satisfiability of S and stop,
goto 3.

3. **Unsatisfiability Check**

i := i+1,
if $H_S^i[S]$ is unsatisfiable
then report unsatisfiability of S and stop
else goto 2.

Procedure 1 stops for finitely satisfiable as well as for unsatisfiable S and runs forever iff S is an axiom of infinity. In the following sections, we propose optimizations of this finite satisfiability check.

5. An Improved Procedure

The efficiency of Procedure 1 can be considerably improved, if an optimization technique is applied that is often called Δ-optimization, for example in recursion theory [BAYE 85]. Since a Herbrand level $H_S{}^i$ contains every smaller level it can be computed recursively according to:

$$H_S{}^i = H_S{}^{i-1} + \Delta_S{}^i$$

Regular term-mappings of Herbrand levels may be obtained recursively as well. Consider a term-mapping σ^i of $H_S{}^i$. By definition of regularity the restriction σ^{i-1} of σ^i to $H_S{}^{i-1}$ is regular, too. Therefore a regular term-mapping δ^i: $\Delta_S{}^i \rightarrow H_S{}^i$ exists such that:

$$\sigma^i = \sigma^{i-1} + \delta^i$$

This equation serves as the basis of an optimized finite satisfiability check where regular term-mappings on level i are systematically constructed by augmenting mappings that have already been constructed on level i-1.

However, not all possible augmentations are acceptable. Consider Herbrand levels $H_S{}^1 = \{a, f(a), g(a)\}$ and $H_S{}^2 = \{a, f(a), g(a), f^2(a), f(g(a)), g(f(a)), g^2(a)\}$ and the following regular term-mapping σ^1 of $H_S{}^1$:

$a \rightarrow a$
$f(a) \rightarrow a$
$g(a) \rightarrow g(a)$

The fact that σ^1 replaces f(a) by a and leaves g(a) unchanged already "predetermines" the assignments of a to $f^2(a)$, and of g(a) to g(f(a)) in any acceptable extension of σ^1. Therefore only replacements for the remaining terms $g^2(a)$ and f(g(a)) have to be chosen when constructing a possible δ^2. We say that δ^2 has to be σ^1-*compatible*. This property is formally defined as follows:

Definition 6:
Let σ^{i-1} be a term-mapping of $H_S{}^i$ and δ^i a term-mapping of $\Delta_S{}^i$.
δ^i is σ^i-*compatible* iff for every term $t = f(t_1,\dots,t_n) \in \Delta_S{}^i$, we have:

$$t' = f(\sigma^{i-1}(t_1),\dots,\sigma^{i-1}(t_n)) \in H_S{}^{i-1} \Rightarrow \delta^i(t) = \sigma^{i-1}(t')$$

The previous remarks lead to the following procedure sound and complete for both unsatisfiability and finite satisfiability. (A term-mapping σ is expressed as a set of pairs (σ(t),t).)

Procedure 2:

1. **Initialization**

M^0 :- $\{(t,t) \mid t \in H_S^0\}$,
i := 0,
if H_S^0 is unsatisfiable
then report unsatisfiability of S and stop
else if $H_S^0 = H_S^1$
  then report finite satisfiability of S and stop
  else goto 2.

2. **Finite Satisfiability Check**

$M^{i+1} := \emptyset$,
for each $\sigma^i \in M^i$
  for each σ^i-compatible and regular term-mapping $\delta^{i+1}: \Delta_S^{i+1} \rightarrow H_S^{i+1}$
    $\sigma^{i+1} := \sigma^i + \delta^{i+1}$,
    if $\sigma\, H_S^i[S]$ is satisfiable
    then report finite satisfiability of S and stop
    else $M^{i+1} := M^{i+1} \cup \{\sigma^{i+1}\}$,
goto 3.

3. **Unsatisfiability Check**

i := i+1,
if $H_S^i[S]$ is unsatisfiable
then report unsatisfiability of S and stop
else goto 2.

This procedure, as opposed to the Herbrand procedure, is no longer linear: It performs in fact a breadth-first search of a tree the nodes of which are the members of the sets M^i.

6. Finite Satisfiability Checking on the Basis of g-Models

Saturations over Herbrand levels are sets of ground clauses and may therefore be checked for unsatisfiability by means of an appropriate decision procedure for propositional calculus. Most of the refutation procedures prior to resolution, such as the tableaux method [BETH 59, SMUL 68] and the Davis-Putnam method [DP 60] are based on the notion of g-model [LOVE 78].

Definition 7:

A *g-model* M of a set S of *ground* clauses is a set of unit clauses such that:

1. M does not contain complementary literals.
2. Every clause in S contains a literal in M.

Combining level saturation and construction of g-models leads to a characterization of unsatisfiability that can be seen as a corollary to the Herbrand's theorem.

Proposition 8:

S is unsatisfiable iff some level saturation $H_S^i[S]$ has no g-model.

In a similar way we characterize finite satisfiability by applying regular term-mappings directly to the g-models of level saturations:

Proposition 9:

S is finitely satisfiable iff there is a level H_S^i, a g-model g^i of $H_S^i[S]$, and a regular term-mapping σ of H_S^{i+1} such that $\sigma(H_S^{i+1}) \subseteq H_S^i$ and $g^i\sigma$ is satisfiable.

It can easily be checked whether application of σ to g^i preserves satisfiability: $g^i\sigma$ is unsatisfiable iff it contains two complementary unit clauses. Furthermore, g-models may also be obtained recursively: Every g-model g^i of $H_S^i[S]$ is the union of a g-model g^{i-1} of $H_S^{i-1}[S]$ and of a g-model d^i of $H_S^i[S] \setminus H_S^{i-1}[S]$.

We conclude this section with a semi-decision procedure for finite satisfiability and unsatisfiability based on g-models.

Procedure 3:

1. **Initialization**

M^0 :- $\{(t,t) \mid t \in H_S^0\}$,
i := 0,
G^0 := set of all g-models of $H_S^0[S]$,
if $G^0 = \emptyset$
then report unsatisfiability of S and stop
else if $H_S^0 = H_S^1$
  then report finite satisfiability of S and stop
  else goto 2.

2. **Finite Satisfiability Check**

$M^{i+1} := \emptyset$,
for each $g^i \in G^i$
  for each $\sigma^i \in M^i$
    for each σ^i-compatible and regular term-mapping δ^{i+1}: $\Delta_S{}^{i+1} \rightarrow H_S{}^{i+1}$
      $\sigma^{i+1} := \sigma^i + \delta^{i+1}$,
      if $\sigma^{i+1}(H_S{}^{i+1}) \subseteq H_S{}^i$ and $g^i\sigma^{i+1}$ is satisfiable
      then report finite satisfiability of S and stop
      else $M^{i+1} := M^{i+1} \cup \{\sigma^{i+1}\}$,
goto 3.

3. **Unsatisfiability Check**

$i := i+1$,
$G^i := \emptyset$,
for each $g^{i-1} \in G^{i-1}$
  for each g-model d^i of $H_S{}^i[S] \setminus H_S{}^{i-1}[S]$
    $g^i := g^{i-1} \cup d^i$,
    if g^i is satisfiable
    then $G^i := G^i \cup \{g^i\}$,
if $G^i = \emptyset$
then report unsatisfiability of S and stop
else goto 2.

As an example consider the following set S of clauses, expressing that every human has an ancestor, nobody is his own ancestor, and there are humans ('a' is a Skolem constant, 'f' is a Skolem function):

not anc(X,X)
not human(X) human(f(X))
not human(X) anc(X,f(X))
human(a)

M^0 consists of the identity mapping on $H_S{}^0$, and G^0 consists of the only g-model of $H_S{}^0$

$$g^0 = \{\text{not anc(a,a), human(a), human(f(a)), anc(a,f(a))}\}$$

There are two possible ways how to map $\Delta_S{}^1 = \{f(a)\}$ on $H_S{}^1 = \{a, f(a)\}$. Both are compatible with the mapping in M^0; thus M^1 contains $\sigma_1{}^1 = \{(a,a),(f(a),a)\}$ and $\sigma_2{}^1 = \{(a,a),(f(a),f(a)\}$. The first of these mappings is not yet sufficient because $g^0\sigma_1{}^1$ contains the complementary unit clauses 'anc(a,a)' and 'not anc(a,a)'. The second is not sufficient as $\sigma_2{}^1(H_S{}^1) = H_S{}^1$ is not a subset of $H_S{}^0$. There is only one possibility how to extend g^0 into

$$g^1 = g^0 \cup \{\text{not anc(f(a),f(a),human(}f^2\text{(a)),anc(f(a),}f^2\text{(a))}\}$$

Now $\sigma_2{}^1$ can be extended into $\sigma_1{}^2 = \{(a,a), (f(a),f(a)), (f^2(a),a)\}$. As $\sigma_1{}^2(H_S{}^2) = H_S{}^1$, and $g^1\sigma_1{}^2$ = {not anc(a,a), human(a), human(f(a)), anc(a,f(a)), anc(f(a),a), not anc(f(a),f(a))} is satisfiable, finite satisfiability has been confirmed: $g^1\sigma_1{}^2$ constitutes a finite model of S.

7. Conclusion

In this article, we have proposed an extension of the Herbrand procedure into a semi-decision method complete for both finite satisfiability and unsatisfiability. This procedure is justified by a new characterization of finite satisfiability based on the finite model lemma of Dreben and Goldfarb. It is shown how the additional feature we propose combines with model building refutation procedures. A practical procedure following this approach is described in [BDM 88]. It has been implemented in Prolog as a component of a database design system. The present paper provides a theoretical justification for this implementation.

Other approaches to finite satisfiability checking are possible. One of them, outlined in [BM 86], relies on resolution. Its main difference with the procedures described here is that it delays instantiation as much as possible as opposed to the "instantiation-first" strategy of Herbrand-like procedures. However the resolution-based approach cannot rely on a linear strategy, but requires a saturation strategy in order to reach all finite models.

Whatever approach is chosen, one has to be aware that the capability to detect finite satisfiability necessarily introduces a severe overhead in case the set of formulas under consideration turns out to be unsatisfiable.

8. Acknowledgement

The authors are grateful to Jean-Marie Nicolas for his patience and support during this research, and to Hervé Gallaire and all ECRC for providing such a stimulating environment.

9. References

[BAYE 85] Bayer, R.
Query Evaluation and Recursion in Deductive Database Systems.
Technical Report TUM-18503, Technical University of Munich, 1985.

[BDM 88] Bry, F., Decker, H. and Manthey, R.
A Uniform Approach to Constraint Satisfaction and Constraint Satisfiability in Deductive Databases.
In *Advanced in Database Technology - Proc. EDBT '88.* Mar., 1988.
Springer-Verlag, LNCS 303.

[BETH 59] Beth, E.W.
The Foundation of Mathematics.
North Holland, Amsterdam, 1959.
cited in [SMUL 68].

[BM 86] Bry, F. and Manthey, R.
Checking Consistency of Database Constraints: A Logical Basis.
In *Proc. 12th Int. Conf. on Very Large Data Bases (VLDB '86).* Aug. 25-28, 1986.

[DG 79] Dreben, B. and Goldfarb, W.
The Decision Problem - Solvable Classes of Quantified Formulas.
Addison-Wesley, Reading, Massachussetts, 1979.

[DP 60] Davis, M. and Putnam, H.
A Computing Procedure for Quantification Theory.
J. of the ACM 7(3), Jul., 1960.

[FV 84] Fagin, R. and Vardi M.Y.
The Theory of Data Dependencies - An Overview.
In *Proc. of ICALP.* 1984.

[GMN 84] Gallaire, H., Minker, J. and Nicolas, J.-M.
Logic and Databases: A Deductive Approach.
ACM Computing Surveys 16(2), Jun., 1984.

[KUHN 67] Kuhns, J.L.
Answering Questions by Computer - A Logical Study.
Rand Memo RM 5428 PR, Rand Corp., Santa Monica, Calif., 1967.

[LOVE 78] Loveland, D.
Automated Theorem Proving: A Logical Basis.
North-Holland, Amsterdam, 1978.

[MB 87] Manthey, R. and Bry, F.
A Hyperresolution Proof Procedure and its Implementation in Prolog.
In *Proc. 11th German Workshop on Artificial Intelligence (GWAI '87).* Sep. 28-Oct. 2, 1987.
Springer-Verlag, IF 152.

[MB 88] Manthey, R. and Bry, F.
SATCHMO: A Theorem Prover Implemented in Prolog.
In *Proc. 9th Conf. on Automated Deduction (CADE '88).* May 23-26, 1988.
Springer-Verlag, LNCS.

[MEND 69] Mendelson, E.
Introduction to Mathematical Logic.
Van Nostrand Reinhold, New York, 1969.

[NG 78] Nicolas, J.-M. and Gallaire, H.
Database: Theory vs. Interpretation.
In *Logic and Databases.* Plenum, New York, 1978.

[REIT 84] Reiter, R.
Towards a Logical Reconstruction of Relational Database Theory.
In *On Conceptual Modelling.* Springer-Verlag, Berlin and New York, 1984.

[SMUL 68] Smullyan, R.
First-Order Logic.
Springer-Verlag, New York, 1968.

[TRAC 50] Trachtenbrot, B.A.
Impossibility of an Algorithm for the Decision Problem in Finite Classes.
Dokl. Acad. Nauk. SSSR 70, 1950.
in Russian, translated into English in Amer. Soc. Trans., Series 2, 23, 1963.

IS SETL A SUITABLE LANGUAGE FOR PARALLEL PROGRAMMING - A THEORETICAL APPROACH

by

Elias Dahlhaus

Department of Computer Science

University of Bonn

1. Introduction:

SETL (Set Language) is a programming language working on higher order objects, where the main data structure is the collection of hereditarily finite sets. It was introduced by J.T. Schwartz [Sch 75]. The main motivation for the development of such a programming language was the implementation of arbitrary mathematical structures. Independently on the development of SETL, logocians were interested in set recursion concepts (see for example [Mo 84], [No 78], and [Rö 64]). SETL has been theoretically discussed in [DM 85a] and [DM 85b] to give a good minimal computationally complete choice of basic constructs. The main motivation of these papers was to extend the results of Chandra and Harel [CH 80] to higher order objects, especially to develop a theoretical concept of directory handling as in UNIX and of object oriented programming in hierarchical data structures (compare also [Ho 83]). All concepts of set recursion and set oriented programming have the replacement construct in common which is nothing else than the execution of the replacement axiom in set theory.
That is a parallel construct. Therefore one might think that SETL-like languages are suitable for parallel programming.

We shall do a closer look to the implementation of NC-algorithms in SETL-like languages. NC (Nick's class) (see for example [Co 85]) is here the class of computation problems solvable in polylog parallel time by polynomially many processors. We shall see that there are fundamental difficulties in implementing NC-algorithms in SETL without marginal time loss.

Section 2 introduces the basic concepts of hereditarily finite sets, complexity classes, and basic constructs of a SETL-like language. Section 3 gives examples of NC-problems not solvable in polylog time in a SETL-like language. Section 4 presents an extension of the replacement construct, which makes it possible to solve the problems of section 3 in polylog time. Section 5 **proves the P-completeness of a** computation problem which can be solved in polylog time and polynomial space using the time measures of the extended SETL-like language of section 4. But this result hints at the unsuitability of SETL for parallel programming.

2. Basic Concepts:

2.1. Sets

We introduce non specified basic elements, so called *urelements* (see for example [Ba 75]). The set of urelements is denoted by D. We assume that D is finite.

Set V_0 := D ("sets" of level 0) and $V_{i+1} := V_i \cup P(V_i)$. Here P(X) is the power set of X. V_i is the collection of all sets of level at most i. The collection of all ***hereditarily finite sets*** over D, denoted by V(D), is the union over all $V_i(D)$.

2.2. Complexity classes

NC is the class of all computation problems solvable by a random access machine in polylog time by polynomially many processors. This is equivalent to the computability by a logspace uniform sequence of switching circuits of polylog depth and polynomial size (see [Co 85]).

2.3. An example of a computationally complete base of SETL-constructs:

OTL (Object Transformation Language) consists of the following basic constructs (see also [DM 85b]):

A *constant* D = set of urelements, a *unary operation* $\cup x$, *binary operations* {x,y} and x-y, the while x = ∅ -construct and the *replacement construct* $\{F(x,\bar{z}) : x \in y\}$ where F is just an OTL-computable function.

This is only an example of a computational base of constructs. But it seems to be a good example of a choice of constructs. In [Mo 84] and [Rö 64] one can find other examples of computationally complete bases.

2.4. Complexity measures on OTL-programs:

We define the execution time of a basic operation and of the while-condition check to be one. The execution time of the replacement construct is defined to be the maximal execution time of its components plus one.
Any set needs as many space as the size of its transitive closure.
Then the definition of the space complexity of an OTL-program is obvious.
We assume, that sets are implemented as directed acyclic graphs (U,E), which satisfy the axiom of extensionality:

$\forall u,v \ ((\forall x \ \ xEu \Leftrightarrow xEv) \Rightarrow u=v).$

Now we can compare complexity classes in the usual sense with OTL-complexity classes.
We can prove the following trivial statement:

Lemma 1. Suppose that the equalities and inequalities of all sets of any transitive closure of a stored set are known. Then each basic function of OTL is in NC and each OTL-program, which needs only a polylog execution time and polynomially many space, is in NC.

But the converse of the second statement of Lemma 1 is not true. An example is the transitive closure.
But in future we shall take the transitive closure operation as a basic construct of OTL.

Recall that the transitive closure is defined as follows:

$TC(x) := \{x\} \cup x \cup \bigcup x \cup \bigcup\bigcup x \cup \ldots$

But we shall see that also under the assumption that TC is a basic construct, the converse of the second statement of lemma 1 is not true.

3. The Mostowski-image, an NC-computable function not computable by an OTL-program in polylog time steps:

Each set theoretician is familiar with the following result.

Theorem of Mostowski. For each wellfounded relation (V,E), which satisfies the axiom of extensionality, there is a set x, called the *Mostowski image*, s.t. its transitive closure is isomorphic to (V,E).

We assume that each ordered pair (x,y) is represented by its *Kuratowski pair* $\{\{x,y\},\{x\}\}$. Then any relation is defined as a pair consisting of its domain and a set of Kuratowski pairs over a domain. The following result is obvious.

Lemma 2. For each Kuratowski pair its first and its second projection are NC-computable. The Mostowski image can be computed in NC.

But on the other hand we can prove the following trivial result for OTL-programs:

Lemma 3. At any time step the maximal level of all stored sets increases by at most one.

Corollary. The Mostowski image cannot be computed by an OTL-program in polylog time.

Remark: We have also much simpler NC-operations, which cannot be executed in polylog time by an OTL-program. Let n' be the n-iterated singleton of the empty set. Then we cannot compute (n+m)' from n' and m' in polylog time by an OTL-program. In the last case we can recognize equalities to old sets in the store provided that the equalities between the old sets are known. In the case of the Mostowski image it is at least not obvious, that we can do so.

In the next section we shall present an extension of the replacement construct which makes it possible to compute the Mostowski image with polynomial space in polylog time.

4. The extended replacement construct:

We call a set $V \subset TC(x)$ *(transtitively) closed,* iff for each $u \in V$ and each v, s.t $u \in v \in TC(x)$ we have $v \in V$.
The *extended replacement construct* is defined as follows:
Let F be an OTL-computable function. Define for each transitively closed subset V of TC(x) a function F', s.t. F' is identical to F on TC(x)-V and for $u \in V$ let $F'(u) := \{F'(v) : v \in u\}$. F'(x) is the result of the extended replacement applied to F, x, and V.
In the extended replacement the immediate predecessors of V in the directed acyclic graph representing the set x are replaced by new elements and the relational structure of V is preserved up to equalities.

Theorem 1. The following ***Mostowski epimorphism*** can be computed with polynomial space in polylog time. by OTL+extended replacement:
Given a well founded relation (V,E). The Mostowski epimorphism is the function f with domain V which satisfies
$f(x) = \{f(y) : (y,x) \in E\}$.

Proof.

We shall state an algorithm which works as follows.

Step 0: For each $x \in V$ let $f'(x) := \{y : (y,x) \in E\}$ and
$U(f'(x) := \{f'(x)\}$

Step 2: Repeat
Apply for each f'(x) and U(f'(x)) the extended replacement, using the function f' and let the result of the extended replacement be the new f'(x).
The new U(f'(x)) consists of the least closed set containing all U(f'(y)), s.t. $y \in TC(f'_{old}(x)) - U(f'_{old}(x))$ and $y \in u$ for at least one $u \in V(f'_{old}(x))$. (Repeatedly the leaves of f'(x) are replaced by their corresponding set).
until
We don't get any new result.

Step 3: Output f: = f'.

It is easily seen that at each recursion step the depth of each U(f'(x)) is multiplied by two. Therefore the loop is repeated only O(log n) times. It is obvious that the algorithm works in polynomial space. The algorithm can easily be transformed into a SETL+extended replacement-program.

Q.E.D.

The next section will show that the extended replacement construct is too powerfull for parallel computation.

5) A P-completeness result:

A P-time computation problem is called P-*complete*, iff each P-time solvable problem can be reduced to it by a logspace reduction. It is a well known trivial result, that the computability of one P-complete problem in NC would imly that P=NC. A well known P-complete problem is the Monotone Circuit Value problem abbreviated also by MCV (see [Go 77]):
Given an and-or-switching circuit and the truth values of its inputs. Is the output of the truth value true ?

We shall prove the following result.

Theorem 2. Computing the Mostowski epimorphism is P-complete.

Proof:

We shall show the P-completeness of the following subproblem by reduction from MCV:
Given a wellfounded relation (V,E) and $x_1, x_2 \in V$. Let f be its Mostowski epimorphism. Is $f(x_1)=f(x_2)$?

But the P-completeness of this decision problem can be checked by the following observation:

1) Simulation of <u>and</u>:

$$x_1=x_2 \text{ and } y_1=y_2 \quad \text{iff} \quad \{\{x_1,x_1\},\{y_1,y_2\}\}=\{\{x_1\},\{y_1\}\}$$

2) Simulation of <u>or</u>:

$$x_1=x_2 \text{ or } y_1=y_2 \quad \text{iff} \quad \{\{\{x_1,x_2\},\{y_1,y_2\}\},\{\{x_1\},\{y_1,y_2\}\},\{\{x_1,x_2\},\{x_2\}\}\} = \{\{\{x_1\},\{y_1,y_2\}\},\{\{x_1,x_2\},\{x_2\}\}\}.$$

It is obvious how to construct a weelfounded relation with two assigned elements x_1, x_2 from a given monotone switching circuit and given truth values of the inputs, s.t. x_1 and x_2 describe the same set iff the output of the switching circuit is true.

Q.E.D.

6. Conclusions:

Extended replacement is not a suitable construct for parallel programming unless P=NC. On the other hand OTL is too weak to cover in polylog time all NC-computable functions, even under the assumption that we have a total ordering on the set of the urelements. The problem of the computation of a canonical labelling on any wellfounded extensional relation in NC remains open. It can easily be done in P. In the case that it is in NC we are also able to check whether two wellfounded relations satisfying the axiom of extensionality desribe the same set. But then NC is the set of all computation problems computable in polylog time and polynomial space by a SETL+Mostowski-image-program. But the actual state of the art is that SETL-like languages are not suitable for parallel programming.

Another aspect is to consider only sets of bounded level, but over an infinite set of urelements. We refer to R. Gandy's pioneer paper [Ga 80] on principles of mechanism. He gave a philosophical background on describing mechanical devices in notions of set theory. A discussion on Gandy's principles of mechanism as a model of parallel computation is due to [DM 88].

References:

Ba 75 J. Barwise, Admissible Sets and Structures, Springer, Berlin 1975

CH 80 A. Chandra, D. Harel, Computable Queries of Relational Data Bases, JCSS 21.2 (1980), p. 156-178.

Co 85 S. Cook, A Taxonomy of Problems with Fast Parallel Algorithms, Information and Control 64 (1985), pp. 2-22.

DM 86a E. Dahlhaus, J. Makowsky, Computable Directory Queries, CAAP 86, LNCS 214, pp. 254-265.

DM 86b E. Dahlhaus, J. Makowsky, The Choice of Programming Primitives in SETL-Like Languages, ESOP 86, LNCS 213, pp. 160-172.

DM 88 E. Dahlhaus, J. Makowsky, Gandy's Principles of Mechanism as a Model of Parallel Computation, to appear in "The Universal Turing Machine, a Half Century Survey", R. Herken ed., Kammerer und Unverzagt, Hamburg.

Ga 80 R. Gandy,Church's Thesis and Principles of Mechanism, in "The Kleene-Symposium", J. Barwise et al. ed, North Holland, Amsterdam 1980, pp. 123-148.

Go 77 L. Goldschlager, The Monotone and Planar Circuit Value Problems are Logspace Complete for P, SIGACT News 9,2 (1977), pp. 25-29.

Ho 83 E. Horowitz, Fundamentals of Programming Languages, Computer Science Press, Rockville 1983.

Mo 84 Y. Moschovakis, Abstract Recursion as a Foundation for the Theory of Algorithms,"Computation and Proof Theory", M. Richter et al. ed., LNM 1104, Springer, Berlin 1984, pp. 289-362.

No 78 D. Norman, Set Recursion, in "Generalized Recursion Theory", J. Fensted et al. ed., North Holland, Amsterdam 1978, 303-320.

Rö 64 D. Rödding, Theorie der Rekusivität über dem Bereich der endlichen Mengen von endlichem Rang, Habilitationsschrift, Universität Münster 1964.

Sch 75 J. Schwartz, On Programming: An Interim Report on the SETL-Project, 2nd Edition, Courant Institute of Mathematics, New York 1975.

LOOSE
DIAGRAMS, SEMIGROUPOIDS, CATEGORIES, GROUPOIDS AND ITERATION

G. Germano and S. Mazzanti
Dip. di Informatica, Universita` di Pisa, 56100 PISA (Italy)
Dip. di Matematica e Informatica, Universita` di Udine, 33100 UDINE (Italy)

In [GM1], semantics of iteration was given in terms of a generalization of the classical inductive closure theory of [MO] and [B]. Computation paths were treated in an elementary way using concatenation, composition, and coalescence, to obtain closure algebras corresponding to **whiles**.
To reformulate that approach in a general algebraic way, we need first a systematic taxonomy of algebraic structures based on arrows. This paper constructs such a taxonomy using the arrow *loosely*, like [E]; this means that we allow that

$$a \xrightarrow{f} b \ , \ a' \xrightarrow{f} b' \quad \text{for} \quad \langle a, b \rangle \neq \langle a', b' \rangle \ .$$

In fact f may transform a into b and a' into b', also for a, b different from a', b' (pressing may transform a sphere into a disk and a cube into a square).
We consider loose diagrams, semigroupoids, categories and groupoids: thus we are able to obtain classes and graphs as special cases of diagrams, to obtain semigroups and transitive graphs as special cases of semigroupoids, to obtain monoids and preorders as special cases of categories, and to obtain groups and equivalences as special cases of groupoids.
The semigroupoid structure (corresponding to the semicategory structure of [GM2]), appears to play a central role, as well from the point of view of the above algebraic taxonomy as from the point of view of semantics of iteration.
In a future paper, we will show that the framework of the above algebraic structures allows us to obtain both inductive closure and semantics of **while** as functors adjoint to the inclusion functor. These functors act on comma semigroupoids or categories constructed on semigroupoids or categories of the computation sequences (histories, paths or processes) we introduce at the end of this paper.

PRELIMINARIES

Homomorphisms

For any relation $\mathscr{R}$ set

$$\operatorname{Arg} \mathscr{R} = \{ x \mid \exists_y \ x \mathscr{R} y \} \ \text{ and } \ \operatorname{Val} \mathscr{R} = \{ y \mid \exists_x \ x \mathscr{R} y \} .$$

For any two structures

$$\mathscr{A} = \langle U_1 , \ldots, U_m , R_1 , \ldots, R_n \rangle \ \text{ and } \ \mathscr{A}' = \langle U_1' , \ldots, U_m' , R_1', \ldots, R_n' \rangle$$

with the same signature:

$\mathscr{R}$ is a *partial homomorphism from* $\mathscr{A}$ *into* $\mathscr{A}'$

iff

$$\forall_{x, x'} \ (x \mathscr{R} x' \ \Rightarrow \ (x \in U_i \Rightarrow x' \in U_i')) ,$$

for $1 \le i \le m$, and

$$\forall_{x_1, \ldots, x_k, x_1', \ldots, x_k'} \ (\bigwedge_{1 \le i \le k} x_i \mathscr{R} x_i' \ \Rightarrow \ (< x_1, \ldots, x_k > \in R_j \Rightarrow \ < x_1', \ldots, x_k' > \in R_j')) ,$$

for $1 \le j \le n$;

$\mathscr{R}$ is a *(total) homomorphism from* $\mathscr{A}$ *into* $\mathscr{A}'$ iff $\mathscr{R}$ is a partial homomorphism from $\mathscr{A}$ into $\mathscr{A}'$ and

$$\cup_i U_i \ \subseteq \operatorname{Arg} \mathscr{R} ;$$

$\mathscr{R}$ is a *(total) homomorphism from* $\mathscr{A}$ *onto* $\mathscr{A}'$ iff $\mathscr{R}$ is a (total) homomorphism from $\mathscr{A}$ into $\mathscr{A}'$ and

$$\cup_i U_i' \subseteq \operatorname{Val} \mathscr{R} .$$

Operations on Sequences

Let $< >$ be the empty sequence and set

$$\operatorname{uni} x = < x > , \qquad \operatorname{emp} x = < > ,$$

$$\operatorname{first} < x_1, \ldots, x_k > = x_1 , \qquad \operatorname{last} < x_1, \ldots, x_k > = x_k ,$$

$$\operatorname{tail} < x > = < > , \qquad \operatorname{tail} < x_1, \ldots, x_k > = < x_2, \ldots, x_k > .$$

For any sequences s and t , let $s + t$ be the concatenation of s and t , so that

$$< > + s = s + < > = s ,$$

$$< x_1, \ldots, x_k > + < y_1, \ldots, y_l > = < x_1, \ldots, x_k, y_1, \ldots, y_l > .$$

For any sequences s and t, set

$$s \oplus t = s + \operatorname{tail} t \qquad \text{if } \operatorname{last} s = \operatorname{first} t ,$$

$$s \oplus t \quad \text{undefined} \qquad \text{otherwise} .$$

We call $s \oplus t$ the "coalescence" of s and t .

Coalescence is used, without name, in [ML] II, 7 and, implicitly, in [E] II, 1; the name was introduced in [GM1]; coalescence is a special case of natural join, see [U] §5.2 .

DIAGRAMS

We consider any two universes V, W and any ternary relation $\longrightarrow$.
We agree that $a, b, c, d \in V$ and $f, g, h \in W$; furthermore that $A, B, C, D \subseteq V$ and $F, G, H \subseteq W$.
We call a, b, c, d " objects ", we call f, g, h " actions " and we word $a \xrightarrow{f} b$ "f transforms a into b".
A structure $\langle V , W , \longrightarrow \rangle$ is a ***diagram*** iff

D1. $\forall_f \exists_{a,b}\ a \xrightarrow{f} b$.

We agree that $\mathscr{D}$ be a diagram .
We set

$$a_1 \xrightarrow{f_1} a_2 \xrightarrow{f_2} a_3 \ldots a_k \xrightarrow{f_k} a_{k+1} \Leftrightarrow a_1 \xrightarrow{f_1} a_2 \wedge a_2 \xrightarrow{f_2} a_3 \wedge \ldots \wedge a_k \xrightarrow{f_k} a_{k+1} .$$

For any structure $\mathscr{A} = \langle V, W, \longrightarrow, R_1, \ldots, R_k \rangle$, set

$$\mathrm{Act}_{\mathscr{A}}(a, b) = \{ f \mid a \xrightarrow{f} b \} , \ \mathrm{Type}_{\mathscr{A}} f = \{ <a, b> \mid a \xrightarrow{f} b \} .$$

and note that

$$f \in \mathrm{Act}_{\mathscr{A}}(a, b) \Leftrightarrow <a, b> \in \mathrm{Type}_{\mathscr{A}} f .$$

Consider a new object Δ and set

$$a^\Delta = \Delta , \ V^\Delta = \{a^\Delta\}_a , \ f^\Delta = f ,$$

$$a^\Delta \xrightarrow[\Delta]{f} b^\Delta \Leftrightarrow a \xrightarrow{f} b , \ R_i^\Delta(x_1^\Delta, \ldots, x_k^\Delta) \Leftrightarrow R_i(x_1, \ldots, x_k) ,$$

$$\mathscr{A}_\Delta = \langle V^\Delta , W , \xrightarrow[\Delta]{} , R_1^\Delta, \ldots, R_k^\Delta \rangle ,$$

consider a new action ∇ and set

$$f^\nabla = \nabla , \ W = \{ f^\nabla \}_f , \ a^\nabla \xrightarrow[\nabla]{f^\nabla} b^\nabla \Leftrightarrow a \xrightarrow{f} b ,$$

$$\mathscr{A}^\nabla = \langle V , W^\nabla , \xrightarrow[\nabla]{} \rangle .$$

CLASSES

A class W can be identified with any diagram $\mathscr{D} = \langle \{a\} , W , \longrightarrow \rangle$, where

$$\forall_f\ a \xrightarrow{f} a .$$

Lemma. For every $\mathscr{D}$: $\mathscr{D}_\Delta$ can be identified with a class ♦

GRAPHS

We consider any binary relation E . Any structure $\langle V , E \rangle$ is a (directed) *graph* .
A graph $\langle V , E \rangle$ can be identified with any diagram $\mathscr{D} = \langle V , E_f , \longrightarrow \rangle$, where

$$E_f = \{ f \} \quad \text{if } \exists_{a,b}\ a E b ,$$

$$E_f = \varnothing \quad \text{otherwise}$$

for some f , and

$$a E b \Leftrightarrow a \xrightarrow{f} b .$$

Lemma. For every $\mathscr{D}$: $\mathscr{D}^\nabla$ can be identified with a graph ♦

EXAMPLES

1.1. Homomorphism Diagrams

For any two structures $\mathscr{A}$, $\mathscr{A}'$ and any relation $\mathscr{R}$, let :

$$\mathscr{A} \xrightarrow[\text{part}]{\mathscr{R}} \mathscr{A}'$$

iff $\mathscr{R}$ is a *partial homomorphism from* $\mathscr{A}$ *into* $\mathscr{A}'$;

$$\mathcal{A} \xrightarrow{\mathcal{R}} \mathcal{A}'$$

iff $\mathcal{R}$ is a *(total) homomorphism from* $\mathcal{A}$ *into* $\mathcal{A}'$;

$$\mathcal{A} \xrightarrow[\text{onto}]{\mathcal{R}} \mathcal{A}'$$

iff $\mathcal{R}$ is a *(total) homomorphism from* $\mathcal{A}$ *onto* $\mathcal{A}'$.

Let Set be the class of all sets, let Rel be the class of all relations, let Fct be the class of all functions, and let Inj be the class of all injections. Then:

$\langle$ Set , Rel , $\xrightarrow[\text{part}]{}$ $\rangle$ is the *diagram of partial relations*,

$\langle$ Set , Rel , $\longrightarrow$ $\rangle$ is the *diagram of (total) relations*,

$\langle$ Set , Fct , $\xrightarrow[\text{part}]{}$ $\rangle$ is the *diagram of partial functions*,

$\langle$ Set , Fct , $\longrightarrow$ $\rangle$ is the *diagram of (total) functions*,

$\langle$ Set , Inj , $\longrightarrow$ $\rangle$ is the *diagram of inclusions*,

$\langle$ Set , Inj , $\xrightarrow[\text{onto}]{}$ $\rangle$ is the *diagram of bijections*.

Let N^i be the set of all sequences of i natural numbers.

Let Pcomp$\{ < N^i, N > \}_i$ be the set of traditional *partial recursive functions*.

Let Tcomp$\{ < N^i, N > \}_i$ be the set of traditional *total recursive functions*.

Let Pcomp$\{ < N^i, N^j > \}_{i,j}$ be the set of *partial computable sequence functions*, see [EE] and [GMS].

Let Tcomp$\{ < N^i, N^j > \}_{i,j}$ be the set of *total computable sequence functions*. Then:

$\langle \{ N^i \}_i$, Comp$\{ < N^i, N > \}_i$, $\xrightarrow[\text{part}]{}$ $\rangle$ is the *diagram of partial recursive functions*,

$\langle \{ N^i \}_i$, Comp$\{ < N^i, N > \}_i$, $\longrightarrow$ $\rangle$ is the *diagram of total recursive functions*,

$\langle \{ N^i \}_i$, Comp$\{ < N^i, N^j > \}_{i,j}$, $\xrightarrow[\text{part}]{}$ $\rangle$ is the *diagram of partial computable sequence functions*,

$\langle \{ N^i \}_i$, Comp$\{ < N^i, N^j > \}_{i,j}$, $\longrightarrow$ $\rangle$ is the *diagram of total computable sequence functions*.

Let Diag be the class of all diagrams and let Fcr_D be the class of all *diagram functors* i.e. functional homomorphisms on diagrams. Then:

$\langle$ Diag , Fcr_D , $\longrightarrow$ $\rangle$ is the *diagram of diagram functors*.

1.2. Local Diagrams

Consider any subdiagram $\mathcal{D} = \langle V, W, \longrightarrow \rangle$ of the diagram of partial relations, such that $\varnothing \notin W$.

For $x, y \in \cup V$ and $R \in W$, set

$$x \xmapsto{R} y \Leftrightarrow \; < x, y > \in R \;.$$

Then loc $\mathcal{D} = \langle \cup V, W, \longmapsto \rangle$ is the *local diagram of* $\mathcal{D}$.

For instance

$$\mathrm{loc}\langle \{ N^i \}_i \;,\; \mathrm{Pcomp}\{ < N^i, N^j > \}_{i,j} \;,\; \xrightarrow[\text{part}]{} \rangle$$
$$= \langle N^* \;,\; \mathrm{Pcomp}\{ < N^i, N^j > \}_{i,j} \;,\; \longmapsto \rangle .$$

Consider any diagram $\mathcal{D}' = \langle V', W', \longrightarrow' \rangle$ and any class $P \subseteq \mathrm{Pow}\, V' = \{ X \mid X \subseteq V' \}$. Set

$$A \;\succ\!\!\xrightarrow{f} B \;\Leftrightarrow\; \forall_{a \in A} \exists_{b \in B} \; a \xrightarrow{f}{}' b \;,$$
$$W'_P = \{ f \in W' \mid \exists_{A, B \in P} \; A \;\succ\!\!\xrightarrow{f} B \;\} .$$

Then $\mathrm{glob}_P \mathcal{D}' = \langle P, W'_P, \succ\!\!\longrightarrow \rangle$ is the *global diagram of* $\mathcal{D}'$ relatively to P.

For instance

$$\mathrm{glob}_{\{ N^i \}} \langle N^* \;,\; \mathrm{Tcomp}\{ < N^i, N^i > \}_{i,j} \;,\; \longmapsto \rangle$$
$$= \langle \{ N^i \} \;,\; \mathrm{Tcomp}\{ < N^i, N^i > \} \;,\; \longrightarrow \rangle .$$

Remark that, for every subdiagram $\mathscr{D}$ of the diagram of total relations, $\text{glob}_V(\text{ loc } \mathscr{D}) = \mathscr{D}$, in so far as

$$X \;\}\!\!\xmapsto{R} Y \Leftrightarrow \forall_{x\in X} \exists_{y\in Y}\; x \xmapsto{R} y$$
$$\Leftrightarrow \forall_{x\in X} \exists_{y\in Y} < x, y > \in R$$
$$\Leftrightarrow X \xrightarrow{R} Y .$$

For instance

$$\text{glob}_{\{\text{N}^i\}_i} \langle \text{N}^* ,\; \text{Tcomp}\{ < \text{N}^i, \text{N}^i > \}_{i,j} ,\; \longmapsto \rangle$$
$$= \langle \{ \text{N}^i \}_i ,\; \text{Tcomp}\{ < \text{N}^i, \text{N}^i > \}_{i,j} ,\; \longrightarrow \rangle .$$

1.3. dom/cod Diagrams

Consider any two functions

$$W \xrightarrow{\text{dom}} V ,\; W \xrightarrow{\text{cod}} V$$

and set

$$a \xrightarrow[\text{dom/cod}]{f} b \Leftrightarrow \text{dom} f = a \wedge \text{cod} f = b .$$

Then $\langle V, W, \xrightarrow[\text{dom/cod}]{} \rangle$ is a diagram , whereas $\langle V, W, \text{dom} , \text{cod} \rangle$ is a diagram in the sense of [G] and [MI] .

In particular, we consider the following special cases of dom/cod diagrams:

$$\langle \text{Set} ,\; \text{Rel} ,\; \xrightarrow[\text{Arg/Val}]{} \rangle = \langle \text{Set} ,\; \text{Rel} ,\; \xrightarrow[\text{onto}]{} \rangle ,$$
$$\langle X ,\; X^* ,\; \xrightarrow[\text{first/last}]{} \rangle ,$$

where X is any class,

$$\langle \text{Pow(Var)} ,\; \text{Prog} ,\; \xrightarrow[\text{In/Out}]{} \rangle ,$$

where Var is a set of variables, Prog is a programming language and the functions

$$\text{Prog} \xrightarrow{\text{In}} \text{Pow(Var)} ,\; \text{Prog} \xrightarrow{\text{Out}} \text{Pow(Var)} ,$$

assign to each program its input variables, respectively its output variables .

If Prog is defined by a grammar like this

<program> ::= <variable>:=<arithmetic expression> | <program>;<program>
| **if** <boolean expression> **then** <program> **endif**
| **while** <boolean expression> **do** <program> **endwhile** ,

then the functions In and Out can be defined in the following way:

In(x:=A) = Var(A) ; Out(x:=A) = $\{x\}$ ∪ Var(A) ;

In(p;q) = In(p) ∪ (In(q) - Out(p)) ; Out(p;q) = Out(p) ∪ Out(q) ;

In(**if** B **then** p **endif**) = Out(**if** B **then** p **endif**) = Var(B) ∪ In(p) ;

In(**while** B **do** p **endwhile**) = Out(**while** B **do** p **endwhile**) = Var(B) ∪ In(p) ,

where A is an arithmetic expression, B is a boolean expression, Var A is the set of variables occurring in A , whereas Var B is the set of variables occurring in B and p, q are programs .

1.4. Class of Actions on one Object

Consider any diagram $\mathscr{D} = \langle V , W , \longrightarrow \rangle$ and any object a .

Then the diagram $\langle \{a\} , \text{Act}_{\mathscr{D}}(a, a) , \longrightarrow \rangle$ can be identified with the class $\text{Act}_{\mathscr{D}}(a, a)$.

1.5. Graph of a Relation

Consider any family of sets $\{ X_i \}_i$, and any relation $R \neq \emptyset$, such that $X_i \xrightarrow{R} X_j$ for some i and j. Then the subdiagram $\langle \{ X_i \}_i , \{ R \} , \longrightarrow \rangle$ of the diagram of relations is the *graph of* R *on* $\{ X_i \}_i$ and the local graph $\langle \cup_i X_i , \{ R \} , \longmapsto \rangle$ is the *local graph of* R *on* $\{ X_i \}_i$.

SEMIGROUPOIDS

Let $\mathrm{Con} = \{ <f, g> \mid \exists_{a,b,c}\, a \xrightarrow{f} b \xrightarrow{g} c \}$. We word $f \,\mathrm{Con}\, g$ " f and g are connected ".
We consider any total operation $\cdot$ from Con into W and we call $f{\cdot}g$ the " composition of f and g ".
An algebra $\langle \mathscr{D} , \cdot \rangle = \langle V , W , \longrightarrow , \cdot \rangle$ is a ***semigroupoid*** iff $\mathscr{D}$ is a diagram and

S1. $\quad \forall_{a,f,b,g,c}\, (a \xrightarrow{f} b \xrightarrow{g} c \Rightarrow a \xrightarrow{f\cdot g} c)$,

S2. $\quad \forall_{a,f,b,g,c,h,d}\, (a \xrightarrow{f} b \xrightarrow{g} c \xrightarrow{h} d \Rightarrow (f{\cdot}g){\cdot}h = f{\cdot}(g{\cdot}h))$.

We agree that $\mathscr{S}$ be a semigroupoid .
We set

$$\begin{array}{ccc} a & \xrightarrow{f_1} & b_1 \\ f_2 \big\downarrow & & \big\downarrow g_1 \\ b_2 & \xrightarrow{f_2} & c \end{array} \Leftrightarrow \quad a \xrightarrow{f_1} b_1 \xrightarrow{g_1} c \wedge a \xrightarrow{f_2} b_2 \xrightarrow{g_2} c \wedge f_1{\cdot}g_1 = f_2{\cdot}g_2 .$$

SEMIGROUPS

We consider any total operation $W \times W \xrightarrow{\cdot} W$.
A structure $\langle W , \cdot \rangle$ is a *semigroup* iff it satisfies the associativity axiom

$$\forall_{f,g,h}\, (f{\cdot}g){\cdot}h = f{\cdot}(g{\cdot}h) .$$

A semigroup $\langle W , \cdot \rangle$ can be identified with any semigroupoid $\langle \{a\} , W , \longrightarrow , \cdot \rangle$ such that

$$\forall_f\, a \xrightarrow{f} a .$$

The composition $f{\cdot}g$ is defined for every f and g , while every f and g are connected, because

$$a \xrightarrow{f} a \xrightarrow{g} a$$

by axiom D1. The associativity axiom turns out to hold by axiom S2 , because

$$a \xrightarrow{f} a \xrightarrow{g} a \xrightarrow{h} a$$

by axiom D1 .

Lemma. For every $\mathscr{S}$: $\mathscr{S}_\Delta$ can be identified with a semigroup ♦

TRANSITIVE GRAPHS

A graph is *transitive* iff it satisfies the transitivity axiom

$$\forall_{a,b,c}\, (a E b \wedge b E c \Rightarrow a E c) .$$

Lemma. For every $\mathscr{S}$: $\mathscr{S}^\nabla$ can be identified with a transitive graph ♦

EXAMPLES

2.1. Homomorphism Semigroupoids

For any two relations $\mathscr{R}_1$ and $\mathscr{R}_2$, set $\mathscr{R}_1 \cdot \mathscr{R}_2 = \{ <x, z> \mid \exists_y\, x \mathscr{R}_1 y \wedge y \mathscr{R}_2 z \}$. Then:

$\langle \mathrm{Set} , \mathrm{Rel} , \xrightarrow[\text{part}]{} , \cdot \rangle$ is the *semigroupoid of partial relations* ,

$\langle \mathrm{Set} , \mathrm{Rel} , \longrightarrow , \cdot \rangle$ is the *semigroupoid of (total) relations* ,

$\langle \mathrm{Set} , \mathrm{Fct} , \xrightarrow[\text{part}]{} , \cdot \rangle$ is the *semigroupoid of partial functions* ,

$\langle \mathrm{Set} , \mathrm{Fct} , \longrightarrow , \cdot \rangle$ is the *semigroupoid of (total) functions* ,

$\langle \mathrm{Set} , \mathrm{Inj} , \longrightarrow , \cdot \rangle$ is the *semigroupoid of inclusions* ,

$\langle$ Set , Inj , $\xrightarrow[\text{onto}]{}$, $\cdot\rangle$ is the *semigroupoid of bijections* .

For any two homomorphisms $\mathcal{R}_1$ and $\mathcal{R}_2$, set

$$\mathcal{R}_1 \circ \mathcal{R}_2 = \mathcal{R}_1 \cdot \mathcal{R}_2 \qquad \text{if } \mathcal{R}_1 \text{ and } \mathcal{R}_2 \text{ are connected ,}$$
$$\mathcal{R}_1 \circ \mathcal{R}_2 \quad \text{undefined} \qquad \text{otherwise .}$$

Then:

$\langle \{ N^i \}_i$, Comp$\{ < N^i, N > \}_i$, $\longrightarrow$, $\cdot\rangle$ is the *semigroupoid of partial recursive functions* ,

$\langle \{ N^i \}_i$, Comp$\{ < N^i, N > \}_i$, $\longrightarrow$, $\circ\rangle$ is the *semigroupoid of total recursive functions* ,

$\langle \{ N^i \}_i$, Comp$\{ < N^i, N^j > \}_{i,j}$, $\longrightarrow$, $\cdot\rangle$ is the *semigroupoid of partial computable sequence functions,*

$\langle \{ N^i \}_i$, Comp$\{ < N^i, N^j > \}_{i,j}$, $\longrightarrow$, $\circ\rangle$ is the *semigroupoid of total computable sequence functions.*

Let Semig be the class of all semigroupoids and let Fcr_S be the class of all *semigroupoid functors* i.e. functional homomorphisms on semigroupoids. Then:

$\langle$ Diag , Fcr_D , $\longrightarrow$, $\circ\rangle$ is the *semigroupoid of diagram functors* ,

$\langle$ Semig , Fcr_S , $\longrightarrow$, $\circ\rangle$ is the *semigroupoid of semigroupoid functors* .

2.2. Local Semigroupoids

Consider any subsemigroupoid $\mathcal{S} = \langle V , W , \longrightarrow , \cdot\rangle$ of the semigroupoid of partial relations, such that $\emptyset \notin W$.

Then loc $\mathcal{S} = \langle \cup V , W , \longmapsto , \cdot\rangle$ is the *local semigroupoid of* $\mathcal{S}$.

For instance

$$\text{loc}\langle \{ N^i \}_i , \text{Pcomp}\{ < N^i, N^j > \}_{i,j} , \xrightarrow[\text{part}]{} , \cdot\rangle$$
$$= \langle N^* , \text{Pcomp}\{ < N^i, N^j > \}_{i,j} , \longmapsto , \cdot\rangle .$$

Consider any semigroupoid $\mathcal{S}' = \langle V' , W' , \longrightarrow' , \cdot'\rangle$ and a class $P \subseteq \text{Pow } V'$.

Then $\text{glob}_P \mathcal{S}' = \langle P , W'_P , \,\}\!\!\longrightarrow , \cdot'\rangle$ is the *global semigroupoid of* $\mathcal{S}'$ relatively to P .

For instance

$$\text{glob}_{\{ N^i \}}\langle N^* , \text{Tcomp}\{ < N^i, N^i > \}_{i,j} , \longmapsto , \circ\rangle$$
$$= \langle \{ N^i \} , \text{Tcomp}\{ < N^i, N^i > \} , \longrightarrow , \circ\rangle .$$

Remark that, for every subsemigroupoid $\mathcal{S}$ of the semigroupoid of total relations, $\text{glob}_V(\text{loc}\,\mathcal{S}) = \mathcal{S}$.

For instance

$$\text{glob}_{\{ N^i \}_i}\langle N^* , \text{Tcomp}\{ < N^i, N^i > \}_{i,j} , \longmapsto , \circ\rangle$$
$$= \langle \{ N^i \}_i , \text{Tcomp}\{ < N^i, N^i > \}_{i,j} , \longrightarrow , \circ\rangle .$$

2.3. dom/cod Semigroupoids

Consider any two functions

$$W \xrightarrow{\text{dom}} V , \; W \xrightarrow{\text{cod}} V$$

and any composition operation $\cdot$ such that

$$\forall_{f,g}(\text{cod} f = \text{dom}\, g \Rightarrow \text{dom}(f\cdot g) = \text{dom} f \wedge \text{cod}(f\cdot g) = \text{cod}\, g) ,$$
$$\forall_{f,g,h}(\text{cod} f = \text{dom}\, g \wedge \text{cod}\, g = \text{dom}\, h \Rightarrow (f\cdot g)\cdot h = f\cdot(g\cdot h)) .$$

Then $\langle V , W , \xrightarrow[\text{dom/cod}]{} , \cdot\rangle$ is a semigroupoid , whereas $\langle V , W , \text{dom} , \text{cod} , \cdot\rangle$ is a semicategory in the sense of [GM] 2 .

In particular, we consider the following special cases of dom/cod semigroupoids:

$$\langle \text{Set} , \text{Rel} , \xrightarrow[\text{Arg/Val}]{} , \cdot\rangle = \langle \text{Set} , \text{Rel} , \xrightarrow[\text{onto}]{} , \cdot\rangle ,$$

where $\cdot$ is the composition operation of 2.1,

$$\langle X \ , \ X^* \ , \ \xrightarrow[\text{first/last}]{} \ , + \rangle \ ,$$

$$\langle X \ , \ X^+ \ , \ \xrightarrow[\text{first/last}]{} \ , \oplus \rangle \ ,$$

where X is any class,

$$\langle \text{Pow(Var)} \ , \ \text{Prog} \ , \ \xrightarrow[\text{In/Out}]{} \ , \ ; \rangle \ .$$

2.4. Semigroupoid of Natural Transformations

Consider any two structures

$$\mathscr{A} = \langle V \ , \ W \ , \ \longrightarrow \ , \ \cdot \ , R_1, \ldots, R_n \rangle \ ,$$

$$\mathscr{A}' = \langle V' \ , \ W' \ , \ \longrightarrow' \ , \ \cdot' \ , R'_1, \ldots, R'_n \rangle \ ,$$

any two homomorphisms

$$\mathscr{A} \xrightarrow{\mathscr{R}_1} \mathscr{A}' \ , \quad \mathscr{A} \xrightarrow{\mathscr{R}_2} \mathscr{A}' \ ,$$

any function

$$V \xrightarrow{\tau} W'$$

and set

$$\mathscr{R}_1 \xrightarrow[\text{nat}]{\tau} \mathscr{R}_2$$

iff

$$\forall_{a,f,b,a_1',f_1',b_1',a_2',f_2',b_2'}$$

$$(a \mathscr{R}_1 a_1' \wedge b \mathscr{R}_1 b_1' \wedge f \mathscr{R}_1 f_1' \wedge a \mathscr{R}_2 a_2' \wedge b \mathscr{R}_2 b_2' \wedge f \mathscr{R}_2 f_2'$$

$$\Rightarrow \quad (a \xrightarrow{f} b \ \Rightarrow \ \begin{array}{ccc} a_1' & \xrightarrow{f_1'} & b_1' \\ {\scriptstyle \tau a}\big\downarrow & & \big\downarrow{\scriptstyle \tau a} \\ a_2' & \xrightarrow{f_2'} & b_2' \end{array})) \ .$$

We word $\mathscr{R}_1 \xrightarrow[\text{nat}]{\tau} \mathscr{R}_2$ "τ is a natural transformation from $\mathscr{R}_1$ to $\mathscr{R}_2$".

Let Hom_S be the class of all semigroupoid homomorphisms and let Nat_S be the class of all natural transformations on semigroupoid homomorphisms.

Then $\langle \text{Hom}_S \ , \ \text{Nat}_S \ , \xrightarrow[\text{nat}]{} \ , \ \cdot \ \rangle$ is the *semigroupoid of natural transformations on semigroupoids* .

2.5. Semigroup of Actions on one Object

Consider any semigroupoid $\mathscr{S} = \langle V \ , \ W \ , \ \longrightarrow \ , \ \cdot \rangle$ and any object a .

Then $\langle \{ a \} \ , \ \text{Act}_{\mathscr{S}}(a, a) \ , \ \longrightarrow \ , \ \cdot \rangle$ can be identified with the semigroup $\langle \text{Act}_{\mathscr{S}}(a, a) \ , \ \cdot \ \rangle$.

2.6. Semigroup of Positive Iterations of a Relation

Consider any set X, any relation R, such that $X \xrightarrow{R} X$, and the composition operation $\cdot$ of 2.1 .

Then $\langle \{ X \} \ , \ \{ R^i \}_{i>0} \ , \ \longrightarrow \ , \ \cdot \rangle$ can be identified with the *semigroup* $\langle \{ R^i \}_{i>0} \ , \ \cdot \ \rangle$ *of positive iterations of* R *on* X .

2.7. Transitive Graph of the less-than Relation

Consider the successor function on natural numbers $\mathrm{N} \xrightarrow{S} \mathrm{N}$ and the composition operation $\cdot$ of 2.1 .

Then the local semigroupoid of $\langle \{ \mathrm{N} \} \ , \ \{ S^i \}_{i>0} \ , \ \longrightarrow \ , \ \cdot \rangle$ is

$$\langle \mathrm{N} \ , \ \{ S^i \}_{i>0} \ , \ \longmapsto \ , \ \cdot \rangle$$

and

$$\langle \mathrm{N}, \{S^i\}_{i\geq 0}, \longmapsto, \cdot\rangle^{\nabla} = \langle \mathrm{N}, \{\nabla\}, \underset{\nabla}{\longmapsto}\rangle$$

can be identified with the transitive graph $\langle \mathrm{N}, < \rangle$.

CATEGORIES

We consider any total operation 1 from V into W and we call $1a$ the " unit of a ".

A structure $\langle \mathcal{S}, 1\rangle = \langle V, W, \longrightarrow, \cdot, 1\rangle$ is a ***category*** iff $\mathcal{S}$ is a semigroupoid and

C1. $\forall_a\ a \xrightarrow{1a} a$,

C2. $\forall_{a,f,b}\ (a \xrightarrow{f} b \Rightarrow (1a)\cdot f = f = f\cdot(1b))$.

We agree that $\mathcal{C}$ be a category .

MONOIDS

We consider any action $e \in W$.

A structure $\langle W, \cdot, e\rangle$ is a *monoid* iff $\langle W, \cdot\rangle$ is a semigroup and satisfies the unity axiom

$$\forall_f\ e\cdot f = f = f\cdot e\ .$$

A monoid $\langle W, \cdot, e\rangle$ can be identified with any category $\langle \{a\}, W, \longrightarrow, \cdot, 1\rangle$ such that

$$\forall_f\ a \xrightarrow{f} a \text{ and } 1a = e\ .$$

The unity axiom turns out to hold by axiom C2 , because $a \xrightarrow{1a} a$, by axiom C1 .

Lemma. For every $\mathcal{C}$: $\mathcal{C}_\Delta$ can be identified with a monoid.♦

PREORDERS

A graph is *reflexive* iff it satisfies the reflexivity axiom

$$\forall_a\ a E a\ .$$

A *preorder* is a transitive and reflexive graph .

Lemma. For every $\mathcal{C}$: $\mathcal{C}^\nabla$ can be identified with a preorder ♦

EXAMPLES

3.1. Homomorphism Categories

For any structure $\mathcal{A} = \langle U_1, \ldots, U_m, R_1, \ldots, R_n\rangle$, let $1\mathcal{A} = \{ <x,x> \mid x \in \cup_i U_i \}$. Then:

$\langle \mathrm{Set}, \mathrm{Rel}, \xrightarrow[\mathrm{part}]{}, \cdot, 1\rangle$ is the *category of partial relations* ,

$\langle \mathrm{Set}, \mathrm{Rel}, \longrightarrow, \cdot, 1\rangle$ is the *category of (total) relations* ,

$\langle \mathrm{Set}, \mathrm{Fct}, \xrightarrow[\mathrm{part}]{}, \cdot, 1\rangle$ is the *category of partial functions* ,

$\langle \mathrm{Set}, \mathrm{Fct}, \longrightarrow, \cdot, 1\rangle$ is the *category of (total) functions* ,

$\langle \mathrm{Set}, \mathrm{Inj}, \longrightarrow, \cdot, 1\rangle$ is the *category of inclusions* ,

$\langle \mathrm{Set}, \mathrm{Inj}, \xrightarrow[\mathrm{onto}]{}, \cdot, 1\rangle$ is the *category of bijections* ,

$\langle \{\mathrm{N}^i\}_i, \mathrm{Pcomp}\{<\mathrm{N}^i, \mathrm{N}^j>\}_{i,j}, \xrightarrow[\mathrm{part}]{}, \cdot, 1\rangle$ is the *category of partial computable sequence functions* ,

$\langle \{\mathrm{N}^i\}_i, \mathrm{Tcomp}\{<\mathrm{N}^i, \mathrm{N}^j>\}_{i,j}, \longrightarrow, \cdot, 1\rangle$ is the *category of total computable sequence functions* ,

$\langle \mathrm{Diag}, \mathrm{Fcr}_{\mathrm{D}}, \longrightarrow, \circ, 1\rangle$ is the *category of diagram functors* ,

$\langle$ Semig , Fcr_S , $\longrightarrow$, $\circ$, 1 $\rangle$ is the *category of semigroupoid functors* .

Let Cat be the class of all categories and Fcr_C be the class of all *category functors* i.e. functional homomorphisms on categories . Then:

$\langle$ Cat , Fcr_C , $\longrightarrow$, $\circ$, 1 $\rangle$ is the *category of category functors* .

3.2. Local Categories

Consider any category $\mathscr{C} = \langle V, W, \longrightarrow, \cdot, 1 \rangle$ of the category of partial relations.

Assume that $\varnothing \notin W$ and that the sets in V are pairwise disjoint.

For $x \in \bigcup V$, let set x be the unique set in V , such that $x \in$ (set x) and let $\mathrm{l}x = 1(\text{set } x)$.

Then loc $\mathscr{C} = \langle \bigcup V , W , \longmapsto , \cdot , \mathrm{l} \rangle$ is the *local category of* $\mathscr{C}$.

For instance

$$\text{loc}\langle \{ N^i \}_i , \text{Pcomp}\{ < N^i, N^j > \}_{i,j} , \xrightarrow[\text{part}]{} , \cdot , 1 \rangle$$
$$= \langle N^* , \text{Pcomp}\{ < N^i, N^j > \}_{i,j} , \longmapsto , \cdot , \text{len} \rangle ,$$

where $\text{len}(n_1, ..., n_i) = 1(N^i)$.

Consider any category $\mathscr{C}' = \langle V' , W' , \longrightarrow' , \cdot' , 1' \rangle$ and any class $P \subseteq \text{Pow } V'$, such that

$$x, y \in X \in P \Rightarrow 1'x = 1'y .$$

Set

$$\text{un } X = \bigcup_{x \in X} 1'x .$$

Then $\text{glob}_P \mathscr{C}' = \langle P, W'_P , \longmapsto , \cdot' , \text{un} \rangle$ is the *global category of* $\mathscr{C}'$ relatively to P .

For instance

$$\text{glob}_{\{ N^i \}} \langle N^* , \text{Tcomp}\{ < N^i, N^i > \}_{i,j} , \longmapsto , \circ , \text{len} \rangle$$
$$= \langle \{ N^i \} , \text{Tcomp}\{ < N^i, N^i > \} , \longrightarrow , \circ , 1 \rangle .$$

Remark that, for every subcategory $\mathscr{C}$ of the category of total relations (with the above properties),

$$\text{glob}_V (\text{loc } \mathscr{C}) = \mathscr{C}.$$

For instance

$$\text{glob}_{\{ N^i \}_i} \langle N^* , \text{Tcomp}\{ < N^i, N^i > \}_{i,j} , \longmapsto , \circ , \text{len} \rangle$$
$$= \langle \{ N^i \}_i , \text{Tcomp}\{ < N^i, N^i > \}_{i,j} , \longrightarrow , \circ , 1 \rangle .$$

3.3. dom/cod Categories

Consider any two functions

$$W \xrightarrow{\text{dom}} V , W \xrightarrow{\text{cod}} V$$

any composition operation $\cdot$ as in 2.3 and any unit operation 1, such that

$$\forall_a \text{dom}(1a) = \text{cod}(1a) = a ,$$
$$\forall_f ((1(\text{dom} f))\cdot f = f = f\cdot(1(\text{cod} f))) .$$

Then $\langle V , W , \xrightarrow[\text{dom/cod}]{} , \cdot , 1 \rangle$ is a category , whereas $\langle V , W , \text{dom} , \text{cod} , \cdot , 1 \rangle$ is a category in the sense of [EML] and [ML].

In particular, we consider the following special cases of dom/cod categories:

$$\langle \text{Set} , \text{Rel} , \xrightarrow[\text{Arg/Val}]{} , \cdot , 1 \rangle = \langle \text{Set} , \text{Rel} , \xrightarrow[\text{onto}]{} , \cdot , 1 \rangle ,$$

where $\cdot$ is the composition operation of 2.1,

$$\langle X , X^* , \xrightarrow[\text{first/last}]{} , + , \text{emp} \rangle ,$$
$$\langle X , X^+ , \xrightarrow[\text{first/last}]{} , \oplus , \text{uni} \rangle ,$$

where X is any class .

3.4. Category of Natural Transformations

Consider any two structures

$$\mathscr{A} = \langle V , W , \longrightarrow , \cdot , 1 , R_1, ..., R_n \rangle ,$$
$$\mathscr{A}' = \langle V', W' , \longrightarrow' , \cdot' , 1' , R'_1, ..., R'_n \rangle ,$$

any two homomorphisms

$$\mathscr{A} \xrightarrow{\mathscr{R}_1} \mathscr{A}' , \mathscr{A} \xrightarrow{\mathscr{R}_2} \mathscr{A}' ,$$

any function

$$V \xrightarrow{\tau} W'$$

and set $\iota = \{ < a, 1'a > \}_a$.

Let $\mathrm{Hom_C}$ be the class of all category homomorphisms and let $\mathrm{Nat_C}$ be the class of all natural transformations on category homomorphisms.

Then $\langle \mathrm{Hom_C} , \mathrm{Nat_C} , \underset{\mathrm{nat}}{\longrightarrow} , \cdot , \iota \rangle$ is the *category of natural transformations on categories* .

3.5. Monoid of Actions on one Object

Consider any category $\mathscr{C} = \langle V , W , \longrightarrow , \cdot , 1 \rangle$ and any object a .

Then $\langle \{ a \} , \mathrm{Act}_{\mathscr{C}}(a, a) , \longrightarrow , \cdot , 1 \rangle$ can be identified with the monoid $\langle \mathrm{Act}_{\mathscr{C}}(a, a) , \cdot , 1a \rangle$.

3.6. Monoid of Iterations of a Relation

Consider any set X , any relation R as in 2.6, the composition operation $\cdot$ of 2.1 , the unit operation 1 of 3.1 and let $R^0 = 1X$.

Then $\langle \{ X \} , \{ R^n \}_{n\geq 0} , \longrightarrow , \cdot , 1 \rangle$ can be identified with the *monoid* $\langle \{ R^n \}_{n\geq 0} , \cdot , 1X \rangle$ *of iterations of* R *on* X .

3.7. Preorder of the less-than-or-equal Relation

Consider the successor function on natural numbers $\mathrm{N} \xrightarrow{S} \mathrm{N}$, the composition operation $\cdot$ of 2.1 and the unit operation 1 of 3.1 . Then the local category of $\langle \{\mathrm{N}\} , \{ S^n \}_{n\geq 0} , \longrightarrow , \cdot , 1 \rangle$ is

$$\langle \mathrm{N} , \{ S^n \}_{n\geq 0} , \longmapsto , \cdot , 1 \rangle$$

and

$$\langle \mathrm{N} , \{ S^n \}_{n\geq 0} , \longmapsto , \cdot , 1 \rangle^{\nabla} = \langle \mathrm{N} , \{ \nabla \} , \underset{\nabla}{\longmapsto} \rangle$$

can be identified with the preorder $\langle \mathrm{N} , \leq \rangle$.

GROUPOIDS

We consider any total $^-$ operation from W into W and we call f^- the " inversion of f ".

An algebra $\langle \mathscr{C}, ^- \rangle = \langle V , W , \longrightarrow , \cdot , 1 , ^- \rangle$ is a ***groupoid*** iff $\mathscr{C}$ is a category and

G1. $\forall_{a,f,b} \, (a \xrightarrow{f} b \Rightarrow b \xrightarrow{f^-} a)$,

G2. $\forall_{a,f,b} \, (a \xrightarrow{f} b \Rightarrow f \cdot f^- = 1a \wedge f^- \cdot f = 1b)$.

We agree that $\mathscr{G}$ be a groupoid.

GROUPS

A structure $\langle W , \bullet , e , ^- \rangle$ is a *group* iff $\langle W , \bullet , e \rangle$ is a monoid and satisfies the inversion axiom

$$\forall_f \; f \bullet f^- = e = f^- \bullet f \; .$$

A group $\langle W , \bullet , e , ^- \rangle$ can be identified with any groupoid $\langle \{a\} , W , \longrightarrow , \bullet , 1 , ^- \rangle$ such that

$$\forall_f \; a \xrightarrow{f} a \text{ and } 1a = e \; .$$

The inversion axiom turns out to hold by axiom G2 , because $a \xrightarrow{f} a$, by axiom D1 .

Lemma. For every $\mathcal{G}$: $\mathcal{G}_\Delta$ can be identified with a group ♦

EQUIVALENCES

A graph is *symmetric* iff it satisfies the symmetry axiom

$$\forall_{a,b} \; (a E b \Rightarrow b E a) \; .$$

An *equivalence* is a symmetric preorder .

Lemma. For every $\mathcal{G}$: $\mathcal{G}^\nabla$ can be identified with an equivalence ♦

EXAMPLES

4.1. Homomorphism Groupoids

For any relation $\mathcal{R}$, let $\mathcal{R}^- = \{ <y, x> \mid x \mathcal{R} y \}$. Then:

$\langle \text{Set} , \text{Inj} , \xrightarrow[\text{onto}]{} , \bullet , 1 , ^- \rangle$ is the *groupoid of bijections* .

Let Grou be the class of all groupoids and let Iso_G be the class of all *groupoid isomorphisms*, i.e. bijective homomorphisms on groupoids. Then:

$\langle \text{Grou} , \text{Iso}_G , \xrightarrow[\text{onto}]{} , \circ , 1 , ^- \rangle$ is the *groupoid of groupoid isomorphisms* .

4.2. Local Groupoids

Consider any subgroupoid $\mathcal{G} = \langle V , W , \xrightarrow[\text{onto}]{} , \bullet , 1 , ^- \rangle$ of the groupoid of bijections.

Assume that $\varnothing \notin W$, and that the sets in V are pairwise disjoint.

Define set x as in 3.2 and let $\mathrm{l}x = 1(\text{set } x)$.

Then $\text{loc}\,\mathcal{G} = \langle \cup V , W , \longmapsto , \bullet , \mathrm{l} , ^- \rangle$ is the *local groupoid of* $\mathcal{G}$.

Consider any groupoid $\mathcal{G}' = \langle V' , W' , \longrightarrow' , \bullet' , 1' , ^{-\prime} \rangle$, any class $P \subseteq \text{Pow } V'$, such that

$$x, y \in X \in P \Rightarrow 1'x = 1'y \; .$$

Define un X as in 3.2 .

Then $\text{glob}_P \mathcal{G}' = \langle P , W'_P , \rightarrowtail , \bullet' , \text{un} , ^{-\prime} \rangle$ is the *global groupoid of* $\mathcal{G}'$ relatively to P .

Remark that, for every subgroupoid $\mathcal{G}$ of the groupoid of bijections (with the above properties),

$$\text{glob}_V (\text{loc}\,\mathcal{G}) = \mathcal{G} \; .$$

4.3. dom/cod Groupoids

Consider any two functions

$$W \xrightarrow{\text{dom}} V \; , \; W \xrightarrow{\text{cod}} V$$

any composition operation $\bullet$ as in 2.3 , any unit operation 1 as in 3.3 and any inversion operation $^-$ such that

$$\forall_f \; (\text{dom}(f^-) = \text{cod}\, f \wedge \text{cod}(f^-) = \text{dom}\, f) \; ,$$

$$\forall_f \; (f \bullet f^- = 1(\text{dom}\, f) \wedge f^- \bullet f = 1(\text{cod}\, f)) \; .$$

Then $\langle V , W , \xrightarrow[\text{dom/cod}]{} , \bullet , 1 , ^- \rangle$ is a groupoid, whereas $\langle V , W , \text{dom} , \text{cod} , \bullet , 1 , ^- \rangle$ is a groupoid in the sense of [HA], [HI] and [ML].

In particular,

$$\langle \text{Set} , \text{Inj} , \xrightarrow[\text{Arg/Val}]{} , \cdot , 1 , ^- \rangle = \langle \text{Set} , \text{Inj} , \xrightarrow[\text{onto}]{} , \cdot , 1 , ^- \rangle .$$

4.4. Groupoids of Natural Transformations

Consider any two structures

$$\mathcal{A} = \langle V , W , \longrightarrow , \cdot , 1 , ^- , R_1, ..., R_n \rangle ,$$

$$\mathcal{A}' = \langle V' , W' , \longrightarrow' , \cdot' , 1' , ^{-'} , R'_1, ..., R'_n \rangle ,$$

any two homomorphisms

$$\mathcal{A} \xrightarrow{\mathcal{R}_1} \mathcal{A}' , \quad \mathcal{A} \xrightarrow{\mathcal{R}_2} \mathcal{A}' ,$$

any function

$$V \xrightarrow{\tau} W'$$

and set $\tau^{\bullet} = \{ < a, (\tau a)^- > \}_a$.

Let Hom_G be the class of all groupoid homomorphisms and let Nat_G be the class of all natural transformations on groupoid homomorphisms .

Then $\langle \text{Hom}_G , \text{Nat}_G , \xrightarrow[\text{nat}]{} , \cdot , \iota , ^{\bullet} \rangle$ is the *groupoid of natural transformations on groupoids*

4.5. Group of Actions on one Object

Consider any groupoid $\mathcal{G} = \langle V, W , \longrightarrow , \cdot , 1 , ^- \rangle$ and any object a .

Then $\langle \{ a \} , \text{Act}_{\mathcal{G}}(a, a) , \longrightarrow , \cdot , 1 , ^- \rangle$ can be identified with the group

$$\langle \text{Act}_{\mathcal{G}}(a, a) , \cdot , 1a , ^- \rangle .$$

4.6. The Trivial Equivalence on Integers Numbers

Consider the successor function on integer numbers $\mathrm{I} \xrightarrow{S} \mathrm{I}$, the predecessor function on integer numbers $\mathrm{I} \xrightarrow{P} \mathrm{I}$, the composition operation $\cdot$ of 2.1 and the unit operation 1 of 3.1 and the inversion operation $^-$ of 4.1 . Then the local groupoid of $\langle \{\mathrm{I}\} , \{ S^n , P^n \}_{n\geq 0} , \longrightarrow , \cdot , 1 , ^- \rangle$ is

$$\langle \mathrm{I} , \{ S^n , P^n \}_{n\geq 0} , \longmapsto , \cdot , \mathrm{I} , ^- \rangle$$

and

$$\langle \mathrm{I} , \{ S^n , P^n \}_{n\geq 0} , \longmapsto , \cdot , \mathrm{I} , ^- \rangle^{\nabla} = \langle \mathrm{I} , \{ \nabla \} , \underset{\nabla}{\longmapsto} \rangle$$

can be identified with the trivial equivalence $\langle \mathrm{I} , \mathrm{I} \times \mathrm{I} \rangle$.

FROM DIAGRAMS TO SEMIGROUPOIDS AND CATEGORIES VIA HISTORIES, PATHS AND PROCESSES

For any structure $\mathcal{A} = \langle V , W , \longrightarrow \rangle$:

$< a >$ is an $\mathcal{A}$*-history* ,

$< a_1, f_1, a_2, ..., a_k, f_k, a_{k+1} >$ is an $\mathcal{A}$*-history* iff $\bigwedge_{1\leq i\leq k} a_i \xrightarrow{f_i} a_{i+1}$;

$< a >$ is an $\mathcal{A}$*-path* ,

$< a_1, ..., a_{k+1} >$ is an $\mathcal{A}$*-path* iff there is an $\mathcal{A}$*-history* $< a_1, f_1, a_2, ..., a_k, f_k, a_{k+1} >$;

$<>$ is an $\mathcal{A}$*-process* ,

$< f_1, ..., f_k >$ is an $\mathcal{A}$*-process* iff there is an $\mathcal{A}$*-history* $< a_1, f_1, a_2, ..., a_k, f_k, a_{k+1} >$.

Let Hist $\mathscr{A}$ be the class of $\mathscr{A}$-histories, let Path $\mathscr{A}$ be the class of $\mathscr{A}$-paths and let Proc $\mathscr{A}$ be the class of $\mathscr{A}$-processes .

For any object a let

$$a \xrightarrow[\text{proc}]{<\ >} a \ ;$$

for any two objects a, b and any $\mathscr{A}$-process $<f_1, ..., f_k>$ let

$$a \xrightarrow[\text{proc}]{< f_1 .. f_k >} b$$

iff there is an $\mathscr{A}$*-history* $< a, f_1, a_2, ..., a_k, f_k, b >$. Then :

$\text{hist}_D\mathscr{A} = \langle V, \text{Hist}\,\mathscr{A}, \xrightarrow[\text{first/last}]{} \rangle$ is the diagram of $\mathscr{A}$-histories ,

$\text{path}_D\mathscr{A} = \langle V, \text{Path}\,\mathscr{A}, \xrightarrow[\text{first/last}]{} \rangle$ is the diagram of $\mathscr{A}$-paths ,

$\text{proc}_D\mathscr{A} = \langle V, \text{Proc}\,\mathscr{A}, \xrightarrow[\text{proc}]{} \rangle$ is the diagram of $\mathscr{A}$-processes .

For any $\mathscr{A}$ -processes s and t , let

$s + t = s + t$ if (last s) Con (first s)

$s + t$ undefined otherwise .

Then :

$\text{hist}_S\mathscr{A} = \langle V, \text{Hist}\,\mathscr{A}, \xrightarrow[\text{first/last}]{}, \oplus \rangle$ is the semigroupoid of $\mathscr{A}$-histories ,

$\text{path}_S\mathscr{A} = \langle V, \text{Path}\,\mathscr{A}, \xrightarrow[\text{first/last}]{}, \oplus \rangle$ is the semigroupoid of $\mathscr{A}$-paths ,

$\text{proc}_S\mathscr{A} = \langle V, \text{Proc}\,\mathscr{A}, \xrightarrow[\text{proc}]{}, + \rangle$ is the semigroupoid of $\mathscr{A}$-processes ,

$\text{hist}_C\mathscr{A} = \langle V, \text{Hist}\,\mathscr{A}, \xrightarrow[\text{first/last}]{}, \oplus, \text{uni} \rangle$ is the category of $\mathscr{A}$-histories ,

$\text{path}_C\mathscr{A} = \langle V, \text{Path}\,\mathscr{A}, \xrightarrow[\text{first/last}]{}, \oplus, \text{uni} \rangle$ is the category of $\mathscr{A}$-paths ,

$\text{proc}_C\mathscr{A} = \langle V, \text{Proc}\,\mathscr{A}, \xrightarrow[\text{proc}]{}, +, \text{emp} \rangle$ is the category of $\mathscr{A}$-processes .

EXAMPLES

5.1. Rewriting systems

Consider any finite " alphabet " Σ and any finite set $P \subseteq \Sigma^* \times \Sigma^*$ of " productions " .

For any two words $w, w' \in \Sigma^*$ and any production $p \in P$, let

$$w \xrightarrow[\text{rew}]{p} w' \ \text{iff} \ \exists_{w_1, w_2} \ (w = w_1 + (\text{ first } p) + w_2 \ \wedge \ w' = w_1 + (\text{ last } p) + w_2) \ .$$

A *rewriting system* is a diagram $\mathscr{R} = \langle \Sigma^* , P , \xrightarrow[\text{rew}]{} \rangle$ and a $\mathscr{R}$*-derivation* is a $\mathscr{R}$-path .

For any two words $w, w' \in \Sigma^*$, we say that " w can be rewritten by $\mathscr{R}$ as w' " iff there is a $\mathscr{R}$-derivation s , such that $w \xrightarrow[\text{first/last}]{s} w'$.

5.2. Automata

A *finite automaton* $\mathscr{A}ut$ consists of a finite set $Q = \{ q_1, ..., q_n \}$ of " states ", a finite " alphabet " Σ and a " transition " table T as follows :

	q_1	q_j	q_n
q_1			
q_i		σ_{ij}	
q_n			

where $\sigma_{ij} \in \Sigma \cup \{ \text{empty} \}$.

We say that the letter $\sigma \in \Sigma$ " causes a transition " from q_i to q_j iff $\sigma_{ij} = \sigma$ and we say that " there is no transition " from q_i to q_j iff σ_{ij} is empty .
Set $T = \{ < q_i, \sigma_{ij}, q_j > \mid \sigma_{ij} \in \Sigma \}$. Then a finite automaton $\mathcal{A}ut$ can be described as a structure $\langle Q , \Sigma , T \rangle$ and turns out to be a particular case of the above structures $\mathcal{A} = \langle V , W , \longrightarrow \rangle$.
Thus, histories, paths and processes for automata can be obtained from the above definitions .
For any (finite) automaton $\mathcal{A}ut$ let res$\mathcal{A}ut = \langle Q , \Sigma' , T \rangle$ be the *restriction* of $\mathcal{A}ut$, where Σ' is obtained from Σ by dropping every letter non occurring in T , and remark that res$\mathcal{A}ut$ is a (finite) diagram.
Now, for every automaton $\mathcal{A}ut$:

Hist $\mathcal{A}ut$ = Hist(res $\mathcal{A}ut$) , Path $\mathcal{A}ut$ = Path(res $\mathcal{A}ut$) , Proc $\mathcal{A}ut$ = Proc(res $\mathcal{A}ut$) .

This means that restricted automata have the same " behaviour " as unrestricted ones.
Therefore, in order to investigate the behaviour of automata, it is more convenient to consider restricted automata or diagrams.
Following [E] , we could generalize finite automata to the infinite case. Then we would obtain the above structures $\langle V , W , \longrightarrow \rangle$ and diagrams as the restrictions of such structures .

HISTORIES, PATHS, PROCESSES AND ITERATION

Consider the successor function on natural numbers S , the graph

$\mathcal{S}uc = \langle \{ \mathrm{N} \} , \{ S \} , \longrightarrow \rangle$,

and its local graph

loc $\mathcal{S}uc = \langle \mathrm{N} , \{ S \} , \longmapsto \rangle$.

Then Hist(loc $\mathcal{S}uc$) comprehends the sequences :

$< 0 >$, $< 1 >$, ...
$< 0, S, 1 >$, $< 1, S, 2 >$, ...
$< 0, S, 1, S, 2 >$, $< 1, S, 2, S, 3 >$, ... ;

Path(loc $\mathcal{S}uc$) comprehends the sequences :

$< 0 >$, $< 1 >$, ...
$< 0, 1 >$, $< 1, 2 >$, ...
$< 0, 1, 2 >$, $< 1, 2, 3 >$, ...

and Proc(loc $\mathcal{S}uc$) comprehends the sequences :

$< >$, $< S >$, $< S, S >$, ...

On the other hand, the local semigroupoid of positive iterations of S is

$\langle \mathrm{N} , \{ S^i \}_{i>0} , \longmapsto , \cdot \rangle$

and that the local category of iterations of S is

$\langle \mathrm{N} , \{ S^i \}_{i\geq 0} , \longmapsto , \cdot , 1 \rangle$.

Now, constructing the semigroupoids of histories, paths and processes of any positive number of " steps " on the local graph of the function S takes to the same goal as constructing the local semigroupoid of positive iterations of S, in so far as

$$m \xrightarrow[\text{first/last}]{< m\ S...S\ m+i >} m+i \Leftrightarrow m \xrightarrow[\text{first/last}]{< m...m+i >} m+i \Leftrightarrow m \xrightarrow[\text{proc}]{< S..S >} m+i \Leftrightarrow m \stackrel{S^i}{\longmapsto} m+i \ ,$$

where i is the length of the sequence $< S, ..., S >$.

Constructing the categories of histories, paths and processes of any non negative number of " steps " on the local graph of the function S takes to the same goal as constructing the local category of iterations of S, in so far as

$$m \xrightarrow[\text{first/last}]{< m >} m \Leftrightarrow m \xrightarrow[\text{proc}]{< >} m \Leftrightarrow m \stackrel{S^0}{\longmapsto} m \ .$$

Note that the program

for v:= 1 **until** i **do** x:= x+1 **endfor** ,

when the variable x has the initial value m, " causes " the history $< m, S, ..., S, m+i >$, " describes " the path $< m, ..., m+i >$, " launches " the process $< S, ..., S >$, and " computes " the iteration S^i of S

Note that the program

for v:= 1 **until** 0 **do** x:= x+1 **endfor** ,

when the variable x has the initial value m, " causes " the history $< m >$, " describes " the path $< m >$, " launches " the process $< >$, and " computes " the iteration S^0 of S.

Thus the construction of semigroupoids and categories from diagrams via histories, paths and processes constitutes the starting point for the algebraic analysis of iteration.

REFERENCES

[B]

G. Birkhoff, Lattice theory, *AMS Colloq. Publ.* 25, (1967).

[E]

S. Eilenberg, Automata, Languages and Machines, Vol. A, New York 1974.

[EE]

1. S. Eilenberg and C.C. Elgot, Iteration and recursion, *Proc. Nat. Acad. Sci.* U.S.A. 61 (1968), 378-379.

2. S. Eilenberg and C.C. Elgot, Recursiveness, NewYork 1970.

[EML]

S. Eilenberg, S. Mac Lane, General theory of natural equivalences, *Trans. Am. Math. Soc.* 58 (1945) 231-294

[G]

A. Grothendieck, Sur quelques points d'algèbre homologique, *Tôhoku Math. J.*, Ser. 2, 9 (1957) 119-221.

[GM]

1. G. Germano and S. Mazzanti, Partial closures and semantics of while: towards an iteration-based theory of data types, Computation and proof theory, *Lecture notes in mathematics* 1104 (1984) 163-174.

2. G. Germano and S. Mazzanti, A setting for generalized computability, Computation theory and logic, *Lecture notes in computer science* 270 (1987) 154-165.

[GMS]

1. G. Germano and A. Maggiolo-Schettini, Markow's algorithms without concluding formulas, *4th Congrss for Logic, Methodology and Philosophy of Science*, Bucharest 1971.

2. G. Germano and A. Maggiolo-Schettini, A characterization of partial recursive functions via sequence functions, *Notices Amer. Math. Soc.* 19 (1972), 332.

3. G. Germano and A. Maggiolo-Schettini, Quelques caracterizations des functions recursives partielles, *C.R. Acad. Sci. Paris*, Sér. A, 276 (1973), 1325-1327.

4. G. Germano and A. Maggiolo-Schettini, Sequence-to-sequence recursiveness, *Information Processing Lett.* 4 (1975), 1-6.

[HA]

M. Hasse, Einige Bemerkung über Graphen, Kategorien und Gruppoide, *Math. Nachr.* 22 (1960) 255-270.

[HI]

1. P.J. Higgins, Presentations of groupoids, with applications to groups, *Proc. Camb. Phil. Soc.* 60 (1964) 7-20.

2. P.J. Higgins, Notes on Categories and Groupoids, London 1971.

[MI]

B. Mitchell, Theory of Categories, New York 1965.

[ML]

S. Mac Lane, Categories for the Working Mathematicians, New York 1971.

[MO]

E.H. Moore, Introduction to a form of general analysis, *AMS Colloq. Publ.* 2 (1910) 1-150.

[U]

J.D. Ullman, Principles of Database Systems, Sec.ed., Rockville 1982.

Algebraic Operational Semantics and Modula-2*

Yuri Gurevich and James M. Morris
Electrical Engineering and Computer Science
University of Michigan
Ann Arbor, MI 48109-2122

0. Introduction

We start with several arguments in favor of operational semantics for imperative programming languages. One important purpose of formal semantics is to help a programmer understand a given language (as opposed to particular programs written in that language). We would claim that, when conceiving a program expressed in an imperative language, a journeyman programmer has in mind an ideal machine that executes the language's commands. That is to say, our fundamental understanding of an imperative programming language is behavioral (or operational).

A semantic description of a programming language should provide an accessible account of *all* of a language's constructs. Languages like Modula-2 that are designed for (among other things) the writing of operating systems include facilities for multiprocessing and facilities for describing interaction with peripheral devices. Specifically, such languages include a means for dealing with hardware interrupts which usually involve both these sorts of facility. Consequently, an adequate semantic account of a language like Modula must treat interrupts. Now, the very notion of interrupt involves the concept of time: an interrupt is an event which occurs at an arbitrary *moment* in a computation. The idea that a computation is a sequence of states unfolding in time is the basis of operational semantics. Therefore, it seems most natural to describe operationally languages which allow one to deal with interrupts. It also seems to be true that programming language constructs for expressing multiprocessing are most straightforwardly described in terms of the behavior they elicit.

A formal semantics for a language should also provide a *basis* for proving the correctness of the language's implementations, for examining the expressive power of the language, for reasoning about programs written in the language, etc. We emphasize that operational semantics provides only a basis rather than methods for accomplishing these tasks. Some of the tasks fall within the purview of a logic or proof system using operational semantics as a foundation. We no not consider operational semantics as a competitor of other approaches, like axiomatic or denotational semantics or temporal logic, but rather as complementing and providing a foundation for them.

* Supported in part by NSF grant DCR 85-03275

The starting point for the development of operational semantics is a consideration of the important problem of what ideal machines are from a mathematical point of view. We do not find the existing solutions (VDL [8], LISP interpreters written in (a subset of) LISP [5], the SECD machine [4], and even Plotkin's transition systems [7]) satisfactory. The approach we shall describe, algebraic operational semantics, was originally proposed in [2]. To assess this new approach, we have worked out an algebraic operational semantics for the programming language Modula-2 (referred to subsequently as Modula) in its entirety. We have chosen Modula as our example because it is, in many ways, a model imperative programming language. It is largely free of extraneous constructs and integrates machine-dependent facilities in an elegant way. This paper gives a self-contained illustration of our approach using Modula as *an* example. A complete description of Modula is found in the Ph.D. dissertation [6]. Semantic accounts of Smalltalk and Occam using algebraic operational semantics are in preparation ([1] and [3], respectively).

So, what is an abstract machine for a programming language from a mathematical point of view? In algebraic operational semantics, it is an *evolving* (or *dynamic*) *algebra* (or *structure*) of a sort, tailored explicitly for the language at hand. What is a dynamic structure? Here we restrict ourselves to sequential evolving structures; in connection with distributive evolving algebras, see [3].

Each state of an evolving structure is what the logician would call a finite, many-sorted, first-order structure. It comprises a number of finite sets called *universes* and functions on Cartesian products of universes. (The presence of a Boolean universe allows one to treat relations as Boolean-valued functions; in that sense the static structures are algebras.) In the case of Modula, the signature (also called vocabulary or language) of the current state does not change during the structure's evolution, but some of the functions and universes may. Accounts of languages other than Modula may require a dynamic signature.

One distinguishing feature of algebraic operational semantics is that its universes are usually (finite and) bounded; in other words, its abstract machines usually have bounded resources. We do not view finite machines necessarily as approximations to infinite ones. For example, a machine equipped with genuine integers will loop forever executing

n := 1 ; WHILE true DO n := 2 * n END,

but no machine with bounded resources will. The initial state of a dynamic structure should reflect all its resource bounds. Thus, given a particular programming language L, algebraic operational semantics defines a family of families of machines. The former are determined by programs written in L and, given a particular L-program Prog, the latter are determined by (the fragment of L used in Prog and) the resource bounds of the dynamic structures for Prog.

Transition rules guide the evolution of a dynamic structure from state to state. We shall give their syntax in a moment. A structure's transition rules should depend only on the language for which the structure provides semantics. Moreover, if the components of the structure have been chosen properly, the changes described by its transition rules should be slight.

For the purposes of this paper, we invoke the principle of separation of concerns and restrict our attention to the dynamic semantics of programs. Towards this end, we assume that a program is represented by its parse tree with respect to a given context-free grammar and that the initial state of an algebra reflects the static semantics of the given program.

1. The Syntax of Transition Rules

We begin with transition rules without parameters (free variables). The basic component of a transition rule is called an *update*. There are three sorts of update. Let S be a state of an evolving algebra M.

(i) Function updates: let f be a function symbol in the signature of M. Suppose that the type of f is $U_1 \times \cdots \times U_k \rightarrow U_0$, where each U_i is a universe name. Let $e_0, \ldots, e_k$ be closed (i.e. without free variables) expressions (terms) of types $U_0, \ldots, U_k$. Then $f(e_1, \ldots, e_k) := e_0$ is a function update. Its meaning is: first compute $e_0, \ldots, e_k$ in S and let $a_0, \ldots, a_k$ be the results, respectively; then assign a_0 to $f(a_1, \ldots, a_k)$. Read and write operations are treated as special forms of function update. A read operation is of the form $f(e_1, \ldots, e_k) := \mathit{Input}(\mathit{channel})$, where f and the e_i are as before and *channel* is a path over which information passes. The meaning of a read operation is: when a value v is obtained from outside M over *channel* (in a given state S), evaluate $e_1, \ldots, e_k$ in S and let $a_1, \ldots, a_k$ be the results, then assign v to $f(a_1, \ldots, a_k)$. A write operation is of the form $\mathit{Output}(\mathit{channel}) := f(e_1, \ldots, e_k)$, where f and the e_i are again as above. The meaning of a write operation is: compute $e_1, \ldots, e_k$ in the given state and let $a_1, \ldots, a_k$ be the results, then transmit $f(a_1, \ldots, a_k)$ outside M over *channel*.

(ii) Contractions of universes: let e be a closed expression, then $\mathit{Dispose}(e)$ is a universe contraction. Its meaning is: compute e in S and let a be the result; then delete a from the universe to which it belongs. The deletion of a may make some functions undefined on some elements of their domains. The usual trick of using dummy elements "undefined", "uninitialized", etc. allows one to deal with total functions only.

(iii) Extensions of universes: let U be a universe name and F be a list of function updates some of which mention a variable *temp*, then

$$\textbf{let } \mathit{temp} = \mathit{New}(U) \textbf{ in } F \textbf{ endlet}$$

is a universe extension. Its meaning is: first add a new element to U and let *temp* name this element temporarily; then perform the function updates in the list F. The scope of *temp* is delimited by the brackets **let** and **endlet**.

Basically, a transition rule is of the form

$$\textbf{if } e \textbf{ then } F \textbf{ endif},$$

where e is a closed Boolean expression and F is a list of updates. The meaning of such a transition depends on the value of e in the given state. If e is false, the rule does not alter the state of the algebra; if e is true, the state of the algebra is altered according to the updates in F. The whole language is described by a finite set of transition rules which are executed simultaneously. A priori, different transition rules or even different updates of the same transition rule can contradict each other; we restrict our attention to (deterministic) consistent evolving algebras.

For brevity and convenience, we allow a slightly more complicated syntax. Let $r_1, \ldots, r_k$ be updates or transition rules and e be a closed Boolean expression, then

$$\begin{array}{l}\textbf{if } e \textbf{ then}\\ r_1, \ldots, r_k\\ \textbf{endif}\end{array}$$

is a transition rule. Its meaning is: perform $r_1, \ldots, r_k$, if e is true in S and do nothing, otherwise.

There are several, tightly circumscribed, situations in a semantic account of Modula where parameterized transition rules are natural. Two such situations occur at block entry and block exit, when a relatively large number of locations must be allocated or deallocated. Modula specifies no ordering of the allocations or deallocations, hence, the natural thing to do is perform them "simultaneously". We express this simultaneity, or better, absence of ordering, by a parameterized transition rule. The meaning of such a rule is: perform the rule for all possible values of its parameters.

2. A State of a Modula Evolving Algebra

Since an evolving algebra for Modula reflects a given program, we give a sample program Prog which will allow us to supply concrete examples of the universes and functions comprising an algebra. The sample program appears in Figure 1.

We now describe the universes, functions and relations that comprise an evolving algebra M(Prog) for Prog. We also mention in passing those components which might be present in an algebra for a Modula program different from Prog but which are unneccessary to an account of Prog's ideal machine. We use *evolving algebra* and *dynamic structure* interchangeably in our account. All universes of a dynamic structure have the equality relation defined on them.

2.1. Integers

Prog declares a record type, Vertex, that includes a field of type integer. Therefore, a dynamic structure M(Prog) will include a universe *int* consisting of all the integers in

```
MODULE Prog;
FROM    Storage IMPORT ALLOCATE;
FROM    InOut   IMPORT ReadInt,Done,WriteInt,WriteLn;
TYPE    Link = POINTER TO Vertex;
        Vertex = RECORD
                   datum:INTEGER;
                   left,right:Link
                 END;
VAR     r,tree:Link;
PROCEDURE Insert(item:Link; VAR subtree:Link);
BEGIN
  IF subtree = NIL THEN
    subtree := item;
    subtree ↑ .left := NIL;
    subtree ↑ .right := NIL
  ELSEIF item ↑ .datum < subtree ↑ .datum THEN
    Insert(item, subtree ↑ .left)
  ELSE
    Insert(item, subtree ↑ .right)
  ENDIF
END Insert;
PROCEDURE Print(subtree:Link);
BEGIN
  IF subtree ↑ .left ≠ NIL THEN Print(subtree ↑ .left);
  WriteInt(subtree ↑ .datum, 6);Writeln;
  IF subtree ↑ .right ≠ NIL THEN Print(subtree ↑ .right)
END Print;
BEGIN
  tree := NIL;
  NEW(r);ReadInt(r ↑ .datum);
  WHILE Done DO
    Insert(r, tree);
    NEW(r);ReadInt(r ↑ .datum)
  END;
  IF tree ≠ NIL THEN Print(tree)
END Prog.
```

Figure 1. An Example Program

the interval [*MinInt*, *MaxInt*]. *MinInt* and *MaxInt* are distinguished elements of *int*. The universe *int* comes equipped with the usual ordering and the partial arithmetic operations +, −, ×, quotient, and remainder.

2.2. Boolean

A structure M(Prog) will include a universe *bool* = {*true*, *false*} equipped with the usual Boolean operations and ordered such that *false* < *true*. The binary Boolean operations are used *only* in transition rules. In Modula, the binary Boolean operations appear in a "conditional" form in which both an operation's arguments are not always evaluated. Consequently, their semantics are given by the transition rules that govern sequencing through the parse trees of Boolean expressions.

2.3. Other Basic Types

The other universes a Modula structure may comprise are a finite ordered set of characters *char*, an initial segment of the natural numbers *card*, and a finite set of real numbers *real*. In general, *char* and its ordering relation differ among Modula structures, but *char* must contain the upper case letters of the Roman alphabet, the digits 0, ..., 9, and certain punctuation marks (cf. The Modula Report [9]). The universe *char* is equipped with operations, *Ord* and *Char*, which give the position in the ordering of one of its elements and the element corresponding to a position in the ordering, respectively. The universe *card* includes those natural numbers less than or equal to *MaxCard*, where *MaxCard* is a constant that differs among Modula structures. The usual ordering and (partial) arithmetic operations are defined on *card*. We omit a description of *real*.

2.4. The Parse Tree

The parse tree of Prog is represented by a universe called *parsetree* with a relatively rich structure plus some additional functions from and to *parsetree*. The elements of *parsetree* are the nodes of the parse tree. The partial functions *Child1*, *Child2*, ... map an element of *parsetree* to its first, second, etc. child, if it has one. The function *Children* indicates how many children a node possesses. The function *Parent* maps an element of *parsetree* to its parent node, if it has one.

An auxiliary universe *grammarsymbol* provides labels for parse tree nodes which indicate the grammatical category to which the subtree under a node belongs. A function *Label* : *parsetree* → *grammarsymbol* represents this correspondence.

There is also a function *Sp* (for specification) that is used to simplify the representation in the parse tree of identifiers and constants. The grammar for Modula includes productions which describe the syntax of identifiers and constants. However, it is more convenient to deal with the identifiers themselves or the values denoted by the constants than with parse sub-trees representing their syntactic analysis. So we allow leaf nodes in our parse trees to be labelled by the non-terminal grammatical symbols 'id' and 'const' and have *Sp* map such a node to the appropriate identifier or value. Nodes labelled 'id' are mapped to a finite universe *ident* of identifiers; *ident* is equipped with the equality relation only. The values to which *Sp* maps constants are taken from universes such as *int*.

For convenience, a Modula evolving algebra comes equipped with a binary relation, *SubTree*, which, for a given parse tree node *n*, indicates which nodes are in the subtree of which *n* is the root. This relation is useful in certain transition rules, as we shall see in section 3.

The are two dynamic distinguished elements of *parsetree*: *AN* and *XN*. *AN*, for "active node", indicates at which node control currently resides. *XN* is an "auxiliary" active node which is used in the transition rules for declarations and procedure calls when there needs to be, in effect, two active nodes because two sub-trees must be traversed in synchronized fashion.

2.5. Raw Variables

Modula evolving algebras include a universe *rawvar* whose elements serve as the denotations of variable identifiers and, hence, play a central role in our account of program variables. However, we must first consider the semantic complication arising from the fact that Modula allows identifiers to be re-used. In our example program, 'subtree' appears in both the procedures Insert and Print. In order to give unique names to variables, procedures, etc., we adopt the convention of prefixing identifiers with the identifiers of the procedures and modules in which their declarations are nested in order from largest to smallest enclosing block. For example, the variable identifiers of Prog become InOut.Done, Prog.r, Prog.tree, Prog.Insert.item, Prog.Insert.subtree, and Prog.Print.subtree. The denotation of each of these extended identifiers is a unique element of *rawvar*, i.e. a raw variable. The denotations of extended identifiers are called raw variables because, in general, a block that is the body of a procedure may be activated recursively creating multiple incarnations of its variables each of which is a variable in its own right. More about this in a moment.

2.6. The Universe of Type Representatives

A Modula structure will include a universe *types* whose elements are tokens which represent the structure's data types. In particular, elements of *types* serve as the denotations of type identifiers. Our example program Prog uses the following types; for each of them, *types* contains a distinct element. INTEGER appears as the type of one of the fields of the record type Vertex; BOOLEAN appears implicitly as the type of the imported variable Done and certain expressions; Vertex is a declared record type; Link is declared of type 'POINTER TO Vertex'. Each of the procedures InOut.ReadInt, InOut.WriteInt, InOut.WriteLn, Prog.Insert, and Prog.Print is of a different procedure type (determined by the types of their parameters and whether they're value or variable) and corresponds to an element of *types*.

2.7. Locations

Modula structures include a universe *loc* whose elements play a dual role. First, they represent the incarnations of raw variables produced by activating the blocks in which the raw variables are introduced. Secondly, they represent the elements of dynamic data structures created by the procedure NEW. The latter role requires that *loc* be a dynamic universe, since the number of calls on NEW to be expected during the execution of a program cannot, in general, be predicted. Since calls on NEW produce locations, it should be apparent that locations are the values which incarnations of pointer variables assume. For example, Prog introduces a number of raw variables of type 'POINTER TO Vertex'; each of these will be mapped, by functions to be described below, to locations which will, in turn, be mapped to values of a universe corresponding to Vertex. Note that our locations are more abstract than those sometimes appearing in theories of programming language semantics. They are not intended to model an ideal computer's "memory": they are not ordered and there are no operations other than the equality relation defined on them. There is no notion of "re-using" locations in our semantics: new locations are created and old locations are dropped, but the story ends there—the new locations created bear no relation to the old ones dropped. However, our structures are *finite* and, moreover, bounded, therefore every structure places a limit on the size of *loc*.

2.8. Structured Data Types

Our example program Prog introduces a record type Vertex. For every record type there exists a dynamic universe which contains an element for every instance of the record type created but not yet deleted at that point. In the case of Prog, let *vertex* refer to the universe of M(Prog) corresponding to the record type of the same name. The denotations of the field names of the record type Vertex will be dynamic functions from *vertex* $\rightarrow$ *loc*: the function corresponding to 'datum' will map elements of *vertex* to locations that assume integer values and the functions corresponding to 'left' and 'right' will map elements of *vertex* to locations that assume values that are themselves locations. These functions are dynamic because transition rules expanding their domains must be applied to them as elements are added to *vertex*. Note that, for each element added to *vertex*, three elements are added to *loc*.

We next consider arrays even though our sample program includes no array types. To an array type corresponds a universe, initially empty, whose elements represent instances of the array type, and an "access" function, which maps pairs consisting of an instance of the array type and an index value to a location. To create a new instance of an array type, one adds a new element to the appropriate universe of array values, one adds new locations to contain the array's components, and one applies a transition rule to the array type's access function to cause it to map pairs consisting of the new array value and an index value to the corresponding new locations.

The components of arrays and records are represented as locations because they may be passed as actual parameters to procedures with variable formal parameters. This means that an array or record component may become an "incarnation" of the raw variable that is the denotation of a variable procedure parameter and the incarnation of a raw variable is a location.

2.9. Command Results and Space

Modula dynamic structures include a universe *result* comprised of three elements: *ok*, *error*, and *uneval* (for unevaluated). The elements of *result* are used to signal the outcome of sub-computations, such as those specified by Modula commands, that don't otherwise produce a result or to indicate that control has yet to visit a sub-parse-tree.

Each dynamic structure will include a universe *space* whose elements are called *units*. What a unit corresponds to varies among structures. A unit may correspond to a bit, a byte of 8 bits, or a word of some number of bits. For each data type a program introduces, a function *Size* tells us how many units of *space* correspond to that type. A Modula dynamic structure will also include a dynamic function *Avail* that indicates, at any given moment, how much space is available.

2.10. The Static Functions *Intro*, *Sig*, and *Type*

Modula allows the reuse of identifiers. However, the declaration or procedure parameter specification introducing the identifier that is in force at any point in the program may be determined by examination of the program's text. Therefore, every identifier occurring in a Modula program can be uniquely associated with an introduction of the identifier. Moreover, this association may be established without executing the program. Consequently, we assume that Modula structures come equipped with a static function, *Intro*, which maps an identifier node in the parse tree to the node representing the same identifier in the appropriate declaration or parameter specification subtree introducing the identifier. For example, in the case of Prog, *Intro* maps occurrences of 'r' in the main body to the occurrence of 'r' in Prog's variable declaration list. It maps occurrences of 'subtree' in the body of Insert to the occurrences of 'subtree' in Insert's formal parameter list and occurrences of 'subtree' in the body of Print to the occurrence of 'subtree' in Print's formal parameter list. *Intro* also maps procedure identifer nodes to the root of the procedure's declaration subtree.

Modula structures also include a static function *Sig* which maps nodes representing defining occurrences of identifiers to their significations. In particular, *Sig* maps identifier nodes in variable declarations or formal parameter specifications to the raw variable that is the denotation of the variable or parameter. Hence, given a variable identifier node, one obtains that variable's denotation by applying the composition of *Intro* and *Sig* to the identifier node. For example, if n is a node labelled 'id' in the subtree for Insert whose specification is the identifier 'subtree', then $Sig(Intro(n))$ is the raw variable Prog.Insert.subtree. In principle, the function *Sig* is unnecessary — raw variables can be identified with the corresponding nodes of the parse tree. However, since raw variables play such an important role, we find it convenient to distinguish them from the corresponding nodes of the parse tree.

Modula structures include a static function *Type* which maps a parse tree node in the range of *Intro* to the element of *types* representing the type of the object introduced at the node.

2.11. The Dynamic Function *Top* and The Predecessor Relation on *loc*

We have seen how the static functions *Intro* and *Sig* take us from a program variable node to the raw variable that is the program variable's denotation. The possibility of recursively activating the block in which a program variable is introduced means that multiple incarnations of the raw variable may exist in some state of a dynamic structure. The problem is to keep track of these incarnations in such a manner that the value of the most recently created one is fetched when needed and that the previous incarnation is restored when control leaves the block in which the program variable was introduced. Consider also the following sort of "variables" which are implicitly part of a Modula structure. In our semantics, a subcomputation ideally corresponds to a traversal of a parse tree. During such a traversal partial results are produced. These partial results are made available by "attaching" them to appropriate parse tree nodes. In this scheme, a parse tree node may be thought of as corresponding to an implicit variable whose value is the result of performing the subcomputation represented by the subtree under the node. The possibility of recursion means that these implicit variables may have multiple incarnations. Therefore, the problems of coping with incarnations mentioned above obtain with them as well. Modula structures include two dynamic functions which solve these problems. The first is *Top*, which maps raw variables and parse tree nodes to locations. Specifically, *Top* maps a raw variable to the location that represents its most recent incarnation and it maps a parse tree node to the most recent incarnation of the implicit variable corresponding to the node. Given a parse tree node n representing a variable, we obtain the most recent incarnation of that variable by applying the composition of *Intro*, *Sig*, and *Top* to n: $Top(Sig(Intro(n)))$. To obtain the most recent incarnation of the implicit variable corresponding to a node, one applies *Top* to the node directly.

When control leaves the block in which a variable is introduced, a transition rule must be applied to *Top* to restore its previous value at the (raw or implicit) variable, if it had one. To remember previous incarnations of variables, Modula structures include a partial dynamic function *Pred*. When applied to a location and raw variable or parse tree node, *Pred* yields the location representing the raw or implicit variable's previous incarnation, if it has one, and is undefined otherwise. *Pred* takes a raw variable as well as a location as argument because it is possible, via aliasing, for a single location to represent an incarnation of more than one raw variable and, hence, to have different predecessors depending on which raw variable one considers. This situation occurs when a program variable is passed as actual parameter in a procedure call for a formal variable parameter.

2.12 The Dynamic Function *Val*

Modula structures come equipped with a dynamic function *Val* which assigns values to locations. The range of *Val* includes those data types used in a program. In the case of Prog, we have:

$$Val : loc \rightarrow int \cup bool \cup loc \cup vertex.$$

For convenience, in the transition rules, we let $Nval(n)$ abbreviate $Val(Top(n))$, where n is an implicit variable. $Nval(n)$ always gives the value of the most recent incarnation of the implicit variable.

2.13 The Procedure Stack

The procedure stack consists of a dynamic universe *pstack* with dynamic distinguished element *PSTop*, a function $PStack : pstack \rightarrow parsetree$, and a relation on *pstack*, *PSPred* (for predecessor). *PSTop* is the "top" element of the stack, *PStack* maps each element of the stack to the root of a procedure call subtree, and *PSPred* records the history of yet-to-be-completed procedure calls.

3. Some Representative Transition Rules

First, we describe the transition rule for assignment statements. The grammar production describing assignment statement subtrees is

$$\text{assignment} \rightarrow \text{desig} := \text{exp}.$$

The semantics of assignments are familiar. Evaluate the designator on the left to obtain a location l; evaluate the expression on the right to obtain a value v; make v the new value of the dynamic function *Val* at l. However, the transition rule for assignments is somewhat complicated by the requirement that one transition rule suffice for all instances, in a parse tree, of a particular grammatical category. Specifically, expressions may appear in a number of contexts; among them are assignment statements and actual parameter lists of procedure calls. There exists a potential conflict between the kind of value required in these two contexts. An expression appearing in an assignment statement should always evaluate to an expression value (sometimes called an ***r-value***). An expression appearing in place of a variable formal procedure parameter should always evaluate to a location (sometimes called an *l-value*). Most expressions pose no problem: if the expression contains operators (other than array indexing, record field selection, and pointer dereferencing) it will always evaluate to an r-value. If the expression consists only of a variable, the transition rules must cause it to evalute to a location. Then, if the expression's context requires an l-value, a location is available; if the expression's context requires an r-value, the location can be coerced to an r-value by an application of *Val*. An auxiliary function *Value* performs the coercion:

$$Value(x) = \begin{cases} Val(x), & \text{if } x \in loc; \\ x, & \text{otherwise.} \end{cases}$$

The transition rule for assignment statements appears in figure 2.

Next, we give the transition rule for procedure call subtrees. The relevant grammar production is:

$$\text{procall} \rightarrow \text{id(explist)}.$$

When AN is labelled 'procall', its first child is the procedure's identifier and its third child is the subtree representing the formal parameter list. The transition rule for 'procall' subtrees consists of three inner transition rules. The first transfers control to the formal parameter list subtree if it has not been evaluated. The second invokes three actions: it updates the procedure stack, it allocates a new location for the implicit variables corresponding to the nodes of the subtree for the procedure being called, and it transfers control to the procedure. The transition rule that creates new incarnations of

```
if Label(AN) = assignment then
  if Nval(Child1(AN)) = uneval then
    AN := Child1(AN)
  endif,
  if Nval(Child1(AN)) ≠ uneval then
    if Nval(Child3(AN)) = uneval then
      AN := Child3(AN)
    endif,
    if Nval(Child3(AN)) ≠ uneval then
      Val(Nval(Child1(AN))) := Value(Nval(Child3(AN))),
      AN := Parent(AN),
      Nval(AN) := ok,
      Nval(Child1(AN)) := uneval,
      Nval(Child3(AN)) := uneval
    endif
  endif
endif.
```

Figure 2. The Transition Rule for Assignment Statements

the procedure's implicit variables is an example of a parameterized transition rule. Its parameter *n* ranges over the nodes in the 'block' subtree that constitutes the body of the procedure being called. When the active node is the root of the procedure call, the root of the subtree for the body of the procedure is given by '$Child3(Intro(Child1(AN)))$'. The transition rule that updates the procedure stack extends the universe *PStack*. The element added is subsequently removed, by the update *Dispose*(*PSTop*), when the called procedure is exited. The third inner rule transfers control to the procedure call's parent after the call has completed. Note here that completion of the call is indicated by '$Nval(AN) \neq uneval$'. The value of this implicit variable is changed just prior to exiting the body of the procedure. The transition rule for 'procall' nodes is given in Figure 3.

4 An Application

In this section we show how our methods of semantic definition may be extended to to certain "low-level" facilities of Modula and then indicate how the correctness of a simple keyboard interrupt handling routine can be proven. In doing so, we shall have to incorporate the interrupt mechanism and input/output channels of a hypothetical computer into our model. We hope to accomplish two purposes: first, to illustrate how connections between semantic models of "official" Modula and its implementations can be made and, second, to show how our semantic models may be used to prove properties of Modula programs. The keyboard interrupt handler we shall use as an example is taken from [9]. It is presented in Figure 4. This program fragment is based on a PDP-11 implementation of Modula, although we do not claim to have formalized the PDP-11 here. Rather, we formalize those properties of an underlying machine required to reason

```
if Label(AN) = procall then
  if Nval(AN) = uneval and Nval(Child3(AN)) = uneval then
    AN := Child3(AN)
  endif,
  if Nval(AN) = uneval and Nval(Child3(AN)) ≠ uneval then
    if Subtree(n, Child3(Intro(Child1(AN)))) then
      let temp = New(loc) in
        Val(temp) := uneval
        Top(n) := temp
        Pred(temp, n) := Top(n)
      endlet
    endif,
    let temp = New(pstack) in
      PStack(temp) := AN,
      PSPred(temp) := PSTop,
      PSTop := temp
    endlet,
    AN := Intro(Child1(AN))
  endif,
  if Nval(AN) ≠ uneval then
    AN := Parent(AN)
  endif
endif.
```

Figure 3. The Transition Rule for Procedure Calls

about the program Wirth presents in [9]. We have chosen an interrupt handling routin as our example program because we believe it demonstrates the utility of our approac to semantics most effectively. The very notion of interrupt involves the concept of time an interrupt is an event which occurs at an arbitrary *moment* in the evolution of computation. And the idea that a computation is a sequence of states unfolding in tim is the basis of operational semantics. Moreover, the state changes which an interrup engenders are not directly connected to any part of a program's text. Therefore, semantic theory which ascribes, for example, mathematical functions to components c program text will not deal readily with interrupts. Yet, interrupts are fundamental, a the right level of detail, to the function of all modern computing machinery.

We shall now describe those aspects of our example program which are not part "official" Modula, i.e. the low-level facilities of which it makes use. The first is the notio of process in general and coroutine in particular. Implementations of Modula are free t adopt a concept of process of the designer's choice. Obviously, this choice will be largel but not entirely, determined by the hardware on which the implementation is to ru On single processor machines, the coroutine concept is attractive. We shall restrict ou attention to coroutines. The basic idea of a coroutine is the quasi-concurrent executio of a number of sequential processes, i.e. at any given moment only one of two or mo sequential processes is executing. An executing process may suspend itself and transf control to another, which then resumes executing where it last left off. Each proce has its own local state information as well as (possibly) access to data structures share

```
MODULE keyboard[4];
  EXPORT fetch, n;
  IMPORT ADR, SIZE, WORD, PROCESS,
         NEWPROCESS, TRANSFER, IOTRANSFER;
  CONST  N = 32;
  VAR    x[777562B] : CHAR; (* keyboard data *)
         s[777560B] : BITSET; (* keyboard status *)
  VAR    n, in, out : CARDINAL;
         buf : ARRAY[0..N - 1] OF CHAR;
         PRO, CON : PROCESS;
         wsp : ARRAY[0..177B] OF WORD;

  PROCEDURE fetch(VAR ch : CHAR);
    BEGIN (* to be called only if n > 0 *)
      IF n > 0 THEN
        ch := buf[out]; out := (out + 1) MOD N;
        n := n - 1
      ELSE ch := 0C
      END
    END fetch;

  PROCEDURE producer; (* acts as coroutine *)
    BEGIN
      LOOP
        IOTRANSFER(PRO, CON, 60B);
        IF n < N THEN
          buf[in] := x; in := (in + 1) MOD N;
          n := n + 1
        END
      END
    END producer;

  BEGIN
    n := 0; in := 0; out := 0;
    NEWPROCESS(producer, ADR(wsp), SIZE(wsp), PRO);
    EXCL(s, 6); TRANSFER(CON, PRO)
  END keyboard.
```

Figure 4. A Keyboard Handler Module (from [9])

with its co-routines. Since coroutines are considered low-level facilities, their associated data type and its operations are imported from the module SYSTEM; the import list in our example program reflects this fact. A process is determined by a parameterless procedure which must be declared in the outermost block of a module. A process may be thought of as an instantiation, created by the pre-defined procedure NEWPROCESS, of the procedure which determines it. This means, among other things, that the process will have its own copies of all the procedure's local data structures. NEWPROCESS is exported by the SYSTEM module. Control is explicitly transferred to and from a process by means of predefined procedures TRANSFER and IOTRANSFER which are also exported from the SYSTEM module. The process in which a call on NEWPROCESS is executed becomes the parent of the created process.

Our example program imports the data type PROCESS from the SYSTEM module. As its name suggests, elements of this data type represent processes. To provide a denotation for this data type, we augment our dynamic structure with a dynamic universe *processes*. The universe of processes has a dynamic distinguished element *AP* (for active process) which indicates which process is currently executing. In the initial state of a dynamic structure *processes* will contain a single element. Elements are added to and deleted from *processes* as processes are created and deleted. As mentioned above, processes are created by calls on the procedure NEWPROCESS. A process is deleted when control reaches the end of the procedure which determines it or when control reaches the end of the procedure which determines one of its parent processes. Since each process must have its own local state space, we must alter the dynamic functions *PSTop*, *Top*, and *Avail* so that they take as additional argument an element of *processes*. Similarly, the dynamic distinguished elements of *parsetree* — *AN* and *XN* — must now become dynamic functions from *processes* into *parsetree*.

The declarations of the variables 'x' and 's' in our example both include an octal constant (777562B in the case of 'x' and 777560B in the case of 's'— the 'B' indicates that the preceding digits are to be interpreted as octal digits) which is meant to be interpreted as a memory address. This is so because the input/output registers of our hypothetical computer are "memory-mapped", i.e. one refers to them as if they were memory cells and, in our example, we wish to use the names 'x' and 's' to refer to the keyboard data and status registers, respectively. Thus, the declarations of 'x' and 's' must indicate the address of the registers with which they are to be associated. In our model 'x' and 's' will be bound to input channels. This is accomplished by adding a new symbol 'ioregister' to *grammarsymbol* to represent such variables and adding new grammatical productions 'factor → ioregister' and 'ioregister → id'. The range of *Sig* must be expanded to include input/output channels. The value of *Sig* at the 'id' node in the declaration for a variable bound to a channel will be initialized to the name of the channel to which the variable is bound. In the case of 'x', for example, this name is the octal constant '777562B'. We give the transition rule for the production 'ioregister → id' when the 'id' node refers to the keyboard data register of our hypothetical computer:

> **if** *Label*(*AN*(*AP*)) = ioregister **and** *Sig*(*Intro*(*Child1*(*AN*(*AP*)))) = 777562B
> **then**
> *Nval*(*AN*(*AP*)) := *Input*(*Sig*(*Intro*(*Child1*(*AN*(*AP*))))),
> *Output*(777560B) := *Input*(777560B) − {6},
> *AN*(*AP*) := *Parent*(*AN*(*AP*))
> **endif**.

This function update '*Output*(777560B) := *Input*(777560B) − {6}' reflects the fact that bit 6 of the keyboard status register of our hypothetical computer is reset when its keyboard data register is read. (The keyboard status register is declared to be of type BITSET and the operator '-' denotes set difference here.)

The pre-defined procedure NEWPROCESS has as its heading:

> PROCEDURE NEWPROCESS(P : PROC, A : ADDRESS,
> n : CARDINAL, VAR new : PROCESS).

In a call on NEWPROCESS, the actual parameter corresponding to 'P' denotes the procedure that determines the process to be created, the actual parameter corresponding to 'A' gives the base address of the workspace in which the processes' local variables are to allocated, the actual parameter corresponding to 'n' gives the size of this workspace, and the actual parameter corresponding to 'new' is a variable of type PROCESS in which a reference to the created process is stored. PROC is a pre-defined data type "parameterless procedure". At the level of abstraction at which we are formalizing our example program we will not need the base address of the new process' workspace. Therefore, we may omit a discussion of how our hypothetical computer's memory is modelled. Calls on NEWPROCESS are characterized by the CFG production

$$\text{predefcall} \rightarrow \text{id(explist)},$$

where the specification of the node labelled 'id' is 'NEWPROCESS'. The corresponding transition rule first prescribes evaluation of the actual parameters of the call. In what follows let 'P', 'new' and 'n' denote the roots of the subtrees in the actual parameter list of a call on NEWPROCESS corresponding to the formal parameters of the same names. A suite of function updates is applied to *Val*, *Avail*, and *AN*. A function update '*Val*(*Nval*(new)) := *temp*' sets the value of the most recent incarnation of the actual parameter corresponding to 'new' to the newly created element of *processes*; this makes this parameter into a reference to the new process, as desired. A function update '*Avail*(*temp*) := *Value*(*Nval*(n))' sets the amount of available storage for the new process. A function update '*AN*(*temp*) := *Value*(*Nval*(P))' sets the active node for the new process. Note that this update does not activate the new process, since the current active process (indicated by *AP*) is the process executing the call on NEWPROCESS; control remains in this latter process and proceeds to the parent node of the call on NEWPROCESS. The root of the pocedure call subtree is marked *ok* to signal successful creation of the new process.

The predefined procedure TRANSFER has the following heading:

> PROCEDURE TRANSFER(VAR source, destination : PROCESS);

In a call on TRANSFER, the actual parameter corresponding to 'source' will be a variable of type PROCESS in which a reference to the process executing the call, i.e. an element of *processes*, will be stored; the actual parameter corresponding to 'destination' will be a variable of type PROCESS in which a reference to the process to be activated is stored. Calls on TRANSFER are described by the same CFG production as calls on NEWPROCESS. In the following let 'source' and 'destination' denote the roots of the subtrees in the actual parameter list of a call on TRANSFER corresponding to the formal parameters of the same names. The function update 'AP := *Val*(*Nval*(destination))' activates the process represented by the value stored in the variable supplied as second actual parameter of the call on TRANSFER. This actual parameter must evaluate to a location (since it corresponds to a VAR formal parameter), hence the appearance of *Val* in the function update. The function update '*Val*(*Nval*(source)) := AP' stores a reference to the current process in the location to which the first actual parameter of the call on TRANSFER evaluated. The two remaining function updates advance control in the about-to-be-deactivated current process to the parent of the call on TRANSFER and mark the root of procedure call subtree *ok*. When this process is later reactivated, execution will resume at the parent of the call subtree.

Before we describe the semantics of calls on the predefined procedure IOTRANSFER, we must describe our model of interrupts. An interrupt is essentially the communication, from outside a dynamic structure, of a value of type CARDINAL. This communication takes place over a channel *interrupt*. The specific CARDINAL value communicated indicates which agent initiated the interrupt; the assignment of values to agents depends on the configuration of the computing system being modelled. Each agent has a priority. Priorities will also be expressed by CARDINAL values. For this purpose we add a static function *IntPriority* to our dynamic structure. *IntPriority* maps a CARDINAL value representing an interrupting agent to the CARDINAL value that expresses its priority: the priority of agent i is greater than that of agent j, if $IntPriority(i) > IntPriority(j)$. Each interrupting agent will have associated with it a process called its *handler*, which is activated, in a manner to be described shortly, whenever the agent interrupts. The element of *processes* that represents a handler will be stored in a location which is obtained by applying a function *IntHandler* to the CARDINAL value representing the agent. For each interrupting agent we must also reserve a location to hold the representative of the process that was executing when the agent interrupted. This is so that control may be returned to this process when the agent's handler has completed its job. We obtain this location by applying a function *IntRetDest* to the CARDINAL value representing the agent. For a particular interrupt i, the value of *IntPriority*(i), *IntHandler*(i), and *IntRetDest*(i) collectively constitute the *interrupt vector* for i.

We must extend the notion of priority to the statements of a Modula program. We shall do so by adding to our dynamic structure a dynamic function *CurPriority* which maps elements of *processes* to CARDINAL values: for each process, *CurPriority* gives the current priority level of the statement executing in that process. Now, how is the current priority established? Note that heading of the declaration of the module 'keyboard' in our example program includes the symbol '[4]'. This assigns a priority of 4 to all the executable statements of the module and its procedures. Otherwise, the statements of a procedure inherit the priority of the program that called the procedure. We represent this situation as follows. To deal with modules with an explicitly declared priority (like 'keyboard' in our example), we augment our dynamic structure with a static, partial function on *parsetree*, *ModulePriority*, which maps all the nodes of such a module to the CARDINAL value that expresses the module's priority. Whenever one of the module's procedures is called, *CurPriority* is set to the value obtained by applying *ModulePriority* to the root of the procedure's declaration subtree. In order to restore the priority of the calling program, we stack the value of *CurPriority* which prevailed during its execution. To accomplish this we need a dynamic function *PriorityStack* which maps elements of *pstack* to CARDINAL values. Moreover, for those procedures that are not part of modules with an explicit priority, *CurPriority* may be set to *PriorityStack*(*PSTop*), i.e. such procedures inherit the calling procedure's priority. The transition rules for 'procall' and 'procdecl' nodes must be modified. The interested reader may consult [6] for details.

The predefined procedure IOTRANSFER has the following heading

PROCEDURE IOTRANSFER(VAR source, dest : PROCESS; va : CARDINAL);

IOTRANSFER is like TRANSFER in that it activates the process whose representative is stored in the actual parameter corresponding to 'dest' and stores the current process's representative in the actual parameter corresponding to 'source'. In addition, it sets the interrupt priority, interrupt handler, and interrupt return destination attributes of the interrupt designated by the value of the actual parameter corresponding to 'va'. In the following let 'source', 'dest' and 'va' denote the nodes of the call subtree corresponding to the formal parameters of the same name. The semantics of IOTRANSFER are expressed by a number of function updates. In the following discussion, we mean by "the interrupt" the interrupt denoted by the value of the actual parameter corresponding to 'va'. The function update

$$IntPriority(Value(Nval(\text{va}))) := ModulePriority(AN(AP))$$

sets the priority of the interrupt to the priority of the call-statement. The function update

$$IntHandler(Value(Nval(\text{va}))) := Nval(\text{source})$$

sets the interrupt's handler to process represented by the value in the location to which 'source' evaluates. The function update

$$IntRetDest(Value(Nval(\text{va}))) := Nval(\text{dest})$$

establishes the contents of the location to which 'dest' evaluates as the process to which control returns when the interrupt's handler has finished executing. We shall see next how an element of *processes* is stored in this location.

We shall now give the transition rule that describes how our dynamic structure changes when an external agent interrupts. When an external agent interrupts, an appropriate CARDINAL value is communicated to our dynamic structure over the channel *interrupt*. The interrogation of this value is indicated in a transition rule by writing '*Input*(*interrupt*)'; this term is undefined in a particular state of a dynamic structure, if no value is present on the channel. Therefore, the occurrence of an interrupt causes the guard '*Input*(*interrupt*) $\neq\perp$' to evaluate to *true*. We then have the following transition rule for interrupts:

> **if** *Input*(*interrupt*) $\neq\perp$ **then**
> **if** *IntPriority*(*Input*(*interrupt*)) $>$ *CurPriority*(*AP*) **then**
> $AP :=$ *Val*(*IntHandler*(*Input*(*interrupt*)))
> *Val*(*IntRetDest*(*Input*(*interrupt*))) $:= AP$,
> **endif**
> **endif**.

Note that an interrupt is ignored if its priority is lower than the priority of the currently executing process. When an interrupt of sufficiently high priority occurs, a TRANSFER operation is effectively performed. The difference is that, in the case of an interrupt there is no associated program text and, hence, no need to alter the active node or *Nval*. In order to make our dynamic structure deterministic, we must embed the transition rules we gave in Chapter 4 in an outer transition rule whose guard is

$$Input(interrupt) = \perp .$$

That is, in the absence of interrupts processing procedes as we have described it in previous sections of this paper.

Let Prog be a program that includes and uses the module 'keyboard' given above. How can one prove that the module 'keyboard' works correctly, i.e. that the characters fetched by Prog are exactly the characters entered from the keyboard. Here is one way. Define in the natural way

(a) sequences of characters *deposit_sequence*, *fetch_sequence*, and *buffer_contents*, and

(b) terms *in*, *out*, *n*, and *N* with values of type CARDINAL

and establish that in all appropriate states

(1) *deposit_sequence* is the concatenation of *fetch_sequence* with *buffer_contents*, and

(2) $in = out + n \; Mod \; N$.

The reader is referred to [6] for details.

References

1. Blakley, Robert and Gurevich, Yuri, "The Algebraic Operational Semantics of Smalltalk", in preparation.

2. Gurevich, Yuri, "Logic and the Challenge of Computer Science", in *Current Trends in Theoretical Computer Science* (ed. E. Boŕger), Computer Science Press, 198., 1–57.

3. Gurevich, Yuri and Moss, Lawrence, "The Algebraic Operational Semantics of Occam", in preparation.

4. Landin, Peter J., "A λ-calculus approach", in *Advances in Programming and Nonnumerical Computation*, L. Fox(ed.), London, Pergamon Press, 1966.

5. McCarthy, John and others, *The Lisp 1.5 Programmer's Manual*, Cambridge, Massachusetts, MIT Press, 1962.

6. Morris, James, *Algebraic Operational Semantics for Modula 2*, Ph.D. dissertation, The University of Michigan, 1988.

7. Plotkin, Gordon, *A Structural Approach to Operational Semantics*, DAIMI FN–19, Aarhus University.

8. Wegner, Peter, "The Vienna Definition Language", *ACM Computing Surveys*, 4(1), 5–63.

9. Wirth, Niklaus, *Programming in Modula-2*, Berlin, Springer-Verlag, 1982.

PROGRAM VERIFICATION USING DYNAMIC LOGIC

M. Heisel, W. Reif, W. Stephan
Universität Karlsruhe
Institut für Logik, Komplexität und Deduktionssysteme
Postfach 6980
D-7500 Karlsruhe

Abstract
This paper describes the use of dynamic logic in a system which provides an environment for the implementation of various verification methods. We concentrate on the logical basis of this system. In particular we discuss the role of so-called uninterpreted reasoning as a means to extend the basic logic by derived rules and tactics which then are used to implement verification strategies.

1 Introduction

In this paper we describe the use of dynamic logic as a logical basis of a system (the Karlsruhe Interactive Verifier), see [HHRS 86], which serves as an environment to implement various verification and program development strategies. Apart from that the KIV System can be used as a proof assistant to generate proofs not following a general verification method. Among the strategies which are currently implemented are BURSTALL's method for proving total correctness assertions [Bu 74], [HRS 87] and GRIES's program development method [Gr 81].

We will concentrate on the logical basis of the KIV System. The formalism we use can be extended freely by derived rules and tactics we need for a given verification strategy. In the case of backward proofs tactics are subgoal generating programs which are programmed entirely in terms of basic and derived rules. As far as the logic is concerned it has turned out that some sort of uninterpreted reasoning (we consider all interpretations of the symbols we use) is required for these purposes. Systems for interpreted reasoning (the symbols of our language are given a fixed meaning), see for example [Ha 79], are designed for a special and in some sense complete verifcation strategy. Since we do not want to stick to a single method we add to the system as much knowledge about our programming language as possible. Systems for uninterpreted reasoning, see for example [Go 82], use infinitary rules in order to obtain completeness. "Reasoning" by means of infinitary rules of course cannot be implemented. In our setting infinitary rules are replaced by inductive arguments. Although we lose completeness for standard interpretations of the programming language constructs the resulting formalism has turned out to be well suited for the type of system we are looking for. A rich collection of derived rules has been programmed in the KIV System, among them being all those which are used in systems of interpreted reasoning and HOARE-like calculi. Known strategies like BURSTALL's "execution and induction strategy" have been extended by simply adding appropriate new rules.

The paper is organized as follows. In chapter two after a brief introduction to Dynamic Logic we discuss general aspects of our axiomatisation. Some of the actual axioms for programming language constructs are presented in chapter three. By two examples we demonstrate the style of reasoning which is supported by our system. In chapter four we give a survey of the KIV System. In particular we will demonstrate how the basic logic can be extended by derived rules and tactics.

2 Dynamic Logic

2.1 General Remarks

Dynamic logic (DL) extends ordinary predicate logic (PL) by formulas $[\alpha]\phi$ where α is a program, let's say a PASCAL-program, and ϕ is again a DL-formula. The intuitive meaning of $[\alpha]\phi$ is: "if α terminates, ϕ holds after execution of α." For PL-formulas ϕ and ψ the formula $\phi \rightarrow [\alpha]\psi$ corresponds to the well known partial correctness assertion $\phi\{\alpha\}\psi$. However, in contrast to HOARE's Logic (HL) we also may express termination of programs by $\neg[\alpha]\neg\phi$, which is abbreviated by $\langle\alpha\rangle\phi$, and program implications like $[\alpha]\phi \rightarrow [\beta]\phi$.

Following the approach of GOLDBLATT [Go 82] a *model* for a Z-sorted *signature* Σ and a Z-sorted system of *variables* **X** is given by a quadruple $\mathbf{M} = (A\ , S\ , v\ , [\![\ \dots\ ]\!])$, where A is a Σ-Algebra, S is a set of states, v associates with each state $s \in S$ and each variable $x \in X_\mu$ an element of A_μ and $[\![\ \dots\ ]\!] : Prog(\Sigma,X) \rightarrow 2^{S\times S}$ is a semantics of our programming language Prog(Σ,X). For box-formulas the relation $\mathbf{M} \Vdash_s \phi$, "ϕ holds in $\mathbf{M}$ in state s" , is defined by: $\mathbf{M} \Vdash_s [\alpha]\psi$ iff for all $t \in S$ $\ s [\![\alpha]\!] t$ implies $\mathbf{M} \Vdash_t \psi$.

Usually we are interested in a fixed semantics of our programming language Prog(Σ,X). The programming language constructs are given their intended meanings by so-called *standard model conditions*.

2.2 Interpreted vs. Uninterpreted Reasoning

In his survey of DL HAREL [Ha 85] makes a distinction between two levels of reasoning: interpreted reasoning and uninterpreted reasoning. In both cases we deal with the same logical language.

Using *interpreted reasoning* we have in mind a fixed interpretation of the function and predica symbols which occur in the formulas. In [Ha 79] HAREL presents surprisingly simple axiom system (for various programming languages) which are *arithmetically complete*. This means that we ca deduce all DL-formulas which are valid in an *arithmetical universe* A if we take as additional axiom all first-order formulas which are A-valid. In other words DL-formulas can be effectively reduced t a set of PL-formulas using these axiom systems. The PL-formulas which are generated by this proces can be viewed as *"verification conditions"* and have to be proved in one way or the other. Howeve due to the limited amount of "dynamic reasoning" which is incorporated in these systems we ar restricted to a single (verification) strategy which uses *invariants* and *convergents*. Even for simp assertions about programs of a simple programming language this restriction is problematic, if we ar interested in practical program verification. Things get worse for program implications and mor sophisticated control structures. But what can we do to obtain a more flexible way of provin assertions about programs?

In *uninterpreted reasoning* we are interested in those DL-formulas which are valid in a structures A. Thus uninterpreted reasoning might be the formalism we are looking for. However, th set of valid formulas is highly inconstructive. Usually this set is given a *syntactic characterisation* b using *infinitary* rules, see for example [Go 82] and [Ha 85]. Obviously this approach is not wel suited for practical applications. In our approach Ω-rules are replaced by an inductive arguments.

To demonstrate this style of reasoning we present an informal example before we go into th details of our axiomatisation. In ordinary PL we may prove $\forall x.P(x,h(x,y)) \rightarrow P(g(x),h(g(x),y))$ (actually in many HILBERT-style axiomatisations this is an axiom). In DL things are a bit more mo complicated. Consider the implication

$\forall x.$ [**while** Q(x,y) **do** y:=f(x,y) **od**] P(x,y) $\rightarrow$ [**while** Q(g(x),y) **do** y:=f(g(x),y) **od**] P(g(x),y)

As in the case of PL this implication holds regardless of the interpretation of P, Q, h, g and f. W present an informal proof of the implication above following the lines of uninterpreted reasoning as it i used in our system. Recall that $[\alpha]\phi$ has to be read "if α terminates ϕ holds after execution of α". $[\alpha]$ holds vacuously in all states where α does not terminate.

$\forall x.\phi$ means that ϕ still holds after having assigned an arbitrary value to x. We conclude tha $\forall x.$[**while** Q(x,y) **do** y:=f(x,y) **od**]P(x,y) implies [x:=g(x)][**while** Q(x,y) **do** y:=f(x,y) **od**]P(x,y) We are left with the problem of proving that [x:=g(x)][**while** Q(x,y) **do** y:=f(x,y) **od**] P(x,y) implie [**while** Q(g(x),y) **do** y:=f(g(x),y) **od**] P(g(x),y) . For a while-loop α we have

$[\alpha]\phi$ if and only if

for all i, if the while-loop terminates after i iterations, then ϕ holds afterwards.

Hence in our case it is sufficient to show that

if after the execution of x:=g(x) the first loop terminates after i iterations, then P(x,y) holds afterward implies

if the second loop terminates after i iterations, then P(g(x),y) holds afterwards.

For the case i=0 the result holds vacuously if we have Q(g(x),y). Let us assume $\neg$Q(g(x),y). I this case we have to show that P(g(x),y) holds. Since $\neg$Q(g(x),y) implies [x:=g(x)]$\neg$Q(x,y) afte execution of x:=g(x) the first loop terminates after 0 iterations. Hence by our assumption we hav [x:=g(x)]P(x,y). But [x:=g(x)]P(x,y) implies P(g(x),y).

Assume that for i the result holds in all states in order to prove it for i+1. If $\neg Q(g(x),y)$ holds then the second loop is not executed and the result is vacuously true. Note that we have to consider only the case where the second loop is executed (i+1)-times which means that the test must be true in the beginning. $Q(g(x),y)$ implies $[x:=g(x)]Q(x,y)$. Thus the first loop is executed at least once after the assignment $x:=g(x)$. Hence according to our assumption if after execution of $x:=g(x)$; $y:=f(x,y)$ the first loop terminates after i iterations, then $P(x,y)$ holds afterwards. Since for arbitrary θ $[x:=g(x)\ ;\ y:=f(x,y)]\theta$ is equivalent to $[y:=f(gx),y)\ ;\ x:=g(x)]\theta$ we conclude that if after execution of $y:=f(gx),y)$ and $x:=g(x)$ the first loop terminates after i iterations, then $P(x,y)$ holds. By the inductive assumption it follows that if after execution of $y:=f(gx),y)$ the second loop terminates after i iterations, $P(g(x),y)$ holds afterwards. Since we have assumed $Q(g(x),y)$ we conclude that if the second loop terminates after i+1 iterations, then $P(g(x),y)$ holds afterwards.

In the proof above we had to use the equivalence $[x:=g(x)\ ;\ y:=f(x,y)]\theta \leftrightarrow [y:=f(gx),y)\ ;\ x:=g(x)]\theta$, where θ was a formalisation of "If the first loop terminates after i iterations, ... ". In our approach this is an instance of an axiom scheme (see chapter three). In systems of interpreted reasoning we only have a single scheme for assignments: $[y:=\tau]\phi \leftrightarrow \phi(\tau/y)$, where ϕ is a PL-formula and $\phi(\tau/y)$ is obtained from ϕ by replacing all free occurrences of y by τ provided that no binding conflict arises. This is only sufficient to prove the equivalence for PL-formulas θ. Hence using the simple axiom systems of interpreted reasoning we will not be able to formalize the proof above. Of course for suitable interpretations of f, g, P and Q the implication above can be proved using interpreted reasoning in the sense of HAREL. However the proof is quite different from the ours. It leads to "verification conditions" which depend on the interpretation we have in mind.

But what's so special about the style of proof we have presented above? Perhaps the experienced reader will already have noticed that our proof can be generalized to a "recipe" which works for *all* implications of the form $[x:=\tau][\alpha]\phi \rightarrow [\alpha][x:=\tau]\phi$, where x does not occur on the left hand side of assignments in α. Following the ML-approach [GMW 79] in our system "recipes" for generating proofs are formulated using a functional metalanguage. The style of reasoning which is supported by systems like the one given by HAREL seem not to be suited for these purposes. On the other hand a metalanguage to formulate "recipes" as the one mentioned above is a means to reduce the complexity of systems of uninterpreted reasoning.

.3 Ω-Rules and Induction

GOLDBLATT gives a syntactic characterisation of the formulas valid in all standard models by using an infinitary rule Ω_{while} to prove admissible statements $\Phi\{...\}$ about while-loops:

$$\frac{\Phi\{\ \phi_n(\varepsilon,\alpha)\ \}\ \text{ for all n}}{\Phi\{\ [\textbf{while}\ \varepsilon\ \textbf{do}\ \alpha\ \textbf{od}]\phi\ \}},$$

where $\phi_0(\varepsilon,\alpha) \equiv \neg\varepsilon \rightarrow \phi$ and $\phi_{n+1}(\varepsilon,\alpha) \equiv \varepsilon \rightarrow [\alpha]\ \phi_n(\varepsilon,\alpha)$.

In our approach infinitary rules are replaced by inductive arguments which are based on built-in datastructures, *counters* in the case of while-loops and *environments* in the case of procedures. I addition to these datastructures our programming language has to be augmented by additiona constructs: loop-programs and units. The resulting formalism is of course no longer complete wit respect to the class of all standard models. To achieve completeness we have to drop at least the critica standard model conditions. However, in this case we have to take into account *non-standar* interpretations of some of our programming language constructs. These interpretations cannot b excluded by axioms. Despite the fact that there are some built-in datastructures this type of formalism i our opinion still covers the basic ideas of "uninterpreted reasoning". After introducing some of th axioms for the programming language we demonstrate this by some examples.

3 Axiomatising Programming Languages

3.1 Axioms for a Simple Programming Language

In this section we will present the axioms for a simple programming language. We will n mention the remaining (logical) axioms of our system which deal with propositional logi quantification and modal logic. A complete list of axioms can be found in [Re 84].

Basic Constructs

$$[x{:=}\tau]\phi \leftrightarrow \phi(\tau/x) \text{ , where } \phi \text{ is a PL-formula ;}$$

$$[x{:=}\tau][x{:=}\sigma]\phi \rightarrow [x{:=}\sigma^{\tau}{}_{x}]\phi \text{ ;}$$

$$[x{:=}\tau][y{:=}\sigma]\phi \rightarrow [y{:=}\sigma^{\tau}{}_{x}][x{:=}\tau]\phi \text{ , where x does not occur in } y{:=}\tau \text{ ;}$$

$$[x{:=}\tau]\phi \vee [x{:=}\tau]\neg\phi \text{ (determinism) ;}$$

$$\neg[x{:=}\tau]\underline{\text{false}} \text{ (termination) ;}$$

$$[\textbf{skip}]\phi \leftrightarrow \phi \text{ ;}$$

$$[\textbf{abort}]\phi \text{ ;}$$

$$[\alpha;\beta]\phi \leftrightarrow [\alpha][\beta]\phi \text{ ;}$$

$$[\textbf{if } \varepsilon \textbf{ then } \alpha \textbf{ else } \beta \textbf{ fi}]\phi \leftrightarrow (\varepsilon \rightarrow [\alpha]\phi) \wedge (\neg\varepsilon \rightarrow [\beta]\phi) .$$

Loop-programs

$$[\textbf{loop } \alpha \textbf{ times } \underline{\text{zero}}]\phi \leftrightarrow \phi \text{ ;}$$

$$[\textbf{loop } \alpha \textbf{ times } \text{next}(\iota)]\phi \leftrightarrow [\alpha][\textbf{loop } \alpha \textbf{ times } \iota]\phi .$$

While-loops

$$[\textbf{while } \varepsilon \textbf{ do } \alpha \textbf{ od}]\phi \leftrightarrow \forall i.\ [\textbf{while } \varepsilon \textbf{ do } \alpha \textbf{ od}{\downarrow}i]\ \phi ,$$

where $\textbf{while } \varepsilon \textbf{ do } \alpha \textbf{ od}{\downarrow}i \equiv \textbf{loop } (\varepsilon!\alpha) \textbf{ times } i \ ; \ \textbf{if } \varepsilon \textbf{ then abort else skip fi}$

and $(\varepsilon!\alpha) \equiv \textbf{if } \varepsilon \textbf{ then } \alpha \textbf{ else abort fi}$.

Apart from the fact that in our setting assignments always terminate the axioms for the basic onstructs are identical to those given by GOLDBLATT.

The expression following the symbol "**times**" in a loop construct is a *counter expression.* ounter expressions, denoted by ι, are made up of the constant zero and the unary function symbol ext. Counters and loop programs have been introduced to admit induction proofs about while-loops. ounter expressions are assumed not to occur in assignments in α. From the remaining axioms for ounters we just mention the *induction* scheme $\forall i.\ (\ \forall j.(\ j<i \rightarrow \phi(j/i)\ ) \rightarrow \phi) \ \rightarrow\ \forall i.\phi$. The axioms or < ("less than") are as usual. A completeness result for the case where nonstandard interpretations of ounters and loop constructs are admitted is given in [Re 86].

In standard models **while** ε **do** α **od**$\downarrow$i is the "i-th *approximation* of **while** ε **do** α **od**" in the ense that we have s $[\![$**while** ε **do** α **od**$\downarrow$i$]\!]$ t iff t can be reached from s by *exactly* v(s,i) iterations f the while-loop. Hence [**while** ε **do** α **od**$\downarrow$i] ϕ is true in some state s iff ϕ holds in all states which an be reached from s by exactly v(s,i) iterations. There is an obvious correspondence between $_{while}$ and the axiom for while-loops. In our formalism for all natural numbers n we can prove $_n(\varepsilon,\alpha) \leftrightarrow$[**while** ε **do** α **od**$\downarrow\iota_n$] ϕ , where $\iota_n \equiv$ next^n(zero). The use of induction on counters will be emonstrated by the example below.

The KIV System is based on a *sequent calculus.*We use "$\Rightarrow$" for the *sequent arrow*. The xioms mentioned above are incorporated as $\Rightarrow \phi_{Ax}$.

.2 Example I

Let $\alpha \equiv$ **while** x$\neq$y **do** x:=suc(x) ; z:=pred(z) **od** . It has been shown be ANTONIOU & PERSCHNEIDER [AS 84] that the partial correctness assertion (x=0 $\wedge$ z=y) $\rightarrow$ [α] z=0 is not rovable in HL if we take as the underlying datastructure $N = \langle$Nat, 0 , λx.x+1 , λx.x-1$\rangle$. Instead of roving the above assertion directly we are going to prove the program implication [β] z=0 $\rightarrow$ [α] =0 , where $\beta \equiv$ **while** x$\neq$y **do** y:=pred(y) ; z:=pred(z) **od.** It is an easy exercise to prove (x=0 $\wedge$ =y) $\rightarrow$ [β] z=0 in HL by using z=y as an invariant. Note that all the rules of HL can be obtained as *erived* rules in our system. We give a top-down proof where *goals* are *reduced* to *subgoals*. The roof-steps presented below are *"macro-steps"* in the sense that they comprise more than a single pplication of a basic rule. In our comments we will mention only the most important axioms which ave to be used. The reader is referred to chapter four for a dicussion of how these "macro-steps" are ctually implemented in the KIV System.

The first goal is $\Rightarrow$ [β] z=0 $\rightarrow$ [α] z=0 .

y the while axiom it is reduced to

$$\Rightarrow\ \forall i.\forall(x,y,z).\ (\ [\beta\downarrow i]\ z=0\ \rightarrow\ [\alpha\downarrow i]\ z=0\ ).$$

sing the induction axiom we get as a subgoal

$$\phi_H\ \Rightarrow\ [\beta\downarrow i]\ z=0\ \rightarrow\ [\alpha\downarrow i]\ z=0,$$

here the *induction hypothesis* is $\phi_H \equiv \forall j.\ (\ j<i \rightarrow \forall(x,y,z).\ (\ [\beta\downarrow j]\ z=0\ \rightarrow\ [\alpha\downarrow j]\ z=0\ )\ )$.

Case analysis yields

$$i=\underline{zero}\,,\ \phi_H \ \Rightarrow\ [\beta\downarrow i]\ z=0 \rightarrow [\alpha\downarrow i]\ z=0$$

and

$$i=next(j_0)\,,\ \phi_H \ \Rightarrow\ [\beta\downarrow i]\ z=0 \rightarrow [\alpha\downarrow i]\ z=0\ .$$

Using the first loop axiom we get

$$i=\underline{zero}\,,\ \phi_H \ \Rightarrow\ [\textbf{if } \varepsilon \textbf{ then abort else skip fi}]\ z=0 \rightarrow [\textbf{if } \varepsilon \textbf{ then abort else skip fi}]\ z=0$$

which is trivial.

To reduce the second goal we use the second loop axiom and the induction hypothesis. To get a appropriate instance of the hypothesis we have to use the axiom: $\forall \mathbf{x}.\phi \rightarrow [\gamma]\phi$, where all variable which occur on the left-hand side of assignments in γ are members of the list **x**. First this axiom is use with $\gamma \equiv j{:=}j_0$ and after that with $\gamma \equiv (x{\neq}y\ !\ \beta_{bdy})$, where. $\beta_{bdy} \equiv y{:=}pred(y)\ ;\ z{:=}pred(z)$. It remains show

$$i=next(j_0)\,,\ \phi_H\ ,\ [(x{\neq}y\ !\ \beta_{bdy})][\alpha\downarrow j_0]\ z=0 \ \Rightarrow\ [\alpha\downarrow i]\ z=0\ .$$

Using the *lemma*

$$\Rightarrow\ [(x{\neq}y\ !\ \beta_{bdy})][\alpha\downarrow k]\ z=0 \rightarrow [(x{\neq}y\ !\ \alpha_{bdy})][\alpha\downarrow k]\ z=0\ ,$$

where $\alpha_{bdy} \equiv x{:=}suc(x)\ ;\ z{:=}pred(z)$, and the second loop axiom we finish the main part of our proof

To prove the lemma we again use induction. Proceeding in the same way as above after som intermediate steps we get

$$k=\underline{zero}\,,\ \psi_H\ ,\ [(x{\neq}y\ !\ \beta_{bdy})]\ [\textbf{if } \varepsilon \textbf{ then abort else skip fi}]\ z=0 \ \Rightarrow$$
$$[(x{\neq}y\ !\ \alpha_{bdy})]\ [\textbf{if } \varepsilon \textbf{ then abort else skip fi}]\ z=0$$

and

$$k=next(j_0)\,,\ \psi_H\ ,\ [(x{\neq}y\ !\ \beta_{bdy})][(x{\neq}y\ !\ \alpha_{bdy})][\alpha\downarrow j_0]\ z=0 \ \Rightarrow\ [(x{\neq}y\ !\ \alpha_{bdy})][\alpha\downarrow k]\ z=0\ ,$$

where $\psi_H \equiv\ \forall j.\ (\,j<k \rightarrow \forall(x,y,z).\ ([(x{\neq}y\ !\ \beta_{bdy})][\alpha\downarrow j]\ z=0 \rightarrow [(x{\neq}y\ !\ \alpha_{bdy})][\alpha\downarrow j]\ z=0)\ )$. We onl demonstrate the proof of the second subgoal. As a *sublemma* for arbitrary θ we use

$$\Rightarrow\ [(x{\neq}y\ !\ \beta_{bdy})][(x{\neq}y\ !\ \alpha_{bdy})]\ \theta \rightarrow [(x{\neq}y\ !\ \alpha_{bdy})][(x{\neq}y\ !\ \beta_{bdy})]\theta$$

and get

$$k=next(j_0)\,,\ \psi_H\ ,\ [(x{\neq}y\ !\ \alpha_{bdy})][(x{\neq}y\ !\ \beta_{bdy})][\alpha\downarrow j_0]\ z=0 \ \Rightarrow\ [(x{\neq}y\ !\ \alpha_{bdy})][\alpha\downarrow k]\ z=0.$$

Application of the induction hypothesis yields

$$k=next(j_0)\,,\ \psi_H\ ,\ [(x{\neq}y\ !\ \alpha_{bdy})][(x{\neq}y\ !\ \alpha_{bdy})][\alpha\downarrow j_0]\ z=0 \ \Rightarrow\ [(x{\neq}y\ !\ \alpha_{bdy})][\alpha\downarrow k]\ z=0\ .$$

Using the second loop axiom we finish the proof of the lemma.

Note that so far we have not used any knowledge about the datastructure we are dealing wit We now turn to the proof of the sublemma.

$$\Rightarrow\ [(x{\neq}y\ !\ \beta_{bdy})][(x{\neq}y\ !\ \alpha_{bdy})]\theta \rightarrow [(x{\neq}y\ !\ \alpha_{bdy})][(x{\neq}y\ !\ \beta_{bdy})]\theta$$

simplifies to

$$[(x{\neq}y\ !\ \beta_{bdy})][(x{\neq}y\ !\ \alpha_{bdy})]\theta \ \Rightarrow\ [(x{\neq}y\ !\ \alpha_{bdy})][(x{\neq}y\ !\ \beta_{bdy})]\theta\ .$$

Application of the conditional axiom yields

$$[(x{\neq}y\ !\ \beta_{bdy})][(x{\neq}y\ !\ \alpha_{bdy})]\theta\ ,\ x{\neq}y \ \Rightarrow\ [\alpha_{bdy}][(x{\neq}y\ !\ \beta_{bdy})]\theta$$

and

$$[(x \neq y \,!\, \beta_{bdy})][(x \neq y \,!\, \alpha_{bdy})]\theta \ , \ \neg x \neq y \quad \Rightarrow \quad [\mathbf{abort}][(x \neq y \,!\, \beta_{bdy})]\theta \ .$$

The second subgoal is trivial. The first one is reduced to

$$[(x \neq y \,!\, \beta_{bdy})][(x \neq y \,!\, \alpha_{bdy})]\theta \ , x \neq y \ , suc(x) \neq y \quad \Rightarrow \quad [\alpha_{bdy}][\beta_{bdy}]\theta$$

and

$$[(x \neq y \,!\, \beta_{bdy})][(x \neq y \,!\, \alpha_{bdy})]\theta \ , x \neq y \ , \neg suc(x) \neq y \quad \Rightarrow \quad [\alpha_{bdy}][\mathbf{abort}]\theta \ .$$

using the conditional axiom and the first assignment axiom. Again the second subgoal is trivial. Simplification of the antecedent yields

$$x \neq y \ , \ suc(x) \neq y \ \Rightarrow \ x \neq y \ ,$$

$$x \neq y \ , \ suc(x) \neq y \ \Rightarrow \ x \neq pred(y) \ ,$$

$$[\beta_{bdy}][\alpha_{bdy}]\theta \ \Rightarrow \ [\alpha_{bdy}][\beta_{bdy}]\theta \ .$$

The last goal can be proved using the assignment axioms. Note that we have not to instanciate θ in this proof. The second subgoal is the only nontrivial "verification condition" which is generated.

3.3 Axioms for Procedures

The programming language we have presented so far is by no means appropriate for an application in the area of *practical* program verification. Work has to be done in two directions. We have to add special built-in *data structures* like arrays, records and pointers, and we have to study more elaborate *control structures*. In this paper we shall indicate briefly how the programming language given above can be augmented by the declaration of *local variables* and *(simple)recursive procedures*. Simple recursive procedures take value and variable parameters but no procedure parameters.

As far as syntax is concerned we add three new constructs to our programming language:

$$\mathbf{var}\ x_1 = \tau_1 \ ; \dots ; x_n = \tau_n \ \mathbf{in}\ \alpha \ ,$$

$$\mathbf{proc}\ p_1 \Leftarrow \lambda(x_1 : y_1).\alpha_1 \ ; \dots ; p_n \Leftarrow \lambda(x_n : y_n).\alpha_n \ \mathbf{in}\ \alpha$$

and

$$\mathbf{call}\ p(\tau : z) \ .$$

In the declaration of local variables x_i is *initialized* to the value of τ_i. $\mathbf{x}_i$ and $\mathbf{y}_i$ are the lists of the *formal* value and variable pramerters respectively and α_i is the procedure body. The construct $\lambda(\mathbf{x}_i, \mathbf{y}_i).\alpha_i$ is called an *abstraction*. In the *procedure call* τ and $\mathbf{z}$ are the lists of the *actual* parameters. The occurrences of variables following the symbols "λ" and "**var**" are *binding occurrences*. The *scope* of these binding occurrences is defined in the usual way. An occurrence of a variable inside the scope of a binding occurrence of that variable is called *bound*.

As in the case of while-loops we have to add a new datastructure and a new construct to axiomatise recursive procedures. Here we consider so-called *units* $(\rho|\alpha)$ which consist of an *environment expression* ρ and a command α. The datastructure of environments is used to record the meaning of the procedure identifiers. Environments are lists of entries of the form $[p/(\rho|\gamma)]$, where ρ is again an environment expression and γ is an abstraction. The environment ρ is used instead of the current environment upon a call of p. Entities of the form $(\rho|\gamma)$ are called *closures*. As counters in th case of while-loops environments belong to our object language. Environment expressions are made u of the constant empty which denotes the empty environment and dyadic function symbols $mod_{p,\gamma}$ $mod_{p,\gamma}(\rho_0,\rho_1)$ denotes the environment which is obtained from ρ_0 by adding a new entry $[p/(\rho_1|\gamma)]$ Note that since (in standard models) environments are *finite* tree-like objects a unit $(\rho|\gamma)$ will allov only a finite number of (recursive) procedure calls. Instead of adding an infinitary rule Ω_{proc}, se [St 85] for an infinitary axiomatisation of this type of recursive procedures, we will prove properties c recursive programs by induction on the structure of environments. The use of induction o environments (also for the case where procedure arguments are allowed) will be described mor detailed in [St 88].

Local variables

$$[(\rho \mid \mathbf{var}\ x_1=\tau_1\ ; \dots ; x_n=\tau_n\ \mathbf{in}\ \alpha)]\phi \leftrightarrow [y_1:=\tau_1] \dots [y_n:=\tau_n]\,[(\rho \mid \alpha(y_1/x_1) \dots (y_n/x_n))]\phi,$$

where $y_1, \dots, y_n$ are pairwise distinct fresh variables.

Procedure declarations

$$[(\rho \mid \mathbf{proc}\ \delta\ \mathbf{in}\ \alpha)]\phi \ \leftrightarrow\ \forall e.\,(\,Adm_\delta(\rho,e) \ \rightarrow [(e \mid \alpha)]\phi\ ,$$

where $\delta \equiv\ p_1 \Leftarrow \lambda(x_1:y_1).\alpha_1\ ; \dots ; p_n \Leftarrow \lambda(x_n:y_n).\alpha_n$ and for each predicate Adm_δ we have

$$Adm_\delta(e_0,e_1) \ \leftrightarrow\ e_1=\underline{empty} \ \ \vee$$

$$\exists e_2.\,(\,Adm_\delta(e_0,e_2) \wedge e_1=e_0[p_1/(e_2 \mid \lambda(x_1:y_1).\alpha_1)] \dots [p_n/(e_2 \mid \lambda(x_n:y_n).\alpha_n)]\,)$$

We have written $\rho_0[p/(\rho_1|\gamma)]$ for $mod_{p,\gamma}(\rho_0,\rho_1)$ to increase readability.

Procedure calls

$$[(\rho_0\ [p/(\rho_1|\ \lambda(x:y).\alpha)] \mid \mathbf{call}\ p(\tau:z))]\phi \ \leftrightarrow\ [u_1:=\tau_1] \dots [u_n:=\tau_n][(\rho_1\ \mid \alpha'(u/x)(z/y))]\phi$$

and

$$[(\underline{empty} \mid \mathbf{call}\ p(\tau:z))]\phi\ ,$$

where $\mathbf{u} \equiv (u_1,\dots,u_n)$ is a vector of pairwise distinct fresh variables and α' is obtained from α by a suitable renaming of the bound variables in α in order to avoid a binding conflict when the elements c $\mathbf{z}$ are substituted for all free occurrences of the elements of $\mathbf{y}$.

3.4 Example II

Consider the following two programs α_{rec} and α_{it}.

```
αrec ≡ proc p ⇐ λ(x:y).  {pbody} var z0=0 ; z1=0 in
                          if x=nil then y:=1
                                else call p(left(x):z0) ; call p(right(x):z1) ; y:=z0+z1
                          fi {endof pbody}
       in call p(tree:ct)
```

nd

$\alpha_{it} \equiv$ {prep} stk:=$\underline{epty}$; ct:=1 {endof prep}

{loop} **while** stk≠$\underline{epty}$ ∨ tree≠$\underline{nil}$

do {body} **if** tree≠$\underline{nil}$

then stk:=push(tree,stk) ;

tree:=left(tree)

else ct:=ct+1 ;

tree:=right(top(stack)) ;

stk:=pop(stk)

fi {endof body}

od {endof loop}

It is easy to see that α_{rec} terminates for all inputs and computes the *number of tips of a binary ree*. For α_{it} this is far less obvious. Hence we might be interested in proving the implication $\langle\alpha_{rec}\rangle$ct=c0 → $\langle\alpha_{it}\rangle$ct=c0 . We use an extension of BURSTALL's method ("Program Proving as and Simulation with a little Induction") [Bu 74]. The "execution" of α_{prep} leads to the subgoal

$$\langle\alpha_{rec}\rangle ct=c0 , stk=\underline{epty} , ct=1 \quad \Rightarrow \quad \langle\alpha_{loop}\rangle ct=c0 .$$

f after some number of iterations we reach a state where tree=$\underline{nil}$ and stk=$\underline{epty}$, then the while-loop erminates. Using the axiom for procedure declarations we can deduce that it is sufficient to prove

$\Rightarrow$ ∀e_1. ∀(ct,stk,tree,rdy,c,s,c0,c1,t1). ($Adm_{p,\lambda (x:y). ...}$($\underline{empty}$, e_1) ∧ $\langle$(e_1 | **call** p(t1:c1)$\rangle$c1=c0 ∧ t1=t ∧ tree=t ∧ stk=s ∧ ct=c+1 → ∃i. $\langle$**loop** (ε ! α_{body}) **times** i$\rangle$(tree=$\underline{nil}$ ∧ stk=s ∧ ct=c+c0)) ,

where ε ≡ stk≠$\underline{epty}$ ∨ tree≠$\underline{nil}$. The proof is by induction on the structure of environments. We have o show

$\langle$(e_1 | **call** p(t1:c1)$\rangle$c1=c0 , $Adm_{p,\lambda (x:y). ...}$($\underline{empty}$, e_1) , t1=t , tree=t , stk=s , ct=c+1 , ϕ_H $\Rightarrow$

∃i. $\langle$**loop** (ε ! α_{body}) **times** i$\rangle$(tree=$\underline{nil}$ ∧ stk=s ∧ ct=c+c0 ,

where ϕ_H is the inductive hypothesis. Due to the axiom for procedure calls the case e_1=$\underline{empty}$ is trivial. or the case e_1=$\underline{empty}$[p/(e_2 | λ(x:y).α_{pbody})] and $Adm_{p,\lambda (x:y). ...}$($\underline{empty}$, e_2) we eliminate the rocedure call, the local variable declaration and the conditional by the corresponding axioms. In the ase of "**else**" we are left with

[t2:=t1][c2:=0][c3:=0]$\langle$(e_2 | **call** p(left(t2):c2); **call** p(right(t2):c3); c1:=c2+c3)$\rangle$c1=c0 ,

$Adm_{p,\lambda(x:y). ...}$($\underline{empty}$, e_2), t1=t , tree=t , stk=s ,ct=c+1 , ϕ_H , t≠$\underline{nil}$ $\Rightarrow$

∃i. $\langle$**loop** (ε ! α_{body}) **times** i$\rangle$(tree=$\underline{nil}$ ∧ stk=s ∧ ct=c+c0) .

implification yields

$\langle$(e_2 | **call** p(t2:c2))$\rangle$c2=c4 , [t2:=t1][c3:=0]$\langle$(e_2 | **call** p(right(t2):c3); c1:=c4+c3)$\rangle$c1=c0 , ...

.... , t2=left(t) , t1=t , ... $\Rightarrow$

∃i. $\langle$**loop** (ε ! α_{body}) **times** i$\rangle$(tree=$\underline{nil}$ ∧ stk=s ∧ ct=c+c0) .

We reduce this subgoal by "executing" (ε ! α_{body}) once. Note that t≠$\underline{nil}$. We get

.. , tree=left(t) , stk=push(s,t) , ... $\Rightarrow$ ∃i. $\langle$**loop** (ε ! α_{body}) **times** i$\rangle$(tree=$\underline{nil}$ ∧ stk=s ∧ ct=c+c0) .

We have now reached a situation where we can apply a suitable instance of the inductive hypothesis. For example we instanciate t1 with t2, c1 with c2, c0 with c4, t with left(t) and s with push(s,t). We get

$[t2:=t1][c3:=0]\langle(e_2 \mid \textbf{call}\ p(right(t2):c3);\ c1:=c4+c3)\rangle c1=c0\ , ...$

$. \ .., t1=t\ , tree=\underline{nil}\ , stk=push(s,t)\ , ct=c+c4 \quad \Rightarrow$

$\exists i.\ \langle \textbf{loop}\ (\varepsilon\ !\ \alpha_{body})\ \textbf{times}\ i\rangle(tree=\underline{nil} \wedge stk=s \wedge ct=c+c0)\ .$

Note that t1, t etc. are not changed by α_{body}. Simplification yields

$\langle(e_2 \mid \textbf{call}\ p(t2:c3))\rangle c3=c5\ , \langle c1:=c4+c5\rangle c1=c0\ , ..., t2=right(t)\ , ... \Rightarrow$

$\exists i.\ \langle \textbf{loop}\ (\varepsilon\ !\ \alpha_{body})\ \textbf{times}\ i\rangle(tree=\underline{nil} \wedge stk=s \wedge ct=c+c0)\ .$

"Executing the body" leads to the subgoal

$..., tree=right(t)\ , stk=s\ , ct=c+c4+1\ , ... \Rightarrow$

$\exists i.\ \langle \textbf{loop}\ (\varepsilon\ !\ \alpha_{body})\ \textbf{times}\ i\rangle(tree=\underline{nil} \wedge stk=s \wedge ct=c+c0)\ .$

Again we have reached a situation where we can apply the inductive hypothesis. This time c i instantiated with c+c4 and c0 with c5. We get

$\langle c1:=c4+c5\rangle c1=c0\ , tree=\underline{nil}\ , stk=s\ , ct=c+c4+c5\ , ... \quad \Rightarrow$

$\exists i.\ \langle \textbf{loop}\ (\varepsilon\ !\ \alpha_{body})\ \textbf{times}\ i\rangle(tree=\underline{nil} \wedge stk=s \wedge ct=c+c0)\ .$

We now finish the induction proof by choosing i=zero

$\langle c1:=c4+c5\rangle c1=c0\ , tree=\underline{nil}\ , stk=s\ , ct=c+c4+c5\ , ... \quad \Rightarrow \quad (tree=\underline{nil} \wedge stk=s \wedge ct=c+c0).$

4 The KIV System

4.1 The Metalanguage PPL

In the preceding chapters we have tried to convince the reader that *in principle* DL on th uninterpreted level is a powerful and flexible logical formalism which can be used for many differe purposes and which supports many proof styles. However it seems to be hopeless to carry out form proofs in a step by step manner using only the basic formalism. Most of the "macro-steps" in examp II require more than ten applications of basic rules. Even a proof checker will not suffice to mak proofs like this one feasible. At least we need a system that allows the user to carry out formal proo (following a given strategy) in just the way we have presented it above. This means that one only ha to type in "execute" , "simplify by ...", "use the induction hypothesis" , etc. , and the system wi carry out the corresponding goal reduction automatically. As a next step the user can be provided wi some bookkeeping facilities which tell him/her what has still to be done and where to step back if wrong decision has been made. An even more ambitious aim is to carry out parts of the proo automatically. For example we might look for heuristics to select the appropriate tactic. For a first ste in this direction the reader is referred to [HRS 87].

Following the ideas of ML [GMW 79] our basic logical formalism is embedded in a function language which can be used to program the construction of proofs. The central data structure of PP (Proof Programming Language) are so-called *proof-trees*: The proven sequent is the root of the tre the axioms and hypothesis are its leaves, and $f_1, ..., f_n$ are sons of a node f iff f can be derived fro

$f_1, \ldots, f_n$ by application of some rule. The sequents which are attached to the nodes may contain *metavariables* for any syntactical category like for example formulas and programs. The use of metavariables enables us to carry out *schematic proofs* , a feature which can be exploited to implement *program development* strategies in the KIV environment.

The basic rule schemes of our formalism are given by elementary proof-trees. The operation mktree can be used to define arbitrary new rules which are called user-defined or derived rules. To guarantee soundness the user has to supply a *validation* for each of them. A validation is either a proof-tree verifying the rule directly, or a PPL function which can be used to generate a (verifying) proof-tree at any time the user wants. Typically a validation is called after the metavariables have been instantiated by a refine or infer operation, see below. However, if for example we deal with schematic programs in program development, validitions can be postponed till the end of the whole process.

Proof-trees are modified by operations infer(τ , $[i_1,\ldots,i_n]$, $[\tau_1,\ldots,\tau_n]$) and refine(σ_1 , i , σ_2). The infer operation performs a *forward* proof-step by using the conclusions of n proof-trees $\tau_1,\ldots,\tau_n$ as premisses of the proof-tree $\Theta(\tau)$ yielding a new conclusion. The refine operation performs a *backward* proof-step by replacing one premise of the proof-tree σ_1 by the proof-tree $\Theta(\sigma_2)$ yielding the premisses of $\Theta(\sigma_2)$ as new subgoals. Both operations use *matching*: The proof-trees τ and σ_2 can be considered as generalized inference rules and thus be instanciated by applying a matcher Θ to some of the metavariables. Θ satisfies the following conditions: the i_k-th premise of $\Theta(\tau)$ is equal to the conclusion of τ_k for k = 1, ..., n in case of the infer operation and $\Theta(\sigma_2)$ is equal to the i-th premise of σ_1 in the case of refine. PPL allows arbitrary combination of forward and backward proof steps.

The control structures of PPL include conditionals, recursion, explicit failure and alternatives. The last two constructs, **or** and **fail**, are used to implement backtracking.

4.2 Derived Rules

Recall the following part of the informal proof in example I. In order to carry out the induction step we had to reduce:

$$i=next(j_0)\ ,\ \phi_H \ \Rightarrow\ [\beta{\downarrow}i]z=0 \rightarrow [\alpha{\downarrow}i]z=0 \quad (+)$$

to

$$i=next(j_0)\ ,\ \phi_H\ ,\ [(x{\neq}y\ !\ \beta_{bdy})][\alpha{\downarrow}j_0]z=0 \ \Rightarrow\ [\alpha{\downarrow}i]z=0\ , \quad (++)$$

where ϕ_H was the induction hypothesis:

$$\forall j.\ (\, j<i \rightarrow \forall(x,y,z).\ ([\beta{\downarrow}\, j]z=0 \rightarrow [\alpha{\downarrow}j]z=0)\,)\ .$$

The reduction comprises some intermediate steps providing the appropriate instance of the hypothesis. This is a simple technical procedure that has to be repeated in every induction proof.

We will now discuss a slightly simplified version of the *derived rule* which plays a central role in the reduction process mentioned above. We present a PPL definition of the rule (named induction_step) including its validation. In PPL metavariables are prefixed by $ to destinguish them from other entities like object variables and PPL identifiers. For example in [**while** $e **do** $b **od**↓i]$$p_1$ $e stands for an arbitrary expression while i denotes an object variable of sort counter. To shorten our

notation we write $[\$e\#\$b{\downarrow}i]\$p_1$ as an abbreviation for [**while** $e **do** $b **od**$\downarrow$i]$\$p_1$. Terms of the objec
language like sequences, formulas and programs are quoted by ".

```
def induction_step =
    letrec
     conclusion  =
    "i=next($t) , ∀j. (j<i → ∀$v.([$e#$b↓j]$p1 → $p2))  ⇒  ([$e#$b↓i]$q1  → $q2)"
    and
    hyp1  =
    "i=next($t) , ∀j.(j<i → ∀$v.([$e#$b↓j]$p1 → $p2)) , [$e ! $b][j:=$t]$p2 ⇒  $q2"
    and
    hyp2  =  "   ⇒  ($q1 → $p1)"
    and
    val  =  lambda (s, s*)
      let
      equation = exp1(s)   (exp1 selects the instance of i=next($t) from s)   and
      ind_hyp  = exp2(s)   (exp2 selects the instance of ∀$v.([$e#$b↓j]$p1 → $p2)
                                from s)   and
      alpha      = exp3(s*)   (exp3 selects the instance of $e! $b from s*)   and
      phi1       = exp4(s)   (exp4 selects the instance of $p1 from s)   and
      theta1     = exp5(s)   (exp5(s) selects the instance of $q1 from s)
      in   letrec
           t1 = specialize_ind_hyp ( ind_hyp, equation)  and
           t2 = apply_α-axiom ( suc (t1), alpha)  and
           t3 = distribute_and_fold (suc (t2))  and
           t4 = reduce (mkstree (mkseq (suc (t3), subst (suc (t3), phi1,theta1))))  and
           t5 = infer (cut, list (1, 2),
                       list (infer (cut, list (1, 2),
                                    list (infer (cut, list (1, 2), list (t1, t2)), t3)), t4))
           in
           infer (cut, list (1, 2),
                 list (t5,
                     reduce (mkstree (mkseq (attach (suc (concl (t5)), ant (concl (t5))),
                                                    suc (conclusion))))))
     in    mktree (mkstree (conclusion), list (mkstree (hyp1), mkstree (hyp2)), val)
```

In the notation of textbooks the rule would take the form:

$$\frac{i=next(\$t)\,,\ \phi_H,\ [\$e!\ \$b][j:=\$t]\$p_2 \Rightarrow \$q_2 \quad \Big| \quad \Rightarrow\ (\$q_1 \rightarrow \$p_1)}{i=next(\$t),\ \phi_H\ \Rightarrow\ ([\$e\#\$b{\downarrow}i]\$q_1\ \rightarrow \$q_2)}$$

where $\phi_H \equiv \forall j.\,(j<i \rightarrow \forall \$v.([\$e\#\$b\downarrow j]\$p_1 \rightarrow \$p_2))$

If this rule is used to reduce (+) we obtain the following instanciations for the metavariables: $\$t \Leftarrow j_0$, $\$v \Leftarrow (x,y,z)$, $\$e \Leftarrow x\neq y$, $\$b \Leftarrow \beta_{bdy}$, $\$q_1,\$p_1 \Leftarrow z=0$, $\$q_2 \Leftarrow [\alpha\downarrow i]z=0$ and $\$p_2 \Leftarrow [\alpha\downarrow j]z=0$. We get the subgoals:

$$i=next(j_0)\,,\ \phi_H\,,\ [(x\neq y\ !\ \beta_{bdy})][j:=j_0][\alpha\downarrow j]z=0 \ \Rightarrow\ [\alpha\downarrow i]z=0 \quad (*)$$

and

$$\Rightarrow\ (z=0 \rightarrow z=0) \quad (**)$$

The first is reduced to (++) by simplification, and the second is trivial. So we are done with our reduction if the validation *val* can be executed successfully for this instantiation of the rule.

In the rest of the section we give a trace of the validation function *val* called with the instantiations given above.

The formal parameter s is bound to (+) and s* to the list made up of (*) and (**). The declarations of the **let**-block in val provide the relevant parts of s and s*. The execution part of this block actually produces the proof. At first the subfunction specialize_ind_hyp yields a proof (t1) of:

(1) $$i=next(j_0)\,,\ \forall j.\,(j<i \rightarrow \forall(x,y,z)([\beta\downarrow j]z=0\rightarrow[\alpha\downarrow j]z=0))\ \Rightarrow$$
$$\forall(x,y,z).\ ([\beta\downarrow j_0]z=0 \rightarrow [\alpha\downarrow j_0]z=0)$$

This is done by specializing the induction hypothesis: j becomes j_0 .

For the next step the validation uses the α-axiom: $\Rightarrow \forall v.\phi \rightarrow [\alpha]\phi$, where the assignment variables of α must be a subset of v. The result (t2) is a proof of

(2) $$\forall(x,y,z).\ ([\beta\downarrow j_0]z=0 \rightarrow [\alpha\downarrow j_0]z=0) \ \Rightarrow\ [x\neq y\ !\ \beta_{bdy}]([\beta\downarrow j_0]z=0 \rightarrow [\alpha\downarrow j_0]z=0)$$

The function distribute_and_fold applies the distribution law of modal logic and the axiom for loops. It generates and binds to t3 a proof of

(3) $$[x\neq y\ !\ \beta_{bdy}]([\beta\downarrow j_0]z=0 \rightarrow [\alpha\downarrow j_0]z=0) \ \Rightarrow\ ([\beta\downarrow next(j_0)]z=0 \rightarrow [x\neq y\ !\ \beta_{bdy}][\alpha\downarrow j_0]z=0)$$

Since both phi1 and theta1 have the value z=0 the argument of the reduce function is trivial. Reduce proves (and binds to t4)

(4) $$([\beta\downarrow next(j_0)]z=0 \rightarrow [x\neq y\ !\ \beta_{bdy}][\alpha\downarrow j_0]z=0) \Rightarrow ([\beta\downarrow next(j_0)]z=0 \rightarrow [x\neq y\ !\ \beta_{bdy}][\alpha\downarrow j_0]z=0)$$

In this case the proof is trivial. In more general cases where phi1 and theta1 are different the function reduce will not be able to prove (4) completely. Instead it will end up with the single unproved subgoal stating that theta1 implies phi1, which is the second premise of the rule.

Putting together (1), (2), (3), (4) by the cut rule we get a proof (bound to t5) for

(5) $$i=next(j_0)\,,\ \forall j.\,(j<i \rightarrow \forall(x,y,z).\ ([\beta\downarrow j]z=0\rightarrow[\alpha\downarrow j]z=0))\ \Rightarrow$$
$$[\beta\downarrow next(j_0)]z=0 \rightarrow [x\neq y\ !\ \beta_{bdy}][\alpha\downarrow j_0]z=0$$

In the execution part of the inner **letrec**-block the function reduce computes a proof of

$$i=next(j_0)\,,\ \forall j.\,(j<i \rightarrow\forall(x,y,z).\ ([\beta\downarrow j]z=0\rightarrow[\alpha\downarrow j]z=0)),$$
$$([\beta\downarrow next(j_0)]z=0 \rightarrow [x\neq y\ !\ \beta_{bdy}][\alpha\downarrow j_0]z=0) \ \Rightarrow\ ([\beta\downarrow i]z=0 \rightarrow [\alpha\downarrow i]z=0) \quad (\S)$$

leaving as an unproved subgoal

$$i=next(j_0)\,,\ \phi_H\,,\ [(x\neq y\ !\ \beta_{bdy})][j:=j_0][\alpha\downarrow j]z=0 \ \Rightarrow\ [\alpha\downarrow i]z=0$$

which is the first premise of the rule. Finally the validation applies the cut rule to t5 and (§), and return a proof for (+) with (*) as an open subgoal. Since the set of the remaining subgoals is a subset of the premisses of the rule the validation terminates successfully, and thus demonstrates the triple (+), (*) (**) to be a sound instance of the rule induction_step.

Note that if we remove the quantifier $\forall$(x,y,z) from the inductive hypothesis the validation *fails* when the α-axiom is used. In this way validations can be used to detect logical errors.

4.3 Tactics and Strategies

Tactics are more general than derived rules in the sense that (in backward proofs) we can generate subgoals by performing a step which cannot be expressed schematically. For example given sequent $x=\tau$, $\Gamma \Rightarrow \Delta$ we might wish to substitute τ for x in Γ and Δ. This can be accomplished by a tactic (which fails if a binding conflict arises). As opposed to derived rules a tactic cannot be applied without running the corresponding PPL program. Hence all formulas which are accessed by a tactic must be fully instanciated. For example we can apply the rule $\Rightarrow$ $[x:=\tau][\alpha]\phi \rightarrow [\alpha][x:=\tau]\phi$ in a given context without running its validation. However, we must be aware of the fact that this is only a "first guess" because the rule might not be valid for this instanciation. This feature of rules is exploited to perform *"schematic proofs"* which are used for example in program development where we have to deal with partly instanciated programs and formulas.

Derived rules and tactics represent the logical building blocks of the verification method we are going to implement in the KIV environment. The nonlogical aspects, like the overall structure of the method, bookkeeping facilities, backtracking and heuristics, are realized by PPL programs we call *strategies*. Step by step we enlarge the degree of automatisation which is incorporated in a strategy. Using heuristics we may try to guess the right instanciation of a induction hypothesis, generate the induction hypothesis automatically (generalization), select tactics and detect dead ends of a proof. If we consider the degree of automatisation, the strategies which are currently implemented, like BURSTALL's method, are still far from systems like the one of BOYER & MOORE [BM 79]. In our system however, all deductions are logically valid with respect to the basic formalism.

References

[AS 84] Antoniou,G./Sperschneider V. Incompleteness of HOARE's Calculus over Simple Datastructures. Interner Bericht 3/84, Fakultät für Informatik, Universität Karlsruhe (1984)

[BM 79] Boyer, R.S./ Moore, J.S. A Computational Logic. Academic Press, New York (1979)

[Bu 74] Burstall, R.M. Program Proving as Hand Simulation with a little Induction. Information Processing 74, North-Holland Publishing Company (1974)

[GMW 79] Gordon,M/Milner,R./Wadsworth,C. Edinburgh LCF. Springer LNCS 78 (1979)

[Go 82] Goldblatt, R. Axiomatising the Logic of Computer Programming. Springer LNCS 130 (1982)

[Gr 81] Gries, D. The Science of Programming, Springer-Verlag (1981)

[Ha 79] Harel, D. First Order Dynamic Logic. Springer LNCS 68 (1979)

[Ha 84] Harel, D. Dynamic Logic. Handbook of Philosophical Logic, D. Gabbay and F. Guenther (eds.), Reidel (1984), Vol. 2, 496-604

[HHRS 86] Hähnle, R./Heisel, M./Reif, W./Stephan, W. An Interactive Verification System Based on Dynamic Logic. Proc. 8-th International Conference on Automated Deduction, J.Siekmann (ed), Springer LNCS 230 (1986), 306-315

[HRS 86] Heisel,M./.Reif, W./Stephan, W. A Functional Language to Construct Proofs. Interner Bericht 1/86, Fakultät für Informatik, Universität Karlsruhe (1986)

[HRS 87] Heisel,M./.Reif, W./Stephan, W. Program Verification by Symbolic Execution and Induction. Proc. 11-th German Workshop on Artificial Intelligence, K. Morik (ed), Informatik Fachberichte 152, Springer-Verlag (1987)

[Re 84] Reif, W. Vollständigkeit einer modifizierten Goldblatt-Logik und Approximation der Omegaregel durch Induktion. Diplomarbeit, Fakultät für Informatik, Universität Karlsruhe (1984)

[Re 86] Reif, W. A Completeness Result in Nonstandard Dynamic Logic. Interner Bericht 27/86, Fakultät für Informatik, Universität Karlsruhe (1986)

[St 85] Stephan, W. A Logic for Recursive Programs. Interner Bericht 5/85, Fakultät für Informatik, Universität Karlsruhe (1985)

[St 88] Stephan, W. Axiomatising Recursive Procedures in Dynamic Logic. Forthcoming (1988)

Induction in the elementary theory of types and names

Gerhard Jäger
Institut für Informatik
ETH Zürich

Type-theoretic concepts play an important role in present day computer science and for the design of modern software tools. They reach from untyped universes of pure lambda calculus and Lisp like languages over monomorphic type structures to polymorphic type systems which are related to programming languages in the style of ML (cf. e.g. [3]).

Type theories are also regarded as a formal device for building up programming environments where programs are developed consistently with formal specifications and based on principles of constructive mathematics. Well known projects which try to bridge the gap between abstract formal treatments of constructive mathematics and practically useful computer applications are for example: de Bruijn's AUTOMATH [6], Constable's proof development system Nuprl [4], the theory of constructions due to Coquand-Huet [5], the work done in Edinburgh in connection with LCF and ML [7], the Swedish attempts to implement Martin-Löf theories [20,22,23] and Feferman's theories of explicit mathematics [8,10] which are the theoretical basis of Hayashi's proof extraction system PX [17].

Although being based on related logical concepts, these approaches are formally fairly diverse such that something like a unifying theoretical basis would be desirable. This survey article is an attempt to establish such a framework. It consists of two parts where the first one presents an elementary theory *ETN* of types and names. *ETN* is built upon a flexible language for the natural development of type structures and may act as a basic link between type theories and subsystems of second order arithmetic.

The second part is dedicated to the representation of inductively defined types within this framework. This is an important aspect of the whole enterprise since induction is very much to the heart of constructive mathematics and computing and has a lot to do with the strength of constructive formalisms. We introduce a series of induction principles of different power and state some specific results concerning these forms of induction in the special case of the type of the natural numbers.

1 The theory *ETN*

In this section we introduce the elementary theory of types and names *ETN*. It is formulated in a 2-sorted language about objects and types. We will assume that the objects form a partial combinatory algebra V and the types are subclasses of V. The novel point in our approach is that we claim that every type $X \subset V$ has a name $n_X \in V$. The identity relation on the objects is intensional whereas identity on the types is extensional; i.e. the types X and Y are identical if they contain the same elements. It is therefore possible that a type X has two different names m_X and n_X.

The elementary theory of types and names is a framework for studying type theories as they are used in present day computer science. Objects are the entities the computer manipulates with. They are directly accessible and explicitly represented in suitable form, possibly as bitstrings in a computer memory. Types, on the other hand, are rather abstract collections of objects. In order to address them, we have to use their names. Hence the name n_X of a type X has to provide enough information such that X can be determined from n_X. If the object a is the name of type X, then the extension $ext(a)$ of a is this (unique) type X. Otherwise $ext(a)$ is not defined.

The language *L(ETN)* of the elementary theory of types and names has as its first order variables the object variables $x, y, z, \ldots$, and as its second order variables the type variables $X, Y, Z, \ldots$. There are also object constants, type constants and relation symbols, to be specified. The object constant include the symbols 0, *true*, *false*, k, s, p, p_L, p_R, d, s_V, p_V and c_n fo all $n < \omega$; the relation symbols include the predicate *name*. The meanin of all these symbols will be explained later.

The principal term formation operation is term application which we writ as $(a \cdot b)$ or often just as ab. In this simplified form we adopt the conventio of association to the left such that $a_1 a_2 \ldots a_n$ stands for $(\ldots(a_1 a_2)\ldots)$. W also use the notation $a(b_1, \ldots, b_n)$ for $ab_1 \ldots b_n$.

The *object terms* $(a, b, c, \ldots)$ of *L(ETN)* are generated as follows:

1. Each object variable is a term.

2. Each object constant is a term.

3. If a and b are terms, then $(a \cdot b)$ is a term.

The *type terms* $(A, B, C, \ldots)$ of *L(ETN)* are generated as follows:

1. Each type variable is a type term.

2. Each type constant is a type term.

3. If $\varphi(x)$ is an elementary formula of *L(ETN)*, then $\{x : \varphi(x)\}$ is a typ term.

The *atomic formulas* of *L(ETN)* are those of the form $a = b$, $A = B$, $a \downarrow$ $a \in B$ and $R(\sigma_1, \ldots, \sigma_n)$ where $\sigma_1, \ldots, \sigma_n$ are object or class terms and R is an n ary relation symbol.

The *formulas* $(\varphi, \psi, \chi, \theta, \ldots)$ of *L(ETN)* are generated as follows:

1. Each atomic formula is a formula.

2. If φ and ψ are formulas, then so are $\neg\varphi$, $(\varphi \wedge \psi)$, $(\varphi \vee \psi)$, $(\varphi \rightarrow \psi$ and $(\varphi \leftrightarrow \psi)$.

3. If φ is a formula, then so are $\forall x\varphi$, $\exists x\varphi$, $\forall X\varphi$ and $\exists X\varphi$.

An *L(ETN)* formula is called *elementary* if it contains no bound type variables and no occurrence of the relation symbol *name*.

We write $\underline{\sigma}$ for finite strings $\sigma_1, \ldots, \sigma_n$ of object and type terms. The notation $\varphi[\underline{\sigma}]$ is used to indicate that all free variables of φ come from the list $\underline{\sigma}$; $\varphi(\underline{\sigma})$ may contain other free variables besides $\underline{\sigma}$.

The logic of explicit mathematics is the classical or intuitionistic logic of partial terms due to Beeson-Feferman as in [1]. The atomic formula $a\downarrow$ is to be read as "a is defined". We assume that every individual variable and individual constant is defined; if a compound term is defined, then each subterm is defined. We also introduce a partial equality $\simeq$ defined by

$$a \simeq b \quad :\Leftrightarrow \quad a\downarrow \vee\, b\downarrow \rightarrow \; a = b.$$

The crucial modifications of ordinary predicate logic are in the quantifier axioms

$$\forall x \varphi(x) \wedge a\downarrow \rightarrow \varphi(a),$$
$$\varphi(a) \wedge a\downarrow \rightarrow \; \exists x \varphi(x).$$

The non-logical axioms of *ETN* can be divided into the following seven classes.

I. **Applicative axioms.**

(1) $kxy = x$

(2) $sxyz \simeq xz(yz) \;\wedge\; sxy\downarrow$

(3) $k \neq s$

II. **Pairing and projection.**

(4) $pxy\downarrow \;\wedge\; p_L x\downarrow \;\wedge\; p_R x\downarrow \;\wedge\; p_L(pxy) = x \;\wedge\; p_R(pxy) = y$

III. **Definition by cases.**

(5) $d(x, y, z)\downarrow \;\wedge\; d(0, y, z) = y \;\wedge\; d(1, y, z) = z$

IV. Successor and predecessor.

(6) $\forall x(s_V x \neq 0 \ \wedge \ p_V(s_V x) = x)$

(7) $(\forall x)(\forall y)(s_V x \simeq s_V y \ \rightarrow \ x \simeq y)$

V. Extensionality of types.

(8) $\forall x(x \in A \leftrightarrow x \in B) \ \rightarrow \ A = B$

VI. Name axioms.

(9) $(\forall X)(\exists y) name(X, y)$

(10) $name(A, c) \wedge name(B, c) \ \rightarrow \ A = B$

VII. Comprehension axioms. Each elementary formula φ is assigned a Gödel number $\lceil\varphi\rceil$ in some standard way; then we write c_φ instead of $c_{\lceil\varphi\rceil}$ If $\underline{A}$ is the sequence of type terms $A_1, \ldots, A_n$ and $\underline{b}$ the sequence of objec terms $b_1, \ldots, b_n$, then $name(\underline{A}, \underline{b})$ stands for $\bigwedge_{i=1}^{n} name(A_i, b_i)$. *Elementar comprehension* (ECA) consists of the two schemes

$$(ECA.1) \qquad (\forall x)(x \in \{y : \varphi(y)\} \ \leftrightarrow \varphi(x))$$

$$(ECA.2) \qquad name(\underline{A}, \underline{b}) \ \rightarrow \ name(\{x : \varphi[\underline{A}, \underline{c}, x]\}, c_\varphi(\underline{b}, \underline{c}))$$

for all elementary formulas $\varphi[\underline{Y}, \underline{z}, x]$ with the the free type variables $\underline{Y} = Y_1, \ldots, Y_m$ and individual variables $\underline{z} = z_1, \ldots, z_n$.

The applicative axioms state that the universe forms a partial combinator algebra. By standard arguments one can show that they prove the theoren about lambda abstraction and the recursion theorem. Pairing and projec tion are as usual. In the following we write $\langle a, b\rangle$ instead of pab. (5) i definition by Boolean cases, a stronger form is definition by cases on th universe (cf. [10]).

The name axioms formalize that every type has a name. This is a natura requirement since in the context of computer science all entities, includin

The subsets of A must not be confused with the subtypes of A. We write $B \subset A$ if every element of type B is an element of type A,

$$B \subset A \quad :\Leftrightarrow \quad \forall x(x \in B \rightarrow x \in A).$$

Every subset f of A induces the subtype $\{x : x \in A \wedge x \varepsilon f\}$ of A, but a subtype B of A need not have a characteristic function. Accordingly, $PP(A)$ is the type of *partial characteristic functions* on A, i.e. the type of *partial subsets* of A.

Warning $A \subset B$ and $a \in P(A)$ do not imply that $a \in P(B)$. From $a \in P(A)$ we only know that $(\forall x \in A)(fx \simeq \mathit{false} \vee fx \simeq \mathit{true})$ but we cannot conclude that f is defined on $B \backslash A$. However, $A \subset B$ and $a \in PP(A)$ imply $a \in PP(B)$.

Elementary comprehension is sufficient to develop monomorphic type structures à la Church. Besides this, type variables are available in ETN and we have the possibility to form all elementary definable subtypes of a given type. It is also true that weak forms of polymorphism can be handled in ETN. In order to reflect the full strength of polymorphism in the sense of Girard [15,16] and Reynolds [24], we have to add further comprehension principles (cf. Feferman [14] and Jäger [19] for similar approaches).

2 Positive inductive definitions

The theory ENT reflects the logical part of our approach. The more mathematical aspects are brought in by adding suitable induction principles. In this section we consider some general forms of positive inductive definitions. The special case of induction over the natural numbers will be considered later.

Definition 1 *Let $\mathcal{A}[X,y]$ be a formula of the language L(ETN) which contains no negative occurrences of the type varaible X. Then we denote the formula*

$$\mathcal{D}[X] \quad :\Leftrightarrow \quad \forall y(\mathcal{A}[X,y] \;\rightarrow\; y \in X)$$

as a positive inductive definition.

In order to emphasize the central ideas and to simplify the notation we will restrict ourselves to the case of non-iterated inductive definitions. The extension of this approach to more general situations should be obvious.

For each positive inductive definition $\mathcal{D}[X]$ we introduce a new type constant $Q_{\mathcal{D}}$ and a new object constant $i_{\mathcal{D}}$ as name for $Q_{\mathcal{D}}$. The meaning of $Q_{\mathcal{D}}$ and $i_{\mathcal{D}}$ is implicitly defined by the following axioms.

Closure axiom for $\mathcal{D}[X]$.

$$\mathcal{D}[Q_{\mathcal{D}}]$$

Name axiom for $\mathcal{D}[X]$.

$$name(Q_{\mathcal{D}}, i_{\mathcal{D}})$$

The closure axiom for $\mathcal{D}$ and the name axiom for $\mathcal{D}$ are augmented by principles of induction on $Q_{\mathcal{D}}$ where we distinguish between five different versions.

Induction axioms for $\mathcal{D}[X]$.

Set–IND$_{\mathcal{D}}$: $\quad a \in P(Q_{\mathcal{D}}) \land D[\hat{a}] \rightarrow (\forall x \in Q_{\mathcal{D}})(x \,\varepsilon\, a)$

Partial–Set–IND$_{\mathcal{D}}$: $\quad a \in PP(Q_{\mathcal{D}}) \land D[\hat{a}] \rightarrow (\forall x \in Q_{\mathcal{D}})(x \,\varepsilon\, a)$

Object–IND$_{\mathcal{D}}$: $\quad D[\hat{a}] \rightarrow (\forall x \in Q_{\mathcal{D}})(x \,\varepsilon\, a)$

Type–IND$_{\mathcal{D}}$: $\quad D[X] \rightarrow Q_{\mathcal{D}} \subset X$

Full–IND$_{\mathcal{D}}$: $\quad D[\varphi] \rightarrow (\forall x \in Q_{\mathcal{D}})\varphi(x)$

for all formulas φ of the corresponding language. Since every subset of N is a partial subset of N, every partial subset of N defines a subtype of N and every subtype of N induces a formula, it is clear that

$$\begin{gathered} \textit{Full-IND}_{\mathcal{D}} \Rightarrow \textit{Type-IND}_{\mathcal{D}} \Rightarrow \textit{Object-IND}_{\mathcal{D}} \\ \Rightarrow \textit{Partial-Set-IND}_{\mathcal{D}} \Rightarrow \textit{Set-IND}_{\mathcal{D}} \end{gathered}$$

The induction schemes *Full–IND*$_{\mathcal{D}}$ and *Type–IND*$_{\mathcal{D}}$ are *external inductions* in the sense that they refer to the whole type structure. They export induction to all types. *Object–IND*$_{\mathcal{D}}$, *Partial–Set–IND*$_{\mathcal{D}}$ and *Set–IND*$_{\mathcal{D}}$, on the other hand, are *internal* with respect to $Q_{\mathcal{D}}$. In these cases induction is applied to arbitrary objects, partial subsets of $Q_{\mathcal{D}}$ or subsets of $Q_{\mathcal{D}}$ but no reference is made to types. Hence the meaning of these induction principles is independent of the type structure and the type existence axioms formulated in the corresponding theory.

It is well known that positive inductive definitions provide a very powerful tool in order to introduce data types. They are fundamental for many branches of mathematical logic and computer science and have been studied from various points of views (cf. e.g. [2,4,18,21]).

The traditional model-theoretic and proof-theoretic approach to inductive definitions concentrates on the versions with full induction and type induction and not much is known about object induction, partial set induction and set induction. Nevertheless is has turned out that internal inductions are of great relevance for studying the relationship between type theories and computer programming.

On the one hand Feferman has shown that internal inductions are sufficient to develop ordinary mathematics to a reasonable extent (cf. e.g. [9,12,13]); on the other hand it is known from standard proof theory that normalization procedures and proof extraction procedures are very sensitive to the inductions which are involved. Hence it is desirable to work in a modular framework of reasonable expressive power with controlable induction principles.

We end this paper with some specific results concerning induction on the natural numbers. In our context the natural numbers can be easily represented as the type $Q_{\mathcal{N}}$ which is induced by the following inductive definition

$$\mathcal{N}[X] \quad :\Leftrightarrow \quad \forall x[x = 0 \lor \exists y(y \in X \land x = s_V y) \quad \rightarrow \quad x \in X].$$

The closure axiom for $N[X]$ makes sure that $Q_{\mathcal{N}}$ contains 0 and is closed under successor. The various induction axioms state that $Q_{\mathcal{N}}$ is a minimal witness for $N[X]$ respect to subsets of $Q_{\mathcal{N}}$, partial subsets of $Q_{\mathcal{N}}$, objects types or arbitrary formulas.

The following theorem relates the elementary theory of types and names with its different induction axioms to well known subsystems of first and second order arithmetic. Detailed proofs will be published elsewhere; similar results are treated for example in Feferman [12,13] and Jäger [19].

Theorem 2 *The following proof-theoretic results have been established:*

1. $ETN + Set\text{–}IND_{\mathcal{N}} \leq PRA$
2. $ETN + Partial\text{–}Set\text{–}IND_{\mathcal{N}} \equiv ETN + Object\text{–}IND_{\mathcal{N}} \equiv PRA$
3. $ETN + Type\text{–}IND_{\mathcal{N}} \equiv PA$
4. $ETN + Full\text{–}IND_{\mathcal{N}} \equiv (\Pi^1_0 - CA)$

References

[1] M.J. Beeson, *Foundations of Constructive Mathematics*, Springer Berlin, 1985.

[2] W. Buchholz, S. Feferman, W. Pohlers, W. Sieg, *Iterated Inductive Definitions and Subsystems of Analysis: Recent Proof-Theoretical Studies*, Lecture Notes in Mathematics 897, Springer, Berlin, 1981.

[3] L. Cardelli and P. Wegner, On understanding types, data abstraction and polymorphism, *Computing surveys 17* (1985).

[4] R.L. Constable, S.F. Allen, H.M. Bromley, W.R. Cleaveland, J.F Cremer, R.W. Harper, D.J. Howe, T.B. Knoblock, N.P. Mendler P.Panangaden, J.T. Sasaki and S.F.Smith, *Implementing Mathematics with the Nuprl Proof Development System*, Prentice-Hall, Englewood Cliffs, NJ, 1986.

[5] Th. Coquand and G. Huet, Constructions: A higher order proof system for mechanizing mathematics, in: *Proceedings EUROCAL 85*, Lecture Notes in Computer Science 203, Springer, Berlin, 1985.

[6] N.G. de Bruijn, A survey of AUTOMATH, in: J.P. Seldin and J.R. Hindley (eds.), *To H.B. Curry: Essays on Combinatory Logic, Lambda Calculus and Formalism*, Academic Press, New York, 1980.

[7] M. Gordon, R. Milner and C. Wadsworth, *Edinburgh LCF*, Lecture Notes in Computer Science 78, Springer, Berlin, 1979.

[8] S. Feferman, A language and axiom for explicit mathematics, in: *Algebra and Logic*, Lecture Notes in Mathematics 450, Springer, Berlin, 1975.

[9] S. Feferman, Theories of finite type, in: J. Barwise (ed.), *Handbook of Mathematical Logic*, North-Holland, Amsterdam, 1977.

[10] S. Feferman, Constructive theories of functions and classes, in: M. Boffa, D. van Dalen, K. McAloon (eds.), *Proceedings of Logic Colloquium '78*, North-Holland, Amsterdam, 1979.

[11] S. Feferman, Iterated fixed-point theories: application to Hancock's conjecture, in: G. Metakides (ed.), *The Patras Symposium*, North-Holland, Amsterdam, 1982.

[12] S. Feferman, A theory of variable types, *Revista Colombiana de Mathemáticas, XIX*, (1985).

[13] S. Feferman, Weyl vindicated: "Das Kontinuum" 70 years later, Preprint, Stanford, 1987.

[14] S. Feferman, The polymorphic typed λ-calculus (and all that) in a type-free axiomatic framework, Preprint, Stanford, 1988.

[15] J.-Y. Girard, Une extension de l'interpretation de Gõdel a l'analyse, et son application a l'elimination des coupures dans l'analyse et la theorie des types, in: *Proceedings 2nd Scandinavian Logic Symposium*, North-Holland, Amsterdam, 1971.

[16] J.-Y. Girard, The system F of variable types, fifeteen years later, *Theoretical Computer Science 45* (1986).

[17] S. Hayashi and H. Nakano, PX a computational logic, Report Research Institute for Mathematical Sciences, Kyoto University, Kyoto, 1987.

[18] G. Huet, Induction principles formalized in the calculus of constructions, in: H. Ehrig, R. Kowalski, G. Levi and U. Montanari (eds.) Proceedings of TAPSOFT '87, Lecture Notes in Computer Science 249, Springer, Berlin, 1987.

[19] G. Jäger, Type theory and explicit mathematics, in: *Proceedings of Logic Colloquium '87*, to appear.

[20] P. Martin-Lõf, Constructive mathematics and computer programming, in: *Proceedings 6th International Congress for Logic, Methodology and Philosophy of Science*, North-Holland, Amsterdam, 1982.

[21] Y.N. Moschovakis, *Elementary Induction on Abstract Structures*, North-Holland, Amsterdam, 1974.

[22] B. Nordstrom and K. Petersson, Types and specifications, in: *Proceedings IFIP '83*, North-Holland, Amsterdam, 1983.

[23] B.Nordstrom and J. Smith, Propositions, types, and specifications in Martin-Lõf's type theory, *BIT 24, n. 3* (1984).

[24] J.C. Reynolds, Towards a theory of type structure, in: *Proceeding Colloque sur la Programmation*, Lecture Notes in Computer Science 19, Springer, Berlin, 1974.

On the computational complexity of quantified Horn clauses

Marek Karpinski
Department of Computer Science
University of Bonn

Hans Kleine Büning
Institut für angewandte Informatik und formale Beschreibungsverfahren
University of Karlsruhe

Peter H. Schmitt
Scientific Center of IBM Germany
Heidelberg

Abstract

A polynomial time algorithm is presented for the evaluation problem for quantified propositional Horn clauses. This answers an open problem posed by Itai and Makowski in (IM 87).

Introduction

The basic idea behind the programming language PROLOG is, that a proof or refutation of Horn formulas can be viewed as an efficient computation from which one extracts an output. Horn formulas (or a program) are conjunctions of Horn clauses, i.e. clauses of the form: $A_1 \wedge A_2 \wedge \ldots A_m \rightarrow B$, where A_i and B are atomic formulas. The computation of the program consists in finding an assignment of values to the variables which satisfies all clauses. Two basic methods used for such a computation are **unification** (to produce assigments) and **resolution** of clauses (as a method of logical inference). The problem of testing a set of Horn formulas for satisfiability , e.g. using unit resolution is known to have linear time solution algorithms, see e.g. (DG 84), (IM 87).

The new development of Prolog query languages, cf. (GR 87), strongly motivated the search for general efficient solutions for quantified Horn clauses. In this paper we present such an efficient solution for the evaluation problem of quantified propositional Horn clauses. The algorithm works in $O(n^3)$ time. We stress in this paper polynomial time solutions for this problem, rather than the design of new data structures to make it work faster. We do hope though to present a linear time or $O(n \log n)$ time algorithm in a subsequent paper. Schäfer in (SCH 78) claimed a polynomial time algorithm for the above problem, but he gives no proof.

It is interesting to note, that the evaluation problem for quantified Boolean formulas, even if restricted to formulas containing at most three literals per clause, is PSPACE-complete , (GJ 79).In (APT 79) a linear time algorithm has been design for the case of quantified Boolean formulas in conjunctive normal form with at most two literals per clause.

Our result in this context entails suprising algorithmic efficiency of the evaluation problem for quantified Horn clauses and opens the possibility of several natural query-like extensions of standard PROLOG.

Terminology

We will mainly deal with propositional and quantified propositional formulas. We denote by **PV** the infinite set of propositional variables. The propositional connectives "and", "or", and "not" are designated by the symbols "$\wedge$", "$\vee$", and "$\neg$". We shall have occasion to deal with the following special sets of propositional formulas: literals, all propositional formulas, clauses, conjuntive normal forms (conjunctions of clauses), Horn clauses (clauses containing at most one positive literal), totally negative clauses (clauses containing only negative literals), negative conjunctive normal forms (conjunctions of totally negative clauses). These will be denoted respectively by **LI, FML, CL, CNF, HC, TNC, NCNF.** In case we allow the propositional constants 0 and 1 to occur, the corresponding sets are indexed by C, e.g. $\mathbf{CNF}_C$, $\mathbf{HC}_C$, etc. .

The universal (existential) quantifier will be denoted by $\forall$ ($\exists$) as usual. For any set Σ of propositional formulas $Q^*\Sigma$ is the set of all formulas of the form $Q_1X_1...Q_nX_n\sigma$ where n is an arbitrary natural number, each Q_i is either $\forall$ or $\exists$, $\sigma \in \Sigma$ and $\{X_1, ..., X_n\}$ is a set of propositional variables. If $\{X_1, ..., X_n\}$ contains all variables occuring in σ, we call $Q_1X_1...Q_nX_n\sigma$ closed. Likewise $\exists^*\Sigma$ is the set of all formulas of the form $\exists X_1, ..., \exists X_n\sigma$ with $\sigma \in \Sigma$.

As usual we distinquish free and bound occurences of variables in quantified propositional formulas. For X $\in$ **PV** and t a constant symbol the formula $\sigma(t/X)$ arises from σ by replacing every free occurence of X in σ by t.

We say that a variable X occurs in a clause ϕ if either X or $\neg X$ is a disjunctive component of ϕ. In contrast we say that X is a literal of ϕ if X is a disjunctive component of ϕ. Thus X occurs in $\neg X \vee Y \vee \neg Z$, but X is not a literal of this clause.

Generalized Unit Resolution

It is well known, that a formula of the form

$$\exists X_1 ... \exists X_k \phi$$

where ϕ is a conjunction of Horn clauses, is true if and only if the empty clause is not derivable from ϕ by unit resolution. We first generalize the operation of unit resolution to the case of arbitrary quantifier prefixes.

Let Φ be a formula of the form

$$\forall \overline{X}_1 \exists \overline{Y}_1 ... \exists \overline{Y}_{k-1} \forall \overline{X}_k \phi$$

where

for all i, $1 \leq i \leq k$ $\overline{X}_i = X_{n_{i-1}+1}, ..., X_{n_i}$ with $n_0 = 0$.

Since we want to treat formulas with arbitrary quantifier prefix, we allow n_1 and n_k to be 0, while for all i, $1 < i < k$ we require $n_i \neq 0$.

For all i, $1 \leq i < k$ $\overline{Y}_i = Y_{m_{i-1}+1}, ..., Y_{m_i}$, where all $m_i \neq 0$.

$\phi = \phi_1 \wedge ... \wedge \phi_r$
where all ϕ_i are Horn clauses.

We may furthermore assume without loss of generality:

for every i, $1 \leq i \leq r$, there is no variable X_j, such that both literals X_j and $\neg X_j$ occur in ϕ_i.

In the given representation of Φ we assume implicitely, that no propositional variable occurs both existentially and universally bound. This is clearly no restriction.

An **X-literal (Y-literal)** is a literal of the form X_i or $\neg X_i$ (resp. Y_i or $\neg Y_i$). A **pure X-clause** is a clause consisting exclusively of X-literals. In particular the empty clause is a pure X-clause.

A clause ϕ_j is called a Y_i **-unit clause** if Y_i occurs positively in ϕ_j and Y_i is the only Y-variable occuring in ϕ_j.

A clause ϕ_j is called a **Y-unit clause** if it is a Y_i-unit clause for some i.

When we say, that the variable X_i is before Y_j, we refer to the order of occurences in the prefix of Φ, i.e. X_i is before Y_j if $n_{p-1} < i \leq n_p$, $m_{q-1} < j \leq m_q$ and $p \leq q$. Analogously we use the phrase X_i is after Y_j.

Let ϕ_p be a Y_i-unit clause and ϕ_q a clause containing the literal $\neg Y_i$. The **resolvent** ψ of ϕ_p and ϕ_q is obtained by

forming the disjunction $\phi_p \vee \phi_q$,

if for some variable X_j both literals X_j and $\neg X_j$ occur in $\phi_p \vee \phi_q$, then stop, no resolvent exists in this case, omitting all occurences both negated and unnegated of the variable Y_l,

omitting all occurences of X-variables, that are not before any Y-variable occuring in the modified disjunction,

A **unit resolution step** on the formula ϕ

$$\forall \overline{X}_1 \exists \overline{Y}_1 ... \exists \overline{Y}_{k-1} \forall \overline{X}_k (\phi_1 \wedge ... \wedge \phi_k)$$

is performed by adding the resolvent ψ of a Y-unit clause ϕ_p and a clause ϕ_q containing the literal $\neg Y$ to the matrix of ϕ, thus obtaining

$$\forall \overline{X}_1 \exists \overline{Y}_1 ... \exists \overline{Y}_{k-1} \forall \overline{X}_k (\phi_1 \wedge ... \wedge \phi_k \wedge \psi)$$

Lemma 1:
Let Σ be obtained from $\Phi = \forall \overline{X}_1 \exists \overline{Y}_1 ... \exists \overline{Y}_{k-1} \forall \overline{X}_k \phi$ by omitting in any clause of ϕ all X-literals for those X, that are not before any Y-variable occuring in this clause, then Σ is true if and only if Φ is true.

Proof: If Σ is true, then Φ is , of course, also true. So let us assume that Φ is true. There are functions f_i for all i, $1 \leq i \leq m_{k-1}$, the number of arguments of f_i equals the number of X-variables that are before Y_i , such that for any sequence $a_1, ..., a_{n_k}$ of 0 and 1 the formula

$$\phi(a_1, ..., a_{n_k}, f_1(\overline{a}^1), ..., f_{m_{k-1}}(\overline{a}^{m_{k-1}}))$$

is true, where $b_i = f_i(a_1, ..., a_n)$ for the appropriate number n of arguments. Let ϕ_l be a clause in the matrix of Φ. Let $\phi_l = \phi_{l,1} \vee \phi_{l,2}$, where $\phi_{l,1}$ contains all Y-literals from ϕ_l and those X-literals of ϕ_l, such that X occurs before Y for some Y-literal in ϕ_l and $\phi_{l,2}$ contains all literals $\neg X_j$ or X_j such that X_j is not before any Y-variable occuring in ϕ_l .

Let us fix an assignment $a_1, ..., a_{n_k}$ of 0 and 1. We will use b_i as an abbreviation for $f_i(\overline{a}^i)$.

We will show, that

$$\phi_{i,1}(a_1, ..., a_{n_k}, f_1(\overline{a}^1), ..., f_{m_{k-1}}(\overline{a}^{m_{k-1}}))$$

is true.

Let $a'_1, ..., a'_{n_k}$ be another assignment of values 0 and 1 to the X-variables which agrees with the fixed assignment except possibly for variables X_j that are not before any Y-variable in ϕ_l. The assignment $\overline{a}'$ is chosen to have the property, that $\phi_{l,2}(\overline{a}', \overline{b}')$ is false. This is possible since by assumption on Φ the pure X-clause $\phi_{l,2}$ contains no complementary pair X_j , $\neg X_j$.

Since ϕ is true under the assignment $a'_1, ..., a'_{n_k}, b'_1, ..., b'_{m_{k-1}}$ $\phi_{l,1}$ has to be true. Since $\phi_{l,1}$ contains only X-variables X_i for which $a_i = a'_i$ and since for all variables Y_j in $\phi_{l,1}$ the function f_j does not have any of the changed X-values among it arguments, $\phi_{p,1}$ is also true under the original assignment $\bar{a}$.

Lemma 2:
Let Σ be obtained from Φ by a resolution step, ,then Σ is true if and only if Φ is true.

Proof: If Σ is true, then Φ is , of course, also true. To prove the converse direction we first observe, that adding to ϕ the ordinary resolvent of two clauses, without omitting any variables leads to a logically equivalent formula ϕ' . Now Lemma 1 is used to pass from $\forall \overline{X}_1 \exists \overline{Y}_1 ... \exists \overline{Y}_{k-1} \forall \overline{X}_k \phi'$ to Σ.

Theorem 3: Let Φ be a formula of the form $\forall \overline{X}_1 \exists \overline{Y}_1 ... \exists \overline{Y}_{k-1} \forall \overline{X}_k \phi$
Φ is true if and only of no pure X-clause can be derived from ϕ by Y-unit resolution.

Proof:

Let Φ' be obtained from Φ by Y-unit resolution, such that the matrix ϕ' of Φ' contains a pure X-clause ψ. By assumption on Φ and the definition of unit resolution ψ cannot contain a complementary pair. Thus Φ' is obviously false. By Lemma 1 also Φ has to be false.

Now let us assume, that no pure X-clause can be derived from ϕ. Let σ be the conjunction of ϕ together with all resolvents, that can be derived by Y-unit resolution and let Σ be the formula with the same prefix as Φ and the matrix σ. We will show that Σ is true, which immediately yields also the truth of Φ.

Let an arbitrary assignment $\bar{a} = a_1, ..., a_{n_k}$ of 0 and 1 be given. We define the assignments b_l for the variables Y_l as follows:

- If there is a Y_l-unit clause in σ that is not already made true under the partial assignment $\bar{a}$, then let b_l equal 1.
- Let b_l equal 0 otherwise.

We prove by induction on the number s of Y-variables in χ, that $\chi(\bar{a}, \bar{b})$ is true, for any clause χ of σ.

If $s = 0$, then χ would consist entirely of X-variables. By assumption this is not possible.

Let $s = 1$. If χ is a Y_l-unit clause, then χ is either already true on the basis of the assignment $\bar{a}$ or b_l has been defined to be equal to 1. So let us assume that the only Y-literal in χ is $\neg Y_l$. If no Y_l-unit clause occurs in

σ, that is not true on the basis of $\bar{a}$ alone, then b_l is equal to 0 and χ is true. Finally it remains to consider the case that σ contains a Y_l-unit clause χ' , that is not already true under the partial assignment $\bar{a}$. By the Horn property all X-literals in χ' are negative. We may therefore draw the conclusion that for all variables X_j in χ' $a_j = 1$. By assumption χ and χ' cannot have a resolvent, i.e. for some j X_j occurs in χ and $\neg X_j$ occurs in χ', which implies that χ is true, since $a_j = 1$.

Induction step. Let χ contain s+1 Y-literals, where we may now assume $s > 1$. By the Horn property χ has to contain a negative Y-literal $\neg Y_l$. If there is no Y_l-unit clause in σ, that is not already true under the assignment $\bar{a}$, then $b_l = 0$ and χ is true. Otherwise let χ' be such a clause. The resolvent ψ of χ and χ' contains s Y-literals and is thus true by induction hypothesis. Since the disjunctive part of ψ stemming from χ' is not true, the part stemming from χ has to be. Thus also χ is true.

Examples

Example 1 Let

$$\Phi = \forall X \exists Y((X \vee \neg Y) \wedge (\neg X \vee Y))$$

The second clause is a Y-unit clause. Its resolvent with the first clause would contain the complementary pair X and $\neg X$ and is thus not performed. No pure X-clause is derivable, Φ is true.

Example 2 Let

$$\Phi = \exists Y \forall X((X \vee \neg Y) \wedge (\neg X \vee Y))$$

Again the second clause is a Y-unit clause. Its resolvent with the first clause is the empty clause since all occurences of X-variables are dropped. Thus the formula is false.

Example 3 Let

$$\Phi = \exists Y_1 \forall X \exists Y_2((\neg Y_1 \vee X \vee \neg Y_2) \wedge (\neg Y_1 \vee \neg X \vee Y_2) \wedge Y_1)$$

The only Y-unit clause is Y_1. The resolvents with the first and second clause are $X \vee \neg Y_2$ and $\neg X \vee Y_2$ respectively.
The second second clause is again a Y-unit clause. No resolution with the first clause is possible, because a complementary pair would arise. This Φ is true.

Example 4 Let

$$\Phi = \forall X_1 \forall X_2 \exists Y_1 \exists Y_2((X_2 \vee \neg Y_2) \wedge (Y_2 \vee \neg Y_1) \wedge (\neg X_2 \vee Y_1) \wedge (\neg X_1 \vee Y_1))$$

Using the Y-unit clauses $\neg X_2 \vee Y_1$ and $\neg X_1 \vee Y_1$ we obtain by resolution with the second clause two new Y-unit clauses $Y_2 \vee \neg X_2$ and $Y_2 \vee \neg X_1$.

Only the second of these can be used to continue resolution with the first clause to obtain $X_3 \vee \neg X_2$. Thus Φ is false.

Lemma 4: Let Φ be a formula of the form $\forall \overline{X} \exists \overline{Y} \phi$. Then Φ is false if and only if for some assignment $\overline{a} = a_1, ..., a_n$ of values 0 and 1 with at most one occurence of 0, the formula $\exists \overline{Y} \phi(a_1, ..., a_n)$ is false.

Proof: One implication of the lemma is trivial. So let us assume that $\forall \overline{X} \exists \overline{Y} \phi$ is false. Let ϕ_0 be the conjunction of ϕ together with all clauses, that can be derived from ϕ by Y-unit resolution. By Lemma 1 $\forall \overline{X} \exists \overline{Y} \phi$ is equivalent to $\forall \overline{X} \exists \overline{Y} \phi_0$. By our assumption the latter formula is false and thus contains by virtue of Theorem 3 a pure X-clause χ. Let $\overline{a} = a_1, ..., a_n$ be an assignment of values 0 and 1 to the X-variables, such that $\chi(a_1, ..., a_n)$ is false. Since χ is a Horn clause, we may choose $\overline{a}$, such that at most one 0 occurs. Obviously $\exists \overline{Y} \phi_0(a_1, ..., a_n)$ is false and therefore by the equivalence stated above also $\exists \overline{Y} \phi(a_1, ..., a_n)$ is false.

Lemma 5: The truth of an $\forall\exists$-quantified conjunction of Horn formulas can be decided in polynomial time.

Proof: Let $\Phi = \forall \overline{X} \exists \overline{Y} \phi$. The algorithm consists in testing for all assigments $\overline{a}$ with at most one 0 the truth of $\exists \overline{Y} \phi(\overline{a})$. There are (number of X-variables) + 1 many assigments $\overline{a}$ with at most one 0. The reduction of $\phi(\overline{a})$ to a conjunction ϕ_1 of Horn clauses not containing the constants 0 and 1 can be affected in linear time. Finally the satisfiability of ϕ_1 can be decided in linear time. Thus the overall running time of the algorithm may be bounded by $(\text{length of input})^2$.

An Algorithm

Let Φ be a formula of the form

$$\forall \overline{X}_1 \exists \overline{Y}_1 ... \exists \overline{Y}_{k-1} \forall \overline{X}_k \phi$$

be given.

Let N_ϕ be the set of clauses in ϕ, that are not pure X-clauses and contain only negative Y-literals. Let P_ϕ be the set of clauses in ϕ, that contain at least one positive Y-literal.

for all clauses C in N_Φ do

let S_C be the set of positive X-literals in C. { Thus S_C may be a singleton set or the empty set }.

if S_C is empty then do

remove all occurences of all X-literals in P_Φ and C obtaining P'_Φ and C'
apply standard unit-resolution to P'_Φ and C' .
if the empty clause can be derived terminate with "Φ is false"
otherwise terminate with "Φ is true".

end if

if $S_C = \{X_r\}$ then do

for all variables X different from X_r remove all X-literals from P_Φ obtaining P'_Φ .
begin 1

letL be the set of Y-unit clauses that may be derived from P'_Φ by standard unit resolution **without** taking the obstacle X_r into consideration and such that Y occurs before X_r in the prefix of Φ.
for all Y ε L remove all occurences of the literal $\neg Y$ in all clauses in P'_Φ
remove all clauses containing a Y-literal, with Y occuring before X_r in the prefix of Φ obtaining P''_Φ
let U be the set of Y-unit clauses in P''_Φ not containing the literal $\neg X_r$
let R be the empty set
while U is not empty do

for Y ε U do
remove all occurences of the literal $\neg Y$ in all clauses in P''_Φ
remove all clauses in P''_Φ containing the literal Y
add new Y-unit clauses not containing $\neg X_r$ to U
remove Y from U
add Y to R
end for

end while

end 1

if all Y-variables in C occur among the variables in L ∪ R, then "Φ is false"
otherwise "Φ is true".

end if

end for

The complexity of the above algorithm is $O(n^3)$ observing that unit-resolution can be performed in linear time.

References

AvE 82 K.R. Apt and M.H. van Emden, Contributions to the Theory of Logic Programming, J. ACM vol. 29, 1982, pp. 841 - 862.

APT 79 B. Aspvall, M. F. Plass, R. E. Tarjan, A linear-time algorithm for testing the truth of certain quantified boolean formulas, Inf. Processing Letters, Vol. 8, 1979, pp. 121 - 123.

DG 84 W.F. Dowling and J.H. Gallier, Linear-Time Algorithms for Testing the Satisfiability of Propositional Horn Formulae, J Logic Programming, vol. 3, 1984, pp. 267 - 284.

GR 87 J.H. Gallier and S. Raatz, HORNLOG: A Graph-Based Interpreter for General Horn Clauses, J. of Logic Programming vol 4, 1987, pp. 119 - 155.

GJ 79 M. R. Garey and D. S. Johnston, Computers and Intractability, A Guide to the Theory of NP-Completeness, W. H. Freeman and Co., San Fransicao, 1979.

IM 87 A. Itai and J. A. Makowsky, Unification as a complexity measure for logic programming, J. Logic Programming, vol. 4, 1987, pp. 105 - 117.

SCH 78 Th. J. Schäfer, The Complexity of Satisfiability Problems. Proc. 10 th. Ann. ACM STOCS 1978, pp. 216 - 226

THE CONJUNCTIVE COMPLEXITY OF QUADRATIC BOOLEAN FUNCTIONS

Katja Lenz * and Ingo Wegener *
Lehrstuhl für Theoretische Informatik II, Universität Dortmund
4600 Dortmund 50, Fed. Rep. of Germany

Abstract

The minimal number of conjunctions in monotone circuits for quadratic Boolean functions, i.e. disjunctions of quadratic monomials $x_i x_j$, is investigated. Single level circuits which have only one level of conjunctions are compared with arbitrary monotone circuits. The computation of the single level complexity is shown to be NP complete. For almost all quadratic functions almost optimal circuits can be computed in polynomial time. The single level conjecture is disproved, i.e. some quadratic function is defined whose single level complexity is larger than its conjunctive complexity.

1. INTRODUCTION

The circuit complexity is known only for a small number of simple functions. On one hand we believe that we can design efficient circuits but on the other hand only poor lower bound techniques have been developped . In this situation one can try to prove new lower bound records or one can try to analyse thoroughly the complexity of all functions in some class of Boolean functions. In this paper we follow the second approach and consider the class of quadratic Boolean functions.

Let $G = (V,E)$ be an undirected graph with the vertex set $V = \{1,\ldots n\}$ and the edge set $E \subseteq \{(i,j) \mid 1 \le i < j \le n\}$.

Definition 1: The quadratic (Boolean) function $f_G^{\vee}$ associated with G is defined by $f_G^{\vee}(x_1, \ldots, x_n) = \bigvee_{(i,j)\in E} x_i x_j$.

Definition 2: The quadratic (Boolean) form $f_G^{\oplus}$ associated with G is defined by $f_G^{\oplus}(x_1, \ldots, x_n) = \bigoplus_{(i,j)\in E} x_i x_j$.

Mirwald and Schnorr [9] have investigated $C_{\wedge}(f_G^{\oplus})$, the multiplicative complexity of quadratic forms, i.e. the minimal number of conjunctions ($\wedge$-gates) in a circuit for $f_G^{\oplus}$ over the basis $\{\oplus,\wedge,0,1\}$, and $C_{\wedge}^1(f_G^{\oplus})$, the multiplicative single level complexity of $f_G^{\oplus}$. Single level circuits are circuits where no path combines $\wedge$-gates. They

*Supported in part by DFG grants No. We 1066/1-2 and Me 872/1-1

could present a complete solution of the problem and proved the following results.

1.) $C^1_\wedge(f^\oplus_G) = C_\wedge(f^\oplus_G)$ for all G and each optimal circuit for $f^\oplus_G$ is a single level circuit. For pairs $(f^\oplus_G, f^\oplus_G)$ of quadratic forms there exists always an optimal circuit which is a single level circuit.
2.) Given G, $C_\wedge(f^\oplus_G)$ can be computed within $O(n^3)$ steps, i.e. in polynomial time.
3.) The hardest quadratic form on n variables has a multiplicative complexity of $\lfloor n/2 \rfloor$.
4.) Almost all quadratic forms have a multiplicative complexity of n/2-o(n) which is almost the complexity of the hardest function.

The first three results did not agree with our intuition. This motivated us to investigate the class of quadratic functions $f^\vee_G$ and its conjunctive complexity $C_\wedge(f^\vee_G)$, the minimal number of $\wedge$-gates in a circuit for $f^\vee_G$ over the basis $\{\vee,\wedge,0,1\}$, and its single level complexity $C^1_\wedge(f^\vee_G)$. These problems have already been considered by Bloniarz [2], Bublitz [3], Chung [4] and Tuza [14].

Our results for quadratic functions differ strongly from the above mentioned results for quadratic forms. By the way, these results agree with our intuition.

In Section 2 we point out what we have learnt about the differences between the bases $\{\oplus,\wedge,0,1\}$ and $\{\vee,\wedge,0,1\}$. Furthermore, we mention how the single level complexity of a quadratic function can be expressed in a purely graph theoretical or combinatorial setting. In Section 3 we analyse the complexity of computing, given G, $C^1_\wedge(f^\vee_G)$ or $C_\wedge(f^\vee_G)$. In Section 4 we discuss the complexity of the hardest function and the complexity of almost all functions. Furthermore, we present an efficient algorithm for the design of almost optimal circuits for almost all functions. In Section 5 we disprove the single level conjecture. For some explicitely defined G we prove that $C^1_\wedge(f^\vee_G) > C_\wedge(f^\vee_G)$. In Section 6 we list some open problems.

2. QUADRATIC FORMS VS.QUADRATIC FUNCTIONS AND A GRAPH THEORETICAL CHARACTERIZATION

First we like to point out some differences between the two models.
i) In the case of the basis $\{\oplus,\wedge,0,1\}$ one works in the Galois field $\mathbb{Z}_2$ and can apply algebraic methods. In particular, $x \oplus x = 0$, hence there exist inverse elements with respect to $\oplus$, but there are no inverse elements with respect to $\vee$.
ii) In the case of the basis $\{\vee,\wedge,0,1\}$ one works in a distributive lattice and it seems to be more appropriate to use combinatorial methods. The so-called law of simplification $xy \vee x = x$ holds over the monotone basis but there is no counterpart in Galois fields.

We leave it at this place to the reader to discuss which properties might be helpful or embarassing for the computation of quadratic form or function.

We show that for some G $f_G^{\oplus}$ is easier than $f_G^{\vee}$ and that for some G' $f_{G'}^{\oplus}$ is harder than $f_{G'}^{\vee}$.

<u>Proposition 1:</u> Let $G = K_3$ be the complete graph on 3 vertices. Then $C_{\wedge}(f_G^{\oplus}) = C_{\wedge}^1(f_G^{\oplus}) = 1$ and $C_{\wedge}(f_G^{\vee}) = C_{\wedge}^1(f_G^{\vee}) = 2$.

<u>Proof</u>: The first part follows from the fact that
$f_G^{\oplus}(x_1,x_2,x_3) = [(x_1 \oplus x_2) \wedge (x_1 \oplus x_3)] \oplus x_1$.
The second part is well-known (see e.g. Bloniarz [2]).

□

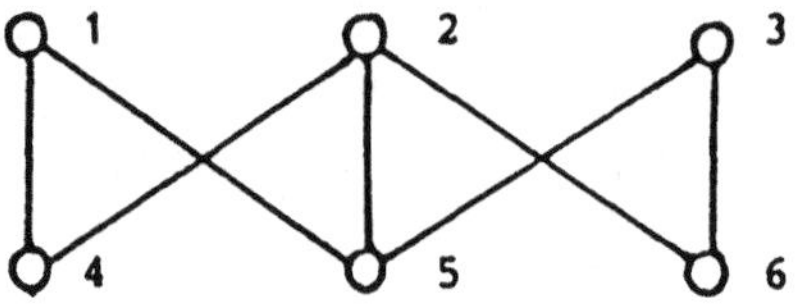

Fig. 1

<u>Proposition 2:</u> Let G be the graph of Fig. 1. Then $C_{\wedge}(f_G^{\oplus}) = C_{\wedge}^1(f_G^{\oplus}) = 3$ and $C_{\wedge}(f_G^{\vee}) = C_{\wedge}^1(f_G^{\vee}) = 2$.

<u>Proof</u>: The first part follows easily from the results of Mirwald and Schnorr [9]. The upper bound of the second part follows since
$f_G^{\vee}(x_1,\dots,x_6) = [(x_1 \vee x_2) \wedge (x_4 \vee x_5)] \vee [(x_2 \vee x_3) \wedge (x_5 \vee x_6)]$.
The lower bound follows by the well-known elimination method. If we replace x_1 by 1 we can eliminate at least one $\wedge$-gate and obtain a circuit for a function which cannot be computed without $\wedge$-gates.

□

The single level complexity of $f_G^{\vee}$ can be expressed in a purely graph theoretical or combinatorial setting. Let g be an $\wedge$-gate, then it has no $\wedge$-gate as predecessor. Hence, its inputs are Boolean sums s_1 and s_2, i.e. disjunctions of Boolean variables. If x_i is a term of s_1 and of s_2, then x_i is also a prime implicant of the output of g. Since in single level circuits only $\vee$-gates are following g, x_i or 1 is a prime implicant of the output of the circuit in contradiction to the fact that the circuit computes a quadratic function. Thus, only disjoint Boolean sums s_1 and s_2 are admissible.

Then $s_1 \wedge s_2$ is the disjunction of all $x_i x_j$ where x_i belongs to s_1 and x_j belongs to s_2. Which graph corresponds to this function? It consists of two disjoint vertex sets V_1 and V_2 corresponding to the variables of s_1 and s_2 resp. and all edges between V_1 and V_2. Such graphs are called <u>complete bipartite graphs.</u>

Fig. 2 shows the graph if $s_1 = x_1 \vee x_2 \vee x_3$ and $s_2 = x_4 \vee x_5$.

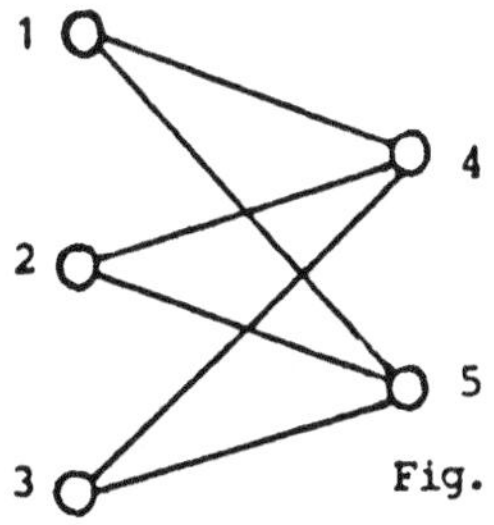

Fig. 2

From these considerations we conclude the following characterization.

Theorem 1: $C^1_\wedge(f^\vee_G)$ is equal to the minimal number of complete bipartite graphs whose union (union of the edge sets) equals G.

3. THE COMPLEXITY OF COMPUTING THE CONJUNCTIVE COMPLEXITY OF QUADRATIC BOOLEAN FUNCTIONS

We know that it is in general difficult to estimate the complexity of some function with respect to some complexity measure. Thus, the result of Mirwald and Schnorr [9], that the multiplicative complexity of quadratic forms can be computed in polynomial time, is surprising. What about the complexity of computing the conjunctive complexity of quadratic functions ?

An instance of the problem is specified by an undirected graph G on n vertices and a number $k \le n$. The problem is to decide whether $C^1_\wedge(f^\vee_G) \le k$ or $C_\wedge(f^\vee_G) \le k$.

Theorem 2: It is an NP complete problem to decide for (G,k) whether $C^1_\wedge(f^\vee_G) \le k$.

Proof: We apply Theorem 1 and a polynomial transformation from the GRAPH K-COLORABILITY-problem via the PARTITION INTO CLIQUES-problem due to Orlin [10] (see also Garey and Johnson [7]).

□

This result emphasizes our intuition that it is in general hard to compute the complexity of a function. The efficient computation of the multiplicative complexity of quadratic forms seems to be an exception. Nevertheless ,we do not know much about the complexity of deciding whether the conjunctive complexity of $f^\vee_G$ is bounded by k. This problem is not known to be in NP (the number of prime clauses may be exponentially large) and not known to be NP hard. The best known result is the following.

Proposition 3: The problem to decide whether the conjunctive complexity of $f^\vee_G$ ist bounded by k is contained in Σ^P_2, the complexity class on the second level in the polynomial time hierarchy.

This result seems to be obvious since the corresponding language can be expressed in the following form:

$\exists$ monotone circuit c with at most k $\wedge$-gates $\forall$ $(a_1, \ldots, a_n) \in \{0,1\}^n$:
the output of c on input a equals $f_G^{\vee}(a)$.

But the input of our problem has only size $\Theta(n^2)$. A circuit c with g gates can be encoded with $O(g \log g)$ bits. Since the number of $\vee$-gates in c is not bounded, not all monotone circuits with at most k $\wedge$-gates can be encoded in polynomial length. We apply ideas of Alon and Boppana [1] (see also Wegener [16]) to bound the number of useful $\vee$-gates. (This result will be applied also in Section 4.)

Lemma 1: If f can be computed in a monotone circuit with $k \geq 1$ $\wedge$-gates, then f can be computed in a monotone circuit with k $\wedge$-gates and altogether at most $kn + \binom{k-1}{2} - 1$ gates.

Proof: Let c be a monotone circuit for f with k $\wedge$-gates and let $f_1, \ldots, f_{k-1}$ be the outputs of the first k-1 $\wedge$-gates and $f_k = f$. It is sufficient to prove that f_i can be computed out of the input set $I_i = \{x_1, \ldots, x_n, f_1, \ldots, f_{i-1}\}$ with $n+i-2$ additional gates, among them at most one $\wedge$-gate. By definition $f_i = s_1 \vee (s_2 \wedge s_3)$ where s_j is the disjunction of some elements in I_i. If t is contained in s_1, t can be cancelled in s_2 and/or s_3. If t is contained in s_2 and s_3, it can be cancelled in s_2 and s_3 and added to s_1. Thus, we may choose s_1, s_2 and s_3 in such a way that each element in I_i is contained in at most one s_j. Finally, f_i can be computed by $n+i-2$ additional gates, among them at most one $\wedge$-gate.

□

Lemma 1 shows that the monotone complexity cannot be large if the conjunctive complexity is small.

Now, Proposition 3 follows easily, since we can restrict ourselves to monotone circuits with at most $kn + \binom{k-1}{2} - 1$ gates, among them at most k $\wedge$-gates.

4. THE COMPLEXITY OF THE HARDEST FUNCTION AND ALMOST ALL FUNCTIONS

Definition 3: Let $C_\wedge(n)$ and $C_\wedge^1(n)$ be the maximum of all $C_\wedge(f_G^{\vee})$ and $C_\wedge^1(f_G^{\vee})$ resp. for graphs on n vertices.

We like to estimate $C_\wedge(n)$ and $C_\wedge^1(n)$. Upper bounds should be proved by efficient algorithms for the construction of circuits with a small number of $\wedge$-gates. It would be nice if we could construct efficiently graphs G such that $f_G^{\vee}$ is of large conjunctive complexity. Finally, we try to estimate the complexity of almost all quadratic functions.

The best lower bound on $C_\wedge(n)$ is due to Bloniarz [2] and can be proved by the elimination method. Let $G(n)$ be a graph on n vertices consisting of $\lfloor n/3 \rfloor$ disjoint triangles. Then $C_\wedge(f^\vee_{G(n)}) = 2\lfloor n/3 \rfloor$. Obviously, $G(n)$ can be constructed efficiently. Although this bound seems to be far away from the correct result, we write it down as a theorem.

<u>Theorem 3</u>: Graphs $G(n)$ where $C_\wedge(f^\vee_{G(n)}) = 2\lfloor n/3 \rfloor$ can be constructed in polynomial time.

The single level complexity is a purely graph theoretical complexity measure (see Theorem 1). Such measures are widely studied (for a general approach see Pudlák, Rödl and Savický [12]). Chung [4] proved that $C^1_\wedge(n) \geq n - n^{3/4}$ for infinitely many n. The graphs she investigates cannot be constructed (until now) in polynomial time. Rödl [13] proved the following result by probabilistic methods.

<u>Theorem 4</u>: The single level complexity of almost all quadratic functions is for some constant c larger than n-clogn. In particular, $C^1_\wedge(n) \geq n - c\log n$ for large n.

If $G = (V,E)$ and $G' = (V',E')$ are graphs on disjoint sets of vertices, $G \cup G' = (V \cup V', E \cup E')$ is the disjoint union of G and G'. From Theorem 1 we can conclude the following result.

<u>Proposition 4</u>: $C^1_\wedge(f^\vee_{G \cup G'}) = C^1_\wedge(f^\vee_G) + C^1_\wedge(f^\vee_{G'})$.

By this result it is easy to construct for given $\alpha < 1$ in polynomial time graphs $G(n)$ on n vertices such that $C^1_\wedge(f^\vee_{G(n)}) \geq \alpha n$ for large n. By systematic search one computes the lexicographically first graph G' on say m vertices such that $C^1_\wedge(f^\vee_{G'}) \geq \alpha m$. Then, let $G(n)$ be the disjoint union of $\lfloor n/m \rfloor$ copies of G'. It is an open problem whether graphs of larger (single level) conjunctive complexity can be constructed in polynomial time.

<u>Theorem 5</u>: For each $c > 4$, the conjunctive complexity of almost all quadratic functions is larger than n/c logn. In particular, $C_\wedge(n) \geq n/c \log n$ for large n.

<u>Proof</u>: We combine Shannon's counting argument and Lemma 1, the result about the limited use of many $\vee$-gates in the presence of only a small number of $\wedge$-gates. For each $d > 4$, the monotone circuit complexity of almost all quadratic functions is not smaller than $n^2/d \log n$ (see Wegener [16]). By Lemma 1, for almost all $G(n)$ and $k = k(G(n)) = C_\wedge(f^\vee_{G(n)})$ it holds that

$$\frac{n^2}{d \log n} \leq kn + \binom{k-1}{2} - 1 \leq kn + k^2.$$

By choosing $d > 4$ in dependence of c small enough, we can conclude that $k \geq n/c \log n$ for large n. □

The best known upper bound for all quadratic functions has been proved by Tuza [14]. We show that this upper bound can be achieved efficiently.

<u>Theorem 6</u>: $C_\wedge(n) \leq C^1_\wedge(n) \leq n - \lfloor \log n \rfloor + 1$.
For a graph G with n vertices and e edges, given by its adjacency lists, a monotone

single level circuit for $f_G^\vee$ with at most $n-\lfloor \log n\rfloor+1$ $\wedge$-gates can be constructed in time $O(en)$.

Proof: Let $G = (V,E)$, $n = |V|$, $e = |E|$ and $2^t + 2^{t-1} \le n$.

We describe an algorithm which constructs a complete bipartite V-covering $G_r = (P_r, Q_r)$ $(1 \le r \le n-t)$ of the graph G, i.e. all G_r are complete bipartite subgraphs of G ($Q_r = \emptyset$ is possible) with edge set $E_r = \{(j,k) \mid j \in P_r, k \in Q_r\}$, E is the union of all E_r and V is the union of all P_r. This last property facilitates the correctness proof due to Erdös and Szekeres [5] and Tuza [14]. We concentrate on the efficient implementation of the algorithm. A star centered at vertex v is the complete bipartite graph connecting v and its neighbors $\Gamma(v)$.

Preprocessing: If $e \le n - \lfloor \log n\rfloor + 1$, cover each edge by a single complete bipartite graph. Otherwise $n = O(e)$. Compute the adjacency matrix. For each edge (i,j) where $i < j$ and each vertex $k > j$ test whether (i,j,k) builds a triangle in G. Produce a linear list of all triangles in lexicographic order. Preprocessing time: $O(en)$.

Call the cover algorithm $C(V,n,t)$ where t is the largest number such that $2^t + 2^{t-1} \le n$. In general $C(V',n',t')$ for some $V' \subseteq V$, $n' = |V'|$, $2^{t'} + 2^{t'-1} \le n'$ returns a complete bipartite V'-covering of G', the subgraph on V' induced by G, with at most $n'-t'$ complete bipartite graphs.
To simplify notation we describe only $C(V,n,t)$.
Step 0: If $t \le 1$, return the stars centered at $1,\dots,n-3$ and a complete bipartite V-covering of the subgraph on the vertices $n-2, n-1, n$ by at most two graphs.
Step 1: Compute in time $O(n+e)$ for all v its degree $d(v)$.
Step 2: Decide which of the 4 cases holds (implementation and time analysis are described later).
Case 1: $\forall v \in V$: $d(v) = n-1$.
Case 2: $\exists v \in V$: $2^{t-1}+2^{t-2} \le d(v) < n-1$.
Case 3: $\exists v \in V$: $d(v) < 2^{t-1}+2^{t-2}$ and v is contained in a triangle (v,w,z).
Case 4: G contains no triangle.
Step 3: Perform the algorithm for the correct case as described below.

Case 1: G is the complete graph K_n on n vertices. We add a dummy vertex n+1 and consider the graph K_{n+1}. It is easy to cover K_{n+1} with $\lceil \log(n+1)\rceil$ complete bipartite graphs such that vertex n+1 is always in the Q-set. We eliminate the dummy variable. This case can be handled, since $e = \binom{n}{2}$, in time $O(n \log n) = O(e)$.

Case 2: Call $C(\Gamma(v), |\Gamma(v)|, t-1)$ which returns (P_i, Q_i') for $1 \le i \le |\Gamma(v)|-(t-1)$. Set $Q_i = Q_i' \cup \{v\}$. The pairs (P_i, Q_i) $(1 \le i \le |\Gamma(v)|-(t-1))$ cover already all edges on $\Gamma(v) \cup \{v\}$ and all vertices in $\Gamma(v)$.
Let $Y = V-(\Gamma(v) \cup \{v\})$. Choose some $y \in Y$. Return (P_i,Q_i) for $1 \le i \le |\Gamma(v)|-(t-1)$, (P,Q) with $P = \{v,y\}$ and $Q = \Gamma(v) \cap \Gamma(y)$, and the stars $(\{y'\},\Gamma(y'))$ centered at $y' \in Y-\{y\}$. This case can be handled in time $O(n+e)$ plus the time for the recursive call.

Case 3: Let $Y = V-(\{v\} \cup \Gamma(v))$. Call $C(Y,|Y|,t-1)$ which returns (P_i,Q_i) $(1 \le i \le |Y|-(t-1))$. Return these pairs and the stars $(\{y\},\Gamma(y)\})$ for all $y \in \Gamma(v)-\{w,z\}$ and $(\Gamma(w),\{w\})$,

$(\Gamma(z),\{z\})$. This case can be handled in time $O(n+e)$ plus the time for the recursive call.

Case 4: Compute ℓ, the largest number such that $\binom{\ell+1}{2} \le n$. Call IS(V), an algorithm computing an independent set I of size at least ℓ. Return $(\{v\},\Gamma(v))$ for $v \notin I$ and $(I,\emptyset)$. IS(V) is a recursive algorithm.
If $\ell = 1$, return $I=\{1\}$. Otherwise sort $d(v)$ for $v \in V$ using the bucket sort. If $d(v) \ge \ell$ for some v, return $I = \Gamma(v)$, which is an independent set because G is free of triangles. Otherwise call $IS(V-(\{1\} \cup \Gamma(1)))$ which returns I'. Return $I = I' \cup \{1\}$. If vertex w is exluded from consideration, the degree of each vertex $z \in \Gamma(w)$ decreases by 1. The sorted order of the vertices with respect to their degree in the currently considered graph can be maintained in time $O(|\Gamma(w)|)$. Thus, this case can be handled in time $O(n+e)$.

We describe how we decide between the four cases. Because we know the degree of all vertices, we can decide in time $O(n)$ whether Case 1 or Case 2 holds. Otherwise, run through the list of triangles and search for the lexicographically first triangle completely included in V', the currently considered set of vertices. So we are able to distinguish between Case 3 and Case 4.
In Case 1 and Case 4 the algorithm terminates. In Case 2 and Case 3 the recursive call investigates a proper subset V" of V' with at most $|V'|-2$ vertices. Hence we have to run through the list of triangles at most once and we may add this time to the preprocessing time.

Let $T(n)$ be the running time of the algorithm without the preprocessing time and the time for the list operations. Then $T(n) \le T(n-2) + O(n+e)$ and
$T(n) = O((n+e)n) = O(en)$. The preprocessing time and the time for the list operations is of the same size.

□

We remark that Case 4 is a crucial part of the algorithm . The computation of a maximum independent set in graphs without triangles is an NP hard problem (Poljak [11]). Furthermore (see also Johnson [8]), no polynomial approximation algorithm for the general maximum independent set problem is known. But in our special situation it is possible to find efficiently an independent set which is large enough.

We know that $C^1_\wedge(n) = n-\Theta(\log n)$ and conjecture that $C^1_\wedge(n) > C_\wedge(n) \ge n-\log n-O(1)$. This would imply that almost all quadratic functions belong with respect to their conjunctive complexity to the class of almost hardest functions (see Theorem 4), but no hard function can be defined explicitely, no important quadratic function seems to be one of the hardest functions. At least almost optimal computation schemes can be computed for almost all quadratic functions by an efficient algorithm (see Theorem 6). This is a typical situation in Boolean complexity theory.

5. DISPROVING THE SINGLE LEVEL CONJECTURE

With some preliminary remarks we try to put the reader into a position that he/she cannot not only verify the counterexamples but understands why the single level conjecture does not hold for monotone circuits although it holds for circuits over $\mathbb{Z}_2$. Because of the inverse element with respect to $\oplus$ one eliminates unintentionally over $\mathbb{Z}_2$ useful monomials of length 2 and because there is no law of simplification over $\mathbb{Z}_2$ it is difficult to eliminate monomials of length 3 or more.

We first want to discuss the situation in monotone circuits where monomials of length 3 and more are eliminated by a "magic trick". Let $G' = (V',E')$ and $G" = (V",E")$ be copies of G on disjoint sets of vertices. By Proposition 4, $C^1_\wedge(f^\vee_{G'\cup G"}) = 2\, C^1_\wedge(f^\vee_G)$. Let $t = C^1_\wedge(f^\vee_G)$ and let $(P_1, Q_1), \ldots, (P_t, Q_t)$ be an optimal covering of G by complete bipartite graphs. Let P'_i, Q'_i and $P"_i$, $Q"_i$ be the copies of P_i, Q_i on V' and V" resp. We compute the Boolean sums p_i and q_i corresponding to $P'_i \cup P"_i$ and $Q'_i \cup Q"_i$ resp. $(1 \le i \le t)$, afterwards $f_i = p_i \wedge q_i$ and $f = f_1 \vee \ldots \vee f_t$. In this way we compute "in parallel" with only t $\wedge$-gates two copies of G together with some interconnecting edges. We eliminate the "wrong" monomials by first lengthening them and then using our magic trick. With $2\lceil \log n \rceil$ $\wedge$-gates we compute the quadratic functions $T_2(V')$ and $T_2(V")$ corresponding to the complete graphs on V' and V" resp. Because of our magic trick

$f^\vee_{G'\cup G"} = f \wedge (T_2(V') \vee T_2(V"))$ and

$C^1_\wedge(f^\vee_G) + 2\lceil \log n \rceil + 1$ $\wedge$-gates would be sufficient for the computation of $f^\vee_{G'\cup G"}$. This number is usually much smaller than $2\, C^1_\wedge(f^\vee_G)$.

<u>Remark:</u> For those readers who are familiar with the theory of slice functions (an important class of functions for which the monotone complexity is not much larger than the circuit complexity, see Wegener [15]), we remark that the magic trick works for the 2-slices of quadratic functions if we allow $\wedge$-gates of fan-in 3 and if we apply the result of Friedman [6] that the threshold function T^n_3 can be computed with $O(\log n)$ $\wedge$-gates.

From these considerations we learn that we have to ensure that it is easy to eliminate all monomials of length 3 or more without eliminating shorter monomials The law of simplification should do this job. We illustrate these ideas by a simple example which has optimal single level and optimal two levels circuits.

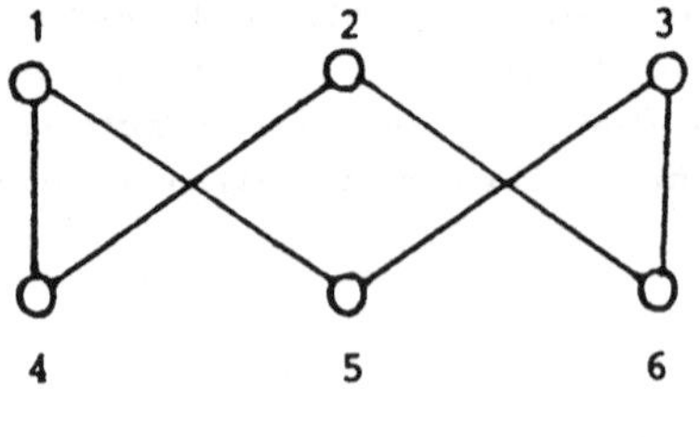

Fig. 3

<u>Proposition 5</u>: Let G be the graph of Fig. 3. Then $C^1_\wedge(f^\vee_G) = 3$ and $f^\vee_G$ can be computed by a two levels circuit with 3 $\wedge$-gates.

<u>Proof</u>: $C^1_\wedge(f^\vee_G) = 3$, since G can be covered by the stars centered at 1,2 and 3 and since G has six edges and each complete bipartite subgraph of G has at most two edges.
Finally $f^\vee_G(x_1,\dots,x_6) = ([(x_1 \vee x_2) \wedge (x_4 \vee x_5)] \vee [(x_2 \vee x_3) \wedge (x_5 \vee x_6)]) \wedge (x_1 \vee x_3 \vee x_4 \vee x_6)$.

□

<u>Theorem 7</u>: The single level conjecture does not hold for quadratic functions with respect to their conjunctive complexity, i.e. there exist graphs G where $C_\wedge(f^\vee_G) < C^1_\wedge(f^\vee_G)$.

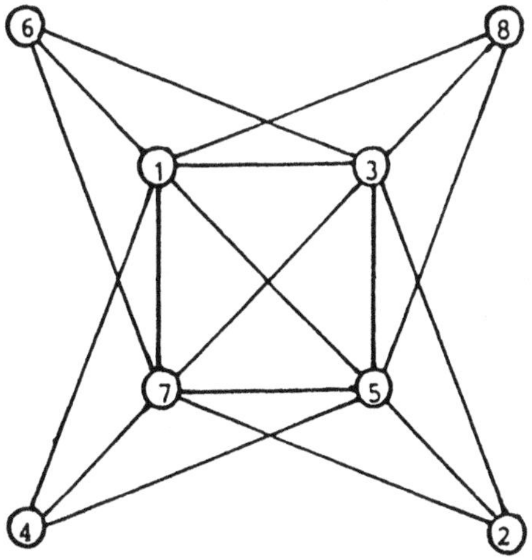

Fig. 4

<u>Proof:</u> Let G be the graph of Fig. 4.
<u>$C_\wedge(f^\vee_G) \le 3$</u> since

$$f^\vee_G(x_1,\dots,x_8) = ([(x_1 \vee x_2 \vee x_3 \vee x_4) \wedge (x_5 \vee x_6 \vee x_7 \vee x_8)] \vee [(x_1 \vee x_2 \vee x_5 \vee x_6) \wedge (x_3 \vee x_4 \vee x_7 \vee x_8)]) \wedge (x_1 \vee x_3 \vee x_5 \vee x_7).$$

<u>$C^1_\wedge(f^\vee_G) = 4$</u>: We denote by $K_{i,j}$ a complete bipartite graph between a set of i vertices and a set of j vertices. We compute all maximal complete subgraphs of G.

<u>Group 1</u>: $K_{2,4}$
1A: 1,3 - 5,6,7,8
1B: 1,5 - 3,4,7,8
1C: 1,7 - 3,4,5,6

1D: 3,5 - 1,2,7,8
1E: 3,7 - 1,2,5,6
1F: 5,7 - 1,2,3,4

Group 2: $K_{1,6}$
2A: 1 - 3,4,5,6,7,8
2B: 3 - 1,2,5,6,7,8
2C: 5 - 1,2,3,4,7,8
2D: 7 - 1,2,3,4,5,6

Group 3: $K_{2,3}$
3A: 1,2 - 3,5,7
3B: 3,4 - 1,5,7
3C: 5,6 - 1,3,7
3D: 7,8 - 1,3,5

It is obvious, that G can be covered by the 4 stars of Group 2. For the lower bound it is sufficient to prove that 3 of the above 14 graphs are not enough to cover G. Because of the symmetry of G we have to analyse much less than the $\binom{14}{3} = 182$ possible cases.

Let us assume that there exists a covering with 3 of the complete bipartite graphs. If the covering contains a graph of Group 1, then because of symmetry w.l.o.g. graph 1A.

1A and 1B(similarly 1C,1D,1E): The star centered at 2 is missing. Thus we need graph 3A. The edge (4,7) is not covered.
1A and 1F: The edges (1,3), (1,4) and (2,3) are not covered and cannot be covered by one further graph.
1A and 2A (similarly 2B): The star centered at 2 is missing. Thus we need graph 3A The edge (4,7) is not covered.
1A and 2C (similarly 2D): The edges (2,3) and (2,7) are not covered and we need graph 3A (or graph 1E, but this case has been considered above). The edge (1,4) is not covered.
1A and 3A (similarly 3B): The star centered at 4 is missing. Thus we need graph 3B The edge (6,7) is not covered.
1A and 3C (similarly 3D): The stars centered at 2 and 4 are missing. They cannot b covered by one graph.

Hence we may use only graphs of Group 2 and Group 3 which have 6 edges each. G has 18 edges. Therefore, we have to look for 3 disjoint graphs, and at least 2 disjoint graphs from Group 2 or from Group 3. It is easy to see that such graphs do not exist.

□

This special counterexample can be generalized by Proposition 4. We do not know what the largest possible value of $C^1_\wedge(f^\vee_G)/C_\wedge(f^\vee_G)$ is. Mirwald and Schnorr [9] have shown for pairs of quadratic forms and their multiplicative complexity, that always optimal single level circuits exist. By Theorem 7 and Proposition 4 such a result cannot hold for quadratic functions and their conjunctive complexity. Nevertheless, we present a class of counterexamples in order to obtain more insight into the structure of the problem.

Let $G' = (V',E')$ and $G'' = (V'',E'')$ be disjoint copies of $G= (V,E)$ where $|V| = n$. Let $h(x)$ and $h(y)$ be the corresponding quadratic functions. Let $T_1(x)$ and $T_1(y)$ be the disjunction of all x-variables and y-variables resp. Finally let
$f_1(x,y) = h(x) \vee (T_1(x) \wedge T_1(y))$ and
$f_2(x,y) = h(y) \vee (T_1(x) \wedge T_1(y))$.

Theorem 8:
i) $C^1_\wedge(f_1,f_2) \geq 2C^1_\wedge(h)$

ii) $C_\wedge(f_1,f_2) \leq C^1_\wedge(h) + 2\lceil \log n\rceil + 3.$

Proof: Let G_1 and G_2 be the graphs corresponding to f_1 and f_2 .
i) Let the complete bipartite graph between P and Q be a part of an optimal single level algorithm for the pair (f_1, f_2). If not only P but also Q contains variables of type x and variables of type y, we cover with this graph edges between x-vertices and y-vertices. Such bipartite graphs are not subgraphs of G_1 or G_2 . Hence, in single level circuits, the two copies of G have to be covered by different graphs.

ii) Let $(P_1, Q_1),\dots,(P_t, Q_t)$ be an optimal covering of G by complete bipartite graphs. Let P'_i,Q'_i,P''_i,Q''_i be the corresponding vertex sets in V' and V" resp. Then we compute with $t = C^1_\wedge(h)$ $\wedge$-gates the union of all complete bipartite graphs $(P'_i\cup P''_i, Q'_i\cup Q''_i)$. Again we compute "in parallel" two copies of G and some interconnecting edges. The corresponding quadratic function g can be written as
$g(x,y) = h(x) \vee h(y) \vee g'(x,y)$ for some quadratic function g' such that
$g'(x,y) \leq T_1(x) \wedge T_1(y)$.
With $2\lceil \log n\rceil$ $\wedge$-gates we compute $T_2(x)$ and $T_2(y)$, the quadratic functions corresponding to the complete graphs on V' and V". With 1 $\wedge$-gate we compute $T_1(x) \wedge T_1(y)$. Then we compute with 2 $\wedge$-gates
$g_1(x,y) = g(x,y) \wedge T_2(x) = h(x) \vee (h(y) \wedge T_2(x)) \vee (g'(x,y) \wedge T_2(x))$ and
$g_2(x,y) = g(x,y) \wedge T_2(y) = (h(x) \wedge T_2(y)) \vee h(y) \vee (g'(x,y) \wedge T_2(y))$.
Finally it is easy to see that
$f_1(x,y) = g_1(x,y) \vee (T_1(x) \wedge T_1(y))$ and $f_2(x,y) = g_2(x,y) \vee (T_1(x) \wedge T_1(y))$.

□

6. OPEN PROBLEMS

We have learnt a lot about the conjunctive complexity of quadratic Boolean functions. Our results are in contrast to the result of Mirwald and Schnorr [9] about the multiplicative complexity of quadratic Boolean forms over $\mathbb{Z}_2$. There are still interesting open problems which we list in the following.

1.) What is the complexity of the following problem? Instance G, an undirected graph, and a number k. Decide whether $C_\wedge(f_G^\vee) \le k$.
2.) What is the exact value of $C_\wedge^1(n)$? $C_\wedge^1(n) = n - \lfloor \log n \rfloor - O(1)$?
3.) $C_\wedge(n) = n - o(n)$?
$C_\wedge(n) = n - O(\log n)$?
$C_\wedge(n) = C_\wedge^1(n)$?
4.) What is the complexity of almost all quadratic functions with respect to $C_\wedge$?
5.) Is it possible to construct in polynomial time one of the hardest quadratic functions on n variables?
6.) Does the single level conjecture hold for quadratic functions and the monotone circuit complexity, i.e. if we count conjunctions <u>and</u> disjunctions?
7.) Compute max $\{C_\wedge^1(f_G^\vee)/C_1(f_G^\vee) \mid G = (V,E), n = |V|\}$.

References

[1] Alon,N. and Boppana,R.: The monotone complexity of Boolean functions, Techn. Rep., 1985.

[2] Bloniarz,P.: The complexity of monotone Boolean functions and an algorithm for finding shortest paths in a graph, Ph.D.Thesis, MIT, 1979.

[3] Bublitz,S.: Decomposition of graphs and monotone formula size of homogeneous functions, Acta Informatica 23, 689-696, 1986.

[4] Chung,F.R.K.: On the covering of graphs, Discrete Mathematics 30, 89-93, 1980.

[5] Erdös,E. and Szekeres,G.: A combinatorial problem in geometry, Compositio Math. 2, 463-470, 1935.

[6] Fiedman,J.: Constructing O(n log n) size monotone formulae for the k-th elementary symmetric function of n Boolean variables, 25. FOCS, 506-515, 1984.

[7] Garey,M. and Johnson, D.: Computers and intractability:A guide to the theory of NP-completeness, W.H.Freeman, 1979.

[8] Johnson, D.: Approximation algorithms for combinatorial problems, Journal of Computer and System Sciences 9, 256-278,1974.

[9] Mirwald, R. and Schnorr, C.P.: The multiplicative complexity of quadratic Boolean forms, 28. FOCS, 1987, submitted to TCS.

[10] Orlin, J.: Contentment in graph theory: covering graphs with cliques, unpublished, 1976.

[11] Poljak, S.: A node on stable sets and coloring of graphs, Comment. Math. Univ Carolinae 15, 307-309, 1974.

[12] Pudlàk, P., Rödl,V. and Savický,P.: Graph complexity, Techn. Rep., Univ. Prague, 1987.

[13] Rödl,V.: private communication (cited in [14]).

[14] Tuza, Z.: Covering of graphs by complete bipartite subgraphs, complexity of 0-1 matrices, Combinatorica 4, 111-116, 1984.

[15] Wegener,I.: On the complexity of slice functions, Theoretical Computer Science 38, 55-68, 1985.

[16] Wegener,I.: The complexity of Boolean functions, Wiley- Teubner, 1987.

On Type Inference for Object-Oriented Programming Languages

Hans Leiß
Siemens AG, ZTI INF 2.3
Otto-Hahn-Ring 6
8000 München 83

Abstract

We present a type inference calculus for object-oriented programming languages. Explicit polymorphic types, subtypes and multiple inheritance are allowed. Class types are obtained by selection from record types, but not considered subtypes of record types. The subtype relation for class types reflects the (mathematically clean) properties of subclass relations in object-oriented programming to a better extend than previous systems did.
Based on Mitchells models for type inference, a semantics for types is given where types are sets of values in a model of type-free lambda calculus. For the sublanguage without type quantifiers and subtype relation, automatic type inference is possible by extending Milners algorithm W to deal with a polymorphic fixed-point rule.

0. Introduction

A class in object-oriented programming languages is a mechanism to generate "objects", i.e. records which may have components for data and functional values. Typically, some of these components are constants, i.e. their value is the same in all the records generated by the class, others are variables, i.e. their value may differ from one record to another. In most systems, the constants will include all the functional values of a record; hence these are given in the class description (the "message protocoll" of the class).

Classes are organized as a hierarchy of subclasses ("inheritance graph"), which amounts to a convention saying that all constants of a superclass which are not mentioned in the subclass description are to be understood as constants for the subclass, too. In this way, the functional components are by default "inherited" from a superclass to its subclasses (which leads to an important amount of code-sharing); but the programmer also may overwrite a functional value in a subclass.

The functional components of a record (or its class description) contain those functions which may be applied to this very record. As a consequence of overwriting, records belonging to a subclass may respond to a function name f in a different way than records of a superclass do. This means that we must not confuse the set of objects generated by a class with a type in the mathematical sense: in general, we cannot restrict a function operating on a class τ to a subclass σ of τ without loosing its familiar meaning.

We would like to impose a type structure onto a class hierarchy to avoid this defect. The aim of this paper is to propose a type system for functional languages which allows for (most of) the advantages of type free object oriented languages and for automatic type inference and correctness tests as well. In particular, we introduce class types as record types with fixed functional components and provide a notion of subtypes which - applied to class types - is more limited than the notion of subclass, but mathematically clean. Important aspects of object-oriented languages can be modelled by objects and class types in our sense. We hope that these types will be useful in building optimizing compilers for the languages in question.

In section 1 we review the type inference calculus behind the functional language ML, which operates with quantifier free type schemes. A closer look shows that it implicitly uses a limited form of universally quantified types and a subtype relation defined in terms of substitution of type variables. We extend the fixed-point rule to a truly polymorphic rule, which seems necessary to type recursively defined objects in the sense of object-oriented languages. Section 2 introduces a type inference calculus where type expressions are explicitly polymorphic (i.e. admit universally quantified type variables), and a subtype relation based on the structure of type terms. We extend these types in sections 3 and 4 to get a notion of class type that is more restrictive than the ones proposed by Cardelli[1984], as we fix the behaviour of a classes objects in the type expression. We also give a semantics where objects are elements and types are subsets of models of type free λ-calculus. Finally, section 5 extends Milners algorithm W to infer types for the sublanguage with type schemes only, but where class types may use the polymorphic fixed-point rule of section 1. We conjecture that we still have principle types, and give partial results in this direction.

1. Type inference calculi for functional languages: from parametric polymorphic types to explicitly polymorphic types

From a practical point of view, the most influential type inference system for functional languages is the one of ML developed by Hindley/Milner/Damas. We present Milners[1978] system as a natural deduction calculus. We show how its inference rules are derived rules of a more general system with subtypes and type quantifiers presented in section 2. The notion of type and term used here will be extended in the following sections. The terms of our toy programming language can be reduced to terms of type free lambda calculus.

Definition 1: A *term* is either an individual variable $x_1, x_2, \ldots$, an application $(f \cdot e)$ of a term f to a term e, an abstraction λxe of a variable x in a term e, a conditional (if e_0 then e_1 else e_2), a let-term (let x be e in t), which binds variable x in term t to e, or a rec-term (rec x e), which binds variable x in term e.
A *type (expression)* is either a type variable $\alpha_1, \alpha_2, \alpha_3, \ldots$, or a type constant $\underline{a}_1, \underline{a}_2, \underline{a}_3, \ldots$, or a function type $(\sigma \rightarrow \tau)$, for given types σ and τ. If a type expression contains free type variables, we sometimes call it a *type scheme*.

We use let- and rec-terms as abbreviations, more precisely, we allow the following term reduction rules:

$$(\text{let } x \text{ be } e \text{ in } t) := (\lambda xt \cdot e), \qquad (\text{rec } x\, e) := (Y \cdot \lambda xe), \quad \text{where } Y := \lambda f.\, (\lambda x.\, f(xx)) \cdot (\lambda x. f(xx)).$$

Y is a fixed-point operator, as we have $f(Yf) = (Yf)$ for any term f, using β-reduction. In particular,

$$(\text{rec } x\, e) = \lambda xe \cdot (\text{rec } x\, e) = e\,[(\text{rec } x\, e)/x].$$

Our notation will follow the usual conventions, dropping brackets and application dots, and using separation dots to indicate missing lambdas and brackets, as in $\lambda xy.z(xy)$ instead of $\lambda x \lambda y(z \cdot (x \cdot y))$.

To define the notion of well-typings, we use a free-variable type inference calculus in natural deduction style (which differs slightly from the system of Damas[1982] having types with ∀-quantifiers prefixes). A *typing statement* $t{:}\tau$ assigns a type τ to a term t; it is *basic* if t is a variable. The calculus uses sequents of the form $\Sigma \vdash \psi$ where Σ is a set of basic typing statements - the undischarged assumptions -, and ψ a typing statement. Σ_x always denotes a set of assumptions that does not contain any typing statement for the variable x.

<u>Currys rules</u>:

$$\text{(Var)}\quad \frac{}{\Sigma \cup \{x:\tau\} \vdash x:\tau} \qquad (\rightarrow \text{I})\quad \frac{\Sigma_x \cup \{x:\sigma\} \vdash e:\tau}{\Sigma_x \vdash \lambda x\, e : (\sigma \rightarrow \tau)} \qquad (\rightarrow \text{E})\quad \frac{\Sigma \vdash f:(\sigma \rightarrow \tau), \quad \Sigma \vdash e:\sigma}{\Sigma \vdash (f{\cdot}e):\tau}$$

<u>Milners rules</u>:

For any types σ and τ, we write $\sigma \le_\Sigma \tau$ if there are type variables $\alpha_1, \ldots, \alpha_n$ which do not occur free in Σ, and types $\tau_1, \ldots, \tau_n$, such that $\tau = \sigma[\tau_1/\alpha_1, \ldots, \tau_n/\alpha_n]$.

$$\text{(let)}\quad \frac{\Sigma_x \vdash e:\sigma, \qquad \Sigma_x \cup \{x:\sigma_1, \ldots, x:\sigma_m\} \vdash t:\tau, \qquad \sigma \le_{\Sigma_x} \sigma_1, \ldots, \sigma \le_{\Sigma_x} \sigma_m}{\Sigma_x \vdash (\text{let } x \text{ be } e \text{ in } t):\tau}$$

$$\text{(rec)}\quad \frac{\Sigma_x \cup \{x:\sigma_1, \ldots, x:\sigma_m\} \vdash e:\sigma, \qquad \sigma \le_{\Sigma_x} \sigma_1, \ldots, \sigma \le_{\Sigma_x} \sigma_m}{\Sigma_x \vdash (\text{rec } x\ e):\sigma}$$

$$\text{(if)}\quad \frac{\Sigma \vdash e_0:\underline{\text{boole}}, \qquad \Sigma \vdash e_1:\sigma, \qquad \Sigma \vdash e_2:\sigma}{\Sigma \vdash (\text{if } e_0 \text{ then } e_1 \text{ else } e_2):\sigma.}$$

A *type assignment* is a set Σ of basic typing statements which assigns at most one type to each variable. A *well-typing of t* is a sequent $\Sigma \vdash t{:}\tau$ which can be derived by the above axioms and rules, where Σ is a type assignment. We often simply write $\Sigma \vdash t{:}\tau$ instead of saying that $\Sigma \vdash t{:}\tau$ is a well-typing.
Note that for both the let- and rec-construct we do not have introduction and elimination rules like the Currys structural rules for λ-abstraction and application. This is clear when looking at the expanded form of the let- or rec-term: it is an application of an abstraction to another term, and hence combines an introduction with an elimination of →.

As has been noted by Howard[1980] in 1969, the types that occur when Currys rules are used to type λ-terms are valid formulas of intuitionistic propositional logic. With Milners rules we still have quantifier free propositional formulas as types. We now are going to give intuitive justifications for the let- and rec-rules. These will lead us to introduce quantifiers on type variables and thereby extend the type expressions to quantified propositional formulas, i.e. second order propositional logic. It also suggests to use a partial order on types.

Discussion of the let- rule:

Milners rules go beyond Currys in that they do not have the subterm property (when seen as λ-terms), i.e. the whole term is assigned a type although some of its subterms may not be typable. For example, using the let-rule we can type as follows (with α not free in Σ_x):

$$\frac{\begin{array}{ll} \Sigma_x \vdash \lambda yy : (\alpha \to \alpha), & \Sigma_x \cup \{x : (\alpha \to \alpha),\ x : ((\alpha \to \alpha) \to (\alpha \to \alpha))\} \vdash (xx) : (\alpha \to \alpha), \\ (\alpha \to \alpha) \leq_{\Sigma_x} (\alpha \to \alpha), & (\alpha \to \alpha) \leq_{\Sigma_x} ((\alpha \to \alpha) \to (\alpha \to \alpha)) = (\alpha \to \alpha)[(\alpha \to \alpha)/\alpha] \end{array}}{\Sigma_x \vdash (\text{let } x \text{ be } \lambda yy \text{ in } (xx)) : (\alpha \to \alpha)}$$

But the subterm $\lambda x(xx)$ of (let x be λyy in (xx)) = $\lambda x(xx) \cdot \lambda yy$ has no type according to the typing rules: In ($\to$ I) we are not allowed to abstract on a variable having different types in the assumptions.
Why then can this be allowed in the let-rule? First note that as the variables $\alpha_1, \ldots, \alpha_n$ do not occur free in Σ_x, from a logical point of view the assumptions in (let) amount to $\Sigma_x \vdash \forall\alpha_1 \ldots \forall\alpha_n (e : \sigma)$, hence in particular $\Sigma_x \vdash e : \sigma_i$ for each i, as σ_i is a substitution of types for type variables $\alpha_1, \ldots, \alpha_n$ in σ. Thus we can say $\Sigma_x \vdash e : \wedge\{\sigma_1, \ldots, \sigma_m\}$ for some kind of intersection type $\wedge\{\sigma_1, \ldots, \sigma_m\}$. Using the assumptions $\{x : \sigma_1, \ldots, x : \sigma_m\}$ in (let) we implicitly assign type $\wedge\{\sigma_1, \ldots, \sigma_m\} \to \tau$ to the subterm λxt. An application of ($\to$ E) then gives $\Sigma_x \vdash$ (let x be e in t) : τ.
But it seems unnatural to view any finite intersection of types to be a type, at least if we think of types as sets of values of similar structure. With this in mind, we restrict intersection of types to families of types of the same form. Definable families of this form are obtained from a type expression by using some of its free variables as parameters.
To be more precise, yet leaving a detailed definiton of models to the following sections, suppose we give meaning to type expressions in such a way that types are sets of objects; let $[[\tau]]\, e$ stand for the denotation of type τ under the type environment e in a model (of type-free λ-calculus). If $\Sigma_x \vdash \forall\alpha_1 \ldots \forall\alpha_n(e : \sigma)$ we want the value of e to belong to type $[[\sigma]]\, \Sigma_x[A_1/\alpha_1, \ldots, A_n/\alpha_n]$, for any types $A_1, \ldots, A_n$. In general, we want to admit new types

$\forall\alpha\,\tau$, with denotation $\quad [[\forall\alpha\tau]]\, e \;=\; \cap\{[[\tau]]\, e[A/\alpha] \mid A \text{ a type in the model}\}$.

Then clearly

$[[\forall\alpha_1 \ldots \alpha_n.\sigma]]\, e \subseteq [[\, \sigma[\tau_1/\alpha_1, \ldots, \tau_n/\alpha_n]\,]]\, e \qquad$ for any type expressions $\tau_1, \ldots, \tau_n$.

This suggests a partial ordering $\leq$ on types which can be seen as a generalization of $\leq_{\Sigma_x}$. In particular it leads to the substitution axiom (sub), corresponding to Milners notion of "generic instantiation":

(sub) $\quad \forall\alpha_1 \ldots \alpha_n.\sigma \leq \forall\beta_1 \ldots \beta_k.\, \sigma[\tau_1/\alpha_1, \ldots, \tau_n/\alpha_n]$,
for any type expressions $\tau_1, \ldots, \tau_n$ and type variables $\beta_1, \ldots, \beta_k$ not free in $\forall\alpha_1 \ldots \alpha_n.\sigma$.

Rule (let) can now best be understood by reducing it to the more expressive calculus of section 2. Using $\forall$ introduction and -elimination rules on type quantifiers (see below), we can substitute an application of (let) by the following derivation:

$$\dfrac{\dfrac{\dfrac{\Sigma_x \vdash e : \sigma}{\Sigma_x \vdash e : \forall a_1 \ldots a_n . \sigma}\,(\forall I) \qquad \dfrac{\dfrac{\dfrac{\dfrac{}{\Sigma_x \cup \{ x : \forall a_1 \ldots a_n . \sigma \} \vdash x : \forall a_1 \ldots a_n . \sigma,}\,(\mathrm{Var}) \qquad \dfrac{\sigma \leq_{\Sigma_x} \sigma_i}{\forall a_1 \ldots a_n . \sigma \leq \sigma_i}\,(\mathrm{sub})}{\Sigma_x \cup \{ x : \forall a_1 \ldots a_n . \sigma \} \vdash x : \sigma_i \qquad \text{for } i = 1, \ldots, m}\,(\mathrm{weak})}{\Sigma_x \cup \{ x : \forall a_1 \ldots a_n . \sigma \} \vdash t : \tau,}\,(*)}{\Sigma_x \vdash \lambda x\, t : (\forall a_1 \ldots a_n . \sigma) \to \tau}\,(\to I)}{\Sigma_x \vdash (\lambda x\, t) \cdot e : \tau}\,(\to E)}{\Sigma_x \vdash (\text{let } x \text{ be } e \text{ in } t) : \tau .}\,(\text{definition of let-terms})$$

At (*) we made use of the assuption $\Sigma_x \cup \{ x : \sigma_1, \ldots, x : \sigma_m \} \vdash t : \tau$ from the let-rule, and weakening. This reduction essentially relies on

$$(**) \qquad \dfrac{\Sigma_x \cup \{ x : \sigma_1, \ldots, x : \sigma_m \} \vdash t : \tau, \qquad \sigma \leq_{\Sigma_x} \sigma_1, \ldots, \sigma \leq_{\Sigma_x} \sigma_m, \qquad (\text{i.e. } \sigma_i = \sigma[\tau_{i1}/a_1, \ldots, \tau_{in}/a_n])}{\Sigma_x \vdash \lambda x\, t \;:\; (\forall a_1 \ldots a_n . \sigma) \to \tau \quad .}$$

We inferred a type for λxt that is $\geq \bigwedge\{\sigma_1, \ldots, \sigma_m\}. \to \tau$ above, as any function applicable to all objects of type $\bigwedge\{\sigma_1, \ldots, \sigma_m\}$ is, by restriction, applicable to all objects of "explicitly polymorphic" type $\forall a_1 \ldots a_n . \sigma$. Clearly, the Milner inference system is incapable of well typing functions like λxt that take polymorphic objects as arguments.

As far as I know, it is still an open problem to extend the Hindley-Milner type inference system to cover explicitly polymorphic types in such a way that it remains quickly decidable whether a term can be typed (cf. Reynolds [1985], Mitchell[1986]). Until this is settled, it may be useful to find out the limits of Milners trick:

Problem 1:

Can the Hindley-Milner type inference system be extended by typing rules that assign types to (useful) complex terms (other than let- or rec-terms) while not all of their subterms can be typed ?

For example, the let-rule implicitly allows to *apply* terms t of type $(\forall a_1 \ldots a_n . \sigma) \to \tau$ to other terms, and it seems to complete the calculus in this respect. But the fixed-point combinator Y may not be the only useful operator $Z : ((\forall a_1 \ldots a_n . \sigma) \to \tau) \to \rho$ which might be added to the system to *be applied to* such terms t. The resulting term Zt should have quantifier free type ρ.

Discussion of the rec-rule:

In the type inference system of Milner[1978] - or rather in the notion of well-typing used there - recursively defined objects get typed according to the simple fixed-point rule

$$(\text{fix}) \qquad \dfrac{\Sigma_x \cup \{ x : \sigma \} \vdash e : \sigma}{\Sigma_x \vdash (\text{rec}\, x\, e) : \sigma .}$$

This obviously is an instance of our more complicated rule (rec). The advantage of (rec) is that in finding a type for e we may assume different types for x, which all have to be instances of a single type scheme. For example, using the rec-rule we can type as follows (with α not free in Σ_x):

$$\frac{\Sigma_x \cup \{x:(\alpha\to\alpha),\ x:\alpha\} \vdash (xx):\alpha, \qquad \alpha \le_{\Sigma_x} \alpha, \qquad \alpha \le_{\Sigma_x} (\alpha\to\alpha) = \alpha[(\alpha\to\alpha)/\alpha]}{\Sigma_x \vdash (\mathrm{rec}\ x\ (xx)):\alpha.}$$

Note that we cannot type (rec x (xx)) using (fix) as we are forced to assume a unique type for x in the fix-rule, which does not suffice to deduce a type for (xx). Thus (rec) is stronger than (fix). Milner (personal communication, Feb.1987) also has a version of (fix) in the spirit of the let-rule, but I don't know its precise form.

To motivate (rec), we assume $\Sigma_x \vdash Y : \forall\alpha((\alpha\to\alpha)\to\alpha)$ and that $\alpha_1, \ldots, \alpha_n$ do not occur free in $\sigma_1, \ldots, \sigma_m$ or Σ_x. Using (**) above and taking $\sigma^* := (\forall\alpha_1\ldots\alpha_n.\sigma)$, we can derive (rec), again using some rules to be given in the following section:

$$\dfrac{\dfrac{\dfrac{\Sigma_x \cup \{x:\sigma_1, \ldots, x:\sigma_m\} \vdash e:\sigma}{\Sigma_x \cup \{x:\sigma_1, \ldots, x:\sigma_m\} \vdash e:\sigma^*,}\,(\forall\, I) \qquad \sigma \le_{\Sigma_x} \sigma_1, \ldots, \sigma \le_{\Sigma_x} \sigma_m}{\Sigma_x \vdash \lambda x\, e : (\forall\alpha_1\ldots\alpha_n.\sigma)\to\sigma^*}\,(**) \qquad \dfrac{\Sigma_x \vdash Y : \forall\alpha((\alpha\to\alpha)\to\alpha)}{\Sigma_x \vdash Y : (\sigma^*\to\sigma^*)\to\sigma^*}\,(\mathrm{weak})}{\dfrac{\Sigma_x \vdash Y\cdot(\lambda x\, e):\sigma^*}{\dfrac{\Sigma_x \vdash (\mathrm{rec}\ x\ e):\sigma^*}{\Sigma_x \vdash (\mathrm{rec}\ x\ e):\sigma.}\,(\mathrm{weak})}\,(\text{def. of rec-terms})}\,(\to E)$$

In the special case of the fix-rule we take $\sigma_1 = \ldots = \sigma_m = \sigma$ and hence can do with (quantifier free) type *schemes* $\Sigma_x \vdash \lambda x\, e : \sigma\to\sigma$ and $\Sigma_x \vdash Y : (\sigma\to\sigma)\to\sigma$ in order to show $\Sigma_x \vdash (\mathrm{rec}\ x\ e):\sigma$.

We have used the assumption that Y has type $\forall\alpha((\alpha\to\alpha)\to\alpha)$, which, however, is not derivable using the Curry/Milner rules. We either may add $Y : \forall\alpha((\alpha\to\alpha)\to\alpha)$ as an axiom to the type inference system Alternatively, we can infer type $(\alpha\to\alpha)\to\alpha$ for Y if we allow types $\beta = (\beta\to\alpha)$, i.e. if we admit recursive types (c.f. MacQueen e.a.[1984]).

The main advantage of Milners original system over more expressive ones (cf. Reynolds[1985], Cardelli and Wegner[1985], Boehm[1985]) lies in the following properties, which establich its practical importance for ML-like languages:

1. Existence of principle types: The set of types which can be inferred for a term t is the set of substitution instances into one single type scheme, which is called the *principle type* of t (cf. Milner[1978] Hindley[1969]), and
2. Decidability of type inference: There is an algorithm (Algorithm W of Milner[1978]) which decides whether a type for t can be inferred, and if so, computes the principle type of t (cf. Damas/Milner[1982]).

As we will model objects for object-oriented languages as recursive records in section 4, we want a typing rule as strong as possible to allow for flexible recursive definitions of objects. In order to build an automatic type inference algorithm for these languages, we would like to have the above properties for well-typings according to the stronger system:

Problem 2:
Do we still have decidability of type inference and computability of principle types for the calculus with (rec) instead of (fix) ?

It is interesting that W can handle applications of (let) - and (fix) - simply by unification of type schemes. This is no longer the case for applications of (rec), although this rule is much in the spirit of (let). We think that Problem 2 has a positive answer, and give more details and a partial result on this in the last section.

2. Polymorphic types and subtyping

In the preceding section, *polymorphism*, i.e. the fact that a term can have several well-typings, has been treated implicitly by means of free type variables, which some people call parameter polymorphism. As we have seen in dealing with (let) and (rec), there is also a need for types that code polymorphism explicitly by binding type variables. In the following we extend the notion of well-typings by adding type quantifiers and corresponding inference rules. The universal quantifiers will be interpreted by intersection of types. Let us call a type expression *explictly polymorphic*, if it can be obtained using the formation rules of definition 1 together with:

If α is a type variable and σ a type, then $\forall\alpha\sigma$ is a type.

From now on, unless stated otherwise, by "type" we mean "explicitly polymorphic type", and well-typings refer to the calculus consisting of (Var), ($\rightarrow$ I), ($\rightarrow$ E) and the following rules ($\forall$ I) - ($\forall$ S), where Σ is supposed to contain typing statements for basic terms, and inequalities for basic type expressions only. As for terms, we tacitly assume a rule for renaming of bound variables in types.

Introduction and elimination rules for universal quantifiers are as follows:

$$(\forall I)\quad \frac{\Sigma \vdash e:\sigma,\ \alpha \text{ not free in } \Sigma}{\Sigma \vdash e:\forall\alpha\,\sigma} \qquad\qquad (\forall E)\quad \frac{\Sigma \vdash e:\forall\alpha\,\sigma}{\Sigma \vdash e:\sigma[\tau/\alpha]}$$

We axiomatize the subtype relation $\leq$ as a partial order which respects derivability and a given theory Σ on types.

$$(\leq_1)\quad \frac{(\sigma \leq \tau) \in \Sigma}{\Sigma \vdash \sigma \leq \tau} \qquad (\leq_2)\quad \frac{\sigma \text{ is a basic type}}{\Sigma \vdash \sigma \leq \sigma} \qquad (\leq_3)\quad \frac{\Sigma \vdash \sigma \leq \tau,\quad \Sigma \vdash \tau \leq \rho}{\Sigma \vdash \sigma \leq \rho}$$

$$(\text{weak})\quad \frac{\Sigma \vdash e:\sigma,\quad \Sigma \vdash \sigma \leq \tau}{\Sigma \vdash e:\tau} \qquad\qquad \frac{\Sigma \vdash \psi \text{ for each } \psi \in \Psi,\quad \Psi \vdash e:\sigma}{\Sigma \vdash e:\sigma}$$

Next we have to fix the relationship between $\leq$ and type constructors:

$$(\rightarrow \leq)\quad \frac{\Sigma \vdash \sigma_1 \leq \sigma_2, \quad \Sigma \vdash \tau_1 \leq \tau_2}{\Sigma \vdash (\sigma_2 \rightarrow \tau_1) \leq (\sigma_1 \rightarrow \tau_2)}$$

$$(\forall \leq)\quad \frac{}{\Sigma \vdash \forall \alpha\, \sigma \leq \sigma[\tau/\alpha]} \qquad \frac{\Sigma \vdash \sigma \leq \tau, \quad \alpha \text{ not free in } \Sigma \cup \{\sigma\}}{\Sigma \vdash \sigma \leq \forall \alpha\, \tau}$$

As we are concerned with total functions, the function space constructor $\rightarrow$ is monotone in its second, but antitone in its first argument.

Quantified types provide us with what might be called semi-recursive types, such as $\beta := \forall\gamma(\gamma \rightarrow \alpha)$, satisfying $\beta \leq (\beta \rightarrow \alpha)$, but they do not give recursive types, defined by, for example, $\beta = (\beta \rightarrow \alpha)$. Thus we can get self-applicable functions $f : \beta \leq (\beta \rightarrow \alpha)$, but cannot yet type Y.

<u>Proposition 1</u>:

a) Axiom scheme (sub) and Milners (let) are derived rules.

b) (fix) and (rec), with $\Sigma_x \vdash \sigma \leq \tau$ instead of $\sigma \leq_{\Sigma_x} \tau$, are equivalent relative to the above calculus, and if $Y: \forall\alpha.(\alpha \rightarrow \alpha) \rightarrow \alpha$ is added, are derived rules.

Proof: Clearly (sub) is obtained using $(\forall \leq)$. From (weak) we get

(***) If $\Sigma_x \cup \{x:\sigma_1, \ldots, x:\sigma_m\} \vdash t:\tau$ and $\Sigma_x \vdash \sigma \leq \sigma_1, \ldots, \sigma \leq \sigma_m$, then $\Sigma_x \cup \{x:\sigma\} \vdash t:\tau$.

Hence it is equivalent whether we add (fix) or (rec). It also follows that (**) of section 1 holds, by

$$\frac{\Sigma_x \cup \{x:\sigma_1, \ldots, x:\sigma_m\} \vdash t:\tau, \qquad \dfrac{\sigma \leq_{\Sigma_x} \sigma_1, \ldots, \sigma \leq_{\Sigma_x} \sigma_m, \quad \text{i.e. } \sigma_i = \sigma[\tau_{i1}/\alpha_1, \ldots, \tau_{in}/\alpha_n]}{\Sigma_x \vdash \forall\alpha_1 \ldots \alpha_n.\sigma \leq \sigma_i \quad \text{for } i = 1, \ldots, n}\,(\forall \leq)}{\dfrac{\Sigma_x \cup \{x: \forall\alpha_1 \ldots \alpha_n.\sigma\} \vdash t:\tau}{\Sigma_x \vdash \lambda x\, t : (\forall\alpha_1 \ldots \alpha_n.\sigma) \rightarrow \tau.}}\,(***)$$

By the reductions in the previous section, (let) and - modulo $Y : \forall\alpha\, ((\alpha \rightarrow \alpha) \rightarrow \alpha)$ - also (rec) is a derived rule of this system.

But note that (***) does not hold for Milners inference system and $\leq_{\Sigma_x}$ instead of $\leq$. We will not deal with (if) in our calculus, adding a constant if : $\forall\alpha(\text{boole} \rightarrow (\alpha \rightarrow (\alpha \rightarrow \alpha)))$ when necessary.

Finally, universal type quantification and function space constructor are related via quantifier scope using $\sigma = \tau$ to abbreviate $\sigma \leq \tau$ and $\tau \leq \sigma$:

$(\forall S)$ $\qquad \Sigma \vdash \forall\alpha(\sigma \rightarrow \tau) = (\sigma \rightarrow \forall\alpha\tau)$, if α does not occur free in σ.

A semantics of typing statements and type inequalities is now given by a simplified form of Mitchells[1986] models of type inference. He avoids mixing the syntax of type expressions with the notion of models at the cost of using a model of typed λ-calculus to provide a syntax-independent domain for [[ ]].

Definition 2: A structure $D = (D, \cdot, \varepsilon, T, [[\ ]])$ is a *model of type inference* if

(i) $D = (D, \cdot, \varepsilon)$ is a λ-model of the untyped λ-calculus,

(ii) T is a family of subsets of D, called the set of *types of D*, and

(iii) $[[\ ]]$: type expressions $\times$ (type variables $\to$ T) $\to$ T is an evaluation function for type expressions, such that for all types σ, τ, ρ, type variables α and type environments e :

(a) $\varepsilon \cdot ([[\sigma]]\,e \to [[\tau]]\,e) \subseteq [[(\sigma \to \tau)]]\,e \subseteq ([[\sigma]]\,e \to [[\tau]]\,e)$,

where $(A \to B) := \{ d \mid d \in D, d \cdot A \subseteq B \}$ is the set of all elements representing functions from A to B, and $d \cdot A := \{ d \cdot a \mid a \in A \}$, for $A, B \subseteq D$ and $d \in D$;

(b) $[[\forall\alpha\sigma]]\,e = \cap\{ [[\sigma]]\,e[A/\alpha] \mid A \in T \}$.

If e is understood we sometimes write D_σ instead of $[[\sigma]]e$. There are two extreme ways to interpret function types: *simple models* are those where in (iii) (a) function type $D_{(\sigma \to \tau)}$ is taken to be the set $(D_\sigma \to D_\tau)$ of *all* elements representing functions from D_σ to D_τ. On the other hand, *F-models (function models)* are those where type $D_{(\sigma \to \tau)}$ is taken to be the set of just the *function* elements of D taking D_σ to D_τ, i.e. the set $\varepsilon \cdot (D_\sigma \to D_\tau) = \{ \varepsilon \cdot d \mid d \in D, d \cdot A \subseteq B \}$. Recall that $\varepsilon \cdot d = [[\lambda y(xy)]]\,[d/x]$ is the unique function element that represents the (unary) function represented by d.

Definition 3:

Let e be an environment assigning elements of D to individual variables and sets from T to type variables. A typing statement *t:τ holds in D with respect to e*, or: $D \models (t : \tau)e$, if $[[t]]e \in [[\tau]]e$. A type inequality *σ≤τ holds in D with respect to e*, or: $D \models (\sigma \leq \tau)e$, if $[[\sigma]]e \subseteq [[\tau]]e$. A statement *holds* in D if it holds in D with respect to every environment.

If Σ is a set of type assignment statements and inequalities between type expressions, we say *D satisfies* Σ, or: $D \models \Sigma$, if each ψ in Σ holds in D with respect to every environment.

Correctness of the above inference rules can be verified by a simple induction on the length of proofs:

Theorem 1

Let Σ be a type assignment, D a simple model of type inference and e an environment such that $D \models \Sigma\, e$.

1. Semantic subtyping: For any types σ and τ, if $\Sigma \vdash \sigma \leq \tau$ is provable, then $D \models (\sigma \leq \tau)\, e$.
2. Soundness of typing: For any term t and type τ, if $\Sigma \vdash t{:}\tau$ is provable, then $D \models (t{:}\tau)\, e$.

The same holds for function models, too, if we drop axiom ($\forall$ S). As Mitchell has shown, $\forall\alpha(\sigma \to \tau) \leq (\forall\alpha\sigma \to \forall\alpha\tau)$ and hence ($\forall$ S) does not hold in all models of type inference. For function models, we still have $\varepsilon \cdot D_{\forall\alpha(\sigma \to \tau)} \subseteq D_{\sigma \to \forall\alpha\tau} \subseteq D_{\forall\alpha(\sigma \to \tau)}$, if α is not free in σ, but $D_{\forall\alpha(\sigma \to \tau)} \subseteq D_{\sigma \to \forall\alpha\tau}$ and hence ($\forall$ S) need not be true. For simple models, $D_{\forall\alpha(\sigma \to \tau)} = D_{\sigma \to \forall\alpha\tau}$ is easily checked.

The theorem does not hold for arbitrary models simply because the denotation of function-type expressions is not a function of the denotation of their subexpressions. The same applies to record- and class-type expressions of the following sections. However, the *semantic* type constructors (function space, intersection, as well as (union,) record building and class selection below) have monotony properties which validate the subtype rules and transfer to simple and function semantics for type expressions.

A completeness theorem, restricted to validity, can be derived from Mitchells results.

Theorem 2

Let Σ be a type assignment and ψ a typing statement or type inequality. Then $\Sigma \vdash \psi$ is provable if and only if $D \models \psi e$ for every simple model $D \models \Sigma e$ and environment e.

Proof: (Sketch)

By reduction to the completeness theorem for calculus $\vdash_{sc}$ of Mitchell[1986]. Axiom schemes of $\vdash_{sc}$ are (sub) and (dist) : $\forall a_1 \ldots a_n.(\sigma \to \tau) \leq (\forall a_1 \ldots a_n.\sigma \to \forall a_1 \ldots a_n.\tau)$, and rules corresponding to (weak$_1$), ($\leq_3$), ($\to \leq$), and

$$(\mathrm{Var})_{\leq} \quad \frac{x:\sigma \in \Sigma, \quad \Sigma \vdash \sigma \leq \tau}{\Sigma \vdash x:\tau}, \qquad (\forall \leq)_{cong} \quad \frac{\Sigma \vdash \sigma \leq \tau, \ a \text{ not free in } \Sigma}{\Sigma \vdash \forall a\sigma \leq \forall a\tau}$$

$$(\to \mathrm{I})_{\forall,\leq} \quad \frac{\Sigma_x \cup \{x:\sigma\} \vdash e:\tau, \quad \Sigma_x \vdash \forall a_1 \ldots a_n.(\sigma \to \tau) \leq \rho, \quad a_1 \ldots a_n \text{ not free in } \Sigma_x}{\Sigma_x \vdash \lambda x\, e : \rho}$$

$$(\to \mathrm{E})_{\forall,\leq} \quad \frac{\Sigma \vdash t: \forall a_1 \ldots a_n.(\sigma \to \tau), \ \Sigma \vdash s: \forall a_1 \ldots a_n.\sigma, \quad \Sigma \vdash \forall a_1 \ldots a_n.\tau \leq \rho}{\Sigma_x \vdash t \cdot s : \rho}$$

We derive (dist) via $\Sigma \vdash \forall a(\sigma \to \tau) \leq (\sigma \to \tau) \leq (\forall a\sigma \to \tau) \leq \forall a\, (\forall a\sigma \to \tau) \leq (\forall a\sigma \to \forall a\, \tau)$, using ($\to \leq$) in the second and ($\forall$ S) (i.e. simple semantics) in the last step. The rules are easily seen to be derivable as well. Hence, if $\Sigma \vdash \psi$ is not provable, it is not provale using $\vdash_{sc}$, and there is a simple model D in Mitchells sense and an environment e with $D \models \Sigma$ e, but not $D \models \psi$ e. But each (simple) model in his sense gives rise to a (simple) model in our sense, satisfying the same statements.

Notes:

1. Simple models are interesting because it seems more likely that principle types exist if we restrict to simple semantics. It might be useful in this respect to add $\exists$-quantifiers, interpreted by union of types, to get type expressions with reduced quantifier scopes, which also might be useful to obtain principle types. For example, the following are valid in simple models:

   ($\forall$ S$_2$) $\quad \Sigma \vdash \exists a(\sigma \to \tau) \leq (\forall a\sigma. \to \tau)$, if a does not occur free in τ

   ($\exists$ S$_1$) $\quad \Sigma \vdash \exists a(\sigma \to \tau) \leq (\sigma \to \exists a\tau)$, if a does not occur free in σ

   ($\exists$ S$_2$) $\quad \Sigma \vdash \forall a(\sigma \to \tau) = (\exists a\sigma. \to \tau)$, if a does not occur free in τ

   $$(\exists \leq) \quad \frac{\Sigma \vdash \sigma \leq \tau, \quad a \text{ not free in } \Sigma \cup \{\tau\}}{\Sigma \vdash \exists a\, \sigma \leq \tau} \qquad \frac{}{\Sigma \vdash \sigma[\tau/a] \leq \exists a\sigma}$$

2. As Cardelli and Wegner[1985] pointed out, bounded quantifiers $\forall a \leq \rho$ are useful in object-oriented programming. For example, by using $f: \forall a \leq \rho.(a \to \tau)$ instead of $f: \rho \to \tau[\rho/a]$, we parameterize the result type of f by the type of the argument, getting better information about the type of (f·e) when e : $a \leq \rho$. Thus, when a zoom-function f defined on rectangles is typed in this way, we may zoom a square and know the result to be a square, not just a rectangle, even if the subclass of squares did not yet

exist when f was defined. However, bounded quantifiers pose some additional problems to automatic type inference, as to what type inequalities have to be removed from the assumptions in an $(\forall\alpha\leq\sigma)$-introduction rule.

3. In section 1 we have seen that $\Sigma \vdash (\text{rec } x\,(xx)) : \alpha$, even for empty Σ, hence $\vdash (\text{rec } x\,(xx)) : \forall\alpha\,\alpha$. Thus the intersection of all types is nonempty in every model with $Y{:}\forall\alpha((\alpha\rightarrow\alpha)\rightarrow\alpha)$. For the existence of such models, see Mitchell[1986] or MacQueen e.a.[1984].

3. Record types and classes of object-oriented programming

In object-oriented programming languages, programs and data are grouped together into objects. An object consists of a storage to keep the data and of a series of functions which may be applied to these data, possibly with further arguments. For example, a stack is an object in this sense: it has a content which is a sequence of data units, functions push and pop to insert data into or extract it from its content, and a test function to check whether its content is empty. The precise definition of these functions may be private to the stack object, and only the names of the functions are public as the interface to the stored information. Thus without knowing its internal structure, we can ask the stack to push a given data unit onto its content, or to pop a data unit from its content. The stack itself knows how to interpret these messages "push <data unit>" and "pop".

We can think of objects as records, i.e. as finite functions from names (labels) to values. Field selection for records is then just function application; yet we use the familiar dot-notation for field selection in the following. We first have to extend the notions of term and type to account for records and record-types.

<u>Definition 4</u>: Let A be an infinite set of new symbols which we call *labels*.

i) If $a_1, \ldots, a_n$ are pairwise distinct labels, and $t_1, \ldots, t_n$ are terms, then $(a_1 = t_1, \ldots, a_n = t_n)$ is a (record-) term. If $(a_1 = t_1, \ldots, a_n = t_n)$ is a record term, then $(a_1 = t_1, \ldots, a_n = t_n).a_i$ is a term, for $i = 1, \ldots, n$.

ii) If $a_1, \ldots, a_n$ are pairwise distinct labels and $\tau_1, \ldots, \tau_n$ are type expressions, then $(a_1{:}\tau_1, \ldots, a_n{:}\tau_n)$ is a (record-) type expression.

In a model D of λ-calculus, for $A_1, \ldots, A_n \subseteq \dot{D}$ and labels $a_1, \ldots, a_n$, we define the record type

$$(a_1 : A_1, \ldots, a_n : A_n) := \{ d \mid d \in D, d\cdot a_i \in A_i \text{ for } i = 1, \ldots, n\}$$

by taking all elements of D which represent functions mapping each a_i to a member of A_i.

To be able to deal with record type expressions in models $D = (D, \cdot, \varepsilon, T, [[\ ]])$ of type inference, add the following condition on the evaluation function $[[\ ]]$:

(iii) (c) For all distinct labels $a_1, \ldots, a_n$, all type expressions $\tau_1, \ldots, \tau_n$ and type environments e:

$$\varepsilon\cdot(a_1{:}\,[[\tau_1]]\,e, \ldots, a_n{:}\,[[\tau_n]]\,e) \subseteq [[(a_1{:}\,\tau_1, \ldots, a_n{:}\,\tau_n)]]\,e \subseteq (a_1{:}\,[[\tau_1]]\,e, \ldots, a_n{:}\,[[\tau_n]]\,e).$$

Again, in a *simple* model we demand $[[(a_1{:}\,\tau_1, \ldots, a_n{:}\,\tau_n)]]\,e$ to be the set $(a_1{:}\,[[\tau_1]]\,e, \ldots, a_n{:}\,[[\tau_n]]\,e)$ of *all* elements of D which represent functions mapping each a_i to a member of A_i, whereas in a *function* model we take the corresponding set $\varepsilon\cdot(a_1{:}\,[[\tau_1]]\,e, \ldots, a_n{:}\,[[\tau_n]]\,e)$ of *function* elements only.

In order to give meaning to a record term $(a_1 = t_1, \dots, a_n = t_n)$ in a model D, we have to choose a particular function mapping a_i onto the value of t_i. In order to do this, we use a theorem of Böhm, Coppo e.a. on separable sets of λ-terms. The theorem says that given distinct closed terms $a_1, \dots, a_n$ in βη-normal form, for any terms $t_1, \dots, t_n$ there is a term t such that $t{\cdot}a_i = t_i$ is provable, for $i = 1, \dots, n$ (cf. Barendregt [1984], Corollary 10.4.14.). Such a term t, call it $B(a_1, \dots, a_n, t_1, \dots, t_n)$, is constructed from $a_1, \dots, a_n$ and $t_1, \dots, t_n$ in the proof of the theorem. Hence from now on we use closed βη-normal forms as labels, and adopt the following term reduction rules:

$$(a_1 = t_1, \dots, a_n = t_n) \quad := \quad B(a_1, \dots, a_n, t_1, \dots, t_n), \quad \text{and}$$

$$(a_1 = t_1, \dots, a_n = t_n).a_i \; := \; (a_1 = t_1, \dots, a_n = t_n){\cdot}a_i \quad \text{for } i = 1, \dots, n.$$

Record terms and field selection terms get types according to the following rules:

$$(\mathrm{RI}) \quad \frac{\Sigma \vdash e_i : \sigma_i, \quad \text{for } i = 1, \dots, n}{\Sigma \vdash (a_1 = e_1, \dots, a_n = e_n) : (a_1{:}\sigma_1, \dots, a_n{:}\sigma_n)} \qquad (\mathrm{RE}) \quad \frac{\Sigma \vdash e : (a_1{:}\sigma_1, \dots, a_n{:}\sigma_n)}{\Sigma \vdash e.a_i : \sigma_i}$$

The notion of subtype is extended to records in such a way that subrecords may contain additional components:

$$(\mathrm{R} \le) \quad \frac{\Sigma \vdash \sigma_i \le \tau_i, \quad \text{for } i = 1, \dots, n}{\Sigma \vdash (a_1{:}\sigma_1, \dots, a_n{:}\sigma_n, a_{n+1}{:}\sigma_{n+1}, \dots, a_m{:}\sigma_m) \le (a_1{:}\tau_1, \dots, a_n{:}\tau_n)}$$

As opposed to Bruce and Wegner[1986] we do not need coercer functions and still have a notion of subrecord which fits well with what is needed in object-oriented programming languages.

4. Classes as types of records with fixed components

Although a record sometimes is seen as a satisfying model of what an object in languages like Smalltalk, Loops, or Lisp Flavors is (cf. Cardelli[1985], Bruce and Wegner[1986]), we think this does not capture all essential aspects of such languages. One point in question is the notion of a class. A class roughly is a description of the structure and behaviour of similar objects, and is used to generate new objects with the same structure and behaviour. As it seems impossible to model functions that create new objects of a given class within a fixed static structure, we only look at the static aspects of classes and think of the collection of objects belonging to a class as a type of our models. In order to describe the behaviour of its objects, a class fixes the values of their functional components. Thus, for example, any two stacks operate the same way, although they may store different information. The class "stack" then will contain defining terms for the functions "push" and "pop". Hence class types are defined relative to individual terms, which describe the fixed functional values.

Definition 5:

i) If $a_1, \dots, a_n, b_1, \dots, b_k$ are pairwise distinct labels, $\sigma_1, \dots, \sigma_n, \tau_1, \dots, \tau_k$ are type expressions and $t_1, \dots, t_k$ are terms, then $((a_1{:}\sigma_1, \dots, a_n{:}\sigma_n, b_1{:}\tau_1, \dots, b_k{:}\tau_k)$ with b_1 by $t_1, \dots, b_k$ by $t_k)$ is a (class-) type expression.

ii) If, moreover, $e_1, \ldots, e_n$ are terms and x is an individual variable, then (obj x $(a_1 = e_1, \ldots, a_n = e_n; b_1 = t_1, \ldots, b_k = t_k)$) is a (object- or instance-) term.

iii) If e is a term and b is a label, then (send b to e) is a (message send-) term.

We only treat messages without further arguments; messages with additional arguments might be handled using (send b $t_1 \ldots t_r$ to e) := (send b to e) $t_1 \ldots t_r$.

In a model D of λ-calculus, we define class types by selection from record types. That is, for distinct labels $b_1, \ldots, b_k$, subset A and elements $d_1, \ldots, d_k$ of D we put

$$(A \text{ with } b_1 \text{ by } d_1, \ldots, b_k \text{ by } d_k) := \{ d \mid d \in A, d \cdot b_1 = d_1 \cdot d, \ldots, d \cdot b_k = d_k \cdot d \}.$$

Then all elements d of a class type have the same behaviour in so far as they all understand the "messages" b_j in the same way: if d is send the message b_j with additional data $s_1, \ldots, s_k$, this is evaluated as $d \cdot b_j \cdot s_1 \cdot \ldots \cdot s_k = d_j \cdot d \cdot s_1 \cdot \ldots \cdot s_k$, i.e. the reciever d interprets the message b_j as the function d_j and applies it to himself and the additional arguments. We have to make d one of d_j's arguments in order to give the function (represented by) d_j access to the data stored within the "object" d.

To evaluate a class type expression in a model $D = (D, \cdot, \varepsilon, T, [[\ ]])$ of type inference, add the following condition on the evaluation function [[ ]].

(iii) (d) For all distinct labels $a_1, \ldots, a_n, b_1, \ldots, b_k$, all type expressions $\sigma_1, \ldots, \sigma_n, \tau_1, \ldots, \tau_n$, terms $t_1, \ldots, t_k$ and environments e:

$$[[((a_1{:}\sigma_1, \ldots, a_n{:}\sigma_n, b_1{:}\tau_1, \ldots, b_k{:}\tau_k) \text{ with } b_1 \text{ by } t_1, \ldots, b_k \text{ by } t_k)]]\, e \ := \ ([[(a_1{:}\sigma_1, \ldots, a_n{:}\sigma_n, b_1{:}\tau_1, \ldots, b_k{:}\tau_k)]]\, e \text{ with } b_1 \text{ by } [[t_1]]\, e, \ldots, b_k \text{ by } [[t_k]]\, e),$$

which in simple models is just

$$((a_1 : [[\sigma_1]]\, e, \ldots, a_n : [[\sigma_n]]\, e, b_1 : [[\tau_1]]\, e, \ldots, b_k : [[\tau_k]]\, e) \text{ with } b_1 \text{ by } [[t_1]]\, e, \ldots, b_k \text{ by } [[t_k]]\, e).$$

Note that we may have free type variables in τ_i and free individual variables in t_j. Hence we can deal with parameterized classes in a smooth manner. As distinct closed βη-normal forms b get distinct values in every model, we simply wrote b instead of [[b]] e.

Finally, the meaning of an object term is given by the term reduction rule

$$(\text{obj } x\, (a_1 = e_1, \ldots, a_n = e_n; b_1 = t_1, \ldots, b_k = t_k)) := (\text{rec } x\, (a_1 = e_1, \ldots, a_n = e_n, b_1 = t_1, \ldots, b_k = t_k)),$$

and the term denotes an instance of the class $((a_1{:}\sigma_1, \ldots, a_n{:}\sigma_n, b_1{:}\tau_1, \ldots, b_k{:}\tau_k)$ with b_1 by $\lambda x t_1, \ldots, b_k$ by $\lambda x t_k)$. Thus instances of classes are, in general, *recursive* records. The bound variable x corresponds to Smalltalks pseudo variable "self". A special notation is needed in order to distinguish syntactically between object and record terms in type inference. Writing x^* for (rec x $(a_1 = e_1, \ldots, a_n = e_n, b_1 = t_1, \ldots, b_k = t_k)$) we get

$$x^* \cdot a_i = (a_1 = e_1, \ldots, a_n = e_n, b_1 = t_1, \ldots, b_k = t_k)[x^*/x] \cdot a_i = e_i[x^*/x], \quad \text{and}$$

$$x^* \cdot b_j = (a_1 = e_1, \ldots, a_n = e_n, b_1 = t_1, \ldots, b_k = t_k)[x^*/x] \cdot b_j = t_j[x^*/x] = (\lambda x t_j) \cdot x^*.$$

If x occurs free in t_j we can define the behaviour of instances uniformly in terms of their internal structure. (Building the fixed components into the instance term is weaker than an explicit pointer from instances to the class definition in Smalltalk etc., but also partially codes the class into its instances.)

In particular, the meaning of send expressions can be given by the reduction rule

$$(\text{send } b \text{ to } e) := e.b,$$

hence message sending is interpreted as field selection, which in turn is function application. But note that field b of e is obtained by applying λxt to e, if $e : (\sigma \text{ with } .., b \text{ by } \lambda xt, \dots)$.

Introduction for class types is allowed in the following form:

$$\text{(C I)}\quad \frac{\Sigma_x \cup \{x:\sigma\} \vdash (a_1 = e_1, \dots, a_n = e_n, b_1 = t_1, \dots, b_k = t_k) : \sigma, \quad \sigma := (a_1{:}\sigma_1, \dots, a_n{:}\sigma_n, b_1{:}\tau_1, \dots, b_k{:}\tau_k)}{\Sigma_x \vdash (\text{obj } x\ (a_1 = e_1, \dots, a_n = e_n; b_1 = t_1, \dots, b_k = t_k)) : (\sigma \text{ with } b_1 \text{ by } \lambda xt_1, \dots, b_k \text{ by } \lambda xt_k),}$$

Note that the assumptions are sufficient to derive $\Sigma_x \vdash (\text{rec } x\ (a_1 = e_1, \dots, a_n = e_n, b_1 = t_1, \dots, b_k = t_k)) : \sigma$. As opposed to arbitrary record terms, object terms can only be used in a rather limited way, as the following rule (C E) will show. Namely, components $b_1, \dots, b_k$ define the interface to the object: the object will only "understand" messages b_j, but "reject" $a_1, \dots, a_n$. (This has been encoded into the object term by the semicolon, thus forcing a type checker not to infer a class type that allows $a_1, \dots, a_k$ as messages, too.) Yet, it is important that the assumptions in (C I) above allow us to treat x as a record, so we can access every component of x using terms $x.a_i$ and $x.b_j$ *within* e_l *and* t_m. (Consequently, depending on the meaning λxt_j given to b_j, by sending b_j to the object we may indirectly be allowed to extract the a_i-component from outside.)

$$\text{(C E)}\quad \frac{\Sigma \vdash e : ((a_1{:}\sigma_1, \dots, a_n{:}\sigma_n, b_1{:}\tau_1, \dots, b_k{:}\tau_k) \text{ with } b_1 \text{ by } \lambda xt_1, \dots, b_k \text{ by } \lambda xt_k)}{\Sigma \vdash (\text{send } b_j \text{ to } e) : \tau_j .}$$

Although we can easily check that in simple or function models, for any environment e and record type $\sigma = (a_1{:}\sigma_1, \dots, a_n{:}\sigma_n, b_1{:}\tau_1, \dots, b_k{:}\tau_k)$, we have

$$[[(\sigma \text{ with } b_1 \text{ by } \lambda xt_1, \dots, b_k \text{ by } \lambda xt_k)]]\, e \subsetneq [[\sigma]]\, e,$$

we do not make the class type (σ with b_1 by $\lambda xt_1, \dots, b_k$ by λxt_k) be a subtype of σ. Otherwise the weakening rules would allow a type inference algorithm to circumvent the objects interface of message sending.

We define the subclass relation different from the corresponding relation in object-oriented languages. A subclass in these languages describes the structure of its members by adding components to the structure of members of a superclass. It also may add or change the behaviour of its members in comparison to the behaviour of members of the superclass.

In our system, a *subclass type* is a subrecord type of the classes record type, which fixes all the components that are fixed by the class - using the very same values -, but may fix some other components, too:

$$(C\leq)\quad \frac{\Sigma\vdash\sigma_i\leq\sigma_i{}^{*}\quad \text{for } i=1,\ldots,n,\qquad \Sigma\vdash\tau_j\leq\tau_j{}^{*}\quad\text{for } j=1,\ldots,k}{\Sigma\vdash((a_1{:}\sigma_1,\ldots,a_{n+m}{:}\sigma_{n+m},b_1{:}\tau_1,\ldots,b_{k+r}{:}\tau_{k+r})\text{ with } b_1 \text{ by } t_1,\ldots,b_{k+r}\text{ by } t_{k+r})\leq ((a_1{:}\sigma_1{}^{*},\ldots,a_n{:}\sigma_n{}^{*},b_1{:}\tau_1{}^{*},\ldots,b_k{:}\tau_k{}^{*})\text{ with } b_1\text{ by } t_1,\ldots,b_k\text{ by } t_k)}$$

The difference to real object-oriented languages is threefold:

1. In Smalltalk, Lisp Flavors etc., the subclass relation is given explicitly, i.e. by pointers from the subclass to its (immediate) superclass(es). We instead do subclassing by comparison of the structure of class types. Consequently, we have "multiple inheritance": a class type can be a subtype of more than one class types.
2. We do not allow to overwrite a fixed value t_j when going to a subclass; instead, we have to install a class of its own. Arbitrary overwriting in our opinion does not fit well to the idea of similar behaviour for objects in the same class.
   The understandability of an object-oriented programming environment depends heavily on how well the subclass relations reflect the behaviour of objects. Yet, in languages like Smalltalk nothing is done to prevent a programmer from arbitrary redefining. Hence the systems understandability relies on name *conventions*.
   Also, in common systems there is a problem in multiple inheritance: if different superclasses of a class have a functional component named f, say, which of the corresponding values is to be inherited to be the value of f in the subclass? If there is no overwriting, there is no such problem.
3. In common object-oriented languages classes *are* objects, which they are not in our system. Of course, to each class type $((a_1{:}\sigma_1,\ldots,a_n{:}\sigma_n,b_1{:}\tau_1,\ldots,b_k{:}\tau_k)$ with b_1 by $t_1,\ldots,b_k$ by $t_k)$ we can associate a record $(a_1=\bot,\ldots,a_n=\bot,b_1=t_1,\ldots,b_k=t_k)$, using some default element $\bot{:}\forall\alpha.\alpha$. But in order to model the dynamic aspects of classes, like creating new or editing existing objects, we had to make these records dynamic, either by using updatable components or by modelling objects in general as streams. Along these lines, it seems possible to model Smalltalks *metaclasses*. This would be more adequate, but forced us to admit recursive types.

Remark:

Still, it is a natural and practical requirement that a subclass may *refine* the behaviour of its objects, compared to those of its superclasses. In order to allow for refinements which cannot be obtained by mere addition of functional components, one has to fix a notion of refined function. In the above framework of subclass types, this can be done using terms $t_i{}^{*}$ instead of t_i in the superclass, and coercion functions from subtypes to supertypes which make the following diagram commute:

$$\begin{array}{ccc} \tau_i & \leq_{\text{coerce}} & \tau_i{}^{*} \\ t_i\uparrow & & \uparrow t_i{}^{*} \\ (a_1{:}\sigma_1,\ldots,a_{n+m}{:}\sigma_{n+m},b_1{:}\tau_1,\ldots,b_{k+r}{:}\tau_{k+r}) & \leq_{\text{coerce}} & (a_1{:}\sigma_1{}^{*},\ldots,a_n{:}\sigma_n{}^{*},b_1{:}\tau_1{}^{*},\ldots,b_k{:}\tau_k{}^{*}). \end{array}$$

Note, however, that in order to ensure commutativity by structure of the class type expressions, we have to introduce a partial order on function *terms* which implies a corresponding partial order on the denoted functions. For given simple coercion functions - such as dropping additional components - this may be possible, but we do not see how to do it in a reasonably general form. But, for example, we think that a limited use of Smalltalks "super" can be modelled along these lines.

Abstract classes of Smalltalk correspond to those class types where all components have predescribed values. These classes do not have (nontrivial) instances, but their subclasses may do. An abstract class can only fix the behaviour of its subclasses instances, possibly in terms of labels which are given meanings in subclasses only.
More generally, it is important that labels are a kind of "top level names" which everybody may use as messages. Their meaning, however, is determined by the object recieving this message, or rather by its class. Thus adding new classes to the system changes the "global" meaning of a label. It seems questionable whether a type system for object-oriented languages has to assign types to labels, and whether it consequently has to view the meaning of a label as a function which is defined by modular, implicit distinction on the recievers class. (By the way, this way of implicit distinction on cases implies much of the flexibility of object-oriented languages.) In this case, labels might get (dynamic) variant types. In the system above, we have decided not to do so: labels need not be typed at all.

It is easy to see that theorem 1 of section 2 on soundness with respect to simple models (or function models, if we omit (∀ S)) also hold when record types and class types are included.

5. Extending Milners Algorithm W

Automatic type inference in the presence of subtypes and type quantifiers is an open problem, and the existence of principle types is not known (cf.Mitchell[1986]). Hence we now return to the quantifier-free system of section 1 in order to extend Milners type infernce algorithm W to deal with (rec) instead of (fix) and show how record and class types are to be treated. Clearly this is a severe restriction in the context of object-otriented languages with parameterized classes. On the other hand, it seems possible to extend the ideas of this section by adding subtyping along the lines of Mitchell[1984].

Let R, S, T be substitutions of types for type variables, e, s, t be terms and ρ, σ, τ be type expressions. Σ is a type assignment and $x, x_1, \ldots, x_n$ are individual variables.

Milners algorithm W takes a term e and a type assignment Σ for the free variables of e, and either fails or returns a substitution S of types for type variables and a type σ, satisfying the following conditions:

(i) If $W(\Sigma, e) = (S, \sigma)$ then $\Sigma S \vdash e : \sigma$ is a well-typing.

(ii) If there is a well-typing $\Sigma^* \vdash e : \sigma^*$ and a substituition T with $\Sigma T\,|_{free(e)} = \Sigma^*\,|_{free(e)}$, then
- $W(\Sigma, e) = (S, \sigma)$ for some S and σ, and
- there is R such that $SR\,|_{free(e)} = T\,|_{free(e)}$ and $\sigma R = \sigma^*$.

(iii) If there is no well-typing $\Sigma^* \vdash e : \sigma^*$ and substituition T with $\Sigma T\,|_{free(e)} = \Sigma^*\,|_{free(e)}$, then $W(\Sigma, e)$ = fail.

Note that, with respect to well-typings, by (i) W is correct and by (ii) is complete and computes principle types. W terminates by (iii) and (ii), and hence it is decidable whether a well-typing instance $\Sigma T \vdash e : \sigma^*$ for (Σ, e) exists.

5.1 Extending W to (rec)

Recall that in this context, types do not contain quantifiers and there is no explicit subtype relation. First note that the calculus does not assume that variables get at most one type in Σ, but W always does, as it deals with type assignments. Hence instead of assuming one variable x with different types we have to substitute each occurrence of x in e by a new variable x_i:

$W(\Sigma, (\text{rec } x\ e)) :=$

$(SR\,|_{free(\Sigma)}, \sigma R)$,

if $W(\Sigma \cup \{x_1{:}\alpha_1, \ldots, x_n{:}\alpha_n\}, e^*) = (S, \sigma)$, where $\alpha, \alpha_1, \ldots, \alpha_n$ are distinct new type variables, $x_1, \ldots, x_n$ are distinct new variables not free in $\Sigma \cup \{e\}$, $e = e^*[x/x_1, \ldots, x/x_n]$, and R is the most general substitution T with $\sigma T \leq_{\Sigma ST} \alpha_i ST$ for $i = 1, \ldots, n$,

fail, else.

Conjecture:

It can be decided whether a most general T with the given properties exists. That is,we conjecture that there is an algorithm $\text{Unify}_{\leq\Sigma}(\sigma; \tau_1, \ldots, \tau_n)$ which either computes a substitution R such that

(a) $\sigma R \leq_{\Sigma R} \tau_i R$ for $i = 1, \ldots, n$, and

(b) for any T with $\sigma T \leq_{\Sigma T} \tau_i T$ for $i = 1, \ldots, n$, there is a substitution U such that $T = RU$ (on the relevant free variables),

or fails, if there is no R satisfying (a).

Note that even if this is not true we get a correct type inference algorithm stronger that Milners simply by testing whether $\sigma \leq_{\Sigma S} \alpha_i S$, instead of looking for a most general T with $\sigma T \leq_{\Sigma ST} \alpha_i ST$, for $i = 1, \ldots, n$.

We now show that given the conjeczture, the extended algorithm W satisfies (i) - (iii). An example and hints on how to define $\text{Unify}_{\leq\Sigma}(\sigma; \tau_1, \ldots, \tau_n)$ are given below.

(i) Correctness of W:

$W(\Sigma \cup \{x_1{:}\alpha_1, \ldots, x_n{:}\alpha_n\}, e^*) = (S, \sigma) \Rightarrow \Sigma S \cup \{x_1{:}\alpha_1 S, \ldots, x_n{:}\alpha_n S\} \vdash e^* : \sigma, \Rightarrow \Sigma SR \cup \{x_1{:}\alpha_1 SR, \ldots, x_n{:}\alpha_n SR\} \vdash e^* : \sigma R, \Rightarrow \Sigma SR \cup \{x{:}\alpha_1 SR, \ldots, x{:}\alpha_n SR\} \vdash e : \sigma R$. As $\sigma R \leq_{\Sigma SR} \alpha_i SR$, we get $\Sigma SR \vdash (\text{rec } x\ e) : \sigma R$ by an application of (rec).

(ii) Completeness of W:

In order to show that $W(\Sigma, (\text{rec } x\ e))$ does not fail, suppose there is a well-typing $\Sigma^* \vdash (\text{rec } x\ e) : \sigma^*$ and a substitution T with $\Sigma T\,|_{free(rec\ x\ e)} = \Sigma^*\,|_{free(rec\ x\ e)}$. To facilitate notation, we may assume $\Sigma T = \Sigma^*$, i.e. disregard typings of variables not free in (rec x e). The last step in proving $\Sigma^* \vdash (\text{rec } x\ e) : \sigma^*$ must have been an application of (rec), and hence there are types $\sigma_1, \ldots, \sigma_n$ such that

a) $\Sigma T \cup \{x{:}\sigma_1, \ldots, x{:}\sigma_n\} \vdash e{:}\sigma^*$ and b) $\sigma^* \leq_{\Sigma T} \sigma_1, \ldots, \sigma^* \leq_{\Sigma T} \sigma_n$ (with x not free in ΣT).

We may assume that n is the number of free occurrences of x in e, and thus $\Sigma T \cup \{x_1{:}\sigma_1, \ldots, x_n{:}\sigma_n\} \vdash e^*{:}\sigma^*$, using a). For fresh type variables $\alpha_1, \ldots, \alpha_n$, by induction we get substitutions S and R such that

c) $W(\Sigma \cup \{x_1{:}\alpha_1, \ldots, x_n{:}\alpha_n\}, e) = (S, \sigma)$ and d) $T = SR$, $\sigma^* = \sigma R$, and $\sigma_i = \alpha_i SR$ for $i = 1, \ldots, n$.

From b) and d) we obtain $\sigma R \leq_{\Sigma SR} \alpha_i SR$ for all i. Take the most general substitution R^* by the (conjectured) algorithm above, and split R into R^*T^* for suitable T^*. Then $W(\Sigma, (\text{rec } x\ e)) = (SR^*, \sigma R^*)$, $(SR^*)T^* = SR = T$ and $(\sigma R^*)T^* = \sigma R = \sigma^*$, which would prove (ii).

(iii) Termination of W and decidability of type inference using (rec):
If for no T and σ^* we have $\Sigma T \vdash (\text{rec } x\ e) : \sigma^*$, then either there is no well typing $\Sigma S \cup \{x_1{:}\alpha_1 S, \ldots, x_n{:}\alpha_n S\}$ $\vdash e^* : \sigma$ - which, by induction, is decidable using W -, or for the most general such (S,σ), equal to $W(\Sigma \cup \{x_1{:}\alpha_1, \ldots, x_n{:}\alpha_n\}, e^*)$, there is no R with $\sigma R \leq_{\Sigma SR} \alpha_i SR$ for i = 1, ..., n. By the conjecture, there is no most general such R, and then $\text{Unify}_{\leq \Sigma S}(\sigma; \alpha_1 S, \ldots, \alpha_n S) = \text{fail}$, hence $W(\Sigma, \text{rec } x\ e) = \text{fail}$.

Example: $\varnothing \vdash (\text{rec } x.\ (\lambda yz.yz)(xx)) : \beta \rightarrow \gamma$ is a well-typing.
First note that

$$W(\varnothing, \lambda yz.yz) = ([/], (\beta \rightarrow \gamma) \rightarrow (\beta \rightarrow \gamma)) \quad \text{and}$$

$$W(\{x_1{:}\alpha_1, x_2{:}\alpha_2\}[/], (x_1 x_2)) = ([(\alpha_2 \rightarrow \alpha_3)/\alpha_1], \alpha_3) \quad \text{for some new type variable } \alpha_3.$$

In computing $W(\{x_1{:}\alpha_1, x_2{:}\alpha_2\}, (\lambda yz.yz)(x_1 x_2))$, type α_3 of $(x_1 x_2)$ is unified with the argument type $(\beta \rightarrow \gamma)$ of $(\lambda yz.yz)$, yielding

$$W(\{x_1{:}\alpha_1, x_2{:}\alpha_2\}, (\lambda yz.yz)(x_1 x_2)) = ([(\alpha_2 \rightarrow (\beta \rightarrow \gamma))/\alpha_1], (\beta \rightarrow \gamma)) =: (S, \sigma).$$

Finally, using $\Sigma = \varnothing = \Sigma SR$ and $R = [(\beta \rightarrow \gamma)/\alpha_2]$ ($= \text{Unify}_{\leq \Sigma}(\beta \rightarrow \gamma; \alpha_2 \rightarrow (\beta \rightarrow \gamma), \alpha_2)$ below), we have

$$\sigma R = (\beta \rightarrow \gamma) \leq_{\Sigma SR} \alpha_1 SR = (\alpha_2 \rightarrow (\beta \rightarrow \gamma))R = (\beta \rightarrow \gamma) \rightarrow (\beta \rightarrow \gamma), \text{ and}$$

$$\sigma R = (\beta \rightarrow \gamma) \leq_{\Sigma SR} \alpha_2 SR = \alpha_2 R = (\beta \rightarrow \gamma).$$

Clearly R is most general, and hence $W(\varnothing, (\text{rec } x.\ (\lambda yz.yz)(xx))) = (SR\restriction_{free(\varnothing)}, \sigma R) = ([/], (\beta \rightarrow \gamma))$. Note that R is needed, since it is not the case that $\sigma \leq_{\Sigma S} \alpha_2 S$.

The example is simple as $\Sigma = \varnothing$. For comparison note $W(\{z{:}(\beta \rightarrow \gamma) \rightarrow (\beta \rightarrow \gamma)\}, (\text{rec } x.\ z(xx))) = \text{fail}$, as from

$$\{z{:}(\beta \rightarrow \gamma) \rightarrow (\beta \rightarrow \gamma)\} \cup \{x_1{:}\alpha_2 \rightarrow (\beta \rightarrow \gamma), x_2{:}\alpha_2\} \vdash z(x_1 x_2) : (\beta \rightarrow \gamma)$$

no substitution R gives $(\beta \rightarrow \gamma)R \leq_{\Sigma SR} (\alpha_2 \rightarrow (\beta \rightarrow \gamma))R$ and $(\beta \rightarrow \gamma)R \leq_{\Sigma SR} \alpha_2 R$, since $\Sigma = \Sigma S = \{z{:}(\beta \rightarrow \gamma) \rightarrow (\beta \rightarrow \gamma)\}$ contains β and γ. But, of course, in the extended system with type quantifiers we get

$$\{z{:}\forall\beta\gamma.(\beta \rightarrow \gamma) \rightarrow (\beta \rightarrow \gamma)\} \cup \{x{:}\forall\beta\gamma.(\beta \rightarrow \gamma)\} \vdash z(xx) : \forall\beta\gamma.\beta \rightarrow \gamma,$$

and then $\{z{:}\forall\beta\gamma.(\beta \rightarrow \gamma) \rightarrow (\beta \rightarrow \gamma)\} \vdash (\text{rec } x.\ z(xx)) : \forall\beta\gamma.\beta \rightarrow \gamma$.

Remark on the conjecture:
It is sufficient to define $\text{Unify}_{\leq \Sigma}(\sigma, \tau)$ instead of $\text{Unify}_{\leq \Sigma}(\sigma; \tau_1, \ldots, \tau_n)$. We then get $\text{Unify}_{\leq \Sigma}(\sigma; \tau_1, \ldots, \tau_n)$ by taking $\text{Unify}_{\leq \Sigma}(f(\sigma, \ldots, \sigma), f(\tau_1, \ldots, \tau_n))$ for some (pseudo-) type constructor f. Let α be a type variable, σ and τ be arbitrary types, and $\text{unify}(\tau_1, \ldots, \tau_n)$ denote ordinary Herbrand/Robinson unification of terms.

$\text{Unify}_{\leq \Sigma}(\alpha, \tau) :=$

- $[/]$, if α is not free in Σ,
- $\text{unify}(\alpha, \tau)$, if α is free in Σ and τ is not a type variable

$\mathrm{Unify}_{\leq\Sigma}(\sigma, \alpha) :=$

$[\sigma'/\alpha, \beta_1''/\beta_1, \ldots, \beta_n''/\beta_n]$,

if α is not free in σ, $\{\beta_1, \ldots, \beta_n\} = \mathrm{free}(\sigma) \setminus \mathrm{free}(\Sigma)$, $\beta_1', \ldots, \beta_n''$ are distinct fresh variables, and $\sigma' := \sigma[\beta_1'/\beta_1, \ldots, \beta_n'/\beta_n]$,

fail, else

$\mathrm{Unify}_{\leq\Sigma}(f(\sigma_1, \ldots, \sigma_n), f(\tau_1, \ldots, \tau_n)) :=$

R, if for $i = 1, \ldots, n$, $R_i := \mathrm{Unify}_{\leq\Sigma}(\sigma_i, \tau_i) \neq \mathrm{fail}$, $\mathrm{dom}(R) := \cup\{\mathrm{dom}(R_i) \mid i = 1, \ldots, n\}$, and for each $\beta \in \mathrm{dom}(R_i)$, $\beta R := \beta R_i\, \mathrm{unify}(\beta R_1, \ldots, \beta R_n) \neq \mathrm{fail}$, and $f(\sigma_1, \ldots, \sigma_n)R \leq_{\Sigma R} f(\tau_1, \ldots, \tau_n)R$,

fail, else.

We can show that $\mathrm{Unify}_{\leq\Sigma}(\alpha, \tau)$ and $\mathrm{Unify}_{\leq\Sigma}(\sigma, \alpha)$ satisfy what we need in the conjecture. On the other hand, we know of more cases than given in the above definition when $\mathrm{Unify}_{\leq\Sigma}(f(\sigma_1, \ldots, \sigma_n), f(\tau_1, \ldots, \tau_n))$ should not fail, but these seem to be hard to state precisely (and do not seeem to occur often in programming). In particular, if R as given satisfies $\sigma_i R \leq_{\Sigma R} \tau_i R$ for all i, it needs not satisfy $f(\sigma_1, \ldots, \sigma_n)R \leq_{\Sigma R} f(\tau_1, \ldots, \tau_n)R$, while a substitution instance of R still might do.

Note: After finishing this paper, H.Schlütter pointed out to me that Mycroft[1984] has given a partial solution to problem 2 of section 1. He showed that in the presence of (a variant of) the rec-rule, each well-typable term has a principle type, which can be computed iteratively. However, he has no decision procedure for the existence of well-typings, and asks for a non-iterating (and terminating) algorithm to compute principle types more efficiently. We think that both can be obtained as outlined by the conjecture above.

5.2 Extending W to record and class types (without type quantification and subtype relation)

The following clauses extending the definition of W do not fit exactly to rules (RI) - (C E) of section 4, as we here do not assume a subtype relation.

$W(\Sigma, (a_1{:}e_1, \ldots, a_n{:}e_n))$:

$W(\Sigma, ()) :=$

$([/], ())$,

$W(\Sigma, r\bullet(a{:}e)) :=$

$(S_r S, \sigma_r S\bullet(a{:}\sigma))$, if $W(\Sigma, r) = (S_r, \sigma_r)$ and $W(\Sigma S_r, e) = (S, \sigma)$,

fail, else,

where $(a_1{:}e_1, \ldots, a_n{:}e_n)\bullet(b_1{:}t_1, \ldots, b_m{:}t_m) := (a_1{:}e_1, \ldots, a_n{:}e_n, b_1{:}t_1, \ldots, b_m{:}t_m)$, and similarly for record type expressions.

$W(\Sigma, e.a_i) :=$

(S, σ_i), if $W(\Sigma, e) = (S, (a_1{:}\sigma_1, \ldots, a_n{:}\sigma_n))$,

fail, else.

$W(\Sigma, (\text{obj } x\ (a_1 = e_1, ..., a_n = e_n; b_1 = t_1, ..., b_m = t_m)) :=$

$(SR\,|_{free(\Sigma)}, (\sigma R \text{ with } b_1 \text{ by } \lambda x t_1, ..., b_m \text{ by } \lambda x t_m)),$

if $W(\Sigma \cup \{x_1:\rho_1, ..., x_k:\rho_k\}, e) = (S, \sigma)$, where $\rho_i := (a_1:\alpha_{i1}, ..., a_n:\alpha_{in}, b_1:\beta_{i1}, ..., b_m:\beta_{im})$ with distinct fresh type variables $\alpha_{i1}, ..., \alpha_{ik}, \beta_{i1}, ..., \beta_{im}$ for $i = 0, ..., k$, and $x_1, ..., x_n$ are distinct fresh variables not free in $\Sigma \cup \{e\}$, such that $(a_1:e_1, ..., a_n:e_n, b_1:t_1, ..., b_m:t_m) = e[x/x_1, ..., x/x_n]$, and R is the most general substitution T with $\sigma T \leq_{\Sigma ST} \rho_i ST$ for $i = 1, ..., k$,

fail, else.

This step corresponds to the following inference rule which is tailored to a quantifier-free type system without explicit subtyping:

$$(CI)'\quad \frac{\Sigma_x \cup \{x:\sigma_1, ..., x:\sigma_k\} \vdash (a_1 = e_1, ..., a_n = e_n, b_1 = t_1, ..., b_m = t_m) : \sigma, \qquad \sigma \leq_{\Sigma_x} \sigma_i \text{ for } i = 1, ..., k}{\Sigma_x \vdash (\text{obj } x\ (a_1 = e_1, ..., a_n = e_n; b_1 = t_1, ..., b_m = t_m)) : (\sigma \text{ with } b_1 \text{ by } \lambda x t_1, ..., b_m \text{ by } \lambda x t_m),}$$

i.e. if $(a_1 = e_1, ..., b_m = t_m)$ can be assigned a record type σ when different occurrences of x in e_i or t_j are seen as records of types weaker than σ, then the recursive record $x = (a_1 = e_1, ..., b_m = t_m)$ gets type σ and can be made an object by specifying an interface $b_1, ..., b_m$.

$W(\Sigma, (\text{send } b \text{ to } e)) :=$

(S, τ_j), if for some record type $\rho = (a_1:\sigma_1, ..., a_n:\sigma_n, b_1:\tau_1, ..., b_m:\tau_m)$ and some terms $t_1, ..., t_m$, $W(\Sigma, e) = (\rho \text{ with } b_1 \text{ by } t_1, ..., b_m \text{ by } t_m)$ and $b = b_j$,

fail, else.

Summary:

In programming languages, polymorphic terms are those that can be assigned various types. In the ML-type discipline, polymorphism comes by type expressions containing free type variables. Implicitly, a limited form of universally quantified types are also allowed. We have shown that, without changing the overall properties of the type system, the recursion operator can be made polymorphic in a way that allows to assign types to terms which have no types in ML.

We have motivated the introduction of a subtype relation as a generalization of the ML substitution of types for type variables. Subtype polymorphism then covers parameter or substitution polymorphism as a special case. Finally, we have modelled classes of object-oriented programming languages using a selection operation on record types. The subtype relation, applied to class types, allows for multiple inheritance, but does not allow to redefine functions in subclasses. It thus covers some important aspects of subclasses of object-oriented languages, but abandons those which do not fit well to the intuitve concept of grouping objects of similar behaviour together.

A type inference calculus has been given to deal with parameterized types, quantified type variables, subtyping and class-types in a uniform manner. We have given semantic account for type inference rules by introducing interpretations based on models of type-free lambda calculus. Whether the set of typings of a term is finitely representable has only been considered for a sublanguage, and has not not been fully answered.

References:

H.Barendregt [1984] : The Lambda Calculus. Its Syntax and Semantics. Revised Edition. Studies in Logic and the Foundations of Mathematics, Vol. 103 North-Holland Publishing Co., Amsterdam 1984

H.J.Boehm [1985] : Partial polymorphic type inference is undecidable. 26th Annual Symposium on Foundations of Computer Science (1985), p.339 - 345

K.B.Bruce, P.Wegner [1986] : An Algebraic Model of Subtype and Inheritance (Extended Abstract). Preprint Sept. 1986, Williams College, Brown University

A.H.Borning, D.H.H.Ingalls [1982] : A Type Declaration and Inference System for Smalltalk. Conference Record of the Ninth Annual ACM Symposium on Principles of Programming Languages (1982), p. 133 - 139

L.Cardelli [1984] : A Semantics of Multiple Inheritance. Proceedings of the International Symposium on Semantics of Data Types, LNCS 173, p. 51 - 67, Springer-Verlag, Berlin 1984

L.Cardelli, P.Wegner [1985] : On Understanding Types, Data abstraction, and Polymorphism. Computing Surveys, vol. 17, no. 4, December 1985, p. 471 - 522

A.Goldberg, D.Robson [1983] : Smalltalk-80: The Language and its Implementation. Addison-Wesley Publishing Company, Reading, Massachusetts 1983

J.R.Hindley [1969] : The Principal Type-Scheme of an Object in Combinatory Logic. Transactions of the AMS 146 (1969), p. 29-60

J.R.Hindley, J.P.Seldin (eds.) [1980] : To H.B.Curry: Essays on Combinatory Logic, Lambda Calculus and Formalism. Academic Press, New York and London, 1980

W.Howard [1980] : The formulae-as-types notion of construction, in: J.R.Hindley, J.P.Seldin (eds.) [1980], p. 479 - 490

R.E.Johnson [1986] : Type-Checking Smalltalk. Proceedings of the First ACM Symposium on Object-Oriented Programming Systems, Languages, and Applications (OOPSLA '86), p. 315 - 321 Special Issue of SIGPLAN Notices vol.21, no.11, Nov. 1986

D.MacQueen, G.Plotkin, R.Sethi [1984] : An ideal model for recursive polymorphic types. Conference Record of the Ninth Annual ACM Symposium on Principles of Programming Languages (1984), p. 165 - 174

R.Milner [1978] : A Theory of Type Polymorphism in Programming. Journal of Computer and System Sciences 17 (1978), p. 348 - 375

J.C.Mitchell [1984] : Type Inference and Type Containment. Proceedings of the International Symposium on Semantics of Data Types. LNCS 173, p. 257 - 277, Springer-Verlag, Berlin 1984

J.C.Mitchell [1986] : Polymorphic type inference and containment (Revised Draft, July 9, 1986). To appear in: Information and Control.

A.Mycroft[1984]: Polymorphic Type Schemes and Recursive Definitions.
Proceedings of the International Symposium on Programming, 6th Colloquium, LNCS 167, p. 217 - 228, Springer-Verlag, Berlin 1984

J.C.Reynolds [1985]: Three Approaches to Type Structure.
TAPSOFT advanced Seminar on the Role of Semantics in Software Development.
LNCS 185, p. 97 - 138, Springer-Verlag, Berlin 1985

N.Suzuki [1981]: Inferring Types in Smalltalk.
Conference Record of the Eighth Annual ACM Symposium on Principles of Programming Languages (1981), p. 187 - 199

Optimization Aspects of Logical Formulas

Ulrich Löwen*

FB 11 – Fachgebiet Praktische Informatik
Universität – GH – Duisburg
D-4100 Duisburg 1 (West-Germany)

Abstract

We consider logical formulas and we are interested in the question whether a clause γ is a consequence of a given formula α. We investigate the problem whether efficiency of an algorithm deciding deducibility $\alpha \models \gamma$ for some clause γ can be improved by learning from queries γ' having been answered by the algorithm before. Thus, instead of α we consider a formula α' being equivalent to α. In the first part of this paper we show a connection of this kind of optimization problem to the P=NP-problem. Afterwards we consider Prolog programs and the Prolog inference strategy under these aspects of optimization presenting various possibilities of optimizing propositional Prolog programs.

1 Introduction

In this paper we consider propositional calculus formulas α and we investigate the problem whether efficiency of an algorithm deciding deducibility $\alpha \models \gamma$ for some clause γ can be improved by learning from queries γ' having been answered by the algorithm before. Thus, we try to find a formula α' after each question γ such that α and α' are equivalent. This formula also has the property that the complexity of the algorithm deciding deducibility has been reduced at least for those queries having been asked for already.

In the next chapter we consider this problem from a more theoretical point of view. First we show various attempts to examine the corresponding optimization problem giving a formal definition of the corresponding approach. Further, we show a connection of these kinds of optimization problems to the P=NP-problem proving that P≠NP if a propositional calculus formula cannot be optimized. Most of these considerations can be found in [KBLö 87] as well.

*The work of the author was supported by the Studienstiftung des Deutschen Volkes

In chapter 3 we consider propositional calculus Prolog programs and the Prolog inference strategy under the aspect of optimizing a logical formula. We present classes of Prolog programs which can be optimized using the well-known inference strategy of Prolog, whereas we can prove on the other side that there are classes of Prolog programs which cannot be optimized. We mention that these results essentially depend on the inference strategy taken as basis as pointed out in chapter 3, too. Some of the results of that chapter can be found in [KBLö 88b] also.

Optimization problems appear in many fields of computer science. Especially in the field of artificial intelligence one needs efficient algorithms due to the size of the search space, because naive generate-and-test procedures with backtracking often result in gross inefficiency or may even make a problem impossible to solve. Therefore various sophisticated search strategies have been considered (see [Nil 82]) or intelligent backtracking strategies have been analyzed like e. g. selective backtracking [PePo 82] or there has been optimized the backtrack search [Nat 87]. Our fundamental statement of the problem however is more general, but our considerations concerning optimization of Prolog programs are analogous to the just mentioned approaches. Another approach of an optimization problem having a formulation of the question related to our basic intention can be found in [GeSm 85].

We assume that the reader is familiar with basic notations and facts from logic. For unexplained terminology, notations, and basic results borrowed from logic we refer to standard textbooks like e. g. [Sho 67] or [Bör 85]. Further, the reader should be well acquainted with the depth-first-search control strategy with backtracking of Prolog. Otherwise the reader should consult Prolog textbooks like e. g. [ClMe 84] or [KBSch 86].

2 The Optimization Problem

2.1 Optimizing Logical Formulas

Concerning with logical formulas we often have to decide the question whether a formula γ is a consequence of a given formula α. Often there are many questions to one fixed formula α, sometimes one inquires for the same question several times. If a program answers $\alpha \models \gamma$ there are deduced in general many consequences of α. Generally these consequences are provisional results and normally they will be generated each time renewed. We assumed that these informations should not be overlooked and that the complexity of the algorithm can be reduced by adding suitable consequences generated during the computation to α. One can expect that by this modification of α various later questions can be answered more efficient. Thus, we investigate the problem whether efficiency of an algorithm deciding $\alpha \models \gamma$ can be improved by learning from queries γ' having been answered before, which outlines briefly the *optimization problem* of logical formulas.

In our approach we restrict ourselves to propositional calculus, further, we restrict attention to queries γ being clauses, i. e. disjunctions of literals, where a literal is an atom or a negated atom. This is no essential restriction. Additionally we assume without loss of generality that $atomset(\gamma) \subseteq atomset(\alpha)$. Thus, the problem whether γ is a consequence of α is coNP-complete, since $\alpha \models \gamma$ if and only if $\alpha \wedge \neg\gamma$ is not satisfiable (see [Coo 71]). This shows that from a practical point of view the problem of deducibility is a hard problem and therefore any kind of optimization is desirable. But there is a difference between inconsistency and the problem of deducibility: Considering deducibility we can distinguish between the formula α being fixed for *each* query and the question γ changing in each instance of the problem, whereas in the case of inconsistency this distinction is not taken into account in the proof of the coNP-completeness.

Now let us present two aspects of optimization, the formal definition of the optimization problem from a more theoretical point of view will be given in the next section. First let us speak about *dynamic optimization*. Let $\mathcal{T}(\alpha, \gamma)$ denote the complexity of an arbitrary but fixed algorithm deciding $\alpha \models \gamma$. Consider a formula α and let γ be a clause being a consequence of α. Obviously, α and $\alpha \wedge \gamma$ are equivalent and most algorithms occurring in practice satisfy

$$\mathcal{T}(\alpha \wedge \gamma, \gamma) \leq \mathcal{T}(\alpha, \gamma).$$

Hence, we can learn from a consequence γ by adding γ to the underlying formula. But unfortunately this approach is not practicable, since the number of consequences γ (satisfying the restrictions mentioned above) of a formula α is exponential in $atomset(\alpha)$ and an exponential increase of space cannot be attended from a practical point of view. Therefore we impose a polynomial bound (in the length of the original formula α) on the length of all formulas taken into consideration. Thus, we have to add *suitable* consequences only or we have to eliminate various redundant clauses from α after each question in such a way that we do not make worse the complexity for those queries having been answered before. This yields to

Problem (dynamic optimization) *For some propositional calculus formula α, a clause γ, and a fixed algorithm deciding $\alpha \models \gamma$ find a formula $opt_d(\alpha, \gamma)$ being equivalent to α satisfying the following conditions: for arbitrary clauses γ_i let*

$$\begin{aligned} \alpha_0 &:\equiv \alpha \\ \alpha_i &:\equiv opt_d(\alpha_{i-1}, \gamma_i) \end{aligned}$$

Then $length(\alpha_i)$ is bounded uniformly by some fixed polynomial in $length(\alpha)$, the algorithm decides $\alpha_i \models \gamma_i$ efficient, and $\mathcal{T}(\alpha_i, \gamma_j) \leq \mathcal{T}(\alpha_{i-1}, \gamma_j)$ for $1 \leq j < i$.

Considering dynamic optimization we should distinguish two cases: In the case that a clause γ is implied by α we could choose $\alpha \wedge \gamma$ for $opt_d(\alpha, \gamma)$. Though this method, if applied ruthlessly, can result in an exponential explosion in the size of the formula, we have at least some intuition how to improve the complexity of $\alpha \models \gamma$ if γ is a consequence of α. In the case that a clause γ is not implied by α we unfortunately have not any idea how to choose $opt_d(\alpha, \gamma)$, which leads to a refinement of the problem of dynamic optimization, where we consider only such clauses γ_i being consequences of α. Thus, we do not demand that a query γ can consequence γ we can decide $\alpha \models \gamma$ efficient even in the case of $\alpha \not\models \gamma$ by returning the answer **FAIL** after $\max\{T(\alpha,\gamma) \mid \alpha \models \gamma\}$ steps of computation.

Another aspect concerns *static optimization*, where we try to find an optimized formula $opt_s(\alpha)$ being equivalent to α such that *each* query can be answered efficient using $opt_s(\alpha)$, formally speaking

Problem (static optimization) *For some propositional calculus formula α and an algorithm deciding $\alpha \models \gamma$ for a clause γ find a formula $opt_s(\alpha)$ being equivalent to α such that length($opt(\alpha)$) is polynomially bounded in length(α) and the algorithm decides $opt_s(\alpha) \models \gamma$ efficient for any clause γ.*

From a practical point of view we can use a preprocessor in the case of static optimization transforming a given formula α to the optimized formula $opt_s(\alpha)$ and afterwards the formula will not be modified any longer, whereas in the case of dynamic optimization the formula is modified during the execution and there will be obtained an optimized formula approximatively. Though for practice the aspects of static and dynamic optimization are very different approaches, let us point out that these two problems are equivalent from a more theoretical point of view: Assume that there exists for any formula α and any clause γ a formula $opt_d(\alpha,\gamma)$ satisfying the conditions of dynamic optimization. Then the problem of static optimization can be solved by choosing

$$opt_s(\alpha) :\equiv opt_d(\ldots opt_d(opt_d(\alpha,\gamma_1),\gamma_2)\ldots,\gamma_n)\ ,$$

where $\{\gamma_1,\ldots,\gamma_n\}$ is the set of all clauses γ satisfying $atomset(\gamma) \subseteq atomset(\alpha)$. Obviously, $opt_s(\alpha)$ defined in such a way satisfies the conditions of static optimization. On the other side assume that there exists for any formula α a formula $opt_s(\alpha)$ satisfying the conditions of static optimization. Then $opt_d(\alpha,\gamma)$ defined by

$$opt_d(\alpha,\gamma) :\equiv opt_s(\alpha)$$

trivially satisfies the conditions of dynamic optimization. Hence, dynamic optimization implies static optimization and vice versa.

2.2 The Optimization Problem and the P=NP-Problem

In this section we define the optimization problem exactly stipulating that *efficient* means decidable deterministically in polynomial time:

Definition (optimization problem) *Given a propositional calculus formula α. Does there exist a formula $opt(\alpha)$ being equivalent to α such that length($opt(\alpha)$) is bounded polynomially in length(α) and $opt(\alpha) \models \gamma$ can be decided deterministically in polynomial time for clauses γ satisfying $atomset(\gamma) \subseteq atomset(\alpha)$?*

Note that we have defined the optimization problem in such a way that we demand an improvement for the *worst-case* complexity of $\alpha \models \gamma$. From a practical point of view results concerning the average complexity would be more desirable, but results for the average complexity of algorithms in logic are very rare, since the arising combinatorial problems are very complex. We refer to [Gol 79], [BrPu 81],

[BrGoPu 82], [BrPu 85], [Spe 87], and [Spe 88], where the average complexity of various algorithms for testing satisfiability of various classes of propositional calculus formulas are investigeated. Concerning average complexity there additionally arises the problem of finding a distribution being relevant for practice.

It is an accepted fact that all problems being decidable in a time justifiable from a practical point of view are decidable deterministically in polynomial time. Therefore, from a practical point of view the complexity of $opt(\alpha)$ should be bounded polynomially in $length(\alpha)$ and we could modify the optimization problem by imposing a bound on the degree of the polynomial. Such a refinement would be desirable for practice, but we do not consider such changes, since we are not able to solve even the optimization problem as formulated above. Perhaps it is more promising to investigate classes of logical formulas having a higher worst-case complexity than propositional calculus such that the size of improvement, which is demanded by the optimization, is in a sense smaller than a worst-case improvement from coNP to P. But up to now we have not succeeded in finding such a class of formulas. For each class of predicate calculus formulas, which we have considered for optimization, there arised similar problems as in the case of propositional calculus.

To see the difficulty of the optimization problem assume that P=NP. In this case let $opt(\alpha) :\equiv \alpha$ and the optimization problem is trivial. Consequently, if we cannot optimize propositional calculus formulas we have proved P$\neq$NP. On the other side it is an open problem whether P$\neq$NP implies that propositional calculus formulas cannot be optimized. These relations reveal the difficulty of the optimization problem and the difficulty becomes perhaps more obvious, if we consider the following modification: we stipulate that $opt(\alpha)$ has the form $\alpha \wedge \gamma$ for some clause γ being a consequence of α. Reasoning intuitively we cannot optimize propositional calculus formulas in this way, but if we could prove this assertion we have proved P$\neq$NP.

The difficulty of the optimization problem has led us to consider modifications of the optimization problem. There are various approaches like considering a fixed algorithm (e. g. resolution) deciding deducibility, or restricting attention to special kinds of queries (e. g. clauses of restricted length), or regarding special classes of formulas. Results concerning the first two approaches can be found in [KBLö 87], where the optimization problem has been strengthened in this way: a polynomial time bound is demanded only for those clauses being a consequence of the formula. This rejects the potential objection that for special procedures we cannot reduce the complexity by considering an equivalent formula, if we ask for a clause which is not a consequence of the underlying formula. This problem has been mentioned already in the previous section. But concerning the last approach we investigate in the next chapter propositional Prolog programs and the Prolog inference strategy under the aspect of optimization.

3 Optimization of Prolog Programs

3.1 Prolog Programs and SLD-Resolution

We briefly introduce some definitions and describe the Prolog inference strategy, which is based on SLD-resolution first described in [Kow 74]. Further details can be found in e. g. [ApEm 82].

We regard a *Prolog program* as a sequence of clauses $A \leftarrow A_1, \ldots, A_n$, where A is called the *head* and $A_1, \ldots, A_n$ the *body* of the clause. For atoms $A, B \in \mathit{atomset}(\pi)$ of a Prolog program π we write $A \prec^1 B$, if there is a clause in π having the head A and a body containing B. Further, let $\prec$ denote the transitive closure of $\prec^1$. Then we say that π contains a *cycle*, if there exists an atom A satisfying $A \prec A$. Without loss of generality we assume that a Prolog program π does not contain any fact, since otherwise π can be reduced to $\pi' \wedge \varphi$, where π' does not contain any fact, φ is a conjunction of facts, and $\mathit{atomset}(\pi') \cap \mathit{atomset}(\varphi) = \emptyset$. Note that our considerations either correspond to π' solely or to φ, which always is a trivial case. A sequence $A_1 \ldots A_n$ of atoms is called a *goal*. The empty goal is denoted by $\sqcup$. For a Prolog program π a goal $A_1 \ldots A_{i-1} B_1 \ldots B_m A_{i+1} \ldots A_n$ is called an *SLD-resolvent* of $A_1 \ldots A_n$, if π contains $A_i \leftarrow B_1, \ldots, B_m$. We write $A_1 \ldots A_n \vdash^{1}_{SLD} A_1 \ldots A_{i-1} B_1 \ldots B_m A_{i+1} \ldots A_n$ in this case. $\vdash_{SLD}$ denotes the reflexive and transitive closure of $\vdash^{1}_{SLD}$ and we say that an atom A can be *refuted* by π if $A \vdash_{SLD} \sqcup$. It is well-known that a Prolog program π implies $A \leftarrow A_1, \ldots, A_n$ if and only if A can be refuted by $A_1 \wedge \ldots \wedge A_n \wedge \pi$.

According to the definition of an SLD-derivation the following choices have to be made in each step of constructing a refutation:

1. We can choose an arbitrary atom in a goal for resolution. It can be proved that this selection function does not influence the completeness of the refutation procedure, see e. g. [ApEm 82]. In Prolog always the first atom of a goal is selected.

2. We can choose an arbitrary clause having a head corresponding to the selected atom in the goal for refutation. In Prolog there is selected in the first instance the first clause (according to the order of the clauses in the Prolog program) and the other alternatives are tried by backtracking in the case that the choice did not succeed.

In the next sections we investigate the optimization problem for Prolog programs when using SLD-resolution to decide $\pi \models A \leftarrow A_1, \ldots, A_n$. We mention that in the worst-case SLD-resolution and especially the Prolog inference strategy are very inefficient, there are even classes of Prolog programs where the average complexity of the Prolog inference strategy is exponential, see [KBLö 88a]. Therefore, our results essentially depend on the inference strategy taken as basis: It is well-known that $\pi \models A \leftarrow A_1, \ldots, A_n$ for a Prolog program π can be decided deterministically in polynomial time, see [JoLa 77], and allowing random access machines there even exist linear-time algorithms, see [DoGa 84]. Thus, considering such an algorithm Prolog programs are optimized according to our definition.

3.2 Optimization of SLD-Resolution

In this section we analyze the optimization problem for Prolog programs using SLD-resolution to decide $\pi \models A \leftarrow A_1, \ldots, A_n$. We allow to choose the atom in a goal and the clause for resolution nondeterministically presenting the following results: If we do not allow to eliminate multiple occurrences of atoms in a goal, then there are classes of Prolog programs which cannot be optimized, otherwise there always exists a refutation bounded linear in the length of the formula. The last result is an immediate consequence of the fact that unit-resolution is complete for Horn-formulas, see [HeWo 74].

Theorem 3.1 *Consider the following Prolog programs*

$$\pi_0 \;:\equiv\; A_0 \leftarrow B_0, A_{-1}, A_{-2} \wedge B_0 \leftarrow C_0, A_{-1}, A_{-2}$$
$$\pi_n \;:\equiv\; A_n \leftarrow B_n, A_{n-1}, A_{n-2} \wedge B_n \leftarrow C_n, A_{n-1}, A_{n-2} \;\wedge\; \pi_{n-1}$$

and let π'_n be arbitrary Prolog programs being equivalent to π_n such that for some polynomial p we have $length(\pi'_n) \leq p(length(\pi_n))$. Then there exist consequences $A^{(n)} \leftarrow A_1^{(n)}, \ldots, A_{i_n}^{(n)}$ of π_n such that the length of any SLD-refutation of $A^{(n)}$ using clauses of $A_1^{(n)} \wedge \ldots \wedge A_{i_n}^{(n)} \wedge \pi'_n$ cannot be bounded polynomially. □

We skip the proof of Theorem 3.1 and refer to [KBLö 87], but we mention that the result is based essentially on the fact that we do not allow to eliminate multiple occurrences of literals. Note that in practice the elimination of multiple occurrences of atoms is very expensive and can be compared with occur-checking [Pla 84] of Prolog which is ommitted in general for the sake of efficiency.

Lemma 3.2 *Let π be a Prolog program and assume that $A \leftarrow A_1, \ldots, A_n$ is a consequence of π. If we allow to eliminate multiple occurrences of atoms in a goal, then there exists an SLD-refutation of A of length bounded linear in $length(\pi)$ using clauses of $A_1 \wedge \ldots \wedge A_n \wedge \pi$.*

Proof: Consider

$$\mathrm{P}_0 \;:=\; \{A_1, \ldots, A_n\}$$
$$\mathrm{P}_k \;:=\; \mathrm{P}_{k-1} \cup \{B \mid B \leftarrow B_1, \ldots, B_s \text{ is a clause of } \pi \text{ and } B_i \in \mathrm{P}_{k-1} \text{ for } 1 \leq i \leq s\}$$

Since $A_1 \wedge \ldots \wedge A_n \wedge \pi \wedge \neg A$ is inconsistent and unit-resolution is complete for Horn-formulas, there is an $r \leq atomset(\pi)$ satisfying $A \in \mathrm{P}_r \backslash \mathrm{P}_{r-1}$. Therefore consider the following SLD-refutation of A:

$$A \vdash^{1}_{SLD} B_1^{(r-1)} \ldots B_{s_{r-1}}^{(r-1)} \vdash_{SLD} B_1^{(r-2)} \ldots B_{s_{r-2}}^{(r-2)} \vdash_{SLD} \cdots \vdash_{SLD} B_1^{(0)} \ldots B_{s_0}^{(0)} \vdash_{SLD} \sqcup$$

where $B_j^{(i)} \in \mathrm{P}_i$ for $0 \leq i \leq r-1$, $1 \leq j \leq s_i$, and the goal $B_1^{(i)} \ldots B_{s_i}^{(i)}$ is obtained from $B_1^{(i+1)} \ldots B_{s_{i+1}}^{(i+1)}$ by resolving each $B_j^{(i+1)} \in \mathrm{P}_{i+1} \backslash \mathrm{P}_i$ and by eliminating afterwards all multiple occurrences of atoms.

In this resolution each clause of $A_1 \wedge \ldots \wedge A_n \wedge \pi$ is used at most once, which yields

3.3 Possibilities of Optimizing Prolog Programs

Now we consider the optimization problem for Prolog programs using the Prolog inference strategy for deciding $\pi \models A \leftarrow A_1, \ldots, A_n$: We select the first atom in a goal and the first clause according to the order in the Prolog program for resolution. The other clauses are tried by backtracking in the case that the choice did not succeed, see [ClMe 84] or [KBSch 86]. Note that the Prolog strategy does not eliminate multiple occurrences of atoms in a goal. Thus, let $\mathcal{T}(\pi, A \leftarrow A_1, \ldots, A_n)$ denote the number of resolutions needed by the Prolog inference strategy for deciding $\pi \models A \leftarrow A_1, \ldots, A_n$ and let

$$\mathcal{T}(\pi) := \max\{\mathcal{T}(\pi, A \leftarrow A_1, \ldots, A_n)\} .$$

Sometimes we additionally consider $\mathcal{T}_{\models}(\pi)$ defined by

$$\mathcal{T}_{\models}(\pi) := \max\{\mathcal{T}(\pi, A \leftarrow A_1, \ldots, A_n) \mid \pi \models A \leftarrow A_1, \ldots, A_n\} .$$

Further, we regard only those programs which do not have any cycle, since otherwise the Prolog inference strategy could enter an infinite loop. Finally, we mention that the facts $A_1 \wedge \ldots \wedge A_n$ are added at the *front* of a program π if we want to decide $\pi \models A \leftarrow A_1, \ldots, A_n$ by refuting A. In the following sections we present examples of optimizable Prolog programs considering various possibilities of optimizing a program.

3.3.1 Changing the Succession of Clauses

Let π be a Prolog program and consider an arbitrary Prolog program ψ obtained from π by reordering the clauses. Obviously, we have $\mathcal{T}(\pi, \gamma) = \mathcal{T}(\psi, \gamma)$ for each clause satisfying $\pi \not\models \gamma$. But in special cases we can reduce $\mathcal{T}(\pi, \gamma)$ for consequences γ by changing the succession of the clauses of π: Consider

$$\begin{aligned} \pi_0 &:\equiv \sqcup \\ \pi_n &:\equiv A_n \leftarrow A_{n-1} \wedge A_n \leftarrow B_n \wedge B_n \leftarrow A_{n-1} \wedge \pi_{n-1} \end{aligned}$$

$\mathcal{T}(\pi_n, A_n)$ satisfies the following recurrence:

$$\begin{aligned} \mathcal{T}(\pi_0, A_0) &= 0 \\ \mathcal{T}(\pi_n, A_n) &= 3 + 2 \cdot \mathcal{T}(\pi_{n-1}, A_{n-1}) \end{aligned}$$

Thus we obtain

$$\mathcal{T}(\pi_n, A_n) = 3 \cdot 2^n - 3$$

and therefore these programs are not optimized:

$$\begin{aligned} \mathcal{T}(\pi_n) &= 3 \cdot 2^n - 3 \\ \mathcal{T}_{\models}(\pi_n) &= \mathcal{T}(\pi_n, A_n \leftarrow B_n) = 3 \cdot 2^{n-1} \end{aligned}$$

Now consider

$$\begin{aligned} \psi_0 &:\equiv \sqcup \\ \psi_n &:\equiv A_n \leftarrow B_n \wedge A_n \leftarrow A_{n-1} \wedge B_n \leftarrow A_{n-1} \wedge \psi_{n-1} \end{aligned}$$

where ψ_n is obtained from π_n by changing the succession of some clauses. We get $\mathcal{T}(\psi_n, \gamma) \leq 2 \cdot n + 1$, if γ is a consequence of π_n. Hence $\mathcal{T}_{\models}(\psi_n)$ is bounded linear in $length(\psi_n)$.

3.3.2 Removing Redundant Clauses

Now let us give an example, where we optimize the programs π_n of the previous section by removing clauses. Consider

$$\begin{aligned} \varphi_0 &:\equiv \sqcup \\ \varphi_n &:\equiv A_n \leftarrow B_n \wedge B_n \leftarrow A_{n-1} \wedge \varphi_{n-1} \end{aligned}$$

and we conclude $\mathcal{T}(\varphi_n, \gamma) \leq 2 \cdot n + 1$ for *any* clause γ.

3.3.3 Adding Consequences

In this section we consider classes Π of Prolog programs, which can be optimized by adding suitable consequences to the programs. Consider for $\mu > 1$

$$\begin{aligned} \pi_{0,\mu} &:\equiv \sqcup \\ \pi_{\nu,\mu} &:\equiv A_\nu \leftarrow B_{\nu,1}, \ldots, B_{\nu,\mu} \wedge \bigwedge_{1 \leq i \leq \mu} B_{\nu,i} \leftarrow A_{\nu-1} \wedge \pi_{\nu-1,\mu} \end{aligned}$$

For each clause $A_\nu \leftarrow C_1, \ldots, C_\ell$ the complexity $\mathcal{T}(\pi_{\nu,\mu}, A_\nu \leftarrow C_1, \ldots, C_\ell)$ satisfies the following recurrence:

$$\begin{aligned} \mathcal{T}(\pi_{1,\mu}, A_1 \leftarrow C_1, \ldots, C_\ell) &\leq 2 \cdot \mu + 1 \\ \mathcal{T}(\pi_{\nu,\mu}, A_\nu \leftarrow C_1, \ldots, C_\ell) &\leq \mu + 1 + \mu \cdot \mathcal{T}(\pi_{\nu-1,\mu}, A_{\nu-1} \leftarrow C_1, \ldots, C_\ell) \end{aligned}$$

For the clauses $A_\nu \leftarrow A_0$ the above mentioned estimations turn into equalities, which yields

$$\mathcal{T}(\pi_{\nu,\mu}) = \mathcal{T}(\pi_{\nu,\mu}, A_\nu \leftarrow A_0) = (\mu + 1) \cdot \frac{\mu^\nu - 1}{\mu - 1} + \mu^\nu \tag{1}$$

Let Π be a class of Prolog programs $\pi_{\nu,\mu}$. Whether such a class Π can be optimized by adding suitable consequences to the programs $\pi_{\nu,\mu}$ depends on the ratio of ν and μ. We prove the following results:

Lemma 3.3 *If ν is bounded uniformly by some constant C, a class Π of formulas $\pi_{\nu,\mu}$ is optimized.*

Proof: In this case the length of any program $\pi_{\nu,\mu}$ is bounded polynomially in μ and because of (1) we conclude

$$\mathcal{T}(\pi_{\nu,\mu}) \leq (\mu + 1) \cdot \frac{\mu^C - 1}{\mu - 1} + \mu^C \in O(\mu^C)$$

which yields the desired result. □

Lemma 3.4 *If ν is bounded by $C \cdot \log \mu$ for some constant C, a class Π of formulas $\pi_{\nu,\mu}$ can be optimized by adding the clauses $A_i \leftarrow A_{i-1}$ for $1 \leq i \leq \nu$ in front of a program $\pi_{\nu,\mu}$.*

Proof: Thus, consider

$$\begin{aligned}\psi_{0,\mu} &:\equiv \sqcup \\ \psi_{\nu,\mu} &:\equiv A_\nu \leftarrow A_{\nu-1} \wedge A_\nu \leftarrow B_{\nu,1},\ldots,B_{\nu,\mu} \wedge \bigwedge_{1\leq i\leq\mu} B_{\nu,i} \leftarrow A_{\nu-1} \wedge \psi_{\nu-1,\mu}\ ,\end{aligned}$$

where $\psi_{\nu,\mu}$ is obtained from $\pi_{\nu,\mu}$ by adding the consequences $A_i \leftarrow A_{i-1}$, $1 \leq i \leq \nu$, in front of $\pi_{\nu,\mu}$. We conclude

$$\begin{aligned}T(\psi_{1,\mu}, A_1 \leftarrow C_1,\ldots,C_\ell) &\leq \mu+2 \\ T(\psi_{\nu,\mu}, A_\nu \leftarrow C_1,\ldots,C_\ell) &\leq \mu+2+2\cdot T(\psi_{\nu-1,\mu}, A_{\nu-1} \leftarrow C_1,\ldots,C_\ell)\end{aligned}$$

which yields

$$T(\psi_{\nu,\mu}, A_\nu \leftarrow C_1,\ldots,C_\ell) \leq (\mu+2)\cdot(2^\nu-1)\ .$$

Consequently, the complexity $T(\psi_{\nu,\mu})$ is bounded polynomially in *length*$(\pi_{\nu,\mu})$ in the case of $\nu \in O(\log\mu)$, which furnishes the assertion. □

Proposition 3.5 *For any program $\varphi_{\nu,\mu}$, which can be obtained from $\pi_{\nu,\mu}$ by adding consequences, and any number κ satisfying $\nu \geq \kappa > 0$ we have*

$$T(\varphi_{\nu,\mu}) \geq \min\{2^{\lfloor\nu/\kappa\rfloor}, \mu^\kappa\}$$

Proof: Without loss of generality we assume that each consequence is added in front of $\pi_{\nu,\mu}$. Otherwise obtain $\varphi'_{\nu,\mu}$ from $\varphi_{\nu,\mu}$ by deleting a clause $C \leftarrow C_1,\ldots,C_\ell$ if there is a clause $C \leftarrow C'_1,\ldots,C'_\ell$ of $\pi_{\nu,\mu}$ occurring before $C \leftarrow C_1,\ldots,C_\ell$. Obviously $T(\varphi_{\nu,\mu}) \geq T(\varphi'_{\nu,\mu})$.

Let us say that an atom C has *index* i if $C \in \{A_i, B_{i,j} \mid 1 \leq j \leq \mu\}$, which is denoted by *index*(C). The clauses of $\pi_{\nu,\mu}$ have the property that each goal in a refutation of an atom C contains only such atoms having an index at most *index*(C). Therefore, if we remove those atoms from the body of a clause $C \leftarrow C_1,\ldots,C_\ell$ of $\varphi_{\nu,\mu}$ having an index greater than *index*(C), the resulting clause is a consequence of $\pi_{\nu,\mu}$ as well. Thus, we can assume without loss of generality that the index of any atom occurring in the body of some clause of $\varphi_{\nu,\mu}$ is less or equal to the index of the corresponding head. Otherwise consider $\varphi'_{\nu,\mu}$ obtained from $\varphi_{\nu,\mu}$ by deleting all atoms from the body of a clause $C \leftarrow C_1,\ldots,C_\ell$ having an index greater than *index*(C). Obviously $\varphi_{\nu,\mu}$ and $\varphi'_{\nu,\mu}$ are equivalent and $T(\varphi_{\nu,\mu}) \geq T(\varphi'_{\nu,\mu})$.

We say that a clause is of *block* i if each atom C occurring in the clause satisfies $(i-1)\cdot\kappa \leq$ *index*$(C) \leq i\cdot\kappa$. We consider two cases:

1. There exists a $1 \leq i \leq \lfloor\frac{\nu}{\kappa}\rfloor$ such that any clause of $\varphi_{\nu,\mu}$, which does not occur in $\pi_{\nu,\mu}$, is not of block i:

We conclude

$$\mathcal{T}(\varphi_{\nu,\mu}) \geq \mathcal{T}(\varphi_{\nu,\mu}, A_{i\cdot\kappa} \leftarrow A_{(i-1)\cdot\kappa}) \geq \mathcal{T}(\pi_{\nu,\mu}, A_{i\cdot\kappa} \leftarrow A_{(i-1)\cdot\kappa}) \,, \tag{2}$$

since in the case that we choose a clause not occurring in $\pi_{\nu,\mu}$ for resolution there is introduced an atom in the goal having an index less than $(i-1)\cdot\kappa$. Such an atom cannot be refuted, hence backtracking causes that another clause is selected. Note that because of (1) we obtain

$$\mathcal{T}(\pi_{\nu,\mu}, A_{i\cdot\kappa} \leftarrow A_{(i-1)\cdot\kappa}) = (\mu+1)\cdot\frac{\mu^\kappa - 1}{\mu - 1} + \mu^\kappa \geq \mu^\kappa \tag{3}$$

2. For each $1 \leq i \leq \lfloor\frac{\nu}{\mu}\rfloor$ there exists a clause $C^{(i)} \leftarrow C_1^{(i)}, \ldots, C_{n_i}^{(i)}$ of $\varphi_{\nu,\mu}$ which is of block i and which does not occur in $\pi_{\nu,\mu}$:
   Let $\{B_1, \ldots, B_m\} := B^{(1)} \cup \ldots \cup B^{(\lfloor\frac{\nu}{\kappa}\rfloor)}$, where $B^{(j)}$ is defined as follows

$$B^{(j)} := \begin{cases} \emptyset & \text{if } C^{(j)} \equiv A_k \text{ for some } k \\ \{B_{k,\ell} \mid 1 \leq \ell \leq \mu\}\backslash C^{(j)} & \text{if } C^{(j)} \equiv B_{k,l} \text{ for some } k, l \end{cases}$$

   Obviously $C^{(i)} \leftarrow B_1, \ldots, B_m, C^{(i-1)}$ is a consequence of $\pi_{\nu,\mu}$, whereas the clause $C^{(i)} \leftarrow B_1, \ldots, B_m$ is not a consequence of $\pi_{\nu,\mu}$. Therefore, in the case of refuting $C^{(i)}$ using clauses of $B_1 \wedge \ldots \wedge B_m \wedge \varphi_{\nu,\mu}$ there is generated a goal containing the atom $C^{(i-1)}$ as first element. There are at least two clauses in $\varphi_{\nu,\mu}$ having the head $C^{(i)}$ and both can be used for resolution to derive a goal having $C^{(i-1)}$ as first atom, wherefore we conclude

$$\mathcal{T}(\varphi_{\nu,\mu}, C^{(i)} \leftarrow B_1, \ldots, B_m) \geq 2 + 2\cdot\mathcal{T}(\varphi_{\nu,\mu}, C^{(i-1)} \leftarrow B_1, \ldots, B_m) \,, \tag{4}$$

   This yields

$$\begin{aligned} \mathcal{T}(\varphi_{\nu,\mu}) &\geq \mathcal{T}(\varphi_{\nu,\mu}, C^{(\lfloor\frac{\nu}{\kappa}\rfloor)} \leftarrow B_1, \ldots, B_m) \\ &\geq 2^{\lfloor\frac{\nu}{\kappa}\rfloor - 1}\cdot\mathcal{T}(\varphi_{\nu,\mu}, C^{(1)} \leftarrow B_1, \ldots, B_m) \\ &\geq 2^{\lfloor\frac{\nu}{\kappa}\rfloor} \end{aligned} \tag{5}$$

The relations (2),(3), and (5) yield the assertion. □

Remark: A more careful analysis of the second case in the proof of Proposition 3.5 yields a similar lower bound for $\mathcal{T}_{\models}(\varphi_{\nu,\mu})$ as well.

Lemma 3.6 *If ν cannot be bounded by $C\cdot\log\mu$ for any constant C, a class Π of programs $\pi_{\nu,\mu}$ cannot be optimized by adding consequences.*

Proof: Because of Proposition 3.5 we obtain for any program $\varphi_{\nu,\mu}$ obtained from $\pi_{\nu,\mu}$ by adding consequences in the case of $\kappa := \lfloor\sqrt{\frac{\nu}{\log\mu}}\rfloor$:

$$\mathcal{T}(\varphi_{\nu,\mu}) \geq \min\{2^{\lfloor\sqrt{\nu\cdot\log\mu}\rfloor}, \mu^{\lfloor\sqrt{\frac{\nu}{\log\mu}}\rfloor}\} \geq c^{\sqrt{\nu\cdot\log\mu}}$$

for some constant $c > 1$. The conditions of Lemma 3.6 yield $\sqrt{\nu} \notin O(\sqrt{\log\mu})$, therefore we obtain $\sqrt{\nu\cdot\log\mu} \notin O(\log\mu)$. Consequently $\sqrt{\nu\cdot\log\mu} \notin O(\log\nu\cdot\mu)$.

Thus, $\mathcal{T}(\varphi_{\nu,\mu})$ cannot be bounded polynomially in $\nu \cdot \mu$. This yields the assertion, since *length*$(\pi_{\nu,\mu})$ is bounded by some polynomial in $\nu \cdot \mu$. □

Finally, let us consider the case where the program $\pi_{(\log \nu)^2,2}$ occurs as a subprogram of a program π_ν of length ν. Because of (1) the complexity $\mathcal{T}(\pi_\nu) \geq \mathcal{T}(\pi_{(\log \nu)^2,2}) = 4 \cdot \nu^{\log \nu} - 3$ cannot be bounded by some polynomial in ν, whereas we can reduce the complexity of $\pi_{(\log \nu)^2,2}$ to be polynomially bounded in ν by adding suitable consequences. Therefore consider

$$\varphi_{\lambda,\mu} :\equiv \bigwedge_{1 \leq i \leq \lambda} A_{i \cdot \mu} \leftarrow A_{(i-1) \cdot \mu} \wedge \pi_{\lambda \cdot \mu, 2}$$

and we estimate

$$\begin{aligned} \mathcal{T}(\varphi_{1,\mu}, A_\mu \leftarrow C_1, \ldots, C_\ell) &\leq \mathcal{T}(\pi_{\mu,2}) + 1 \\ \mathcal{T}(\varphi_{\lambda,\mu}, A_{\lambda \cdot \mu} \leftarrow C_1, \ldots, C_\ell) &\leq \mathcal{T}(\pi_{\mu,2}) + 1 + 2 \cdot \mathcal{T}(\varphi_{\lambda-1,\mu}, A_{(\lambda-1)\cdot\mu} \leftarrow C_1, \ldots, C_\ell) \end{aligned}$$

and we conclude

$$\mathcal{T}(\varphi_{\lambda,\mu}) \leq (\mathcal{T}(\pi_{\mu,2}) + 1) \cdot (2^\lambda - 1) \tag{6}$$

Obviously, $\varphi_{\log \nu, \log \nu}$ is obtained from $\pi_{(\log \nu)^2,2}$ by adding suitable consequences and because of (6) and (1) we get

$$\mathcal{T}(\varphi_{\log \nu, \log \nu}) \leq 4 \cdot 2^{\log \nu} \cdot (2^{\log \nu} - 1) \in O(\nu^2) ,$$

which yields the desired result.

3.4 Extended Prolog Programs

Let us call a program π' an *extension* of π if for any clause $\gamma \equiv A \leftarrow A_1, \ldots, A_n$ satisfying $\{A, A_1, \ldots, A_n\} \subseteq$ *atomset*(π) we have $\pi \models \gamma$ if and only if $\pi' \models \gamma$. Now we allow to consider arbitrary extensions π' of a program π to optimize π. Note that the considerations of the previous sections are special cases of optimizing by extension. Similar aspects can be found in [ŠtŠt 84], where complexity measures for And/Or-graphs are studied and there are presented transformations to other graphs representing extensions such that the complexity is reduced. We only want to give few examples demonstrating the power of optimizing by extension.

Consider the following programs $\phi_{\nu,\mu}$:

$$\phi_{\nu,\mu} :\equiv \bigwedge_{1 \leq i_1 < \ldots < i_\mu \leq \nu} A \leftarrow A_{i_1}, \ldots, A_{i_\mu}$$

We immediately get that *length*$(\phi_{\nu,\mu})$ is bounded polynomially in $\binom{\nu}{\mu}$. Now regard the following extension $\phi'_{\nu,\mu}$ of $\phi_{\nu,\mu}$:

$$\begin{aligned} \phi'_{\nu,\mu} :\equiv\ & A \leftarrow X_{1,0} \\ & \wedge \bigwedge_{1 \leq i < \nu} \big(\bigwedge_{1 \leq j < \mu} X_{i,j-1} \leftarrow A_i, X_{i+1,j} \big) \wedge X_{i,\mu-1} \leftarrow A_i \\ & \wedge \bigwedge_{\substack{1 \leq i < \nu \\ 0 \leq j < \mu}} X_{i,j} \leftarrow X_{i+1,j} \end{aligned}$$

where the first index i of an atom $X_{i,j}$ denotes that A_i may be generated and the second index j denotes the number of atoms A_ℓ, $1 \leq \ell < i$, generated already. Obviously, $length(\phi'_{\nu,\mu})$ is bounded polynomially in $\nu \cdot \mu$ and we conclude that the length of $\phi'_{\nu,\nu/2}$ is bounded polynomially in $\log(length(\phi_{\nu,\nu/2}))$. This reduction of length can be generalized to various classes of programs, which become optimized by applying a similar reduction of length.

To give further intuition of optimizing by extension we mention that the programs π'_n defined recursively als follows

$$\begin{aligned} \pi'_0 &:\equiv A_0 \leftarrow B_0, X_0 \ \wedge\ B_0 \leftarrow C_0, X_0 \ \wedge\ X_0 \leftarrow A_{-1}, A_{-2} \\ \pi'_n &:\equiv A_n \leftarrow B_n, X_n \ \wedge\ B_n \leftarrow C_n, X_n \ \wedge \\ & X_n \leftarrow A_{n-1}, A_{n-2} \ \wedge\ X_n \leftarrow Y_n, X_{n-1} \ \wedge \\ & Y_n \leftarrow A_{n-1} \ \wedge\ Y_n \leftarrow B_{n-1} \ \wedge\ Y_n \leftarrow C_{n-1} \ \wedge\ \pi'_{n-1} \end{aligned}$$

are extensions of the programs π_n in Theorem 3.1. It is easy to prove that for any consequence $Z \leftarrow Z_1, \ldots, Z_\ell$ of π_n there exists a refutation of Z using clauses of $Z_1 \wedge \ldots \wedge Z_\ell \wedge \pi_n$ having length bounded polynomially in n. Hence, Theorem 3.1 becomes false when considering extended programs also. But notice that using the Prolog inference strategy $T_\models(\pi'_n)$ cannot be bounded by any polynomial in n.

We have not yet succeeded in giving a characterization for arbitrary Prolog programs whether they can be optimized by extension or not, but considering 2-Prolog programs only, i. e. each clause contains exactly two literals, we have given in [KBLö 88b] the following characterization:

Theorem 3.7 *Let π be a minimal (i. e. π does not contain any fact or any redundant clause) 2-Prolog program having no cycle, let π' be a Prolog program which is an extension of π having no cycle as well. Then $T(\pi') \geq T_\models(\pi') > \frac{1}{2} \cdot T(\pi)$.*

Thus, a 2-Prolog program π can be optimized by extension if and only if $min(\pi)$, which denotes the unique 2-Prolog program being minimal and equivalent to π, is optimized.

4 Conclusions

We have investigated the problem whether a propositional calculus formula α can be optimized with regard to questions of deducibility if we consider a formula α' being equivalent to α. The difficulty of this problem becomes evident when relating the optimization problem to the P=NP-problem. It remains open whether the optimization problem and the P=NP-problem are equivalent. Considering Prolog programs under this point of view we have presented classes of programs which can be optimized, on the other side there are formulas which cannot be optimized. Regarding Prolog programs having at most two literals per clause we have given necessary and sufficient conditions whether a class of Prolog programs can be optimized, whereas the situation becomes more complicated when considering programs having more than two literals per clause, since now there are more aspects and possibilities of optimizing a program. We try to obtain for arbitrary classes of propositional Prolog programs also a similar classification whether the class can be optimized or not.

References

[ApEm 82] K. R. Apt, M. H. van Emden: Contributions to the Theory of Logic Programming, *J. of the ACM* **29** (1982), pp. 841–862

[Bör 85] E. Börger: *Berechenbarkeit, Komplexität, Logik*, Vieweg-Verlag, Braunschweig 1985 (English translation in preparation)

[BrGoPu 82] C. Brown, A. Goldberg, P. Purdom: Average Time Analysis of Simplified Davis-Putnam Procedures, *Information Processing Letters* **15** (1982), pp. 72–75

[BrPu 81] C. A. Brown, P. W. Purdom: An Average Time Analysis of Backtracking, *SIAM J. Computing* **10** (1981), pp. 583–593

[BrPu 85] C. A. Brown, P. W. Purdom: The pure literal rule and polynomial average time, *SIAM J. Computing* **14** (1985), pp. 943–953

[ClMe 84] W. F. Clocksin, C. S. Mellish: *Programming in Prolog*, Springer-Verlag, Berlin 1984

[Coo 71] S. A. Cook: The Complexity of Theorem-proving Procedures, *Proc. Third ACM Symp. on Theory of Computing* (1971), pp. 151–158

[DoGa 84] W. F. Dowling, J. H. Gallier: Linear-Time Algorithms for Testing the Satisfiability of Propositional Horn Formulae, *J. Logic Programming* **1** (1984), pp. 267–284

[GeSm 85] M. R. Genesereth, D. E. Smith: Ordering Conjunctive queries, *Artificial Intelligence* **26** (1985), pp. 171–215

[Gol 79] A. Goldberg: Average case complexity of the satisfiability problem, *Proc. Fourth Workshop on Automated Deduction* (1979), pp. 1–6

[HeWo 74] L. Henschen, L. Wos: Unit Refutation and Horn Sets, *J. of the ACM* **21** (1974), pp. 590–605

[JoLa 77] N. D. Jones, W. T. Laaser: Complete Problems for Deterministic Polynomial Time, *Theoretical Computer Science* **3** (1977), pp. 105–117

[KBLö 87] H. Kleine Büning, U. Löwen: Optimizing Propositional Calculus Formulas with Regard to Questions of Deducibility, *Technical Report* **178** (1987), Universität Karlsruhe, Institut für Angewandte Informatik und Formale Beschreibungsverfahren

[KBLö 88a] H. Kleine Büning, U. Löwen: Towards Average Complexity of Propositional Binary Prolog Programs, *Preprint* (1988)

[KBLö 88b] H. Kleine Büning, U. Löwen: Optimization Aspects for Special Prolog Programs, *Preprint* (1988)

[KBSch 86] H. Kleine Büning, S. Schmitgen: *Prolog*, B. G. Teubner, Stuttgart 1986

[Kow 74] R. Kowalski: Predicate Logic as Programming Language, *Information Processing* 74, J. Rosenfeld (ed.), North-Holland, Amsterdam 1974, pp. 556–574

[Nat 87] K. S. Natarajan: Optimizing Backtrack Search for all Solutions to Conjunctive Problems, *Proc. Tenth Int. Joint Conf. on Artificial Intelligence* (1987), pp. 955–958

[Nil 82] N. J. Nilsson: *Principles of Artificial Intelligence,* Springer-Verlag, Berlin 1982

[PePo 82] L. M. Pereira, A. Porto: Selective Backtracking, *Logic Programming*, K. Clark and S. Tärnlund (eds.), Academic Press, New York 1982, pp. 107–114

[Pla 84] D. Plaisted: The Occur-Check Problem in Prolog, *Proc. Int. Symp. on Logic Programming* (1984), pp. 272–280

[Sho 67] J. R. Shoenfield: *Mathematical Logic*, Addison-Wesley, London 1967

[Spe 87] E. Speckenmeyer: Classes of CNF-Formulas with Backtracking Trees of Exponential or Linear Average Order for Exact Satisfiability, *Technical Report* **47** (1987), Universität - GH - Paderborn, Fachbereich Mathematik-Informatik

[Spe 88] E. Speckenmeyer: On the Average Case Complexity of Backtracking for the Exact Satisfiability Problem, *this volume*

[ŠtŠt 84] P. Štěpánek, O. Štěpánková: Transformations of Logic Programs, *J. Logic Programming* **1** (1984), pp. 305–318

LOGIC OF APPROXIMATION REASONING

Helena Rasiowa
University of Warsaw, Institute of Mathematics
PKiN 9th floor, 00-901 Warsaw, Poland

ABSTRACT

An algebraic and set-theoretical approach to approximation reasoning as proposed in [10] and [5] leads to a formulation of a class of first order logics. They are certain intermediate logics equipped with approximation operators d_t for $t \in T$ - where $(T, \leq)$ is a poset establishing a type of logic under consideration - and with modal connectives C_t of possibility and I_t of necessity, $t \in T$ and possibly with C_T and I_T. Their semantics is based on the idea that a set of objects to be recognized in a process of an approximation reasoning is approximated by means of a family of sets covering this set and by their intersection. Approximating sets with equivalence classes of equivalence relations, as connected with Pawlak's rough sets methods (see [8], [7], [12], [13]) is an additional tool. The main task of this paper is to formulate and prove the completeness theorem for the logics under consideration. For that purpose a theory of plain semi-Post algebras as introduced and developed in [3] has been applied. These algebras replace more complicated semi-Post algebras occurring in [10].

Introduction

An approach to approximation reasoning to be discussed in this paper is based on the following observation. An approximation reasoning may be considered as a gradual approximating of a set of objects to be recognized, by a family of sets covering this set, and by their intersection. This point of view has been presented in [10] and [5]. Two examples of such reasonings will be quoted from [5].

<u>Example 1</u>. Consider a game of two players: a questioner Q and a responder R. The task of Q is to guess in a given number of questions

what R is thinking about. Assume R is thinking about Kurt Gödel. The following dialogue leads to the win of Q.
Q: is this a human being? R: yes. Q: is this a man? R: yes. Q: is he famous? R; yes. Q: is he a scientist? R: yes. Q: is he a specialist in philology? R: no. Q: is he a mathematician? R: yes. Q: is his field mathematical logic? R: yes. Q: is he alive? R: no. Q: was his 80th anniversary celebrated in 1986? R: yes. Q: Kurt Gödel? R: yes.

Example 2. A detective D looking for killers of a person X would be interested to obtain answers on the following queries:
q_1: Y was near the place of the crime at the time of this crime.
q_2: Y doesn't have alibi.
q_3: Y has been interested in the death of X .
q_4: Y is a man (if it is known that a woman was not a killer).
q_5: Y looks like a murderer of X according to a description of a witness.
Assume that $u_1,\dots,u_{10}$ satisfy q_1; $u_3,\dots,u_{10}$ satisfy q_2; $v_1,v_2,u_3,\dots,u_7$ satisfy q_3; v_1,u_6,u_7 satisfy q_4; v_1,u_7 satisfy q_5. Then sets $\{u_1,\dots,u_{10}\}$, $\{u_3,\dots,u_{10}\}$, $\{v_1,v_2,u_3,\dots,u_7\}$, $\{v_1,u_6,u_7\}$, $\{v_1,u_7\}$ approximate a set of killers.
The intersection $\{u_7\}$ of these sets suggests that u_7 is mostly suspect to be a killer.

Investigations concerning an attempt to construct first order logics dealing with approximation reasonings of that kind have been progressively developed in papers [12], [13], [7], [9], [10], [5], giving more and more general approaches. Starting with a modal logic ([12] corresponding to approximating by equivalence classes of one equivalence relation) through a multimodal one ([13]) and ω^+-valued multimodal ([9] corresponding to approximating by descending sequences of sets and equivalence classes of a descending sequence of equivalence relations) - all of them with special semantics - the most general approach has been proposed in [10]. It is based on the following idea. Let $\underline{T} = (T, \leq)$ be an arbitrary enumerable poset (partially ordered set). Intuitively it can be treated as a set of queries in a data base, or a set of consistent finite subsets of objects in a Scott's information system, a partially ordered set of informations etc. It may be taken as a type for approximation reasonings. With $\underline{T} = (T, \leq)$ there is associated a Heyting algebra $\underline{LT} = (LT, \cup, \cap, \Rightarrow, \neg)$ formed of all $\underline{T}$-ideals (i.e. non-empty subsets S of T such that if $s \in S$ and $t \leq s$ then $t \in S$) and $\emptyset$.
For convenience $\underline{T}$ is treated as a subposet of $\underline{LT}$. The least element in LT is $\emptyset$ to be denoted by $\wedge$ and the greatest element

in LT is T, to be denoted by $\vee$.
Roughly speaking plain semi-Post algebras (briefly psP-algebras) of type $\underline{T} = (T,\leq)$ are Heyting algebras with a unit $e_\vee$ and a zero $e_\wedge$, with Post constants e_s for $s \in LT$, such that $s \leq t$ implies $e_s \leq e_t$ and with one-argument operations d_t, $t \in T$, satisfying certain conditions. Among them we have $d_t a \leq d_s a$ for $s \leq t$ and for any a, $a = \bigcup_{t \in T}(d_t a \cap e_t)$. This representation is unique. Plain semi-Post algebras $\underline{ELT}$ of type $\underline{T}$, consisting of elements e_t, $t \in LT$ are called basic sP-algebras of type $\underline{T}$. Functions $f : U \longrightarrow ELT$ (where $ELT = \{e_t : t \in LT\}$), to be called $\underline{T}$-functions are taken as representing algebraically predicates. They determine uniquely descending T-sequences $(Sd_t f)_{t \in T}$ of subsets of U (i.e. such that $t \leq s$ implies $Sd_s f \subset Sd_t f$) which form a psP-algebra. $Sd_t f \overset{df}{=} \{u \in U: d_t f(u) = e_\vee\}$. The set $Sf = \{u \in U : f(u) = e_\vee\}$ is covered by $Sd_t f$, $t \in T$ and $Sf = \bigcap_{t \in T}(Sd_t f)$. Thus the sets $Sd_t f$, $t \in T$ approximate Sf.

Among $\underline{T}$-functions over $U \neq \emptyset$ there are two-argument $\underline{T}$-functions which determine descending $\underline{T}$-sequences of equivalence relations $(\cong_t)_{t \in T}$ and $\cong_T = \bigcap_{t \in T} \cong_t$ over U. Least unions of equivalence classes $[a]_t$ $([a]_T)$ of $\cong_t$ $(\cong_T)$ covering $X \subset U$ are taken as closures $C_t X$ $(C_T X)$ of X. These closure operations are extended on descending T-sequences $(Sd_t f)_{t \in T}$ and induce analogous operations on $d_t f$ for $t \in T$ and on T-functions $f : U \longrightarrow ELT$.

Given an enumerable well founded poset $\underline{T} = (T, \leq)$ there are introduced first order predicate languages $\underline{L}_T$ of type $\underline{T}$, additionally equipped with propositional constants $\underline{e}_t$, $t \in LT$, approximation connectives d_t, $t \in T$, and modal operators C_t, $t \in T$ and C_T as well as with an equivalence predicate $\underline{e}$ and its classical counterpart $\underline{e}^*$. A notion of a semantic model of $\underline{L}_T$ in $U \neq \emptyset$ is introduced and a relationship of such a model with a corresponding algebraic realization is established. A formal consequence operation is introduced by means of axiom schemes and rules of inference and the completeness theorem is proved on applying a theory of plain semi--Post algebras.

1. Plain semi-Post algebras and their representation

Semi-Post algebras have been introduced and examined in [1] and [2]. Plain semi-Post algebras (briefly psP-algebras) are semi-Post algebras of a special simpler form. They have been discussed in [3]. In order to make the paper self-contained, in this section the notion of a psP-algebra will again be presented and fundamental properties necessary to our investigations summerized.

Let $\underline{T} = (T, \leq)$ be an arbitrary enumerable poset (partially ordered set). We shall assume in this paper that $\underline{T}$ is well founded, i.e. that for every $t \in T$ the set $\{s \in T : s \leq t\}$ is finite. A subset S of T is said to be an ideal of $\underline{T}$ or a $\underline{T}$-ideal if $S \neq \emptyset$ and for every $t \in S$, if $s \leq t$ then $s \in S$. Thus every ideal is a finite set. The set consisting of $\emptyset$ and of all ideals of $\underline{T}$ will be denoted by LT. It is also a poset with respect to the inclusion which in this case will be denoted by $\leq$, too. Clearly LT is a complete set lattice uniquely determined by $\underline{T}$. For the sake of simplicity we shall in the sequel identify any $t \in T$ with the ideal generated by t, i.e. with the set $\{s \in T : s \leq t\}$. By this identification $(T, \leq)$ can be treated as a subposet of $(LT, \leq)$. Then every element s in LT has the following representation

(1) $$s = \bigcup \{t \in T : t \leq s\}.$$

The greatest element in LT, which is equal to T, will be denoted by $\vee$ and the least element equal to $\emptyset$ will be denoted by $\wedge$. Clearly $\wedge \notin T$.

For any poset $\underline{T} = (T, \leq)$ we shall define psP-algebras of type $\underline{T}$.

An algebra $\underline{P} = (P, \cup, \cap, \Rightarrow, \neg, (d_t)_{t \in T}, (e_s)_{s \in LT})$ is said to be a psP-algebra of type $\underline{T} = (T, \leq)$ provided that for any $a, b \in P$, $t, w \in T$, $s \in LT$ the following conditions are satisfied:

(p_0) $(P, \cup, \cap, \Rightarrow, \neg, e_\wedge, e_\vee)$ is a pseudo-Boolean algebra with the zero element $e_\wedge$ and the unit element $e_\vee$,

(p_1) $d_t(a \cup b) = d_t a \cup d_t b$,

(p_2) $d_t(a \cap b) = d_t a \cap d_t b$,

(p_3) $d_t(a \Rightarrow b) = \bigcap_{w \leq t} (d_w a \Rightarrow d_w b)$,

(p_4) $d_t \neg a = \bigcap_{w \leq t} \neg d_w a$,

(p_5) $d_w d_t a = d_t a$,

(p_6) $$d_t e_s = \begin{cases} e_\vee & \text{if } t \leq s \\ e_\wedge & \text{otherwise} \end{cases},$$

(p_7) $d_t a \cup \neg d_t a = e_\vee$,

(p_8) $a = (\underline{P}) \bigcup_{t \in T} (d_t a \cap e_t)$ where $(\underline{P}) \bigcup$ denotes l.u.b. in $\underline{P}$. If $\underline{P}$ is established we shall sometimes write $\bigcup$ instead of $(\underline{P}) \bigcup$.

Constants e_t, $t \in LT$ are called Post constants and e_t, $t \in T$ primitive ones. The operations d_t, $t \in T$ can be conceived to be projections of an element of P into components t of $\underline{P}$. It follows from (p_5), (p_7) that $d_t a$ for $a \in P$ and $t \in T$ are complemented (Boolean) elements having all projections equal. They will be called cylindrical elements in P. We shall denote by B_P the set of all cylindrical elements in P. Thus

(2) $$B_P = \{d_t a : a \in P, t \in T\}.$$

The set of all complemented elements in P will be denoted by BP. Obviously $B_P \subset BP$. It can be proved that in general $B_P \neq BP$.
The simplest and very important example of a psP-algebra of type $\underline{T} = (T, \leq)$ is offered by a basic semi-Post algebra $\underline{LT} = (LT, \cup, \cap, \Rightarrow, \neg, (d_t)_{t \in T}, (e_s)_{s \in LT})$, where $(LT, \cup, \cap)$ is a complete set lattice determined by $\underline{T}$, for any $t, s, w \in LT$ the operations $\Rightarrow$ of relative pseudocomplement and $\neg$ of pseudocomplement exist and

$$w \leq s \Rightarrow t \text{ iff } s \cap w \leq t, \quad \neg w = w \Rightarrow \wedge ,$$

$$e_s \overset{df}{=} s \text{ for } s \in LT \qquad d_t e_s = \begin{cases} e_\vee & \text{if } t \leq s \\ e_\wedge & \text{otherwise} . \end{cases}$$

It is easy to verify that axioms (p_0) - (p_8) are satisfied.
The algebra $\underline{LT}$ and every algebra isomorphic to $\underline{LT}$ is said to be a basic semi-Post algebra of type $\underline{T}$. In particular, given any psP-algebra $\underline{P} = (P, \cup, \cap, \Rightarrow, \neg, (d_t)_{t \in T}, (e_s)_{s \in LT})$ of type $\underline{T}$ the subalgebra $\underline{ELT} = (ELT, \cup, \cap, \Rightarrow, \neg, (d_t)_{t \in T}, (e_s)_{s \in LT})$ of $\underline{P}$, where $ELT = \{e_s\}_{s \in LT}$, formed of all Post constants of $\underline{P}$ is isomorphic to $\underline{LT}$.

Basic semi-Post algebras of type $\underline{T}$ play in the class of all psP-algebras of the same type a role analogous to that of two-element Boolean algebra in the class of all Boolean algebras. They will be admitted as a basis to define a semantics for logic of approximation reasoning.

<u>Example</u> Let $T = \{t_1, t_2, t_3\}$ and assume $t_i \leq t_i$ for $i=1,2,3$ and $t_2 \leq t_3$ define a partial order in $\underline{T} = (T, \leq)$. Then $LT = \{\emptyset, \{t_1\}, \{t_2\}, \{t_2, t_3\}, \{t_1, t_2\}, \{t_1, t_2, t_3\}\}$. We set $\wedge = \emptyset$, $\vee = T$.

The algebra

$\underline{ELT} = (\{e_t\}_{t \in LT}, \cup, \cap, \Rightarrow, \neg, (d_t)_{t \in T}, (e_s)_{s \in LT})$

where $e_s = s$ for $s \in LT$, $d_t e_s = e_\vee$ for $t \le s$ and $d_t e_s = e_\wedge$ if non $t \le s$, $e_t \Rightarrow e_s = e_\vee$ if $t \le s$, $e_t \Rightarrow e_s = e_s$ if $s \ne \wedge$ and non $t \le s$, $e_t \Rightarrow e_\wedge = \neg e_t$, $\neg e_\vee = e_\wedge$, $\neg e_{\{t_1,t_2\}} = e_\wedge$, $\neg e_{\{t_2,t_3\}} = e_{t_1}$, $\neg e_{t_2} = e_{t_1}$, $\neg e_{t_1} = e_{\{t_2,t_3\}}$.

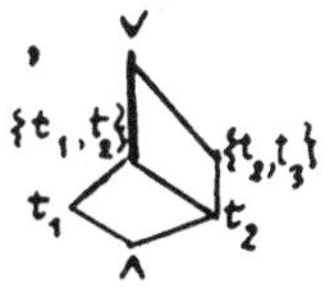

Notice that the following fundamental properties of psP-algebras of type $\underline{T} = (T, \le)$ are easy to prove.

(3) $a \le b$ iff $d_t a \le d_t b$ for every $t \in T$,

(4) $a = b$ iff $d_t a = d_t b$ for every $t \in T$,

(5) if $t \le s$, then $e_t \le e_s$ for $t, s \in LT$,

(6) if $t \le s$, then $d_s a \le d_t a$ for $t, s \in T$, $a \in P$,

(7) if $a \in BP$, then $d_t \neg a = \neg d_t a$,

(8) if $a \in BP$, then $d_t \neg d_s a = \neg d_s a$, $t, s \in T$.

The following theorems have been proved in [3].

1.1 (Theorem 2 (iv), Corollary 1 in Sec. 3 in [3]). Given a psP-algebra $\underline{P} = (P, \cup, \cap, \Rightarrow, \neg, (d_t)_{t \in T}, (e_s)_{s \in LT})$ of type $\underline{T} = (T, \le)$, the basic semi Post algebra $\underline{ELT} = (ELT, \cup, \cap, \Rightarrow, \neg, (d_t)_{t \in T}, (e_s)_{s \in LT})$, where $ELT = \{e_s\}_{s \in LT}$, is a complete lattice and for every $S \subset LT$

$$(\underline{P}) \bigcup_{s \in S} e_s = (\underline{ELT}) \bigcup_{s \in S} e_s, \quad (P) \bigcap_{s \in S} e_s = (\underline{ELT}) \bigcap_{s \in S} e_s .$$

Moreover for any set $\{a_w : w \in W\}$ of elements in P, and $t \in T$

$$(\underline{P}) \bigcup_{w \in W} d_t a_w = (\underline{B_P}) \bigcup_{w \in W} d_t a_w \quad \text{and} \quad (\underline{P}) \bigcap_{w \in W} d_t a_w = (\underline{B_P}) \bigcap_{w \in W} d_t a_w ,$$

i.e. the infinite join (meet) in $\underline{P}$ exists if and only if the infinite join (meet) in $\underline{B_P}$ exists and they are equal.

1.2 (Generalization of Epstein's lemma, Theorem 2(v) in [3]). For any $a \in P$ and a set $\{a_w : w \in W\}$ of elements in $\underline{P}$,

$$a = (\underline{P}) \bigcup_{w \in W} a_w \qquad (a = (P) \bigcap_{w \in W} a_w) \text{ if and only if}$$

$$d_t a = (\underline{B_P}) \bigcup_{w \in W} d_t a_w \qquad (d_t a = (\underline{B_P}) \bigcap_{w \in W} d_t a_w) \text{ for all } t \in T .$$

All psP-algebras of a well founded enumerable type $\underline{T} = (T, \leq)$ can be obtained up to isomorphism applying the following method.

Let $U \neq \emptyset$ be an arbitrary space and let $\underline{B}(U) = (B(U), \cup, \cap, \Rightarrow, -)$ be a field of subsets of U. Let DS(B(U)) be the set of all descending $\underline{T}$-sequences

$$Y = (Y_t)_{t \in T} \quad \text{of sets} \quad Y_t \quad \text{for} \quad t \in T \quad \text{in} \quad B(U) ,$$

i.e. satisfying the condition

$$t \leq s \quad \text{implies} \quad Y_s \subset Y_t \quad \text{for all} \quad t, s \in T .$$

Let us define an ordering relation $\leq$ over DS(B(U)) componentwise, i.e. for $Y = (Y_t)_{t \in T}$ and $Z = (Z_t)_{t \in T}$,

$$Y \leq Z \text{ if and only if } \quad Y_t \subset Z_t \quad \text{for all} \quad t \in T .$$

Put for every $s \in LT$, $X = (X_t)_{t \in T}$, $Y = (Y_t)_{t \in T}$: $E_s = (Z_t)_{t \in T}$, where $Z_t = U$ for $t \leq s$ and $Z_t = \emptyset$ if non $t \leq s$,

$$X \cup Y = (X_t \cup Y_t)_{t \in T} \quad , \quad X \cap Y = (X_t \cap Y_t)_{t \in T} ,$$

$$X \Rightarrow Y = (Z_t)_{t \in T} \quad , \text{ where } \quad Z_t = \bigcap_{s \leq t} (X_s \Rightarrow Y_s) ,$$

$$\neg X = (Z_t)_{t \in T} \quad , \text{ where } \quad Z_t = \bigcap_{s \leq t} - X_s ,$$

$$d_s X = (Z_t)_{t \in T} \quad , \text{ where } \quad Z_t = X_s \quad \text{for every} \quad t \in T , s \in T .$$

It can be proved by an easy verification that all axioms (p_0) - (p_8) are satisfied. Thus

$$\underline{\underline{DS}}(B(U)) = (DS(B(U)), \cup, \cap, \Rightarrow, \neg, (d_t)_{t \in T}, (E_s)_{s \in LT})$$

and all its psP-subalgebras (i.e. subsets of DS(B(U)) which contain all E_s for $s \in LT$, and are closed with respect to operations $\cup$, $\cap$, $\Rightarrow$, $\neg$, d_s for $s \in T$) are psP-algebras of type $\underline{T}$. $\underline{\underline{DS}}(B(U))$ is called full to emphasize that it is constructed of all descending $\underline{T}$-sequences of sets in $\underline{B}(U)$.

The following representation theorem is fundamental in this paper.

1.3. For every non-degenerate psP-algebra $\underline{P}$ there is a monomorphism h from $\underline{P}$ into a full psP-algebra $\underline{DS}(B(U))$ of all descending $\underline{T}$-sequences of sets in $B(U)$. Moreover, it can be assumed that for any enumerable set (Q)

$$\text{(Q)} \qquad a_n = (\underline{P}) \bigcup_{k \in K_n} a_{nk} \qquad\qquad b_n = (P) \bigcap_{m \in M_n} b_{nm}$$

of infinite joins and meets in $\underline{P}$, h preserves infinite joins and meets in (Q) and in (DQ), where

$$\text{(DQ)} \qquad d_t a_n = (\underline{B}_P) \bigcup_{k \in K_n} d_t a_{nk} \qquad d_t b_n = (\underline{B}_P) \bigcap_{m \in M_n} d_t b_{nm} \text{ for all } t \in T .$$

Sketch of a proof. Let U be the set of all prime filters in $\underline{B}_P$ preserving infinite joins and meets in (DQ).
Put $h_o(d_t a) = \{\nabla_o \in U : d_t a \in \nabla_o\}$. Then h_o is an isomorphism from $\underline{B}_P$ onto the field $B(U) = \{h_o(d_t a) : a \in P \text{ and } t \in T\}$.
Let $h(\bar{a}) = (h_o(d_t a))_{t \in T} \in DS(B(U))$. Because if $t \leq s$, then $d_s a \leq d_t a$ and hence $h_o(d_s a) \subset h_o(d_t a)$. It can be proved that h is a monomorphism from $\underline{P}$ into $\underline{DS}(B(U))$ and preserves infinite joins and meets in (Q) and in (DQ).

The following theorem results from theorems proved in [3].

1.4 Let ∇_o be any prime filter in $\underline{B}_P$ preserving infinite joins and meets in (DQ). Let

$$(9) \qquad \nabla = \{a \in P : d_t a \in \nabla_o \text{ for all } t \in T\} .$$

Put for any $a,b \in P$, $a \cong_\nabla b$ iff $a \Rightarrow b \in \nabla$ and $b \Rightarrow a \in \nabla$.
Then the following conditions are satisfied:

(i) ∇ is a prime filter in $\underline{P}$,

(ii) $\nabla \cap B_P = \nabla_o$,

(iii) $a \in \nabla$ iff $d_t a \in \nabla$ for all $t \in T$,

(iv) $b_n \in \nabla$ iff $b_{nm} \in \nabla$ for all $m \in M_n$,

(v) $\cong_\nabla$ is a congruence in $\underline{P}$,

(vi) $\underline{P}/\nabla$ is isomorphic to a basic psP-algebra $\underline{ELT}$ of type $\underline{T}$ and for any $a,b \in P$

(10) $|a| = |e_\vee|$ iff $a \in \nabla$, where $|a|$ is the equivalence class

of $\tilde{=}_{\nabla}$, determined by a ,

(11) if $a \in \nabla$ and $a \Rightarrow b \in \nabla$, then $b \in \nabla$,

(vii) ∇ preserves infinite joins and meets in (DQ) and in (Q), i.e.

(12) $$|d_t a_n| = (\underline{P}/\nabla) \bigcup_{k \in K_n} |d_t a_{nk}| , \quad |d_t b_n| = (\underline{P}/\nabla) \bigcap_{m \in M_n} |d_t b_{nm}|, \quad t \in T, \quad n \in N ,$$

(13) $$|a_n| = (\underline{P}/\nabla) \bigcup_{k \in K_n} |a_{nk}| , \quad |b_n| = (\underline{P}/\nabla) \bigcap_{m \in M_n} |b_{nm}| , \quad n \in N .$$

(14) $$|a| = \underline{P}/\nabla \bigcup_{t \in T} |d_t a| \cap |e_t| .$$

2. $\underline{T}$-functions vs. descending $\underline{T}$-sequences of sets

Let $\underline{T} = (T, \leq)$ be an enumerable well founded poset and consider a basic sP-algebra of type $\underline{T}$, $\underline{ELT} = (ELT, \cup, \cap, \Rightarrow, \neg, (d_t)_{t \in T}, (e_s)_{s \in LT})$.

Let $U \neq \emptyset$ be any space, $\underline{B}(U)$ - the field of all subsets of U and let us take under consideration the set ELT^U of all functions

(1) $$f : U \longrightarrow \{e_s\}_{s \in LT} .$$

They will be said to be $\underline{T}$-functions over U. To every $f \in ELT^U$ let as assign Boolean functions $d_t f$ for $t \in T$, which according to the axiom (p_6) in Sec.1 are defined thus:

(2) $$d_t f(u) = \begin{cases} e_{\vee} & \text{if } f(u) \geq e_t \\ e_{\wedge} & \text{otherwise} \end{cases} .$$

By (p_8) in Sec.1

(3) $$f(u) = (\underline{ELT}) \bigcup_{t \in T} (d_t f(u) \cap e_t) , \quad \text{for every } u \in U .$$

In this sense we write

(4) $$f = \bigcup_{t \in T} (d_t f \cap e_t) .$$

Clearly functions $d_t f$, $t \in T$ can be treated as characteristic

functions of some subsets of U. Let us denote by $S(d_t f)$, $t \in T$ sets such that their characteristic functions are $d_t f$, $t \in T$, respectively.
This yields

(5) $$S(d_t f) = \{ u \in U: d_t f(u) = e_\vee \} = \{ u \in U: f(u) \geq e_t \}.$$

By (6) in Sec.1 ,

(6) $t \leq s$ implies $S(d_s f) \subset S(d_t f)$ for any $t, s \in T$.

Thus

(7) $S(d_t f)_{t \in T}$ is a descending $\underline{T}$-sequence of sets in $\underline{B}(U)$.

It is easy to prove that a mapping $\varphi : ELT^U \longrightarrow DS(B(U))$ assigning to each $f = \bigcup_{t \in T} (d_t f \cap e_t)$ the descending $\underline{T}$-sequence $S(d_t f)_{t \in T}$ of sets in $B(U)$ is one-to-one and maps ELT^U onto $DS(B(U))$.

3. Approximation spaces of type $\underline{T} = (T, \leq)$ and approximation operators

Let $EQ(U)$, $U \neq \emptyset$ be the set of all $\underline{T}$-functions $eq : U^2 \longrightarrow \{ e_s \}_{s \in LT}$ satisfying the following conditions:

(1) $eq(u,u) = e_\vee$, (2) $eq(u_1,u_2) = eq(u_2,u_1)$,

(3) $eq(u_1,u_2) \cap eq(u_2,u_3) \leq eq(u_1,u_3)$,

where $\cap$ is the meet operation in $\underline{ELT}$.

Notice that $d_t eq : U^2 \longrightarrow \{ e_\vee, e_\wedge \}$ for $t \in T$ are in $EQ(U)$ provided that $eq \in EQ(U)$ and

(4) $t \leq s$ implies $d_s eq(u_1,u_2) \leq d_t eq(u_1,u_2)$ for $t, s \in T$.

It is easy to see that

3.1. Every $eq \in EQ(U)$ determines equivalence relations $\cong_t$ for $t \in T$ and $\cong_T$ on U by adopting

(5) $u_1 \cong_t u_2$ iff $d_t eq(u_1, u_2) = e_V$, for $t \in T$,

(6) $u_1 \cong_T u_2$ iff $d_t eq(u_1, u_2) = e_V$, for all $t \in T$.

Relations $\cong_j$ for $j \in T$ and $j = T$ can be extended on U^n , $n = 1, 2, \ldots$, as follows

(7) $(u_1, \ldots, u_n) \cong_j (u_1', \ldots, u_n')$ iff $u_i \cong_j u_i'$ for all $i=1, \ldots, n$

Moreover,

(8) $s \leq t$ implies $\cong_t \subset \cong_s$ for any $t, s \in T$,

(9) $\cong_T = \bigcap_{t \in T} \cong_t$.

An approximation space of type $\underline{T} = (T, \leq)$ determined by $eq \in EQ(U)$ is a system $\underline{A} = (U, (\cong_t)_{t \in T}, \cong_T)$, where $\cong_t$ for $t \in T$ and $\cong_T$ are equivalence relations defined by (5) and (6). This approximation space will also be denoted by $\underline{A} = (U, eq)$.
Every equivalence relation $\cong_j$, for $j \in T$ or $j = T$ in $\underline{A}$ defines a topology $\mathcal{O}_j$ in U^n by adopting the family of all unions of equivalence classes of $\cong_j$ and the empty set $\emptyset$ as a basis for the open sets of topology $\mathcal{O}_j$ in U^n .
The closure operation C_j in $\mathcal{O}_j$ assigns to any $X \subset U^n$ the set $C_j X$ being the union of equivalence classes of $\cong_j$ which are not disjoint with X and the interior operation I_j in $\mathcal{O}_j$ associates with every $X \subset U^n$ the set $I_j X$ being the union of equivalence classes of $\cong_j$ which are contained in X . It follows that for every $X \subset U^n$, $j \in T$ or $j = T$

(10) $u \in C_j X$ iff there is $u' \in U^n$ such that $u \cong_j u'$ and $u' \in X$,

(11) $u \in I_j X$ iff for every $u' \in U^n$, if $u \cong_j u'$ then $u' \in X$.

Of course

$$C_j X = - I_j - X .$$

For every $X \subset U^n$, $C_j X$ for $j \in T$ or $j = T$ are adopted as upper approximations of X and $I_j X$ for $j \in T$ or $j = T$ as lower approximations of X. Operators C_j and I_j for $j \in T$ or $j = T$

are algebraic counterparts of modal propositional connectives of the possibility and of the necessity, respectively.

The next task is to define C_j and I_j, $j \in T$ or $j = T$, on descending $\underline{T}$-sequences of subsets of U^n and also on $\underline{T}$-functions in ELT^{U^n}.

It is quite natural to adopt

$$C_j(X_t)_{t \in T} \overset{df}{=} (C_j X_t)_{t \in T}, \quad \text{for } j \in T \text{ or } j = T,$$

$$I_j(X_t)_{t \in T} \overset{df}{=} (I_j X_t)_{t \in T}, \quad \text{for } j \in T \text{ or } j = T.$$

Now, consider any $\underline{T}$-function $f : U^n \longrightarrow \{e_t\}_{t \in LT}$ having a unique representation

$$f = \bigcup_{t \in T} (d_t f \cap e_t)$$

and

$$\mathcal{C}(f) = (Sd_t f)_{t \in T}.$$

According to the previous establishments we extend C_j and I_j for $j \in T$ or $j = T$ on $\mathcal{C}(f)$ as follows :

(13) $$C_j(Sd_t f)_{t \in T} \overset{df}{=} (C_j Sd_t f)_{t \in T}, \quad \text{for } j \in T \text{ or } j = T.$$

(14) $$I_j(Sd_t f)_{t \in T} \overset{df}{=} (I_j Sd_t f)_{t \in T}, \quad \text{for } j \in T \text{ or } j = T.$$

Let us set for $j \in T$ or $j = T$

(15) $$C_j d_t f(u) = \begin{cases} e_\vee & \text{if there is } u' \in U^n \text{ such that } u \cong_j u' \text{ and } d_t f(u') = e_\vee \\ e_\wedge & \text{otherwise}, \end{cases}$$

(16) $$I_j d_t f(u) = \begin{cases} e_\vee & \text{if for each } u' \in U^n, \text{ if } u \cong_j u' \text{ then } d_t f(u') = e_\vee \\ e_\wedge & \text{otherwise}. \end{cases}$$

Notice that $C_j d_t f \geqq C_j d_s f$ if $t \leqq s$ and

$I_j d_t f \geqq I_j d_s f$ if $t \leqq s$.

Let us set for every $j \in T$ and $j = T$

(17) $C_j f \overset{df}{=} \bigcup_{t \in T} (C_j d_t f \cap e_t)$ and $I_j f \overset{df}{=} \bigcup_{t \in T} (I_j d_t f \cap e_t)$.

By the uniqueness of representations of any $f \in ELT^{U^n}$, we obtain

(18) $d_t C_j f = C_j d_t f$ and $d_t I_j f = I_j d_t f$.

Notice that (13), (14), (15), (16), (17), (18) yield for $j \in T$ and $j = T$

(19) $\mathcal{C}(C_j f) = C_j(\mathcal{C} f)$ and $\mathcal{C}(I_j f) = I_j \mathcal{C}(f)$.

If f is a zero-argument function, then we set

(20) $I_j d_t f = C_j d_t f = d_t f$ for $j \in T$ and $j = T$, $t \in T$.

Hence by (18)

(21) $I_j f = \bigcup_{t \in T} (d_t I_j f \cap e_t) = \bigcup_{t \in T} (d_t f \cap e_t) = f$

and

(22) $C_j f = \bigcup_{t \in T} (d_t C_j f \cap e_t) = \bigcup_{t \in T} (d_t f \cap e_t) = f$.

4. Logic of approximation reasoning of type $\underline{T} = (T, \leq)$

Let $\underline{T} = (T, \leq)$ be any enumerable well founded poset. It can be considered as an information system.

Consider a countable first order predicate language $\underline{L}_T$ constructed as follows. Assume that Var is the set of all individual variables in $\underline{L}_T$. The set F_{at} of atomic formulas consists of propositional constants $\underline{e}_s$, $s \in LT$, and of formulas $\underline{e}(x,y)$, $\underline{e}^*(x,y)$, $p_i(x_1,\dots,x_{n(i)})$ for any $x,y,x_1,\dots,x_{n(i)} \in$ Var and $i = 1,\dots,q$, where p_i is a n(i)-ary predicate for $i = 1,\dots,q$. Other formulas are built of atomic ones by means of propositional connectives $\cup$, $\cap$, $\Rightarrow$, $\neg$, approximation operators d_t for $t \in T$, modal operators C_j and I_j for $j \in T$ and $j = T$, quantifiers $\exists$, $\forall$ and parentheses Instead of $(A \Rightarrow B) \cap (B \Rightarrow A)$ we write $A \Leftrightarrow B$. Let F be the set of all formulas in $\underline{L}_T$. Another, simpler version $\underline{L}_T^-$ of $\underline{L}_T$ is obtained from $\underline{L}_T$ by eliminating $\underline{e}^*(x,y)$ for $x,y \in$ Var from F_{at} and by eliminating modal connectives C_T , and I_T .

Formulas d_tA for $t \in T$, according to the intuitive meaning, could be read "A is approximated by t". For instance if A(x) is interpreted as "to be Kurt Gödel" and t(x) is a query in T "to be a logician" then $d_tA(x)$ would be interpreted as "to be Kurt Gödel is approximated by to be a logician".

Formulas C_tA for $t \in T$ (C_T) could be read "A is possible towards t (T)" and formulas I_tA for $t \in T$ (I_T) could be read "A is necessary towards t (T)".

By a model M of $\underline{L}_T$ we shall mean any structure of the following form

(1) $\quad M = (U, (\cong)_{t \in T}, \cong_T, (S_{1t})_{t \in T}, \ldots, (S_{qt})_{t \in T})$

where $(\cong)_{t \in T}$ is a T-sequence of equivalence relations over U, $\cong_T = \bigcap_{t \in T} \cong_t$, and $(S_{it})_{t \in T}$ for $i = 1, \ldots, q$ are T-sequences of n(i)-ary relations in U. T-sequences in M are descending.
Let Val be the set of all valuations of individual variables in U, i.e. the set of functions $v : Var \longrightarrow U$. We are going to define the notion of satisfiability of any formula $A \in F$ in M for a valuation v.
Let $M, v \models A$ stands for "valuation v satisfies A in M". For any $A \in F$ let Var A denotes the set of all free individual variables in A.

(2) $\quad M, v \models d_t e_s$ iff $t \leq s$, $t \in T$, $s \in LT$,

(3) $\quad M, v \models d_t \underline{e}(x, y)$ iff $v(x) \cong_t v(y)$, $t \in T$

(4) $\quad M, v \models d_t \underline{e}^{*}(x, y)$ iff $v(x) \cong_T v(y)$ i.e. iff $v(x) \cong_t v(y)$ for all $t \in T$,

(5) $\quad M, v \models d_t p_i(x_1, \ldots, x_{n(i)})$ iff $(v(x_1), \ldots, v(x_{n(i)})) \in S_{it}$

(6) $\quad M, v \models d_s d_t A$ iff $M, v \models d_t A$

(7) $\quad M, v \models d_t(A \cup B)$ iff $M, v \models d_t A$ or $M, v \models d_t B$

(8) $\quad M, v \models d_t(A \cap B)$ iff $M, v \models d_t A$ and $M, v \models d_t B$

(9) $\quad M, v \models d_t(A \rightarrow B)$ iff for every $s \leq t$: non $M, v \models d_s A$ or $M, v \models d_s B$

(10) $M,v \models d_t \neg A$ iff for every $s \preceq t$: non $M,v \models d_s A$,

(11) $M,v \models d_t C_j A(x_1,\ldots,x_n)$ where $\mathrm{Var}\, A = \{x_1,\ldots,x_n\}$, $j \in T$ or $j = T$ iff there are $u_1,\ldots,u_n \in U$ such that $u_i \cong_j v(x_i)$, $i=1,\ldots,n$ and $M,v_{u_1 \ldots u_n} \models d_t A(x_1 \ldots x_n)$ where $v_{u_1 \ldots u_n}(x_i)=u_i$ for $i=1,\ldots,n$, $v_{u_1 \ldots u_n}(y) = v(y)$ for $y \neq x_1,\ldots,x_n$.

(12) $M,v \models d_t C_j A$, where $\mathrm{Var}\, A = \emptyset$ and $j \in T$ or $j = T$, iff $M,v \models d_t A$,

(13) $M,v \models d_t I_j A(x_1 \ldots x_n)$, where $\mathrm{Var}\, A = \{x_1,\ldots,x_n\}$, $j \in T$ or $j = T$ iff for every $u_1,\ldots,u_n$ such that $u_i \cong_j v(x_i)$, $i = 1,\ldots,n$, $M,v_{u_1 \ldots u_n} \models d_t A(x_1,\ldots,x_n)$, where $v_{u_1 \ldots u_n}$ is defined as in (11) ,

(14) $M,v \models d_t I_j A$, where $\mathrm{Var}\, A = \emptyset$ and $j \in T$ or $j = T$, iff $M,v \models d_t A$,

(15) $M,v \models d_t(\forall x)A(x)$ iff for each $u \in U$, $M,v_u \models d_t A(x)$,

(16) $M,v \models d_t(\exists x)A(x)$ iff there is $u \in U$ such that $M,v_u \models d_t A(x)$,

(17) $M,v \models A$ iff for every $t \in T$, $M,v \models d_t A$.

A model M of $\underline{L}_T$ is a model of a set $\Sigma \subset F$ if for every valuation $v \in \mathrm{Val}$, and every $A \in \Sigma$, $M,v \models A$.

Given a model M being a structure (1) it determines uniquely an algebraic realization R of $\underline{L}_T$.

(18) $R = (U, eq, eq^*, f_1,\ldots,f_q)$,

where $eq \in EQ(U)$, $eq^* \in EQ(U)$, $f_i : U^{n(i)} \to \{e_s\}_{s \in LT}$ are T-functions defined as follows

(19) $$d_t eq(u_1,u_2) = \begin{cases} e_\vee & \text{if } u_1 \cong_t u_2 \text{ in } M \\ e_\wedge & \text{otherwise} \end{cases},$$

(20) $$eq(u_1 u_2) = (\underline{ELT}) \bigcup_{t \in T} (d_t eq(u_1,u_2) \cap e_t) ,$$

$$(21)\quad eq^{*}(u_1,u_2) = d_t eq^{*}(u_1,u_2) = \begin{cases} e_{\vee} & \text{if } u_1 \cong_T u_2 \text{ in } M \\ e_{\wedge} & \text{otherwise} \end{cases}$$
for every $t \in T$,

$$(22)\quad d_t f_i(u_1,\ldots,u_{n(i)}) = \begin{cases} e_{\vee} & \text{if } (u_1,\ldots,u_{n(i)}) \in S_{it} \text{ in } M \\ e_{\wedge} & \text{otherwise} \end{cases}$$

$$(23)\quad f_i(u_1,\ldots,u_{n(i)}) = (\underline{ELT}) \bigcup_{t\in T} (d_t f_i(u_1,\ldots,u_{n(i)}) \cap e_t), i=1,\ldots,q$$

It is easy to see, that eq and eq^{*} determine T-sequence $(\cong_t)_{t\in T}$ of equivalence relations in U according to the establishments in Sec.3 and $\cong_T = \bigcap_{t\in T} \cong_t$.
Moreover, it follows from (22), (23) and (5) in Sec.3 that

$$(24)\qquad (Sd_t f_i)_{t\in T} = (S_{it})_{t\in T} \quad .$$

A realization R assigns to propositional connectives $\cup, \cap, \Rightarrow, \neg$, d_t for $t \in T$ the corresponding operations in <u>ELT</u>, to operations I_j, C_j for $j \in T$ and $j = T$ corresponding operations on T-functions (see Sec.3, (15), (16), (17)), and to quantifiers $\forall$, $\exists$ infinite meets and joins in <u>ELT</u>, respectively. For any formula $A \in F$, a realization of A by valuation v will be denoted by $A_R(v)$.

The following theorem is easy to prove by inductive argument with respect to the length of formulas.

4.1 For every formula $A \in F$, any model M in U, valuation $v \in Val$ and realization R defined by (18) - (23)

$$M,v \models A \quad \text{iff} \quad A_R(v) = e_{\vee} \quad .$$

Adopt as logical axioms in $\underline{L_T}$: all formulas in F which are substitutions of axioms of the intuitionistic propositional calculus and moreover the following axiom schemes for predicate calculus of type $\underline{T}$, being counterparts of axioms (p_1) - (p_8) in Sec.1

$$(\text{ax } 1)\quad d_t(A \cup B) \Leftrightarrow (d_t A \cup d_t B), \quad t \in T,$$

$$(\text{ax } 2)\quad d_t(A \cap B) \Leftrightarrow (d_t A \cap d_t B), \quad t \in T,$$

$$(\text{ax } 3)\quad d_t(A \Rightarrow B) \Leftrightarrow \bigcap_{s\leq t} (d_s A \Rightarrow d_s B), \quad s,t \in T,$$

(ax 4) $d_t(\neg A) \Leftrightarrow \bigcap_{s \leq t} \neg d_s A \qquad s,t \in T$,

(ax 5) $d_t d_s A \Leftrightarrow d_s A$, $\qquad s,t \in T$,

(ax 6) $d_t \underline{e}_s$ for $t \leq s$ and $\neg d_t \underline{e}_s$ for t,s such that non $t \leq s$ and $s \in LT$,

(ax 7) $d_t A \Rightarrow d_s A$ for $s \leq t$, $\quad s,t \in T$,

(ax 8) $\underline{e}_{\vee}$

(ax 9) $d_t A \cup \neg d_t A$, $\quad t \in T$,

(ax 10) $(d_t A \cap \underline{e}_t) \Rightarrow A$, $\quad t \in T$,

axioms for predicates $\underline{e}$ and $\underline{e}^*$

(ax 11) $\underline{e}(x,x)$,

(ax 12) $\underline{e}(x,y) \Rightarrow \underline{e}(y,x)$,

(ax 13) $(\underline{e}(x,y) \cap \underline{e}(y,z)) \Rightarrow \underline{e}(x,z)$,

(ax 14) $\underline{e}^*(x,y) \Rightarrow d_t \underline{e}(x,y)$, $\quad t \in T$,

(ax 15) $\underline{e}^*(x,y) \Leftrightarrow d_t \underline{e}^*(x,y)$, $\quad t \in T$,

and the following axiom schemes for I_j , C_j where $j \in T$ or $j = T$,

(ax 16) $I_j A \Leftrightarrow A$ if $\mathrm{Var}\, A = \emptyset$,

(ax 17) $\forall y_1 \ldots \forall y_n((\underline{e}^*(x_1,y_1) \cap \ldots \cap \underline{e}^*(x_n,y_n)) \Rightarrow d_t A(y_1,\ldots,y_n)) \Leftrightarrow$
$I_T d_t A(x_1,\ldots,x_n)$, where
$\mathrm{Var}\, A = \{x_1,\ldots,x_n\}$,

(ax 18) $\forall y_1 \ldots \forall y_n((d_j \underline{e}(x_1,y_1) \ \ldots \ d_j \underline{e}(x_n,y_n)) \Rightarrow d_t A(y_1,\ldots,y_n))$
$\Leftrightarrow I_j d_t(A(x_1,\ldots,x_n))$, where $\mathrm{Var}\, A = \{x_1,\ldots,x_n\}$,

(ax 19) $d_t I_j A \Leftrightarrow I_j d_t A$,

(ax 20) $d_t C_j A \Leftrightarrow C_j d_t A$,

(ax 21) $C_j d_t A \Leftrightarrow \neg I_j \neg d_t A$, $\quad j \in T$ or $j = T$.

Rules of inference for intuitionistic predicate calculi are adopted and moreover the following ones:

$(r_1)\quad \frac{A}{d_t A}$ for $t \in T$, $\quad (r_2)\quad \frac{\{d_t A\}_{t \in T}}{A}$,

$(r_3)\quad \frac{\{A \Rightarrow d_t \underline{e}(x,y)\}_{t \in T}}{A \Rightarrow \underline{e}^*(x,y)}$.

Notice that (ax 17) and (r_3) are omitted in formalizing of the logic of approximation reasoning built on the basis of the language $\underline{L}_T^-$. We shall write $\sum \vdash A$ for any $\sum \subset F$ and $A \in F$ if F is provable from $\sum$.

We shall sketch an algebraic proof of the following

4.2 Completeness Theorem. A formula A_o in F is provable from a set $\sum \subset F$ if and only if every model M of $\sum$ is also a model of A_o.

If follows from 4.1 that it is sufficient to prove that this holds for realizations of $\underline{L}_T$, i.e. a formula A_o is provable from $\sum \subset F$ if and only if for every realization R, if R is a model of $\sum$ then R is a model of A_o.

First of all it follows from axioms and rules of inference that for any $\sum \subset F$ and $A,B \in F$:

(25) if $\sum \vdash A \Rightarrow B$, then $\sum \vdash I_j A \Rightarrow I_j B$ and $\sum \vdash C_j A \Rightarrow C_j B$

for $j \in T$ and $j = T$,

(26) if $\sum \vdash A$, then $\sum \vdash I_j A$ for $j \in T$ and $j = T$,

(27) $\vdash I_j A \Rightarrow A$ for $j \in T$ and $j = T$.

Soundness, i.e. implication: if $\sum \vdash A_o$, then $\sum \models A_o$ is easy to prove by verifying logical axioms and rules of inference.

Given $\sum \subset F$, consider a relation $\equiv$ over F, defined by adopting $A \equiv B$ iff $\sum \vdash A \Rightarrow B$ and $\sum \vdash B \Rightarrow A$.
It follows from the intuitionistic axioms, (ax 3), (ax 4), rule (r_1) and (25), that $\equiv$ is a congruence relation on the algebra of formulas. Let

$$\underline{F}/\equiv\; = (F/\equiv, \cup, \cap, \Rightarrow, \neg, (d_t)_{t \in T}, (\underline{e}_t)_{t \in LT}, (I_j)_{j \in T}, (C_j)_{j \in T}, I_T, C_T)$$

be the quotient algebra consisting of equivalence classes $|A|$ for

$A \in F$. Let $\underline{P}$ be the reduct of $\underline{F}/\equiv$ obtained by the elimination of I_j, I_T, C_j, C_T for $j \in T$. Then $\underline{P}$ is a psP-algebra of type $\underline{T}$, and

(28) $|A| = |\underline{e}_\vee| = e_\vee$ iff $\sum \vdash A$, $|A| \leq |B|$ iff $\sum \vdash A \Rightarrow B$, $|\underline{e}_t| = e_t$ for $t \in LT$,

(29) $|A| = \bigcup_{t \in T} (|d_t A| \cap |\underline{e}_t|)$ for every $A \in F$,

(Q) $|(\forall y)A(y)| = (\underline{P}) \bigcap_{x \in Var} |A(y/x)|$, $|(\exists y)A(y)| = (P) \bigcup_{x \in Var} |A(y/x)|$,
$|\underline{e}^*(x,y)| = (\underline{P}) \bigcap_{t \in T} |d_t(\underline{e}(x,y))|$

(DQ) $d_t|(\forall y)A(y)| = (\underline{B}_{\underline{P}}) \bigcap_{x \in Var} d_t|A(y/x)|$,
$d_t|(\exists y)A(y)| = (\underline{B}_{\underline{P}}) \bigcup_{x \in Var} d_t|A(y/x)|$,
$d_t|e^*(x,y)| = (\underline{B}_{\underline{P}}) \bigcap_{t \in T} |d_t \underline{e}(x,y)|$,

for x not being in a scope of any quantifier in $A(y)$.

Assume non $\sum \vdash A_o$. Then by (28), $|A_o| \neq |\underline{e}_\vee|$. Hence, by (4) in Sec.1 and (p_6) in Sec.1 there is $t \in T$ such that $d_t|A_o| \neq |\underline{e}_\vee|$. On account of lemma 9.2 in [11] there is a prime filter ∇_o in the Boolean algebra $\underline{B}_{\underline{P}}$, which preserves all infinite joins and meets (DQ) and such that

$$|d_t A_o| \notin \nabla_o .$$

By 1.4 in Sec.1,

$$\nabla = \{|A| \in F/\equiv : |d_s A| \in \nabla_o \quad \text{for all} \quad s \in T\}$$

is a prime filter in $\underline{P}$, preserving infinite joins and meets in (Q) and (DQ) and such that

(30) $|A_o| \notin \nabla$.

Moreover, the quotient algebra $\underline{P}/\nabla$ is isomorphic to a basic psP-algebra $\underline{ELT}$ of type $\underline{T} = (T, \leq)$ and

(31) $\|A\| = \|\underline{e}_{\vee}\|$ iff $|A| \in \nabla$.

It follows from (30) and (31) that

(32) $\|A_0\| \neq \|\underline{e}_{\vee}\|$.

Now we are going to define a canonical realization R of the language $\underline{L}_T$ as usually . Assume $Val = Var^{Var}$ and

$$R = (Var, eq, eq^*, p_{1R},\dots,p_{qR}) \quad , \quad \text{where}$$

(33) $eq(x,y) \overset{df}{=} \|\underline{e}(x,y)\|$ for $x,y \in Var$,

(34) $eq^*(x,y) \overset{df}{=} \|\underline{e}^*(x,y)\|$ for $x,y \in Var$,

(35) $p_{iR}(x_1,\dots,x_n) \overset{df}{=} \|p_i(x_1,\dots,x_n)\|$.

Then

(36) $x_1 \cong_t x_2$ iff $d_t\|\underline{e}(x,y)\| = \|\underline{e}_{\vee}\|$ iff $d_t|\underline{e}(x,y)| \in \nabla$,

(37) $x_1 \cong_T x_2$ iff $\|\underline{e}^*(x,y)\| = \|\underline{e}_{\vee}\|$ iff $|\underline{e}^*(x,y)| \in \nabla$.

The following lemma can be proved by inductive argument with respect to the length of a formula:

<u>Lemma</u>. For each $A \in F$ and valuation $v : Var \longrightarrow Var$

(38) $A_R(v) = \|vA\|$,

where vA is a formula obtained from A by the simultaneous replacement of each free individual variable x by $v(x)$ if $v(x)$ is not in a scope of a quantifier. For atomic formulas (38) follows from (33), (34), (35) and the realization of $\underline{e}_t$, $t \in LT$ given by $\underline{e}_{tR} = \|\underline{e}_t\|$ for $t \in LT$.
In the case of formulas $B \cup D$, $B \cap D$, $B \Rightarrow D$, $\neg B$, d_tB for $t \in T$, $(\forall x)A(x)$, $(\exists x)A(x)$ proofs are standard on applying the definition of the realization of formulas, (Q), (DQ) and the fact that in $\underline{P}/_{\nabla}$ all infinite joins and meets in (Q) and (DQ) are preserved (cf. (12), (13) in Sec.1).

Now assume $\operatorname{Var} A = \{x_1,\dots,x_n\}$ and

(39) $d_tA(x_1,\dots,x_n)_R(v) = \| v d_tA(x_1,\dots,x_n)\|$ for $t \in T$ and $v \in \mathrm{Val}$.

Claim

(40) $I_j d_tA(x_1,\dots,x_n)_R(v) = \| v I_j d_tA(x_1,\dots,x_n)\|$ for $j \in T$ or $j = T$.

It follows from (p_6) in Sec.1 (16), (18) in Sec.3, (ax 19), (ax 6) that both sides of (40) can only admit Boolean values $e_\vee = \|\underline{e}_\vee\|$, $e_\wedge = \|\underline{e}_\wedge\|$. Thus to prove (40) it is sufficient to show that the left-hand side is equal $\|e_\vee\|$ iff the right-hand side is equal $\|\underline{e}_\vee\|$.
Assume $\| vI_Td_tA(x_1,\dots,x_n)\| = \|\underline{e}_\vee\|$.
By (31) $| vI_Td_tA(x_1,\dots,x_n)| \in \nabla$. Assume $v(x_i) \cong_T y_i$, $i=1,\dots,n$. Then by (37) $|\underline{e}^*(v(x_i),y_i| \in \nabla$ for $i=1,\dots,n$. Hence applying (ax 17) and the property (11) in Sec.1 and 1.4(iv) of ∇ we obtain $|v'd_tA(x_1,\dots,x_n)| \in \nabla$ for valuation v' such that $v'(x_i) = y_i$ for $i = 1,\dots,n$ and $v'(x) = v(x)$ for $x \neq x_1,\dots,x_n$. By (39) $d_tA(x_1,\dots,x_n)_R(v') = d_tA(y_1,\dots,y_n)_R(v) = \|\underline{e}_\vee\|$. This and (16) in Sec.3 yield $I_Td_tA(x_1,\dots,x_n)_R(v) = \|\underline{e}_\vee\|$.
In a similar way, applying (ax 18) instead of (ax 17) it can be proved that the assumption $\| vI_jd_tA(x_1,\dots,x_n)\| = \|\underline{e}_\vee\|$ implies

$I_jd_tA(x_1,\dots,x_n)_R(v) = \|\underline{e}_\vee\|$ for $j \in T$.

Now assume $I_Td_tA(x_1,\dots,x_n)_R(v) = \|\underline{e}_\vee\|$. This implies by (16) in Sec. 3 that: for all $y_1,\dots,y_n \in \mathrm{Var}$, if $v(x_i) \cong_T y_i$ for $i = 1,\dots,n$, then $d_tA(x_1,\dots,x_n)_R(v') = \|\underline{e}_\vee\|$ where $v'(x_i) = y_i$, $i = 1,\dots,n$ and $v'(x) = x$ for $x \neq x_1,\dots,x_n$. Hence by (39) and (31), (37) for all $y_1,\dots,y_n \in \mathrm{Var}$, $|v'd_tA(x_1,\dots,x_n)| \in \nabla$ provided $|\underline{e}^*(v(x_1),y_1)|,\dots,|\underline{e}^*(v(x_n),y_n| \in \nabla$.

Hence on applying (ax 15) and the definition of ∇ it follows that

$$| v'd_tA(x_1,\dots,x_n)| \in \nabla_0 \quad \text{if} \quad |\underline{e}^*(v(x_1),y_1|,\dots,|\underline{e}^*(v(x_n),y_n)| \in \nabla_0.$$

Since ∇_0 is a prime filter in $\underline{B}_P$ preserving (DQ), we infer that

$$|\forall y_1 \dots \forall y_n(\underline{e}^*(v(x_1),y_1) \cap \dots \cap \underline{e}^*(v(x_n),y_n) \Rightarrow v'd_tA(x_1 \dots x_n)| \in \nabla_0 \subset \nabla .$$

This and (ax 17), (31), as well as (11) in Sec.1 yield

$$|vI_T d_t A(x_1,\ldots,x_n)| \in \nabla \quad , \text{ i.e. } \quad \| vI_T d_t A(x_1,\ldots,x_n) \| = \| \underline{e}_V \| \; .$$

In the case of $j \in T$ a proof is quite similar applying (ax 18) instead of (ax 17).
In the case of $\mathrm{Var}\, A = \emptyset$, $I_j d_t A_R(v) = d_t A_R(v) = \| vd_t A \| = \| vI_j d_t A \|$ by (21) in Sec.3, an inductive argument and (ax 16).
The inductive step for $C_j d_t A$, $j \in T$, $j = T$, $t \in T$, is based on (15), (16) in Sec.3, the inductive step for $I_j d_t A$ just proved and (ax 21).
To prove (38) for $I_j A$ and $C_j A$ for $j \in T$ and $j = T$, $v \in \mathrm{Val}$ we apply as inductive arguments $I_j d_t A_R(v) = \| vI_j d_t A \|$, $C_j d_t A_R(v) = | vC_j d_t A |$ for all $t \in T$, (p_8) in Sec.1 for $\underline{P}/_\nabla$, (18) in Sec.3, (ax 19) which yields

$$I_j A_R(v) = (\underline{P}/_\nabla) \bigcup_{t \in T} (I_j d_t A_R(v) \cap \| \underline{e}_t \|) = (\underline{P}/_\nabla)_{t \in T} (\| vI_j d_t A \| \cap \| \underline{e}_t \|) =$$

$$= \bigcup_{t \in T} \| vd_t I_j A \cap \underline{e}_t \| = \| vI_j A \| \; .$$

Analogously on applying (ax 20) instead of (ax 19) we get $C_j A_R(v) = \| vC_j A \|$.
This completes the sketch of a proof of Lemma.

It follows from Lemma that R is a model of $\sum$. But by the identical valuation v_0 such that $v_0(x) = x$ for $x \in \mathrm{Var}$, $A_{0R}(v_0) = \| A_0 \| \neq e_V$, which follows from (32). Let M be the canonical model of $\underline{L}_T$ determined by R, i.e.

$$M = (\mathrm{Var}, (\cong_t)_{t \in T}, \cong_T, (S_{1t})_{t \in T}, \ldots, (S_{qt})_{t \in T})$$

where relations $\cong_t$, $t \in T$ and $\cong_T$ are defined by (36), (37) and

$$(x_1,\ldots,x_n) \in S_{it} \text{ iff } \| p_i(x_1,\ldots,x_n) \| = \| \underline{e}_V \| \text{iff } | p_i(x_1,\ldots,x_n) | \in \nabla \, .$$

Then by 4.1, M is a model of $\sum$ in which A_0 is not valid.

References

[1] Ng. Cat Ho and H. Rasiowa, Semi-Post algebras, Studia Logica 46, 2 (1987), 147-158
[2] Ng. Cat Ho and H. Rasiowa, Subalgebras and homomorphisms of semi-Post algebras, ibidem, 159-173

[3] Ng. Cat Ho and H. Rasiowa, Plain semi-Post algebras and their representations, manuscript to be published elsewhere

[4] M.J. Cresswell and G.E. Hughes, An introduction to modal logic, London: Methuen and Co Ltd., 1980

[5] G. Epstein and H. Rasiowa, Approximation Reasoning and Scott's Information Systems, Proc. 2-nd Int. Symp. on Methodologies for Intelligent Systems, ISMIS'87; Charlotte, NC, USA, North Holland, 33-42

[6] Y. Halpern, Reasoning about knowledge, Ed. Y. Halpern, Morgan, Kaufman, 1986

[7] W. Marek and H. Rasiowa, Approximating Sets with Equivalence Relations, Theoretical Computer Science, 48 (1986), 145-152

[8] Z. Pawlak, Rough Sets, Int. Journal of Computer and Information Science 11(5), 1982, 341-356

[9] H. Rasiowa, Logic approximating sequences of sets, invited lecture, Proc. Advanced Int. School and Symp. on Mathematical Logic and its Applications, Drushba, Bulgara 1986, Plenum Press 1987, 167-186

[10] H. Rasiowa, An algebraic approach to some approximate reasonings, Invited lecture, Proc. ISMVL'87, Boston, USA, IEEE Computer Society Press, 342-347

[11] H. Rasiowa and R. Sikorski, The Mathematics of Metamathematics, 3rd Ed. 1970

[12] H. Rasiowa and A. Skowron, Rough concepts logic, in: Computation Theory, ed. A. Skowron, LNCS 208 (1985), 288-297

[13] H. Rasiowa and A. Skowron, Approximation logic, in: Mathematical Methods of Specification and Synthesis of Software Systems'85, ed. . Bibel and K.P. Jantke, Mathematical Research 31, Akademie Verlag, Berlin, 123-139

[14] D. Scott, Domains for denotational semantics, A corrected and expanded version of a paper prepared for ICALP 1982 Aarhus, Denmark 1982

Deciding the Path- and Word-Fair Equivalence Problem

Ralf Rehrmann and Lutz Priese *Fachbereich Mathematik-Informatik
Universität-Gesamthochschule Paderborn
4790 Paderborn Warburgerstr.100

1 Introduction

The notion of fairness has attracted much attention in recent years. The common feature of all different approaches to fairness in the literature is the requirement that in a fair process any component of a system that is enabled infinitely often must be activated eventually.

A first definition - starvation-freeness - is probably due to Dijkstra. Most research on fairness has been done in programming languages, see e.g. [AO83], [DH86], [Har86], [LPS81], or the nice book of Francez [Fra86]. Several people have looked for fairness concepts in different formal models for distributed computation, such as Petri-nets (see e.g. [Bes84]), Milner's CCS (see e.g. [Mil80], [CS84], [Dar85]), transition-systems (see e.g. [QS83]), finite automata-like CCS terms (see e.g. [GN87]), or within finite transition-systems , that means within automata theory as in [Par84] and our approach in [PRW87b], [PRW87a] .

In this paper we follow the lines of our papers [PRW87b], [PRW87a] and present several new results. The structure of this paper is as follows:

In chapter 2 we introduce the formal approach to automata and fairness in automata. A path of an automaton is called *edge-fair (path-fair)* if every edge (path) that is touched infinitely often must also be used infinitely often. If we could use some letter (i.e. a name of an edge) infinitely often and have thus to do so we speak about *letter-fairness* . If we have to use any finite sequence of letters (i.e. words) that could be used infinitely often, we speak about *word-fairness* . We thus distinguish carefully between edges and their names in the graph-structure of an automaton and result with different fairness notions, as has been seen also before in the literature, e.g. [QS83].

Our formal model allows this distinction but is simply another version of a classical nondeterministic automaton. Any sequence of names (labels) of some fair path of A belongs to the *fair language* of the automaton A. We thus do not require a further acceptance condition for a "successful" fair path as would be done in Muller- or Büchi-automata. However, all our results do also hold for such additional acceptance properties, as it is shown in [PRW87b]. Thus we will not deal with Muller- or Büchi-automata in this paper. Also chapter 2 presents some few results (mainly for path- and word-fairness) of [PRW87a]. Path-fairness is not only of interest because it is a "limit" of "finite" fairness notions (i.e. n-fairness , see e.g. [Bes84], [PRW87a]). Dealing with path-fairness yields to interesting languages, namely which consist of highly acyclic infinite words. Although the class of these languages leaves the theory of ω-regular events one can prove a "main-theorem" similar to Kleene's theorem or Büchi/McNaughton's $Rec^{\omega} = Rat^{\omega}$.

In chapter 3 and 4 we present new results. In chapter 3 we prove that any path-fair language is also a word-fair language (of some different automaton in general) and vice versa and present an ω-deterministic normalform for automata accepting path- and word-fair languages.

Chapter 4 connects our research on fairness to the semantics of concurrent systems. We present a relation $\sim_{wM}$ which is a weaker version of Milner's bisimulation (applied to finite systems) . Remember that $s \sim_{Bis} s'$ (i.e. s and s' are equivalent modulo bisimulation) holds if any computation of s to some state s_1 can be simulated by a computation from s' to a state s'_1 s.t. $s_1 \sim_{Bis} s'_1$ holds again (and vice versa). The resulting semantic is quite strong as the processes from s and s' have to be algebraically very

*This research has been partially supported by a grant of the DFG

similar. We say that $s \sim_{wM} s'$ holds if the above requirements are fulfilled for a continuation of suc a computation. This is a weaker requirement. Unfortunately $\sim_{wM}$ is no equivalence relation any more However, for automata within ω-deterministic normalform $\sim_{wM}$ coincides with the equality of path-fai languages. With this technique we are able to decide the equality of the path-fair (or word-fair) languages c two given automata. Also this chapter gives some links to one of our interests in fairness, namely its stron connection to the semantics of distributed systems via "state-equivalence" relations like the mentione bisimulation or testing-equivalences [HdN84]. For an overview of such researchs see e.g. [Pom84], [PW86

Such a strong relation of path-fairness to a weaker form of Milner's bisimulation is essentially neede to decide the fair-language equality problem and these connections should be studied further.

2 Basic Definitions, Automata and Fairness

We frequently use standard mathematical abbreviations. E.g. $\forall x(p(x))$: ... reads: for all x with th property p(x) there holds ... , $\exists\, x$: ... reads: there exists an x s.t. ... . Additionally we write $\exists^\omega\, x$: .. for: there exist infinitely many x s.t. ... .

For any set A the cardinality is denoted $|A|$. The powerset of A is written as 2^A. $\mathbb{N}$ is the set of a positive $\mathbb{N}_0$ the set of all nonnegative integers.

For set inclusion we use $\subseteq$, and $\subset$ for proper set inclusion.

For an alphabet Σ let Σ^* (Σ^ω respectively) denote the set of all finite (infinite) sequences or *words* ov Σ (Σ^* is the free monoid). The *empty sequence* is denoted λ, $\Sigma^+ := \Sigma^* - \{\lambda\}$. For an alphabet Σ an $\epsilon \notin \Sigma$ let $\Sigma_\epsilon := \Sigma \cup \{\epsilon\}$.

$|w|$ denotes the length of a word w, so if $w = x_1...x_n \in \Sigma^*$ ($x_i \in \Sigma$ *for* $i \in \{1,...,n\}$) $|w| := n$ and $w \in \Sigma^\omega$ we let $|w| = \infty$, where $\infty > n\ \forall n \in \mathbb{N}$. The empty sequence has length 0.

We identify words $w \in \Sigma^*$ with sequences of letters of Σ. w(i) is the i-th element of the sequen w if $|w| \geq i$, and remains undefined otherwise. With w[i] we denote the *prefix* of length i, so we l $w[i] := w(1)...w(i)$ *if* $|w| \geq i$ and $w[i] := w$ otherwise.

The set of arbitrary long sequences is $\Sigma^\infty := \Sigma^* \cup \Sigma^\omega$. For $v \in \Sigma^*$ *and* $w \in \Sigma^\infty$ the *concatenation* $v \circ$ (usually written as vw if no confusion will arise) is defined as the word u that is uniquely determined b u(i)=v(i) for $i \leq |v|$, and otherwise u(i)=w(i-|v|). For $v \in \Sigma^\omega$ and $w \in \Sigma^\infty$ vw remains undefined.

An ω-language (∞-language, *-language respectively) is a subset of Σ^ω (Σ^∞, Σ^*). In the sequel we u the word *language* to denote a *-language, ω-language or ∞-language.

For $v \in \Sigma^*$, v^ω denotes the string $u \in \Sigma^\omega$, where for all $n \in \mathbb{N}_0$ $u(n|v| + i) = v(i)$. Let $(w_i)_{i\in\mathbb{N}}$ be sequence of finite words on Σ. We write $u = w_1..w_n..$ for the uniquely determined word $u \in \Sigma^\omega$ determine by the equation $u[\sum_{i=1}^{n} |w_i|] = u[\sum_{i=1}^{n-1} |w_i|] \circ w_n$, that is the successive concatenation of the words w_i.

On Σ^∞ we define a partial order $\leq$ by setting $v \leq w$ iff there exists an $i \in \mathbb{N}$, s.t. $v = w[i]$. We w write $v < w$ if $v \leq w$ and $v \neq w$. If $v \leq w$ ($v < w$) v is a (proper) *prefix* of w. The set of all prefixes of word w is abbreviated as *Pref(w)*, i.e. $Pref(w) := \{u \in \Sigma^* | u \leq w\}$. For a sequence $(w_i)_{i\in\mathbb{N}}$ of words Σ^* with the property $w_i < w_{i+1}$ we define $w := \lim_{i\to\infty} w_i$ to be the uniquely determined word $w \in \Sigma^\omega$ s. $\forall i \in \mathbb{N} :\ w_i < w$. For $v, w \in \Sigma^\infty$ we say v is a *sub-word* of w (v$\subseteq$w for short) iff $\exists u \in \Sigma^*$ *s.t.* $uv \leq w$. a subword (i.e. segment) occurs infinitely often, i.e. if $\exists J \subseteq \mathbb{N}\ |J| = \omega$, *s.t.* $\forall j \in J :\ w[j]v < w$ we w write $v \subseteq_\omega w$. If $|v| = 1$ we sometimes write $v \in w$ ($v \in_\omega w$) instead of $v \subseteq w$ ($v \subseteq_\omega w$).

For any language M over Σ we define the following sets: $Pref(M)$, the *prefix language* of M , the union of all Pref(w) where $w \in M$. By the way note that Pref(M) is always a *-language, i.e. language in the classical sense. The set $\overline{M}$ is called the *closure* or ω-*closure* of M and is defined $\overline{M} := \{w \in \Sigma^\omega | \exists (w_i)_{i\in\mathbb{N}} :\ \forall i\ w_i \in M \text{ and } w_i < w_{i+1} \text{ and } w = \lim_{i\to\infty} w_i\}$.

Further the *adherence* of M is $adh(M) := \overline{Pref(M)}$.

Additionally for any *-language M the *infinite iteration* is defined as $M^\omega := \{w \in \Sigma^\omega | \exists (w_i)_{i\in\mathbb{N}} :\ w_i$ $(M - \{\lambda\})^i$ *and* $w_i < w_{i+1}$ *and* $w = \lim_{i\to\infty} w_i\}$ for $M \notin \{\emptyset, \{\lambda\}\}$ and $\emptyset^\omega := \{\lambda\}^\omega := \{\lambda\}$. Also we l $M^\infty := M^\omega \cup M^*$.

For convenience, we now introduce a model of computation, the multi-graph, which is strongly relat to classical notions like 'automaton' or 'transition-system'. The notion of automaton, as used later in th paper is based on this multigraph. Indeed there is only one essential difference to classical automata (edg with the special label ϵ), but the formalization chosen is really helpful, when dealing with fairness.

Definition 2.1

A *finite multi-graph* G is a tuple G=(V,E,μ) , where

- V is a finite set of vertices,
- E is a finite set of edges and
- $\mu : E \longrightarrow V \times V$ is a mapping.

If $\mu(e) = (v_1, v_2)$ we say that e is an edge from vertex v_1 to v_2.

A *path* p in G is a finite or infinite sequence $(e_i)_{i\in I}$ of edges $e_i \in E$, s.t. $\forall i : \mu(e_i) = (v_i, v_{i+1})$ implies $\mu(e_{i+1}) = (v_{i+1}, v_{i+2})$ We thus regard a path as a word $p \in E^\infty$ and define $P^* \subseteq E^*$ to be the set of all finite paths in G and $P^\omega \subseteq E^\omega$ to be the set of all infinite paths in G

We will use the standard technical terms for graphs. As $\mu(e_1) = \mu(e_2)$ for $e_1 \neq e_2$ may hold we allow multiple arcs between vertices of a multigraph.

Definition 2.2

An *automaton* A is a tuple $A = (S, \Sigma, E, \mu, \Phi, s)$ of finite sets S (of states), Σ (of labels), and E of edges, s.t.

- (S,E,μ) is a multi-graph,
- Σ is an alphabet with $\epsilon \notin \Sigma$,
- $\Phi : E \longrightarrow \Sigma_\epsilon$ is a weight-function and
- s is an initial state.

- A path p in an automaton A is a path in the included multi-graph.
- A path $(e_i)_{1\leq i\leq n}$ with $\mu(e_i) = (s_i, s_{i+1})$ *starts from* s_1, *passes* (or *touches*) s_i ($i \in \{2, ..., n\}$) and *ends* in s_{n+1} and is called finite.
- An infinite paths is a path corresponding to an infinite sequence of edges.
- A path ending in some state s is called *final* if there exists no path starting in s (s is a sink-state).
- A subpath of a path p is a finite subword (segment) of p$\in P^* \cup P^\omega$.
- A infinite path $p = (e_i)_{i\in \mathbb{N}} \in P^\omega$ *passes* (or *touches*) a state $s \in S$ infinitely often iff $\forall j \in \mathbb{N}\ \exists i \geq j, s_i\ :\ \mu(e_i) = (s_i, s)$.
- A infinite path $p = (e_i)_{i\in \mathbb{N}} \in P^\omega$ uses an edge e infinitely often iff $\forall j \in \mathbb{N}\ \exists i \geq j,\ :\ e_i = e$.
- $S^\omega(p) := \{s \in S | p\ passes\ s\ infinitely\ often\}$
- $E^\omega(p) := \{e \in E | p\ uses\ e\ infinitely\ often\}$.
- We extend the mapping Φ to a fine homomorphism $\Phi : E^\infty \longrightarrow \Sigma_\epsilon^\infty$ via

$$\Phi(\lambda) := \lambda \text{ and } \Phi(e \circ p) := \Phi(e) \circ \Phi(p).$$

Let $\Lambda : \Sigma_\epsilon^\infty \longrightarrow \Sigma^\infty$ be the homomorphism which maps ϵ onto λ and is the identity otherwise.
From this we derive a homomorphism $\Phi^\lambda : E^\infty \longrightarrow \Sigma^\infty$, via $\Phi^\lambda(p) := \Lambda(\Phi(p))$.

The definitions of a subpath and the infinity sets are for technical reasons only. The definitions of the paths and the final paths are very important, because they are used to define the computational abilities of an automaton. Note that ϵ is used as a special label in this definition and should not be mixed up with the empty word!

With this formal apparatus we now can give a precise definition of several fairness concepts :

Definition 2.3

Let $A = (S, \Sigma, E, \mu, \Phi, s_A)$ be an automaton. The infinite path p is called:

edge-fair (ef)

iff $\forall s \in S^\omega(p) : \forall e \in E : (\exists s' \in S : e = (s, s') \Longrightarrow e \in_\omega p)$

path-fair (pf)

iff $\forall s \in S^\omega(p) : \forall p_0 \in E^+ : (p_0\ starts\ from\ s \Longrightarrow p_0 \subset p)$

letter-fair (lf)

iff $\forall s \in S^{\omega}(p) : \forall e \in E : (\exists s' \in S : e = (s, s') \Longrightarrow \Phi(e) \in_{\omega} \Phi(p))$

word-fair (wf)

iff $\forall s \in S^{\omega}(p) : \forall p_0 \in E^{+} : (p_0 \textit{ starts from } s \Longrightarrow \Phi(p_0) \subset \Phi(p))$

Further any final path p is called x-fair for every x∈ {edge, path, letter, word}.

In contrast to edge- and letter-fairnesses it suffices to state $p_0 \subset p$ $(\Phi(p_0) \subset \Phi(p))$ for path- and word-fairness as this implies the $\subset_{\omega}$ relation obviously. As we used the homomorphism Φ in the fairness definitions we also allow a path to use arcs with ϵ-labels infinitely often if he touches them infinitely often. However, these names ϵ will not be seen in the accepted language.

Definition 2.4

Let $A = (S, \Sigma, E, \mu, \Phi, s_A)$ be an automaton and s,t $\in$ S. The *languages* induced by A are defined as follows:

$L(A) := \{w \in \Sigma^{*} | \exists p \in P^{*}$ final and starting in s_A, s.t. $w = \Phi^{\lambda}(p)\}$

$L_{s,t}(A) := \{w \in \Sigma^{*} | \exists p \in E^{*}$ starting in s and ending in t s.t. $w = \Phi^{\lambda}(p)\}$

$L^{\omega}(A) := \{w \in \Sigma^{*} | \exists p \in P^{\omega}$ starting in s_A s.t. $w = \Phi^{\lambda}(p)\}$

$L^{\infty}(A) := L^{\omega}(A) \cup L(A)$

$L^{xf}(A) := \{w \in \Sigma^{\infty} | \exists p \in P^{\infty}$ x-fair, starting in s_A, s.t. $w = \Phi^{\lambda}(p)\}$, where x-fair denotes one of the fairness notions from above.

To get an idea of the fair languages of an automaton we refer to the discussion and examples in [PRW87a]. From the results in [PRW87a] we first mention :

Theorem 2.1

Let A and B be automata. There holds:

1. $L^{pf}(A) \subseteq L^{wf}(A)$
2. $L^{ef}(A) \subseteq L^{lf}(A)$
3. $\exists A' : L^{lf}(A) = L^{ef}(A')$
4. The questions $L^{ef}(A) = L^{ef}(B)$? and $L^{lf}(A) = L^{lf}(B)$? are decidable.

The ef- (lf-) equivalence problem is decidable as it is possible to embed the theory of ef- (lf-) languages into the theory of ω-regular languages. Unfortunately this strategy fails for path- and word-fairness.

Dealing with path-fairness one can transform (constructively) every automaton A into an equivalent ϵ-free automaton B (s.t. $L^{pf}(A) = L^{pf}(B)$). Thus in the theory of path-fairness one may manage without ϵ-edges. However, they are useful as some transformations on automata become more evident.

Very important parts of an automaton are the *final* subautomata. Here a subautomaton A' of A is called final if its graphical representation is strongly connected and there exists no arc leaving A'. Note that a sink-state is a (trivial) final subautomaton too. Several final subautomata may induce the same final subgraph as they may differ only in their initial states.

The importance of final subautomata is based on the property that every path-fair path in A yield into some final subautomaton of A. If p is a final path he will yield into some sink-state (and will end there) ; if p is an infinite path-fair path he will yield into some final subautomaton (and will behave path-fair within this final subautomaton).

Without loss of generality we only deal with final subautomata which contain at least one edge labeled by an element of Σ. If all edges are labeled by ϵ we replace this subautomaton by a sink-state. Thus all finite fair words are related to sink-states and all infinite fair words are related to well-labeled final subautomata. For word-fair paths one can act analogously.

As pointed out in [PRW87a] one can decompose the pf-language of an automaton A into several sub-languages resulting from the final parts of A. If Fin(A) is the set of all final subautomata of A and if A_t is an element of Fin(A) with an initial state t there holds :

$$L^{pf}(A) = \sum_{A_t \in Fin(A)} L_{s_A,t}(A) \circ L^{pf}(A_t).$$

Further in [PRW87a] we presented a kind of Kleene's Main Theorem for fairness, namely that the automata theoretical approach coincides with an algebraical one. Therefore define :

Definition 2.5

Let M be a language with M $\neq M^*$. Then

$$M^{pf} := M =: M^{wf} \text{ and } \{\lambda\}^{pf} := \{\lambda\} =: \{\lambda\}^{wf}.$$

Let M be a $*$−invariant language (i.e. $\{\lambda\} \neq M = M^*$). Then

$$M^{wf} := \{w \in adh(M) \mid \forall u \in M : u \subseteq w\}$$

$$M^{pf} := \{w \in M^\omega \mid \exists (w_i)_{i \in N} : \forall i : (w_i < w_{i+1} \text{ and } w_i \in (M - \{\lambda\})^i) \text{ and } \lim w_i = w \text{ and } \forall u \in M\ \exists k, l \in N : w_k = w_l u\}$$

From this one gets the classes of path- and word-fair regular expressions, where the expressions are interpreted as languages over an alphabet Σ:

Definition 2.6

The set of languages defined by regular expressions Rat_Σ is defined as usual :

1. $0 \in Rat_\Sigma$, $\forall a \in \Sigma : a \in Rat_\Sigma$
2. $\forall x, y \in Rat_\Sigma : (x + y)$, $(x \circ y)$, $x^* \in Rat_\Sigma$

For xf $\in$ {pf , wf } Rat_Σ^{xf} is defined analogously :

1. $Rat_\Sigma \subseteq Rat_\Sigma^{xf}$
2. $\forall x, y \in Rat_\Sigma^{xf}\ \forall z \in Rat_\Sigma : (x + y)$, $(z \circ x)$, $z^{xf} \in Rat_\Sigma^{xf}$

Definition 2.7

The set of languages recognized by automata is also defined canonically:
Rec_Σ^{xf} (and $Rec_{\Sigma,\epsilon-free}^{xf}$) denotes the set of all x-fair languages (for x $\in$ {edge, letter, path, word}) accepted by some (ϵ-free) automaton over Σ.

In [PRW87a] a lot of different results for fair regular languages are shown. A short collection is presented in the next theorem. For the proof see [PRW87a] .

Theorem 2.2

1. For every final automaton A = $(S, \Sigma, E, \mu, \Phi, s_A)$there holds: $L^{pf}(A) = (L_{s_A, s_A}(A))^{pf}$.
2. For every ϵ-free final automaton A = $(S, \Sigma, E, \mu, \Phi, s_A)$it holds: $L^{wf}(A) = (L_{s_A, s_A}(A))^{wf}$.
3. $Rec_\Sigma^{pf} = Rat_\Sigma^{pf}$.
4. $Rec_\Sigma^{pf} = Rec_{\Sigma,\epsilon-free}^{pf}$.
5. Let M , N be $*$-invariant languages over Σ. Then

$$M^{wf} = N^{wf} \ iff \ Pref(M) = Pref(N)$$

It follows from 2.2.1 that the formal definition of the pf-operator is compatible to the underlying idea Hence a natural result is $Rec_\Sigma^{pf} = Rat_\Sigma^{pf}$ which is nicely comparable to Kleene's theorem or " $Rat_\Sigma^\omega = Rec_\Sigma^\omega$". Furthermore 2.2.1 implies 2.2.4.

Unfortunately the analog result 2.2.2 for the wf-operator presented in [PRW87a] is not as general as it should be. Note that 2.2.2 is valid only for ϵ-free automata. The reason for this is the different kind of definition of $.^{pf}$ and $.^{wf}$. Path-fairness (and the pf-operator) is a more constructive property because some activities take place at certain states, whereas word-fairness is a more analytic property. Hence dealing with word-fairness leads to some difficulties on automata as the inquired activities may occur anywhere in the automaton. On the other hand is the definition of the wf-operator much easier and nicer than the definition of $.^{pf}$ and allows more results within the theory of *regular* fair events (see 2.2.5). The missing link between word-fairness as a property of paths and the word-fairness operator on languages is inquired in the following section.

3 About the Coincidence of Rec_Σ^{pf} , Rec_Σ^{wf} , Rat_Σ^{pf} and Rat_Σ^{wf}

From now on we present new results that have not been published before. First we need one definition fo the following technical proofs (or proof ideas).

Definition 3.1 Let A = $(S, \Sigma, E, \mu, \Phi, s_A)$be an automaton ; s,t $\in$ S . The following notations are use in the sequel:

$s \xrightarrow{p}_A$ iff p is a path starting from s .
$s \xrightarrow{p}_A t$ iff p is a path from s to t .
$s \xrightarrow{w}_A$ iff w is a word starting from s .
$s \xrightarrow{w}_A t$ iff p is a word from s to t .
$s\ {}_\omega\!\xrightarrow{v}_\omega$ iff the word v is taken infinitely often during the execution of the word w.
$s \not\xrightarrow{p}_A$ iff p is not a path starting from s .
And all other negations analogously.

Theorem 3.1

Let A=$(S_A, \Sigma, E_A, \mu_A, \Phi_A, s_A)$ be a final automaton, then $L^{pf}(A) = L^{wf}(A)$.

Proof

We prove the following inclusions :

$$L^{pf}(A) \subseteq L^{wf}(A) \subseteq L^{wf}(A_{det}) \subseteq L^{pf}(A_{det}) \subseteq L^{pf}(A)$$

ad 1: $L^{pf}(A) \subseteq L^{wf}(A)$ is a trivial consequence of our definitions as any pf path p in an automaton A is also a word-fair path.
ad 2: $L^{wf}(A) \subseteq L^{wf}(A_{det})$. Here A_{det} is the canonical deterministic closure of A (not complete in general) obtained by the subset state construction ($S_{A_{det}} \subseteq 2^{S_A}$), where also ϵ-edges are eliminated. Thus e is an edge with name a from state S_1 to S_2 in A_{det} if there exist states s_1, s_1', s_2, s_2' in S_A, two paths from s_1 to s_1' and from s_2' to s_2 with only ϵ-labels and from s_1' to s_2' an edge with name a s.t. $s_1 \in S_1$ and $s_2 \in S_2$ hold. Obviously, every infinite path p in A defines uniquely a path $\bar{p}$ in A_{det} with $\Phi^\lambda(\bar{p}) = \Phi(p)$. In addition, if p is word-fair then $\bar{p}$ is easily seen to be word-fair too.
ad 3: $L^{wf}(A_{det}) \subseteq L^{pf}(A_{det})$. We can prove a more general inclusion, namely:
$\forall B$ deterministic and ϵ-free: $L^{wf}(B) \subseteq L^{pf}(B)$.
Note that in B every word w and state s defines uniquely a path p starting from s with $\Phi^\lambda(p)$=w. Take some w $\in L^{wf}(B)$ with a word-fair path p starting at the initial state s.t. $\Phi^\lambda(p)$=w. We have to show that p is also path-fair.
Therefore take any $s_1 \in S^\omega(p)$ and an arbitrary finite path q starting from s_1. We have to prove that $s_1{}_\omega\!\xrightarrow{q}_\omega$ holds. Thus suppose $s_1{}_\omega\!\not\xrightarrow{\Phi(q)}_\omega$(we identify q with $\Phi(q)$ here ,as the state is fixed). As w is word-fair it is easily seen that $\Phi(q) \subseteq_\omega$w has to hold.
Thus there exists some state $s_2 \in S^\omega(p)$ ($s_2 \neq s_1$) s.t. $s_2{}_\omega\!\xrightarrow{\Phi(q)}_\omega$ holds. As $s_1, s_2 \in S^\omega(p)$ there exist v_2, s_2' s.t. $s_2 \xrightarrow{\Phi(q)} s_2' \xrightarrow{v_2} s_1$. (Let v:= $\Phi(q)$). Thus $s_1{}_\omega\!\not\xrightarrow{vv_2v}_\omega$and $s_2{}_\omega\!\not\xrightarrow{vv_2v}_\omega$.
Again $vv_2v \subseteq_\omega$w has to hold and this implies the existance of a state $s_3 \in S^\omega(p)$ with $s_3{}_\omega\!\xrightarrow{vv_2v}_\omega$.
Applying the same argument we find a word v_3 s.t. with u:=vv_2vv_3v $s_i{}_\omega\!\not\xrightarrow{u}_\omega$holds for i=1,2,3 , but $s_4{}_\omega\!\xrightarrow{u}_\omega$ for some $s_4 \in S^\omega(p)$.
As $S^\omega(p)$ is a finite set this kind of argument leads to a contradiction.
ad 4: $L^{pf}(A_{det}) \subseteq L^{pf}(A)$. Now things become complicated and we can give only rough ideas. Define an auxiliar automaton A_{help} that has the same (state-)structure as A_{det} but may have multiple arcs between two states (say S_1, S_2) with the same name (say a); for any pair $s_1 \in S_1$, $s_2 \in S_2$ s.t. $s_1 \xrightarrow{a}_A s_2$ take one arc labeled with a from S_1 to S_2 in A_{help} . In a first step one proves quite easily $L^{pf}(A_{det}) = L^{pf}(A_{help})$.
It remains to prove that for every path-fair path p in A_{help} exists a path-fair path $\bar{p}$ in A with $\Phi(p) = \Phi(\bar{p})$. (Let us ignore ϵ-edges for the moment). Now the inherent difficult can be seen:

Every path q in A_{help} defines canonically a sequence $\hat{q}$ of edges in A with $\Phi(\hat{q}) = \Phi(q)$, but $\hat{q}$ may be no path at all in A. However, one can (quite easily) construct for any $n \in \mathbb{N}$ a path $\bar{p}[n]$ in A with $\Phi(\bar{p}[n]) = \Phi(p[n])$ and result thus in an infinite path $\bar{p}$ in A with $\Phi(\bar{p}) = \Phi(p)$. But now $\bar{p}$ is generally not path-fair any more. Therefore the construction of $\bar{p}[n]$ has to be done very carefully, using glueing-techniques and a diagonalization argument to obtain the infinite path $\bar{p}$, s.t. every finite path of A - here we need the fact that A is final ! - is a subpath of some $\bar{p}[n]$.

■

Corollary 3.1

Let A=$(S_A, \Sigma, E_A, \mu_A, \Phi_A, s_A)$ be a final automaton, then $L^{pf}(A) \;=\; L^{pf}(A_{det})$.

A first consequence of theorem 3.1 is the following

Theorem 3.2

$$Rec_\Sigma^{pf} = Rec_\Sigma^{wf}$$

Proof

As $Rec_\Sigma^{pf} = Rec_{\Sigma,\epsilon-free}^{pf}$ let A be an ϵ-free automaton s.t.

$$L^{pf}(A) \;=\; \Sigma_{A_t \in Fin(A)}\, L_{s_A,t}(A) \circ L^{pf}(A_t) \;=\; \Sigma_{A_t \in Fin(A)}\, L_{s_A,t}(A) \circ L^{wf}(A_t) \;\; (by\ 3.1)$$

Now add for every automaton A_t an identical copy A_t' to A, include an ϵ-edge from an arbitrary state of A_t to the related state in its copy and call the automaton constructed in this manner B. As the ϵ-edges force every word-fair path into some A_t' and by 3.1 it holds:

$$L^{wf}(B) = \Sigma_{A_t' \in Fin(B)} L_{s_B,t'}(B) \circ L^{wf}(A_t') \;=\; L^{pf}(A).$$

For the second inclusion 3.1 leads to $L^{wf}(A) = \Sigma_{A_t \in StrFin(A)}\, L_{s_A,t}(A) \circ L^{wf(pf)}(A_t)$, where $StrFin_{wf}(A)$ is the set of all maximal strongly connected components of A in which a word-fair path may yield forever. With a "copy-trick" as above one gets an automaton B s.t. $L^{pf}(B) = L^{wf}(A)$.

■

Note that the transformations of theorem 3.2 are effective as one can find all elements of StrFin(A) algorithmically. Hence the pf-equivalence problem (Is it decidable whether $L^{pf}(A) = L^{pf}(B)$ holds?) is equivalent to the wf-equivalence problem. Another corollary of theorem 3.1 identifies the wf-operator on *-invariant regular languages with the pf-operator.

Corollary 3.2

1. For a (classical) regular *-invariant language M it holds $M^{pf} = M^{wf}$.
2. Let A be a final automaton. Then $L^{wf}(A) = (L_{s_A,s_A}(A))^{wf}$.

Proof

1) Let B be a final ϵ-free automaton s.t. $L_{s_B,s_B}(B) = M$ (such a B exists !!)
$\Longrightarrow M^{wf} = (L_{s_B,s_B}(B))^{wf} = L^{wf}(B) = L^{pf}(B) = (L_{s_B,s_B}(B))^{pf} = M^{pf}$.
2) $L^{wf}(A) = L^{pf}(A) = (L_{s_A,s_A}(A))^{pf} = (L_{s_A,s_A}(A))^{wf}$ (by 1.)

■

Note that the second statement doesn't yield to $Rec_\Sigma^{wf} = Rec_{\Sigma,\epsilon-free}^{wf}$ as difficulties for $a^* \in Rec_\Sigma^{wf}$ arise outside final parts. But one can immediately verify the following theorem, as the identity of $.^{pf}$ and $.^{wf}$ on regular *-invariant languages leads to $Rat_\Sigma^{pf} = Rat_\Sigma^{wf}$.

Theorem 3.3

$$Rec_{\Sigma}^{pf} = Rat_{\Sigma}^{pf} = Rat_{\Sigma}^{wf} = Rec_{\Sigma}^{wf}$$

A last important corollary of corollary3.2 and theorem2.2.5 is

Corollary 3.3

Let A and B be final automata. Then

$$L^{pf}(A)=L^{pf}(B) \text{ iff } \mathrm{Pref}(L_{s_A,s_A}(A)) = \mathrm{Pref}(L_{s_B,s_B}(B)).$$

In the proof of 3.1 deterministic automata play an important part. Although it is not true tha $Rec_{\Sigma}^{pf} = Rec_{\Sigma,det}^{pf}$ (only deterministic automata) one can state $Rec_{\Sigma}^{pf} = Rec_{\Sigma,\omega det}^{pf}$ where $Rec_{\Sigma,\omega det}^{pf}$ is th class of languages generated by automata in an ω-deterministic normal form (ωDNF),i.e. where all *fin* subautomata are deterministic.

Definition 3.2

An automata A is in ω-deterministic normalform (ωDNF) iff all *final* subautomata of A are deterministic.

4 Handling the Path-Fair Behavior

The main difference between path-fair (resp. word-fair) languages is the lack of a cyclic description of th infinite behavior of path-fair words, as it is done for words of ω-regular languages. However, this motivat the introduction of highly acyclic languages (as $L^{pf}(A)$), but dealing with path-fair languages , mar problems arise by this difference.

Introducing a new kind of regular languages requires an answer of the question : "Is it decidable wheth two languages of this class are identical ?", i.e. is it decidable whether for two given automata "$L^{pf}(A)$ $L^{pf}(B)$ " holds. This will be done in the sequel.

Definition 4.1
Let A=$(S_A, \Sigma, E_A, \mu_A, \Phi_A, s_A)$ and B=$(S_B, \Sigma, E_B, \mu_B, \Phi_B, s_B)$ be automata.
Define the following relations on $(S_A \cup S_B)^2$.

1. $s \sim_{St} t$ iff Pref(s) = Pref(t) =: $\{ w \in \Sigma^* \mid t \xrightarrow{w} \}$ (St for "Starke").
2. $s \sim_{pf} t$ iff the pf-languages starting from s and t are identical.
3. A relation $\sim \subseteq (S_A \cup S_B)^2$ is called a *weak* relation iff $s \sim t$ implies :
$\forall w \in \Sigma^*, s'' \in S_A \cup S_B : s \xrightarrow{w} s''\ \exists v \in \Sigma^*, s', t' : s \xrightarrow{w} s'' \xrightarrow{v} s'$ and $t \xrightarrow{wv} t'$ and $s' \sim t'$
and
$\forall w \in \Sigma^*, t'' \in S_A \cup S_B : t \xrightarrow{w} t''\ \exists v \in \Sigma^*, t', s' : t \xrightarrow{w} t'' \xrightarrow{v} t'$ and $s \xrightarrow{wv} s'$ and $s' \sim t'$.
4. $s \sim_{wM} t$ iff there exists a weak relation $\sim$ s.t. $s \sim t$ (wM for "weak Milner").
5. Let $w \in \Sigma^{\infty}$.
$s\ syn_w\ t$ iff $\exists w' < w : s_A \xrightarrow{w'} s$ and $s_B \xrightarrow{w'} t$.

Note that $\sim_{St}$ and $\sim_{pf}$ are equivalences whereas $\sim_{wM}$ and syn_w are not transitive in general. $\sim_{w}$ may be regarded as a weaker version of Milner's concept of bisimulation (applied to finite automat where a computation need not reach "equivalent" states immediately but maybe prolonged to such state Applying the last corollary one can easily obtain

Lemma 4.1

Let s and t be states of two (or one) *final* automata. There holds:

$$s \sim_{pf} t \text{ iff } s \sim_{St} t.$$

Proof

Regard s and t as initial states of final automata and use corollary 3.3.

■

Lemma 4.2

1. $\sim_{wM}$ is a weak relation.
2. Let A = $(S_A, \Sigma, E_A, \mu_A, \Phi_A, s_A)$ and B = $(S_B, \Sigma, E_B, \mu_B, \Phi_B, s_B)$ be automata and s $\in S_A$, t $\in S_B$ s.t. $s \sim_{wM} t$. It holds:
   (a) $\forall w \in \Sigma^*, r \in S_A : s \xrightarrow{w} r$
   $\exists$ states s' (t') within some final part of A (resp. B) s.t. $s' \sim_{wM} t'$ and
   $\exists v \in \Sigma^* : s \xrightarrow{w} r \xrightarrow{v} s'$ and $t \xrightarrow{wv} t'$.
   (b) analog for t .
3. $\sim_{wM} \subseteq \sim_{St} \not\subseteq \sim_{wM}$.

Part 1 of lemma 4.2 is obvious. The second property follows directly by the fact that from every state exists a path to a final subautomaton.
The following main technical lemma yields to the strong relation between $\sim_{pf}$ and $\sim_{wM}$.

Lemma 4.3 (Main Technical Lemma)

Let A = $(S_A, \Sigma, E_A, \mu_A, \Phi_A, s_A)$ be a final automaton, B = $(S_B, \Sigma, E_B, \mu_B, \Phi_B, s_B)$ a *deterministic* ϵ-free automaton and w $\in L^{pf}(A) \cap L^{\omega}(B)$, w = Φ^{λ}(p) for a path-fair path p of A. It holds:

$$\forall s \in S_A \;\; \exists\, T_s \subseteq S_B \;\; \forall t \in T_s \;\; \forall q\text{: finite paths from s to s in A:}$$
$$|\{\, p'<p \mid s_A \xrightarrow{p'}_A s \xrightarrow{q}_A \text{ and } s_B \xrightarrow{\Phi^{\lambda}(p')}_B t \xrightarrow{\Phi^{\lambda}(q)}_B \text{ and } p'q < p\}| = \omega.$$

Proof

Let $P_{s,s}$ be the set of all paths from s to s in A and define the set of all infinitely often synchronous to s reached (resp. p) states of B by :

$$T_0 := \{t \in S_B \mid \exists^{\omega} p' < p \text{ s.t. } s_A \xrightarrow{p'}_A s \text{ and } s_B \xrightarrow{\Phi(p')}_B t\ \}$$

Define a mapping $f : P_{s,s} \times T_0 \longrightarrow \mathbb{N}_0 \cup \{\omega\}$ by

$$f(q, t_0) := |\{p' < p \mid s_A \xrightarrow{p'}_A s \xrightarrow{q}_A \text{ and } s_B \xrightarrow{\Phi(p')}_B t_0 \xrightarrow{\Phi(q)}_A \text{ and } p' \circ q < p\}|$$

Starting from T_0 define a sequence $(T_i)_{i \in \mathbb{N}_0}$ of sets $T_i \subseteq T_0$ under the assumption (*) that for all T_i with an even index there holds:

$$\exists q_i \in P_{s,s},\ t_i \in T_i \text{ s.t. } f(q_i, t_i) < \infty.$$

and define

$$T_{i+1} := \{t \in T_i \mid f(q_i, t) = \infty\} \text{ and}$$
$$T_{i+2} := \{t' \in T_0 \mid \exists t \in T_{i+1} : t \xrightarrow{\Phi^{\lambda}(q_i)}_B t'\}$$

As p is path-fair and $w \in L^{\omega}(B)$ induction on i leads to : $T_i \neq \emptyset\ \forall i \in \mathbb{N}_0$.
As B is deterministic there holds: $|T_{2i+1}| \geq |T_{2(i+1)}|\ \forall i \in \mathbb{N}_0$.
By the assumption (*) it follows $|T_{2i}| > |T_{2i+1}|\ \forall i \in \mathbb{N}_0$.
Thus $(|T_{2i}|)_{i \in \mathbb{N}}$ is a strictly decreasing sequence starting at the bounded value of $|T_0|$ which never reaches 0. Hence the assumption (*) fails for some $n \in \mathbb{N}_0$.

$$\Longrightarrow \exists k \in \mathbb{N}_0\ \forall t \in T_{2k}\ \forall q \in P_{s,s}\text{: } f(q,t) = \omega.$$

■

Corollary 4.1

Under the assumption of lemma 4.3 there holds:

1. $\forall s \in S_A\ \exists t \in S_B : Pref(s) \subseteq Pref(t)$ and $s\ syn_w\ t$
2. $\forall s \in S_A\ \exists t \in S_B, w_t < w : \forall v \in \Sigma^*$: $s \xrightarrow{v}_A \exists w_v \in \Sigma^*$ s.t.

   i) $w_t w_v v < w$

   ii)$s_A \xrightarrow{w_t}_A s \xrightarrow{w_v}_A s \xrightarrow{v}_A$ and $s_B \xrightarrow{w_t}_B t \xrightarrow{w_v}_B t \xrightarrow{v}_B$.

Theorem 4.1

$$\sim_{wM} \subseteq \sim_{pf}$$

Proof

Let A=$(S_A, \Sigma, E_A, \mu_A, \Phi_A, s_A)$ and B=$(S_B, \Sigma, E_B, \mu_B, \Phi_B, s_B)$ be automata and assume without loss of generality $s_A \sim_{wM} s_B$. We have to show "$L^{pf}(A) = L^{pf}(B)$". Therefore let w$\in L^{pf}(A)$.
If w is finite it will end at a sink-state of A. As $s_A \sim_{wM} s_B$ implies $(s_A \xrightarrow{w}_A sink_A \Longrightarrow \exists sink_B \in S_B\ :\ s_B \xrightarrow{w}_B sink_B)$ it follows $w \in L^{pf}(B)$.
If w is an infinite word consider the automaton B_{det}. As $s_A \sim_{wM} s_B$ it follows $s_A \sim_{St} s_B$ and hence w$\in L^{\omega}(B) \cap L^{\omega}(B_{det})$. Now the path-fair word w yields into some final subautomaton A' of A with an initial state s_1. ($s_A \xrightarrow{w_0}_A s_1$ and $w = w_0 \circ w_\infty$).
Let T_1 be the state of B_{det} s.t. $\{s_B\} \xrightarrow{w_0}_{B_{det}} T_1$ and let $B_{det}(T_1)$ be the part of B_{det} reachable from T_1 . Hence $w_\infty \in L^{pf}(A') \cap L^{\omega}(B_{det}(T_1))$, A' final and $B_{det}(T_1)$ is deterministic. Corollary 4.1 implies:

$$\exists T \in S_{B_{det}},\ w_T < w\ : \forall v \in \Sigma^*\ : s_1 \xrightarrow{v}_A \exists w_v \in \Sigma^* \text{ s.t. } w_T w_v v\ <\ w$$
$$\text{and } s_1 \xrightarrow{w_T}_A s_1 \xrightarrow{w_v}_A s_1 \xrightarrow{v}_A \text{ and } T_1 \xrightarrow{w_T}_{B_{det}} T \xrightarrow{w_v}_{B_{det}} T \xrightarrow{v}_{B_{det}} T'.$$

Now choose a special $v \in \Sigma^*$ namely which exists because of lemma 4.1.2 where $s_A \sim_{wM} s_B$ implies that there exists a $v \in \Sigma^*$ and a state t' within some *final* subautomaton of B s.t. $s_A \xrightarrow{w_0 w_T} s_1 \xrightarrow{v} s'$ and $s_B \xrightarrow{w_0 w_T v}_B t'$ and $s' \sim_{wM} t'$. Then t' must be an element of T' and $s' \sim_{wM} t'$ implies $s' \sim_{St} t'$ and hence by 4.1 $s' \sim_{pf} t'$ as s' and t' are both within final subautomata .
Let $A'_{s'}$ and $B'_{t'}$ be these subautomata where s' and t' are regarded as their initial states.

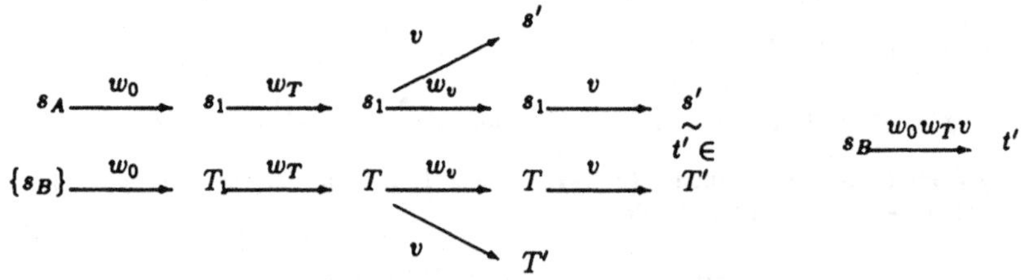

Thus $w \in (w_0 \circ w_T \circ w_v \circ v \circ L^{pf}(A'_{s'})) \cap (w_0 \circ w_T \circ w_v \circ v \circ L^{pf}(B'_{t'})\ )) \subseteq L^{pf}(B)$.
By symmetry this proves theorem 4.1.

■

The relation between $\sim_{wM}$ and $\sim_{pf}$ is much closer as pointed out in the preceding theorem. Within the class of all automata in ωDNF, which is as mighty as the class of arbitrary automata, they are identical. The next theorem shows that for ωDNF-automata $\sim_{pf}$ is a weak relation itself. For this a lemma is used which emphasizes the confluent (modulo$\sim_{St}$-equivalent states) behavior of path-fair words in ωDNF-automata.

Lemma 4.4

Let A and B be automata in ω-DNF and $w \in L^{pf}(A) \cap L^{pf}(B)$. Then there exists a state s of a final subautomaton of A and a state t of a final subautomaton of B s.t. $s\ syn_w t$ and $s \sim_{St} t$.

Proof

For finite w, lemma 4.4 is obvious. Therefore let w be an infinite word. As w yields into final subautomata A' and B' of A and B let $w = w_0 \circ w_\infty$ s.t. $s_A \xrightarrow{w_0}_A s'$ and $s_B \xrightarrow{w_0}_B t'$ where s' and t' are regarded as the initial states of A' and B'.
$\Longrightarrow w_\infty \in L^{pf}(A') \cap L^{pf}(B')$ and A' and B' are both deterministic.
Denote ($s\ syn_w t$ and $Pref(s) \subseteq Pref(t)$) by $s \longrightarrow t$
Then corollary 4.1 leads to a graphical representation where for every $s \in S_{A'}$ exists $t \in S_{B'}$ s.t. $s \longrightarrow t$ and the other way round. As this graphical representation contains no sink-state it is no DAG and has a cycle . Hence lemma 4.4 is proved.

■

Theorem 4.2

Within the class of all automata in ω-DNF there holds: $\sim_{pf} = \sim_{wM}$.

Proof

Without loss of generality consider again only the initial states s_A and s_B of two given automata to be pf-equivalent. The claim of the proof is to show that $\sim_{pf}$ is a weak relation. Suppose $s_A \sim_{pf} s_B$ and let $w \in \Sigma^*, r \in S_A$ s.t. $s_A \xrightarrow{w}_A r$. Now w maybe prolonged by a $w' \in \Sigma^*$ into a final part of A ($s_A \xrightarrow{w}_A r \xrightarrow{w'}_A s_1$ a state within a final part of A). If s_1 is a sink state, $s_A \sim_{pf} s_B$ implies that there exists a sink state t_1 of B s.t. $s_B \xrightarrow{ww'} t_1$ and as both s_1 and t_1 are sink states one gets $s_1 \sim_{pf} t_1$. If s_1 is a state of a non-trivial final subautomaton consider the word $ww'w_\infty \in L^{pf}(A)$ where w_∞ is a path-fair word starting at s_1. Hence $ww'w_\infty \in L^{pf}(A) = L^{pf}(B)$ and lemma 4.4 implies that there are states s,t within final subautomata s.t. s $\sim_{St}$ t and s $syn_{ww'w_\infty}$ t. Moreover it is easy to verify from the proof of lemma 4.4 that s maybe chosen out of the same final subautomaton as s_1.
Thus there exists a w_2 s.t. $s_A \xrightarrow{w}_A r \xrightarrow{w_2}_A s$ and $s_B \xrightarrow{ww_2} t$ and s $\sim_{St}$ t. As s and t are states of final subautomata lemma 4.1 leads to $s \sim_{pf} t$. Hence $\sim_{pf}$ is a weak relation and therefore $\sim_{pf} \subseteq \sim_{wM}$. $\Longrightarrow$ $\sim_{pf} = \sim_{wM}$.

■

For finite models (as our concept of automata) the test whether for two states $s \sim_{wM} t$ holds can be done algorithmically. If additionally the automata are in ω-DNF one has to test the following conditions (*) (analog for t):

$\forall w \in \Sigma^*, r \in S_A$ s.t. $s \xrightarrow{w}_A r\ \exists w' \in \Sigma^*$. s',t' within final subautomata s.t.
$s \xrightarrow{w}_A r \xrightarrow{w'}_A s'\ t \xrightarrow{ww'}_B t'$ and $s' \sim_{St} t'$.

Thus the p-f equivalence problem is decidable within the class of all ω-deterministic automata.

Theorem 4.3

Let A and B be arbitrary automata. The following problems are decidable:

1. $L^{pf}(A) = L^{pf}(B)$
2. $L^{wf}(A) = L^{wf}(B)$

Proof

As pointed out in section 3 , 1. and 2. are equivalent. A decision-algorithm for problem 1 is based on the following strategy :

1. Detect all final subautomata of A and B . (i.e. all maximal strongly connected components of the graphical representation of A and B with no arc leaving).
2. Construct automata A_1, B_1 in ω-DNF s.t. $L^{pf}(A_1) = L^{pf}(A)$ and $L^{pf}(B_1) = L^{pf}(B)$ using corollary 3.1 .
3. Test $s_{A_1} \sim_{wM} s_{B_1}$ by the conditions (*) above.

■

Acknowledgement
It is a pleasure to acknowledge the helpful discussions about various issues in this paper with Uwe Willecke Klemme.

References

[AO83] K. R. Apt and E. R. Olderog. Proof rules and transformation dealing with fairness. *Science Computer programming*, 3:65 – 100, 1983.

[Bes84] Eike Best. Fairness and conspiracies. *Information Processing Letters*, 18:215 – 220, 1984.

[CS84] Gerardo Costa and Colin Stirling. A fair calculus of communicating systems. *Acta Informatica* 21:417 – 441, 1984.

[Dar85] Ph. Darondeau. About fair asynchrony. *Theoretical Computer Science*, 37:305 – 336, 1985.

[DH86] Ido Dayan and David Harel. Fair termination with cruel schedulers. *Fundamenta Informatica* IX:1–12, 1986.

[Fra86] N. Francez. *Fairness*. Springer-Verlag, 1986.

[GN87] Irène Guessarian and Wafaa Niar. *An Automaton Characterization of Fairness in SCCS*. Report, CNRS-LITP, 1987.

[Har86] David Harel. Effective transformation on infinite trees, with application to high undecidability dominoes and fairness. *Journal of the ACM*, 33:224 – 248, 1986.

[HdN84] M. Hennessy and R. de Nicola. Testing equivalences for processes. *Theoretical Computer Science*, 34:83 – 133, 1984.

[LPS81] P. Lehmann, A. Pnueli, and J. Stavi. Impartiality, justice and fairness. In *Proceedings of the 8. ICALP, LNCS 115*, pages 264–277, 1981.

[Mil80] Robin Milner. *A Calculus of Communicating Systems. Lecture Notes in Computer Science 9* Springer-Verlag, 1980.

[Par84] David Park. Concurrency and automata on infinite sequences. In *Proceedings of the 5th G conference on Theoretical Computer Science*, pages 167 – 183, Springer-Verlag, 1984.

[Pom84] Lucia Pomello. *Some Equivalence Notions for Concurrent Systems*. Technical Report 10 GMD, July 1984.

[PRW87a] Lutz Priese, Ralf Rehrmann, and Uwe Willecke-Klemme. An introduction to the regular theory of fairness. *Theoretical Computer Science*, 53, 1987.

[PRW87b] Lutz Priese, Ralf Rehrmann, and Uwe Willecke-Klemme. Some results on fairness - the regular case. In *Proceedings of the 5th Symposium on Theoretical Aspects of Computer Science* pages 383 – 395, EATCS, Springer-Verlag, 1987.

[PW86] Lutz Priese and Uwe Willecke-Klemme. *On State Equivalence Relations in Nondeterministic or Concurrent Systems*. Technical Report 34, Universität GH Paderborn, Dezember 1986.

[QS83] J.P. Queille and J. Sifakis. Fairness and related properties in transition systems — a temporal logic to deal with fairness. *Acta Informatica*, 19:195 – 220, 1983.

Learning by teams from examples with errors

Reinhard Rinn and Britta Schinzel

Aachen Technical University
Lehrgebiet Theoretische Informatik, Ahornstr. 55
D - 5100 Aachen, West Germany

Introduction

The model of learning studied here was introduced by M. Gold [5] in a recursion theoretic setting. It uses an algorithmic device, called inductive inference machine, which takes as input the graph of a function, pair by pair and synchronously outputs program hypotheses. The machine correctly identifies the function if it converges to some fixed hypothesis, which is program for the function. C. Smith [9] extended the original definition to inference of programs working incorrectly on a finite number of instances of the example sequence and G. Richter-Schäfer [8] introduced input anomalies, i.e. multi-valued example sequences. We will study the conjunction of all these inference devices, i.e. we allow teams of machines to work in parallel on input sequences with finitely many multivalued arguments and to output programs, which denote one function given by the input sequence, but possibly with finitely many erraneous values.

Notations

Let f,g,... be functions from $\mathbb{N}$ (natural numbers) into $\mathbb{N}$; $\Gamma(f \cup g)=\Gamma(f) \cup \Gamma(g)$ (this operation being possible only if $f|_{\text{dom } f \cap \text{dom } g} = g|_{\text{dom } f \cap \text{dom } g}$).

$SEQ=\bigcup_{n \in \mathbb{N}} (\mathbb{N} \times \mathbb{N})^n$; $SEQ! \subset SEQ$ the set of one-valued sequences, i.e. if $\sigma \in SEQ!$, then (x,y) and (x,z) in σ implies $y=z$; for $\sigma, \tau \in SEQ$ $\sigma \hat{} \tau$ is the concatenation of σ with τ. If not causing confusion we sometimes identify sequences with finite functions, i.e. we neglect the order of the sequence.

Let $\lambda ix\varphi(i,x)$ be a Gödel numbering of $\mathbb{P}$, the set of partial recursive functions, $\mathbb{R} \subseteq \mathbb{P}$ the set of total recursive functions. Partial recursive functions M: $SEQ \to \mathbb{N}$, called inference machines or strategies, will be considered as well; convergence of M on σ is denoted by $M(\sigma)\downarrow$, divergence by $M(\sigma)\uparrow$. If σ is introduced as finite function and fed into M, then it should be thought as the sequence in natural order concatenating the elements of $\Gamma(\sigma)$. (In anticipation of the following, identification via feeding in natural order does not cause loss of generality in case of identification of total recursive functions see Blum & Blum [2]). a.e. (almost everywhere) and $\overset{\infty}{\forall}$ is short for "all but finitely many"; i. o. (infinitely often) for "infinitely many". For sets A,B $A \# B$ iff $A \not\subseteq B$ and $B \not\subseteq A$.

In the first chapter the basic definitions on inference and erraneous identification and some very basic results are given. The latter are proved in simplified versions. Here we want to thank Martin Ziegler [10] for valuable discussions. The second chapter introduces input errors and lists some results from [5] and [6] Chapter three deals with teams of inference machines working in parallel on sequences with input errors and gives some results from [5].

I. Basic Definitions and Results

Definition 1 (Gold, Blum & Blum): The IIM M EX-identifies $f \in P$ ($f \in EX(M)$), iff for all enumerations $a_o, a_1, \ldots$ of $\Gamma(f)$ it holds that $\forall n \in N$ $M((a_o, \ldots, a_n))\downarrow$ and if $n \to \infty$ then $M((a_o, \ldots, a_n))$ converges to an index, say i, of an extension of f: $\varphi_i \supseteq f$. Moreover EX:= $\{U \subseteq P \mid \exists M$ IIM such that $U \subseteq EX(M)\}$.

It has been proved already by Mark Gold [5], that the set of total recursive functions R cannot be identified in the above sense:

Theorem 1 (Gold): $R \notin EX$.

A proof of this theorem follows later.

Definition 2 (Barzdin): M BC-identifies $f \in P$ ($f \in BC(M)$), iff for all enumerations $a_o, a_1, \ldots$ of $\Gamma(f)$ it holds that $\forall n \in N$ $M((a_o, \ldots, a_n))\downarrow$ and $\overset{\infty}{\forall} n \in N$ $\varphi_{M((a_o, \ldots, a_n))} \supseteq f$.

BC:= $\{U \subseteq P \mid \exists M$ IIM such that $U \subseteq BC(M)\}$.

Definition 3: (Case, Smith) (Let $a \in N$, M EX^a-identifies $f \in P$ ($f \in EX^a(M)$) iff for all enumerations $a_o, a_1, \ldots$ of $\Gamma(f)$: $\forall n \in N$ $M((a_o, \ldots, a_n))\downarrow$ and, if $n \to \infty$ then $M((a_o, \ldots, a_n))$ converges to some i such that $f \subseteq^a \varphi_i$ (i.e. f differs from a subfunction of φ_i for at most a argument/value-pairs, that means $f(x)\downarrow$ and either $\varphi_i(x)\downarrow$ and $\varphi_i(x) \neq f(x)$ or $\varphi_i(x)\uparrow$. EX^a:= $\{U \subseteq P \mid \exists M, U \subseteq EX(M)\}$.

Theorem 2 (Barzdin): $R \notin BC$.

Again the proof follows later.

Definition 4: EX*-identification is defined analogously, but instead of $f \subseteq^a \varphi_i$ f needs only to be some finite variant of a subfunction of φ_i: $f \subseteq^* \varphi_i$.

<u>**Theorem 3:**</u> $\mathbb{R} \notin EX^*$.

<u>**Proof of Theorems 1-3:**</u> Let M EX-(BC-, EX*-) identify the a.e. constant functions, then we can construct some $f \in \mathbb{R}$ which M cannot identify.

<u>**Lemma 1:**</u> Let σ, τ, ϱ be finite fuctions on initial segments. To each σ there exists $\varrho \supset \sigma$ such that for some τ, $\sigma \subseteq \tau \subseteq \varrho$ and some $x \in dom(\varrho \setminus \sigma)$ $\varphi_{M(\tau)}(x) \neq \varrho(x)$.

<u>**Proof of Lemma 1:**</u> Let g be the total 0-continuation of σ, then M must identify f. So there must be some τ, $\sigma \subseteq \tau \subset g$ and $M(\tau)$ is index for g (index for a finite variant of g in case of EX*). Also there must be some $x \in Dom(g \setminus \tau)$ such that $\varphi_{M(\tau)}(x) = g(x) = 0$. Let ϱ be the 0-continuation of τ until argument x-1 and with $\varrho(x)=1$. ■

Finding this ϱ to σ is an r.e. condition.

Application of the Lemma:

Starting with the nowhere defined function and iterating the Lemma with $\varrho=\sigma$ gives a growing sequence of σ's building up f.

The construction also delivers a growing sequence of τ_i's and a sequence of growing x_i's such that $\varphi_{M(\tau_i)}(x_i) \neq f(x_i)$.

Now M cannot BC-identify f, because all $\varphi_{M(\tau_i)}$ differ at least for one x_i from f. M cannot EX*-identify f, because if the $M(\tau_i)$ converge, then $\varphi_{M(\tau_i)}$ i.o. differs from f. ■

<u>**Definition 5:**</u> M <u>BC*-identifies</u> $f \in P$ iff for all enumerations $a_0, a_1, \ldots$ of $\Gamma(f)$ it holds that: $\forall n \in \mathbb{N}$ $M((a_0, \ldots, a_n))\downarrow$ and for $\overset{\infty}{\forall} n \in \mathbb{N}$ $M((a_0, \ldots, a_n))$ is index for an extension of a finite variant of f(i.e. $\varphi_{M((a_0,\ldots,a_n))} \supseteq^* f$; Note: variant and extension may vary with n.

__Theorem 4__ (Harrington in Case & Smith [3]): $P \in BC^*$.

__Proof:__ Let $\sigma \in SEQ$ be of length s. $M(\sigma)$ is defined by the following procedure: Let $e_1 < e_2 < \ldots < e_s$ be the first s indices, for which $\varphi_{e_1}^s, \ldots, \varphi_{e_s}^s$ do not contradict σ. We now enumerate the graph of a p.r.f. φ_e by $\varphi_e^{t+1} := \varphi_e^t \cup \{(\varphi_{a_1}^t \cup \ldots \cup \varphi_{a_n}^t)|_{N \setminus dom(\varphi_e^t)}\}$ where $a_1, \ldots, a_n$ are those indices from $e_1, \ldots, e_s$ not cancelled by the rule: e_i is cancelled, if for some $j<i$ $\varphi_{e_j}^t$ contradicts $\varphi_{e_i}^t$. Let now $\{e'_1, \ldots, e'_m\} := \{e_i | 1 \le i \le s$, where $\forall j<i$ φ_{e_i} is compatible with $\varphi_{e_j}\}$.
Then $\varphi_e =^* \varphi_{e'_1} \cup \ldots \cup \varphi_{e'_m}$.
$M(\sigma) := e$.
Let $f \in P$, then M identifies f: for let e^* be some index for f. Choose $\sigma \subset f$ big enough, such that e^* appears in the list $e_1, \ldots, e_s$ and such that $\forall e < e^*$: if φ_e contradicts f, then it contradicts σ. Then $e^* \in \{e'_1, \ldots e'_m\}$ and $\varphi_e \supseteq^* \varphi_{e^*} = f$. ∎

__Theorem 5__ (Harrington and Case & Smith [3]): $BC \setminus EX^* = \emptyset$

__Proof:__ Let $S := \{f \in R | \overset{\infty}{\forall} x\ \varphi_{f(x)} = f\}$, then $S \in BC$ with $M(\sigma) :=$ last value of σ. But $S \notin EX^*$, for let M be an IIM EX^*-identifying S. ∎

__Lemma 5.1:__ Let $f \in P$, then to each $\sigma \in SEQ$! either

a) some $x \notin dom(\sigma)$ with $\varphi_{M(\sigma)}(x)\downarrow$ can be found, or

b) some $\varrho \supset \sigma$ can be found with $M(\sigma) * M(\varrho)$ and the new values of ϱ are indices of the function ϱ extended by f (on the complement of $dom(\varrho)$).

__Proof of Lemma 5.1:__ Using the recursion theorem we can find $\varphi_e \supset \sigma$ with the following property: if for all finite initial segments τ_i of g, where g is the constant extension of σ with values e $M(\tau_i) = M(\sigma)$, then $\varphi_e = g$, else let i be minimal such that $M(\tau_{i+1}) * M(\sigma)$ and

$\varphi_e = \tau_{i+1}\widehat{\ }f|\overline{dom(\tau_{i+1})}$.

Then either an x like in a) can be found, or in enumerating g into M a mindchange occurs, for if not the latter then M(σ) is an index for a finite variant of $g=\varphi_e \in S$. Consequently $\varphi_{M(\sigma)}$ is nearly total, so there is an x like in a). ■

Proof of Theorem 5: Let $f \in P$, e_1, e_2 be different indices of f, we construct $f' \in R$ by $f' = \sigma_0 \cup \sigma_1 \cup \ldots$, such that $\forall i \in N$

a) $\exists x \in dom(\sigma_{i+1}) \setminus dom(\sigma_i)$ with $\varphi_{M(\sigma_i)}(x)\downarrow \neq \sigma_{i+1}(x)$ and the new values of σ_{i+1} are from $\{e_1, e_2\}$, or

b) $M(\sigma_{i+1}) \neq M(\sigma_i)$ and the new values of σ_{i+1} are indices of σ_{i+1} continued by f.

Using the recursion theorem we can find some f=f' with the above property and $f \in S$, because only values e_1, e_2 are used in a) and only values being indices of f' are used in b). M cannot EX*-identify f, for if b) occurs infinitely often, then M diverges; and if a) occurs infinitely often and M converges to some i, then $\varphi_i(x) \neq f(x)$ for infinitely many x. ■

II. Erraneous and ambiguous Inputs

Definition 1: A multivalued function $A \subset N^2$ is a b-(resp. b,*-) variant of f, if dom A = dom f, $f \subseteq A$ and there are at most b arguments where A is properly multivalued with arbitrarily (resp. finitely) many values.

Definition 2: M ${}^{b}EX$-(resp. ${}^{b,*}EX$-) identifies $f \in P$ ($f \in {}^{b}EX(M)$ resp. ${}^{b,*}EX(M)$) iff for all b-(b,*-) variants A of f and all enumerations (a_i) of A:

$\forall n \in N$ $i_n := M((a_o, \ldots, a_n))\downarrow$ and for n large enough both $i := i_n = i_{n+k}$ for all $k \in N$ and $\varphi_i|_{dom\ f} \subseteq A$ with $dom\ \varphi_i \supseteq dom\ f$.

<u>**Definition 3:**</u> M ${}^{b}BC$-(resp. ${}^{b,*}BC$-) identifies $f \in P$ ($f \in {}^{b}BC(M)$) iff for all b-(b,*-) variants A of f and all enumerations (a_i) of A: $\forall n \in \mathbb{N}$ $i_n := M((a_o,\dots,a_n))\downarrow$ and for n large enough both $\varphi_i|_{\mathrm{dom}\, f} \subseteq A$ and dom $\varphi_{i_n} \supseteq$ dom f.

<u>**Definition 4:**</u> M <u>${}^{b}EX^{c}$-identifies $f \in P$</u> ($f \in {}^{b}EX^{c}(M)$), iff for all b-variants A of f and all enumerations (a_i) of A: $\forall n \in \mathbb{N}$ $M((a_o,\dots,a_n))\downarrow =: i_n$ and for n large enough both $i := i_n = i_{n+k}$ for all $k \in \mathbb{N}$ and $\varphi_i|_{\mathrm{dom}\, f} \subseteq^{c} A$ and dom $\varphi_i \supseteq^{c}$ dom f.
Analogously <u>${}^{b,*}EX^{c}$-identification</u> is defined via b,*-variants A of f.

<u>**Definition 5:**</u> M <u>${}^{b}BC^{c}$-identifies $f \in P$</u> ($f \in {}^{b}BC^{c}(M)$) iff for all b-variants A of f and for all enumerations (a_i) of A it holds, that: $\forall n \in \mathbb{N}$ $i_n := M((a_o,\dots,a_n))\downarrow$ and for n large enough $\varphi_{i_n}|_{\mathrm{dom}\, f} \subseteq^{c} A$ and dom $\varphi_{i_n} \supseteq^{c}$ dom f.
Again <u>${}^{b,*}BC^{c}$-identification</u> is defined via b,*-variants of f.
The following seven Theorems are proved in [7], [8].

<u>**Theorem 1:**</u> $\forall a \in \mathbb{N}$ ${}^{a}BC \supsetneq {}^{a}EX$.

<u>**Theorem 2:**</u> $\forall a \in \mathbb{N}$ a) ${}^{a}BC \supsetneq {}^{a+1}BC$. and
b) ${}^{a,*}BC \subsetneq {}^{a+1,*}BC$.

<u>**Theorem 3:**</u> $\forall a,b \in \mathbb{N}$ ${}^{a}EX^{b} \subsetneq {}^{a}BC^{b}$.

<u>**Theorem 4:**</u> $\forall b \in \mathbb{N}$ ${}^{*}BC^{b+1} \setminus BC^{b} \neq 0$.

<u>**Theorem 5:**</u> $\forall a,b \in \mathbb{N}$ ${}^{a(,*)}BC^{b+1} \supsetneq {}^{a(,*)}BC^{b}$.

<u>**Theorem 6:**</u> $\forall a,b \in \mathbb{N}$ ${}^{a}BC^{b} \supsetneq {}^{a+1}BC^{b}$.

<u>**Theorem 7:**</u> If a>b and n>m, then ${}^{a}BC^{n} \# {}^{b}BC^{m}$ and ${}^{a,*}BC^{n} \# {}^{b,*}BC^{m}$

<u>III. On Input Anomalies with Teams of Inference Machines.</u>

Teams of Inference Machines want to model independent parallel investigation of learning devices on the same problems. Evidently for a fixed team the class of functions identified by it is the union of the classes identified by each single machine. But following Carl Smith [9] we ask, given $n \in \mathbb{N}$, how large is the problem class, that can be learned by any team of n machines?

A different kind of teamwork for learning has been defined by Osherson et al. [6].

<u>Definition 3.1</u> : Let I be any identification criterion (EX, BC,...) and M_1, M_2, ... be inference machines, then

$I(M_1,\dots,M_n) := \bigcup_{i=1,\dots,n} I(M_i)$ and

$C(n,I) := \{U \subseteq P \mid \exists\, M_1,\dots,M_n, U \subseteq I(M_1,\dots,M_n)\}$.

Carl Smith [9] has investigated team-identification for EX, BC EX^a, BC^a; for ${}^bEX$, ${}^bBC$, ${}^bEX^a$, ${}^bBC^a$ this will be done in the following.

<u>Theorem 3.1:</u> For all $a,n \in \mathbb{N}$ ${}^aBC \setminus C(n+1,EX^*) \neq \emptyset$

The <u>proof</u> proceeds using S from Theorem 1.5 as witness in a modification of Harringtons proof for $S \in C(n+1,EX^*)$. But $S \in {}^aBC$ by a strategy that always outputs the value of the largest argument from the input set of argument/value-pairs being single valued. ∎

<u>Corollary 3.2:</u> For all $n,a,b \in \mathbb{N}$, $n>0$ $C(n,{}^bBC^a) \supsetneq C(n,{}^bEX^a)$.

<u>Theorem 3.3:</u> For all $n,a,b \in \mathbb{N}$, $n>0$ ${}^bEX^a \setminus C(n,{}^{b+1}BC) \neq \emptyset$.

<u>Proof:</u> Let ${}^bS^a := \{f \in R \mid \forall x \le b[f(x)=f(0)$ and $f =^a \varphi_{f(o)}]\}$

${}^bS^a \in {}^bEX^a$: For each b-variant of $f \in {}^bS^a$ at least one argument in $\{o,\dots,b\}$ is single valued. A strategy which searches for this and outputs the value will identify f with up to a errors.

${}^bS^a \notin C(n,{}^{b+1}BC^a)$: for if not then it can be shown that $P \in C(n,{}^{b+1}BC^a)$

contradicting $C(n,BC^a)\subsetneq C(n+1,BC^a)$ in Smith [9].

We code $f\in P$ into a b+1-variant of some function in ${}^bS^a$ by shifting each value to argument+b+1 and adding all pairs (o,m),(1,m) ...(b,m), $\forall m\in\mathbb{N}$, which must be ${}^{b+1}BC^a$-identified by some team of n machines. But then a modified team can identify f by coding, simulating the old one and decoding. ■

<u>Corollary 3.4:</u> For all $n,a,b\in\mathbb{N}$, $n>0$

a) $C(n,{}^{b+1}EX^a)\subsetneq C(n,{}^bEX^a)$

b) $C(n,{}^{b+1}BC^a)\subsetneq C(n,{}^bBC^a)$

<u>Theorem 3.5:</u> For all $n,a,b\in\mathbb{N}$, $n>0$

$C(n,{}^bBC^a)\subsetneq C(n,{}^bBC^{a+1})$.

<u>Proof:</u> As $BC^a\subseteq BC^{a+1}$, also $C(n,{}^bBC^a)\subseteq C(n,{}^bBC^{a+1})$. To show $C(n,{}^bBC^{a+1})\setminus C(n,{}^bBC^a)$ we use a proof-idea from C. Smith [9].

For each n we separate $\mathbb{N}$ into n classes $N_k^n=\{x\mid x\equiv k \bmod n\}$, $k\in\{0,\dots,n-1\}$ and use one of them for selfdefining arguments of $S_n^m:=\{f\in R\mid \exists k\in\{0,\dots,n-1\}$ such that $\forall x\in N_k^n\ \varphi_{f(x)}={}^mf\}$ Now $S_n{}^a\in C(n,{}^bBC^a)$ for all $b\in\mathbb{N}$: each team machine works in one class N_k^n and outputs the image of the biggest one-valued argument there.

$S_n^a\notin C(n,{}^bBC^{a-1})$: we use a <u>Theorem of Daley [1</u>.

$\forall d, 0\le d<a$, if $m<n\cdot\left\lceil\frac{a+1}{d+1}\right\rceil$, then $S_n^a\notin(m,BC^d)$.

Let $d:=a-1$ and $m:=\frac{n}{2}\cdot\left\lceil\frac{a+1}{d+1}\right\rceil$, then $\forall a\in\mathbb{N}$, $a>0$ it holds that $\left\lceil\frac{a+1}{d+1}\right\rceil=2$ and therefore $m=n$, consequently $S_n^a\notin C(n,BC^{a-1})\supseteq C(n,{}^bBC^{a-1})\forall b\in\mathbb{N}$. ■

From Theorems 3.4 and 3.5 we can draw the picture for $n,a,b\in\mathbb{N}$:

$$\begin{array}{ccccc} & \ne\cap & & \ne\cap & \\ \supsetneq & C(n,{}^{b}BC^{a}) & \supsetneq & C(n,{}^{b+1}BC^{a}) & \supsetneq \dots \\ & \ne\cap & & \ne\cap & \\ \supsetneq & C(n,{}^{b}BC^{a+1}) & \supsetneq & C(n,{}^{b+1}BC^{a+1}) & \supsetneq \dots \\ & \ne\cap & & \ne\cap & \end{array}$$

Corollary 3.6: $\forall n, a_1, a_2, b_1, b_2 \in \mathbb{N}$, $a_1<a_2$, $b_1<b_2$
$C(n,{}^{b_2}BC^{a_2})\setminus C(n,{}^{b_1}BC^{a_1} \neq \emptyset$.

Proof: $S_n^{a_2} \in C(n,{}^{b_2}BC^{a_2})\setminus C(n,{}^{b_1}BC^{a_1})$. ■

From Theorem 3.3 also follows

Corollary 3.7: For all $a,b,n_1,n_2 \in \mathbb{N}$ and $0<n_1<n_2$
$C(n_1,{}^{b}EX^{a})\setminus C(n_2,{}^{b+1}EX^{a}) \neq 0$ and $C(n_1,{}^{b}BC^{a})\setminus C(n_2,{}^{b+1}BC^{a}) \neq \emptyset$.
In analogy to Smith's investigation [9], wether a bigger team helps to identify more exactly (less output errors) and vice versa, we now ask wether a bigger team helps to cope with more input anomalies and vice versa.
In order to show also a converse property we introduce a witness set T_n, defined by C. Smith [9]. ■

Notation: For $f \in \mathbb{R}$ let <u>D(f)</u> $= \{x \in \mathbb{N} \mid x>0$ and $f(x)<f(x-1)\}$ the set of points, where f is decreasing; moreover for $f \in \mathbb{R}$, $j,n \in \mathbb{N}$, $j<n$ we pull out f on N_j^n, called the <u>j-th n-ply of f:</u> $\lambda x f(n,x+j)$; T_n consists of all functions, some n-ply of which has only finitely many decreasing points, the last of which is selfdefining: $\underline{T_n}$:= $\{f \in \mathbb{R} \mid \exists j<n$ and g is j-th n-ply of f, such that D(g) is finite and $\varphi_{g(\max(D(g)))} = f\}$

Lemma 3.8: $T_n \in C(n,{}^{a,*}EX) \cup C(n,{}^{1}EX)$ for all $a \in \mathbb{N}$.

Proof: $T_n \in C(n, {}^{a,*}EX)$.

Let $f \in T_n$ and A be a,*-variant of f. Each one of the n strategies $M_j (o \le j < n)$ works through A on the domain N_j^n. The set of decreasing points is $D(A) = \{x \mid \exists (x,y) \in A$ and $\exists (x-1,z) \in A$ with $y < z\}$. Because $D(f|_{N_j} n)$ is finite, also $D(A|_{N_j} n)$ is finite and the selfdefining argument must be either the largest one valued decreasing point or some multivalued decreasing point above it. Let these candidates for selfdefinition be $y_1, \ldots, y_k$. There must be some step n, where M_j already has got to know all of them. On input $A|_{N_j} n$ M_j can find φ_{y_m} with the smallest $m \in \{1, \ldots, k\}$ which is thread through A by enumeration and comparison, if the j-th n-ply is selfdefining. Therefore one of the n machines M_j must ^{a,*}-identify f correctly. ∎

$T_n \in C(n, {}^1EX)$:

In a 1-variant A of $f \in T_n$ there is only one input anomaly with possibly infinitely many values but only finitely many decreasing points add to those of f. Therefore again the above strategy will work. ∎

Note: If two infinite input anomalies lie on consecutive arguments, then infinitely many decreasing points are added making the inference impossible.

Therefore the witness T_n is modified:

$T_{n,p} :=$ $\{f \in \mathbb{R} \mid \exists i \in \{0, \ldots, n-1\}$ such that $\forall j \in \{0, \ldots, p-1\}$, if g_{ij} is the i.p+j-th n.p-ply of f, then $D(g_{ij})$ is finite and $\varphi_{g_{ij}}(\max(D(g_{ij}))) = f\}$.

Among these classes $N_k^{n.p} := \{x \in \mathbb{N} \mid x \equiv k \bmod n.p\}$ there are p consecutive ones: $N_{i.p}^{n.p}, N_{i,p+1}^{n.p}, \ldots, N_{(i+1).p-1}^{n.p}$, where f has only finitely many decreasing points, the last of which always gives a selfdefining value.

Theorem 3.9: For all $n,m,p\in\mathbb{N}$ and $n>0$

$$T_{n,p}\in C(n,{}^{p-1}EX)\setminus C(n-1,BC^m).$$

Proof: $T_{n,p}\in C(n,{}^{p-1}EX)$: On input A being a p-1-variant of $f\in T_{n,p}$ each one of the n machines M_i works on $N_{i.p+j}$ for $j\in\{0,\ldots,p-1\}$ and searches for the first j_o such that the $i.p+j_o$-th n.p-ply of A is free of anomalies. If j_o is found, M_j works on $N_{i.p+j_o}$ to find the last decreasing point. For some i M_i must be successful on A.

$T_{n,p}\notin C(n-1,BC^m)$:

The proof is a slight modification of the proof that $T_n\notin C(n-1,BC^m)$ [9]. We therefore omit it here. ∎

Corollary 3.10: For all $n,m,p\in\mathbb{N}$ and $n>0$

a) $C(n+1,{}^{p+1,*}EX^m)\setminus C(n,{}^{p,*}EX^m)\neq\emptyset$

b) $C(n+1,{}^{p+1,*}BC^m)\setminus C(n,{}^{p,*}BC^m)\neq\emptyset$.

Proof: This follows from Theorems 3.5 and 3.9 with

$$S_{n+1}=S_{n+1,0}\notin C(n,BC^m).$$ ∎

Corollary 3.11: For all $n,m\in\mathbb{N}$

$$P\notin C(n,BC^m).$$

Proof: It follows from Theorem 3.9. ∎

Corollary 3.12: For all $n,m,p\in\mathbb{N}$ and $n>0$

a) $C(n+1,{}^{p}EX^m) \supsetneq C(n,{}^{p}EX^m)$

b) $C(n+1,{}^{p,*}EX^m) \supsetneq C(n,{}^{p,*}EX^m)$

c) $C(n+1,{}^{p}BC^m) \supsetneq C(n,{}^{p}BC^m)$

d) $C(n+1,{}^{p,*}BC^m) \supsetneq C(n,{}^{p,*}BC^m)$.

Proof: Theorem 3.9 proves this.

Therefore we can draw the following 3-dimensional picture:

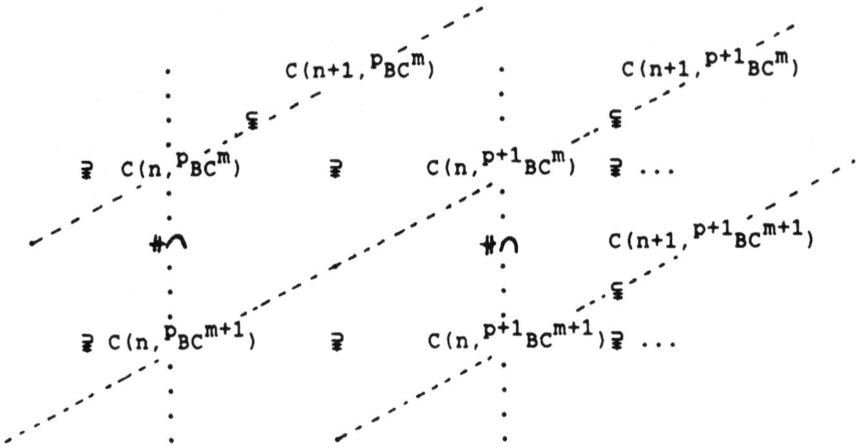

References:

[1] Barzdin, J.M.: Two theorems on the limiting syntheses of functions, Latv. Gos. Univ. Uce. Zap- 210 (1974) 82-88 (in Russian).

[2] Blum & Blum: Toward a Mathematical Theory of Inductive Inferencde, Inform. & Control 28 (1975), 125-155.

[3] Case & Smith: Comparision of Identification Criteria for Machine Inductive Inference, Theoret. Comput. Sc. 25 (1983), 193-220.

[4] Daley, R.: On the Error Correcting Power of Pluralism in BC-Type Inductive Inference, Theoret. Comput. Sc. 24 (1983), 95-104.

[5] Gold, M.: Language identification in the limit, Information & Control 10 (1967) 447-474.

[6] Osherson, Stob, Weinstein: Aggregating Inductive Expertise, Inf. & Control 70, (1986) p. 69-95.

[7] Rinn, R: Über Eingabeanomalien bei verschiedenen Inferenzmodellen, Aachener Informatikberichte 87-5.

[8] Schäfer-Richter, G.: Über Eingabeabhängigkeit und Komplexität von Inferenzmodellen, Dissertation, RWTH Aachen 1984.

[9] Smith, C. H.: The power of Pluralism for Automatic Program Synthesis, J.ACM 29 (1982), 1144-1165.

[10] Ziegler, Martin: private communication

A Survey of Rewrite Systems

P. H. Schmitt

IBM Deutschland GmbH

Wissenschaftliches Zentrum Heidelberg

Wilckensstraße 1a

6900 Heidelberg

Introduction

The purpose of this paper is to give a short introduction into the most important results, methods and open problems in the theory of rewriting systems. In preparing this survey we could draw upon earlier survey papers on the subject or on special aspects of it, most notably these were (Buchberger Loos 1982), (Buchberger 1987), (Derschowitz 1987) and (Huet Oppen 1980). As this survey is an extension of a talk presented at the first German Conference on Logic in Computer Science, emphasis is placed on a consise explanation of the basic facts in a way that exhibits the close links between these two sciences. We have tried to focus the interest, that logicians and computer scientist may have in rewriting systems, by stating three explicit problem areas. We would be very pleased, if both parties would find these open questions interesting.

As a consequence of the general plan for this paper some issues had to be neglected, e.g. associative-commutative rewriting, the unfailing Knuth-Bendix algorithm , application to theorem proving in equational logic, to mention the topics the author would have liked to include.

Thanks are due to the participants of the Conference on Logic in Computer Science for valuable comments and critisism, in particular to Corrado Böhm and Petr Stepanek.

Confluence and Termination

The most general way to look at rewrite rules is to represent them by an abstract binary relation R. We will use the more suggestive notation $a \rightarrow b$ instead of R(a,b), whenever this is conveniently possible. We sometimes write $a \leftarrow b$ for $b \rightarrow a$. Since there is no point in rewriting an element by itself, we assume that for all a in the field of $\rightarrow$ the relation $a \rightarrow a$ is false. A binary relation with this property we call a **rewrite relation**.

We denote by $\xrightarrow{*}$ the transitive, reflexive closure of $\rightarrow$, i.e. $a \xrightarrow{*} b$ if there is a natural number n and there are elements $a = a_1, a_2, ..., a_{n-1}, a_n = b$, such that for all i, $1 \leq i < n$ $a_i \rightarrow a_{i+1}$. Since n may be 0, we have in particular $a \xrightarrow{*} a$ for every a.

A rewrite relation $\rightarrow$ is called **confluent**, when for any three elements a, b_1 and b_2, such that $a \xrightarrow{*} b_1$ and $a \xrightarrow{*} b_2$, there is a fourth element c satisfying $b_1 \xrightarrow{*} c$ and $b_2 \xrightarrow{*} c$.

A rewrite relation $\rightarrow$ is **locally confluent** if for any tripel a, b_1, b_2 of elements, such that $a \rightarrow b_1$ and $a \rightarrow b_2$ there is a fourth element c satisfying $b_1 \xrightarrow{*} c$ and $b_2 \xrightarrow{*} c$.

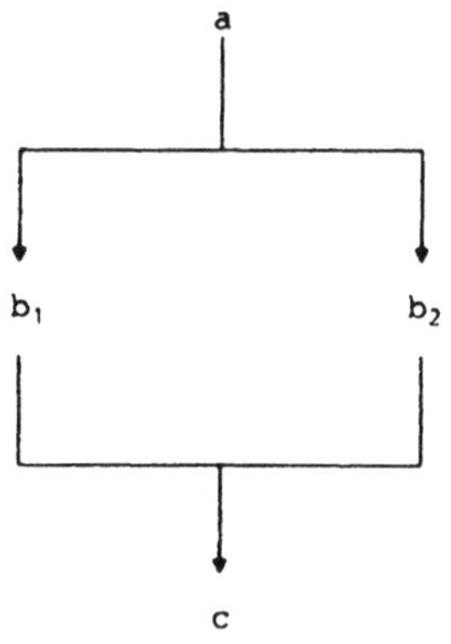

Abbildung 1. Confluence

A rewrite relation $\rightarrow$ is called **Nötherian (or terminating or wellfounded)** if there is no infinite sequence $a_1 \rightarrow a_2 \rightarrow \ldots \rightarrow a_n \rightarrow \ldots$.

With every rewrite relation $\rightarrow$ there is an associated equivalence relation, the reflexive, transitive, symmetric closure of $\rightarrow$ denoted by $\overset{*}{\leftrightarrow}$. Thus $a \overset{*}{\leftrightarrow} b$ if there is a natural number $n \geq 0$ and there are elements $a = a_1, a_2, \ldots, a_{n-1}, a_n = b$ such that for alle i , $1 \leq i < n$ either $a_i \rightarrow a_{i+1}$ or $a_i \leftarrow a_{i+1}$.
We use t $\downarrow$ s, to abbreviate the relation: there exists an element u, such that $t \overset{*}{\rightarrow} u$ and $s \overset{*}{\rightarrow} u$.

Obvioulsy the rewrite relation is confluent if and only of $\downarrow$ is transitive.

An element a is called **irreducible** with respect to the rewrite relation $\rightarrow$, if there is no element b, such that $a \rightarrow b$. An element a_0 is called a **normal form of a** if a_0 is irreducible and $a \overset{*}{\rightarrow} a_0$.

There are two easy results that can be formulated at the present level of abstraction:

Theorem 1 Let $\rightarrow$ be a Nötherian rewrite relation. Then $\rightarrow$ is confluent iff $\rightarrow$ is locally confluent.

This result can be traced back to (Newman 1942). The following figure shows, that the assumption on the well-foundedness of $\rightarrow$ cannot be dropped.

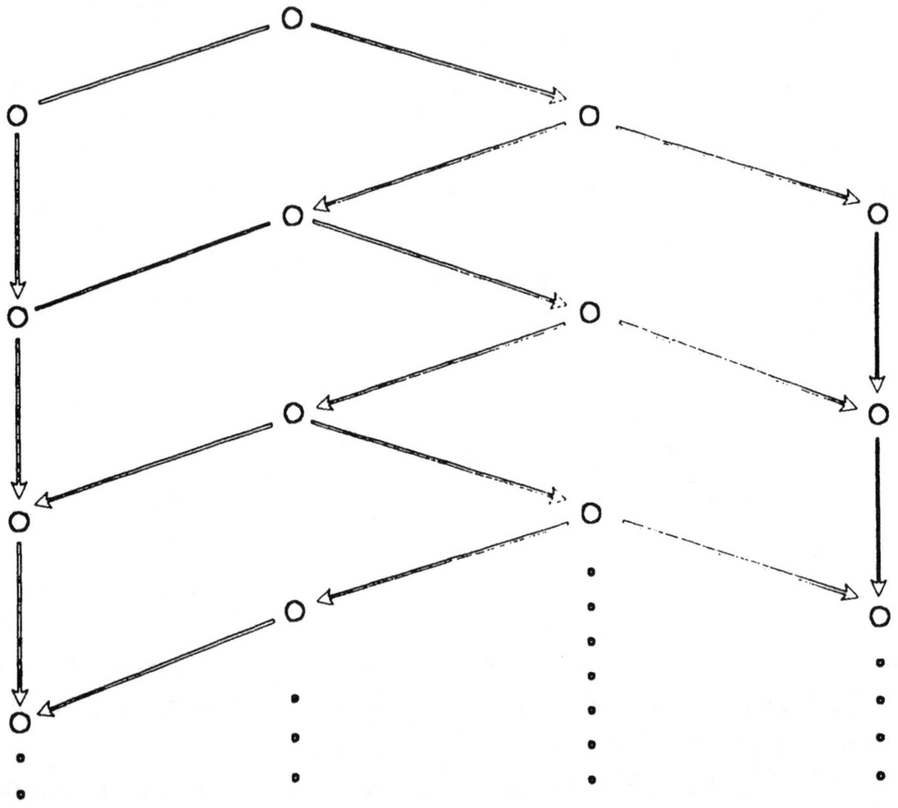

Abbildung 2. A locally confluent but not confluent relation

Theorem 2:

1. If $\rightarrow$ is confluent, then $t_1 \overset{*}{\leftrightarrow} t_2$ if and only if there is a term s such that $t_1 \overset{*}{\rightarrow} s$ and $t_2 \overset{*}{\rightarrow} s$.

2. If $\rightarrow$ is a Nötherian and confluent rewrite relation, then every equivalence class of $\overset{*}{\leftrightarrow}$ contains a unique normal form with respect to $\rightarrow$.

Examples of rewrite relations

Example 1: Equational Term Rewriting

Let Σ be a set of equations between terms over some fixed set F of function and constant symbols.

We represent terms as trees, whose nodes are labeled with function, constant or variable symbols. A node labeled by a constant or variable symbol is a leaf, i.e. does not have a successor. A node N labeled by an k-ary function symbol has k successor nodes. The edges leading from N to its successors are numbered from 1 to k. The nodes in the tree are named by sequences of natural numbers. The empty sequence denotes the root. If the sequence $<n_1,...,n_{r-1}>$ denotes the node N, then $<n_1, ..., n_{r-1}, n_r>$ denotes the successor N_r of N, that is reached via the edge with label r from N. Every node in the tree representing a term t is the root of a tree representing a subterm of t, which we will denote by t/u . We also say that a sequence of natural numbers u denotes a subterm occurence of t.
If t and s are terms and u denotes a subterm occurence of t, then $t[u \leftarrow s]$ is the term obtained from t by replacing the subterm occurence u of t by the term s.

With Σ we associate the rewrite relation $\rightarrow_\Sigma$ as follows:

For terms t and s over F the relation $t \rightarrow_\Sigma s$ holds true, if there is a subterm occurence u of t, an equation $e_1 = e_2$ in Σ and a substitution σ, such that

$$t/u = \sigma(e_1)$$

and

$$s = t[u \leftarrow \sigma(e_2)]$$

Less formally $t \rightarrow_\Sigma s$ if s is obtained from t by replacing a subterm occurence t_1 of t by a term equal to t_1 on the basis of Σ.

It should be noted that the relation $\rightarrow_\Sigma$ depends on the way the equations in Σ are oriented, i.e. the equation $e_1 = e_2$ enables different rewrite rules than $e_2 = e_2$. To emphasize this point Σ is sometimes called a set of oriented equations.

Termination and confluence of $\rightarrow_\Sigma$ depend strongly on the particular set Σ of equations. If $\rightarrow_\Sigma$ is confluent, then $\overset{*}{\leftrightarrow}$ conincides with the equivalence relation induced by the equational theory Σ.

The only general statement, that can be made is, that wellfoundedness and confluence of $\rightarrow_\Sigma$ imply the decidability of the equivalence problem for Σ,. since in this case two terms are equal if their respective normal forms are identical.

Example 2: Reducing Multivariate Polynomials Modulo An Ideal

Let F be a field, then the ring $F[X_1, ..., X_n]$ of polynomials in the indeterminates $X_1, .., X_n$ over F consists of the formal object of the form $m_1 + ... + m_r$, where each monomial m_i is of the form $c_i \times pp_i$ with c_i a non-zero element of F and each pp_i a power product, i.e. $pp_i = X_1^{e_{i,1}} \times ... \times X_n^{e_{i,n}}$ with $e_{i,j}$ natural number ≥ 0. The obvious operations are defined to turn $F[X_1, ..., X_n]$ into a ring.

Let < be an **admissible** ordering on the set of monomials, i.e. an order relation satisfying for all monomials s, t and u:

if s < t , then $s \times u < t \times u$

1 < t

The lexicographical ordering is a typical example of an admissible ordering.

Let B be a set of polynomials in $F[X_1, ..., X_n]$. The rewrite relation $\rightarrow_B$ on $F[X_1, ..., X_n]$. is definied as follows:
$f \rightarrow_B g$ if there is a monomial $c_1 \times m_1$ of f , there is a polynomial h = $c_2 \times m_2 + h_0$ in B with $c_2 \times m_2$ the greatest monomial in h with respect to < and there is a power product m, such that

$$m \times m_2 = m_1$$

$$g = (f - c_1 \times m_1) + (c_1 \times c_2^{-1}) \times m \times h_0$$

The rewrite relation $\rightarrow_B$ is Nötherian for every choice of B. Furthermore there is for any given B a set G of polynomials, such that B and G generate the same ideal in $F[X_1, ..., X_n]$ and $\rightarrow_G$ is confluent. G may be computed from B by Buchberger's algorithm.

For an easy introduction to Buchberger's algorithm see (Buchberger 1985).

Example 3: Reduction of λ-Terms

Let the set Λ of **λ-terms** be defined as follows:

x ε Λ for every variable symbol x.

if M ε Λ, then also (λxM) ε Λ for every variable symbol x.

if M ε Λ and N ε Λ, then (MN) ε Λ.

There is an obvious notion of a bound variable in λ-terms: The occurence of a variable x in M is **bound** if it is within a subterm N of M of the form (λxK). Two λ-terms are called **α-congruent**, if they can be made identical by renaming of bound variables. We will follow common practice and identify α-congruent terms. So the real object of our investigations is the set Λ/α-congruence.

The **β-reduction** relation $\rightarrow_\beta$ on Λ is defined by:
$M \rightarrow_\beta N$ if there is a subterm $(\lambda xM')N'$ of M and N arises from M by replacing this subterm by the term $M'\{x:=N'\}$. It is assumed that no free variable occurence in N' becomes bound after this replacement.

The β-reduction relation is confluent. (See e.g. (Barendregt 1984), section 3.2.)

The β-reduction relation is not well-founded, there are even λ-terms without normal form, e.g. $(\lambda x.xx)$.

The β-reduction of λ-terms is only a very special case. More general reduction relations on more complex sets of λ-terms have been studied and proved to be confluent. See e.g. (Ruckert 1985), where also further refeerences may be found.

Example 4: String rewriting

Let S a be an **alphabet** , i.e. an arbitrary set of symbols, $S^\times$ the set of all strings of symbols from S including the empty string. A **string rewriting** system R is a set of pairs (s,r) of strings. The rewrite relation $u \rightarrow_R v$ for u, v ε $S^\times$ holds true if u = xsy , v = xry and (s,r) ε R.

The difference to term rewriting is, that in string rewriting there are no variables and hence no substitutions involved and furthermore the internal structures of stings of symbols is much poorer than the internal structure of terms.

The central object of study in string rewriting is the monoid M_R , which is obtained by considering $S^\times$ as a monoid under string composition and factoring it by the congruence relation $\overset{*}{\leftrightarrow}_R$.

A comprehensive survey of string rewriting systems may be found in (Book 87).

Problem:
Find an abstract setting covering these examples that allows
to prove confluence
formulate confluence tests
formulate algorithms for testing confluence

A modest beginning has been made in section 2 of (Bauer 1981), where some properties of the set Term(F) of terms with respect to substitution are proved in the abstract setting of a monoid **O** operating on a set M.

There have also been numerous attempts to unify the Knuth-Bendix Algorithm and Buchberger's Algorithm at different levels of generality, see (Buchberger 1987) pp. 24/25 for further references.

Critical Pairs

Let us return to our first example of a rewrite relation, i.e. rewriting with respect to a set Σ of oriented equations.

Is the problem of deciding wether $\rightarrow_\Sigma$ is confluent algorithmically decidable ?

The following considerations will show that this is the case, when $\rightarrow_\Sigma$ is Nöthe-rian. In this case it suffices to test for local confluence. The main idea is to reduce the potenially infinitely many situations, where an element can be rewritten in two different ways, to a finite number of test situations. The central definition is that of a **critical pair** of the set Σ of oriented equations.

A substitution σ satisfying $\sigma(t_1) = \sigma(t_2)$ for two terms t_1 and t_2 is called a **unifier** of t_1 and t_2. If furthermore for any other unifier μ of t_1 and t_2 there is a substitution ρ, suchthat $\mu = \sigma * \rho$ (i.e. μ is obtained by first applying σ and then ρ) then

σ is called a **most general unifier** of t_1 and t_2. It is well known, that whenever a unifier for two terms t_1, t_2 exists, then there exists also a most general unifier, which is unique upto renaming of variables. There is furthermore an algorithm, which computes the most general unifier of two given terms or returns the message that the terms are not unifiable.

Let $s_1 = t_1$ and $s_2 = t_2$ be two oriented equations in Σ, which may without loss of generality be assumed to contain no common variables. Let u be a subterm occurence in s_1, such that s_1 /u is not a variable and unifiable with s_2 Let σ be the most general unifier of s_1/u and s_2, then $\sigma(s_1[u \leftarrow t_2])$, $\sigma(t_1)$ is called a **critical pair** of Σ.

Example of a Critical Pairs

Let the oriented equations

$$f(e,X) = X$$

$$f(\ f(U,V),W\ ) = f(\ U,f(V,W)\ )$$

be given

The left-hand-side of the first equations can be unified with the subterm f(U,V) of the left-hand-side of the second equation by the most general unifier σ:
$\sigma(U) = e$ and $\sigma(V) = X$
This yields the critical pair:

$$f(X,W)\ ,\ f(\ e,f(X,W)\ )$$

There are obviously only finitely many critical pairs for Σ.

Theorem 3:

If for every critical pair t_1, t_2 of Σ there is a term t, such that $t_1 \overset{*}{\to}_\Sigma t$ and $t_2 \overset{*}{\to}_\Sigma t$, then $\to_\Sigma$ is locally confluent.

The first version of this theorem appeared in (Knuth Bendix 1967), the presented formulation is taken from (Huet 1977).

Termination Orderings

The problem to decide wether an arbitrary equational term rewriting system is Nötherian, is undecidable. This has been proved in (Huet Lankford 1978) by associating uniformly with every Turing maschine M a term rewriting system R_M, such that R_M is Nötherian iff there is no instantaneous description, that leads to an infinite computation of M. This variation of the halting problem has been proved to be undecidable of degree 0″ in (Herman 1971). The construction of Huet and Lankford uses only unary functions symbols and constants and the rewrite rules of R_M contain only one variable. It is shown in the same paper that termination for finite systems of rules without variables is decidable.

Given the undecidability of the termination problem for term rewriting systems in general, the best we can do is to look for criteria sufficient for termination, that work in as many cases as possible. Much has been done in this direction. The starting point is the next Lemma.

First we need to fix some terminology.
By an ordering relation, $\leq$, we understand a **partial ordering** relation, i.e. a transitive, reflexive, and antisymmetric relation. If we want $\leq$ to have the property, that for all elements a,b either $a \leq b$ or $b \leq a$ we call $\leq$ a **total ordering**. As usual we write $a < b$ for $a \leq b$ and $a \neq b$. An ordering relation $\leq$ is **Nötherian** or **well-founded** if there is no infinite descending sequence $a_1 > a_2 ... > a_n > ...$.
We will also encounter **quasi-orderings**, these are partial orderings, $\leq$, that do not necessarily satisfy the antisymmetry requirement, i.e. $a \leq b$ and $b \leq a$ may be true for elements $a \neq b$. With a quasi-ordering $\leq$ we associate the equivalence relation $a \sim b$, defined by $a \leq b$ and $b \leq a$. Thus a quasi-ordering $\leq$ is an ordering exactly if $\sim$ equals the identity relation. If $\leq$ is a quasi-ordering, we write $a < b$ for $a \leq b$ and not $a \sim b$.

For quasi-orderings $\leq$ there is a stronger notion than well-foundedness. We call $\leq$ a **well-quasi-ordering** if for any infinite sequence $a_1, a_2, ..., a_n, ...$ there exist indices $j < k$ such that $a_j \leq a_k$.

It is easily verfied that a quasi-ordering $\leq$ is a well-quasi-ordering iff $\leq$ is well-founded and contains no infinite set of pairwise incomparable elements.

Definition: A quasi-ordering $\leq$ on the set Term(F) of terms over a set F of function symbols is **monotonic** if for all term t,s and all function symbols

$$t < s \quad \text{implies} \quad f(t_1, ...t..., t_n) < f(t_1, ...s..., t_n)$$

Lemma 4: Let $\leq$ be a monotonic well-quasi-ordering on Term(F) and R a system of rewrite rules over F. If for all rules $t \to s$ in R and all substitutions σ

$$\sigma(t) > \sigma(s)$$

is true, then R is Nötherian.

Proof: Let t' be a term, that can be reduced to the term s' by the rule $t \to s$ in R. Then for some occurence u in t' and some substitution σ we have $t'/u = \sigma(t)$ and $s' = t[u \leftarrow \sigma(s)]$. By assumption we have $\sigma(t) > \sigma(s)$ and monotonicity yields $t' > s'$. This shows that $t' \xrightarrow{*} s'$ implies $t' > s'$, which ensures termination of the system R.

A monotonic quasi-ordering, which satisfies for a given system of rewrite rules R the condition of Lemma 4 is called a **termination quasi-ordering** for R.

An easy way to ensure, that a quasi-ordering on Term(F) is a well-quasi-ordering, is to require the subterm property.

Definition: An ordering relation $<$ on the set Term(F) is said to have the **subterm property** if for all terms $f(t_1, ..., t_n)$

$$f(t_1, ..., t_i, ..., t_n) > t_i$$

is true. Following (Dershowitz 1982) we call monotonic quasi-orderings with the subterm property **simplification quasi-orderings**.

Theorem 5: A simplification quasi-ordering on Term(F) for finite F is a well-quasi-ordering.

We will present the proof of a sligthly more general result.

Theorem 6: Let $\leq$ be a simplification quasi-ordering on Term(F), let $\preccurlyeq$ be a well-quasi-ordering on the set F satisfying the **operator replacement condition** with respect to $\preccurlyeq$, i.e.

for all f,g in F with arities n and m respectively

f $\succcurlyeq$ g and n $\geq$ m implies for all tupels of terms $t_1, ..., t_n$ and $s_1, ..., s_m$, such that there are indices $1 \leq j_1 < ... < j_m \leq n$ with $t_{j_i} = s_i$

$$f(t_1, ..., t_n) \;\geq\; g(s_1, ..., s_m)$$

is a well-quasi-ordering.

Note, that Theorem 5 is the special case of Theorem 6 where $\preccurlyeq$ is the identity relation.

The proof of theorem 6 makes use of Kruskal's tree embedding theorem. In the generality sufficient for our purposes this result may be described as follows. Let $\preccurlyeq$ be a quasi-ordering on a set F of function symbols. Kruskal's quasi-ordering relation $\leqq(\preccurlyeq)$ on Term(F) is definied by:

s = $g(s_1, ..., s_m) \leqq(\preccurlyeq)$ t = $f(t_1, ..., t_n)$

if and only if

- s = t

or

- $g \leq f$ and there are indices $1 \leq j_1 < ... < j_m \leq n$ such that for all i, $1 \leq i \leq m$ $s_i \leqq(\preccurlyeq) t_{j_i}$

or

- $s \leqq(\preccurlyeq) t_j$ for some j.

Theorem 7(Kruskal's Tree Theorem): The relation $\leqq(\preccurlyeq)$ on Term(F) is a well-quasi-ordering

iff

$\preccurlyeq$ is a well-quasi-ordering on F.

A proof may be found in (Kruskal 1960) or (Nash-Williams 1963).

As a second incredients for the proof of Theorem 6 we need:

Theorem 8 Let $\preccurlyeq$ be a quasi-ordering on F and $\leq$ an arbitrary simplification quasi-ordering on Term(F) satisfying the operator replacement condition with respect to $\preccurlyeq$, then for all terms t,s:

$$t \leq s \text{ implies } t \leqq(\preccurlyeq)\, s$$

Proof: By induction on the complexity of the pair (t,s).

Proof of Theorem 6: Assume there is an infinite descending sequence $t_1 > \ldots > t_n > \ldots$. By Kruskal's Tree Theorem there are indices i < j such that $t_i \leqq(\preccurlyeq)\, t_j$. By Theorm E this implies $t_i \leq t_j$, contradicting $t_i > s_j$.

The subterm property is not a neccessary condition for a monotonic ordering to be well-foundend. But it is easily shown that:

Lemma 9: If $\leq$ is a total monotonic ordering on Term(F), then $\leq$ is well-founded iff $\leq$ has the subterm property.

As a concrete example of a simplification ordering we want to present the class of **recursive path orderings**. As a preparation we need the notion of a multiset ordering.

For a sequence s of elements from a Set S and an element a from S s - a denotes the sequence obtained from s by deleting one occurence of a in s, for definiteness let us say the first occurence from left.

Let an arbitrary ordering relation < on a set S be given. The relation $\preccurlyeq_m$ on the set of finite sequences of elements from S is definied as follows:

$$< t_1, \ldots, t_n > \ \succ_m\ < s_1, \ldots, s_m >$$

if

n > 0 and m = 0.

or

for all j, $1 \leq j \leq m$, there is some i, $1 \leq i \leq n$, such that $t_i > s_j$.

or

there exist i and j such that $t_i \sim_m s_j$ and $<t_1, ..., t_n> - t_i \gg_m <s_1, ..., s_m> - s_j$

The relation $t \sim_m s$ is definied by $t \gtrsim_m s$ and $s \gtrsim_m t$. For example f(X,Y) $\sim_m$ f(Y,X).

Many other simplification orderings have been studied. Surprisingly all of them are closed under substitutions. This is an important point. The test, that for all rules $t \rightarrow s$ of a rewrite system R and all substitutions σ the relation σ(t) > σ(s) holds true, is automatically decidable, when the order relation > is closed under substitutions.

Problem:

Give a classification of all possible

- monotonic ordering
- simplification orderings
- monotonic ordering closed under substitutions
- simplification orderings closed under substitutions

The Knuth-Bendix Completion Algorithm

Theorem 3 provides the basis for a simple confluence test. Let R be a terminating, finite system of rewrite rules. The set CP(R) of critical pairs of R is also finite. For every pair (t,s) in CP(R) we can form the normal forms t' of t and s' of s. If for all (t,s) ε CP(R) $t' = s'$, then R is confluent, otherwise not.

This idea can be carried further. If R is not confluent and (t',s') are the normal forms of a critical pair, one could try to add either $t' \rightarrow s'$ or $s' \rightarrow t'$ to R. By iterating this process one might hope to obtain finally a confluent set of rewrite rules. If in this process a confluent and terminating set $\hat{R}$ is reached, $\hat{R}$ is called a **completion** of R. One important problem with this procedure is to ensure termination of the enlarged sets of rewrite rules. The simplest solution is to fix a termination quasi-ordering for R $\leq$ in advance, and add a new rule only, when it is compatible with this given ordering. This leads to the following algorithm, first proposed in (Knuth Bendix 1967). We present the algorithm in its simplest form. A refined version will be discussed in the next section.

The Algorithm

input:

R a set of rewrite rules

$<$ a termination quasi-ordering for R

LET CP = CP(R) be the set of critical pairs of R.

WHILE CP is not empty, do
select (t,s) ε CP
remove (t,s) from CP
reduce (t,s) to normal forms (t', s')
IF $t' \neq s'$, then do
IF for all substitutions σ we get $\sigma(t') > \sigma(s')$, then
add to CP all critical pairs between R and $t' \rightarrow s'$
add $t' \rightarrow s'$ to R
IF for all substitutions σ we get $\sigma(s') > \sigma(t')$, then
add to CP all critical pairs between R and $s' \rightarrow t'$
add $s' \rightarrow t'$ to R
ELSE
terminate with "non-orientable equation encountered"
END IF
END IF
END WHILE
"R is the completion of the input system"

END

Examples of Completions

For simplicity we omit a detailed description of the orderings which have been used in computing the following completions.

The standard example of a successful completion are the following axioms of **groups theory**:

m(,) binary multiplication
i(,) unary inversion
e() neutral element

m(m(X,Y), Z) = m(X, m(Y,Z)).
m(e(),X) = X.
m(i(X),X) = e().

This system is not confluent. Here is a completion:

i(m(V1,V2)) = m(i(V2),i(V1)) .
m(V1,m(i(V1),V2)) = V2 .
m(V1,e()) = V1 .
m(V1,i(V1)) = e() .
i(i(V1)) = V1 .
i(e()) = e() .
m(i(V1),m(V1,V2)) = V2 .
m(m(V1,V2),V3) = m(V1,m(V2,V3)) .
m(i(V1),V1) = e() .
m(e(),V1) = V1 .

As a second example let us consider **group theory**, formulated **with left and right division.**

m binary multiplication
r binary right division
l binary left division

in terms of the inversion function i the division functions can be defined as

r(X,Y) = m(X,i(Y))

l(X,Y) = m(i(X),Y)

We start with the axioms:

m(X , l(X,Y)) = Y.

m(r(X,Y) , Y) = X.

l(X , m(X,Y)) = Y.

r(m(X,Y) , Y) = X.

The following is a completion:

r(V1,l(V2,V1)) = V2 .

m(V1,l(V1,V2)) = V2 .

l(r(V1,V2),V1) = V2 .

m(r(V1,V2),V2) = V1 .

l(V1,m(V1,V2)) = V2 .

r(m(V1,V2),V2) = V1 .

Here is another simple example. The following one element set

f(f(V1)) = g(V1) .

is not complete. A completion is:

f(g(V1)) = g(f(V1)) . f(f(V1)) = g(V1) .

Knuth-Bendix Completion Algorithm: Refined Version

The following refined version of the completion algorithm was first proposed in (Huet 1981) and is now the basis for most existing implementations.

The algorithm uses sets E_i of unordered equations and sets R_j of directed equations, or rewrite rules. The objective is to turn unordered equations into directed ones. The algorithm will terminate if E_i becomes empty. The critical pairs arising in the course of the algorithm are added to the set of undirected equations. Furthermore every rewrite rule in R_i is labeled by an natural number and may be marked or unmarked, to keep track of which critical pairs have allready been considered.

The refined algorithm

Input:

a (finite) set of equations E

a (computable) termination ordering

```
        LET E_0 = E
        LET R_0 = the empty set
        LET i = 0, p = 0
LOOP

    WHILE E_i ≠ empty do,
        select equation t=s in E_i
        let t', s' be an R_i-normal form of t , resp. s.

        IF t' = s',
            THEN E_{i+1} = E_i-{t = s}, R_{i+1} = R_i , i = i+1.
            ELSE
                IF t' > s' or s' > t' , then
                  BEGIN
                  Let (λ, ρ) = (t', s') or (λ, ρ) = (s', t') according to wether
                  t' > s' or s' > t' is true
                  let K be the set of labels k of rules in R_i whose left-hand side
                  λ_k is reducible by λ → ρ , say to λ'_k
                  E_{i+1} = E_i-{t = s} ∪ {λ'_k = ρ_k:λ_k → ρ_k ε R_i with kεK}
                  p = p+1
                  λ_p = λ , ρ_p = ρ
                  R_{i+1} = {λ_j → ρ'_j:λ_j → ρ_j ε R_i with j∉K} ∪ {λ_p → ρ_p} where
                  ρ'_j is the normal form of ρ_j using R_i ∪ {λ → ρ}
                  the rules coming from R_i are marked or unmarked as they
                  were in R_i, the new rule λ → ρ is unmarked.
                  i = i+1
                  END
                  ELSE exit loop "unorientable equation"
                ENDIF
        ENDIF
    END WHILE
END LOOP
```

Despite the importance and widespread use of this algorithm not much is known about its behaviour, let alone abouts its computational complexity. The algorithm may stop with success

abort, i.e. find an unorientable equation

run for ever

A criterion for the termination of the algorithm is given in (Avenhaus 1984), where also an example of a set R of equations and a termination ordering $\leq$ for R is presented, such that there is a finite completion of R compatible with the given ordering, but the algorithm fails to find it.

Existence of Completions

If for a set Σ of equations there exists a finite terminating and confluent system R of rewrite rules, such that $\overset{*}{\leftrightarrow}_R$ coincides with $=_\Sigma$, the the equational theory Σ is decidable. The reverse implication is not true, as the following example shows.

Let ASSI be the theory consisting of the associative and idempotent law:

$$(X \bullet Y) \bullet Z = X \bullet (Y \bullet Z))$$
$$X \bullet X = X$$

An ASSI-term t is in normal form, if

- it is bracketed to the left and
- when t_0 is the string obtained from t by deleting all brackets, then t_0 contains no two identical consecutive non-empty substrings.

Obviously every term in ASSI can by algorithmically transformed into an equivalent normal form. Since two normal forms are equivalent in ASSI iff they are identical, this shows that ASSI is a decidable equational theory.

We claim, that the following set R_0 of rules is a terminating and confluent, though infinite, system of rewrite rules for ASSI:

$$(X \bullet Y) \bullet Z = X \bullet (Y \bullet Z)$$

$$X \bullet X = X$$

$$X \bullet (X \bullet Y) = X \bullet Y$$

$$X \bullet (Y \bullet (X \bullet Y)) = X \bullet Y$$

$$X \bullet (Y \bullet (X \bullet (Y \bullet Z))) = X \bullet (Y \bullet Z)$$

$$X \bullet (Y \bullet (Z \bullet (X \bullet (Y \bullet Z)))) = X \bullet (Y \bullet Z)$$

$$X \bullet (Y \bullet (Z \bullet (X \bullet (Y \bullet (Z \bullet U))))) = X \bullet (Y \bullet (Z \bullet U))$$

.

.

$$X_1 \bullet (X_2 \bullet ...(X_n \bullet (X_1 \bullet (X_2 \bullet ...(X_{n-1} \bullet X_n))))...) = (X_1 \bullet (X_2 \bullet ...(X_{n-1} \bullet X_n))...)$$

$$X_1 \bullet (X_2 \bullet ...(X_n \bullet (X_1 \bullet (X_2 \bullet ...(X_n \bullet U))))...) = (X_1 \bullet (X_2 \bullet ...(X_n \bullet U))...)$$

.

.

Let t be an ASSI-term. We will convince ourselves, that t can be transformed into normal form using R_0. First, we may transform t into left-bracketed form t_1 by repeated application of the associativity rule. Let $t_{1'}$ be the string obtained from t_1 by omitting all parentheses and let r a string such that rr is a substring of $t_{1'}$. Let r be of length n. Then, depending on wether rr is a final segment of $t_{1'}$ or not, we may use

$$X_1 \bullet (X_2 \bullet ...(X_n \bullet (X_1 \bullet (X_2 \bullet ...(X_{n-1} \bullet X_n))))...) = (X_1 \bullet (X_2 \bullet ...(X_{n-1} \bullet X_n))...)$$

or

$$X_1 \bullet (X_2 \bullet ...(X_n \bullet (X_1 \bullet (X_2 \bullet ...(X_n \bullet U))))...) = (X_1 \bullet (X_2 \bullet ...(X_n \bullet U))...)$$

to reduce $t_{1'}$. In the second case the variable U will be instantiated with the left-bracketed term t_2, where rrt_2 is a final segment of $t_{1'}$. Since any application of a rewrite rule decreases the sum of

number of not left-bracketed subterms

plus

number of variable symbols

R_0 is terminating. Summing up, R_0 is confluent and terminating and $\downarrow_{R_0}$ equals $=_{ASSI}$. Let $R_{0'}$ be a finite subset of R_0 Then for some n the rule

$$X_1 \bullet (X_2 \bullet ...(X_n \bullet (X_1 \bullet (X_2 \bullet ...(X_{n-1} \bullet X_n))))...) = (X_1 \bullet (X_2 \bullet ...(X_{n-1} \bullet X_n))...)$$

is not in $R_{0'}$ and the term

$$X_1 \bullet (X_2 \bullet ...(X_n \bullet (X_1 \bullet (X_2 \bullet ...(X_{n-1} \bullet X_n))))...)$$

is irreducible in $R_{0'}$ This shows that for no finite subset $R_{0'}$ the relation $\downarrow_{R_{0'}}$ equals $=_{ASSI}$.

The following general considerations prove, that there is no confluent and terminating system R of rewrite rules with $\downarrow_R = =_{ASSI}$ at all.

Lemma 10: Let R be an arbitrary set of rewrite rules. If $t \xrightarrow{*}_R s$, then there is a finite subset R_0 of R, such that $t \xrightarrow{*}_{R_0} s$.

Lemma 11: Let R_1, R_2 be two systems of rewrite rules, R_2 is assumed to be confluent. If for every rule $t \rightarrow_{R_1} s$ in R_1 $T \downarrow_{R_2} s$ is true, then for every reduction $t \xrightarrow{*}_{R_1} s$ $t \downarrow_{R_2} s$ is true.
If furthermore R_1 is finite, then there is a finite subset $R_{2'}$ of R_2, such that $t \xrightarrow{*}_{R_1} s$ implies $t \downarrow_{R_{2'}} s$.

Proof: Easy.

Theorem 12: Let E be an equivalence relation on a set T of terms. Let R be a confluent and terminating system of rewrite rules, such that $\downarrow_R = E$ and there is no finite subset R_0 of R, which is confluent and terminating and $\downarrow_{R_0} = E$. Then there no finite confluent and terminating rewrite system R_1 satisfies $\downarrow_{R_1} = E$.

Proof: Assume for the sake of a contradiction, that there is a finite confluent and terminating system of rewrite rules $R_1 = \{t_1 \rightarrow s_1, ..., t_n \rightarrow s_n\}$ satisfying $\downarrow_{R_1} =$ E. There is thus a finite subset R_0 of R, such that for all i $t_i \downarrow_{R_0} s_i$. By Lemma 11 this entails the contradiction $\downarrow_{R_1} = \downarrow_{R_0} = E$.

Problem:

What is so special about equational theories, that can be presented by a confluent and terminating set of equations ?

Much progress has been made in answering this problem for string rewriting systems. Parallel to the example given above in the case of term rewriting it was quickly realized, that decidability of the word problem for M_R for a string rewriting system R on the alphabet S, does not imply the existence of a completion of R on S, see e.g. (Jantzen 1985) and (Kapur & Narendran 1985). But for all known examples one could find another alphabet F_0 and a confluent and terminating string rewriting system R_0 on F_0, such that M_{R_0} was isomorphic to M_R and the conjecture arose, that this might perhaps be a general fact. It was recently shown, that this is not the case in (Otto Squier 1987). The most interesting result in Squier and Otto's work is the theorem:

Theorem 13: If R is a confluent and terminating string rewriting system, then M_R is an $(FP)_3$-monoid.

Being $(FP)_3$ is a complicated homological condition on the monoid M_R (not depending in a particular presentation of this monoid), see e.g. (Bieri 1976) for a definition and back ground information on $(FP)_3$-monoids.

The above conjecture could now be refuted by exhibiting a finitely presented monoid M with decidable word problem, that does not have the $(FP)_3$- property.

The question wether any decidable $(FP)_3$-monoid can be presented by a complete system of rewrite rules over an appropriate alphabet is still open.

References

Avenhaus 1984

Avenhaus, Jürgen,
On the Termination of the Knuth-Bendix Completion Algorithm
Technical Report 120/84 , Universität Kaiserslautern, Fachbereich Informatik, 1984.

Barendregt 1984

The Lambda Calculus, Studies in Logic, Vol. 103, North-Holland Publ. Co. 1984.

Bauer 1981

Bauer, G.
Zur Darstellung von Monoiden durch konfluente Regelsysteme.
Dissertation, Universität Kaiserslautern, Fachbereich Informatik, 1981.

Bieri 1976 Bieri, R.
Homological Dimension of Discrete Groups
Queen Mary College Mathematics Notes, London, 1976.

Book 1987

Book, R.V.
Thue Systems as Rewriting Systems
J. of Symbolic Computation, Vol. 1 & 2, 1987, pp.39 - 68.

Bose 1985 Bose, N.K. (ed.)
Recent Trends in Multidimensional systems Theory
Reidel Publ. Co., 1985

Book 1980

Book, Ronald, V.
Formal Language Theory,
Academic Press, 1980.

Buchberger Loos 1982

Buchberger, B., Loos, R.
Algebraic Simplification,
in (Buchberger et al. 1982) pp. 11 - 43.

Buchberger et al. 1982

Buchberger, B., Collins, G. Loos, R. (eds.),
Computer Algebra - Symbolic and Algebraic Computation,
Springer Verlag, 1982.

Buchberger 1985

Buchberger, B.
Gröbner Bases: An Algorithmic Method in Polynomial Ideal Theory
in (Bose 1985) pp.

Buchberger 1987

Buchberger, Bruno
History and Basic Features of the Critical-Pair/Completion Procedure
J. Symbolic Computation, vol. 3, 1987, pp. 3 - 38

Dershowitz 1982

Dershowitz, Nachum.
Orderings for Term-Rewriting Systems,
Theoretical Computer Science, vol. 17, 1982, pp. 279 - 301.

Dershowitz 1987

Dershowitz, Nachum.
Termination of Rewriting
J. Symbolic Computation, vol. 3, 1987, pp. 69 - 116.
(revised version of the contribution in (Jouannaud 1985))

Dietrich 1985

Dietrich, Roland.
Eine Programmierumgebung für Termersetzungssysteme,
Arbeitspapiere der GMD, Nr. 130, Gesellschaft für Mathematik und Datenverarbeitung mbH, Schloß Birlinghofen, Postfach 1240, 5205 Sankt Augustin 1.

Herman 1971

Herman, G.
Strong computability and variants of the uniform halting problem
Zeitschrift f. Math. Logik Grundl. Math. vol. 17, 1971, pp. 115 - 131.

Huet 1977 Huet, Gérard,
Confluent Reductions: Abstract Properties and Applications to Term Rewriting Systems,
18 th. IEEE Symposium on Foundations of Compoter Science, 1977, pp. 30 - 45.

Huet Lankford 1978

Huet, Gérard and Lankford, Dallas,
On the Uniform Halting Problem for Term Rewriting Systems
Rapport de Recherche No 283, 1978, IRIA (Institute de Recherche d'Informatique et d'Automatique),
Rocquencourt, BP 105 78150 Le Chesnay, France.

Huet Oppen 1980

Huet, Gérard and Oppen, Derek, C.
Equations and Rewrite Rules,
in (Book 1980), pp. 349 - 405.

Huet 1981 Huet, Gérard,
A Complete Proof of Correctness of the Knuth-Bendix Completion Algorithm
J. of Computer and Systems Science, vol. 23, 1981, pp. 11 - 21.

Jantzen 1985

Jouannaud, M.
A note on a special one-rule semi-Thue system Conference in Dijon, May 1985
Inf. Proc. Letters 21 (1985), 135 - 140.

Jouannaud 1985

Jouannaud, Jean-Pierre (ed.)
Rewriting Techniques and Applications, Proceedings of the Conference in Dijon, May 1985
Springer Lecture Notes in Computer Science, Vol. 202, 1985

Kapur Narendran 1985

Kapur, D., Narendran, P.
A finite Thue system with decidable word problem and without equivalent finite canonical system
Theoret. Comput. Science 35 (1985) 337 - 344.

Knuth Bendix 1967

Knuth, D. E. and Bendix, P.B.,
Simple Word Problems in Universal algebra,
in: (Leech 1967), pp. 263 - 297.

Kruskal 1960

Kruskal, J. B.
Well-quasi-orderings, the Tree Theorem, and Vazsonyis's Conjecture
Trans. Amer. Math. Soc. Vol. 95, 1960, pp. 210 - 225.

Leech 1967

Leech, J. (ed.)
Computational Problems in Abstract,
Pergamon Press, Cambridge, 1967.

Lescanne 1987

Lescanne, Pierre (ed.)
Rewriting Techniques and Applications, Proceedings of the Conference in Bordeaux, May 1987
Springer Lecture Notes in Computer Science, Vol. 256, 1987

Nash-Williams 1963

Nash-Williams, C. St. J.A.
On well-quasi-ordering finite trees.
Proc. Cambridge Philos. Soc. vol. 59, 1963, pp. 833 - 835.

Newman 1942

Newman, M.H.A.
On Theories with a Combinatorial Definition of "Equivalence",
Annals of Math., vol. 43, 1942, pp. 223 - 243.

Otto Squier 1987

Otto, Fr. and Squier, C.
The Word Problem for Finitely Presented Monoids and Finite Canonical Rewrite Systems
in: (Lescanne 1987) pp. 74 - 82.

Ruckert 1985

Ruckert, Martin
Church-Rosser Theorem 12nd Normalisierung für Termkalküle mit unendlichen Termen unter Einschluß permutativer Reduktionen
Dissertation, Fakultät für Mathematik, Ludwig-Maximilian-Universität München, 1985.

Interfacing a logic machine

Wolfgang Schönfeld
Heidelberg Scientific Center
IBM Germany
Wilckensstr. 1a
D-6900 Heidelberg
EARN: SCHFELD at DHDIBM1

Abstract

We specify a certain proof search strategy TC based on classical tableau calculus which extends PROLOG to full first order predicate logic. This is meant in the strong algorithmic sense: For the special case of a definite Horn clause knowledge base Σ and an atomic goal α, TC finds a proof for α from Σ if and only if (standard) PROLOG finds that proof. We motivate TC, describe its theoretical background and design, and indicate some principal ways how to interface TC with the outside system.

Introduction

By *logic machine* we mean the central processor of an expert system. There are at least two different principal types, rule-based and logic-based. Depending on the knowledge representation language they interpret, the former can be characterized as *non-deterministic procedural* whereas the latter are purely *declarative*. We will concentrate on the latter since they can be more easily subjected to a firm theoretical foundation based on mathematical logic.

Prolog is a typical representative of this type. Not only can it be implemented very efficiently ([Colmerauer73]). There also exist theoretical results on complexity ([Shapiro84]) and insufficiency ([Horn51]). The latter states that not every property expressible by first order formulas is expressible by definite Horn clauses. What is missing is classical negation, and negation as failure ([Clark78]) does not fill that hole. Horn clauses may suffice in certain applications, but explicit exclusion of properties occurs in many contexts. Hence, the research in the area of logic machines for full first order predicate logic (then called *theorem provers*) is well motivated.

Most theorem provers are of resolution type, based on the ideas of [Robinson65]. One might say that theorem proving is identified with resolution calculus. This can be easily explained: Only one rule is required which works on a simple normal form of formulas, and there are efficient strategies to apply this rule. So why look for other proof search principles?

A lot of motivation can be extracted from articles like [Bibel83], [Bledsoe77], [Oppacher86], and [Wrightson84]. The resolution rule appears quite unnatural in some contexts. Its position among other reasoning principles is well clarified by the classical article [Gentzen34]. There, the *cut* is only one (and, by the way, dispensable) rule in a whole system of rules. And resolution is just cut rule equipped with an ingenious mechanism (*unification*) to find appropriate substitutions. If one assumes conjunctive normal (*clausal*) form, no other rule is required, thus reaching at a very small proof system.

It should be mentioned at this point that Prolog is usually called resolution-based. But this is only one side of the whole. In [Schönfeld85], a Gentzen-type proof systems based on classical tableau calculus ([Smullyan68]) and a corresponding strategy was developed which generalizes Prolog from definite Horn clauses to full first order logic. This means that certain Resolution- and Gentzen-type proof search procedures coincide in the Prolog case.

In the paper on hand, we will introduce the principles of that proof system by relying on a graphical representation of formulas. Most of the ideas can be shown within propositional logic. The treatment of quantifiers is the same as that of Prolog: We apply unification to find appropriate substitutions. On this basis, we consider the problem of how to integrate a logic machine in an existing software environment. The LEX system ([Blaser85]) is a typical example. We learned in that project that an appropriate paradigm is to assume the knowledge base to be dynamically extendable by some outer *sources*. Then, the task of communication can be partitioned into synchronization and data transfer between logic machine and these sources.[1]

An example in propositional logic

We will demonstrate tableau calculus by the following example. §4(1) of the German law of marriage states that

> *Marriage between brother and sister is forbidden.*

Let us check: *Can my brother be my brother-in-law ?* A non-formal consideration might be:

> *Suppose that he is my brother-in-law.*
> *1. He is my sister's husband. Then she is also his sister, contradicting §4(1).*
> *2. He is my wife's brother. Then she is also my sister, contradicting §4(1).*

For a description in propositional logic, let us abbreviate in the following way:

> *he_me* : He and me are siblings.
> *x_me_marr* : X and me are married.
> *he_me_inlaw* : He and me are siblings-in-law.
> *he_me_br_m_wi* : He is a brother of my wife.
> *he_me_hu_m_si* : He is the husband of my sister.
> Others similarly.

The following is a knowledge base which solves that problem:

> *1: he_me_inlaw.*
> *2: he_me.*
> *3: he_me_inlaw* → *he_me_br_m_wi* ∨ *he_me_hu_m_si.*
> *3a: he_me_br_m_wi* → *x_me_marr.*
> *3b: he_me_br_m_wi* → *he_x.*
> *3c: he_me_hu_m_si* → *y_me.*
> *3d: he_me_hu_m_si* → *he_y_marr.*
> *4: x_me* ← *he_me* ∧ *he_x.*
> *5: he_y* ← *he_me* ∧ *y_me.*
> *6: x_me* → ¬ *x_me_marr.*
> *7: he_y* → ¬ *he_y_marr.*

One gets a good overview if one draws a bipartite graph, called *graph of the knowledge base.* It consists of just one node for each formula number and for each propositional variable. An arrow points from a formula number to a variable if the latter occurs positively in (the clausal form of) the formula. For negative occurrences, the arrow is reversed.

---

[1] We are are convinced that an optimal solution of that problem together with a well understandable reasoning principle lies at the heart of the acceptance of any logic machine, much more than efficiency.

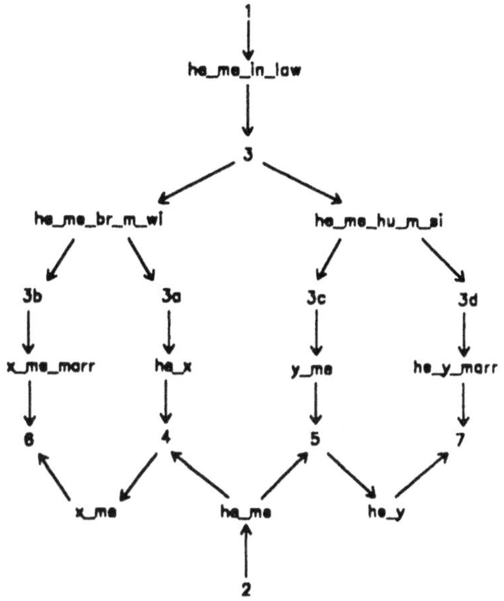

We investigate satisfiability of the knowledge base by coloring its graph. Given a valuation *h* assigning truth values *T*,*F* to the propositional variables, we label nodes and edges of the graph as follows:

1. A variable node gets the label defined by *h*.
2. An edge pointing to a variable gets the same label as the variable. If it parts from a variable, then it gets the complementary label.
3. A number node gets the label *T* iff at least one of the adjacent edges is labelled *T*.

Theorem.
A knowledge base is satisfied by a truth assignment iff all number nodes are labelled T in the corresponding graph.

Proof search for propositional logic

Let us now formulate an alternating (see [Chandra81]) algorithm TC which tries to label a given graph such that all number nodes get the truth value *T* . It labels the edges proceeding along the paths, taking into account that numbers (resp. variables) are 'or'- ('and'-)nodes.

1. Choose the number node of the hypothesis as the current node.
2. Let the current node be a number. There are three cases concerning adjacent edges.
   a. If there is one already labelled *T*, then stop with success.
   b. If there is no one already labelled *T* and at least one unlabeled, then choose one *existentially*, label it *T*, and let the adjacent variable be the current node.
   c. If all adjacent edges are labelled *F*, then stop with fail (= contradiction).
3. Let the current node be a variable and assume that the adjacent edge was just labelled.
   a. If this label contradicts the label of another adjacent edge, then stop with fail.
   b. Otherwise, choose *universally* a reversed adjacent edge, label it complementarily (if not yet done), and let the adjacent number be the current node.

The computation tree of this algorithm corresponds to the unfolding of the graph, with the goal node 1 as root.

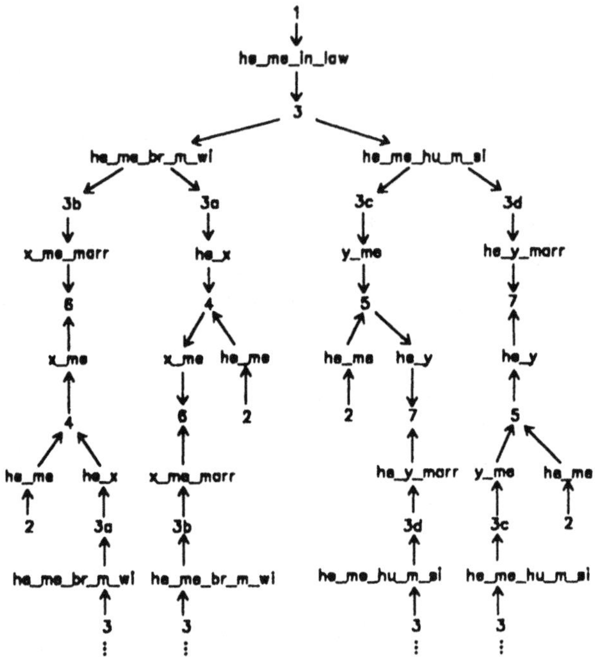

We call it a *tableau* since it has the main feature of the corresponding construction in [Smullyan68] - it is a tree of literals.

Note that all branches are closed by contradiction. E.g. the leftmost branch is contradictory since the edge 2 → *he_me* gets the label *F*, causing the unsatisfiability of 2. We call this a *direct* contradiction, coming from 2.c. in the specification of TC. A contradiction by 3.a. occurs in the second branch from the left. Here, we are forced to assign the label *F* to the last edge 3 → *he_me_br_m_wi* whereas the same edge got *T* above. This is a *circular* contradiction since it results from a circle in the graph. Altogether, we have proved that any attempt to satisfy the assumption has led to contradiction. Hence it has to be rejected. Stated otherwise, we have shown

My brother is never my brother-in-law.

In order to demonstrate the unsatisfiability, we need not consider all of the tableau. It suffices to look for a subtree which verifies the non-acceptance by the alternating machine. This means that it has to contain all successors of any 'or'-node and at least one successor of any 'and'-node. In the above example, we may remove one of the two subtrees adjacent to *he_me_br_m_wi* resp. *he_me_hu_m_si*. The remainder may be called a *formal proof* of the unsatisfiability of the knowledge base. Under certain obvious assumptions concerning connectivity of the knowledge base, correctness and completeness of the thus defined formal calculus can be proved.

Readers with a background in proof systems might like to relate our approach with classical tableau calculus as described in [Smullyan68]. We prefered a more non-traditional presentation just for the sake of clarity and in order to use graph theoretic and computer science terminology. Let us summarize our modifications and extensions as follows:

- During its construction, a tableau does not contain the intermediate steps, only the literals as the final results of working out formulas.
- Instead of a single formula, a knowledge base is assumed.
- Strategy is considered only at the level of the knowledge base, not inside a clause. A nearly trivial mechanism generates the tableau of a single clause. (See [Schmitt87] for a more elaborate construction. That paper uses a more traditional approach to tableau calculus.)
- A formula is built into the tableau only if there is at least one *connection*, i.e. at least one of the resulting branches leads to contradiction.
- If there are several connected formulas, the first one is chosen, and the rest is marked for backtracking. (Here, additional strategy considerations might be used.)
- Unification is applied to compute appropriate substitutions.

- If a finite branch cannot be closed by contradiction, backtracking occurs.
- No formula is applied twice on the same branch (loop check).
- No normal form is required (except in this paper for the sake of clearer representation).

Forward chaining

Our example might suggest that the search be started with the assumption. But this is not necessarily so. We get a *forward-chaining* proof if we let (e.g.) formula 2 be the root of the tableau.

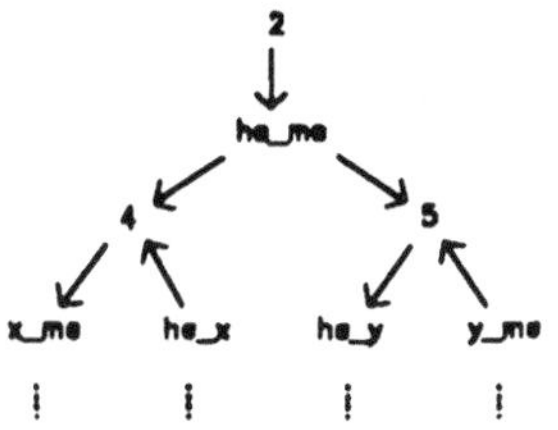

If we remove formula 1 (the goal), we get a tableau in which *he_me_in_law* occurs on all non-contradictory branches. We interpret this in the following way: TC has *verified* the knowledge base by generating a tableau with at least one non-contradictory branch. Since these branches correspond to models of the knowledge base, we know that *he_me_in_law* is true in all models, i.e. follows from the knowledge base.

This verification property is also very useful during knowledge acquisition. We not only know that, but also why, the search failed. This means that we are able to prove (and understand) consistency of knowledge base. In the LEX implementation, this feature is extensively used. Loop check is crucial for this kind af application.

The special case of Prolog

Let us consider the Prolog case - a knowledge base of definite Horn clauses and an atomic goal. Then, any tableau generated by TC has all its edges directed upwards. Hence, only direct and no circular contradictions may arise. An implementation designed for this case need not check for circular contradictions, resulting in a usual Prolog interpreter (for propositional logic).

This also shows the way how to extend TC to predicate logic. Instead of 'connections', we now have to consider 'connections modulo appropriate substitutions'. These can be computed, just in the same way as for Prolog, by unification. We indicate this by

An example in predicate logic

Let us consider the above example. Note that it cannot be formulated by Horn clauses. The law of marriage now reads

sibling(X,Y) ∧rarrow. ¬ married(X,Y)

The following could be a knowledge base to solve that problem:

1. *in_law(he,me) (the assumption)*
2. *sibling(he,me)*
3. *in_law(Y,Z) ∧rarrow. sibling(Y,spouse(Z)) ∧or. sibling(spouse(Y),Z)*
4. *married(X,spouse(X)) ∧ married(spouse(X),X)*
5. *sibling(X,Y) ∧ sibling(Y,Z) ∧rarrow. sibling(X,Z)*
6. *sibling(X,Y) ∧ → sibling(Y,X)*
7. *sibling(X,Y) ∧ → ¬ married(X,Y)*

Note that this is not an optimal formulation since a symmetric and transitive relation may cause loops during proof search. Its graph is

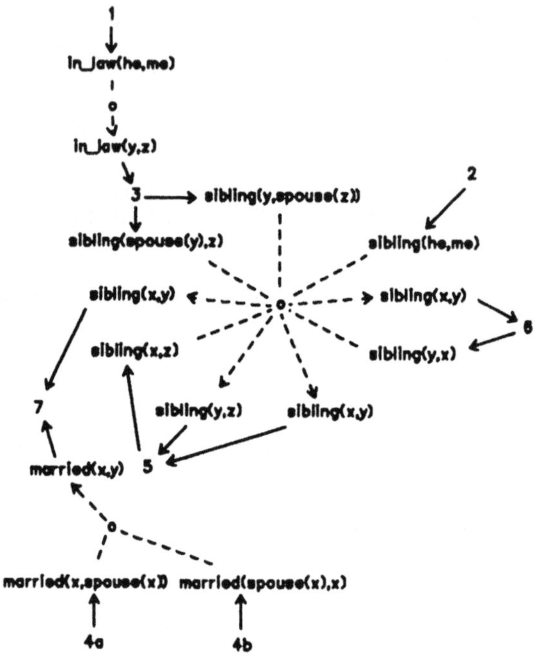

where now the dotted lines indicate possible connections. Its unfolding contains as subtree the following proof

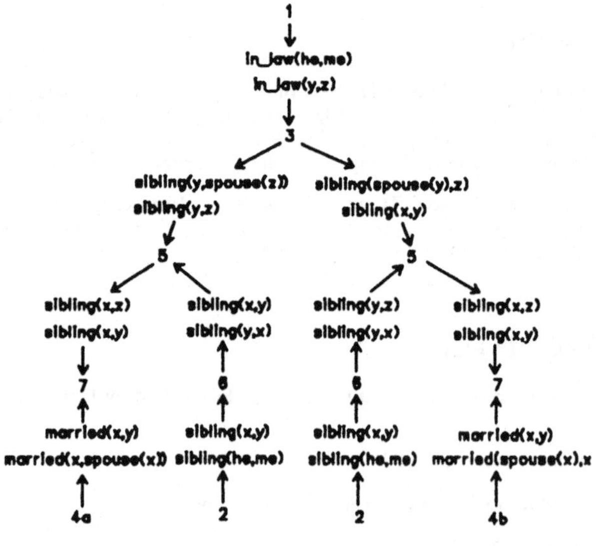

Communicating with the outside world

A logic machine running in total isolation makes no sense. It could do interesting things, but we had no influence on and no insight in what it does. Any existing logic machine supports at least the interfaces

start in a certain state (evoked by the outer system) and
stop with the result (returned to the outer system).

Most classical theorem provers behave this way since their knowledge base is a fixed and stationary mathematical theory. In expert systems, this is quite different. There, the inference engine not only reasons, but also serves as a knowledge acquisition tool. This means that it has to modify its knowledge base during proof search. We will not consider here how to *change* knowledge on line (believe revision) but how to *add* knowledge. The reason is simply that classical logic is monotonic: What is a proof remains a proof.

$$\Sigma \vdash \alpha \ \wedge \ \Sigma \subset \Sigma' \ \Rightarrow \ \Sigma' \vdash \alpha$$

But note that the proof search space may be affected: Unprovability may vanish. Our aim is to avoid this since otherwise a previous *fail* could conflict with a later *success* for one and the same formula.

This clearly depends on the proof search strategy. Hence, let $\vdash_{TC}$ denote provability via the strategy developed above. Given Σ, we want to find out for which extensions Σ' we have

$$\Sigma' \vdash_{TC} \alpha \ \Rightarrow \ \Sigma \vdash_{TC} \alpha$$

If the new knowledge is a complicated proposition containing lots of literals, the proof search space might be highly affected. We believe that the naive user of, say, an expert system should not be allowed to do such radical changes on line. If the knowledge to be added is a literal, there might be hope to perform that extension consistently with the proof search strategy. Note that new search paths may arise which must be taken into account not only in the actual but also in previous and later search states.

Note that, if we relate 'program' of classical programming with 'rules' and 'data' with 'facts', the end user must not change the program. But note also that there might be applications where on-line changes of non-facts make sense. A typical example is a *controversy* in a legal expert system: The user decides on which rule set the logic machine should base its conclusions. We will not pursue this question here since it seems not yet clear to us when to activate this decision. More precisely, we don't know whether the literal-driven activation (see below) is appropriate.

Tableau calculus is literal-oriented: At each step, it tries to prove that a single literal is true. Either the literal is in the knowledge base (modulo unification) or it can be derived. We adopt the standpoint that

There are sources of factual knowledge outside the knowledge base.

The inference engine can ask these sources (or better: oracles) *Do you know whether literal q holds?*[2]

As an example, consider arithmetic. Instead of proving $\exists X$:sum(1,2,X) , we could simply compute the sum and assign it to X.

In our application, the following sources make sense.

call	procedure call to the underlying implementation language
file	parts of the knowledge base in CMS files
thes	thesaurus in CMS file (in a syntax different from logic)
sql	tightly coupled SQL data base
user	user input from terminal
cons	consistency check: If q is consistent with the knowledge base, assume q.
sepa	separate proof search (useful if p must be proved more than once)

In **call**, the new knowledge is computed. Access to remote data sources takes place in **file**, **thes**, and **sql**. In case of **user**, the source of data is the user via his terminal. The last two cases **cons** and **sepa** consist of a recursive call of the logic machine, new and independent from the ongoing proof search. **cons** is a very special (and crude) case of induction. In fact, it is the dual of *negation as failure (to prove)* ([Clark78]) and could hence be called *affirmation as failure to disprove*.

We should note at this point that we will not discuss here the question of how the inference engine could control the outside world. This means to call outside sources should not cause side effects in

---

[2] Maybe, the following standpoint is more appropriate: There is a totality of knowledge spread over different storage media, one of them being the knowledge base.

the outside world. We could admit that if the user had ways to describe in the knowledge base prerequisites and consequences of such side effects.

Declaration of interactions by meta predicates

It is obvious that not all literals should be treated the same way. Since the designer of an inference engine cannot foresee all details, it is better to support a *meta language* in which the user (more precisely, the knowledge engineer) can specify the interactions of the logic machine. Note that its internal behavior could be specified in the same way, leading to a general *programming language for logic machines*, a task which will not be pursued here. The general problem behind this is the critical question: How much of the implementation of a system should be visible to and modifiable by the user?

We assume that all meta knowledge is specified positively. This means that we can formulate e.g. *p holds if p is known in the SQL data base*, but not *p holds if q is not known in the SQL data base*. The justification for this restriction is that it is difficult to define what 'negation of an oracle' means.[3] Here is, again, a general problem: Which special kinds of knowledge modifications should (or can) be performed when the reasoning process is still running?

This leads to the following

Definition. A *meta predicate* is an expression *source*(*literal*) where *source* is one of the above source identifiers and *literal* a usual literal. A *meta rule* is a proposition s.t. there is at least one occurrence of a meta predicate and all such occurrences are negative.

Meta rules are handled in the same way as normal formulas, e.g. are put into the knowledge base at any place and evaluated as usual, more precisely:

Definition. If (and only if) the inference engine is about to look for a connection to $\neg$*source*(*literal*), ordinary proof search is suspended, and the external source is activated (with the given variable valuation) and asked whether it knows that *source*(*literal*) holds. If it returns *true* (possibly with some further variables instantiated), the actual branch is closed by contradiction. If not (meaning *I don't know*), then there is no connection to $\neg$*source*(*literal*). In both cases, proof search resumes as usual.

Remember that questioning some sources may have the side effect that the (positive) answer is actually added to the knowledge base (see below).

By meta rules, the user can specify relations between ordinary predicates and external sources. Default reasoning is a special example. $p \leftarrow q \wedge cons(p)$ means that p holds if q can be proved and p is consistent with the knowledge base.

Storing answers

Note that, in principle, any source may be asked for the same literal, say $p(a)$, more than once. But for some sources, it is useful to store $p(a)$ if the source responds *true* so that the logic machine can make use of this knowledge at later steps, too. This holds e.g. if the knowledge can be regained only with large efforts. We decided to apply that principle to **sepa** (since this feature serves just that purpose) and **user**.

The answer to a request $p(X)$ will in general be $\{p(a_1), \ldots, p(a_n)\}$ where $n \geq 0$. The logic machine proceeds depth-first, and the answers are taken into account one after another. Hence, the sources must deliver the answers just in this way, choosing the next one on backtracking. But some sources cannot be *synchronized*. In this case, the inference engine has to *buffer* all answers by placing them in the knowledge base. Note that some outer sources maintain a buffer, themselves.

Special care must be taken for the order in which the dynamically acquired knowledge is placed inside the knowledge base. Remember that meta rules evoke the acquisition process and that we

---

[3] **cons** might indicate the way since the answer is *yes* just if the logic machine (as an oracle) cannot derive inconsistency. In other words, we adopt here negation as failure on the meta level, or, the logic machine assumes its own completeness.

adopted the Prolog strategy for selecting applicable rules: Among the connected (and hence, applicable) rules, try the first one first. If we have e.g. the meta rule $p \leftarrow user(p)$ and store the user's positive answer by inserting p behind the evoking meta rule, the inference engine would later on make no use of the stored knowledge and, instead, ask the user again and again. (This indicates that we should better adopt the strategy to apply facts before rules or, more generally, to choose according to the minimal branching degree in the tableau.)

The following table summarizes the above considerations

	call	**file**	**thes**	**sql**	**user**	**sepa**	**cons**
buffer answer set	no	yes	yes	no	no	no	no
store positive answer	no	no	no	no	yes	yes	yes

Negative and don't-know answers

If the source does not positively answer a request, then this could mean either *no* or *don't know*. We decided to assume the latter and to store nothing in this case. We could store $\neg p$ if it is known (e.g. by user input), but the proof search procedure makes no use of this knowledge as it tries to prove p. To record a failed request inside the inference engine would require a logic with the three truth values *yes, no, don't know*. In [Carnielli87], a systematic way is described how to achieve that for tableau calculus.

In our implementation, the dialog component outside the logic machine records *don't know* for **user** in order to avoid repeated questioning. The logic machine makes no use of this dialog knowledge.

Recursive calls of the logic machine

Note that such calls lie at the heart of **sepa** and **cons**. Like for any other recursion, infinite loops may easily arise. A radical solution would be to exclude recursion over meta rules at all. But this would also exclude useful applications like the following: Suppose that we have a meta rule $p \leftarrow sepa(p)$ meaning that the logic machine has to start a separate proof search for p before it continues with the main search process (in order to precompute fact p). During this intermediate search, another predicate q may play a central rôle at different places in the prospective proof. Why not apply here the same preprocessing principle and let the logic machine evaluate a second meta rule $q \leftarrow sepa(q)$?

Let us consider how to avoid infinite loops. Suppose the machine has started to apply meta rule $p \leftarrow sepa(p)$, this rule is still present and could be applied during the intermediate search, resulting in an intermediate intermediate search and so on. We discuss the following two solution.

The first is to let the loop checker also catch meta rules, just in the same way as for ordinary formulas. More precisely, imagine that recursive calls of the logic machine result in a *nesting* of tableaux. For this nested tableau, too, apply the principle

On any branch, no ground formula must occur more than once.

Note that this is as incomplete as in the case of pure predicate logic. Recursion over e.g. $p(X) \leftarrow cons(p(f(Y)))$ could not be recognized.

The second solution makes use of the modularization of the knowledge base. The knowledge engineer specifies in the meta rules the applicable parts of the knowledge base by $p \leftarrow sepa(meta1,p)$ and $q \leftarrow sepa(meta2,q)$ meaning that a separate proof search for p may use the part named 'meta1', likewise for q. If the first rule is contained neither in 'meta1' nor in 'meta2', and the second one in 'meta1' only, then these rules will not cause a loop.

Let us mention here a problem of parallelizing proof search. On the one hand, **sepa** and **cons** represent good points where to start a parallel proof search since the nested search is quite independent. But this would exclude the possibility to catch loops automatically: Recursive calls of the logic machine would cause an infinite amount of (virtual) machines working in parallel.

VM/Prolog as an example

call, **sql**, and (partly) **cons** are known in VM/Prolog: There, a procedural attachment *call(p)* is just written *p*. Instead of trying to prove *p*, the corresponding procedure is called. The Prolog interpreter maintains a table of procedure identifiers, built-in or user defined, and hence knows what to do. Syntax for SQL access is *sql(p)* where *p* is an arbitrary predicate and *sql* is a built-in procedure which tries to satisfy *p* by looking in the SQL data base. Default reasoning occurs as the well-known negation as failure. All other functions must be programmed by the user in assembly language, the implementation language of VM/Prolog. We claim that this integration problem can be more easily solved if the interpreter is coded in a higher level language.

References

[Bibel83] W. Bibel, Matings in Matrices, Communications of the ACM 26(1983), 844-852

[Blaser85] A. Blaser, B. Alschwee, He. Lehmann, Hu. Lehmann, W. Schönfeld, Ein Expertensystem mit natürlichsprachlichem Dialog - Ein Projektbericht, in: W. Brauer, R. Radig (Hrsg.), Wissensbasierte Systeme, GI-Kongreß 1985, Informatik-Fachberichte 112, Springer-Verlag, Berlin 1985, 42-57

[Bledsoe77] W.W.Bledsoe, Non-resolution theorem proving, Artificial Intelligence 9(1977), 1-35

[Carnielli87] W.A. Carnielli, Systematization of finite many-valued logics through the method of tableaux, J. Symbolic Logic 52.2 (1987), 473-493

[Chandra81] A.K. Chandra, D.C. Kozen, L.J. Stockmeyer, Alternation, J. ACM 28(1981), 114-133

[Clark78] K. Clark, Negation as failure, in: H. Gallaire e.a. (eds.), Logic and data bases, Plenum Press, New York 1978

[Colmerauer73] A. Colmerauer, H. Kanoui, R. Pasero, P. Roussel, Un système de communication homme-machine en français, Rapport Groupe Intelligence Artificielle, Marseille 1973.

[Gentzen34] G. Gentzen, Untersuchungen über das logische Schliessen, Math. Zeitschr. 39 (1934), 167-210, 405-431

[Horn51] A. Horn, On sentences which are true of direct unions of algebras, J. Symbolic Logic 16(1951), 14-21.

[Oppacher86] F. Oppacher, E. Suen, Controlling deduction with proof condensation and heuristics, Proc. 8th Conf. Automated Deduction, 384-393

[Robinson65] J.A. Robinson, A machine-oriented logic based on the resolution principle, J. ACM 12(1965), 23-41

[Schönfeld85] W. Schönfeld, PROLOG extensions based on tableau calculus, Proc. 9th Int. Conf. Artificial Intelligence, Aug. 1985, Los Angeles, Ca., Vol. 2, 730-732

[Schmitt87] P.H. Schmitt, The THOT Theorem Prover, TR 87.09.007 , IBM Wissenschaftliches Zentrum Heidelberg (1987)

[Shapiro] Ehud H. Shapiro, Alternation and the Computational Complexity of Logic Programs, J. Logic Programming 1(1984), 19-33

[Smullyan68] R.M. Smullyan, First-order logic, Springer-Verlag, Berlin-Heidelberg-New York 1968

[Wrightson84] G. Wrightson, Semantic tableaux, unification, and links, Technical Report CSD-ANZARP-84-001, University of Wellington, 1984

COMPLEXITY CORES AND HARD-TO-PROVE FORMULAS

Uwe Schöning
EWH Koblenz, Informatik
Rheinau 3-4, D5400 Koblenz
West Germany

Abstract. Extending the theory of complexity cores, it is proved, assuming NP ≠ co-NP, that there exist collections of tautologies of exponential density which have only non-polynomially long proofs under every sound proof system.

1. INTRODUCTION

Several authors already observed the strong interrelationships between the NP =? co-NP problem and the existence of proof systems for the tautologies in propositional logic which always have polynomially long proofs (dubbed "super proof systems" in [1]). Of course, these observations are nothing else than exploiting the facts that TAUT (the set of tautologies) or UNSAT (the set of unsatisfiable formulas) are co-NP-complete [2], and that NP can be considered to consist exactly of those languages having succinct (i.e. polynomially long) proofs under certain proof systems. Hence NP = co-NP if and only if super proof systems for the tautologies exist. Stated more formally, we observe the following (cf. [1]):

Proposition 1. NP = co-NP if and only if there exists a sound proof system S and a polynomial p such that every tautology f has a proof of length at most $p(|f|)$ in S if and only if there exists a sound refutation proof system S and a polynomial p such that every unsatisfiable formula f has a refutation in S of length at most $p(|f|)$.

Much work has been done in finding particular (e.g. unsatisfiable) formula classes which have only non-polynomially long proofs under certain (refutation) proof systems (like resolution). E.g., in [3,4] an infinite collection of unsatisfiable formulas is constructed - based on certain encodings of expander graphs - which have only exponentially long resolution refutations, but the formulas turn out to have polynomially long proofs under the standard "Frege systems" Similar research for specific proof systems can be found in [5,6,7].

This paper takes a more abstract and general point of view. We ask the question whether there exist collections of formulas (tautologies or dually, unsatisfiable formulas) which have only long proofs under which proof system whatsoever. We will show (in a certain non-constructive way) that such "uniformly hard-to-prove" formula classes exist, and we further analyze how "dense" such classes can be (cf. also [12]).

These issues are closely related to the study of (polynomial) complexity cores which has been initiated by Lynch [8] and further developed in [9,10,11]. The complexity core notion is tailored for the question P =? NP rather than NP =? co-NP. The purpose of this paper is to transform and also to strengthen some of the results from [10] into the context of "proof length complexity". The strengthening concerns an assertion about the density of such complexity cores. The stronger result is possible because NP $\neq$ co-NP is a stronger assumption than P $\neq$ NP.

By the above proposition, it is clear that, assuming NP $\neq$ co-NP, for every specific proof system S and any given polynomial p there are infinitely many tautologies f which do not have a proof of length $p(|f|)$ in S. (If there were only finitely many such formulas, then we could "patch" S with those formulas as additional axioms and we get TAUT $\in$ NP, hence NP = co-NP, contradicting our assumption). We will show that under the assumption NP $\neq$ co-NP there exists an infinite collection of tautologies F which is uniformly hard to prove, in the sense that for every sound proof system S and every polynomial p there are at most finitely many formulas f in F which have proofs in S of length at most $p(|f|)$. Moreover, the density of the formula collection F is exponential infinitely often, that is, for some $\epsilon > 0$, and infinitely many n, the number of formulas in F of size n exceeds $2^{\epsilon n}$.

2. PRELIMINARIES

All our sets are languages over the fixed alphabet $\Sigma = \{0,1\}$. For a set $A \subseteq \Sigma^*$, $\bar{A} = \Sigma^* - A$ is the complement of A, and for a class of sets C, co-C is the class $\{ A \mid \bar{A} \in C \}$. For a string $w \in \Sigma^*$, $|w|$ denotes its length, and for a set A, $|A|$ denotes its cardinality.

The classes of sets that can be accepted by polynomial-time deterministic (nondeterministic, resp.) Turing machines are denoted by P and NP, resp. The well-known major open problem in this context is to prove the conjecture P $\neq$ NP. An even stronger conjecture is NP $\neq$ co-NP. That is, NP $\neq$ co-NP trivially implies P $\neq$ NP whereas the inverse implication is unknown (i.e. it might be the case that P $\neq$ NP and NP = co-NP).

Cook [2] proved that the set of (encodings of) satisfiable Boolean formulas, SAT, is NP-complete. A set A is called NP-complete if A $\in$ NP and for every B $\in$ NP there is a polynomial-time computable function f such that $f^{-1}(A) = B$. This notion has the consequence that for any NP-complete set A, A $\in$ P if and only if P = NP.

More interesting for this paper are the co-NP-complete sets, i.e. the complements of the NP-complete sets, like TAUT, the set of tautologies, or UNSAT, the set of unsatisfiable formulas. For any co-NP-complete set A, A $\in$ NP if and only if NP = co-NP. As mentioned in Proposition 1, sound super proof systems for the tautologies are essentially the same as polynomial-time nondeterministic Turing machines accepting a subset of TAUT.

Research about the density of such complete languages was initiated by Berman and Hartmanis [13]. For a set A, let $dens_A : N \to N$ be the function $dens_A(n) = \| \{ x \in A \mid |x| = n \} \|$. A set A is called sparse if for some polynomial p, $dens_A(n) \leq p(n)$.

Berman and Hartmanis [13] showed that the following two statements are equivalent:

(1) A set A is p-isomorphic to SAT, i.e. there exists a polynomial time computable bijection f such that A = f(SAT) (hence, SAT = $f^{-1}(A)$) such that also f^{-1} is computable in polynomial time.

(2) A has a padding function, i.e. there is a polynomial-time computable and injective function pad : $\Sigma^* \times \Sigma^* \to \Sigma^*$ such that pad^{-1} is also computable in polynomial time with the property that for all x and y $\in \Sigma^*$, x $\in$ A if and only if pad(x,y) $\in$ A.

In a sense, a padding function provides a method of producing many variants of an input x, syntactically different from x, having the same status as x w.r.t. membership in A. Since all "natural" NP-complete sets do have padding functions, they also satisfy clause (1) above, i.e they are p-isomorphic to SAT.

Similar statements hold for TAUT and the "natural" co-NP-complete sets. In particular, TAUT has a padding function. This fact will be used later.

3. MAIN RESULT

From NP $\neq$ co-NP follows immediately that TAUT $\notin$ NP, and this implies that for any polynomial-time nondeterministic Turing machine M with L(M) $\subseteq$ TAUT there are infinitely many tautologies f such that f $\in$ TAUT - L(M). (If there were only finitely many such formulas, then M could be "patched" to accept TAUT exactly). An analogous statement holds for all sound proof systems for the tautologies: for each such proof system and each polynomial p there are infinitely many tautologies f which cannot be proved in this system within p(|f |) steps.

The following lemma improves on this statement. It additionally asserts that such tautologies occur frequently. A similar result appears in Kleine Büning [14].

Lemma 2. (Assuming NP $\neq$ co-NP)
There is a constant $\varepsilon > 0$ such that for every polynomial-time nondeterministic Turing machine M with L(M) $\subseteq$ TAUT, the density of TAUT - L(M) exceeds $2^{\varepsilon n}$ for infinitely many n.

Proof. By the fact that TAUT has a padding function, there is an injective and polynomial-time computable function pad such that for all x and y, x $\in$ TAUT if and only if pad(x,y) $\in$ TAUT. Moreover, this padding function for TAUT has the property that $|pad(x,y)| \leq |x| + c\cdot|y|$ for some constant c.

Now, suppose for every $\varepsilon>0$ there is a polynomial-time nondeterministic Turing machine M = M(ε) with L(M) $\subseteq$ TAUT and $dens_{TAUT-L(M)}(n) \leq 2^{\varepsilon n}$ for almost every n. Consider the following nondeterminstic algorithm for TAUT.

On input f,
guess a string y, |y| = |f|, and run
M on input pad(f,y).

This algorithm accepts TAUT nondeterministically in polynomial time if

$$(\# \text{ of } y\text{'s}) = 2^n > dens_{TAUT-L(M)}(n+cn) .$$

This inequality holds if

$$n > \varepsilon(n+cn),$$

that is, if $\epsilon < 1/(c+1)$. That means, using the machine $M(1/(c+2))$ in the above algorithm leads to TAUT $\in$ NP, hence NP = co-NP, a contradiction to the assumption. #

Stating the lemma in terms of proof systems, the assertion is that for every sound proof system S and for every polynomial p the number of tautologies f of size n which has no proof in S of length p(n) exceeds $2^{\epsilon n}$ for infinitely many n.

This statement is still non-uniform, in the sense that for every proof system there are "many" hard-to-prove formulas under this particular system. These formulas can be different for each proof system. In the following, we make this statement uniform, such that there is one uniform "dense" collection of formulas which is hard to prove under each proof system.

This uniformization process is typical for arguments in connection with the construction of complexity cores (as in [10]), with the difference that the complexity core notion applies to (the nonexistence of) P-subsets of a given set - instead NP-subsets as in the above lemma. On the other hand, the statement of the lemma is stronger than the corresponding statement (which is also made "uniform" in [10]), namely that no NP-complete set has an algorithm running in polynomial time except on a sparse set of the inputs (cf. [15]).

__Theorem 3__. (Assuming NP $\neq$ co-NP)
There is a constant $\epsilon > 0$ and a collection F of tautologies of density at least $2^{\epsilon n}$ for infinitely many n, such that for every sound proof system S for the tautologies and for every polynomial q, the shortest proof of f in S has length more than $q(|f|)$ for almost every $f \in F$.

__Proof__. Let $S_1, S_2, \ldots$ be an enumeration of all sound proof systems for the tautologies. (This enumeration is not effective). Let $p_1, p_2, \ldots$ be an increasing enumeration of polynomials such that for every polynomial q there is an index i such that for all n and $j \geq i$, $q(n) \leq p_j(n)$. (The sequence $p_i(n) = n^i + i$ will do). Let ϵ be the constant provided by the lemma. Then, by the lemma, for each i and j there is a set of tautologies $F_{i,j}$ such that no $f \in F_{i,j}$ is provable in S_i within $p_j(|f|)$ steps. Furthermore, for infinitely many n, $dens_{F_{i,j}}(n) > 2^{\epsilon n}$.

Now, we construct the desired set of tautologies F which is "uniformly hard-to-prove", i.e. a "complexity core" w.r.t. efficient provability, as follows. The set F is defined in stages such that $F := \emptyset$ is set in stage 0, and in each further stage elements are added to F.

<u>stage 0</u>: $F := \emptyset$;

$n_0 := 0$;

<u>stage k > 0</u>:

n_k := the smallest natural number such that

$n_k > n_{k-1}$ and $dens_{F_{1,k} \cap \ldots \cap F_{k,k}}(n_k) > 2^{\varepsilon n_k}$;

$F := F \cup \{ f \in F_{1,k} \cap \ldots \cap F_{k,k} \mid n_{k-1} < |f| \leq n_k \}$;

First we need to show that the construction can always proceed and doesn't get "stuck", i.e. the smallest number n_k to be determined in stage k always exists. Suppose there is some stage k such that for all $n > n_{k-1}$,

$$dens_{F_{1,k} \cap \ldots \cap F_{k,k}}(n) \leq 2^{\varepsilon n} \quad .$$

Now, take the combination of the proof systems $S_1, \ldots, S_k$ into a single one, say S. The above inequality means that the number of tautologies f not provable in S within $p_k(|f|)$ steps is at most $2^{\varepsilon n}$ for almost every n. This implies the existence of a polynomial-time nondeterministic Turing machine M, $L(M) \subseteq TAUT$, such that

$$dens_{TAUT-L(M)}(n) \leq 2^{\varepsilon n}$$

for almost every n, contradicting the lemma.
By the fact that the construction can always proceed, it is clear now, that for infinitely many n (namely $n = n_k$, $k=1,2,\ldots$) we get $dens_F(n) > 2^{\varepsilon n}$.

Now let S be any sound proof system for the tautologies, and let q be any polynomial. Then there are indices i and j such that $S = S_i$ and $q(n) \leq p_{j'}(n)$ for all n and $j' \geq j$. Then, no formula f in $F_{i,j}$ ($\supseteq F_{i,j+1} \supseteq F_{i,j+2} \supseteq \ldots$) is provable in S_i within $p_j(|f|)$ steps. By construction of F, only such formulas are added to F after stage max(i,j). Hence there are at most finitely many $f \in F$ that have a proof in S of $q(|f|)$ steps. ∎

4. DISCUSSION

We have shown that, in principle, there exist "dense" collection of tautologies which behave "badly" for every sound proof syste for the tautologies (provided NP ≠ co-NP). The above proof doe not reveal any information how such formulas might look like. Th proof of the theorem is non-constructive, since it is based on the noneffective enumeration of all proof systems S_1, S_2, ... Using the same approach as in [10], the proof can be based, though, on a different enumeration which is effective, such that it is possible to bring the complexity of the constructed set F in Theorem 3 down to NEXPTIME. Since such a possible technical refinement does not seem to bring any further insight, it is omitted here.

Also note that the statement of the lemma and the theorem hold just as well for refutation proof systems and the unsatisfiable formulas, UNSAT, by the obvious connection between tautologies and unsatisfiable formulas.

Another remark is that the machinery developed in [16] is applicaple to "proof length complexity" so that it is the case that there is no maximal (w.r.t. inclusion and modulo finite variations) set F as in Theorem 3. That is, for each set of tautologies F having the properties as claimed in Theorem 3, there is another set F' having also these properties, and F' contains infinitely many more formulas than F. This means also, that for every sound proof system S there is still another proof system S' under which infinitely many more formulas can be proved to be tautologies efficiently.

REFERENCES

[1] S.A. Cook and R. Reckow, On the length of proofs in the propositional calculus, Proc. 6th ACM STOC, 1974, 135-148. Corrections in SIGACT News 6, No. 3 (1974), 15-22.

[2] S. A. Cook, The complexity of theorem proving procedures, Proc. 3rd ACM STOC, 1971, 151-158.

[3] A. Haken, The intractability of resolution, Theor. Comput. Sci. 39 (1985), 297-308.

[4] A. Urquhart, Hard examples for resolution, Journ. Assoc. Comput. Mach. 34 (1987), 209-219.

[5] G. S. Tseitin, On the complexity of derivations in the propositional calculus, Structures in Constructive Math. Logic, Part II, A.O. Slisenko (ed.), 1968, 115-125.

[6] Z. Galil, On the validity and complexity of bounded resolution, Proc. 7th ACM STOC, 1975, 72-82.

[7] Z. Galil, On enumeration procedures for theorem proving and integer programming, 3rd ICALP 1976, Edinburgh University Press, S. Michaelson and R. Milner (eds.), 355-381.

[8] N. Lynch, On reducibility to complex or sparse sets, Journ. Assoc. Mach. 22 (1975), 341-345.

[9] S. Even, A.L. Selman, and Y. Yacobi, Hard-core theorems for complexity classes, Journ. Assoc. Comput. Mach. 32 (1985), 205-217.

[10] P. Orponen and U. Schöning, The density and complexity of polynomial cores for intractable sets, Information and Control 70 (1986), 54-68.

[11] D.Z. Du and R.V. Book, The existence and density of generalized complexity cores, Journ. Assoc. Comput. Mach. 34 (1987), 718-730.

[12] B. Krishnamurthy and R.N. Moll, Examples of hard tautologies in the propositional calculus, Proc. 13th ACM STOC, 1981, 28-37.

[13] L. Berman and J. Hartmanis, On isomorphism and density of NP and other complete sets, SIAM Journ. on Computing 6 (1977), 305-322.

[14] H. Kleine Büning, Some remarks on polynomial algorithms for the satisfiability problem, manuscript 1981.

[15] A.R. Meyer and M.S. Paterson, With what frequency are apparently intractable problems difficult?, Techn. Report, MIT/LCS/TM-126, Feb. 1979.

[16] P. Orponen, D.A. Russo, and U. Schöning, Optimal approximations and polynomially levelable sets, SIAM Journ. on Computing 15 (1986), 399-408.

ON THE AVERAGE CASE COMPLEXITY OF BACKTRACKING FOR THE EXACT-SATISFIABILITY PROBLEM

Ewald Speckenmeyer
Fachbereich Mathematik-Informatik, Universität-GH Paderborn
Postfach 16 21, D-4790 Paderborn

ABSTRACT: We analyse the average case performance of a simple backtracking algorithm for determining all exact-satisfying truth assignments of boolean formulas in conjunctive normal form with r clauses over n variables. A truth assignment exact-satisfies a formula, if in each clause exactly one literal is set to true. We show: If formulas are chosen by generating clauses independently, where each variable occurs in a clause either unnegated with probability p or negated with probability q or none of both with probability $1-p-q$ ($p,q>0$, $p+q\leq 1$), then the average number of nodes in the backtracking trees of formulas from these classes is bounded by a constant, for all $n\in\mathbb{N}$, if $r\geq \ln 2/(pq)$ is chosen. (In case of $p=q=1/3$ the result holds for all $r\geq 6$.)

1. INTRODUCTION

In this paper we consider the problem of determining all truth assignments t of some boolean formula F in conjunctive normal form (CNF) such that every clause c of F (a clause is a disjunction of literals and a literal is a boolean variable a or its negation $\bar{a}$) contains exactly one literal x, which is set to true by t. Such a truth assignment t is called exact-satisfying (x- satisfying).

The problem of deciding whether a given CNF-formula has an x-satisfying truth assignment, i.e. whether F is x-satisfiable, is known to be NP-complete, even if all clauses consist of exactly three literals and no negated variables occur in F, see [4], problem LO 4.

This exact-satisfiability problem, which may look artificial at first, turns out to be an immediate extension of the set partitioning problem, one of the most important problems from operations research with a wide area of applications, see [1]. In fact the set partitioning problem is precisely the exact-satisfiability problem for formulas without negated variables, see e.g. [7].

In [6] a sophisticated backtracking algorithm is developed, which decides in $O(r2^{n/4})$ steps whether a CNF-formula with n variables and r clauses is x-satisfiable. This is a substantial improvement over the naive algorithm, which starts enumerating all truth assignments one by one until a first x-satisfying one has been found or the search ends unsuccessfully, whose running time is bounded by $O(|F|2^n)$ steps.

We will consider the average running time of a simple backtracking algorithm for enumerating all x-satisfying truth assignments of CNF-formulas. In order to be more precise we first will introduce some notions and notations.

Let $L=\{a_1,\bar{a}_1,\ldots,a_n,\bar{a}_n\}$ be the set of literals over the set $V=\{a_1,\ldots,a_n\}$ of boolean variables and let $cl(n)=\{x_{i_1}+\ldots+x_{i_k} \mid 1\leq i_1<\ldots<i_k\leq n,\ k\geq 0,\ x_{i_j}\in\{a_{i_j},\bar{a}_{i_j}\}\}$ be the set of

clauses (disjunctions of literals) over V. A clause $c=x_{i_1}+\ldots+x_{i_k}\in cl(n)$ is represented by the set $\{x_{i_1},\ldots,x_{i_k}\}$ of its literals. By $cl(n)^r$ the set of CNF-formulas consisting of r clauses from cl(n), where repetitions of clauses in a formula are possible, is de noted. Formulas are represented by ordered multisets of clauses.

We will consider formulas from $cl(n)^r$ under a class of instance distributions defined as follows.

The p-q-distribution (Constant density model)

Let $p,q>0$ such that $p+q\leq 1$. The p-q-distribution for $cl(n)^r$ is induced by generating formulas as follows. The r clauses of a formula F are generated independently and for each $a\in V$ and $c\in F$ either $a\in c$ holds with probability p or $\bar{a}\in c$ with probability q or none of both with probability 1-p-q. (Note that in case of $p=q=1/3$ we deal with the uniform distribution for $cl(n)^r$.)

A (partial) function $t:V\rightarrow L$ such that $t(a_i)\in\{a_i,\bar{a}_i\}$ in case where $t(a_i)$ is defined, is called a (partial) truth assignment of V. Here $t(a_i)=a_i$ ($\bar{a}_i$) means that a_i is set t true (false) under t. We will identify t with the set $\{t(a_i)\mid a_i\in V,\ t(a_i)\text{ is defined}\}$, and we set $\bar{t}=\{\overline{t(a_i)}\mid t(a_i)\in t\}$ (as usual we set $\bar{\bar{a}}=a$).

Let c be a clause from cl(n) and let t be a (partial) truth assignment of the variable from V. Then t x-satisfies c and we will write $t_x(c)=\text{true}$ iff $|t\cap c|=1$ and $|\bar{t}\cap c|=|c|-$ If $|t\cap c|\geq 2$ or $c\subseteq\bar{t}$ then we say t x-falsifies c and we will write $t_x(c)=\text{false}$. If t neither x-satisfies c nor x-falsifies c then $t_x(c)$ is undefined and in this case eith $t\cap c=\emptyset$ and $c\not\subseteq\bar{t}$ or $|t\cap c|=1$ and $|\bar{t}\cap c|\leq|c|-2$ holds.

These notions are extended to CNF-formulas canonically. Let $F\in cl(n)^r$. Then t x-satisfies F and we write $t_x(F)=\text{true}$ iff $t_x(c)=\text{true}$ holds for all clauses $c\in F$. If there is some clause $c\in F$ s.t. $t_x(c)=\text{false}$ then t x-falsifies F and we write $t_x(F)=\text{false}$. If t neither x-satisfies F nor x-falsifies F then $t_x(F)$ is undefined.

F is called x-satisfiable iff there is some truth assignment t s.t. $t_x(F)=\text{true}$. An x-satisfying truth assignment t of F with $|t|=n$ is called a solution of F. Note that F may not contain all variables from V. In that case there is some x-satisfying parti truth assignment t of F with $|t|<n$, if F is x-satisfiable. Such a t will not be calle a solution of F. But each extension t' of t with $|t'|=n$ is a solution!

The following backtracking algorithm XSAT determines all solutions t of formulas $F\in cl(n)^r$. XSAT uses a stack, which stores (partial) truth assignments t of V_n with $t_x(F)\neq\text{false}$. We also will call such truth assignments admissible.

Algorithm XSAT

1. read input formula F;
2. push $t=\emptyset$ on the stack;
3. <u>repeat</u>
4. pop top-assignment $t=\{x_i\mid n\geq i\geq n-j+1\}$, $j\geq 0$, from the stack;
5. <u>if</u> $t_x(F)=\text{true}$ <u>and</u> $|t|=n$ <u>then</u> output "t is a solution"

```
    else if |t|<n then
    begin
        t1:=t∪{a_{n-j}}; t2:=t∪{ā_{n-j}};
        for i:=1 to 2 do
            if t_{i,x}(F) is not false then push t_i on the stack
    end
until stack is empty;
```

It is easy to see that XSAT determines all solutions of F. The backtracking tree T(F) produced by XSAT applied to F is a binary tree with admissible (partial) truth assignments of the form $t=\{x_n,\ldots,x_{n-k+1}\}$, $0\le k\le n$, $x_i \in \{a_i, \bar{a}_i\}$, as node values.
The running time of XSAT applied to F mainly depends on $|T(F)|$, the number of nodes in T(F). Then we obtain the following

Lemma 1:

XSAT determines all solutions of a formula $F\in cl(n)^r$ in $O((n+|F|)\cdot|T(F)|)$ steps. □

In order to determine the average case running time of XSAT in the constant density model we will concentrate on the average number of nodes in the corresponding backtracking trees.

The next figure shows the backtracking tree T(F) of $F=\{\{\bar{x}_2\}, \{x_1,x_2\}, \{x_1,\bar{x}_3\}\}\in cl(3)^3$ under XSAT, where T(F) is a subtree of the complete binary tree T_3 of depth 3. The bold lines are the edges of T(F), and the admissible truth assignments pushed on the stack of XSAT are written at the nodes. The dashed lines represent that part of T_3, which is cut off because it corresponds to (partial) truth assignments violating some constraints. The truth assignment $t=\{x_1,\bar{x}_2,x_3\}$ is the only solution of F.

Figure 1

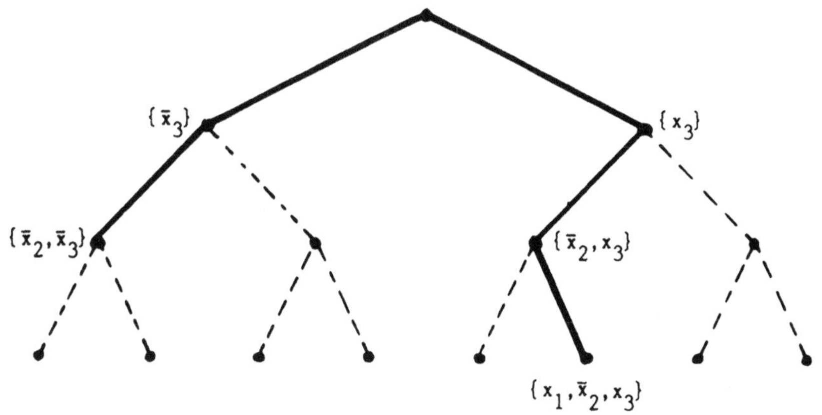

E.g. the node of T_3 corresponding to the partial truth assignment $t=\{x_2,\bar{x}_3\}$ does not belong to T(F), because the clause $c=\{\bar{x}_2\}\in F$ satisfies $c\subseteq\bar{t}$, and the node corresponding to $t=\{x_1,\bar{x}_2,\bar{x}_3\}$ does not belong to T(F), because $c=\{x_1,\bar{x}_3\}\in F$ satisfies $|c\cap t|=2$.

We will show in this paper that the average number of nodes in backtracking trees produced by XSAT applied to $cl(n)^r$ under the p-q-distribution is bounded by a constant, for all $n \in N$, provided that $r \geq \ln(2)/(pq)$. In case of $p=q=1/3$ the result holds, if $r \geq 6$. A similar surprising result has been obtained for the k-coloring problem of graphs in the constant density model, see [2]. We come to this result later on.
Similar investigations for the satisfiability problem in the constant density model can be found in [3] and [5].
In [7] the average case behaviour of XSAT in the constant degree model is studied (i.e for the subset $cl(n,s)^r$ of formulas from $cl(n)^r$, with all clauses of length s, under the uniform instance distribution). It is shown there, e.g., that the average running time of XSAT applied to $cl(n,3)^r$, with $r=O(n)$, is exponentially growing in n.

2. AVERAGE CASE BEHAVIOUR OF XSAT IN THE CONSTANT DENSITY MODEL

We will prove the following main result of this paper.

THEOREM 2:

Let $p,q>0$ s.t. $p+q \leq 1$ and let $r>-2/\log(1-2pq)$. (1)

Then the average number of nodes in backtracking trees of XSAT applied to $cl(n)^r$ unde the p-q-distribution is bounded by $O(1)$, for all $n \in N$. □

We can make the growth of the lower bound on r of (1) explicit by using the well know estimation of $\ln(1+x) \leq x$. Then

$$-2/\log(1-2pq) = -2\ln(2)/\ln(1-2pq) \leq \ln(2)/(pq).$$

This estimation deviates only a little from the estimated function. I.e. the lower bound on (1) is growing linearly in $(pq)^{-1}$.

An immediate consequence of this theorem is the following

Corollary 3:

Let p,q and r as in theorem 2.
Then the probability that a formula drawn from $cl(n)^r$ under the p-q-distribution is x-satisfiable is going to 0, for growing values of n. □

A result similar to theorem 2 has been obtained in a paper by Bender and Wilf, see [2 for the k-colorability problem of graphs in the constant density model. Bender and Wi show that the average number of nodes in backtracking trees under BACKTRACK for deter mining all admissible k-colorings of a graph in the model, where the edges of a graph are generated independently with probability p, is bounded by a constant for graphs with an arbitrary number of nodes.
In order to get a feeling for this surprising result, think of the well known propert that a graph containing a (k+1)-clique is not k-colorable on the one hand. But on the other hand node-induced subgraphs of random graphs in the constant density model, wh by itself are random graphs in the constant density model, too, contain a (k+1)-cliq with high probability already for subgraphs induced by a small number of nodes. It i

not hard to derive this result by using probabilistic methods.
This property of random graphs in the constant density model however is not explicitly used in Bender's and Wilf's proof.

We will show next a simple property, which has to be satisfied by any two clauses of a formula from $cl(n)^r$ in order to be x-satisfiable. This property has for the exact satisfiability problem a similar importance as (k+1)-cliques have for the k-colorability problem.
For a clause $c\in cl(n)$ let $\bar{c}=\{\bar{x}_i \mid x_i\in c\}$.

Lemma 4:

Let $c_1,c_2\in cl(n)$ be two arbitrary clauses. Then there is a truth assignment t simultaneously x-satisfying c_1 and c_2 iff $|c_1\cap\bar{c}_2|\le 2$ and if $|c_1\cap\bar{c}_2|=1$ then $c_1-\{x_i\}\ne c_2-\{\bar{x}_i\}$, where $x_i\in c_1$ and $\bar{x}_i\in c_2$.

Proof:

Suppose $|c_1\cap c_2|\ge 3$. Then there are three literals $x_i,x_j,x_k\in c_1$ s.t. $\bar{x}_i,\bar{x}_j,\bar{x}_k\in c_2$ and so for every truth assignment t either $|t\cap\{x_i,x_j,x_k\}|\ge 2$ or $|t\cap\{\bar{x}_i,\bar{x}_j,\bar{x}_k\}\ge 2$ holds.
I.e. t does not x-satisfy c_1 and c_2.
Now suppose $\{x_i\}=c_1\cap\bar{c}_2$ and $c_1-\{x_i\}=c_2-\{\bar{x}_i\}$.
Then there cannot exist a truth assignment t s.t. $|t\cap c_1|=|t\cap c_2|=1$ holds.

For the inverse direction we consider three cases.

(i) If there are exactly two literals $x_i,x_j\in c_1$ s.t. $\bar{x}_i,\bar{x}_j\in c_2$ then set $t(a_i)=x_i$ and $t(a_j)=\bar{x}_j$ and for all the other literals x_k from $c_1\cup c_2$ set $t(a_k)=\bar{x}_k$. The rest of t is arbitrary. Then obviously $|t\cap c_1|=|t\cap c_2|=1$. I.e. t x-satisfies c_1 and c_2.

(ii) If there is just one literal $x_i\in c_1$ s.t. $\bar{x}_i\in c_2$ and $c_1-\{x_i\}\ne c_2-\{\bar{x}_i\}$ then there is w.l.o.g. a literal $x_j\in c_1$ s.t. neither x_j nor $\bar{x}_j\in c_2$. Define t by $t(a_i)=\bar{x}_i$, $t(a_j)=x_j$ and for all other literals x_k from $c_1\cup c_2$ set $t(a_k)=\bar{x}_k$. The remaining part of t is arbitrary. Then $|t\cap c_1|=|t\cap c_2|=1$. Thus t x-satisfies c_1 and c_2.

(iii) If $c_1\cap\bar{c}_2=\emptyset$ then there is obviously a truth assignment t x-satisfying c_1 and c_2 simultaneously. □

We will apply this lemma in order to prove the following

Lemma 5:

The average number of nodes in backtracking trees produced by XSAT applied to formulas from $cl(n)^r$ with the p-q-distribution is bounded by

$$1+\sum_{k=1}^{n} 2^k\left[\sum_{i=0}^{2}\binom{k}{i}(2pq)^i(1-2pq)^{k-i}\right]^{\lfloor\frac{r}{2}\rfloor}. \qquad (2)$$

Proof:

Let F $cl(n)^r$ be chosen under the p-q-distribution and let c,c' be two of the r clauses in F, arbitrarily chosen. Then the probability that for $a_i\in V$ holds $x_i\in c$ and $\bar{x}_i\in c'$, for $x_i\in\{a_i,\bar{a}_i\}$, is 2pq.

Suppose XSAT has already assigned k values $x_n,\ldots,x_{n-k+1}$ to the variables $a_n,\ldots,a_{n-k+1}$ and under this partial truth assignment t holds $t_x(F)\neq$false. Then by lemma 4 every two clauses $c,c'\in F$ contain at most two complementary literals corresponding to $a_n,\ldots,a_{n-k+1}$ and the probability that c and c' contain at most two complementary literals corresponding to $a_n,\ldots,a_{n-k+1}$ is

$$\sum_{i=0}^{2}\binom{k}{i}(2pq)^i(1-2pq)^{k-i}\quad .$$

Then the probability that no two clauses of F contain more than 2 complementary literals corresponding to $a_n,\ldots,a_{n-k+1}$ is at most

$$\left[\sum_{i=0}^{2}\binom{k}{i}(2pq)^i(1-2pq)^{k-i}\right]^{\lfloor\frac{r}{2}\rfloor}\quad . \tag{3}$$

This formula as well is an upper bound for the expectation that the node in the complete binary tree T_n at depth k, corresponding to $t=\{x_n,\ldots,x_{n-k+1}\}$, belongs to the backtracking tree T(F) of some formula $F\in cl(n)^r$ chosen under the p-q-distribution. Because formula (3) only depends on k, p and q, but not on the individual choice of t, the average number of nodes at depth k in backtracking trees produced by XSAT applied to $cl(n)^r$ under the p-q-distribution is at most

$$2^k\left[\sum_{i=0}^{2}\binom{k}{i}(2pq)^i(1-2pq)^{k-i}\right]^{\lfloor\frac{r}{2}\rfloor}\quad . \tag{4}$$

Summing up (4), for all $0\leq k\leq n$, finally yields the upper bound of (2) as claimed in the lemma. □

It should be mentioned that the bound of (3) for the expectation that some fixed node at depth k of T_n belongs to the backtracking tree of some formula $F\in cl(n)^r$ is not optimal. This is because we take into account for the fact that F is not falsified by $t=\{x_n,\ldots,x_{n-k+1}\}$ the property that after the r clauses from F are grouped into $\lfloor\frac{r}{2}\rfloor$ pairs of clauses, none of these pairs is allowed to contain more than two complementary literals corresponding to $a_n,\ldots,a_{n-k+1}$. But this property also has to be fulfilled by all $\binom{r}{2}$ possible pairs of clauses. Here lies a key for substantially improving the bound on r of (1). Unfortunately the exponent of $\lfloor\frac{r}{2}\rfloor$ in formula (3) cannot simply be replaced by $\binom{r}{2}$, because there are dependencies between the events that the pairs of clauses from F contain more than two complementary literals in the actually considered initial segment.

The next lemma provides the desired lower bound on r.

<u>Lemma 6</u>:

Let p, q and r be as in theorem 2. Then formula (2) is bounded by a constant, for all $n\in N$.

Proof:

For reasons of simplicity we will assume r to be even. Then formula (4) can be written as follows:

$$\left[\sum_{i=0}^{2}\binom{k}{i}\,(2^{\frac{2}{r}}\cdot 2pq)^{i}(2^{\frac{2}{r}}-2^{\frac{2}{r}}\,2pq)^{k-i}\right]^{\frac{r}{2}}$$

$$=\left[(2^{\frac{2}{r}}-2^{1+\frac{2}{r}}\,pq)^{k}+k(2^{1+\frac{2}{r}}\,pq)(2^{\frac{2}{r}}-2^{1+\frac{2}{r}}\,pq)^{k-1}+\frac{k(k-1)}{2}(2^{1+\frac{2}{r}}\,pq)^{2}(2^{\frac{2}{r}}-2^{1+\frac{2}{r}}pq)^{k-2}\right]^{\frac{r}{2}}$$

$$=(2^{\frac{2}{r}}-2^{1+\frac{2}{r}}pq)^{\frac{r}{2}(k-2)}\cdot\left[(2^{\frac{2}{r}}-2^{1+\frac{2}{r}}pq)^{2}+k2^{1+\frac{2}{r}}pq(2^{\frac{2}{r}}-2^{1+\frac{2}{r}}pq)+k(k-1)2^{1+\frac{4}{r}}p^{2}q^{2}\right]^{\frac{r}{2}}.$$

In order to estimate the last formula, we will first determine a lower bound on r s.t.

$$2^{\frac{2}{r}}-2^{1+\frac{2}{r}}pq<1 \quad\text{iff}\quad 2^{-\frac{2}{r}}>(1-2pq) \quad\text{iff}\quad r>-2\log^{-1}(1-2pq).$$

Note that this is precisely the lower bound of (1).(In case of $p=q=1/3$, e.g., each $r\geq 6$ satisfies this bound.)

It is not hard to see that

$$\left[(2^{\frac{2}{r}}-2^{1+\frac{2}{r}}pq)^{2}+k2^{1+\frac{2}{r}}pq(2^{\frac{2}{r}}-2^{1+\frac{2}{r}}pq)+k(k-1)2^{1+\frac{4}{r}}p^{2}q^{2}\right]^{\frac{r}{2}}<k^{r}$$

holds.

Note that $2^{\frac{2}{r}}-2^{1+\frac{2}{r}}pq$ is strictly decreasing in r. So for every r satisfying (1) there is some $0<\delta<1$, s.t.

$$(2^{\frac{2}{r}}-2^{1+\frac{2}{r}}pq)^{\frac{r}{2}}=\delta.$$

Therefore we obtain the following upper bound of

$$O(1)+\sum_{k=2}^{n}\delta^{k-2}\,k^{r}\;\leq\;O(1)+\delta^{-2}\sum_{k=2}^{\infty}(\delta\cdot k^{\frac{r}{k}})^{k} \tag{5}$$

for formula (2).

Because $k^{\frac{r}{k}}\to 1$, if $k\to\infty$, there are some $0<\varepsilon<1$ and some $k'\in N$, s.t. $\delta k^{\frac{r}{k}}<\varepsilon$, for all $k>k'$. So the right side of (5) is bounded by

$$O(1)+\delta^{-2}\left[\sum_{k=2}^{k'}(\delta k^{\frac{r}{k}})^{k}+\sum_{k=k'+1}^{\infty}\varepsilon^{k}\right]=O(1).$$

We thus have completed the proof of the lemma. □

The statement of theorem 2 now immediately follows from the lemmas 5 and 6.

3. REMARKS

Some comments should be made on theorem 2. It shows that the exact-satisfiability problem in the constant density model can in the average be solved very easily. One reason for this is that formulas in this model are not x-satisfiable with probability going to 1, and a backtracking algorithm testing a formula for exact-satisfiability can stop computing after few iterations only, because whole branches from the backtracking tree are cut off very early, because of the property formulated in lemma 4. Note however that the result of theorem 2 is guaranteed only for classes of $cl(n)^r$ under the p-q-distribution, for which $r \geq \ln(2)/(pq)$. In case of $p=q=0.01$, $r \geq 6931$ must be chosen, e.g.. If we could replace however the exponent of $\frac{r}{2}$ in (3) by $\binom{r}{2}$, as mentioned in the discussion following the proof of lemma 5, then we would obtain a lower bound, which is only the square root of the old bound. We expect that theorem 2 also holds for this bound on r.

Two more interesting special classes in the constant density model are $cl(n)^1$ and $cl(n)^2$. While backtracking trees for $cl(n)^1$ have exponentially many nodes in the average (this is because formulas from $cl(n)^1$ do not contain $(1-p-q)\cdot n$ many variables of V in the average, for which the corresponding predecessor nodes in the backtracking trees always have two successor nodes), the question is open for $cl(n)^2$. We expect however that the average number of nodes in backtracking trees of $cl(n)^2$ in the constant density model is polynomially bounded in n, because of lemma 4.

4. REFERENCES

[1] E. Balas and M.W. Padberg, Set partitioning - A survey, in: N. Christofides, et al. eds., Combinatorial Optimization, Wiley, Chichester, 1979

[2] E.A. Bender and H.S. Wilf, A theoretical analysis of backtracking in the graph coloring problem, J. Algorithms, 6, (1985) 275 - 282

[3] J. Franco, On the probabilistic performance of algorithms for the satisfiability problem, Inform. Process. Lett., 23, (1986) 103 - 106

[4] M.R. Garey and D.S. Johnson, Computers and Intractability: A guide to the theory of NP-completeness, Freeman, San Francisco/CA, 1979

[5] A. Goldberg, P. Purdom, and C. Brown, Average time analyses of simplified Davis-Putnam procedures, Inform. Process. Lett., 15, (1982) 72 - 75

[6] B. Monien, E. Speckenmeyer, and O. Vornberger, Upper bounds for covering problems, Methods of Operations Research, 43, (1982) 419 - 431

[7] E. Speckenmeyer, Classes of CNF-formulas with backtracking trees of exponential or linear average order for exact-satisfiability, Bericht Nr. 47, Reihe Theoretische Informatik, Paderborn 1987

On Functions Computable in Nondeterministic Polynomial Time: Some Characterizations

Dieter Spreen[1]

Siemens AG - Corporate Research and Technology - ZTI DES 1
Otto-Hahn-Ring 6 - D-8000 München 83 - West Germany

ABSTRACT

As it is well known, the class **DTIMEF(Pol$_\Sigma$)** of functions computable in deterministic polynomial time is the smallest class of functions that contains the projection functions, zero functions of arities zero and one, successor functions and length multiplication, and is closed under substitution and limited recursion. In this paper it is shown that by adding one more basic function or a further closure operator one obtains the class **NTIMEF(Pol$_\Sigma$)** of functions computable in *nondeterministic* polynomial time. The additional basic function one has to take is the guess function. The operators that are studied are nondeterministic branching, bounded unordered search, which is a generalization of bounded minimization, and limited inversion. Except in the case of nondeterministic branching, with respect to the guess function and each of these operators the functions in **NTIMEF(Pol$_\Sigma$)** possess a normal form which says that they can be generated from functions in **DTIMEF(Pol$_\Sigma$)** by only one application of this additional function or operator.In order to obtain a characterization of **NTIMEF(Pol$_\Sigma$)** that does not use limited recursion, time and space bounded versions of the iteration operator and the operator of taking the reflexive and transive closure of a function are considered. It is shown that **NTIMEF(Pol$_\Sigma$)** is also the smallest class of functions that contains the length multiplication and projection, zero and successor functions and is closed under substitution, nondeterministic branching, the operation of taking the limited inverse and one of these operators. If in their definition the time restriction is skipped, one obtains a characterization of the functions computable in nondeterministic polynomial space, and if, moreover, instead of length multiplication length addition is taken as basic function, then the functions computable in nondeterministic linear space are characterized. A normal form theorem is derived which implies that in any of these cases the characterized functions can be generated by only one application of these limited iteration and/or closure operators from functions computable in nondeterministic linear time.

---

[1]Parts of this work have been done while the author was visiting the Department of Computer Science of the University of Pisa, supported by a grant of the Consiglio Nazionale delle Ricerche and the Siemens Corporate Laboratories for Research and Technology.

1. INTRODUCTION

This paper is part of an investigation of the functions computed by a nondeterministic Turing machine i polynomial time. In a first paper (Spreen, Stahl 1987) the subclass of functions has been considered that ar computed by nondeterministic Turing machines the computation trees of which not only have the propert that the length of each converging path is polynomially bounded but also that any two converging path yield the same result. In the present paper this additional requirement is dropped. As a consequence of thi the functions f we are going to consider are multivalued: for any Turing machine T computing f and any y $\in$ f(x) just if there is a converging path in the computation tree of T on input x for which y is the fin content of T's output tape. If no finite path exists, f(x) is undefined. It is the aim of this paper to give som machine independent characterizations of the class **NTIMEF(Pol$_\Sigma$)** of these functions.

As has been shown by Cobham (1965) and Weihrauch (1973), the class **DTIMEF(Pol$_\Sigma$)** of functio which are computable in deterministic polynomial time is the smallest class of functions that is closed und substitution and limited recursion and contains the length multiplication, the projection and success functions and the zero functions of arities zero and one. After fixing some notation in section 2, in section we shall deal with the question which basic functions or closure operators have to be added in order obtain the class **NTIMEF(Pol$_\Sigma$)**. Since substitution and limited recursion do not lead out of the domain deterministic, i.e. single-valued functions, these additional functions or operators have to be multivalued. one thinks of the usual interpretation of nondeterministic acceptance in formal language theory which say first guess a word of bounded length and then verify that it has a certain property, it is obvious that t guess function is an appropriate candidate. As we shall see, this is indeed the case: **NTIMEF(Pol$_\Sigma$)** is t smallest class that contains the above mentioned basic functions and in addition the guess function, and closed under substitution and limited recursion.

Other characterizations of this type are obtained, if instead of the guess function one of the followi additional closure operators is taken: nondeterministic branching, bounded unordered search, limit inversion and parametric limited inversion. The unbounded unordered search operator has been introduc by Moschovakis (1969) in his studies on higher type computability as a generalization of the minimizati operator. He calls it ν-operator. Whereas the minimization operator looks for the smallest element in a we ordered set which satisfies a certain condition, the ν-operator searches only some element that fulfils t condition. If the search space is bounded, then an obvious nondeterministic algorithm for the computati of this operator runs as follows: guess an element in this space and verify that it meets the given conditic Thus there is strong connection between bounded ν-operator and guess function.

The limited inversion operator first inverts a given function and then restricts the range of this invers limiting the length of its elements according to a given bound. The parametric limited inversion opera does the same. But whereas the limited inversion operator is defined only for unary functions, t parametric limited inversion operator can be applied also in the other cases, the additional variables treated as fixed parameters. In recursion theory there are also other applications of inversion operato Eilenberg and Elgot (1970) use unlimited inversion in a characterization of the partial recursive multivalu word functions over a finite alphabet, and in her famous 1950 paper J. Robinson utilizes an inversi operator in order to characterize the unary partial recursive functions on natural numbers. (An application of this operator to a function f yields a right inverse g of f such that g(x) is the smallest y with f(y)=x.) The result by Eilenberg and Elgot was the motivation for some characterizations presented in section 4. The operators applied in these characterizations are limited versions of the operators used there.

In the case of the partial recursive functions it is well known that these functions can be put into a normal form. This result is due to Kleene (1936). One of its consequences is that the partial recursive functions can be generated from some special primitive recursive functions by only one application of the minimization operator. A similar result can also be derived for **NTIMEF(Pol$_\Sigma$)**. We shall present normal form theorems which imply that the functions in this class can be generated from certain functions in **DTIMEF(Pol$_\Sigma$)** by only one additional application of the guess function, the ν-operator and/or the limited inversion operator. For cardinality reasons such a result cannot hold in the case of nondeterministic branching.

In the characterizations presented in section 3 the limited recursion operator is responsible for the function growth. In section 4 we shall look for other operators with the same effect, which can be taken instead of this operator in order to characterize **NTIMEF(Pol$_\Sigma$)**. In their already mentioned characterization of the partial recursive multivalued word functions Eilenberg and Elgot use the operator of forming the transitive closure of a function to accomplish this task. Beside of this they use nondeterministic branching and inversion as closure operations. We shall prove a subrecursive analogue of their result. To this end a limited version of the transitive closure forming operator will be defined by restricting the length of the elements and the length of the chains in the transitive closure. Then it will be shown that **NTIMEF(Pol$_\Sigma$)** is the smallest class of functions which contains the same initial functions as they are used in the characterizations given in section 3 and is closed under this limited transitive closure forming operator, limited inversion and nondeterministic branching. As we shall see, this characterization remains true, if instead of the limited transitive closure forming operator a limited iteration operator is used where the number of iterations and the length of the words generated during the iteration is restricted.

Contrary to the limited operators considered in section 3, in the limited version of the iteration operator and the transitive closure forming operator not only the length of the words generated during the iteration and /or the process of forming the transitive closure is restricted but also the number of iteration steps and/or the length of the chains in the transitive closure. Therefore the question arises whether this additional restriction is really necessary in order to obtain the above mentioned characterization results. As we shall see, this is indeed the case. If in these characterizations instead of the twofold limited iteration or transitive closure forming operator a version of these operators is applied where only the word lengths are restricted, then one obtains a characterization of the functions computable in nondeterministic polynomial space. If moreover, instead of length multiplication one uses length addtion as a basic function, then the class of functions computable in nondeterministic linear space is characterized.

As has already been mentioned, with respect to certain operators which we shall deal with in section 3 the functions considered in this paper possess a normal form from which it follows that these functions can be generated from functions in **DTIMEF(Pol$_\Sigma$)** by only one application of one of these operators. We shall see that a similar result is true for the just mentioned funtion classes and restrictions of the iteration and the transitive closure forming operator. A normal form theorem is derived which implies that these function can be generated from functions computable in nondeterministic linear time by only one application of on of the limited iteration and/or transitive closure forming operators. In the case of the partial recursiv functions on natural numbers a normal form result of this kind has been shown by Buchberger (1974).

2. PRELIMINARIES

Let $\Sigma=\{a_1,\ldots,a_r\}$ be a fixed alphabet with more than one symbol ($r>1$). Σ^* is the set of finite word over Σ, and ε is the empty word. For a string $w\in\Sigma^*$, $|w|$ is the length of w, for $\mathbf{x}\in(\Sigma^*)^n$, where $\mathbf{x}$ $(x_1,\ldots,x_n)$, $|\mathbf{x}| = \sum_{1\le i\le n} |x_i|$, and for $Z\subseteq\Sigma^*$, $|Z| = \{|x| \mid x\in Z\}$. Moreover, for sets A and B of natur numbers, $A \le B$ iff for all $n\in A$ there is some $m\in B$ such that $n \le m$.

In this paper we shall study classes of partial functions $f\colon (\Sigma^*)^n \to 2^{\Sigma^*}$ ($n\ge 0$). Let $\mathbf{MF}^{(n)}$ be the class all such functions which have arity n, $\mathbf{MF} = \bigcup_{n\ge 0}\mathbf{MF}^{(n)}$ and for $K\subseteq\mathbf{MF}$, $K^{(n)} = K\cap\mathbf{MF}^{(n)}$. For tw functions $f,g\in\mathbf{MF}^{(n)}$, $(f,g)\colon (\Sigma^*)^n \to 2^{\Sigma^*}\times 2^{\Sigma^*}$ is the function defined by $(f,g)(\mathbf{x}) = f(\mathbf{x})\times g(\mathbf{x})$. Moreover, f functions $k_1,\ldots,k_n\in\mathbf{MF}^{(m)}$ and $h\in\mathbf{MF}^{(n)}$, the *substitution* $\mathrm{SUB}(h,k_1,\ldots,k_n)$ of $k_1,\ldots,k_n$ in h is defined by

$$\mathrm{SUB}(h,k_1,\ldots,k_n)(\mathbf{x}) = h(k_1(\mathbf{x}),\ldots,k_n(\mathbf{x})) = \bigcup\{h(\mathbf{y}) \mid \mathbf{y}\in k_1(\mathbf{x})\times\ldots\times k_n(\mathbf{x})\},$$

for all $\mathbf{x}\in(\Sigma^*)^m$ such that $k_i(\mathbf{x})$ is defined, for $i=1,\ldots,n$. In any other case $\mathrm{SUB}(h,k_1,\ldots,k_n)(\mathbf{x})$ remai undefined. A further operator that will be used in the next section is *limited recursion* LR. Let $g_0\in\mathbf{MF}^{(}$ $g_1,\ldots,g_r\in\mathbf{MF}^{(n+2)}$ and $b\in\mathbf{MF}^{(n+1)}$. Then $\mathrm{LR}(g_0,g_1,\ldots,g_r,b)$ is the uniquely determined function $h\in\mathbf{MF}^{(n+}$ which satisfies conditions (i), (ii) and (iii):

(i) $h(\mathbf{x},\varepsilon) = \{z\in g_0(\mathbf{x}) \mid |z| \le |b(\mathbf{x},\varepsilon)|\}$, if $g_0(\mathbf{x})$ and $b(\mathbf{x},\varepsilon)$ are both defined and this set is nonempty,

(ii) for $i=1,\ldots,r$, $h(\mathbf{x},ya_i) = \{z\in g_i(\mathbf{x},y,h(\mathbf{x},y)) \mid |z| \le |b(\mathbf{x},ya_i)|\}$, if $h(\mathbf{x},y)$, $g_i(\mathbf{x},y,h(\mathbf{x},y))$ and $b(\mathbf{x},y$ are defined and this set is nonempty,

(iii) in any other case $h(\mathbf{x},y)$ is undefined.

If $f_1,\ldots,f_n\in\mathbf{MF}$ and $\mathrm{OP}_1,\ldots,\mathrm{OP}_m$ are operators on $\mathbf{MF}$, then $[f_1,\ldots,f_n;\ \mathrm{OP}_1,\ldots,\mathrm{OP}_m]$ denotes t smallest subclass of $\mathbf{MF}$ containing $f_1,\ldots,f_n$ and closed under $\mathrm{OP}_1,\ldots,\mathrm{OP}_m$.

An important subclass of **MF** is the class **F** of single-valued functions $f\colon (\Sigma^*)^n \to \Sigma^*$ ($n\ge 0$). (Note th we identify $a\in\Sigma^*$ with its singleton $\{a\}$.) Some special single-valued functions which we shall use in t sequel are the *successor functions* S_i ($i=1,\ldots,r$) with $S_i(x) = xa_i$, the *zero functions* N_0 and N_1 of arities and 1, respectively, defined by $N_0 = \varepsilon$ and $N_1(x) = \varepsilon$, the *projection functions* $pr_j^{(m)}$ ($m\ge 0$; $1\le j\le m$) w $pr_j^{(m)}(x_1,\ldots,x_n) = x_j$, and the *length multiplication function* M, defined by $M(x,y) = a_1^{|x|\cdot|y|}$ $(x,y,x_1,\ldots$ $x_n\in\Sigma^*)$. Let **BF** be the class of these functions and set $id = pr_1^{(1)}$.

Our model of computing machines are multitape nondeterministic Turing machines. Such a machine h some number $n \ge 0$ read-only input tapes, some number $m \ge 0$ work tapes and one write-only output ta

The tape alphabet of input, work and output tape is Σ. A Turing machine T of this type computes a multivalued partial function namely the function $f_T \in \mathbf{MF}^{(n)}$ with $f_T(\mathbf{x}) = \{y \mid$ there is a finite computation of T on input $\mathbf{x}$ for which y is the final contents of T's output tape$\}$, if this set is nonempty; otherwise $f_T(\mathbf{x})$ is undefined. For $B_1, B_2 \subseteq \mathbf{TOT} = \{f \in \mathbf{F} \mid f \text{ is total}\}$ let **NSPACE-TIMEF**(B_1,B_2) be the class of all functions f_T computable by some Turing machine T for which there exists functions $b_1 \in B_1$ and $b_2 \in B_2$ such that for all $\mathbf{x} \in (\Sigma^*)^n$ and any finite computation z of T on input $\mathbf{x}$,

(i) the length of z is not greater than $|b_2(\mathbf{x})|$ and

(ii) the length of the longest word that is written on one of T's tapes during the computation z is not greater than $|b_1(\mathbf{x})|$.

Moreover, let **DSPACE-TIMEF**(B_1,B_2) be the class of all functions that can be computed by a Turing machine of this type which in addition is deterministic. In the next sections we shall be interested in complexity classes where only the time or the space is bounded. Therefore, for $B \subseteq \mathbf{TOT}$ we define

$$\mathbf{NTIMEF}(B) = \mathbf{NSPACE\text{-}TIMEF}(B,B), \quad \mathbf{DTIMEF}(B) = \mathbf{DSPACE\text{-}TIMEF}(B,B)$$

$$\mathbf{NSPACEF}(B) = \mathbf{NSPACE\text{-}TIMEF}(B,\mathbf{TOT}), \quad \mathbf{DSPACEF}(B) = \mathbf{DSPACE\text{-}TIMEF}(B,\mathbf{TOT})$$

The classes of bounds which we shall use are the classes $\mathbf{Lin}_\Sigma$ and $\mathbf{Pol}_\Sigma$ of functions $f \in \mathbf{F}$ of some arity $n \geq 0$ for which there is some linear function p or some polynomial p, respectively, such that $f(\mathbf{x}) = a_1^{p(|\mathbf{x}|)}$, for all $\mathbf{x} \in (\Sigma^*)^n$.

3. STARTING FROM DETERMINISM

In this section we present some characterizations of the class **NTIMEF**$(\mathbf{Pol}_\Sigma)$ by extending a well known characterization of the class **DTIMEF**$(\mathbf{Pol}_\Sigma)$. As has been shown by Cobham (1965) and Weihrauch (1973)

THEOREM 3.1. **DTIMEF**$(\mathbf{Pol}_\Sigma) = [\mathbf{BF}; \text{SUB}, \text{LR}]$.

The problem we are concerned with now is the question whether we will obtain a characterization of **NTIMEF**$(\mathbf{Pol}_\Sigma)$ by adding certain functions and operators to **BF** and $\{\text{SUB}, \text{LR}\}$, respectively. To this end we have to look for suitable functions and operators. Since the functions in **BF** are single-valued, and substitution and limited recursion do not lead out of the domain of single-valued functions, these functions and operators must be multivalued. From the usual interpretation of nondeterministic acceptance in formal language theory which says: first guess a word of bounded length and then verify that it has a certain property, it follows that the *guess function* $G: \Sigma^* \to 2^{\Sigma^*}$, defined by $G(x) = \{y \mid |y| \leq |x|\}$, may be appropriate. The next normal form theorem shows that this interpretation holds for nondeterministi polynomial time computations in general.

THEOREM 3.2. (G-NORMAL FORM). Let $f \in \mathbf{NTIMEF}(\mathbf{Pol}_\Sigma)^{(n)}$, for some $n \geq 0$. Then there is som $g \in \mathbf{DTIMEF}(\mathbf{Lin}_\Sigma)^{(n+1)}$ and some $p \in \mathbf{Pol}_\Sigma^{(n)}$ such that for all $\mathbf{x} \in (\Sigma^*)^n$

$$f(\mathbf{x}) = g(\mathbf{x}, G(p(\mathbf{x}))).$$

PROOF. Let T witness $f \in \mathbf{NTIMEF}(\{q\})^{(n)}$, for some $q \in \mathbf{Pol}_\Sigma^{(n)}$. The idea of the proof is to construc a deterministic Turing machine T_1 with n+1 input tapes. If $\mathbf{x}$ is the contents of its first n input tapes, then a input on its last input tape, T_1 aspects a finite computation of T on input $\mathbf{x}$. Each such computation is sequence of configurations in which for each time point in which the machine is working the state of th machine, the inscription of its tapes and the position of its heads is recorded. Without restriction, let $\{a_1{}^i \mid 1 \leq i \leq m\}$ be the state set of T. Then every finite computation of T is a string over $\Sigma \cup \{\$\}$ where \$ is som separation symbol that is not in Σ. Since T_1 can only read symbols in Σ, we have to encode $(\Sigma \cup \{\$\})^*$ i Σ^*. There are several ways to do this. An easy encoding C can be obtained as follows. Set $C(\$) = a_2a_2$ an $C(a_i) = a_1a_i$, for i=1,...,r, and then extend C recursively to $(\Sigma \cup \{\$\})^*$ such that $C(\varepsilon) = \varepsilon$. With this encodin the length of each coded finite computation of T on input $\mathbf{x}$ is bounded by $2 \cdot |q(\mathbf{x})| \cdot (|q(\mathbf{x})| \cdot (n+n'+1) + m +$ where n' is the number of working tapes of T and c the number of \$'s used in each configuration. L $p \in \mathbf{Pol}_\Sigma^{(n)}$ be defined by $p(\mathbf{x}) = a_1{}^{2 \cdot |q(\mathbf{x})| \cdot (|q(\mathbf{x})| \cdot (n+n'+1) + m + c)}$. Then T_1 works in the following way: o input $\mathbf{x}$,y it locally decodes y and tests whether y is the coding of a finite computation of T on input $\mathbf{x}$. this is the case, it writes the final contents of T's output tape on its own output tape. Otherwise it diverge Obviously, T_1 can be constructed such that it works in linear time. Let g be the function computed by T Then $g \in \mathbf{DTIMEF}(\mathbf{Lin}_\Sigma)^{(n+1)}$ and for all $\mathbf{x} \in (\Sigma^*)^n$, $f(\mathbf{x}) = g(\mathbf{x}, G(p(\mathbf{x})))$.

As a consequence of this result we have

COROLLARY 3.3. $\mathbf{NTIMEF}(\mathbf{Pol}_\Sigma) \subseteq [\mathbf{BF} \cup \{G\}; \text{SUB}, \text{LR}]$.

It is well known that the class of computable functions can be characterized in a machine independe way with the help of the minimization operator. In his studies on higher type computability Moschoval (1969) introduced a generalization of this operator, the ν-operator. Whereas the minimization operator loo for the smallest element in a well-ordered set which satisfies a certain condition, the ν-operator search only some element that fulfils this condition. Here we consider the *bounded ν-operator* which is defined functions $f, b \in \mathbf{MF}$ of arity n+1 and n, respectively, for any $n \geq 0$. Let $\mathbf{x} \in (\Sigma^*)^n$, then

$$\nu(f,b)(\mathbf{x}) = \{y \mid |y| \leq |b(\mathbf{x})| \wedge \varepsilon \in f(\mathbf{x},y)\},$$

if this set is nonempty. Otherwise $\nu(f,b)(\mathbf{x})$ is undefined. There is an easy relationship between the gue function and the bounded ν-operator: $G = \nu(\text{SUB}(N_1, pr_1^{(2)}), id)$. Hence,

LEMMA 3.4. $[\mathbf{BF} \cup \{G\}; \text{SUB,LR}] \subseteq [\mathbf{BF}; \text{SUB,LR},\nu]$.

A further candidate for an extension of **BF** and/or {SUB,LR} is the *nondeterministic branching operator* $\cup$: **MF**×**MF** → **MF** which is defined only for functions f,g of the same arity. If $f(\mathbf{x})$ and $g(\mathbf{x})$ are both defined, then $\cup(f,g)(\mathbf{x}) = f(\mathbf{x}) \cup g(\mathbf{x})$. Moreover, $\cup(f,g)(\mathbf{x}) = f(\mathbf{x})$, if only $f(\mathbf{x})$ is defined, and $\cup(f,g)(\mathbf{x}) = g(\mathbf{x})$, if only $g(\mathbf{x})$ is defined. In the remaining case that $f(\mathbf{x})$ and $g(\mathbf{x})$ are both undefined, $\cup(f,g)(\mathbf{x})$ is also undefined. Note that sometimes we write $f \cup g$ instead of $\cup(f,g)$.

LEMMA 3.5. $[\mathbf{BF}; \text{SUB,LR},\nu] \subseteq [\mathbf{BF}; \text{SUB,LR},\cup]$.

PROOF. We have to show that $[\mathbf{BF}; \text{SUB,LR},\cup]$ is closed under ν. Let to this end $f,b \in [\mathbf{BF}; \text{SUB,LR},\cup]$ with arities n+1 and n, respectively. Moreover, let pcond$\in \mathbf{F}^{(3)}$ such that pcond(a,a',x) = x, if a = a', and is undefined, otherwise. Let $k(\mathbf{x},y) = \text{pcond}(\varepsilon,f(\mathbf{x},y),y)$ and $g(y,z) = \{ya_1,\ldots,ya_r,z\}$. Then pcond$\in$ $\mathbf{DTIMEF}(\mathbf{Pol}_\Sigma) = [\mathbf{BF}; \text{SUB,LR}]$, $k,g \in [\mathbf{BF}; \text{SUB,LR},\cup]$ and $\text{LR}(N_0,g,\ldots,g,id) = G$. Since $\nu(f,b)(\mathbf{x}) = k(\mathbf{x},G(b(\mathbf{x})))$, it follows that $[\mathbf{BF}; \text{SUB,LR},\cup]$ is closed under ν.

Since moreover $[\mathbf{BF}; \text{SUB,LR},\cup] \subseteq \mathbf{NTIMEF}(\mathbf{Pol}_\Sigma)$, we have thus shown

THEOREM 3.6. $\mathbf{NTIMEF}(\mathbf{Pol}_\Sigma) = [\mathbf{BF} \cup \{G\}; \text{SUB,LR}] = [\mathbf{BF}; \text{SUB,LR},\nu] = [\mathbf{BF}; \text{SUB,LR},\cup]$.

As we have seen in the beginning of this section, the functions in $\mathbf{NTIMEF}(\mathbf{Pol}_\Sigma)$ possess a normal form with respect to the guess function. The same is true with respect to the bounded ν-operator.

THEOREM 3.7 (ν-NORMAL FORM). There is a total function $h \in \mathbf{DTIMEF}(\mathbf{Lin}_\Sigma)^{(1)}$ such that for any function $f \in \mathbf{NTIMEF}(\mathbf{Pol}_\Sigma)$ of some arity $n \geq 0$ there exists another total function $g \in \mathbf{DTIMEF}(\mathbf{Lin}_\Sigma)^{(n+1)}$ and a polynomial $p \in \mathbf{Pol}_\Sigma^{(n)}$ so that for all $\mathbf{x} \in (\Sigma^*)^n$

$$f(\mathbf{x}) = h(\nu(g,p)(\mathbf{x})).$$

PROOF. Let $p \in \mathbf{Pol}_\Sigma^{(n)}$ such that $f \in \mathbf{NTIMEF}(\{p\})^{(n)}$, and let this be witnessed by T. Define h and g as follows. If y is the coding of a finite sequence $z_1,\ldots,z_m$ of Turing machine configurations, then let h(y) be the contents of the output tape recorded in z_m. Otherwise let $h(y) = a_1$. Set $g(\mathbf{x},y) = \varepsilon$, if y is the coding of a finite computation of T on input $\mathbf{x}$, and $g(\mathbf{x},y) = a_1$, otherwise. Then $h,g \in \mathbf{DTIMEF}(\mathbf{Lin}_\Sigma)$ and $f(\mathbf{x}) = h(\nu(g,p)(\mathbf{x}))$, for $\mathbf{x} \in (\Sigma^*)^n$.

This theorem is a subrecursive analogue of Kleene's normal form theorem for the partial reursive functions (cf. Kleene 1936). Kleene's result is a bit stronger than ours, since the functions in his normal form do not depend on some given function and/or Turing machine: the function corresponding to g in this result aspects the coding of a Turing machine as a further argument. Such a stronger result can also be shown in our case. Let $un^{(n)} \in \mathbf{MF}^{(n+1)}$ be a universal function for **NTIMEF(Pol$_\Sigma$)** and T be a Turin machine computing $un^{(n)}$. Moreover, let $pol^{(n)} \in \mathbf{MF}^{(n+1)}$ such that for all $v \in \Sigma^*$ and $\mathbf{x} \in (\Sigma^*)^n$,

(i) $\lambda \mathbf{y}.pol^{(n)}(v,\mathbf{y}) \in \mathbf{Pol}_\Sigma{}^{(n)}$ and

(ii) the length of any finite computation of T on input $(v,\mathbf{x})$ is not greater than $|pol^{(n)}(v,\mathbf{x})|$.

Then by constructing g with respect to this T in the above proof we obtain

THEOREM 3.8 (PARAMETERIZED ν-NORMAL FORM). There exist total functions h **DTIMEF(Lin$_\Sigma$)$^{(1)}$** and $g \in$ **DTIMEF(Lin$_\Sigma$)$^{(n+2)}$**, for each $n \geq 0$, such that for all $v \in \Sigma^*$ and $\mathbf{x} \in (\Sigma^*)^n$

$$un^{(n)}{}_v(\mathbf{x}) = h(\nu(g_v, pol^{(n)}{}_v)(\mathbf{x}))$$

where for $f \in \mathbf{MF}^{(m+1)}$ $(m \geq 0)$, $f_v = \lambda \mathbf{y}.\ f(v,\mathbf{y})$.

In the same way a parameterized G-normal form theorem can be derived. As follows from these norm form results, the functions in **NTIMEF(Pol$_\Sigma$)** can be obtained from functions in **DTIMEF(Pol$_\Sigma$)** by on one application of the guess function or the bounded ν-operator. Such a result does not hold in the case nondeterministic branching. The guess function, e.g., cannot be generated by applying this operator to on single-valued functions. Its cardinality grows exponentially with the length of x, whereas for two functio $f,g \in \mathbf{F}$, $\cup(f,g)(x)$ has at most cardinality 2.

As we have seen in the case of the bounded ν-operator, in order to obtain machine independe characterizations of **NTIMEF(Pol$_\Sigma$)** it can be helpful to study subrecursive analogues of operators that ha been used in characterizations of the partial recursive functions. In 1950 J. Robinson obtained characterization of the unary partial recursive functions with the help of a special inversion operator. Let therefore consider a subrecursive version of the inversion operator, the *limited inversion operator* LIN. F $f,b \in \mathbf{MF}^{(1)}$ and $x \in \Sigma^*$,

$$\text{LIN}(f,b)(x) = \{y \mid |y| \leq |b(x)| \wedge x \in f(y)\},$$

if this set is nonempty. Otherwise LIN(f,b)(x) remains undefined. As follows from this definition, LIN defined only for unary functions. Since we are dealing with functions of arbitrary finite arity, we would li to have some kind of inversion operator which is defined also for nonunary functions. Let $f,b \in \mathbf{MF}^{(n+}$ for some $n \geq 0$, and $(\mathbf{x},z) \in (\Sigma^*)^{n+1}$. Then we set

$$\text{PLIN}(f,b)(\mathbf{x},z) = \{y \mid |y| \leq |b(\mathbf{x},z)| \wedge z \in f(\mathbf{x},y)\},$$

if this set is nonempty. In the other case we let PLIN(f,b)($\mathbf{x}$,z) be undefined. PLIN is called *parameteri limited inversion.*

THEOREM 3.9. **NTIMEF(Pol$_\Sigma$)** = [**BF**; SUB,LR,PLIN].

PROOF. By Theorem 3.6 it suffices to show that [**BF**; SUB,LR,ν] = [**BF**; SUB,LR,PLIN]. Let $f\in$ **MF**$^{(n+1)}$ and $b\in$ **MF**$^{(n)}$, for some $n\geq 0$, and define $b_1\in$ **MF**$^{(n+1)}$ by $b_1(\mathbf{x},z) = b(\mathbf{x})$, for $(\mathbf{x},z)\in(\Sigma^*)^{n+1}$. Then $\nu(f,b)(\mathbf{x}) = \text{PLIN}(f,b_1)(\mathbf{x},\varepsilon)$. Thus, [**BF**; SUB,LR,PLIN] is closed under ν, which implies that [**BF**; SUB, LR,ν] $\subseteq$ [**BF**; SUB,LR,PLIN]. In order to show the converse inclusion let $eq\in$ **F**$^{(2)}$ with $eq(a,a') = \varepsilon$, if $a = a'$, and being undefined, otherwise. Moreover, set $g(\mathbf{x},z,y) = eq(f(\mathbf{x},y),z)$, for $\mathbf{x}\in(\Sigma^*)^n$ and $y,z\in\Sigma^*$. Then $\text{PLIN}(f,b) = \nu(g,b)$. Since $eq\in$ **DTIMEF(Pol$_\Sigma$)** = [**BF**; SUB,LR], it follows that [**BF**; SUB,LR,ν] is closed under PLIN. Hence, we also have that [**BF**; SUB,LR,PLIN] $\subseteq$ [**BF**; SUB,LR,ν].

After this result the question comes up whether also the limited inversion operator LIN can be used to characterize the functions in **NTIMEF(Pol$_\Sigma$)**. As has already been said, LIN is defined for less functions than PLIN.

THEOREM 3.10 (LIN-NORMAL FORM). Let $n\geq 0$. There are total functions $h,k\in$ **DTIMEF(Lin$_\Sigma$)** with arities 1 and n, respectively, such that for any function $f\in$ **NTIMEF(Pol$_\Sigma$)**$^{(n)}$ there exists another function $g\in$ **DTIMEF(Lin$_\Sigma$)**$^{(1)}$ and a polynomial $q\in$ **Pol$_\Sigma$**$^{(1)}$ so that for all $\mathbf{x}\in(\Sigma^*)^n$

$$f(\mathbf{x}) = h(\text{LIN}(g,q)(k(\mathbf{x}))).$$

PROOF. Let $\langle\cdot,\cdot\rangle\in$ **F**$^{(2)}$ be the pairing function defined by $\langle x,y\rangle = a_1^{|x|}a_2xa_1^{|y|}a_2y$, and let π_1 and π_2 be the corresponding decodings with $\pi_i(z) = \varepsilon$ $(i=1,2)$, if z is not in the range of $\langle\cdot,\cdot\rangle$. Let $\langle\cdot,\cdot\rangle$ be extended to any arity $n\geq 2$ in the usual way. For n=0,1, respectively, set $\langle\ \rangle = N_0$ and $\langle\cdot\rangle = id$. Then $\langle\cdot,\ldots,\cdot\rangle,\pi_1,\pi_2\in$ **DTIMEF(Lin$_\Sigma$)**. Now, let T witness $f\in$ **NTIMEF(Pol$_\Sigma$)**$^{(n)}$. Then $g\in$ **F**$^{(n)}$ is defined as follows. If y is the coding of a finite computation of T on input $\mathbf{x}\in(\Sigma^*)^n$ and z is the final contents of T's output tape with respect to this computation, then $g(\langle y,z\rangle) = \langle\mathbf{x}\rangle$. In any other case g is undefined. As it is easy to see, $g\in$ **DTIMEF(Lin$_\Sigma$)**. Let $p\in$ **Pol$_\Sigma$**$^{(n)}$ be as in the proof of Theorem 3.2 and t be a polynomial such that $p(\mathbf{v}) = a_1^{t(|\mathbf{v}|)}$, for all $\mathbf{v}\in(\Sigma^*)^n$. Then $|y|\leq t(n\cdot|x|)$, if $g(\langle y,z\rangle) = x$. Hence, $|\langle y,z\rangle|\leq 4\cdot t(n\cdot|x|)+n$. Set $q(x) = a_1^{4\cdot t(n\cdot|x|)+n}$. Then $f(\mathbf{x}) = \pi_2(\text{LIN}(g,q)(\langle\mathbf{x}\rangle))$, for all $\mathbf{x}\in(\Sigma^*)^n$.

From this Theorem we obtain that **NTIMEF(Pol$_\Sigma$)** $\subseteq$ [**BF**; SUB,LR,LIN]. In order to see that the converse inclusion also holds, let eq be the partial equality test from the proof of Theorem 3.9, $f,b\in$ **MF**$^{(1)}$ and set $d(x,y) = eq(x,f(y))$, for $x,y\in\Sigma^*$. Then $\text{LIN}(f,b) = \nu(d,b)$. Because of Theorem 3.6 we have thus shown

THEOREM 3.11. **NTIMEF(Pol$_\Sigma$)** = [**BF**; SUB,LR,LIN].

4. ITERATION AND TRANSITIVE CLOSURE

In the preceding section we started from a characterization of **DTIMEF(Pol$_\Sigma$)** in order to obtai characterizations of **NTIMEF(Pol$_\Sigma$)**. In these cases the limited recursion operator was responsible for th growth of the functions. Eilenberg and Elgot (1970) give a characterization of the partial recursiv multivalued word functions which uses transitive closure, inversion and nondeterministic branching a closure operators. In what follows we present a subrecursive version of this result. Let $f_1,\ldots,f_r$ $b,t,h \in$ **MF**$^{(n)}$, for some $n \geq 1$, and $\mathbf{x} \in (\Sigma^*)^n$. Moreover, let

$$LC(f_1,\ldots,f_n,b,t,h)(\mathbf{x}) = h(\ \{\mathbf{y} \in (\Sigma^*)^n \mid \exists\, m \leq |t(\mathbf{x})|\ \exists\, \mathbf{v}_0,\ldots,\mathbf{v}_m \in (\Sigma^*)^n \quad \mathbf{v}_0 = \mathbf{x} \wedge \mathbf{v}_m = \mathbf{y}$$
$$\wedge\ \forall i \leq m\ \ |\mathbf{v}_i| \leq |b(\mathbf{x})| \ \wedge\ \forall i < m\ \ \mathbf{v}_{i+1} \in (f_1,\ldots,f_n)(\mathbf{v}_i)\}\ ),$$

if this set is nonempty. In any other case let $LC(f_1,\ldots,f_n,b,t,h)(\mathbf{x})$ be undefined. LC is called *limite transitive closure*. If $f,b,t \in$ **MF**$^{(1)}$ and $x \in \Sigma^*$ such that $|f^i(x)| \leq |b(x)|$, for all $i \leq |t(\mathbf{x})|$, then $LC(f,b,t,id)(x)$ $\bigcup\{f^i(x) \mid i \leq |t(\mathbf{x})|\}$.

LEMMA 4.1. **NTIMEF(Pol$_\Sigma$)** is closed under LC.

PROOF. For $n \geq 0$ and $i=1,\ldots,n+3$, let $f_i \in$ **NTIMEF(Pol$_\Sigma$)**$^{(n)}$. Moreover, let p_i be a polynomial bour on the running time of the Turing machine computing f_i.

PROCEDURE 4.2.

Input: $\mathbf{x}$

begin $m := |f_{n+2}(\mathbf{x})|+1$; (1)
  $\mathbf{y} := \mathbf{x}$;
  while $m \neq 0 \wedge |\mathbf{y}| \leq |f_{n+1}(\mathbf{x})|$ **do** (2)
    begin $m := m-1$; (3)
      begin output $f_{n+3}(\mathbf{y})$ and halt **or** (4)
        $\mathbf{y} := (f_1,\ldots,f_n)(\mathbf{y})$ (5)
      end
    end;
  diverge
end.

The assignment statements in lines (1) and (4) mean: Nondeterministically evaluate the right-hand side a assign the value thus obtained to the left-hand side. Obviously this nondeterministic procedure comput $LC(f_1,\ldots,f_{n+3})$. Let us observe that it runs in polynomial time. If the computations in lines (1), (2) and (are finite, they can be done in polynomial time. Since $|\mathbf{y}| \leq |f_{n+1}(\mathbf{x})| \leq p_{n+1}(|\mathbf{x}|)$, the running time of ea finite computation in lines (4) and (5) is bounded by $p_{n+3}(p_{n+1}(|\mathbf{x}|))+\Sigma_{1 \leq i \leq n}\, p_i(p_{n+1}(|\mathbf{x}|))$. The while-loop executed at most $p_{n+2}(|\mathbf{x}|)+1$ times. Thus, the length of each finite computation of this procedure is bound by a polynomial of $|\mathbf{x}|$. This shows that $LC(f_1,\ldots,f_{n+3}) \in$ **NTIMEF(Pol$_\Sigma$)**.

As we have seen in section 3, **NTIMEF(Pol$_\Sigma$)** is also closed under LIN and $\cup$. Hence

COROLLARY 4.3. [**BF**; SUB,$\cup$,LIN,LC] $\subsetneq$ **NTIMEF(Pol$_\Sigma$)**.

An operator that is strongly related to transitive closure is iteration. Again we introduce a restricted version of this operator, *limited iteration* LIT. For some $n\geq 1$, let $f_1,\ldots,f_n,g,b,t,h \in \mathbf{MF}^{(n)}$ and $\mathbf{x} \in (\Sigma^*)^n$. Then

$$\mathrm{LIT}(f_1,\ldots,f_n,g,b,t,h)(\mathbf{x}) = h(\,\{\mathbf{y} \in (\Sigma^*)^n \mid \varepsilon \in g(\mathbf{y}) \wedge \exists m \leq |t(\mathbf{x})|\ \exists \mathbf{v}_0,\ldots,\mathbf{v}_m \in (\Sigma^*)^n\ \ \mathbf{v}_0 = \mathbf{x} \wedge \mathbf{v}_m = \mathbf{y} \wedge \forall i \leq m\ \ |\mathbf{v}_i| \leq |b(\mathbf{x})| \wedge \forall i < m\ \ \mathbf{v}_{i+1} \in (f_1,\ldots,f_n)(\mathbf{v}_i) \wedge g(\mathbf{v}_i) \cap (\Sigma^* \setminus \{\varepsilon\}) \neq \emptyset\}\,),$$

if this set is nonempty. Otherwise, $\mathrm{LIT}(f_1,\ldots,f_n,g,b,t,h)(\mathbf{x})$ remains undefined. As we shall see next, LIT can be expressed by LC. Let to this end $\mathrm{div}(x) = \mathrm{LIN}(S_1,\mathrm{id})(N_1(x))$. Then div is the nowhere defined function. Moreover, for $a \in \Sigma^*$ let $\mathrm{cond}_a \in \mathbf{F}^{(3)}$ with $\mathrm{cond}_a(x,y,z) = y$, if $x = a$, and $\mathrm{cond}_a(x,y,z) = z$, otherwise.

LEMMA 4.4. For each $a \in \Sigma^*$, $\mathrm{cond}_a \in [\{pr_1^{(1)}, pr_2^{(2)}, pr_j^{(3)}, S_i, N_1 \mid 1\leq j\leq 3,\ 1\leq i\leq r\};\ \mathrm{SUB},\cup,\mathrm{LIN}]$.

PROOF. For $f_1,\ldots,f_m \in \mathbf{MF}^{(n)}$ ($m\geq 2, n\geq 0$), let $\bigcup_{1\leq j\leq m} f_j = f_1 \cup \ldots \cup f_m$. Then we have that

$$\mathrm{cond}_\varepsilon = \mathrm{SUB}(pr_2^{(2)}, \mathrm{SUB}(\mathrm{LIN}(N_1,\mathrm{id}),pr_1^{(3)}), pr_2^{(3)}) \cup \mathrm{SUB}(pr_2^{(2)}, \mathrm{SUB}(\textstyle\bigcup_{1\leq j\leq r} \mathrm{LIN}(S_j,\mathrm{id}),pr_1^{(3)}), pr_3^{(3)})$$

and

$$\mathrm{cond}_{aa_i} = \mathrm{SUB}(\mathrm{cond}_a, \mathrm{SUB}(\mathrm{LIN}(S_i,\mathrm{id}),pr_1^{(3)}), pr_2^{(3)}, pr_3^{(3)}) \cup \mathrm{SUB}(pr_2^{(2)}, \mathrm{SUB}(\mathrm{LIN}(N_1,\mathrm{id}) \cup \textstyle\bigcup_{1\leq j\leq r,\ j\neq i} \mathrm{LIN}(S_j,\mathrm{id}),pr_1^{(3)}), pr_3^{(3)}),$$

for all $1\leq i\leq r$.

Now, let $f_1,\ldots,f_n,g,b,t,h \in \mathbf{MF}^{(n)}$, $\mathbf{x}=(x_1,\ldots,x_n) \in (\Sigma^*)^n$ and $x,y \in \Sigma^*$. Then we define $f'_1,\ldots,f'_{n+1},b',t',h' \in \mathbf{MF}^{(n+1)}$ and $g' \in \mathbf{MF}^{(n)}$ by $f'_i(\mathbf{x},y) = f_i(\mathbf{x})$ ($i=1,\ldots,n$), $b'(\mathbf{x},y) = S_1(b(\mathbf{x}))$, $t'(\mathbf{x},y) = t(\mathbf{x})$, $h'(\mathbf{x},y) = \mathrm{cond}_{a_1}(y,h(\mathbf{x}),\mathrm{div}(y))$, $g'(\mathbf{x}) = \mathrm{cond}_\varepsilon(g(\mathbf{x}),a_1,a_2)$ and $f'_{n+1}(\mathbf{x},y) = \mathrm{cond}_{a_2}(y,g'(\mathbf{x}),\mathrm{div}(y))$. Then $\mathrm{LIT}(f_1,\ldots,f_n,g,b,t,h)(\mathbf{x}) = \mathrm{LC}(f'_1,\ldots,f'_{n+1},b',t',h')(\mathbf{x},g'(\mathbf{x}))$. Note that all auxiliary functions which we have used in these definitions are in [**IF**; SUB,$\cup$,LIN] where $\mathbf{IF} = \{pr_j^{(m)}, S_i, N_1, N_0 \mid m\geq 0,\ 1\leq j\leq m,\ 1\leq i\leq r\}$. Thus

LEMMA 4.5. [**IF**; SUB,$\cup$,LIN,LIT] $\subsetneq$ [**IF**; SUB,$\cup$,LIN,LC].

With respect to limited iteration the computable funcions in **MF** possess a normal form. For $n,n'\geq 0$ and $b,t \in \mathbf{TOT}^{(n)}$, let $\mathbf{NSPACE\text{-}TIMEF}(\{b\},\{t\})^{(n,n')}$ be the class of those functions in $\mathbf{NSPACE\text{-}TIMEF}(\{b\},\{t\})^{(n)}$ for which this membership is witnessed by a Turing machine with n' working tapes.

THEOREM 4.6 (ITERATIVE NORMAL FORM). Let $n,n'\geq 0$ and $m=3n+3n'+2$. Then there are to[tal] functions $in_1,\ldots,in_m,out\in$ [IF; SUB,$\cup$,LIN] such that for all $b,t\in \mathbf{TOT}^{(n)}$ and $f\in$ **NSPACE-TIMEF**$(\{b\},\{t\})^{(n,n')}$ there exist further total functions $d_1,\ldots,d_m,g\in$ [IF; SUB,$\cup$,LIN]$^{(m)}$ so that for all $\mathbf{x}\in(\Sigma^*)^n$

$$f(\mathbf{x}) = \mathrm{LIT}(d_1,\ldots,d_m,g,b,t,out)(in_1(\mathbf{x}),\ldots,in_m(\mathbf{x})).$$

PROOF. Let us first define the auxiliary functions $b_1,b_2\in\mathbf{TOT}^{(1)}$ and $b_3\in\mathbf{TOT}^{(3)}$. If $x = aa_j$, for som[e] $1\leq j\leq r$, then $b_1(x) = a$, $b_2(x) = a_j$ and $b_3(x,y) = ya_j$. Otherwise $b_1(x) = b_2(x) = \varepsilon$ and $b_3(x,y) = y$. Since [b_1] $= \mathrm{LIN}(N_1,N_1)\cup\bigcup_{1\leq j\leq r}\mathrm{LIN}(S_j,id)$, $b_2 = \mathrm{LIN}(N_1,N_1)\cup\bigcup_{1\leq j\leq r}\mathrm{SUB}(S_j,\mathrm{SUB}(N_1,\mathrm{LIN}(S_j,id)))$ and b_3 [=] $\mathrm{SUB}(pr_2^{(2)},\mathrm{SUB}(\mathrm{LIN}(N_1,id),pr_1^{(2)}),pr_2^{(2)})\cup\bigcup_{1\leq j\leq r}\mathrm{SUB}(S_j,\mathrm{Sub}(pr_2^{(2)},\mathrm{Sub}(\mathrm{LIN}(S_j,pr_1^{(2)}),pr_2^{(2)}))$[)] we have that $b_1,b_2,b_3\in$ [IF; SUB,$\cup$,LIN] $\cap$ **TOT**.

We shall now describe the single-step function of the Turing machine T witnessing $f\in$ **NSPAC[E]-TIMEF**$(\{b\},\{t\})^{(n,n')}$ by functions $d_1,\ldots,d_m$. For the sake of simplicity we assume that $n=n'=1$. Moreove[r] without loss of generality we suppose that T has nondeterministic fan-out r, so that each situation in [a] computation of T has at most r successors. T is defined by the transition function δ: $S\times\Sigma'\times\Sigma'$ [→] $\{1,\ldots,r\}\times S\times\Sigma'\times\Sigma'\times V\times V$ where S is the set of states of T, $\Sigma' = \Sigma\cup\{\varepsilon\}$ and $V = \{+,0,-\}$. If $\delta(s,c_1,c_2)$ [=] (i,s',c_3,c_4,v_1,v_2), then this means that if T is in state s, its read-only head scans c_1 and its read/write he[ad] scans c_2, then the ith alternative of what T may do is to change into state s', print c_3 on its work and c_4 [on] its output tape, and move the heads on its input and its work tape respectively according to v_1 and v_2.

Let us assume that the sets S, V and $\{1,\ldots,r\}$ are coded in $\Sigma^*\backslash\{\varepsilon\}$ and let "·" be the coding functio[n]. Then δ: $(\Sigma^*)^3\to(\Sigma^*)^6$. Define Δ: $(\Sigma^*)^3\to(\Sigma^*)^6$ by $\Delta(x_1,x_2,x_3) = \delta(x_1,x_2,x_3)$, if $\delta(x_1,x_2,x_3)$ is define[d] and $\Delta(x_1,x_2,x_3) = (\varepsilon,\ldots,\varepsilon)$, otherwise. Since the domain of δ is a finite set, each component $\Delta_j = pr_j^{(6)}\circ$ [Δ] $(1\leq j\leq 6)$ of Δ can be expressed with the help of the functions $cond_a$ and some constant functions.

Each situation of T can be described by some $\mathbf{z}=(z_1,\ldots,z_8)\in(\Sigma^*)^8$: z_1 is the word on the left-hand si[de] of T's read-only head, z_2 is the symbol scanned by this head and z_3 is the reversal of the word on the rig[ht] hand side of this head; z_4, z_5, z_6 have the corresponding meaning with respect to the working tape ot T, [z_7] is the contents of T's output tape and z_8 is the state of T. For $\mathbf{y}\in(\Sigma^*)^8$ we define functions $k_1,\ldots,k_8$ wi[th] the help of which we can define the components $d_1,\ldots,d_8$ of T's single-step function. The values of the[se] functions depend on the values of Δ_1 and Δ_5 and/or Δ_6.

Let $\Delta_1(y_8,y_2,y_5)$ = "i", for some $1\leq i\leq r$. Then the values of $k_1(\mathbf{y}),\ldots,k_6(\mathbf{y})$ can be taken from [the] following tables:

	$\Delta_5(y_8,y_2,y_5)$ = "0"	$\Delta_5(y_8,y_2,y_5)$ = "-"	$\Delta_5(y_8,y_2,y_5)$ = "+"
$k_1(\mathbf{y})$	$S_i(y_1)$	$S_i(b_1(y_1))$	$S_i(b_3(y_2,y_1))$
$k_2(\mathbf{y})$	$S_i(y_2)$	$S_i(b_2(y_1))$	$S_i(b_2(y_3))$
$k_3(\mathbf{y})$	$S_i(y_3)$	$S_i(b_3(y_2,y_3)$	$S_i(b_1(y_3))$

	$\Delta_6(y_8,y_2,y_5)$ = "0"	$\Delta_6(y_8,y_2,y_5)$ = "-"	$\Delta_6(y_8,y_2,y_5)$ = "+"
$k_4(\mathfrak{y})$	$S_i(y_4)$	$S_i(b_1(y_4))$	$S_i(b_3(\Delta_3(y_8,y_2,y_5),y_4))$
$k_5(\mathfrak{y})$	$S_i(\Delta_3(y_8,y_2,y_5))$	$S_i(b_2(y_4))$	$S_i(b_2(y_6))$
$k_6(\mathfrak{y})$	$S_i(y_6)$	$S_i(b_3(\Delta_3(y_8,y_2,y_5),y_6))$	$S_i(b_1(y_6))$

Moreover

$$k_7(\mathfrak{y}) = S_i(b_3(\Delta_4(y_8,y_2,y_5),y_7))$$

$$k_8(\mathfrak{y}) = S_i(\Delta_2(y_8,y_2,y_5))$$

In any other case, $k_j(\mathfrak{y}) = y_j$, for $1 \le j \le 8$.

Now, we define $d_1,\ldots,d_8$. For $j=1,\ldots,8$,

$$d_j = \bigcup_{1 \le j \le r} \mathrm{SUB}(k_j, \mathrm{SUB}(\mathrm{LIN}(S_i,id),pr_1^{(8)}),\ldots, \mathrm{SUB}(\mathrm{LIN}(S_i,id),pr_8^{(8)})).$$

Moreover, we set $out = \bigcup_{1 \le j \le r} \mathrm{SUB}(pr_7^{(8)}, \mathrm{SUB}(\mathrm{LIN}(S_i,id),pr_1^{(8)}),\ldots, \mathrm{SUB}(\mathrm{LIN}(S_i,id),pr_8^{(8)}))$.

The function g shall express the halting condition of the Turing machine T which says that T halts in a situation $\mathfrak{z}$, if $\delta(z_8,z_2,z_5)$ is undefined, i.e., $\Delta_j(z_8,z_2,z_5) = \varepsilon$, for $1 \le j \le 6$. Thus, we set $g(\mathfrak{z}) = \varepsilon$, if $\Delta_j(z_8,z_2,z_5) = \varepsilon$, for $1 \le j \le 6$, and $g(\mathfrak{z}) = a_1$, otherwise.

In the initial situation of a computation of T the read-only head scans the last symbol of the input string, the work tape and the output tape are both empty, and T is in its initial state s_0. Therefore we define the components $in_1,\ldots,in_8$ of the input function by $in_1(x) = b_1(x)$, $in_2(x) = b_2(x)$, $in_8(x)$ = "s_0" and for $j=2, \ldots,7$, $in_j(x) = \varepsilon$.

Since the functions $k_1,\ldots,k_8$ can be expressed with the help of the functions $cond_a$, it follows that $in_1,\ldots, in_8, out, d_1,\ldots,d_8, g \in$ [**IF**; SUB,$\cup$,LIN]. Moreover, $f(x) = \mathrm{LIT}(d_1,\ldots,d_8,g,b,t,out)(in_1(x),\ldots,in_8(x))$, for all $x \in \Sigma^*$.

As we have already seen, LIT can be expressed by LC. Therefore a similar normal form result holds with respect to LC. In the case of the partial recursive functions such a normal form theorem has been proved by Buchberger (1974).

Note that [**IF**; SUB,$\cup$,LIN] $\subseteq$ **NTIMEF(Lin$_\Sigma$)**. In order to see that **NTIMEF(Lin$_\Sigma$)** is closed under limited inversion, let f,b$\in$ **NTIMEF(Lin$_\Sigma$)$^{(1)}$**. Moreover, let p and q respectively be linear bounds on the running time of the Turing machines computing f and b.

PROCEDURE 4.7.

Input: x

begin m := |b(x)|; (1)

guess some $y \in \Sigma^*$ with $|y| \le m$; (2)

z := f(y); (3)

if x = z **then** output y and halt

else diverge

end.

Obviously this nondeterministic procedure computes LIN(f,b). If the computation in line (1) converges, it length is bounded by q(|x|). Then also the length of the computation in line (2) is bounded by q(|x|), an each finite computation in line (3) is not longer than p(q(|x|)). Thus, the length of every finite computatio of this procedure is linearly bounded in |x|.

As a consequence of Corollary 4.3, Lemma 4.5 and the above result we obtain a further characterizatio of **NTIMEF**($\mathbf{Pol}_\Sigma$).

THEOREM 4.8. **NTIMEF**($\mathbf{Pol}_\Sigma$) = [**BF**; SUB,∪,LIN,LIT] = [**BF**; SUB,∪,LIN,LC].

Now, we study a further restricted version of the transitive closure and/or the iteration operator, namel *space-bounded transitive closure* SC and *space-bounded iteration* SIT. Both operators are defined in th same way as LC and LIT, but without restricting the number m of iterations. As we shall see in the ne theorem, we obtain a characterization of **NSPACEF**($\mathbf{Lin}_\Sigma$) and **NSPACEF**($\mathbf{Pol}_\Sigma$), if we use these opera tors instead of LC and LIT. Let to this end $A \in \mathbf{F}^{(2)}$ with $A(x,y) = a_1^{|x|+|y|}$ be the *length addition function.*

THEOREM 4.9. (a) **NSPACEF**($\mathbf{Lin}_\Sigma$) = [**IF** ∪ {A}; SUB,∪,LIN,SIT] = [**IF** ∪ {A}; SUB,∪,LIN,SC
(b) **NSPACEF**($\mathbf{Pol}_\Sigma$) = [**BF**; SUB,∪,LIN,SIT] = [**BF**; SUB,∪,LIN,SC].

PROOF. As it follows from the corresponding proofs, Lemma 4.5 and Theorem 4.6 also hold wi respect to SC and SIT. Thus, it remains to show that **NSPACEF**($\mathbf{Lin}_\Sigma$) and **NSPACEF**($\mathbf{Pol}_\Sigma$) are clos under LIN and SC. In order to see that they are closed under LIN, consider Procedure 4.7 and assume that and q respectively are space bounds for the Turing machines computing f and b.Then the length of eve word generated in any finite computation of this procedure is bounded by q(|x|)+p(q(|x|)), which is a line function and/or a polynomial of |x|, depending on whether p and q are linear functions or polynomials.

If Procedure 4.2 is slightly modified (delete lines (1) and (3) and the test "$m \neq 0$" in line (2)), then follows in a similar way that both classes are also closed under SC.

The results in this theorem show that in order to obtain a characterization of **NTIMEF**($\mathbf{Pol}_\Sigma$) based iteration or transitive closure, it is necessary to consider limited versions of these operators in which r only the growth of the function values but also the number of iterations is restricted.

ACKNOWLEDGEMENT

Thanks are due to Egon Börger, Giorgio Germano, Rutger Verbeek and Paul Young for useful discussions. In addition, I would like to thank the Computer Science Department of the University of Pisa for its hospitality. It was the pleasant atmosphere at Pisa which made it possible to finish the work on this paper. Moreover, I am indebted to the Consiglio Nazionale delle Ricerche and the Siemens Corporate Laboratories for Research and Technology for supporting my stay at Pisa.

REFERENCES

Buchberger, B. (1974). On certain decompositions of Gödel numberings. *Archiv f. math. Logik u. Grundlagenforsch.* **16**, p. 85-96.

Cobham, A. (1965). The intrinsic computational difficulty of functions. *Logic, Methodology and Philosophy of Science* (Bar-Hillel, Y., ed.), p. 24-30. North-Holland, Amsterdam.

Eilenberg, S. and C. C. Elgot (1970). *Recursiveness*. Academic Press, New York.

Kleene, S. C. (1936). General recursive functions of natural numbers. *Math. Ann.* **112**, p. 727-742.

Moschovakis, Y. N. (1969). Abstract first order computability. I. *Transact. Amer. Math. Soc.* **138**, p. 427-464.

Robinson, J. (1950). General recursive functions. *Proc. Amer. Math. Soc.* **1**, p. 703-718.

Spreen, D. and H. Stahl (1987). On the power of single-valued nondeterministic polynomial time computations. *Computation and Logic* (Börger, E., ed.), p. 403-414. Lec. Notes Comp. Sci. 270. Springer-Verlag, Berlin.

Weihrauch, K.(1973). *Teilklassen primitiv-rekursiver Wortfunktionen*. Bericht Nr. 91, Gesellschaft f. Mathematik u. Datenverarbeitung, St. Augustin.

DEVELOPING LOGIC PROGRAMS: COMPUTING THROUGH NORMALIZING

Olga Štěpánková
Institute of Computational Techniques, ČVUT,
Horská 3, 128 00 Praha 2

Petr Štěpánek
Department of Computer Science, Charles University,
Malostranské náměstí 25, 118 00 Praha 1,
Czechoslovakia

Abstract
It is shown that most transformations used in developing recursive programs (Burstall and Darlington 1977, Tamaki and Sato 1984) are particular cases of normalizing. A general method for normalizing pure logic programs (Ochozka et al. 1987) preserves the length of computations and data flow. It is argued that more specific domain-dependent transformations are needed that change not only the logical structure of the program but its control and data flow, as well. An illustrative example of program development is given.

Introduction.

The idea of Normal Forms or Normalizing Programs goes back to Harel (1980a,b). He defined a simple tree-like language of so called And/Or Schemes and proved that every such scheme can be transformed to a canonical form with at most one node called by recursion and at most two alternations of And- and Or-nodes on every branch. Harel was motivated to define a language embodying the concept of Alternation due to Chandra and Stockmeyer (1977). Shapiro (1984) showed that such a language already existed by simulating computations of Alternating Turing Machines by pure logic programs and vice versa. Independently, the authors of the present paper (1983) proved that every And/Or Scheme is equivalent to a logic program and lifted the Harel Normal Form Theorem to pure logic programs. More precisely, they showed (1984) that every pure logic program can be transformed to its normal form by a finite sequence of local structure transformations. However, there were no upper bounds on the length of computations of normal forms for And/Or Schemes or for logic programs.

Recently, Ochozka et al. (1987) described a simple and uniform method that transforms every pure logic program to its normal form without changing the length of computatations and the data flow during computation. By the end of the 1970's, Burstall and Darlington (1977) studied transformations of recursive programs that improve their computational behaviour. They introduced a system of rules for transforming programs in the form of recursive equations. Their unfol/fold method allows one that "an initially very simple, lucid and hopefully correct program is transformed into a more efficient one by alternating the recursive structure". In their paper, "illustrative examples of program transformations are given, and a tentative implementation is described. Alternative structures for programs are shown, and possible initial phase for an automatic or semiautomatic program manipulation system is indicated". Thier method was adopted to logic programs by Hogger (1978), an later by Tamaki and Sato (1984) and others.

We are going to show that most transformations used in developing recursive programs are particular cases of normalizing:these transformations make the structure of the program closer to its normal form or improve efficiency of programs that are in normal form. We shall show that the above cited result of Ochozka et al. presents theoretical background for developing logic programs. Since the underlying normalizing method is conservative with respect to the length of computations and data flow, it is argued that more specific domain dependent transformations are necessary. It is shown by an illustrative example that such transformations can be developed by a more general version of unfold/fold technique and that such transformations should change not only the logical structure of the program, but its control and data flow, as well.

The paper is organized as follows:in Section 1, the concept of computation trees is recalled along with the definition of normal forms of logic programs. Section 2 shows that the classical examples of program transformations due to Burstall and Darlington are particular cases of normalizing programs. Section 3 presents an example of program development and conclusions.

1. COMPUTATION TREES AND NORMAL FORMS OF PURE LOGIC PROGRAMS

We shall use the concept of computation trees of logic programs introduced in one of our previous papers (1984). However, the reader need not look there for the definition, since the particular cases of such trees we are going to use in this paper are rather self-explaining.

Let us consider the following simple program reversing lists.

Program 1.

```
(1)      reverse ([],[]).
(2)      reverse([H|T],R)     :-  reverse(T,S), append(S,[H],R).
(3)      append([],P,P).
(4)      append([H|T],K,[H|M])  :- append(T,K,M).
```

Its computation tree on Figure 1 contains two nodes called by recursion (1), (3) and two calling lists △2 and △4. The root of the tree is an Or-node labelled by the atom 'reverse L,R'. Its successors are two And-nodes labelled by two clauses of the program describing the relation 'reverse'. The left-hand successor is labelled by the boundary condition /1/. It is an And-list of the tree. The right-hand suc-

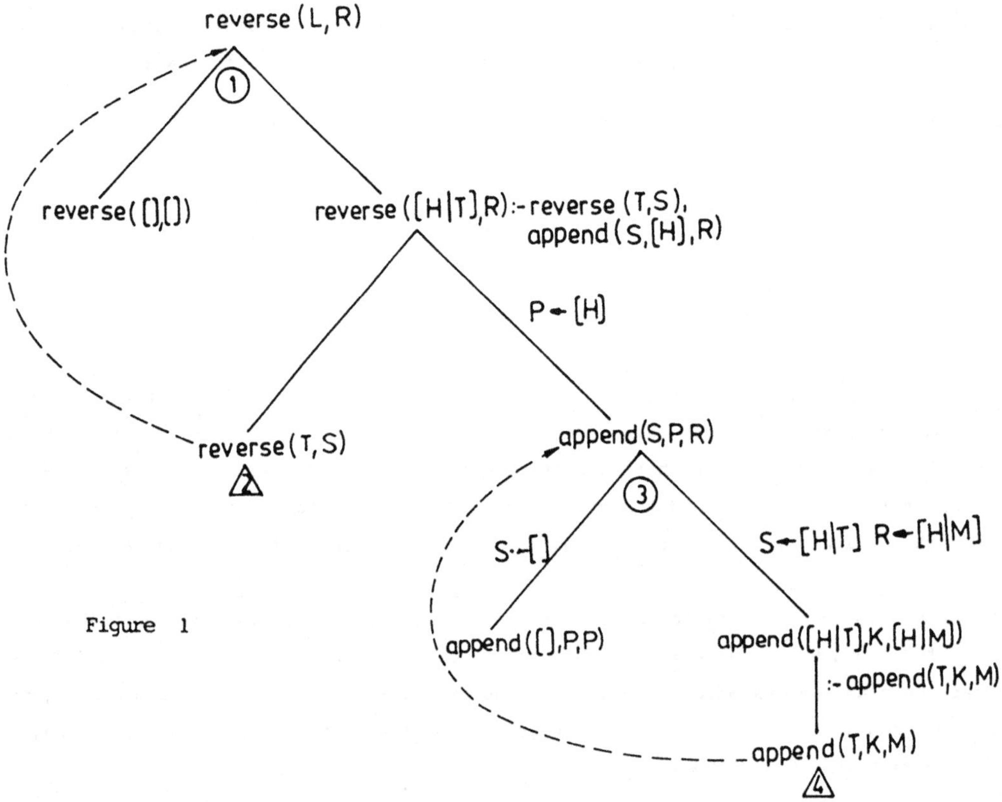

Figure 1

cessor labelled by the conditional statement /2/ has two Or-successors labelled by the atoms corresponding to the two goals in the body of /2/. The left-hand successor is an Or-list calling the root of the tree by recursion. The right-hand successor is an Or-node that is the root of the subtree describing the computations of the relation 'append'. This subtree can be described in a similar way.

A more efficient algorithm for reversing lists is described by the following well-known program

Program 2.

/5/ reverse(L,R) :- rev(L,[],R).

/6/ rev([],R,R).

/7/ rev([H|T],Q,R) :- rev(T,[H|Q],R).

It is not difficult to see that for any two lists L, R , Program 1 solves the goal ´reverse(L,R)´ iff Program 2 solves the goal ´rev(L,[ ],R)´. Hence the clauses /6/ and /7/ define a /more general/ relation ´rev´ from which the relation ´reverse´ is definable as a projection of a subset. For this reason, we may say that the relation ´rev´ is an extension of the relation ´reverse´ and that the program consisting of clauses /6/ and /7/ extends the program 1. We shall return to this later and give a precise definition.

The computation tree of the program consisting of clauses /6/ and /7/ is shown on Figure 2. It has one called node and one calling leaf only, and at most one altern-

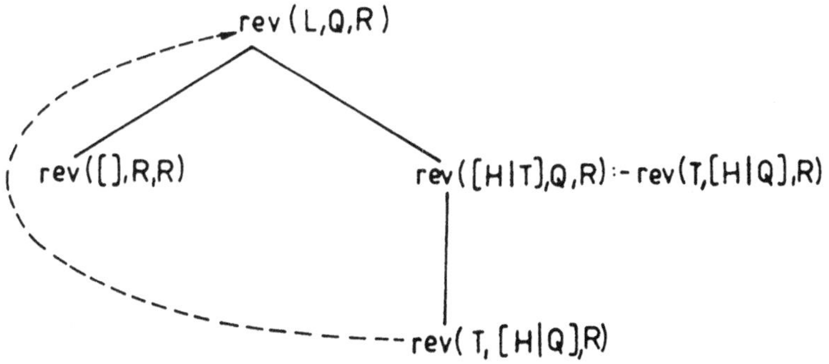

Figure 2

ation of And- and Or-nodes on every branch. We say that a pure logic program is in normal form if it has a computation tree with at most one called node and with at most two alternations of And- and Or-nodes on every branch. Obviously, the Program 2 is in normal form and the same applies to its subprogram shown on Figure 2. Note that Program 2 computes the same ´reverse´ relation as Program 1 and that the computation tree of Program 2 has at most two And/Or alternations on every branch. On the other hand, its subprogram consisting fo clauses /6/ and /7/ computes an extension ´rev´ of the ´reverse´relation and its computation tree /see Figure 2/ has at most one And/Or alternation on every branch.

<u>1.1 Definition</u> We say that a logic program P´ extends a logic program P if the following conditions hold

/i/ the language of P´ contains all constants and function symblols of the language of P. Thus all terms of P are terms of P´ , too.

/ii/ the predicate symbols of P are mapped onto the predicate symbols of P´ in the following manner: the primitive predicates i.e. the predicate symbols that are not defined by P are the same in both programs.

If p is an n-ary predicate defined by P , then there is a natural number k , an /n+k/-ary predicate p´ and terms $s_1,\ldots,s_k$ in the language of P´

such that

/8/ P solves the goal $p(t_1,\ldots,t_n)$ iff P´ solves $p´(t_1,\ldots,t_n,s_1,\ldots)$

for arbitrary terms $t_1, \ldots, t_n$ in the language of P. We say that p´ is an extension of p, that t_i´s are the corresponding arguments and s_j´s are the extending arguments in the corresponding goals $p(t_1, \ldots, t_n)$ and $p´(t_1, \ldots t_n, s_1, \ldots, s_k)$.

Note that the extending arguments s_j depend on the predicate symbol p and not on the terms t_i in /8/. Consequently, the relations defined by the original program P are projections of definable subsets of the corresponding relations computed by P´.

<u>1.2 Theorem</u> /Ochozka, Štěpánková, Štěpánek 1987/ There is an extension in normal form of an arbitrary pure logic program P such that for every pair G , G´ of corresponding goals, we have

/i/ P´ solves G´ in the same number of steps as P solves G ,

/ii/ the corresponding arguments of G and G´ receive identical values at every step of computation.

/iii/ there is at most one alternation of And/Or-nodes on every branch of the computation tree of P´.

Hence the transformation of P to its normal form P´ described by the Theorem preserves the length of computations and the data flow. Moreover, the number of alte nations of And- and Or-nodes in the computation tree of P´ is the least possible.

The normal form obtained by an application of the above theorem from Program 1 reads as follows

Program 3.

```
/1´/    rv([],[],Q,reverse).
/2´/    rv([H|T],R,Q,reverse) :-  rv(T,S,Q,reverse), rv(S,[H],R, append).
/3´/    rv([],K,K, append).
/4´/    rv([H|T],K,[H|M], append)  :-  rv(T,K,M , append .
```

Note that the clauses /1´/ - /4´/ of the resulting normal form are obtained by a simple translation from clauses /1/ - /4/ of Program 1. Since there were no pi mitive relations in Program 1, the resulting Program 3 computes only one relation ´rv´ from which both relations ´reverse´ and ´append´ are definable. The rela ´rv´ has one more argument than the relation ´append´ with the maximal arity i

Program 1 . This auxilliary argument indicates which relation is computed. Note that the variable Q is dummy in the clauses /1´/ and /2´/ and that it may receive some values only when some of the clauses /3´/ or /4´/ is used. Figure 3 shows the computation tree of Program 3 , and the nodes corresponding to the nodes 1 - 4 in the computation tree of Program 1 are indicated by the same numbers. Note that the called node (3) in Figure 1 corresponds to the calling leaf △3 in Figure 3 , since the subtree describing the computations of the ´append´ relation is attached to the root of the computation tree in Figure 3 .

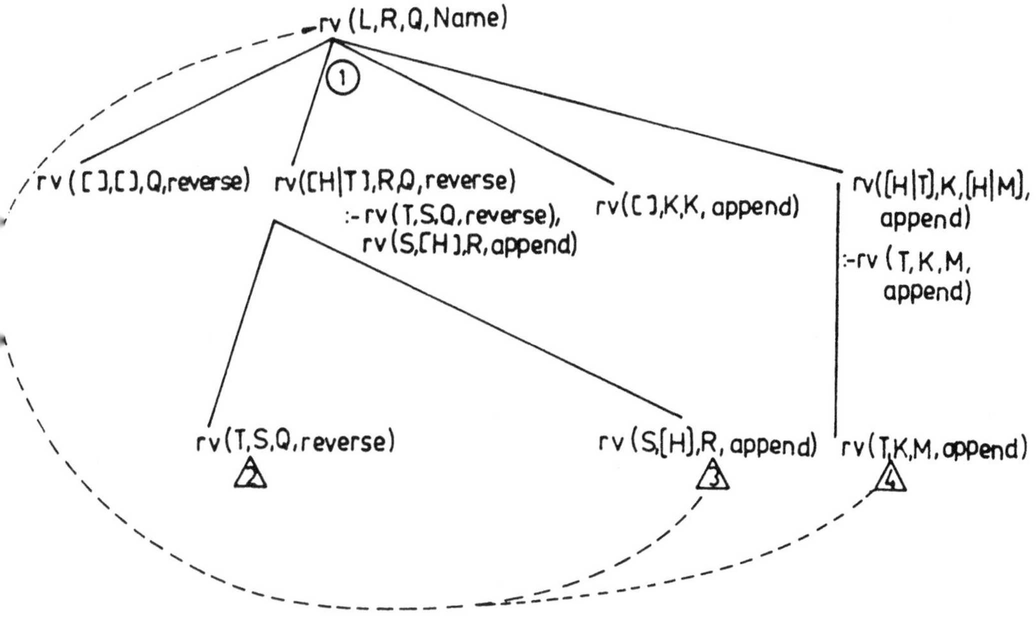

Figure 3

Illustrated by the above example, the transformation described by Theorem 1.2 is simple and uniform. It does not take into account any specific properties of the relations of Program 1. As a result, the computations of Program 3 are imitating step by step the computations of the original program. We may call such transformations conservative. The resulting normal form program is not worse in the length of computations than the original program but it is not better. There is,however, certain overhead in computations of Program 3 that is due to longer strings of the atomic formulas that delays unification. Some of it may be removed by changing the order of the arguments and putting the name of the relation on the first place.

2. DOMAIN DEPENDENT TRANSFORMATIONS

Referring to the well-known Kowalski´s doctrine ALGORITHM = Logic + Control , we may say that the transformation described in Section 1 changes logic of the algorithm while preserving its control and data flow. The normal form program is obtained simply by attaching every proper subtree of the original computation tree to the root of the new computation tree. The root of the tree thus constructed is labelled by an extension of all relations defined by the original program and it becomes the only node of the tree called by recursion. The other called nodes of the original tree are turned to leaves calling the root. The normalizing transformation does not make use of any particular property of relations defined by the original program and thus it disregards possible sources of improvement of the program´s efficiency.

It is not difficult to see that it was associativity of the ´append´ relation that made it possible to transform Program 1 using $O(n^2)$ steps to reverse a list of n items to Program 2 that can do the same in linear time. We borrowed this example from Burstall and Darlington /1977/ and we are going to use some other of their examples to illustrate that their transformations are normalizing programs "by introducing useful interactions between what were originally separated parts of the program".

2.1 Let us consider the following program computing the descending list of factorials

Program 4

```
/8/     faclist(0,[]).
/9/     faclist(N+1, M|L)  :-  fact(N+1,M), faclist(N,L).
/10/    fact(0,1).
/11/    fact(N+1,M)  :-  fact(N,P), M is (N+1)*P .
```

It computes the relation ´faclist´ , where the atom ´faclist(N,L)´ states "L is the list of factorials of N , N-1, ... , 1 " , using the relation ´fact´ . The computation tree of Program 4 /see Figure 4/ has two called nodes and two calling leaves. Given an arbitrary natural number n , Program 4 solves the goal ´faclist(n,L)´ in $O(n^2)$ steps since each of the factorials is computed afresh. By interwining the computations of the two goals in the body of /9/ , we get a new program computing the same goal in linear time.

Program 5

```
/12/    faclist(N,L)  :-  g(N,F,L).
/13/    g(0,1,[]).
/14/    g(N+1,V,[P|K])  :-  g(N,P,K), V is (N+2)*P .
```

Note that Program 4 solves the goal ´faclist(N,L)´ iff Program 5 solves the corresponding goal ´g(N,F,L)´ and that the relation g extends the relation faclist. It follows from /14/ that g does not extend the relation fact since g(N,F,L) implies that F is the factorial of N+1 and not the factorial of N. However, the factorial relation is definable from g . If we insisted that the resulting program computes an extension of both relations faclist and fact , it would suffice to keep the value of the factorial of N as an extra argument of g .

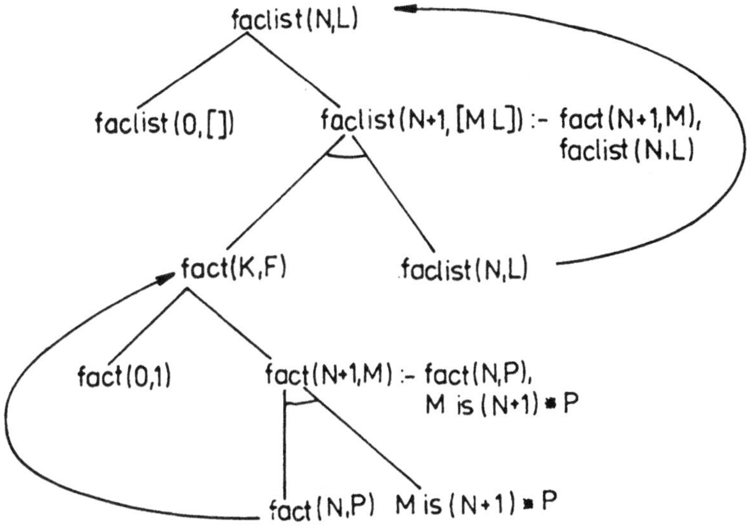

Figure 4

Figure 5 shows that the computation tree of Program 5 is in normal form with one called node and one calling list. We have already seen that the subprogram consist-

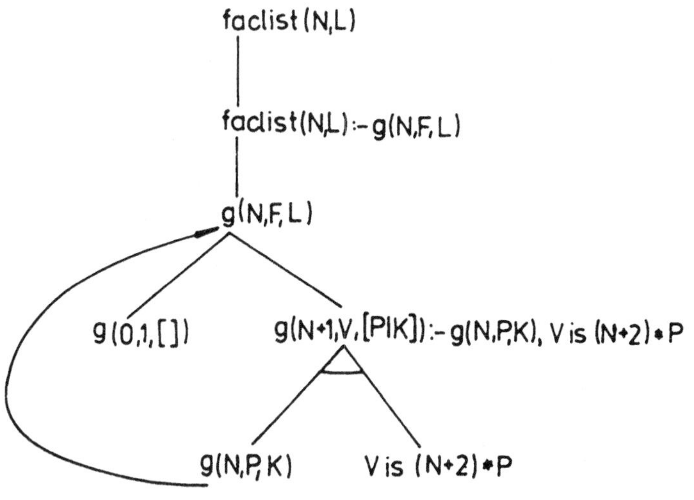

Figure 5

ing of clauses /13/, /14/ computes the extension of the faclist relation. The above example shows that two nested loops may be combined in a single one.

2.2 The following program computes the Fibonacci numbers by binary recursion.

Program 6

```
/15/      fib(0,1).
/16/      fib(1,1).
/17/      fib(N+2,F)  :-   fib(N,F0), fib(N+1 , F1), F is  F0 + F1 .
```

Its computation tree on Figure 6 is in normal form with one called node and two calling leaves.

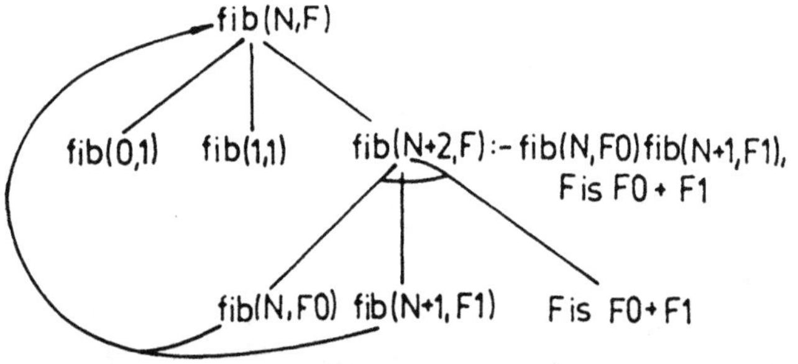

Figure 6

It can be shown that for any natural number n , Program 6 solves the goal fib(n,F) in more than $2^{n/2}$ steps. The exponential time complexity is due to the fact that top-down execution of binary recursion is in this case redundant. The same goal may be solved several times afresh. As shown by Burstall and Darlington, it is possible to remedy this by replacing binary recursion by iteration. Introducing the extension f of the original fib relation , where the atom ´f(M,F,G)´ states " F is the N-th and G is the (N+1)-th Fibonacci number" ,we may transform the program to a new one with only one called node. By this way, we removed binary recursion.

Program 7

```
/18/      fib(N,F)   :-   f(N,F,G).
/19/      f(0,1,1).
/20/      f(N+1, F1, G1)   :-   f(N,K,F1), G1 is  K + F1 .
```

Its computation tree on Figure 7 has only one called node and one calling leaf. Hence we improved computational behaviour of a program in normal form by decreasing the number of calling leaves. Note that /20/ is the only recursive conditional statement of the program and that the first argument of the predicate ´f´ , which is the only in put argument of the loop, has higher value in the head of /20/ than that of the only input argument in its body. It was proved by Ochozka /1987/ that under such conditions, the length of computation is a linear function of the input value. It is not difficult to check that these conditions are satisfied by the recursive conditional statements of Program 2 and Program 5, as well.

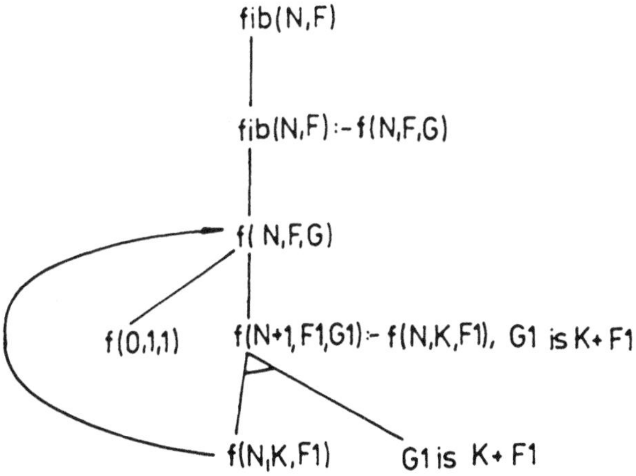

Figure 7

2.3 We shall conclude this Section by another example from the above cited paper of Burstall and Darlington. We assume that a binary tree is either a tip of a natural number or a tree consisting of two trees joined by the constructor functor t . The following program computes the sum and the product of tips of an arbitrary tree thus constructed.

Program 8

```
/21/    tipsum(T,T)   :-   tip(T).
/22/    tipsum(t(T1,T2),S)   :-   tipsum(T1,S1), tipsum(T2,S2), S is S1 + S2 .
/23/    tipprod(T,T)  :-   tip(T).
/24/    tipprod(t(T1,T2),P)  :-   tipprod(T1,P1), tipprod(T2,P2), P is P1*P2 .
```

Figure 8 shows the corresponding computation tree with two independent binary recursion loops defined by the conditional statements /22/ and /24/. In the tree, there are two nodes called by recursion by two calling leaves each. Given a binary tree T, the program solves the goals ´tipsum(T,S)´ and ´tipprod(T,P)´ independently. It is, however, easy to combine both recursive loops in one. It suffices to introduce a common extension tsp of relations tipsum and tipprod by the following definition. For arbitrary tree T and natural numbers S , P , we put

/25/ tsp(T,S,P) iff tipsum(T,S) and tipprod(T,P)

As a consequence of the above definition and of Program 8, we get a new program.

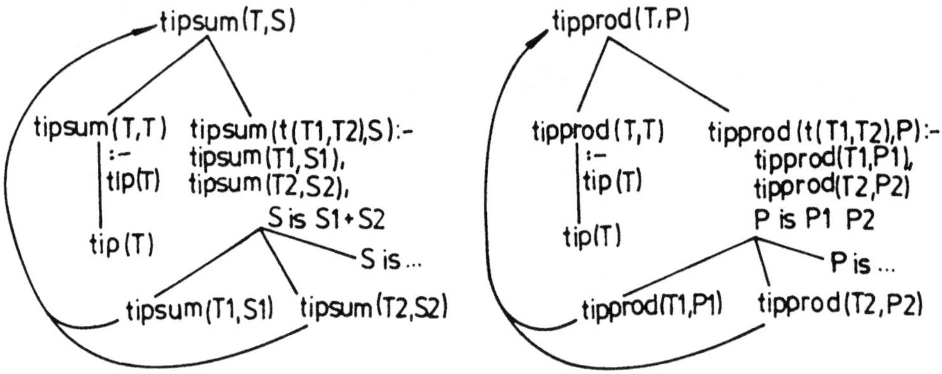

Figure 8

Program 9

/26/ tsp(T,T,T) :- tip(T).

/27/ tsp(t(T1,T2),S,P) :- tsp(T1,S1,P1), tsp(T2,S2,P2),
S is S1 + S2 , P is P1 * P2 .

Its computation tree /Figure 9/ is in normal form with two calling leaves instead of four in Program 8.

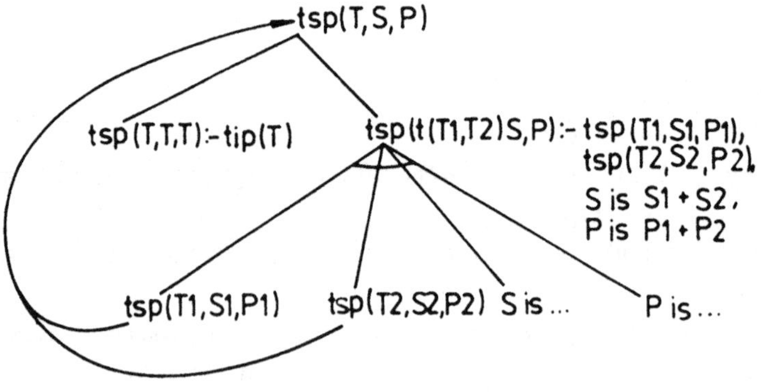

Figure 9

Given a binary tree T , Program 9 cuts by one half the length of computation of the sum S and the product P of tips of T executed by Program 8.

All the above examples show that the transformations obtained by Burstall and Darlington /1977/ by means of their unfold/fold method are normalizing the computation tree, i.e. decreasing the number of its called nodes and/or decreasing the number of calling leaves. These examples also show the role of the concept of common extensions of relations defined by a logic program. According to the Normal Form Theorem 1.2, a common extension of all relations defined by an arbitrary logic program exists and it is computed by a normal form program preserving the length of computation and data flow for any pair of correspondning goals. We call such normal forms conservative. We are going to show in the next Section that normal forms improving computational behaviour of logic programs can be obtained by an extended version of the unfold/fold method.

3. UNFOLD/FOLD TRANSFORMATIONS

In their pioneering paper, Burstall and Darlington /1977/ introduced six types of inference rules for transforming programs defined by a set of recursive equations. These are Definition of a new function, Instantiation, Abstraction, Laws, Unfolding and Folding. Although defined in terms of equations in a functional setting, their bearings are more general. These transformations can be easily adapted to logic programs as well as to other formal descriptions of algorithms.

We are not going to describe these transformations in detail, we note that the names of the first two are rather self-explanatory. The next one, Abstraction combines previously separate functions into one new function returning tuples of values of the original functions. It was used e.g. in 2.3 to combine two recursive loops of Program 8 to one of Program 9. So called Laws transformations make use of particular properties /associativity, commutativity etc./ of functions computed by the program and Unfold transformation amounts to executing one single step of computation. All these transformations are rather obvious except Folding that can be seen as an attempt to speed-up the computation by replacing several steps of computation /due to several equations/ by one new equation.

A formal description of these transformations in the context of logic programs can be found in Tamaki and Sato /1984/ , where these transformations are used in formal reasoning about programs. Tamaki and Sato introduced some new transformations based on replacing of goals or introducing new goals to goal clauses and conditional statements. In the above cited paper, Tamaki and Sato point out that the power of the transformational system depends on the heuristics used in search of the space state generated by the set of transformation rules.

In this Section we present in detail one example of developing a logic program to show that the choice of transformations that are normalizing the computation tree guided by a systematic analysis of computation of the original program is a powerful heuristic in developing more efficient versions of the original program. It turns out that some new specific transformations can emerge during the proces.

3.1 The following program computes common sublists of two lists. Given two lists [a,b,c,d] , [c,b,a,d,f] , the list [b,d] is /the longest/ sublist of the previous two.

Program 10

```
/28/    csub(X,Y,Z)  :-  sub(X,Y), sub(X,Z).
/29/    sub([],Y).
/30/    sub([A|X],[A|Y])  :-  sub(X,Y).
/31/    sub(X,[A|Y])  :-  sub(X,Y).
```

Note that the subprogram consisting of clauses /29/ - /31/ is in normal form. It is due to the clause /28/ that under the standard execution strategy , Program 10 behaves as a ´generate and test´ program. Given two lists k1, k2 and the goal ´csub C,k1,k2 ´, Program 10 tries first to satisfy the goal

/32/ sub(C,k1)

by generating a sublist c of k1 and then trying to satisfy the second goal in the instantiated body of /28/, it tests whether c is also a sublist of k2. In most cases, the sublist c of k1 does not satisfy the second goal enforcing thus new attempts to resatisfy the goal /32/ until a common sublist is found. This is an obvious souce of inefficiency.

Although the relation csub is not defined recursively in /28/, the Normal Form Theorem 1.2 guarantees that there is an extension of this relation recursively defined by a logic program in normal form. One such extension of csub relation may be extracted from the proof of the theorem. However, we already know that this extension is conservative, i.e. that the resulting normal form program preserves the length of computation and dataflow.

We are going to show that a more efficient program computing an extension of the csub relation can be obtained by a systematic examination of computations of Program 10 and of its descendants by means of the unfold/fold method.

3.2 Let us recall that the computation of a logic program P starting with the initial goal clause

/33/ ?- G1, ... , Gn.

can be represented as a sequence of goal clauses, each step of computation generating a new goal clause as a resolvent of the previous one and a clause of the program P. Analyzing these sequences, we are not obliged to follow the standard leftmost-depth-first strategy of execution of logic programs. Instead, we may resolve upon an arbitrary goal of the current goal clause using an arbitrary applicable clause in P . By this way, we are changing control of the algorithm, but we have a good reason to do so. During the process, a tree rather than a sequence of goal clauses is generated since to a single goal to be solved, several clauses of the program may be applicable. We shall call the resulting tree the proof tree of the program determined by the initial goal clause. Every successor of a node of the proof tree is generated by one resolution step that we call unfolding.

<u>3.3 Definition</u> Let P be a logic program and let

/34/ A :- B1,B2, ... , Bk /k $\geq$ 0/

be one of the clauses of P applicable to a goal G_j in /33/. We say that the goal clause

/35/ ?- $G_1\vartheta$, ... , $G_{j-1}\vartheta$, $B_1\vartheta$, ... , $B_k\vartheta$, $G_{j+1}\vartheta$, ... , $G_n\vartheta$

where ϑ is the most general unifier of G_j and A , is obtained by unfolding the goal clause /33/ by /34/ upon the goal G_j .

It follows from the semantics of logic programs that the unfolding /35/ of the goal clause /33/ gives a sufficient condition to satisfy the instance

/33´/ ?- $G_1\vartheta$, ... , $G_n\vartheta$.

of the goal clause /33/. The proof tree on Figure 10 shows some unfoldngs of the goal clause

/35/ ?- csub(C,L,M).

by clauses of Program 10. The goals unfolding is based upon are underlined and the edges of the proof tree are labelled by the corresponding unifiers.

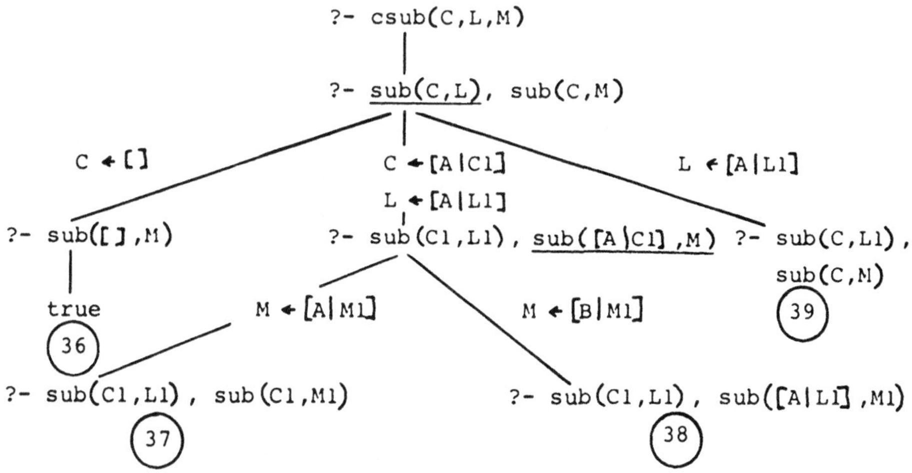

Figure 10

Let us examine the goal clauses labelling the leaves of the proof tree on Figure 10. They indicate various iterated unfoldings of the original goal /35/. If any of these goal clauses is satisfied, then the same holds for the instance of /35/ obtained by the composition of all substitutions labelling the edges of the path from the leaf to the root of the proof tree.

Every branch of the proof tree represents a sequence of successive steps of computation of Program 10. Each sequence can be compressed to one step determined by one of the following new clauses /their reference numbers are corresponding to the numbers attached to the leaves/.

```
/36/   csub([],L,M).
/37/   csub([A|C1],[A|L1], [A|M1])  :-  sub(C1,L1), sub(C1,M1).
/38/   csub([A|C1],[A|L1], [B|M1])  :-  sub(C1,L1), sub([A|L1],M1).
/39/   csub(C,[A|L1],M)  :-  sub(C,L1), sub(C,M).
```

To get a new recursive definition of the csub relation, we should try to express the bodies of the new clauses in terms of csub. Note that we could do that with all the clauses except /38/ , where two different lists L1 and [A|L1] occur as the first arguments of sub.

This indicates that an extension of the csub relation is needed, that would allow to keep the value of A in one auxilliary argument. We define a new relation dsub as follows. For arbitrary lists B, C, L, M , we put

/40/ dsub(B,C,L,M) iff $\exists$D(sub(C,L) and append(B,C,D) and sub(D,M)).

It is not difficult to see that for every item A and arbitrary lists C, L, M the following follows from /28/ and the above definition.

/41/ dsub([],C,L,M) iff csub(C,L,M)

/42/ dsub([A],C,L,M) iff sub(C,L) and sub([A|C],M)

Using /41/ and /42/ , we can express the clauses /36/ - /39/ as follows

```
/36'/   dsub([],[],L,M).
/37'/   dsub([],[A|C1],[A|L1],[A|M1])  :-  dsub([],C1,L1,M1).
/38'/   dsub([],[A|C1],[A|L1],[B|M1])  :-  dsub([A],C1,L1,M1).
/39'/   dsub([],C,[A|L1],M)  :-  dsub([],C,L1,M1).
```

We call this transformation folding, since in each clause /36/ - /39/, we replaced a sequence of goals by one goal from which the previous sequence can be recovered by unfolding using /41/, /42/ and clauses of Program 10.

However, the specification of dsub relation by clauses /36'/ - /39'/ is not complete with respect to the original relation csub. More precisely, the above specification of dsub does not allow to compute the csub relation, since it provides no tools to solve goals

/43/ ?- dsub([A],C,L,M).

that may be generated by /38'/ and,as we have already seen, occur in the proof tree on Figure 10 according to /42/.

The missing clauses to specify dsub relation completely can be obtained by applying the unfol/fold method once more. According to /42/, the goal /43/ is equivalent to the goal clause

/44/ ?- sub(C,L), sub([A|C],M).

that can be unfolded by the original Program 10. The appropriate proof tree is shown on Figure 11.

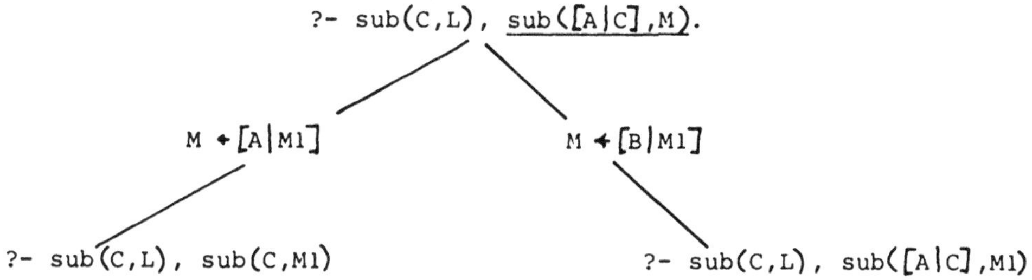

Figure 11

Two missing clauses specifying the dsub relation are obtained from the two branches of the proof tree by folding. They read as follows

/45/ dsub([A],C,L,[A|M1]) :- dsub([],C,L,M1).
/46/ dsub([A],C,L,[B|M1]) :- dsub([A],C,L,M1).

The if-part of /41/ and clauses /36'/ - /39'/ , /45/ and /46/ complete a normal form program computing the original csub relation.

Program 11

/41'/ csub(C,L,M) :- dsub([],C,L,M).
/36'/ dsub([],[],L,M).
/37'/ dsub([],[A|C1],[A|L1],[A|M1]) :- dsub([],C1,L1,M1).
/38'/ dsub([],[A|C1],[A|L1],[B|M1]) :- dsub([A],C1,L1,M1).
/39'/ dsub([],C,[A|L1],M) :- dsub([],C,L1,M1).
/45/ dsub([A],C,L,[A|M1]) :- dsub([],C,L,M1).

/46/ dsub([A],C,L,[B|M1]) :- dsub([A],C,L,M1).

Given two lists l, m as input, Program 11 solves the goal

?- csub(C,l,m).

in a more deterministic way than the original Program 10. Each new item of C suggested by l is immediately tested for m and according to the result, one or both of the lists l, m are made shorter.

Using their own version of unfold/fold method, Tamaki and Sato /1984/ transformed Program 10 to the following

Program 12

```
csub([],L,M).
csub([A|C],[A|L],M)  :-  csubl(A,C,L,M).
csub(C,[A|L],M)  :-  csub(C,L,M).
csubl(A,C,L,[A|M])  :-  csub(C,L,M).
csubl(A,C,L,[B|M])  :-  csubl(A,C,L,M).
```

The resulting program has more complicated structure than Programs 10 and 11. Program 12 defines its relations csub and csubl by multiple recursion. As a result of this, its computation tree has two called nodes and three calling leaves. It is not in normal form. Comparing the length of computations, Program 12 is considerably better than Program 10 . Its performance is close to that of Program 11 although it does not exceed it.

References

Burstall, R.M. and Darlington, J. , A Transformation System for Develop- 1977 ing Recursive Programs , Journal ACM 24 /1977/,44 - 67

Chandra, A.K. , Stockmeyer,L. J., Alternation, Proc IEEE Symp. on Found- 1977 ations of Computer Science, Providence, R.I. 1977,95-99

Harel, D. , And/Or Programs: A New Approach to Structured Programming, 1980a ACM Transactions on Programming Languages and Systems 2 /1980/, 1-17

1980b On And/Or Schemes, in: Math. Foundations of Computer Science 1980, P. Dembinski /editor/, Lecture Notes in Comp. Science, Vol 88, Springer-Verlag Berlin

Hogger, C. , Program Synthesis in Predicate Logic, in: Proc. AISB/GI 1978 Conf. on AI, Hamburg, pp 18 - 20

Ochozka, V. , Štěpánková, O., Štěpánek, P. , Normal Forms and Complex- 1987 ity of Computations of Logic Programs, TR 2 ,1987

Shapiro, E. , Alternation and the Computational Complexity of Logic Pro-
1984 grams, J. Logic Programming 1 /1984/, 19-33

Štěpánková, O. , Štěpánek, P. , And/Or Schemes and Logic Programs, in:
1983 Colloquia Math. Soc. J. Bolyai Vol. 42, Algebra, Combinatorics and Logic in Computer Science, Györ /Hungary/ pp 765 - 776

1984 Transformations of Logic Programs, J. Logic Programming 1 /1984/, 305 - 318

Tamaki, H. , Sato, T. , Unfold/fold Transformations of Logic Programs,
1984 in: Proc. 2nd Intern. Logic Programming Conf. Uppsala 1984, S.A. Tärnlund /Editor/, pp. 127-138

MODEL THEORY OF DEDUCTIVE DATABASES

Hugo Volger
Fakultät für Mathematik und Informatik, Universität Passau
Innstr. 27 , D 8390 Passau

0.Introduction

A relational database may be described as a relational structure $\mathcal{A}$ whereas a deductive database may be described as theory T (cf. Gallaire, Minker,Nicolas [7]). The relational database $\mathcal{A}(T)$ associated with the deductive database T should then be a uniquely determined canonical model of the theory T, the intended relational database. Clearly, this restricts the class of theories which can be used. If one wants to represent disjunctive information in the database then one has to drop the uniqeness requirement for the canonical models. This is the situation we want to study in this paper.

To be more precise let A be a term structure i. e. a structure where each element is denoted by a term of the language considered. Then a relational database on A is a relational structure $\mathcal{A}$ on A . In this case the facts of the database are explicitly given and consist of the atomic formulas containing elements from A which are valid in $\mathcal{A}$. A deductive database on A is a theory T on A . In this case the facts of the database are implicitly given and consist of the atomic formulas containing elements from A which are provable with the help of the axioms of T . This determines an associated relational structure $\mathcal{A}(T)$ on T. This relational structure is generic for T in the sense that the valid facts are just the facts which are provable from T . Now one requires that $\mathcal{A}(T)$ is a canonical model of T. The genericity of $\mathcal{A}(T)$ is often called the Closed World Assumption (cf. Reiter[13]) since is used to define negation in the deductive database.

Disjunctive facts i. e. disjunctions of atomic formulas have different canonical models. In each of them just one disjunct is true and the other disjuncts are false. This shows that the uniqueness requirement for the canonical models has to be dropped.

Usually one considers logic programs i. e. universal Horn theories without equations. In this case it suffices to consider Herbrand structures i. e. term structures where each element is denoted by a unique term. These theories have a uniquely determined minimal model which coincides with the generic structure $\mathcal{A}(T)$. Evaluation of queries is handled by a theorem prover i. e. an interpreter for logic programs.

More generally one can consider universal Horn theories. They have a uniquely determined term model which is initial and it coincides with the generic structure. A model said to be initial if there is a unique homomorphism into any other model of the theory. Thus 'initial' replaces 'minimal' and 'term structure' replaces 'Herbrand structure' in this case. Moreover, it is well known that the universal Horn theories can be characterized by this property i. e. a theory is a universal Horn theory iff the theory and all its consistent extensions by new facts posess a term model which is initial (cf. Malcev [10],Makowsky [9],Volger [15]). The prize to be paid for this generalization is a more general and hence less efficient theorem prover for evaluating the queries.

In order to deal with disjunctive facts one has to consider generalized logic programs i. e. arbitrary universal theories without equations as in Minker [11] and Yahya, Henschen [16]. In this case all the minimal Herbrand models of the theory are jointly generic and the Generalized Closed World Assumption has to be used. Again the prize to be paid is a more general and hence less efficient theorem prover.

We shall show that their results can be extended to arbitrary universal theories. They have term models which are h-core models and the set of all term models which are h-core models is jointly generic. A model is said to a h-core model if any homomorphism from a model into it has a right inverse. This new notion is the correct generalization of initial models. In addition, we prove a decomposition theorem which yields theories which admit initial models.

Actually, we shall use a slightly more general set up where 'pseudo term structures' replace 'term structures' as in Makowsky [9] and Volger [16]. The elements of a pseudo term structure are definable by means of existential primitive positive formulas. In this set up the structure of the results comes out more clearly. The results on universal theories can then be obtained by an obvious specialization. The question whether the characterization of Malcev [10] of the universal Horn theories can be extended to a decomposition theorem which yields universal Horn theories remains open.

In the following T will always be a L-theory for a first order language L with identity. At will denote the set of atomic formulas of L and $\Delta_{At}(A)$ will denote the corresponding diagram of a L-structure A. In addition, let $\exists^+ = \exists\bigvee\bigwedge At$ resp. $\exists\bigwedge At$ be the set of positive existential resp. positive existential primitive formulas. Dually, let $\forall^- = \forall\bigvee\bigwedge\neg At$ resp. $\forall\bigwedge\neg At$ be the set of negative universal resp. negative universal primitive formulas. For a set Σ of sentences the relation $\Rightarrow_\Sigma$ between L-structures is defined as follows: $A \Rightarrow_\Sigma B$ iff $Th(A) \cap \Sigma \subseteq Th(B)$. The corresponding equivalence relation is denoted by $\equiv_\Sigma$.

1.Canonical models of theories

The notion of a canonical model of a theory T can be made precise in several different ways. Therefore let A be a T-model.

The following notion and its weakenings express a minimality condition. A is said to be an *initial structure* for T , if for every T-model B there exists a unique homomorphism from A to B . This states that A is an initial object in the category of T-models and homomorphisms. Note that initial structures for T are unique up to isomorphism. A is said to be a *h-core model* for T if any homomorphism $h : B \to A$ from a T-model B is a retraction. This is a generalization of the notion of e-core model considered below. Note that a T-model which is a retract of a h-core model for T is a again a h-core model. A is said to be a *e-core model* for T if any embedding $e : B \to A$ of a T-model B is a retraction and hence an isomorphism (cf. Kueker [8]). A is said to be *relation minimal* for T if any bijective homomorphism $f : B \to A$ from a T-model B is an isomorphism.

The following weaker notions are related to the existence condition in the definition of initial structures. A is said to be a *prime structure* for T if for every T-model B there exists a homomorphism from A to B. Let Σ be a set of sentences. Then the *closed world assumption* for T with respect to Σ is the set $CWA_\Sigma(T) = \{\neg\sigma : \sigma \in \Sigma, T \not\vdash \sigma\}$. $CWA_{\bigwedge At}$ was introduced by Reiter in [18]. A is said to be Σ*-generic* for T , if $A \models T \cup CWA_\Sigma(T)$ i.e. for every σ in Σ we have: $A \models \sigma$ implies $T \vdash \sigma$. Finally the *generalized closed world assumption* for T with respect to Σ is the set $GCWA_\Sigma(T) = \{\neg\sigma : \sigma \in \Sigma, \text{for all } \mu \in \bigvee\Sigma : T \cup \{\neg\mu\} \not\vdash 0 \text{ implies } T \cup \{\neg\mu\} \not\vdash \sigma\}$. $GCWA_{\bigwedge At}$ was introduced by Minker in [11]. A is said to be Σ*-quasigeneric* for T , if $A \models T \cup GCWA_\Sigma(T)$.

The following notions are related to the uniqueness condition in the definition of initial structures as we shall see later. The set of T-definable elements plays a key role in this context. In particular, it contains all elements denoted by a term.

Let B be a T-model, C be a subset of B and let Φ be a set of formulas. $Tm(C, B)$ is the substructure of B

generated by C i.e. the substructure of those elements b in B for which there exist a term $t(\bar{x})$ and $\bar{c}$ in C such that $B \models t(\bar{c}) \equiv b$. $Def_T^{\exists}(C,B)$ resp. $! - Def_T^{\exists}(C,B)$ is the substructure of B of those elements b for which there exist $\mu(\bar{x},y)$ in Φ and $\bar{c}$ in C such that $B \models \mu(\bar{c},b)$ and $T \vdash \forall \bar{x}\, \exists^{\leq 1} y\, \mu(\bar{x},y)$ resp. $T \vdash \forall \bar{x}\, \exists^1 y\, \mu(\bar{x},y)$.

It can be shown that $Tm(-,B)$,$! - Def_T^{\exists^+}(-,B)$ and $Def_T^{\exists \bigwedge At}(-,B)$ define closure operators on the set of substructures of B. Clearly, we have $Tm(C,B) \leq ! - Def_T^{\exists^+}(C,B) \leq Def_T^{\exists \bigwedge At}(C,B)$.

A is said to be a *term structure* if $A = Tm(\emptyset, A)$ i.e. all elements of A are denoted by variablefree terms. In addition, a term structure A is called a *Herbrand structure* if each element of A is denoted by a unique term. A is said to be a *pseudo term structure* for T if $A = Def_T^{\exists \bigwedge At}(\emptyset, A)$. i.e. for every a in A there exists $\mu(x)$ in $\exists \bigwedge At$ such that $A \models \mu(a)$ and $T \vdash \exists^{\leq 1} \mu(x)$. A is called a *strong pseudo term structure* for T if $A = ! - Def_T^{\exists^+}(\emptyset, A)$ i.e. for every a in A there exists $\mu(x)$ in $\exists^+$ such that $A \models \mu(a)$ and $T \vdash \exists^1 x\, \mu(x)$.

The lemma below collects the known implications between the above notions:

Lemma 1. *For any T-model A we have the following implications:*

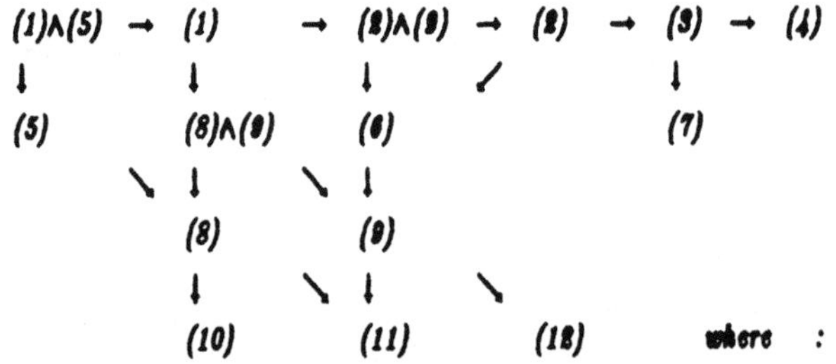

where :

(1) A is an initial structure for T *(2) A is a prime structure for T*

(3) A is $\exists \bigwedge At$-generic for T *(4) A is $\bigwedge At$-generic for T*

(5) A is a term structure

(6) A is a unique h-core model for T up to isomorphism

(7) A is $\exists \bigwedge At$-quasigeneric for T

(8) A is a strong pseudo term structure for T *(10) A is a pseudo term structure for T*

(9) A is a h-core model for T *(11) A is an e-core model for T* *(12) A is a relation minimal model for T*

Only the non obvious implications (2) → (3), (3) → (7), (1) → (8), (1) → (9), (2) → (6), (5) → (8), (8) → (11 need to be proved.

(2) → (3): For any σ in $\exists \bigwedge At$ we have to show that $A \models \sigma$ implies $T \vdash \sigma$. But (2) yields for every T-model B a homomorphism from A to B which preserves σ .

(3) → (7): T is consistent since A is a T-model. Therefore we may use the empty disjunction 0 to prove $T \nvdash \sigma$

(1) → (8): The uniqueness property for homomorphisms from A can be used to show that the following theor $T \cup \Delta_{At}(A) \cup \Delta_{At}(A') \cup \{a \equiv a'\}$ is inconsistent , where A' is a copy of A and a' is a copy of a. A compactnes argument yields a defining formula $\mu(x)$ for the element a in A . This shows $A = Def_T^{\exists \bigwedge At}(\emptyset, A)$ and hence (1) → (10). Now the implication (1) → (3) can be used to verify that A is even a strong pseudo term structure for T .

(1) → (9): Let $h : B \to A$ be a homomorphism from a T-model B . Because A is initial there exists a homomorphis $k : A \to B$ and the composition $h \cdot k$ must be the identity.

(2) → (6): Let B be another h-core model for T. There exists a homomorphism $h : A \to B$ since A is a prim structure. Then there exists a homomorphism $k : B \to A$ with $h \cdot k = id_B$ since B is a h-core model. In addition, ther exists a homomorphism $g : A \to B$ with $k \cdot g = id_A$ since A is a h-core model. Thus h is an isomorphism.

(5) → (8): Let A be a term structure. An element a of A which is denoted by a variablefree term t has $x \equiv t$ as defining formula.

(8) → (11): For a substructure B of A which is a T-model we have $! - Def_T^{\exists^+}(\emptyset, B) = ! - Def_T^{\exists^+}(\emptyset, A) = A$. Here $! - Def_T^{\exists^+}(\emptyset, A)$ is the substructure of those elements a in A for which there exists $\mu(x)$ in $\exists^+$ such that $A \models \mu(a)$ and $T \vdash \exists^1 x\, \mu(x)$. This yields $A \simeq B$ as required.

The following lemma is basic for the following results. It contains a characterization of initial structures as structures which are pseudo term structures which are $\exists \bigwedge At$-generic. Moreover, it explains the role of the pseudo term structures which are h-core models. Later on they will serve as quasiinitial structures.

Lemma 2. *Let A, B be T-models:*

(1) If A is a pseudo term structure for T then: $A \Rightarrow_{\exists \bigwedge At} B$ iff there exists a unique $h: A \to B$ iff there exists $h: A \to B$

(2) If A is a pseudo term structure for T then: A is $\exists \bigwedge At$-generic iff A is initial for T iff A is prime for T. (cf. Makowsky [9])

(3) If A is a pseudo term structure then A is rigid i.e. there is at most one endomorphism on A.

(4) If A is a pseudo term structure and B is a h-core model for T then: $A \Rightarrow_{\exists \bigwedge At} B$ iff $A \simeq B$ iff $A \equiv_{\exists \bigwedge At} B$.

To prove (1) it suffices to construct a homomorphism $h: A \to B$. By $A = Def_T^{\exists \bigwedge At}(\emptyset, A)$ there is a defining formula $\mu(x)$ in $\exists \bigwedge At$ for each element a in A. Let $h(a)$ be the unique solution of $\mu(x)$ in B, which must exist because of $A \Rightarrow_{\exists \bigwedge At} B$. This property can again be used to show that h is well defined and a homomorphism. Clearly, any homomorphism $gA \to B$ must map a onto the the uniqe solution of $\mu(x)$ in B and hence g coincides with h.

Now (2) is a consequence of (1) since A is $\exists \bigwedge At$-generic iff $A \Rightarrow_{\exists \bigwedge At} B$ holds for all T-models B. (3) follows from (1) because of $A \Rightarrow_{\exists \bigwedge At} A$. (4) follows from (1) and (3). (1) yields a homomorphism $h: A \to B$ which has a right inverse g as B is a h-core model. By (3) gh is the identity on A and thus h is an isomorphism. Let A be a h-core model and hence an e-core model for T. Whenever $A_0 = Def_T^{\exists \bigwedge At}(\emptyset, A)$ is again a T-model then A is isomorphic to A_0. Hence we obtain the following corollary of lemma 2.

Corollary 3. *Let T be a theory whose class of models is closed under $Def_T^{\exists \bigwedge At}$:*

(1) If A is a h-core model for T then A is also a pseudo term structure for T

(2) If A,B are h-core models for T then: $A \Rightarrow_{\exists \bigwedge At} B$ iff $A \simeq B$

2.Generic models and irreducible components of theories

The characterization of theories which admit generic structures makes use of the following irreducibility property of a theory. A theory T is called *irreducible with respect to* Σ (cf.Pinter [12]) if for all $(\alpha_i : i = 1, \ldots, n)$ in Σ we have : $T \vdash \bigvee(: \alpha_i : i = 1, \ldots, n)$ implies $T \vdash \alpha_i$ for some i in I.

Proposition 4. *For any theory T the following are equivalent:*

(1) T admits a model which is Σ-generic

(2) T is irreducible with respect to Σ .

The implication (1) → (2) is obvious. The converse implication is proved as follows. The set $T \cup \Delta^-$ is consistent, where $\Delta^- = \{\neg\delta : \delta \in \Sigma, T \nvdash \delta\}$. Otherwise we would have $T \vdash \delta'_1 \vee \ldots \vee \delta'_m$ with $\delta'_1, \ldots, \delta'_m$ in Δ^-. By assumption this implies $T \vdash \delta'$ for some j and hence $\delta'_j \in T$, a contradiction. But any model B of $T \cup \Delta^-$ will be Σ-generic.

This motivates the introduction of the irreducible components of a theory as in Pinter [12]. They can used to obtain a decomposition of the theory into irreducible theories.

Therefore let Σ be a set of sentences closed under disjunctions and conjunctions. A set P of sentences is called an *irreducible ideal of* Σ if P is a deductively closed subset of Σ such that $(\varphi_1 \vee \varphi_2) \in P$ implies $\varphi_1 \in P$ or $\varphi_2 \in P$. A set P of sentences is called an Σ-*component* of a theory T if P is a minimal irreducible ideal of Σ extending $T_\Sigma = T \cap \Sigma$. We shall consider the cases $\Sigma = \exists^+$ and $\Sigma = \forall^-$ whereas Pinter in [12] considered the cases $\Sigma = \exists$ and $\Sigma = \forall$. The reason for this is that we want to consider homomorphisms rather than embeddings between structures. For $P \subseteq \exists^+$ we define as in Pinter [12] $^*P$ as the set of α in $\forall^-$ such that $\neg\alpha$ does not belong to P. Similarly, for $Q \subseteq \forall^-$ we define $^*Q$ as the set of β in $\exists^+$ such that $\neg\beta$ does not belong to Q.

The following lemma on properties of $\exists^+$-components is a special case of a general lemma on Σ-components (cf. Pinter [12]).

Lemma 5. *Let P resp. Q be an irreducible ideal of $\exists^+$ resp. $\forall^-$:*

(1) $^*P$ resp. $^*Q$ is an irreducible ideal of $\forall^-$ resp. $\exists^+$.
(2) $^*Q \subseteq P$ iff $^*P \subseteq Q$, and hence $^{**}P = P$ and $^{**}Q = Q$.
(3) $(T \cap \exists^+) \subseteq P$ iff $T \cup {}^*P$ is consistent , and dually $(T \cap \forall^-) \subseteq Q$ iff $T \cup {}^*Q$ is consistent .
(4) P is an $\exists^+$-component of T iff $^*P$ is a maximal irreducible ideal of $\forall^-$ consistent with T .
(5) If P is an $\exists^+$-component then $T \cup {}^*P \vdash P$ and hence $T \cup {}^*P \cup P$ is consistent.

(1) To prove that $^*P$ is deductively closed assume $^*P \vdash \alpha \in \forall^-$. Then there exist $\delta_1, \ldots, \delta_m \in (\forall^- - P)$ such that $\delta_1 \wedge \ldots \wedge \delta_m \vdash \alpha$ and hence $\neg\alpha \vdash \neg\delta_1 \vee \ldots \vee \neg\delta_m$. If $\alpha \notin {}^*P$ i. e. $\neg\alpha \in P$ then $\neg\delta_1 \vee \ldots \vee \neg\delta_m \in P$ since P is deductively closed. However this contradicts the irreducibility of P . To prove the irreducibility of $^*P$ assume $(\alpha_1 \vee \alpha_2) \in {}^*P$ and hence $\neg(\alpha_1 \vee \alpha_2) = (\neg\alpha_1 \wedge \neg\alpha_2) \notin P$. If $\alpha_1 \notin {}^*P$, $\alpha_2 \notin {}^*P$ then $\neg\alpha_1, \neg\alpha_2 \in P$ and hence $(\neg\alpha_1 \wedge \neg\alpha_2) \in P$, a contradiction. A dual proof yields the result for $^*Q$.

(2) If we assume $^*Q \subseteq P$ then $\alpha \in {}^*P$ implies $\neg\alpha \notin P$ and hence $\neg\alpha \notin {}^*Q$ and finally $\alpha \in Q$ as required. A dual proof yields the other implication. Applying this result to $^*P \subseteq {}^*P$ yields $^{**}P \subseteq P$. To prove $P \subseteq {}^{**}P$ assume $\beta \in P$. This implies $\neg\beta \notin {}^*P$ and hence $\beta \in {}^{**}P$. The proof for $Q = {}^{**}Q$ is analogous.

(3) First assume $(T \cap \exists^+) \subseteq P$ and $T \cup {}^*P \vdash 0$. By compactness there exist $\neg\alpha_1, \ldots, \neg\alpha_n \notin P$ such that $T \cup \{\alpha_1, \ldots, \alpha_n\} \vdash 0$ and hence $T \vdash \neg(\alpha_1 \wedge \ldots \wedge \alpha_n) = (\neg\alpha_1 \vee \ldots \vee \neg\alpha_n) \in (T \cap \exists^+) \subseteq P$. This implies $\neg\alpha_i \in P$ for some i , a contradiction. — Now assume $T \cup {}^*P \nvdash 0$ and $(T \cap \exists^+) - P \neq \emptyset$. Then there exists $\alpha \in (T \cap \exists^+) - P$. This implies $\neg\alpha \in {}^*P$ and $\alpha \in T$ and thus $T \cup {}^*P \vdash 0$, a contradiction. The dual result follows by dualization.

(4) Let P be an $\exists^+$-component of T . By (3) we know already that $T \cup {}^*P$ is consistent. Now let $T \cup Q$ be consistent with $^*P \subseteq Q$. Then by (2) and (3) we obtain $(T \cap \exists^+) \subseteq {}^*Q \subseteq P$. By the minimality of P we have $^*Q = P$ and thus $Q = {}^*P$, as required. — Now let $^*P$ be a maximal irreducible ideal of $\forall^-$ consistent with T . By (3) we know already $(T \cap \exists^+) \subseteq P$. Now assume $(T \cap \exists^+) \subseteq Q \subseteq P$. Then by (2) and (3) we see that $^*P \subseteq {}^*Q$ and $T \cup Q$ is consistent. By the maximality of Q we have $^*P = {}^*Q$ and thus $P = Q$,as required.

(5) If $T \cup {}^*P \not\vdash P$ then there exists β in P such that $T \cup {}^*P \not\vdash \beta$. Hence $\neg\beta \notin {}^*P$ and $T \cup {}^*P \cup \{\neg\beta\}$ is consistent. Let $\mathcal{B}$ be a model of $T \cup {}^*P \cup \{\neg\beta\}$. Then $Q = Th(\mathcal{B}) \cap \forall^-$ is an irreducible ideal in $\forall^-$ consistent with T satisfying ${}^*P \subseteq Q$. By (4) we conclude ${}^*P = Q$. This implies $\neg\beta \in {}^*P$ and hence $\beta \notin P$, a contradiction.

As a consequence we obtain the following characterization of theories with exactly one $\exists^+$-component.

Lemma 6. *For a theory T the following are equivalent:*

(1) T has exactly one $\exists^+$-component
(2) $T \cap \exists^+$ is a $\exists^+$-component
(3) T is irreducible w.r.t. $\exists^+$.

The implication (2) → (1) is obvious. To prove the converse take $\epsilon \in Q - (T \cap \exists^+)$ with $\epsilon \in \exists^+$ where Q is the uniqe $\exists^+$-component of T. Then there exists $\mathcal{B}$ with $\mathcal{B} \models T \cup \{\neg\epsilon\}$ since $T \cup \{\neg\epsilon\}$ is consistent. Then $Th(\mathcal{B}) \cap \forall^-$ is an irreducible ideal in $\forall^-$ containing $\neg\epsilon$. But by lemma 5 ${}^*Q$ is the unique maximal irreducible ideal in $\forall^-$ consistent with T. Thus we have $\neg\epsilon \in {}^*Q$ and hence $\epsilon \notin Q$, a contradiction. The equivalence of (2) and (3) is obvious by the definitions.

As a consequence we obtain a first decomposition result for theories.

Proposition 7. *Let $(Q_i : i \in I)$ be the set of $\exists^+$-components of T. Then we have the following results:*

(1) The theories $T \cup {}^*Q_i$ and $T \cup Q_i$ are irreducible with respect to $\exists^+$
(2) $Mod(T \cup Q_i) \supseteq Mod(T \cup {}^*Q_i)$ for $i \in I$ and $Mod(T) = \bigcup_{i \in I} Mod(T \cup Q_i) \supseteq \bigcup_{i \in I} Mod(T \cup {}^*Q_i)$
(3) $Mod(T \cup {}^*Q_{i_1}) \cap Mod(T \cup {}^*Q_{i_2}) = \emptyset$ for $i_1 \neq i_2$

To prove the first part of (1) take ϵ_1, ϵ_2 in $\exists^+$ with $T \cup {}^*Q_i \vdash \epsilon_1 \vee \epsilon_2$. Now assume $T \cup {}^*Q_i \not\vdash \epsilon_k$ for $k = 1, 2$. Then we have $\neg\epsilon_k \in {}^*Q_i$ and hence $\epsilon_k \notin Q_i$ for $k = 1, 2$ by the maximality of ${}^*Q_i$ from (4) in lemma 5. However, we have $\neg(\epsilon_1 \vee \epsilon_2) \notin {}^*Q_i$ and hence $(\epsilon_1 \vee \epsilon_2) \in Q_i$. This contradicts the irreducibility of Q_i.

To prove the second part of (1) take ϵ_1, ϵ_2 in $\exists^+$ with $T \cup Q_i \vdash \epsilon_1 \vee \epsilon_2$. Because of $T \cup {}^*Q_i \vdash Q_i$ in lemma 5 this implies $T \cup {}^*Q_i \vdash \epsilon_1 \vee \epsilon_2$. Now assume $T \cup Q_i \not\vdash \epsilon_k$ for $k = 1, 2$. Then we have $\epsilon_k \notin Q_i$ and hence $\neg\epsilon_k \in {}^*Q_i$ for $k = 1, 2$. But this implies $T \cup {}^*Q_i \vdash (\neg\epsilon_1 \wedge \neg\epsilon_2) = \neg(\epsilon_1 \vee \epsilon_2)$, a contradiction.

The inclusions $Mod(T) \supseteq Mod(T \cup Q_i) \supseteq Mod(T \cup {}^*Q_i)$ follow from $T \cup {}^*Q_i \vdash Q_i$ due to (5) in lemma 5. This yields the easy inclusions in (2). It remains to show that each T-model $\mathcal{A}$ is a model of some Q_i. Note that $Th(\mathcal{A}) \cap \exists^+$ is an irreducible ideal in $\exists^+$ containing $T \cap \exists^+$. An application of Zorn's lemma yields a minimal irreducible ideal Q of $\exists^+$ satisfying $T \cap \exists^+ \subseteq Q \subseteq Th(\mathcal{A}) \cap \exists^+$. Then $Q = Q_i$ for some i and $\mathcal{A} \models Q_i$.

$T \cup {}^*Q_{i_1} \cup {}^*Q_{i_2}$ is inconsistent by the maximality of ${}^*Q_{i_1}$. This yields the statement (3)

3. Semantical characterization of the generalized closed world assumption

The lemma below explains the usefulness of the pseudo term structures and the operator $Def_T^{\exists \wedge At}(-, \mathcal{B})$ (cf. Bacsich [1-3], Volger [14]). It follows by a straightforward diagram argument.

Lemma 8. *$b \in Def_T^{\exists \wedge At}(C, \mathcal{B})$ iff for all T-models D and homomorphisms f_1, $f_2 : \mathcal{B} \to D$ with $f_1|C = f_2|C$ we have $f_1(b) = f_2(b)$. In particular $\mathcal{B} = Def_T^{\exists \wedge At}(\emptyset, \mathcal{B})$ iff there is at most one homomorphism into any other T-model.*

In the following we shall restrict our attention to theories T whose class of models is closed under the operator $Def_T^{\exists}\bigwedge^{At}(-,-)$. It should be recalled that under this assumption each h-core model for T is also a pseudo term structure for T (cf. (1) in lemma C). The following results from Volger [14] provide a syntactical characterization of this assumption and consequences of it.

Lemma 9. *Let T be an arbitrary theory:*

(1) The class of T-models is closed under $Def_T^{\exists}\bigwedge^{At}$ iff it is closed under equalizers of homomorphisms.

(2) If the class of T-models is closed under $! - Def_T^{\exists^+}$ then it is closed under equalizers and it has the intersection property i.e. the non-empty intersection of substructures of a given T-model which are T-models is again a T-model.

(3) If the class of T-models is closed under equalizers of homomorphisms then it is closed under filtered limits and colimits of homomorphisms.

(4) The class of T-models is closed under filtered colimits of homomorphisms iff the class of T-models is closed under $\exists^+$- substructures iff T can be axiomatized by a set Δ of sentences of the form $\forall \mathbf{x}\,(\alpha(\mathbf{x}) \rightarrow \exists \mathbf{y}\,\beta(\mathbf{x},\mathbf{y}))$ with $\alpha(\mathbf{x}),\beta(\mathbf{x},\mathbf{y})$ in $\bigvee\bigwedge At$.

(5) The class of T-models is closed under $Def_T^{\exists}\bigwedge^{At}$ iff T can be axiomatized by a set Δ of sentences of the form $\forall \mathbf{x}\,(\alpha(\mathbf{x}) \rightarrow \exists \mathbf{y}\,\beta(\mathbf{x},\mathbf{y}))$ with $\alpha(\mathbf{x}),\beta(\mathbf{x},\mathbf{y})$ in $\bigvee\bigwedge At$ and for any such axiom there exist $\mu_1(\mathbf{x},\mathbf{y})\ldots\mu_k(\mathbf{x},\mathbf{y})$ in $\exists\bigwedge At$ such that $T \vdash \forall \mathbf{x}\,(\alpha(\mathbf{x}) \rightarrow \exists \mathbf{y}\,(\beta(\mathbf{x},\mathbf{y}) \wedge \bigvee_{i=1}^{k} \mu_i(\mathbf{x},\mathbf{y})))$ and $T \vdash \forall \mathbf{x}\,\exists^{\leq 1}\mathbf{y}\,\mu_i(\mathbf{x},\mathbf{y})$

Note that A is a $\exists^+$-substructure of B iff the inclusion preserves and reflects the validity of formulas from $\exists^+$. — The proofs of (1),(3),(4),(5) can be found in Volger [14]. The first claim in (2) is due to $! - Def_T^{\exists^+}(C, A) \leq Def_T^{\exists}\bigwedge^{At}(C, A)$. To prove the second claim in (2) one verifies $! - Def_T^{\exists^+}(N, M) \leq N$ for the intersection N of the T-models N_i which are substructures of a given T-model M. The unique solutions a_i in N_i must coincide and yield a solution a in N since they all lie in M.

The following result shows the existence of sufficiently many h-core models for a theory whose class of models is closed under equalisers.

Proposition 10. *If $Mod(T)$ is closed under equalisers then for every T-model B there exist a h-core model A of T and a homomorphism $h: A \rightarrow B$. If B is a pseudo term structure for T then h is surjective.*

The proof has two parts. First we show that for each T-model B there exist a relation minimal T-model B_r on B such that the identity is a homomorphism. This generalizes a result of Bossu and Siegel in [4].

Let $(B_\lambda : \lambda \in \Lambda)$ be the set of T-models on B such that the identity is a homomorphism into B. The family may be ordered by the requirement that the identity is a homomorphism. A minimal element with respect to this ordering is a relation minimal structure for T.

By an application of Zorn's lemma it suffices to show that each totally ordered subfamily $(B_\lambda : \lambda \in \Lambda')$ has a lower bound in the family. Let $\tilde{B}$ be the structure whose relations are the intersection of the relations of the structures in the subfamily. With the help of a transfinite induction it can be shown that $\tilde{B}$ can be represented as the limit of a descending chain of bijective homomorphisms involving a subfamily of the subfamily considered. Our assumption on T implies by lemma 9 that $\tilde{B}$ is again a T-model, as required.

Applying the first part to $B_0 = Def_T^{\exists}\bigwedge^{At}(\emptyset, B)$ we obtain a relation minimal pseudo term structure B_0 for T and an injective homomorphism from B_0 to B. Note that the relation minimal structure will be again a pseudo term structure since the identity is a homomorphism. For the following we fix such a structure B_0.

Now let $(\mathcal{A}_\lambda : \lambda \in \Lambda)$ be the set of relation minimal pseudo term structures $\mathcal{A}_\lambda$ for T which posess a homomorphism $r_\lambda : \mathcal{A}_\lambda \to \mathcal{A}_0 = \mathcal{B}_0$. Note that the homomorphism r_λ is uniquely determined since $\mathcal{A}_\lambda$ is a pseudo term structure. Let $PsTm(T)$ be the set of formulas of the form $\mu(x)$ in $\exists \bigwedge At$ satisfying $T \vdash \exists^{\leq 1} x\, \mu(x)$. The sets A_λ can be represented as quotients of the form Z_λ/Q_λ with canonical projections $q_\lambda : Z_\lambda \to A_\lambda$, where Z_λ is a subset of $PsTm(T)$. Clearly we have $r_\lambda \cdot q_\lambda = q_0|Z_\lambda$. The family is ordered by factorization i. e. by inclusion of the equivalence relations. A minimal element $\mathcal{A}_{\lambda^*}$ with respect to this ordering is a h-core model for T. To see this let $h : \mathcal{C} \to \mathcal{A}_{\lambda^*}$ be a homomorphism from a T-model $\mathcal{C}$. By the first part of the proof there exists a relation minimal pseudo term structure $\mathcal{C}'$ for T and an injective homomorphism $i : \mathcal{C}' \to \mathcal{C}$. Thus $\mathcal{C}'$ must be of the form $\mathcal{A}_\lambda$ and we have $h \cdot i = r_{\lambda,\lambda^*}$. By the minimality $h \cdot i$ is an isomorphism and hence h is right invertible.

Again by an application of Zorn's lemma it suffices to show that each totally ordered subfamily $(\mathcal{A}_\lambda : \lambda \in \Lambda')$ has a lower bound in the family. Let $\tilde{\mathcal{A}}$ be the structure whose equivalence relation $\tilde{Q}$ is the intersection of the equivalence relations of the structures in the subfamily. With the help of a transfinite induction it can be shown that $\tilde{\mathcal{A}}$ can be represented as the limit of a descending chain of homomorphisms involving a subfamily of the subfamily considered. Our assumption on T implies by lemma 9 that $\tilde{\mathcal{A}}$ is again a T-model, as required.

The following results generalize results on equation free universal theories in Yahya,Henschen [16]. The first result states that the set of h-core models of a theory are jointly $\exists \bigwedge At$-generic for the theory (cf. lemma 1 in Yahya,Henschen [16]).

Proposition 11. *Let T be a theory whose class of models is closed under equalizers and let ϵ be a sentence in $\exists \bigwedge At$. Then the following are equivalent:*

(1) $T \vdash \epsilon$

(2) For all h-core models $\mathcal{B}$ for T we have: $\mathcal{B} \models \epsilon$

The implication (1) → (2) is obvious. To prove (2) → (1) let $\mathcal{B}$ be an arbitrary T-model. Then by proposition 10 there exists a h-core model $\mathcal{A}$ for T together with a homomorphism $h : \mathcal{A} \to \mathcal{B}$. By assumption we have $\mathcal{A} \models \epsilon$ and hence $\mathcal{B} \models \epsilon$, as required.

As a consequence we obtain the following characterization of theories which admit initial structures (cf. theorem 9 in Yahya,Henschen [16]).

Proposition 12. *Let T be a consistent theory whose class of models is closed under equalizers . Then the following are equivalent:*

(1) T is irreducible with respect to $\exists \bigwedge At$

(2) T admits a $\exists \bigwedge At$-generic model

(3) T admits an initial structure

(4) T admits up to isomorphism exactly one h-core model

The equivalence of (1) and (2) is due to lemma 4. To prove the implication (2) → (3) let $\mathcal{A}$ be an $\exists \bigwedge At$-generic model of T . Then by the assumption on T the structure $\mathcal{A}_0 = Def_T^{\exists \bigwedge At}(\emptyset, \mathcal{A})$ is a pseudo term structure which is a T-model and which is again $\exists \bigwedge At$-generic. Hence $\mathcal{A}_0$ is an initial structure for T by (2) in lemmma 2. The implication (3) → (4) follows from the implication (1) → (6) in lemma 1. The implication (4) → (2) follows by proposition 11 since there is only one h-core model for T .

The following proposition yields a semantical characterisation of the generalised closed world assumption by means of h-core models which are also pseudo term structures (cf. theorem 14 in Yahya,Henschen [16])

Proposition 13. *Let T be a consistent theory whose class of models is closed under equalisers and let ϵ be a sentence in $\exists\bigwedge At$. Then the following are equivalent:*

(1) There exists a h-core model A for T such that $A \models \epsilon$

(2) $\neg\epsilon$ does not belong to $GCWA_{\exists\bigwedge At}(T)$ i. e. there exists $\mu \in \exists^+$ such that $T \cup \{\neg\mu\} \nvdash 0$ and $T \cup \{\neg\mu\} \nvdash \epsilon$

(3) $\neg\epsilon$ does not belong to the intersection of all maximal irreducible ideals of $\forall^-$ consistent with T i. e. there exists an $\exists^+$-component P of T such that $\epsilon \in P$

(1) → (2): If A is the only h-core model for T then we have $T \vdash \epsilon$ by proposition 11. Thus we may use $\mu = 0$ to get (2). Otherwise let $(A_i : i < \alpha)$ be a set of representatives of the other h-core models for T. By (5) in lemma 2 we have $A_i \not\Rightarrow_{\exists\bigwedge At} A$ for $i < \alpha$. Hence there exist $\mu_i \in \exists\bigwedge At$ such that $A_i \models \mu_i$ and $A \models \neg\mu_i$ for $i > \alpha$. By proposition 11 we can conclude $T \vdash \epsilon \vee \mu$ where $\mu = \bigvee_{i<\alpha} \mu_i$. By a compactness argument we obtain a finite subdisjunction μ' of μ such that $T \vdash \epsilon \vee \mu'$. But we have $T \nvdash \mu'$ because of $A \models \neg\mu'$.

(2) → (1): Let B be a model of $T \cup \{\neg\mu\}$. By proposition 10 there exists a h-core model A for T together with a homomorphism $h : A \to B$. This yields $A \models \neg\mu$ and hence $A \models \epsilon$ because of $T \vdash \mu \vee \epsilon$.

(2) → (3): Let $^*P$ be a maximal irreducible ideal of $\forall^-$ consistent with T and containing $\neg\mu$. By proposition 5 we know that P is a $\exists^+$-component of T which satisfies $T \cup {}^*P \vdash P$. Assuming $\epsilon \notin P$ we obtain $\neg\epsilon \in {}^*P$ and hence $T \cup {}^*P \vdash \neg\epsilon$ contradicting $T \cup {}^*P \vdash \epsilon$. Therefore we have $\epsilon \in P$, as required.

(3) → (2): By proposition 5 we know $T \cup {}^*P \vdash P$ and hence $T \cup {}^*P \vdash \epsilon$. By compactness there exist $\mu_1, \ldots, \mu_k \in \exists^+$ such that $\mu_1, \ldots, \mu_k \notin P$ and $T \cup \{\neg\mu\} \vdash \epsilon$ where $\mu = \mu_1 \vee \ldots \vee \mu_k$. Moreover, $T \cup \{\neg\mu\}$ is consistent since $T \cup {}^*P$ is consistent.

The following proposition can be considered as a generalization of the syntactical characterization of initial structures in (2) in lemma 2. It yields a syntactical characterization of h-core models which are pseudo term structures (cf. theorem 16 in Yahya,Henschen [16]).

Proposition 14. *Let T be a consistent theory whose class of models is closed under equalisers and let A be a T-model. Then the following are equivalent:*

(1) A is a h-core model for T

(2) A is a pseudo term structure for T which is $\exists\bigwedge At$-quasigeneric for T i. e. $A \models T \cup GCWA_{\exists\bigwedge At}(T)$

$\neg$(2) → $\neg$(1): There exists $\epsilon \in \exists\bigwedge At$ such that $\neg\epsilon \in GCWA_{\exists\bigwedge At}(T)$ and $A \models \epsilon$. By proposition 13 this yields $\neg\epsilon \notin GCWA_{\exists\bigwedge At}(T)$, a contradiction.

(2) → (1): Assume that A is not a h-core model for T. By proposition 10 there exists a h-core model A_0 for T together with a homomorphism $h : A_0 \to A$. This implies $A_0 \Rightarrow_{\exists\bigwedge At} A$. By assumption A is not a retract of A_0 because a retract of a h-core model for T is again a h-core model. Moreover, we have $A \not\Rightarrow_{\exists\bigwedge At} A_0$. Otherwise lemma 2 would yield a homomorphism $g : A \to A_0$ such that $g \cdot h$ is the identity on A_0 since there is at most one homomorphism from A_0. Since embeddings between pseudoterm structures are isomorphisms the embdeding h must be an isomorphism, a contradiction. Thus there exists $\epsilon_0 \in \exists\bigwedge At$ such that $A \models \epsilon_0$ and $A_0 \models \neg\epsilon_0$. Let $(A_i : 0 < i < \alpha)$ the family of h-core models for T which satisfy $A_i \models \epsilon_0$. By (5) in lemma 2 $A_i \not\cong A_0$ for $i \neq 0$ yields $\epsilon_i \in \exists\bigwedge At$ with $A_0 \models \epsilon_i$ and $A_i \models \neg\epsilon_i$.

Now we claim $\neg\epsilon' \in GCWA_{\exists\bigwedge At}(T)$ for a finite subdisjunction ϵ' of $\epsilon = \bigwedge_{i<\alpha} \epsilon_i$. If this is not the case there exists by compactness $\mu \in \exists^+$ such that $T \vdash \mu \vee \epsilon$ and $T \not\vdash \mu$. As a consequence we have $A_i \models \mu$ for all $i < \alpha$. As all other h-core models B for T satisfy $B \models \epsilon_0$ we obtain by proposition 11 then $T \vdash \mu$, a contradiction. However, $\neg\epsilon' \in GCWA_{\exists\bigwedge At}(T)$ implies $A \models \neg\epsilon'$ and hence $A_0 \models \neg\epsilon'$. In addition, $A_0 \models \epsilon_i$ for $i \neq 0$ yields $A \models \epsilon_i$ and hence by definition of ϵ finally $A \models \neg\epsilon_0$, a contradiction, as required.

We want to add two characterizations of $CWA_{\exists\bigwedge At}(T)$ and $GCWA_{\exists\bigwedge At}(T)$ as maximal extensions of T.

Proposition 15. *Let T be a theory such that $CWA_{\exists\bigwedge At}(T)$ is consistent. Then $T \cup CWA_{\exists\bigwedge At}(T)$ is the maximal consistent extension of T by sentences from $\forall^-$ which yields no new sentences from $\exists^+$ i. e.*

(1) $CWA_{\exists\bigwedge At}(T) \subseteq \forall^-$
(2) For all ϵ in $\exists^+$: $T \cup CWA_{\exists\bigwedge At}(T) \vdash \epsilon$ implies $T \vdash \epsilon$
(3) For all α in $\forall^-$: $\alpha \in (\forall^- - CWA_{\exists\bigwedge At}(T))$ implies $T \cup CWA_{\exists\bigwedge At}(T) \cup \{\alpha\} \vdash 0$

(1) follows from the definition. (2) is obvious since a T-model is $\exists\bigwedge At$-generic iff it is a model of $T \cup CWA_{\exists\bigwedge At}(T)$. To prove (3) note that α satisfies $T \vdash \neg\alpha$ and hence $T \cup \{\alpha\} \vdash 0$.

Proposition 16. *Let T be a theory which is consistent and whose class of models is closed under equalizers. Then $T \cup GCWA_{\exists\bigwedge At}(T)$ is the maximal extension of T by sentences from $\forall^-$ which yields no new sentences from $\exists^+$ i. e.*

(1) $GCWA_{\exists\bigwedge At}(T) \subseteq \forall^-$
(2) For all ϵ in $\exists^+$: $T \cup GCWA_{\exists\bigwedge At}(T) \vdash \epsilon$ implies $T \vdash \epsilon$
(3) For all α in $\forall^-$: if $\alpha \in (\forall^- - GCWA_{\exists\bigwedge At}(T))$ then there exists ϵ in $\exists^+$ such that $T \not\vdash \epsilon$ and $T \cup GCWA_{\exists\bigwedge At}(T) \cup \{\alpha\} \vdash \epsilon$

(1) follows from the definition. To prove (2) note that $T \cup GCWA_{\exists\bigwedge At}(T)$ is consistent by proposition 10 and theorem 14. Then the claim follows by an application of proposition 11. (3) follows again from the definition of $GCWA_{\exists\bigwedge At}(T)$.

4.A stronger decomposition result

For theories T whose class of models are closed under equalizers we shall prove a stronger decomposition result. The lemma below yields a one-to-one correspondence between the h-core models of T and the duals of the $\exists^+$-components of T.

Lemma 17. *Let T be a theory whose class of models is closed under equalizers and Q be an $\exists^+$-component of T and let A a model of $T \cup {}^*Q$:*

(1) The class of models of $T \cup {}^*Q$ is closed under equalizers
(2) A is h-core model for T iff A is h-core model for $T \cup Q$ iff A is h-core model for $T \cup {}^*Q$
(3) $Mod(T \cup {}^*Q)$ contains up to isomorphism exactly one h-core model for T

(1) follows from ${}^*Q \subseteq \forall^-$. The easy implications in (2) follow from $T \cup {}^*Q \vdash T \cup Q \vdash T$. Now let A be a h-core model for $T \cup {}^*Q$ and let $h : B \to A$ be a homomorphism from a T-model B. But B is also a model of ${}^*Q \subseteq \forall^-$.

This yields the required right inverse for the remaining implication in (2). By proposition 10 the class $Mod(T \cup {}^*Q)$ contains a h-core model. Moreover, it is unique up to isomorphism by the propositions 7 and 12. This proves (3).

We need another assumption on the theory T. A theory T is said to have the *joint source property* if for any T-models A_1, A_2 there exist a T-model B and homomorphisms $f_1 : B \to A_1$, $f_2 : B \to A_2$. Clearly, any theory which admits an initial structure has the joint source property. In addition, any theory whose class of models is closed under binary products has the joint source property. Moreover, if a theory has the joint source property then is irreducible with respect to $\exists \bigwedge At$.

A theory T is said to have the *conditional joint source property* if for any T-models A_1, A_2, C and homomorphisms $h_1 : A_1 \to C$, $h_2 : A_2 \to C$ there exist a T-model B and homomorphisms $f_1 : B \to A_1$, $f_2 : B \to A_2$. A dual of the latter property for embeddings rather than homomorphisms was used in Pinter [12]. Clearly, a theory whose class of models is closed under binary pullbacks of homomorphisms has the conditional source property. The next proposition shows that the models of $T \cup Q$ for an $\exists^+$-component Q belong to the same connected component of the class of T-models.

Proposition 18. *Let T be a theory whose class of models is closed under equalizers and Q be an $\exists^+$-component of T and let A be a h-core model for $T \cup {}^*Q$:*

(1) For every model B of $T \cup {}^*Q$ there exists a homomorphism $h : A \to B$. Hence the $T \cup {}^*Q$ has the joint source property.

(2) For every model C of $T \cup Q$ there exists a homomorphism $h : A \to C'$ and an elementary embedding $f : C \to C'$. Hence $Mod(T \cup Q)$ is connected.

To prove (1) apply proposition 10 to the structure B and then use (2) of lemma 17. The proof of (2) relies on the following observation. $C \models T \cup Q$ implies $(Th(C) \cap \forall^-) \subseteq {}^*Q$ since $C \models \alpha \in \forall^-$ implies $\neg\alpha \notin Q$ and hence $\alpha \in {}^*Q$. However, this yields $A \models T \cup (Th(C) \cap \forall^-)$. In this situation a compactness argument yields a homomorphism $h : A \to C'' \equiv C$ and hence the required result.

The following lemma will be used in the stronger decomposition theorem.

Lemma 19. *Let T be a theory whose class of models is closed under equalisers and which has the conditional joint source property. In addition, let Q_1,Q_2 be $\exists^+$-components of T and let A_1 resp. A_2 be a h-core model for $T \cup {}^*Q_1$ resp. $T \cup {}^*Q_2$. Then we have:*

(1) If there exists a T-model B and homomorphisms $h_1 : A_1 \to B$, $h_2 : A_2 \to B$ then $Q_1 = Q_2$

(2) If A_1 and A_2 are connected by T-models i. e. there exist T-models $B_1, \ldots, B_n$ and homomorphisms $f_1, \ldots, f_{n+1}$ such that $A_1 \xrightarrow{f_1} B_1 \xleftarrow{f_2} \cdots \xleftarrow{f_n} B_n \xleftarrow{f_{n+1}} A_2$ then $Q_1 = Q_2$

(1) An application of the joint source property of T yields a T-model C and homomorphisms $f_1 : C \to A_1$, $f_2 : C \to A_2$. Then $C \models {}^*Q_1$ because of ${}^*Q_1 \subseteq \forall^-$. Since A_2 is an h-core model for T by (2) in Lemma 17 there exist an embedding $e_2 : A_2 \to C$ and thus $A_2 \models {}^*Q_1$. This implies ${}^*Q_1 = {}^*Q_2$ by the maximality of ${}^*Q_1$.

(2) Applying proposition 10 we obtain h-core models $C_1, \ldots, C_n$ and for $T \cup {}^*Q_1$ and homomorphisms $f_1 : C_1 \to B_1, \ldots, C_n \to B_n$. Now iterated application of part (1) yields the desired result.

The decomposition result below should be compared with the result in Pinter [12] for theories with the intersection property.

Proposition 20. *Let T be a theory whose class of models is closed under equalizers and which has the conditional joint source property. In addition, let $(Q_i : i \in I)$ be the set of $\exists^+$-components of T and let $(A_i : i \in I)$ be a family of T-models such that A_i is a h-core model for $T \cup {}^*Q_i$ for $i \in I$. Then we have:*

(1) $Mod(T \cup Q_i)$ and $Comp_T(A_i)$, the connected component of A_i in $Mod(T)$, coincide.

(2) $Mod(T)$ is the disjoint union of the connected components $Mod(T \cup Q_i)$ for $i \in I$.

(3) The class of models of $T \cup Q_i$ is closed under equalizers for $i \in I$.

(4) A_i is an initial structure for $T \cup Q_i$. In particular, $T \cup Q_i$ has the joint source property.

In particular this result applies to theories whose class of models is closed under connected limits i. e. equalizers and arbitrary pullbacks

(1) and (2) are immediate consequences of proposition 7 and the previous lemma. (3) follows from (1) of lemma 17, whereas (4) is obtained by an application of proposition 12 to (3) in lemma 17.

It is well known that a theory T is universal iff its class of models is closed under substructures i. e. closed under the operator $Tm(-,-)$. The previous results can be specialized to results about universal theories as follows. The results so far remain true if we replace everywhere

$\exists \bigwedge At$	by	$\bigwedge At$
$\exists^+$	by	$\bigvee \bigwedge At$
$\forall^-$	by	$\bigvee \bigwedge \neg At$
pseudo term structure	by	term structure
equalizer of homomorphisms	by	substructure

The results about universal theories can be specialized to the results of Yahya,Henschen [16] about universal theories without equations if term structures are replaced by Herbrand structures and h-core structures are replaced by relation minimal structures. Note that the class of models of theories which have equation free axioms are closed under structures induced by inverse images along surjective maps.

5.Summary and comments

We have shown that the results of Yahya,Henschen in [16] on the generalized closed world assumption for universal theories without equations can be extended to universal theories and even theories whose class of models are closed under equalizers. The minimal Herbrand structures have to replaced by term structures respectively pseudo term structures which are h-core models. If there is up to isomorphism just one such structure it is initial.

In addition, we have proved a decomposition theorem in the style of Pinter [12] for these theories. They can be decomposed into theories which admit term structures respectively structures which are initial. The role of the conditional joint source property in this result should be clarified.

The following question remains open. Malcev in [10] has characterized universal Horn theories as theories for which all consistent extensions of the theory by new facts admit term structures which are initial. The corresponding more general characterization was proved in Makowsky [9] resp. Volger [15]. This yields theories whose class of models are closed under arbitrary limits. One might ask if the decomposition theorem could extended to yield a decomposition into universal Horn theories resp. limit theories.

It should be possible to transform the results in this paper into results concerning embedding rather than homomorphisms. The resulting decomposition theorem should be the result on convex theories in Pinter [12].

References:

[1] Bacsich,P.D.: Defining algebraic elements, J.Symb.Logic. 38(1973), 93–101

[2] Bacsich,P.D.: Model theory of epimorphisms, Canad.Math.Bull. 17 (1974), 471–477

[3] Bacsich.P.D.,Rowlands-Hughes,D.: Syntactic characterisations of amalgamations, convexity and related properties, J.Symb.Logic 39(1974), 433–451

[4] Bossu,G.,Siegel,P.: Saturation, nonmonotonic reasoning and the closed world assumption, Artificial Intelligence 25(1985), 13–63

[5] Cherlin,G.L.,Volger,H.: Convexity properties and algebraic closure operators, in: Models and Sets, Proc.Logic Colloq.'83, Aachen, part 1, Lecture Notes in Math. 1103, Springer Verlag 1984, 113–146

[6] Clark,K.L.: Negation as failure, in: Logic and Databases, (Gallaire,H.,Minker,J.,eds.), Plenum Press 1978, 293–324

[7] Gallaire,H.,Minker,J.,Nicolas,J.-M.: Logic and databases: a deductive approach, Computing Surveys 16(1984), 153–185

[8] Kueker,D.W.: Core structures for theories, Fund.Math. 89(1975), 155–171

[9] Makowsky,J.A.: Why Horn formulas matter in computer science: initial structures and generic examples, J.C.S.S. 34(1987), 266–292

[10] Malcev,A.I.: Algebraic Systems, Akademie Verlag, Berlin 1973, english translation from russian original, Nauka Moskwa 1968

[11] Minker,J.: On indefinite databases and the closed world assumption, Proc.6th Conf. on Automated Deduction,Lecture Notes in Comp.Sci. 138, Springer Verlag 1982, 292–308

[12] Pinter,C.: A note on the decomposition of theories with respect to amalgamation, convexity and related properties, Notre Dame J.Formal Logic 19(1978),115–118

[13] Reiter,R.: On closed world databases, in: Logic and Databases, (Gallaire,H.,Minker,J.,eds.), Plenum Press 1978, 55–76

[14] Volger,H.: Preservation theorems for limits of structures and global sections of sheaves of structures, Math.Z. 166(1979), 27–53

[15] Volger,H.: On theories which admit initial models, MIP 8708, Univ.Passau 1987, 12 pages

[16] Yahya,A.,Henschen,L.J.: Deduction in non-Horn databases, J. Automated Reasoning 1(1985), 141–160

ALGORITHMS FOR PROPOSITIONAL UPDATES

Andreas Weber
Fachgebiet Wirtschaft, Fachhochschule Flensburg
Kanzleistr. 91–93, 2390 Flensburg

1 Introduction

Many papers have been written on the definition or processing of queries against databases. From todays point of view, however, one of the seminal papers on this subject has been written by C.C. Green [Gr69] as a result of doing research in artificial intelligence. In his work he applied J.A. Robinson's resolution method for automated theorem proving [Ro65] to question answering systems. He thus established a close relationship between this "systems problem" and its foundation in formal logic.

In database theory this relationship has not been so obvious. One year after Green's paper E.F. Codd published his famous paper on structuring large shared databases [Co70] and in the sequel database theory developed rather independently. Although there have been some researchers investigating the relationship between logic and databases [GM78] this approach has not generally been accepted. One of the reasons might be that the main problem in database theory is updating. The updating problem and the corresponding anomalies have actually been the driving force behind the introduction and development of the relational data model, but there seems to be no real counterpart in at least classical logic.

Two authors who have investigated database updates and logic are R. Fagin et. al. [FUV83], [FKUV86] and M. Winslett-Wilkens [Wi86a], [Wi86b]. R. Fagin uses the maximum principle to save as much information as possible in case of inconsistency, but his approach takes the maximum over a set of clauses. So the result of an update is highly dependent on how the knowledge is represented and how the update is communicated. M. Winslett's approach avoids this for the knowledge representation side but not for the update formula. In artificial intelligence research the update problem has been investigated under headings like "belief revision", "truth maintenance" or "non monotonic reasoning", see for example [Bo80], [McDo82], [BoSi84] or [Mo85]. The approach in this paper has in part been published in [We85], a full description and many more algorithms are give in [We87].

The remainder of the paper is organized as follows: Section 2 contains an analysis of the problem and states some requirements on updates. From these requirements a specification has been developed in section 3 that has some satisfying properties. Section 4 gives complexity results and discusses a number of algorithmic approaches in the light of a typical applicative setting.

2 Statement of the Problem

In this paper we consider propositional formulas φ, μ over some atomset $\Lambda \cup \{0, 1\}$. The set of formulas over Λ is denoted by $\Sigma(\Lambda)$, the set of atoms within a formula φ by $\Lambda(\varphi)$. The semantics of the formula is explained by subsets of Λ, that is models over the universe Λ. The set of models of a formula φ is denoted by Mod (φ). For $\varphi, \mu \in \Sigma(\Lambda)$ we define $\varphi \models \mu$ as usual by every model of φ is a model of μ. Identity on $\Sigma(\Lambda)$ is denoted by $=$, logical equivalence by $\equiv$. Algorithms are sketched in a hypothetical programming language with obvious meaning.

Now let $\varrho, \varphi, \mu \in \Sigma(\Lambda)$. A query ϱ posed to a system that knows φ may be identified with the problem "Is ϱ derivable from φ or not?". The corresponding answer will be "yes" or "no". Quite analogously an update μ posed to a system that knows φ will result in an answer "accepted" or "not accepted". This answer is accompanied by a corresponding state change in the knowledge from some φ to some φ updated by μ, denoted by $\varphi \circ \mu$. The first obvious problem is to characterize $\varphi \circ \mu$ such that the intuitive meaning of an update is met.

First of all we should always have what is sometimes called a consistent system state. So in our formalization we require $\varphi \not\equiv 0$ and for every μ $\varphi \circ \mu \not\equiv 0$ again. Secondly, we would like the result of an update to be dependent only on what information is represented by the formulas and not on how this knowledge is actually described. So for $\varphi \equiv \varphi'$ and $\mu \equiv \mu'$ we expect $\varphi \circ \mu \equiv \varphi' \circ \mu'$. Thirdly, by our intuition of an accepted update we require $\varphi \circ \mu \models \mu$. But note that for $\mu \equiv 0$ this would contradict our first requirement, so we may require $\varphi \circ \mu \models \mu$ if and only if $\mu \not\equiv 0$. In other words every satisfiable update is accepted and unsatisfiable updates are rejected. So we do not consider integrity constraints here which would further restrict the acceptable updates. If $\{\varphi, \mu\}$ is consistent the above requirements are easily satisfied by letting

$$\varphi \circ \mu = \begin{cases} \varphi \wedge \mu, & \text{if } \mu \not\equiv 0; \\ \varphi, & \text{else.} \end{cases}$$

But if $\{\varphi, \mu\}$ is inconsistent we have to modify φ before conjoining μ.

Example 2.1

$$\varphi = it's\_raining$$

$$\mu = \neg it's\_raining$$

a) One reason for the inconsistency could be that the propositions have been stated unprecisely and should rather be

$$\varphi = it's\_raining\_in\_Karlsruhe$$

$$\mu = \neg it's\_raining\_in\_California$$

This is somewhat outside our formal methods and will not be considered here.

b) A variant of a) is the fact that things have simply changed. So we change φ to

$$\sigma = it\_has\_been\_raining$$

and let

$$\varphi \circ \mu = \sigma \wedge \mu = it\_has\_been\_raining \wedge \neg it's\_raining$$

A formal way to treat this kind of updating is to use version numbers or time stamps and has been proposed for database systems.

c) Finally we can just drop the old proposition, change φ to

$$\sigma = 1$$

and let

$$\varphi \circ \mu = \sigma \wedge \mu = \neg it's\_raining$$

This is the most common way of updating by change.

In this paper we shall mostly consider updating by change although some results may be applied to updating by version. In example 2.1.c all old knowledge has been dropped but in general some old knowledge should be retained. So we obtain our fourth requirement stating $\varphi \circ \mu \equiv \sigma \wedge \mu$ where $\varphi \models \sigma$. Of course we would like σ to be maximal and if $\{\varphi, \mu\}$ is consistent we can have $\sigma \models \varphi$, i.e. $\sigma \equiv \varphi$. But if $\{\varphi, \mu\}$ is inconsistent this would violate our first requirement. The choice of σ and especially the choice of an ordering to find a maximum is an open question. The following example explains some alternatives.

Example 2.2

$$\varphi = a \wedge b$$

$$\mu = \neg a \vee \neg b$$

a) Assume $\sigma = a$, then $\sigma \wedge \mu \equiv a \wedge \neg b$.

b) Assume $\sigma = b$, then $\sigma \wedge \mu \equiv \neg a \wedge b$.

c) From a) and b) we observe that in each alternative σ is in some sense maximal, but the resulting knowledge after update will be drastically different depending on some rather arbitrary choice. So instead of choosing randomly we could drop all old knowledge, i.e. let $\sigma = 1$, so that

$$\varphi \circ \mu \equiv \neg a \vee \neg b.$$

d) Finally we can choose a formula that represents a maximal set of consequences being consistent with the update. In this example this set is unique and one such formula is $\sigma = a \vee b$. This results in

$$\varphi \circ \mu \equiv (a \vee b) \wedge (\neg a \vee \neg b)$$

In this paper we will mainly use the approach indicated by a, b and c. The rationale behind that is that we need some concept of local inconsistency. Two formulas are considered to be consistent somewhere and inconsistent somewhere else. This concept is given by atomsets; φ and μ are considered to be consistent on either a or b but not on both. We sum up the

Requirements:

1. $\varphi \not\equiv 0$ and for every μ: $\varphi \circ \mu \not\equiv 0$
2. $\varphi \equiv \varphi'$ and $\mu \equiv \mu' \Rightarrow \varphi \circ \mu \equiv \varphi' \circ \mu'$
3. $\mu \not\equiv 0 \Rightarrow \varphi \circ \mu \models \mu$
4. $\mu \not\equiv 0 \Rightarrow \varphi \circ \mu \equiv \sigma \wedge \mu$ where $\varphi \models \sigma$
5. σ should be maximal
6. for mutually excluding maximal σ_1, σ_2 either
    - choose σ arbitrarily or
    - choose the minimum for all maximal σ_i

3 Specification

In this section we repeat some of the definitions, theorems and examples from [We85]; the proofs and additional results may be found there. A slight change in notation has been made by replacing the term agreeing on by consistent on a set of atoms.

The general approach taken is as follows: We specify the models of the still hypothetical formula $\varphi \circ \mu$ depending on the models of φ and the models of μ. This will automatically satisfy requirement 2. A concept of local consistency is provided by the following definition.

Definition 3.1
Let $\varphi, \mu \in \Sigma(\Lambda)$ and $\Lambda' \subseteq \Lambda$.

(φ, μ) *consistent on* Λ'
$:\Leftrightarrow \exists \mathcal{A} \in \text{Mod}(\varphi) \exists \mathcal{B} \in \text{Mod}(\mu) : \mathcal{A} \cap \Lambda' = \mathcal{B} \cap \Lambda'$.

(φ, μ) *inconsistent on* Λ'
$:\Leftrightarrow (\varphi, \mu)$ not consistent on Λ'.

Given formulas φ and μ we say that Λ' *is consistent for* (φ, μ) if and only if (φ, μ) is consistent on Λ'. If (φ, μ) is inconsistent on some set $\Lambda', (\varphi, \mu)$ may be consistent on some proper subset $\Lambda'' \subseteq \Lambda$. Quite naturally we ask for *maximally consistent sets* Λ', that is sets $\Lambda' \subseteq \Lambda$ such that Λ' is consistent and all proper supersets $\Lambda' \subset \Lambda'' \subseteq \Lambda$ are inconsistent for (φ, μ). Maximally consistent sets are not unique in general and the set of all maximally consistent sets is denoted by $\Gamma(\varphi, \mu)$. Dually one can introduce *minimally inconsistent sets*. Again, given φ and μ, these sets are not unique and the set of all minimally inconsistent sets is denoted by $\Omega(\varphi, \mu)$. As maximally consistent sets are not unique, we cannot assign the property to single atoms. However, if the choice of a maximally consistent set is arbitrary, we can apply the mimimum principle, i.e. use the intersection of all maximally consistent sets. In this case we obtain a partitioning of Λ into those atoms that are involved in the consistency and those that are not.

Theorem 3.1
Let $\varphi, \mu \in \Sigma(\Lambda)$, $\varphi \not\equiv 0$, $\mu \not\equiv 0$. Then

$$\begin{aligned} \Lambda = &\ \bigcap\nolimits_{\Gamma \in \Gamma(\varphi,\mu)} \Gamma \cup \bigcap\nolimits_{\Omega \in \Omega(\varphi,\mu)} \Omega \\ \emptyset = &\ \bigcap\nolimits_{\Gamma \in \Gamma(\varphi,\mu)} \Gamma \cup \bigcap\nolimits_{\Omega \in \Omega(\varphi,\mu)} \Omega \end{aligned}$$

Based on the notion of local consistency we now define the semantics of $\varphi \circ \mu$. At first, to satisfy requirment 3, we have to choose a subset of Mod (μ). To satisfy 4 we have to incorporate some of the information that is contained in φ. We choose those models $\mathcal{A}$ of μ for which there is a model $\mathcal{B}$ of φ that coincides with $\mathcal{A}$ on at least some atoms Λ'. This may be thought of as the result of an imaginary agreement process where φ and μ agree upon the meaning of some atoms and disagree upon others.

Definition 3.2
Let $\varphi, \mu \in \Sigma(\Lambda)$ and $\Lambda' \subseteq \Lambda$.

$$\text{Mod}_{\Lambda'}(\varphi, \mu) := \{\mathcal{B} \in \text{Mod}(\mu) \mid \exists \mathcal{A} \in \text{Mod}(\varphi) : \mathcal{A} \cap \Lambda' = \mathcal{B} \cap \Lambda'\}$$

The choice of Λ' is apparent. Depending on the intended alternatives one chooses Λ' to be one of the maximally consistent sets or their intersection. The following example illustrates the ideas.

Example 3.1

$$\begin{aligned} \Lambda = &\ \{a, b, c, d\} \\ \varphi = &\ a \rightarrow b \wedge b \leftrightarrow c \wedge c \rightarrow d \\ \mu = &\ b \not\leftrightarrow c \end{aligned}$$

$\{a,b,c,d\}$

inconsistency

$\{a,c,d\}$ $\{a,b,d\}$ $\{a,b,c\}$ $\{b,c,d\}$

$\{a,b\}$ $\{a,c\}$ $\{a,d\}$ $\{b,d\}$ $\{c,d\}$ $\{b,c\}$

$\{a\}$ $\{b\}$ $\{c\}$ $\{d\}$

consistency

$\emptyset$

$$\begin{aligned}\mathrm{Mod}(\varphi) &= \{\emptyset,\{d\},\{a,d\},\{b,c\},\{b,c,d\},\{a,b,c,d\}\}\\ \mathrm{Mod}(\mu) &= \{\{b\},\{c\},\{a,b\},\{a,c\},\{b,d\},\{c,d\},\{a,b,d\},\{a,c,d\}\}\end{aligned}$$

We have $\Gamma(\varphi,\mu) = \{\{a,b,d\},\{a,c,d\}\}$ and $\bigcap_{\Gamma\in\Gamma(\varphi,\mu)}\Gamma = \{a,d\}$.

So, if we choose $\Lambda' = \{a,d\}$, we obtain

$$\begin{aligned}\mathrm{Mod}_{\Lambda'}(\varphi,\mu) &= \{\{b\},\{c\},\{b,d\},\{c,d\},\{a,b,d,\},\{a,c,d\}\}\\ &= \mathrm{Mod}(a \to d \wedge b \not\leftrightarrow c)\end{aligned}$$

So we have really saved all consequences involving a and d, dropped those that caused the inconsistency and conjoined the new information. This can be stated more precisely. We first show how to delete all information on a particular atom from a formula.

Definition 3.3
Let $\varphi \in \Sigma(\Lambda)$ and $\alpha \in \Lambda$. Define $\varphi|\underline{\alpha}$ and $\varphi|\overline{\alpha}$ by:

$$\text{Replace } \alpha \text{ in } \varphi \text{ by } \begin{Bmatrix}1\\0\end{Bmatrix} \text{ to obtain } \begin{Bmatrix}\varphi|\underline{\alpha}\\ \varphi|\overline{\alpha}\end{Bmatrix}.$$

$\varphi|\underline{\alpha}$ may be called φ given α is true, $\varphi|\overline{\alpha}$ may be called φ given α is false. The deletion of all information concerning a particular atom α is consequently given by

Definition 3.4
Let $\varphi \in \Sigma(\Lambda)$ and $\alpha \in \Lambda$.

$$\mathrm{del}_\alpha(\varphi) := \varphi|\underline{\alpha} \vee \varphi|\overline{\alpha}$$

$\mathrm{del}_\alpha(\varphi)$ is called the deletion of α from φ. The deletion has exactly the properties stated above.

Theorem 3.2
Let $\varphi \in \Sigma(\Lambda)$, $\alpha \in \Lambda$ and $\sigma = \mathrm{del}_\alpha(\varphi)$.

(a) $\Lambda(\sigma) = \Lambda(\varphi) - \{\alpha\}$

(b) $\varphi \models \sigma$

(c) $\varrho \in \Sigma(\Lambda(\sigma))$ and $\varphi \models \varrho \Rightarrow \sigma \models \varrho$

(d) Let $\sigma_1, \sigma_2 \in \Sigma(\Lambda)$ satisfy (a)–(c), then $\sigma_1 \equiv \sigma_2$.

The theorem shows that $\mathrm{del}_\alpha(\varphi)$ really deletes some consequences from a formula while preserving others. The following theorem relates the semantic definition given earlier to the more syntactic characterization given here.

Theorem 3.3
Let $\varphi, \mu \in \Sigma(\Lambda), (\alpha_1,\ldots,\alpha_n)$ be a sequence of $\alpha_i \in \Lambda$, and $\Lambda' = \Lambda - \{\alpha_1,\ldots,\alpha_n\}$. Then

$$\mathrm{Mod}_{\Lambda'}(\varphi,\mu) = \mathrm{Mod}(\mathrm{del}_{(\alpha_1,\ldots,\alpha_n)}(\varphi) \wedge \mu)$$

4 Algorithms

Given two formulas φ and μ we would like to have algorithms to compute $\varphi \circ \mu$. Depending on whether a maximally consistent set or their intersection is chosen theorem 3.3 suggests the following two approaches:

1. Compute some maximally consistent set Γ. For some sequence $(\alpha_1, \ldots, \alpha_n)$, where $\alpha_i \in \Lambda - \Gamma$, compute $\mathrm{del}_{(\alpha_1,\ldots,\alpha_n)}(\varphi)$. Conjoin μ.

2. Compute $\Omega^* = \bigcup_{\Omega \in \Omega(\varphi,\mu)} \Omega$. For some sequence $(\alpha_1, \ldots, \alpha_n)$, where $\alpha_i \in \Omega^*$, compute $\mathrm{del}_{(\alpha_1,\ldots,\alpha_n)}(\varphi)$. Conjoin μ.

In any case three problems have to be solved.

- Search for one or all maximally (minimally) consistent (inconsistent) sets.
- Compute the deletion of some α from φ.
- Conjoin μ

At first we investigate the worst-case-complexity of the first problem. For simplicity we assume that φ and μ are boolean expressions and that $\Lambda = \Lambda(\varphi) \cup \Lambda(\mu)$. Let $\Lambda' \subseteq \Lambda$, the corresponding decision problems are:

CONSISTENT SET: Are (φ, μ) consistent on Λ'?

INCONSISTENT SET: Are (φ, μ) inconsistent on Λ'?

MAXIMALLY CONSISTENT SET: Are (φ, μ) maximally consistent on Λ'?

MINIMALLY INCONSISTENT SET: Are (φ, μ) minimally inconsistent on Λ'?

For the first two problems we obtain:

Theorem 4.1

(a) CONSISTENT SET is NP-complete.

(b) INCONSISTENT SET is co-NP-complete.

Proof:

(a) To see that CONSISTENT SET is in NP we show that every (φ, μ, Λ') - problem is transformable to SATISFIABILITY:

Given φ, μ and Λ', rename every $\alpha \in \Lambda(\varphi) \cap \Lambda(\mu)$ within μ into some new $\alpha' \notin \Lambda(\varphi) \cup \Lambda(\mu)$. Let the new formula be μ' and let

$$\sigma = \varphi \wedge \mu' \wedge \bigwedge_{\alpha \in \Lambda(\varphi) \cap \Lambda(\mu) \cap \Lambda'} (\neg\alpha \vee \alpha') \wedge (\neg\alpha' \vee \alpha)$$

Then σ is satisfiable if and only if (φ, μ) are consistent on Λ'. The transformation is polynomial in the length of $|\varphi| + |\mu| + \#\Lambda'$ and therefore CONSISTENT SET is transformable to SATISFIABILITY and thus in NP.

To see that CONSISTENT SET is NP-complete transform from SATISFIABILITY. Let σ be a boolean expression, then

$$\sigma \text{ is satisfiable} \iff (1, \sigma) \text{ are consistent on } \emptyset.$$

(b) INCONSISTENT SET is the complement of CONSISTENT SET. ◇

For updating that preserves as much as possible old information we need maximally consistent or minimally inconsistent sets. The corresponding decision problems are NP-easy.

Theorem 4.2

(a) MINIMALLY INCONSISTENT SET is in P^{NP}.

(b) MAXIMALLY CONSISTENT SET is in P^{NP}.

Proof:

(a) The proof is by Turing reduction on CONSISTENT SET. Let

$$agree(\varphi, \mu, \Lambda') = \begin{cases} true, & \text{if } (\varphi, \mu) \text{ is consistent on } \Lambda'; \\ false, & \text{else.} \end{cases}$$

be an oracle for CONSISTENT SET. Then the following OTM-program-sketch computes the required decision:

```
if agree(φ, μ, Λ')
   then write ('no')
   else {(φ, μ) are inconsistent on Λ'}
        minimal := true;
        for each α ∈ Λ' loop
            if not agree(φ, μ, Λ' − {α})
              then minimal := false
            end if
        end loop;
        if minimal
            then write ('yes')
            else write ('no')
        end if
end if
```

agree is called $\#\Lambda' + 1$ – times at most so that the number of calls is trivially limited by the input length. Thus the reduction is polynomial.

(b) Analogous to (a) using the Turing-reduction:

```
if not agree(φ, μ, Λ')
   then write ('no')
   else {(φ, μ) are consistent on Λ'}
        maximal := true;
        for each α ∈ (Λ(φ) ∪ Λ(μ)) − Λ' loop
            if agree(φ, μ, Λ' ∪ {α})
              then maximal := false
            end if
        end loop;
        if maximal
            then write ('yes')
            else write ('no')
        end if
end if
```

From theorems 4.1 and 4.2 it is obvious that all search problems in updating like "Find a maximally consistent set" etc. will be NP-hard. For the variant using the intersection of the maximally consistent sets problems may even be harder at least if the intersection has to be computed in that way.

Computation of the del-Operation right from the definition will double formula length on every deletion; thus improvements like replacing $0 \wedge \sigma$ by 0 etc. are required and a special version may be given for conjunctive normal forms. Some problems are however inevitable, just consider the deletion of b from $\bigwedge_{1 \leq i \leq n}(a_i \rightarrow b) \wedge \bigwedge_{1 \leq j \leq m}(b \rightarrow c_j)$.

Even the last step, that is conjunction of μ, is not trivial. For example for $\varphi = a \vee b$ and $\mu = a$ we might expect $\varphi \circ \mu = a$ and this requires additional improvement steps. Generally speaking the space problems that arise from a too long formula φ may be much more serious than some worst-case time problems look.

Nevertheless, we suspect that every reasonable updating method will have to detect inconsistency in one way or another and will thus probably lead to worst-case exponential algorithms. To check the pragmatics of our update definition and also to get experience on typical application problems we develop some algorithms.

The proof in theorem 4.1 immediately suggest an algorithm to find a maximally consistent set. The algorithm is explained by continuing example 3.1.

Example 4.1

$$\begin{aligned} \Lambda &= \{a, b, c, d, \} \\ \varphi &= a \rightarrow b \wedge b \leftrightarrow c \wedge c \rightarrow d \\ \mu &= b \not\leftrightarrow c \end{aligned}$$

Rename the common atoms in μ to obtain:

$$\mu' = b' \not\leftrightarrow c'$$

Test $\varphi \wedge \mu'$ for satisfiability

$$\varphi \wedge \mu' = a \rightarrow b \wedge b \leftrightarrow c \wedge c \rightarrow d \wedge b' \leftrightarrow c' \not\equiv 0$$

$\varphi \wedge \mu$ is satisfiable. Otherwise, because there are no common atoms, $\varphi \equiv 0$ or $\mu \equiv 0$. By requirement 1 and assuming a correct update method $\varphi \not\equiv 0$, so $\mu \equiv 0$. Thus, if $\varphi \wedge \mu' \equiv 0, \mu$ has to be rejected. Continuing the example conjoin $b \leftrightarrow b'$ and test

$$\varphi \wedge \mu' \wedge (b \leftrightarrow b') \not\equiv 0$$

which is still satisfiable. Now conjoin $c \leftrightarrow c'$ and test

$$\varphi \wedge \mu' \wedge (b \leftrightarrow b') \wedge (c \leftrightarrow c') \equiv 0$$

which is unsatisfiable, so $\{a, b, d\}$ is a maximally consistent set. If there are more maximally consistent sets, they may be obtained by conjoining the equivalences in different order.

The complete algorithm is given by

Algorithm 4.1

```
begin
    compute △ = Λ(φ) ∩ Λ(μ)
    for α in △ loop
        rename α within φ into some α' ∉ Λ(φ) ∪ Λ(μ)
    end loop
    φ := φ ∧ μ
    if not sat(φ) then
        {φ ≡ 0 or μ ≡ 0}
    else
        Γ := ∅
        for α in △ loop
            φ := φ ∧ (¬α' ∨ α) ∧ (α' ∨ ¬α)
            if sat(φ) then
              Γ := Γ ∪ {α}
            else
              delete the last two clauses from φ
            end if
        end loop
    end if
end
```

From algorithm 4.1 we can easily develop an algorithm for updating by version. All that is necessary is to rename the common atoms within φ to α' and conjoin as many equivalences $\alpha \leftrightarrow \alpha'$ as possible. This algorithm is depicted in

Algorithm 4.2

```
begin
    △ := Λ(φ) ∩ Λ(μ)
    for α in △ loop
        rename α within φ into some α' ∉ Λ(φ) ∪ Λ(μ)
    end loop
    φ := φ ∧ μ
    if not sat(φ) then
        {reject update}
    else
        for α in △ loop
            φ := φ ∧ (¬α' ∨ α) ∧ (α' ∨ ¬α)
            if sat(φ) then
              rename α' within φ into α
            end if
            delete the last two clauses from φ
        end loop
    end if
end
```

Although these algorithms compute the desired function they are not practically usefull. In a database or knowledge base application φ represents the database and μ represents the update. For suchlike applications we can generally assume the following background: φ consists of a large number of relatively short clauses. μ is short and the number of common atoms of φ and μ is very small (say, below 10). These assumptions are satisfied in many cases; it should be noted, however, that if μ is long it may be impossible to divide one update into a sequence of shorter ones, i.e. $\varphi \circ (\mu_1 \wedge \mu_2) \not\equiv (\varphi \circ \varphi_1) \circ \varphi_2$, see [We87] pp. 50-52.

Under the above assumptions it is obvious that finding Δ or a loop over Δ is not the main problem. Instead it is impractical to repeatedly establish satisfiability of the whole database. Assuming $\varphi \not\equiv 0$ we thus restrict testing on those parts of the database that are concerned. This is known as set-of-support-strategy in mechanical theorem proving.

Moreover, we know that the satisfiability test will involve equivalences $\alpha' \leftrightarrow \alpha$ and this knowledge may be used to further improve the algorithm. Our algorithm will search for models $\mathcal{A} \models \varphi$ and $\mathcal{B} \models \mu$ and instead of adding equivalences for some atoms we ensure by the algorithm that $\mathcal{A}$ and $\mathcal{B}$ coincide on these atoms.

The algorithm presupposes that $\varphi \not\equiv 0$ and uses a candidate Γ for a maximally consistent set and a candidate Ω for its complement in Δ. Then for every $\alpha \in \Delta - (\Gamma \cup \Omega)$ it is tested whether Γ may be extended to contain α or not. To test whether Γ is a consistent set we search for two models $\mathcal{A} \models \varphi$ and $\mathcal{B} \models \mu$ such that this conincide on Γ.

Algorithm 4.3

```
begin
      if not sat(μ) then
         {μ ≡ 0, reject}
      else
         Δ := A(φ) ∩ A(μ)
         Γ := ∅
         Ω := ∅
         loop
               choose α ∈ Δ − (Ω ∪ Γ)
               exit when no choice possible
               Γ := Γ ∪ {α}
               finddouble(Γ, found)
               if not found then
                  Γ := Γ − {α}
                  Ω := Ω ∪ {α}
               end if
         end loop
      end if
end
```

The procedure finddouble $(\Gamma, found)$ is assumed to return true if and only if there are $\mathcal{A} \models \varphi$ and $\mathcal{B} \models \mu$ such that $\mathcal{A} \cap \Gamma = \mathcal{B} \cap \Gamma$. To implement finddouble an algorithm may be developed as follows. We search for models $\mathcal{A}$, $\mathcal{B}$; so during computation we know for every α whether $\alpha \in \mathcal{A}, \alpha \notin \mathcal{A}$ or we have not yet considered α. These partial models are written for example $\mathcal{A} = \lfloor \underline{a}, \overline{b}, \underline{c} \rfloor$ to denote that $a \in \mathcal{A}$, $b \notin \mathcal{A}$, $c \in \mathcal{A}$ and all other atoms have not been established. The algorithm is a backtracking algorithm that searches for $\mathcal{A}$, $\mathcal{B}$ reading clauses from φ or μ and roughly sketched by the following example.

Example 4.2

Let $\Gamma = \{a, d\}$. Assume we have already computed $\mathcal{A} = \lfloor \underline{a}, \overline{b}, \underline{c} \rfloor$ and $\mathcal{B} = \lfloor \underline{a}, \underline{b} \rfloor$ and clause κ has been read from φ. Then there are four cases:

a) $\kappa = a \vee b$. Both partial models satisfy κ, so we may mark κ and read the next clause

b) $\kappa = \neg a \vee b$. $\mathcal{A}$ may not be extended to satisfy κ, so we track the algorithm back to a clause that caused the setting of a or b.

c) $\kappa = \neg a \vee d$. Because $\alpha \in \mathcal{A}$ and $\alpha \in \mathcal{B}$ this enforces $\mathcal{A} = [\underline{a}, \bar{b}, \underline{c}, \underline{d}]$ and because $d \in \Gamma$ also $\mathcal{B} = [\underline{a}, \underline{b}, \underline{d}]$.

d) $\kappa = \neg a \vee e$. Again because $\alpha \in \mathcal{A}$ this enforces $\mathcal{A} = [\underline{a}, \bar{b}, \underline{c}, \underline{d}]$ but because $e \notin \Gamma$ $\mathcal{B}$ is left unchanged.

The algorithm may stop if no more clauses from φ match $\mathcal{A}$ and no more clauses from μ match $\mathcal{B}$ (set-of-support). It may occasionally happen, that $\mathcal{A}$ and $\mathcal{B}$ conincide on more than just Γ; so we return Γ to improve the average case efficiency of algorithm 4.3. A full formal treatment of these algorithms is given in [We87] which also contains material on the computation of the del-operation and improvements over the conjunction of μ.

Conclusions

We have introduced and analysed propositional updating. It turns out that there are a number of different solutions to that problem and the selection of a method may depend on the pragmatics of the application. As had to be expected computional problems are NP-hard. Heuristics may not be applied in this situation so we have developed algorithms having typical applications in mind. This will allow us to test the method for acceptance before refining the algorithms.

References

[Bo80] Bobrow, D.G. (ed.): Special issue on non-monotonic logic. *Artif. Intell.* **13**, 1/2 (1980).

[BoSi84] Bossu, G.; Siegel, P.: Non-monotonic reasoning and databases. *Advances in Database Theory* **2**, Plenum Press (1984), 239–284.

[Co70] Codd, E.F.: A relational model for large shared data banks. *Comm. ACM* **6** (1970), 377–387.

[FKUV86] Fagin, R.; Kuper, G.M.; Ullmann, J.P.; Vardi, M.Y.: Updating logical databases. *Advances in Computing Research*, Vol. **3** (1986), 1–18.

[FUV83] Fagin, R.; Ullmann, J.D.; Vardi, M.Y.: On the semantics of updates in databases. *Proc. 2nd ACM Symp. on Princ. of Database Syst.* (1983), 352–365.

[GM78] Gallaire, H.; Minker, J.: Logic and Databases. Plenum Press, New York, London (1978).

[Gr69] Green, C.C.: Theorem Proving by Resolution as a Basis for Question Answering Systems. *Mach. Intell.* **4** (1969), 183–208.

[McDo82] McDemott, D.; Doyle, J.: Non-monotonic logic II: Non-monotonic modal theories. *J. ACM* **29** (1982), 33–57.

[Mo85] Moore, R.C.: Semantical considerations on non-monotonic logic. *Artif. Intell.* **25** (1985), 75–94.

[Ro65] Robinson, J.A.: A Machine Oriented Logic Based on the Resolution Principle. *J. ACM* **12** (1965), 25–41.

[We85] Weber, A.: Updating propositional formulas. *TR#160* Institut für Angewandte Informatik und Formale Beschreibungsverfahren, Universität Karlsruhe, (1985), auch: *Proc. of the 1st Int. Conf. on Expert Database Syst.* (1986), 373–386.

[We87] Weber, A.: Eine Methode zur Aktualisierung Aussagenlogischer Wissensbasen. Dissertation, Universität Karlsruhe, Karlsruhe (1987).

[Wi86a] Winslett, M.: A Model Theoretic Approach to Updating Logical Databases. *Proc. 5th ACM Symp. on Principles of Database Syst.* (1986), 224–234.

[Wi86b] Winslett, M.: Updating Logical Databases Containing Null Values. *Proc. Int. Conf. on Database Theory, LNCS 243*. Springer, Berlin (1986), 421–435.

Vol. 296: R. Janßen (Ed.), Trends in Computer Algebra. Proceedings, 1987. V, 197 pages. 1988.

Vol. 297: E.N. Houstis, T.S. Papatheodorou, C.D. Polychronopoulos (Eds.), Supercomputing. Proceedings, 1987. X, 1093 pages. 1988.

Vol. 298: M. Main, A. Melton, M. Mislove, D. Schmidt (Eds.), Mathematical Foundations of Programming Language Semantics. Proceedings, 1987. VIII, 637 pages. 1988.

Vol. 299: M. Dauchet, M. Nivat (Eds.), CAAP '88. Proceedings, 1988. VI, 304 pages. 1988.

Vol. 300: H. Ganzinger (Ed.), ESOP '88. Proceedings, 1988. VI, 381 pages. 1988.

Vol. 301: J. Kittler (Ed.), Pattern Recognition. Proceedings, 1988. VII, 668 pages. 1988.

Vol. 302: D.M. Yellin, Attribute Grammar Inversion and Source-to-source Translation. VIII, 176 pages. 1988.

Vol. 303: J.W. Schmidt, S. Ceri, M. Missikoff (Eds.), Advances in Database Technology – EDBT '88. X, 620 pages. 1988.

Vol. 304: W.L. Price, D. Chaum (Eds.), Advances in Cryptology – EUROCRYPT '87. Proceedings, 1987. VII, 314 pages. 1988.

Vol. 305: J. Biskup, J. Demetrovics, J. Paredaens, B. Thalheim (Eds.), MFDBS 87. Proceedings, 1987. V, 247 pages. 1988.

Vol. 306: M. Boscarol, L. Carlucci Aiello, G. Levi (Eds.), Foundations of Logic and Functional Programming. Proceedings, 1986. V, 218 pages. 1988.

Vol. 307: Th. Beth, M. Clausen (Eds.), Applicable Algebra, Error-Correcting Codes, Combinatorics and Computer Algebra. Proceedings, 1986. VI, 215 pages. 1988.

Vol. 308: S. Kaplan, J.-P. Jouannaud (Eds.), Conditional Term Rewriting Systems. Proceedings, 1987. VI, 278 pages. 1988.

Vol. 309: J. Nehmer (Ed.), Experiences with Distributed Systems. Proceedings, 1987. VI, 292 pages. 1988.

Vol. 310: E. Lusk, R. Overbeek (Eds.), 9th International Conference on Automated Deduction. Proceedings, 1988. X, 775 pages. 1988.

Vol. 311: G. Cohen, P. Godlewski (Eds.), Coding Theory and Applications 1986. Proceedings, 1986. XIV, 196 pages. 1988.

Vol. 312: J. van Leeuwen (Ed.), Distributed Algorithms 1987. Proceedings, 1987. VII, 430 pages. 1988.

Vol. 313: B. Bouchon, L. Saitta, R.R. Yager (Eds.), Uncertainty and Intelligent Systems. IPMU '88. Proceedings, 1988. VIII, 408 pages. 1988.

Vol. 314: H. Göttler, H.J. Schneider (Eds.), Graph-Theoretic Concepts in Computer Science. Proceedings, 1987. VI, 254 pages. 1988.

Vol. 315: K. Furukawa, H. Tanaka, T. Fujisaki (Eds.), Logic Programming '87. Proceedings, 1987. VI, 327 pages. 1988.

Vol. 316: C. Choffrut (Ed.), Automata Networks. Proceedings, 1986. VII, 125 pages. 1988.

Vol. 317: T. Lepistö, A. Salomaa (Eds.), Automata, Languages and Programming. Proceedings, 1988. XI, 741 pages. 1988.

Vol. 318: R. Karlsson, A. Lingas (Eds.), SWAT 88. Proceedings, 1988. VI, 262 pages. 1988.

Vol. 319: J.H. Reif (Ed.), VLSI Algorithms and Architectures – AWOC 88. Proceedings, 1988. X, 476 pages. 1988.

Vol. 320: A. Blaser (Ed)., Natural Language at the Computer. Proceedings, 1988. III, 176 pages. 1988.

Vol. 322: S. Gjessing, K. Nygaard (Eds.), ECOOP '88. European Conference on Object-Oriented Programming. Proceedings, 1988. VI, 410 pages. 1988.

Vol. 323: P. Deransart, M. Jourdan, B. Lorho, Attribute Grammars. IX, 232 pages. 1988.

Vol. 324: M.P. Chytil, L. Janiga, V. Koubek (Eds.), Mathematical Foundations of Computer Science 1988. Proceedings. IX, 562 pages. 1988.

Vol. 325: G. Brassard, Modern Cryptology. VI, 107 pages. 1988.

Vol. 326: M. Gyssens, J. Paredaens, D. Van Gucht (Eds.), ICDT '88. 2nd International Conference on Database Theory. Proceedings, 1988. VI, 409 pages. 1988.

Vol. 327: G.A. Ford (Ed.), Software Engineering Education. Proceedings, 1988. V, 207 pages. 1988.

Vol. 328: R. Bloomfield, L. Marshall, R. Jones (Eds.), VDM '88. VDM – The Way Ahead. Proceedings, 1988. IX, 499 pages. 1988.

Vol. 329: E. Börger, H. Kleine Büning, M.M. Richter (Eds.), CSL '87. 1st Workshop on Computer Science Logic. Proceedings, 1987. VI, 346 pages. 1988.